Managing Information Resources and Technology:

Emerging Applications and Theories

Mehdi Khosrow-Pour
Information Resources Management Association, USA

Information Science
REFERENCE

Managing Director:	Lindsay Johnston
Editorial Director:	Joel Gamon
Book Production Manager:	Jennifer Yoder
Publishing Systems Analyst:	Adrienne Freeland
Development Editor:	Development Editor
Assistant Acquisitions Editor:	Kayla Wolfe
Typesetter:	Christina Henning
Cover Design:	Jason Mull

Published in the United States of America by
Information Science Reference (an imprint of IGI Global)
701 E. Chocolate Avenue
Hershey PA 17033
Tel: 717-533-8845
Fax: 717-533-8661
E-mail: cust@igi-global.com
Web site: http://www.igi-global.com

Library of Congress Cataloging-in-Publication Data

Managing information resources and technology: emerging applications and theories / Mehdi Khosrow-Pour, editor.
pages cm
Includes bibliographical references and index.
Summary: "This book highlights the rising trends and studies in the information technology field, offering interesting perspectives on common problems as well as suggestions for future improvement"--Provided by publisher.
ISBN 978-1-4666-3616-3 (hardcover) -- ISBN 978-1-4666-3617-0 (ebook) -- ISBN 978-1-4666-3618-7 (print & perpetual access) 1. Information technology--Management. 2. Information resources management. I. Khosrowpour, Mehdi, 1951-
HD30.2.M3636 2013
658.4'038--dc23

2012045938

British Cataloguing in Publication Data
A Cataloguing in Publication record for this book is available from the British Library.

Associate Editors

List of Reviewers

Table of Contents

Detailed Table of Contents

Governance of the information security function is critical to effective security. In this paper, the authors present a conceptual model for security governance from the perspective of decision rights allocation. Based on Da Veiga and Eloff's (2007) framework for security governance and two high-level information security documents published by the National Institute of Standards and Technology (NIST), the authors present seven domains of information security governance. For each of the governance domains, they propose a main decision type, using the taxonomy of information technology decisions defined by Weill and Ross (2004). This framework recommends the selection of decision rights allocation patterns that are proper to those decision types to ensure good security decisions. As a result, a balance can be achieved between decisional authority and responsibility for information security.

Business Process Management (BPM) maximizes firm performance by transforming isolated functional activities into streamlined, cross-functional processes. Being a relatively new discipline, disagreement exists regarding the position structure and qualifications required for success. However, certain individual differences have been associated with job performance, both in general and for specific occupations. Because BPM initiatives can be expensive and risky, understanding these individual differences may help practitioners improve their chances for BPM job success. Two models of job performance have dominated organizational research; one argues that personality traits are the chief determinants, while the other argues that intelligence and experience are most important. This paper uses logistic regression to examine the efficacy of each model in predicting job performance among BPM professionals. Results indicate that intelligence, conscientiousness, and openness to experience are the most important differentiators of BPM job performance.

The widespread applications of information and communication technologies have attracted many countries to e-government. Nonetheless, setting appropriate goals for e-government initiatives is an important factor for the success of these projects. This study provides a context-based framework for understanding e-government initiatives in different countries, including degree of e-government readiness, degree of transparency, and level of democratization. According to these determinants, 141 countries are categorized using Parson's generic strategy of IT. Classification of countries in this framework shows significant correlations between these determinants and GDP index, which is an important outcome for country performance. This framework provides a roadmap for policymakers to formulate goals for their e-government initiatives commensurate with their respective environments.

Preface

Information Resources Management (IRM) is driven largely by the steady evolution and advancement of Information and Communication Technologies (ICTs), such as mobile ad-hoc networks, Web 2.0, and online virtual communities. This book presents current research in the ICT field, providing organizations and individuals with the tools and knowledge they require to effectively manage the latest online technologies while avoiding common pitfalls and shortcomings inherent in those technologies. In the following chapters, readers will find a useful reference source for the successful implementation of information technologies in their everyday practices and endeavors, each one a quality contribution to the unfolding discourse amongst professionals and researchers actively engaged in the field.

R. P. Sundarraj and Nick Manochehri begin the discussion with "Application of an Extended TAM Model for Online Banking Adoption: A Study at a Gulf-Region University." The understanding of factors leading to the acceptance or rejection of information systems (IS) is important and relevant. Although there have been studies examining the adoption of Internet Banking (IB), research on this topic in the Gulf context and from an IS perspective is lacking, even though societal factors are acknowledged as having an impact on technology adoption. To fill this gap, the authors use a version of the Technology Acceptance Model (TAM), extended by the compatibility and trust constructs. An empirical study, using students from a large university in the region, validates the research model.

Research indicates that rapidly evolving technology and markets do not provide a first mover strategic advantage but favor the second mover. In "Visible IT in Credit Unions: Strategic Advantage and Disadvantage in Two Web Eras," H. James Nelson introduces a third variable: hype. In a time of rapid technology and market evolution, hype overrides the expected results and gives the first mover a strategic advantage. This chapter examines a homogeneous set of medium-sized information-dependent and information-intensive organizations as they implement visible information technology in two eras: during a time of intense hype and during a more normal time where technology has become commonplace. One hundred matched triples of credit unions were examined as they chose to remain offline, implement an informational website, or implement a transactional website during the highly hyped Internet expansion time of 1998 through 2002. One hundred matched pairs of credit unions were then examined during the more normal time from 2003 through 2007. Results indicate that credit unions that embraced the hyped technology gained significant strategic advantage. Second-moving credit unions that waited for the more mature technology survived, whereas the credit unions that did not adopt the technology were at a significant strategic disadvantage.

Governance of the information security function is critical to effective security. In the next chapter, "Governing Information Security: Governance Domains and Decision Rights Allocation Patterns," Yu "Andy" Wu and Carol Saunders present a conceptual model for security governance from the perspective of decision rights allocation. Based on Da Veiga and Eloff's (2007) framework for security governance and two high-level information security documents published by the National Institute of Standards and Technology (NIST), the authors present seven domains of information security governance. For each of the governance domains, they propose a main decision type, using the taxonomy of information technology decisions defined by Weill and Ross (2004). This framework recommends the selection of decision rights allocation patterns that are proper to those decision types to ensure good security decisions. As a result, a balance can be achieved between decisional authority and responsibility for information security.

Chapter 4, "Antecedents to Job Success in Business Process Management: A Comparison of Two Models" by Richard J. Goeke and Yvonne L. Antonucci, presents a method by which Business Process Management (BPM) maximizes firm performance by transforming isolated functional activities into streamlined, cross-functional processes. Being a relatively new discipline, disagreement exists regarding the position structure and qualifications required for success. However, certain individual differences have been associated with job performance, both in general and for specific occupations. Because BPM initiatives can be expensive and risky, understanding these individual differences may help practitioners improve their chances for BPM job success. Two models of job performance have dominated organizational research; one argues that personality traits are the chief determinants, while the other argues that intelligence and experience are most important. This chapter uses logistic regression to examine the efficacy of each model in predicting job performance among BPM professionals. Results indicate that intelligence, conscientiousness, and openness to experience are the most important differentiators of BPM job performance.

The widespread applications of information and communication technologies have attracted many countries to e-government. Nonetheless, setting appropriate goals for e-government initiatives is an important factor for the success of these projects. "An Integrated Strategic Framework for E-Government Initiatives" by Fatemeh Saghafi *et al.* provides a context-based framework for understanding e-government initiatives in different countries, including degree of e-government readiness, degree of transparency, and level of democratization. According to these determinants, 141 countries are categorized using Parson's generic strategy of IT. Classification of countries in this framework shows significant correlations between these determinants and GDP index, which is an important outcome for country performance. This framework provides a roadmap for policymakers to formulate goals for their e-government initiatives commensurate with their respective environments.

In "What Drives Malaysian E-Government Adoption? An Empirical Analysis," Alain Yee-Loong Chong investigates the factors that affect the adoption of e-government in Malaysia. Variables like perceived usefulness, perceived ease of use, compatibility, trust, and demographic profiles of users are included in this research. Data was collected from 418 respondents, and multiple regression analysis is employed to test the research model. The results show that perceived usefulness, perceived ease of use, compatibility, trust, and age have significant relationships with e-government adoption. The results from this study are useful for Malaysian government in formulating appropriate strategies to improve the adoption of e-government applications in Malaysia.

Armin Sharafi *et al.* present "Bundling Processes between Private and Public Organizations: A Qualitative Study." Businesses are aching under the burdens entailed by public reporting duties while public administrations are faced with rising cost pressures. Fostered by the diffusion and maturation of information technology, businesses put forth growing demands in regard to the quality, integration, and usability of public services. An effective means of meeting these challenges is through the identification and bundling of processes caused by reporting duties. Incorporating corresponding concepts from the business sector, the authors develop an approach for process bundling tailored to public organizations. The authors demonstrate the approach on waste management reporting duties. This chapter provides guidance for practitioners striving to optimize information flows and reduce redundancies within B2G contacts. As a result, both public administrations and businesses benefit from a more straightforward and cost-efficient provision of public services.

Next, Wen-Jang Jih explores the "Impact of e-CRM on Website Loyalty of a Public Organization's Customers." Web-enabled customer relationship management, or e-CRM, is able to simultaneously achieve the conflicting goals of strategic flexibility and operational efficiency in developing and executing innovative e-commerce marketing strategies. A multi-disciplinary field, involving such areas as marketing, economics, business strategy, information systems, social psychology and consumer behavior, e-CRM strengthens customer relationships via a portfolio of trust-building practices with the support of powerful information technologies. While most literature in e-CRM has examined how firms formulate and implement e-CRM initiatives, there is little information on the overall quality of an e-commerce firm's e-CRM practices from the consumer point of view. This chapter proposes such a consumer-oriented concept, e-CRM value, based on existing e-CRM research, and examines the effect of e-CRM value on website loyalty. An empirical study is conducted to validate the theoretical model. Customers' perceptions of e-CRM value have positive causal effects on their website loyalty. Valuable implications can be derived from this finding for public organizations in managing their customer relationships.

Researchers have attempted to integrate the fields of management and ethics for the past 50 years. Although the moral aspects of knowledge management have been studied, its philosophical attitude has been overshadowed. In "Success of Public Knowledge Management in the Light of the Rossian Ethics," Mehdi Shami Zanjani *et al.* design a philosophical background—in moral philosophy—for public knowledge management. To achieve the research goal, the relationships between human critical success factors of knowledge management and moral duties are discussed. These moral duties are based on the Rossian ethical framework. The authors recommend moral duties to public organizations that try to manage knowledge successfully. The results show that "beneficence" is the most significant to knowledge management success in the public sector. In this chapter, the authors integrate knowledge management with the Rossian ethical framework to increase successful knowledge management in public organizations.

"Challenges Faced by Megacities in the Future" by Ali Assadian and Mostafa Nejati explores the advancement of science, industry, and digital technologies, which has shaped the lives of many people and has encouraged more people to live in cities. Since 2007, the urban population has exceeded the rural, and this amount is estimated to increase up to 60% of world habitants by 2030, according to the United Nations. Considering that these changes in people's lifestyle can create various challenges to society, identifying and managing the potential future challenges is a vital step to ensure a dignified living without conflicts. This chapter studies the challenges that cities and megacities may face in the future and provides solutions to manage and handle them. Reports and statistics from international organizations and the authors' critical analysis have been applied to collect the necessary data. The research findings emphasize the importance of enhanced competitiveness and the quality of life and environment on the development of the city. Moreover, the major infrastructural problems facing cities in the digital world are discussed and the importance of strategic planning and sustainable approach toward resolving urban issues are emphasized.

Effective information systems security management combines technological measures and managerial efforts. Although various technical means have been employed to cope with security threats, human factors have been comparatively neglected. Xin (Robert) Luo *et al.* examine, in "Social Engineering: The Neglected Human Factor for Information Security Management," human factors that can lead to social engineering intrusions. Social engineering is a technique used by malicious attackers to gain access to desired information by exploiting the flaws in human logic known as cognitive biases. Social engineering is a potential threat to information security and should be considered equally important to its technological counterparts. This chapter unveils various social engineering attacks and their leading human factors, and discusses several ways to defend against social engineering: education, training, procedure, and policy. The authors further introduce possible countermeasures for social engineering attacks. Future analysis is also presented.

In Chapter 12, Sathiadev Mahesh develops "A Decision Table for the Cloud Computing Decision in Small Business." An issue facing the manager of a small business is the use of cloud computing to meet the information technology (IT) needs of the firm. These businesses typically have limited in-house IT capabilities and often outsource much of their IT. This chapter discusses this rapidly evolving technology and provides a framework for businesses to decide on harnessing the power of cloud computing. It recommends the appropriate decision based on the way in which IT is currently used in the enterprise and future needs to meet competitive challenges. The potential cost savings, technology insurance from cloud computing, and security risks are discussed and factored into the decision.

The following chapter, "Information Technology and Supply Chain Collaboration: Examining the Contingent Role of Environmental Uncertainty" by Karthik N. S. Iyer, explores the utilization of advanced information technologies (IT) in interfirm collaboration—a thematic element in current IT literature. Although conventional wisdom perceives that IT systems facilitate supply chain collaboration, this chapter provides an alternative perspective. Drawing on resource-based view and contingency fit theory, the study investigates a model of relationships that specify how environmental uncertainty factors influence the nature of the association of two critical but distinctive IT capabilities with collaboration. Findings corroborate the positive association between collaboration and B2B e-commerce and IT analytic capability. However, demand unpredictability enhances the IT analytic capability-collaboration relationship while detracting from the B2B e-commerce-collaboration association. Notably, the study did not find any moderating influence of another critical uncertainty factor, technological turbulence. The findings reveal the complex nature of IT-collaboration relationships and provide managers a framework for understanding the uncertainty contexts under which specific information technologies with various functionalities may be more appropriately leveraged to derive benefits.

Oualid (Walid) Ben Ali and Samar Mouakket follow this with "Integrating OLAP/SOLAP in E-Business Domains: An Empirical Study." E-business domains have been considered killer domains for different data analysis techniques. Most researchers have examined data mining (DM) techniques to analyze the databases behind E-business websites. DM has shown interesting results, but this technique presents some restrictions concerning the content of the database and the level of expertise of the users interpreting the results. In this chapter, the authors show that successful and more sophisticated results can be obtained using other analysis techniques, such as Online Analytical Processing (OLAP) and Spatial OLAP (SOLAP). Thus, the authors propose a framework that fuses or integrates OLAP with SOLAP techniques in an E-business domain to perform easier and more user friendly data analysis (non-spatial and spatial) and improve decision making. In addition, the authors apply the framework to an E-business website related to online job seekers in the United Arab Emirates (UAE). The results can be used effectively by decision makers to make crucial decisions in the job market of the UAE.

In "The Evolution of the Massively Parallel Processing Database in Support of Visual Analytics," Ian A. Willson explores the evolution of the Massively Parallel Processing (MPP) database, focusing on trends of particular relevance to analytics. The dramatic shift of database vendors and leading companies to utilize MPP databases and deploy an Enterprise Data Warehouse (EDW) is presented. The inherent benefits of fresher data, storage efficiency, and most importantly accessibility to analytics are explored. Published industry and vendor metrics are examined that demonstrate substantial and growing cost efficiencies from utilizing MPP databases. The author concludes by reviewing trends toward parallelizing decision support workload into the database, ranging from within database transformations to new statistical and spatial analytic capabilities provided by parallelizing these algorithms to execute directly within the MPP database. These new capabilities present an opportunity for timely and powerful enterprise analytics, providing a substantial competitive advantage to those companies able to leverage this technology to turn data into actionable information, gain valuable new insights, and automate operational decision making.

Sofia Kyratzi and Nickolas S. Sapidis, in "3D Object Modeling Using Sketches," present a new algorithm for constructing a solid model when the given input is only one partial-view sketch (natural sketch). This algorithm is a two-step process, where first a complete (wireframe) sketch is derived, which is then transformed into a 3D polyhedron. The chapter details topological and geometric aspects of the process, as well as the essential "user-interaction" components dealing with cases where the sketch-to-solid problem does not have a unique solution.

In the case of certain applications in which a need exists to visualize and interact with voluminous data sets and complex 3-D geometrical models, the conventional computer interface inhibits key human-computer interaction processes. In "On Volume Based 3D Display Techniques" by Barry G. Blundell, several deficiencies of the standard interface are identified with emphasis on a failure to make optimal use of the complex human sensory systems. Various general forms of interaction modality are outlined together with several types of image space. This provides a basis for brief discussion of emerging creative 3-D display systems with emphasis on computational holography, varifocal techniques, and volumetric systems.

Next, Stephen K. Callaway and Saad M. Alflayyeh present a chapter on "Understanding Critical Distance Learning Issues: Toward a Comprehensive Model Predicting Student Satisfaction." Distance education has been the topic of a substantial amount of research. However, prior studies have shown mixed results when trying to determine if a difference exists in student satisfaction between students in distance courses versus traditional courses. Prior empirical studies have been too narrow in scope, and a more comprehensive model is needed to better explain the factors influencing student satisfaction. Therefore, this chapter includes student demographic factors, comprehensive measures of student motivation, and course format, as well as specific course features included, to fully explain student satisfaction. Structural equation modeling is used to test the model. Results indicate a positive association between demographics and motivation, between motivation and course format, between one demographic factor and course format, between course format and preferred features, between course format and satisfaction, and between course features and satisfaction.

The final chapter, "Organizational Citizenship Behavior of Information System Personnel: The Influence of Leader-Member Exchange" by Tzy-Yuan Chou *et al.,* investigates leader-member exchange (LMX), which represents the quality of interaction between leaders and members of a work unit, such as the information system function within an organization. LMX is expected to improve organizational citizenship behavior, beneficial behaviors not explicitly rewarded, but prior research has failed to establish this link satisfactorily. To determine the influence of LMX in the IS environment, a model is developed based on the background in the IS and management literature that considers LMX an important contributor to job satisfaction and organizational commitment. In turn, organizational commitment influences both work quality and organizational citizenship behaviors in a beneficial way. The model is confirmed with a sample of IS professionals in Taiwan. The results show that effective communication and coordination is crucial between leaders and subordinates at levels within the organization not previously considered.

Chapter 1
Application of an Extended TAM Model for Online Banking Adoption:
A Study at a Gulf-Region University

R. P. Sundarraj
IIT Madras, India

Nick Manochehri
Qatar University, Qatar

ABSTRACT

The understanding of factors leading to the acceptance or rejection of information systems (IS) is important and relevant. Although there have been studies examining the adoption of Internet Banking (IB), research on this topic in the Gulf context and from an IS perspective is lacking, even though societal factors are acknowledged as having an impact on technology adoption. To fill this gap, this paper uses a version of the Technology Acceptance Model (TAM), extended by the compatibility and trust constructs. An empirical study, using students from a large university in the region, validates the research model.

INTRODUCTION

Since the mid-1990s, an increasing number of banks, including those in the Gulf Cooperation Countries (GCC[1]), have expanded to provide their services over the Internet. Internet Banking (IB), also referred to as online banking, is defined as a system in which customers use an Internet browser to conduct various banking transactions (e.g., transferring of funds). The changes by banks have spawned behavioral changes in society as well, in the sense that customers no longer need to visit a bank to undertake routine transactions, owing to anytime, anywhere nature of Internet banking. Sophisticated customers, who are usually the more profitable clients, value this service most (Suh & Han, 2002). As a result, there is evidence of Internet banking obtaining significant adoption in developed and developing countries (Migdadi, 2008).

DOI: 10.4018/978-1-4666-3616-3.ch001

IB adoption in the GCC is facilitated by the upgrading of telecommunication infrastructure, as well as by the changing attitudes of the population—a survey found that almost 20% of the customers are willing to move to another financial institution, if their current bank fails to offer online banking services (Guru et al., 2003). Despite this, there are no studies directly relating to IB-adoption in the region. In addition, even in the non-Gulf context, adaptations of IS theories to study IB-adoption are beginning to emerge (Suh & Han, 2002; Sundarraj & Wu, 2005). Given the IS interface that is part of IB, such theories can help with the identification of the reasons (or antecedents) behind IB adoption.

Information Technology (IT) acceptance research has yielded many competing models, each with different set of acceptance determinants. This research adopts the Technology Acceptance Model (TAM) (Davis, 1989) that has been used to explain individual acceptance in a variety of contexts. TAM is tailored to information Systems (IS) context and has been widely applied to a diverse set of technologies and users within the IS domain (Venkatesh et al., 2003). Based on TAM prior research has extended with a number of constructs; including trust and compatibility (Suh & Han, 2002; Venkatesh et al., 2003). In this research, TAM is extended with two constructs trust and compatibility that has been found to be applicable to the Internet domain. Furthermore, the societal context of this study is in the GCC region which never been considered in prior research of IB. This is particularly significant owing to the knowledge-based financial growth facilitated in the region. The extended TAM model is tested with an empirical survey of students from a large university in the region. Data from the survey is then used to validate the proposed model using statistical analyses.

In the next section, background literature is surveyed and the contributions of this paper are identified. The research model and the resulting hypotheses are discussed, and design of the empirical study is given. The results are then presented. Finally, the implications of this research and the conclusions of the paper, respectively, are given.

CUSTOMER ADOPTION MODELS

One approach to IB is a pure stand-alone model, which is followed mainly by small- and medium-size institutions. The more prevalent offering, as of this writing, is an integrated approach consisting of branch services as well as Internet-based services. IB services have expanded considerably in Saudi Arabia, Qatar, Kuwait and UAE. While all these services indicate the level of importance that banks place on IB, they do not provide any hints concerning customer acceptance. Thus, the remainder of this section surveys models related to technology-adoption.

One model that has been consistently used in adoption-studies is the Technology Acceptance Model (TAM) (Davis, 1989). A short list of application of TAM include: Wu and Wang (2005) for mobile commerce, Kleijnen et al. (2004) for wireless finance, Mallet (2006) for mobile ticketing services, Deane et al. (1998) for log date estimate of ISs, Hung et al. (2003) for Wireless Application Protocol (WAP), Moon and Kim (2001) for WWW usage, and Adamson and Shine (2003) for the banking sector.

In addition to these applications to general IS, studies of IB from an Information Systems (IS) perspective are beginning to emerge (see Suh & Han, 2002; Guru et al., 2003; Migdadi, 2008; Tan & Teo, 2000; Liao et al., 1999; Van Der Heijden, 2004; Teo & Pok, 2003), even though researchers (e.g., Paré, & Elam, 1995) have underlined the importance of studying new information systems.

Suh and Han (2002) modified TAM and introduce the trust construct; however, their model and empirical validation is slightly different from ours research. Sundarraj and Wu (2005) use a parsimonious version of TAM to study IB adoption.

Tan and Teo (2000) and Liao et al. (1999) study usage-intention of IB using an alternate model, namely, the Theory of Planned Behavior (TPB). The first study found that certain attributes of the attitude and perceived behavioral control constructs to be significant to adoption intention. Subjective norm was not significant to intention, and R^2 value for adoption intention was not reported. In Liao et al. (1999), the subjective norm construct did not have adequate reliability. Hence, that construct was not used, but instead, attitude and perceived behavioral control was regressed on adoption intention, and found to be significant. However, R^2 for intention was 0.056.

Contributions

This study differs from the above in a couple of ways.

- First, while Sundarraj and Wu (2005) consider a reduced TAM model, and Suh and Han (2002) extend TAM with the trust construct, this paper differs from both these studies in that it considers both the compatibility and trust constructs within the context of TAM.
- Second, the societal context of the study is different. Previous studies were set in the Far East or North America, but this research is based in the GCC which has not been considered in the literature on IB-adoption. This is especially important on account of the knowledge-based economic growth facilitated in the region.

RESEARCH MODEL AND HYPOTHESES

This section first describes the use of a modified version of TAM as the research model of this paper. This is followed by a very brief description of the hypotheses stemming from the research model.

Research Model

Technology Acceptance Model (TAM)

TAM is relevant to this study[2], because a number of Internet-allied technologies, of which IB is an example, have successfully used TAM or its constructs. These include: Wu & Wang (2005) for mobile-commerce acceptance; Deane et al. (1998) for electronic log-on data of healthcare workers; and Klejnen et al. (2004) for WAP (Wireless Adoption Protocol) adoption in the financial sector.

TAM is a model based on the theory of reasoned action (TRA) (Ajzen, 1985) and consists of six constructs (Davis, 1989): system use, behavioral intention to use, attitude toward using, PU, PEOU and external characteristics. Two constructs, namely external characteristics and actual system use, were introduced to encapsulate observable components of technology adoption. TAM then postulates how external characteristics affect the potential adopter's attitudes and perceptions, leading to the use of the system (Agarwal & Karahanna, 2000). Two relationships borrowed from TRA include the direct effect of behavioral intention on actual system usage, and the direct effect of attitude on behavioral intention.

The two behavioral beliefs introduced by TAM are PEOU and PU. The complexity of a system has a direct effect on PEOU. In turn, PEOU has an effect on attitude; for example, if individuals view a system to be fairly free of effort, effects with regards to using the system will increase. PEOU of a system can also contribute to increased performance; thus, ease of use has a direct effect on PU. PU is also considered to have a positive direct effect on attitude toward the system, as well as on the behavioral intention; that is, when a system delivers useful outcomes, attitude, intention to use and use are all increased. It should be pointed out that for first-time IB users, *intention* indicates whether they would start using an IB system, while for respondents having an IB facility, this indicates whether they would continue to use the system.

While the foregoing discussion shows how TAM can be used as a robust building block for examining IB-adoption, there is also growing evidence of the need to extend it. A number of extensions have been proposed (e.g., Agarwal & Karahanna, 2000; Moon & Kim, 2001; Venkatesh & Davis, 2000; Chau & Hu, 2001; Suh & Han, 2002; Wu & Wang, 2005). Two extensions, as given below, are considered.

Extending with Compatibility

In innovation-diffusion (Rogers, 1995), compatibility refers to whether an innovation is consistent with the needs and past experiences of potential adopters (Moore & Benbasat, 1991). According to Agarwal & Karahanna (1998), compatibility refers to consistency with a person's values, and with existing practices, preferred styles and prior experiences.

Compatibility is one of the characteristics that influences the acceptance of innovation (Moore & Benbasat, 1991; Rogers, 1995; Taylor & Todd, 1995; Straub & Chervany, 1999; Venkatesh & Davis, 2000; Chau & Hu, 2001), and lack of consistency with one's needs can lead to failure; for example, in the mid-1960s, a variety of rice developed by the Rice Research Institute failed to be adopted by rice farmers, since it did not taste the same as previous rice varieties (Rogers, 1995). The importance of compatibility has been observed in the IS domain as well. For example compatibility was one of the critical factors in the use of online learning courses (Wu & Chen, 2005).

Compatibility has also been used along with TAM constructs by a number of researchers (Agarwal & Karahanna, 2000; Chau & Hu, 2001; Venkatesh & Davis 2000; Agarwal & Karahanna, 1998; Wu & Wang, 2005). These studies provide the theoretical grounding to use compatibility in this research. Specific hypothesis relating to compatibility will be put forth in a later section.

Extending with Trust

Trust can be defined as the prediction of confidence on an action, based on what a party knows about another party. According to Zucker (1986), there are three different modes that produce trust: (1) characteristics of parties; (2) prior experiences and (3) institutional guidelines, practices and rules. The characteristics of trust comprise ability, integrity and benevolence (Suh & Han, 2002, 2003; Chau & Hu, 2001; Moore & Benbasat, 1991). Ability refers to the capability of the trustee to deliver on whatever needs to be done, benevolence refers to the trustee wanting to do good, and integrity means whether the trustee will act in good-faith.

Trust is a defining and determining attribute of a relationship, and is considered more important than economic factors such as cheaper price (Gefen et al., 2003). With the global outreach of the Internet, trust has become a crucial construct in technology-adoption studies, because the parties concerned are far away and cannot be verified (Gefen et al., 2003; Suh & Han, 2003; Pavlou, 2003). This is also true of IB, which can be viewed as a type of Internet technology.

Several studies have embedded trust with TAM (Gefen et al., 2003; Jarvenpaa & Todd, 1997; Gefen et al., 2003; Pavlou, 2003; Suh & Han, 2003). Trust was successfully introduced within the TAM framework, in online shopping context, both as a direct antecedent of purchase intention (Gefen et al., 2003), and as a direct antecedent of intended use and PU (Gefen et al., 2003). Pavlou (2003) worked on consumer acceptance of electronic commerce, integrating trust and risk with the technology acceptance model and as an antecedent of intention, PU and PEOU. Jarvenpaa and Todd's (1997) research involving trust dealt with electronic shopping on the Web. In contrast to the above, Suh and Han (2003) considered IB and conducted the impact of customer trust and perception of security control on the acceptance of IB; they concluded that trust has a significant impact on the acceptance of IB. Furthermore, in the initial adoption of online tax, Wu and Chen (2005) worked on an extension of both TAM and TPB with the trust construct, and concluded their model was a comprehensive one to understand behavioral intention.

Based on these studies, trust is introduced into the TAM framework. A summary of the foregoing discussion leads to the research model presented in Figure 1.

Trust and Compatibility. While the model in Figure 1 treats compatibility and trust as independent constructs, it is plausible for one to take the view that if trust is lacking, then compatibility will also be affected. With this perspective, some elements of trust could be viewed as a sub-construct of compatibility. This aspect will be examined empirically later in the paper.

Hypotheses

There is a large body of research that supports the hypotheses stemming from TAM. The studies considered varied systems, including, for example, general office-productivity software (Davis, 1989), specific business software (Venkatesh & Davis, 2000), telemedicine software (Chau & Hu, 2001), and online systems such as IB (Suh & Han, 2002) and online tax systems (Wu & Chen, 2005). Based on these prior research works:

Figure 1. Research Model to Study IB-adoption

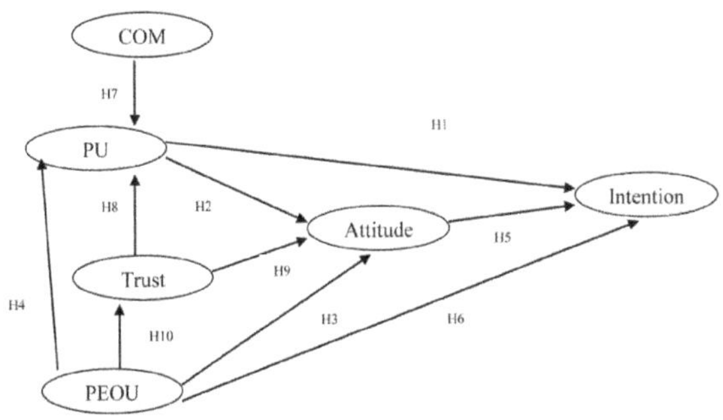

H1: PU has a positive effect on intention to use IB
H2: PU has a positive effect on attitude toward IB
H3: PEOU has a positive effect on attitude toward IB
H4: PEOU has a positive effect on PU
H5: Attitude has a positive effect on intention
H6: PEOU has a positive effect on intention

Comments. First, this paper is based on TAM, since it is a well-tested theory. This way, the application to a new setting would be on firmer foundation. Second, despite the widespread application of the overall explanatory power of TAM, different researchers have reported conflicting results on some of the hypotheses. For example, contrary to the findings of Venkatesh (1999), Chau (2001) did not find PEOU to have a significant on PU and attitude. Thus, it is necessary to know the extent to which specific hypotheses gel with the literature.

As alluded to earlier in this paper, compatibility is a construct stemming from the diffusion of innovation theory proposed in 1983 (Rogers, 1995) and has since then been used in a number of studies related to technology adoption (e.g., Tornatsky & Klein, 1982; Chau & Hu, 2001). Venkatesh and Davis (2000) indirectly used compatibility in extending TAM: they posited that job relevance, output quality and result demonstrability (all of which are related to the compatibility construct used herein) have an impact on PU. Moore and Benbasat (1991) found a strong positive relationship between compatibility and relative advantage, which is considered (see Chau & Hu, 2001) to be similar to PU in the TAM context. Compatibility has been found to influence PU of health care information systems (Chau & Hu, 2001) and online courses (Wu & Wang, 2005). Based on these findings, it can be stated:

H7: Compatibility has a positive effect on PU

Models by Pavlou (2003), Wu and Chen (2005), and Gefen et al. (2003), indicate that trust is an antecedent of PU, especially in an online environment. If consumers trust a system, they will believe it to be useful (Gefen et al., 2003; Wu & Chen, 2005); however, no matter how good an IS appears to be, a lack of trust either in the organization or in the transmission of the transaction negatively impacts the usefulness of the system. In a similar vein, trust can directly influence people's attitude toward the system (Bandura, 1982; Davis, 1989). Therefore:

H8: Trust has a positive effect on PU
H9: Trust has a positive effect on attitude

On the other hand, if users interact with a system and find it to be easy to use, social cognitive theory posits that cognition is improved (Bandura, 1982; Gefen et al., 2003). In turn, cognition-based trust is impacted. Hence:

H10: PEOU has a positive impact on Trust

RESEARCH METHOD

The data for this study was gathered by a questionnaire survey. The next section discusses the survey instrument used, while the following sections deal with the survey administration, descriptive statistics, instrument validity and factor analysis, respectively.

Survey Instrument

The questionnaire used has two sections:

1. Demographic information: including questions on age, gender, educational level, marital status, and whether participants have a bank account and an IB account.
2. Perception questions: Five-point Likert-scale questions pertaining to attitude, intention to use, PU, PEOU, compatibility, subjective norm and perceived behavior control.

The questions for measuring PU, PEOU, attitude and intention are adapted from the TAM literature (e.g., Davis, 1989; Venkatesh & Davis, 2000; Suh & Han, 2003). For trust, two of its characteristics (Mayer, 1995), namely, benevolence, and ability are used. Five questions were used from Suh and Han (2003). Finally, for the compatibility construct, three questions are adapted from Taylor and Todd (1995). Table 1 gives the questions relating to the constructs.

It must be pointed out that one difficulty arises with these questions, because some of the participants may not be familiar with IB features owing to lack of IB experience, while other respondents may have exposure to IB systems. To handle this difference, before administering the survey, a demo of IB features was first provided. Nevertheless, it is possible for the responses to the questions to be biased by a user's prior experience.

Survey Administration and Response Results

A pilot study was first conducted with five people. The pilot was administered to both employees and students of the university. These respondents felt that survey was a little difficult to complete. Based on this feedback, changes were made to the layout of the questionnaire, with a view to improve readability and to reduce the amount of time to answer the survey.

The survey participants were employees and students at a large university in the Gulf region. Participants were informed that the survey was anonymous, participation was entirely voluntary, and response will be secured per confidentiality policy. Overall 220 questionnaires were distributed, and 145 were returned, achieving an overall response rate of over 60%. Among 145 responses, eighteen people missed significant parts of the survey (i.e., perception and/or demographic questions). After excluding these responses, a valid sample of 127 was used for the analysis below.

Table 1. Survey questionnaire used to study internet banking acceptance

Const	Construct/Measure	Mean	S.D.
ATT	1. Using Internet banking is a good idea	4.02	1.054
	2. Using Internet banking system is a wise idea	3.97	.934
	3. Using Internet banking is a pleasant idea	3.90	.919
	4. Using Internet banking is a positive idea	4.11	.779
	5. Using Internet banking is an appealing idea	3.79	.882
Int.	1. I intend to use Internet Banking	3.81	3.81
	2. I expect to use Internet Banking	4.04	.877
	3. I will frequently use Internet Banking	3.75	1.027
	4. I will strongly recommend Internet Banking to others	3.92	.985
Trust	1. Internet Banking systems are trustworthy	3.12	1.136
	2. I trust in the benefits of the decisions of Internet Banking systems	3.72	.925
	3. Internet Banking systems keep the my best interest in mind	3.77	.856
	4. Internet Banking systems would do the job right even if it is not monitored	3.03	1.124
	5. I trust Internet Banking systems	3.28	1.036
PU	1. Using Internet Banking enhances the productivity of my banking activities	3.94	.796
	2. Using Internet banking implies a critical role in supporting my banking activities	3.85	.780
	3. Using Internet banking makes it easier to do my banking activities	4.13	.748
	4. Using Internet Banking enables me to accomplish banking activities more quickly	4.16	.983
	5. I find Internet Banking useful for my banking activities	3.90	.911
PEOU	1. It is easy for me to learn how to utilize Internet Banking	3.87	.975
	2. I will find it easy to get Internet Banking systems to do what I want it to do	4.05	.987
	3. My interaction with Internet Banking systems will be clear and understandable	3.92	.869
	4. I will find Internet banking systems to be easy to use	3.90	.844
COM	1. Using Internet banking fits with the way I perform banking activities	3.84	.830
	2. Using Internet banking does not fit with my banking preferences	3.45	.915
	3. Using Internet banking fits with my service needs.	3.84	.840

Descriptive Statistics

Of the 127 usable responses, 53% were male and 47% were female. Large percentage of participants (74%) were aged under 26 years old while 11% were aged between 26-30, 5% between 31-40 years old, and the remaining 10% were over 40 years old. Furthermore, 8% of participants had high school diploma while 85% were either college students or had Bachelor's degree, and 7% had master's degree or higher. Meanwhile, 71% of participants were single and 26% married. Further, 92% were aware of the existence of IB services. Finally, 74% of participants had a bank account, and 29% of those account holders also used internet banking. Thus, it should be pointed out in this regard that the participants' responses may be biased by the system that they are using.

Descriptive statistics such as mean and standard deviation for the items are in Table 1. In the following section reliability and validity issues are discussed.

Table 2. Cronbach Alphas for instrument items

Variable	Cronbach's Alpha
Trust	.670
PEOU	.730
PU	.759
Attitude	.730

Reliability Analysis

Reliability is a measure of consistency. Reliability analysis gives the properties of measurement scales and the items that make them up. It provides information about the relationship between individual items in the scale, and tests the extent to which a set of questionnaire items accurately measures the same variables. The Cronbach'a Alpha coefficient was used (Hill & Lewicki, 2006). Reliability of Trust, PEOU, PU and Attitude are in Table 2. Since Alpha-values of more than 0.70 are usually considered acceptable in research (Straub, 1989), it can be seen from the table that the items for the attitude, trust, PEOU and PU constructs can be considered to be reliable or close enough to the threshold.

Factor Analysis

Next, factor analysis was conducted for each of the constructs of the model. Principal components analysis with Varimax rotation was used. The results are shown in Table 3, wherein the numbers correspond to the item numbers given in Table 1. All the items of each construct loaded properly.

RESULTS

Four sets of regressions were conducted to test the research model, as described below (See Table 4).

Explaining PU. Regressing the independent variables PEOU, COM and trust on the dependent variable PU yielded an R^2-value of 0.51. This means that 51% of PU's variance is explicable by PEOU, COM and trust. Furthermore, the regression was significant at $p = 0.001$. It can also be seen from the regression coefficients that COM, PEOU and trust all significantly impact PU (hypotheses 4, 7, and 8).

Explaining attitude. This regression used PU, PEOU and trust as independent variables. Results indicate a R^2-value of 0.65, implying that these independent variables explain 65% of the variation in attitude. Standardized coefficients indicate that trust is significant to attitude at $p = 0.004$, to PU at 0.000 and PEOU at 0.004, thereby verifying hypotheses 2, 3 and 9.

Explaining trust. From Table 4, it can be noted that the regression is statistically significant ($p = 0{,}000$) and that hypothesis 10 is satisfied.

Explaining intention. Finally, the regression on Intention, with attitude and PU as the independent variable, was significant ($p = 0{,}000$) and explained 63% of the variation. Hypotheses 1, 5 and 6 were verified at $p = 0.000$.

Trust and compatibility. As indicated earlier, some elements of trust could be a part of compatibility. To assess this, three different regressions were conducted on: (1) a regression with only T1, T2 and T5 questions for trust (T3 and T4 appear

Table 3. Factor Analysis of each of the construct

Items^	Com	PU	PEOU	Trust	Attitude	Intention
1	.802	.790	.716	.729	.595	.839
2	.617	.629	.710	.605	.658	.856
3	.755	.725	.740	.575	.691	.770
4		.688	.816	.565	.814	.802
5		.745		.798	.742	

^ Item numbers for each construct correspond to those in questionnaire table (Table 1)

Table 4. Results of regression analysis

	Dependent Variable	Independent Variables	Coefficients (Significance), Hyp.
1	PU (Adj. R^2 = 0.51, p = 0.000)	COM	0.227 (p = 0.006), H7
		PEOU	0.356 (p = 0.000), H4
		Trust	0.282 (p = 0.001), H8
2	Attitude (Adj. R^2 = 0.65, p = 0.000)	PU	0.497 (p = 0.000), H2
		Trust	0.210 (p = 0.004), H9
		PEOU	0.224 (p = 0.004), H3
3	Trust (Adj. R^2 = 0.30, p = 0.000)	PEOU	0.554 (p = 0.000), H10
4	Intention (Adj. R^2 = 0.66, p = 0.000)	Attitude	0.248 (p = 0.007), H5
		PU	0.423 (p = 0.000), H1
		PEOU	0.249 (p = 0.001), H6

to overlap with COM); (2) a model without trust; and (3) a stepwise regression. The first two regressions yielded a much lower explanatory power, and in the third, the addition of trust provided a significant increase in R^2.

In other words, the model that viewed trust as a sub-construct of compatibility or the one that eliminated the conceptual overlap between trust and compatibility were weaker than the third stepwise-regression model in which trust was added separately. Thus, the empirical results (in the sense of R-squared) indicate that trust is not a sub-construct of compatibility and must be viewed as an independent factor.

IMPLICATIONS

Research Implications. This study used a TAM model extended with the compatibility and trust constructs to study IB adoption. The confirmation of the questionnaire items using reliability and factor analyses affirms that the instruments adapted from prior research (e.g., Agarwal. & Karahanna, 2000; Moon & Kim, 2001; Venkatesh & Davis, 2000; Chau & Hu, 2001; Suh & Han, 2002; Wu & Wang, 2005) can be used.

Consistent with the long-standing TAM literature (e.g., Agarwal & Karahanna, 2000; Moon & Kim, 2001; Venkatesh & Davis, 2000; Chau & Hu, 2001; Suh & Han, 2002; Wu & Wang, 2005), this research found that attitude influences intention, usefulness influences attitude and intention, and ease-of-use influences usefulness. Furthermore, the additional constructs of trust and compatibility have a significant impact on usefulness. Thus, both the extensions to TAM as well as the instruments to assess the model are valid for a relatively new setting—online banking in the GCC region. What is also significant to note from the results is the explanatory power yielded by the model. For example, R^2-value of 0.63 for intention is comparable to that obtained by Wu and Wang (2005) (R^2 = 0.69), and Suh and Han (2002) (R^2-value = 0.65), and is favorable as compared to 0.42 obtained by Chau and Hu (2001) and to 0.52 by Bhattacharjee (2000). This is the case with attitude as well (R^2-value of 0.65, is somewhat lower that Suh and Han's result of 0.75, comparable to Wu and Wang's (2005) 0.59, but much higher compared to 0.01 in Chau and Hu (2001).

Managerial Implications. The survey results showed that a significant proportion of the subjects intend to use online banking: mean for intention questionnaire items is 3.88, as opposed to Chau and Hu (2001) in which the mean was less that 3.5. This augers well for the usage and proliferation of IB in the Gulf region.

The fact that TAM constructs PU and PEOU are significant to adoption implies that IB systems must be made more useful, applicable and user-friendly for customers. In addition, compatibility and trust are used as two antecedent-factors to PU.

Validation of the Com -> PU relationship implies that in order for the system to be considered useful, customers want the system to be relevant to their activities, in addition to it providing appropriate quality and results.

As for trust, the results show that participants have an acceptable level of trust in banking systems, as reflected in the descriptive statistics (mean for trust-items are 3.38). The relationship between trust and PU was validated. Since the conceptual model of trust encompasses benevolence and ability, what this result signifies is that banks might want to be empathetic to customer needs and put together an appropriate system (technology, people and policies) that can deliver on the services, with due regard to security/privacy concerns that are pertinent to online systems.

Implications if the hypotheses are not validated. Notwithstanding the results obtained, it might be possible for some of the hypotheses to be not statistically significant. A general explanation for such phenomena would be that user might consider the particular construct (or relationship) to be not so important, or they could perceive themselves to have a general superior competence with respect to that construct. Explanations of this sort have been adduced in the literature (for example, Chau, 2001). For example, if the trust-PU relationship is not found to be significant, then perhaps participants feel confident about managing their security well; or it could also mean that participants are not aware of the security issues posed by banking systems and therefore do not feel trust to be important. Likewise, if relationship with respect to PEOU is not validated, then may be respondents consider IB to be only mildly useful; as a result, no amount of PEOU can compensate for low usefulness. Alternatively, it could be that IB systems are so easy to use with respect to users' IS competence that PEOU no longer plays a role in determining usage intention

CONCLUSIONS AND LIMITATIONS

This study considered the user-adoption of IB systems. A well-known technology acceptance model was expanded by bringing in two constructs, namely, compatibility (the extent of consistency with users' needs) and trust (the extent to which the user is able to rely on the system). To assess this model, a survey was conducted using students at a university in the GCC region. The results indicate that TAM constructs and hypotheses were verified, and that compatibility and trust are both significant antecedents to the adoption of IB.

The significant points of this study are as follows. First, the research model used has not only considered traditional IS constructs, but also newer ones that are becoming increasingly pertinent to online situations. Second, the results obtained validated this research model, and furthermore, in a societal domain that has not been considered in past studies. Third, a number of GCC countries have been investing heavily into facilitating technology-based services as a way to diversify their economies away from oil-and-gas industries. The user-acceptance found in this study is not only pertinent to the potential for IB in the region, but also speaks, albeit indirectly, about other allied Internet-based services (e.g., e-government) that are advertised and offered in a prominent manner, although there is the need for rigorous validation.

The limitations of this work are as follows. While the theory is grounded in the literature, comparison with other candidate research models would be a useful extension. Models featuring antecedents of the constructs considered herein, as well as models based on other theories (e.g., innovation diffusion) can help explain the reasons for, and variance of, user-acceptance. The second limitation pertains to different aspects of sampling: Using 127 participants for six constructs could pose problems with the analysis. Likewise, the sample demographic (in terms of age and location) is a limitation, even though studies reveal that younger generations are more likely users of

Internet services. Thus, a larger sample drawn from different groups and countries would be a useful extension. Third, since some participants might have IB experience, the responses they provide may be particular to the system they use. Despite some efforts to mitigate this problem, it must be pointed out that the questions may be biased due to a user's prior experience. Fourth, there is research suggesting differences between behavior and intention, and also between self-reported behavior and actual objective behavior. While objective data is hard to obtain and may be unavailable for non-IB users, the lack of objective data is a limitation of this paper. Finally, one could view IB as one of the many technologies of today relevant to the knowledge-based industry. This provides motivation for extensions that determine how the GCC population takes to Internet-based services as a whole (e.g., e-government, etc.).

REFERENCES

Adamson, I., & Shine, J. (2003). Extending the New Technology Acceptance Model to Measure the End User Information Systems Satisfaction in a Mandatory Environment: A Bank's Treasury. *Technology Analysis & Strategic Management*, *15*(4), 441-455.

Agarwal, R., & Karahanna, E. (1998). On The Multi-Dimensional Nature Of Compatibility Beliefs In Technology Acceptance. In *Proceedings of the Annual Meeting of the Diffusion Interest Group in Information Technology (DIGIT),* Tulsa, OK (pp. 1-16). Retrieved May 16, 2008, from http://disc-nt.cba.uh.edu/chin/digit98/first.pdf

Agarwal, R., & Karahanna, E. (2000). Time flies when you're having fun: cognitive absorption and beliefs about information technology usage. *Management Information Systems Quarterly*, *24*(4), 665–694. doi:10.2307/3250951

Ajzen, I. (1985). From Intention to actions: a theory of planned behavior. In Kuhl, J., & Beckmann, J. (Eds.), *Action control: from cognition to behavior* (pp. 11–39). New York: Springer-Verlag. doi:10.1007/978-3-642-69746-3_2

Bandura, A. (1982). Self-efficacy mechanism in human agency. *The American Psychologist*, *37*(2), 122–147. doi:10.1037/0003-066X.37.2.122

Behrens, S., Jamieson, K., Jones, D., & Cranston, M. (2005). *Predicting System Success using the Technology Acceptance Model: A Case Study.* Paper presented at the 16th Australasian Conference on Information Systems Predicting Success using TAM, Sydney, Australia.

Bhattacherjee, A. (2000). Acceptance of e-commerce services: the case of electronic brokerages. *IEEE Transactions on Systems, Man, and Cybernetics. Part A, Systems and Humans*, *20*(4), 411–420. doi:10.1109/3468.852435

Chau, P. Y. K., & Hu, P. J. (2001). Information technology acceptance by individual professionals: a model comparison approach. *Decision Sciences*, *32*(4), 699–717. doi:10.1111/j.1540-5915.2001.tb00978.x

Davis, F. D. (1989). Perceived usefulness, perceived ease of use, and user acceptance of information technology. *Management Information Systems Quarterly*, *13*(3), 319–339. doi:10.2307/249008

Deane, F., Podd, J., & Henderson, R. (1998). Relationship between self-report and log data estimates of information system usage. *Computers in Human Behavior*, *14*(4), 621–636. doi:10.1016/S0747-5632(98)00027-2

Gefen, D., Karahanna, E., & Straub, D. W. (2003). Trust and TAM in online shopping: an integrated model. *Management Information Systems Quarterly*, *27*(1), 51–90.

Guru, B., Shanmugam, B., Alam, N., & Perera, C. (2003). An evaluation of Internet banking sites in Islamic countries. *Journal of Internet Banking and Commerce*, *8*(2), 3–11.

Hill, T., & Lewicki, P. (2006). *Statistics. Method and applications: A comprehensive reference for science, industry and data mining*. Retrieved May 21, 2008, from http://www.statsoft.com/textbook/stathome.html

Hung, S.-Y., Ku, C.-Y., & Chang, C.-M. (2003). Critical factors of WAP services adoption: an empirical study. *Electronic Commerce Research and Applications*, *2*(1), 42–60. doi:10.1016/S1567-4223(03)00008-5

Jarvenpaa, S. L., & Todd, P. A. (1997). Consumer reactions to electronic shopping on the world wide web. *International Journal of Electronic Commerce*, *1*(2), 59–88.

Kleijnen, M., Wetzels, M., & de Ruyter, K. (2004). Consumer acceptance of wireless finance. *Journal of Financial Services Marketing*, *8*(3), 206–217. doi:10.1057/palgrave.fsm.4770120

Liao, S., Shao, Y. P., Wang, H., & Chen, A. (1999). The adoption of virtual banking: an empirical study. *International Journal of Information Management*, *19*(1), 63–74. doi:10.1016/S0268-4012(98)00047-4

Mayer, R. J., Davis, J. H., & Schoorman, F. D. (1995). An integrative model of organizational trust. *Academy of Management Review*, *20*(3), 709–734.

Migdadi, Y. K. A. (2008). Quantitative Evaluation of the Internet Banking Service Encounter's Quality: Comparative Study between Jordan and the UK Retail Banks. *Journal of Internet Banking and Commerce*, *13*(2), 1–8.

Moon, J., & Kim, W. Y. G. (2001). Extending the TAM for World Wide Web Context. *Information & Management*, *38*(4), 217–230. doi:10.1016/S0378-7206(00)00061-6

Moore, G. C., & Benbasat, I. (1991). Development of an Instrument to Measure the Perceptions of Adopting an Information Technology Innovation. *Information Systems Research*, *2*(3), 192–223. doi:10.1287/isre.2.3.192

Paré, G., & Elam, J. J. (1995). Discretionary use of personal computers by knowledge workers: testing of a social psychological theoretical model. *Behaviour & Information Technology*, *14*(4), 215–228. doi:10.1080/01449299508914635

Pavlou, P. A. (2003). Consumer acceptance of electronic commerce: Integrating trust and risk with the technology acceptance model. *International Journal of Electronic Commerce*, *7*(3), 101–131.

Rogers, E. M. (1995). *Diffusion of Innovations* (4th ed.). New York: Free Press.

Straub, D. W. (1989). Validating Instruments in MIS Research. *Management Information Systems Quarterly*, *13*(2), 147–167. doi:10.2307/248922

Suh, B., & Han, I. (2002). Effect of trust on customer acceptance of Internet banking. *Electronic Commerce Research and Applications*, *1*(4), 247–263. doi:10.1016/S1567-4223(02)00017-0

Sundarraj, R. P., & Wu, J. (2005). Using information-systems constructs to study online- and telephone-banking technologies. *Electronic Commerce Research and Applications*, *4*(4), 427–443. doi:10.1016/j.elerap.2004.12.001

Tan, M., & Teo, T. (2000). Factors influencing the adoption of Internet banking. *Journal of the Association for Information Systems*, *1*(5), 1–42.

Taylor, S., & Todd, P. (1995). Understanding information technology usage: A test of competing models. *Information Systems Research*, *6*(2), 144–176. doi:10.1287/isre.6.2.144

Teo, T. S. H., & Pok, S. H. (2003). Adoption of WAP-enabled Mobile Phones Among Internet Users. *Omega*, *31*(6), 483–498. doi:10.1016/j.omega.2003.08.005

Tornatzky, L. G., & Klein, R. J. (1982). Innovation characteristics and innovation adoption-implementation: A meta-analysis of findings. *IEEE Transactions on Engineering Management*, *29*(1), 28–45.

Van Der Heijden, H. (2004). User acceptance of hedonic information systems. *Management Information Systems Quarterly*, *28*(4), 695–704.

Venkatesh, V., & Davis, F. D. (2000). A theoretical extension of the technology acceptance model: Four longitudinal field studies. *Management Science*, *46*(2), 186–204. doi:10.1287/mnsc.46.2.186.11926

Venkatesh, V., Morris, M., Davis, G., & Davis, F. (2003). User Acceptance Of Information Technology: Toward A Unified View. *Management Information Systems Quarterly*, *27*(3), 425–437.

Wu, I. L., & Chen, J. L. (2005). An extension of Trust and TAM model with TPB in the initial adoption of on-line tax: An empirical study. *International Journal of Human-Computer Studies*, *62*(6), 784–808. doi:10.1016/j.ijhcs.2005.03.003

Wu, J.-H., & Wang, S.-C. (2005). What drives mobile commerce? An empirical evaluation of the revised technology acceptance model. *Information & Management*, *42*(5), 719–729. doi:10.1016/j.im.2004.07.001

Zucker, L. G. (1986). Production of trust: institutional source of economic structure, 1840–1920. In Staw, B. M., & Cummings, L. L. (Eds.), *Research in Organizational Behavior* (pp. 53–111). Greenwich, CT: JAI Press.

ENDNOTES

1. Includes Bahrain, Kuwait, Oman, Qatar, Saudi Arabia and UAE.
2. The research model initially featured a comparison between extensions of TAM and TPB. As will be seen, the TPB part was dropped.

This work was previously published in the Information Resources Management Journal, Volume 24, Issue 1, edited by Mehdi Khosrow-Pour, pp. 1-13, copyright 2013 by IGI Publishing (an imprint of IGI Global).

Chapter 2
Visible IT in Credit Unions:
Strategic Advantage and Disadvantage in Two Web Eras

H. James Nelson
Southern Illinois University Carbondale, USA

ABSTRACT

Research indicates that rapidly evolving technology and markets do not provide a first mover strategic advantage but favor the second mover. This paper introduces a third variable: hype. In a time of rapid technology and market evolution, hype overrides the expected results and gives the first mover a strategic advantage. This study examines a homogeneous set of medium-sized information dependent and information-intensive organizations as they implement visible information technology in two eras: during a time of intense hype and during a more normal time where technology has become commonplace. One hundred matched triples of credit unions were examined as they chose to remain offline, implement an informational website, or implement a transactional website during the highly hyped Internet expansion time of 1998 through 2002. One hundred matched pairs of credit unions were then examined during the more normal time from 2003 through 2007. Results indicate that credit unions that embraced the hyped technology gained significant strategic advantage. Second-moving credit unions that waited for the more mature technology survived, whereas the credit unions that did not adopt the technology were at a significant strategic disadvantage.

INTRODUCTION

In a surprisingly short period of time the primary source of economic output in developed countries has evolved from agriculture to manufacturing to services to today's significant shift into an information economy (Karmakar & Apte, 2007). High quality and timely information has always been an important component of economic and social life, and the collection, manipulation, and control of information has been seen as a source of competitive advantage over other organizations (Porter &

DOI: 10.4018/978-1-4666-3616-3.ch002

Millar, 1985). Industries whose primary output is information itself rather than physical goods have risen to dominate the economic landscape.

These industries include banking and credit agencies, security and commodity brokers, insurance carriers, holding and investment offices, business services, legal services, central administrative and government offices, and so on. These information-intensive and information-dependent industries have been major consumers of information technology (IT), traditionally used for process integration and optimization, service bundling, and economies of scale (Nehmzow, 1997). These "inward looking" IT projects were justified solely on the basis of return on investment with direct cost savings and higher productivity (Clemons & Weber, 1990). Far from being a strategic advantage, IT was a strategic necessity. In order to transform IT from a strategic necessity to a strategic advantage a radically new technology and new strategic philosophy needed to be developed. Enter the "outward looking" information technology of the Internet.

The introduction of a new, breakthrough technology carries with it tremendous opportunity. Organizations that can "get there first" and exploit the new technology can achieve and maintain a strategic advantage over later entrants (Porter & Millar, 1985). Organizations that wait and do not adopt the new technology lose market share, are seen as technologically backwards, and risk failure (Tushman & Anderson, 1990).

For the first mover, any new technology also carries with tremendous risk. First movers bear the costs of initial development, user training, and convincing potential customers of the advantages of their product. Second movers can take advantage of significant incremental advancements based on the original innovation. For information technology-driven industries, followers win (Hidding, Wilson, Williams, & Kuncheria, 2008).

Organization management has an important strategic decision to make: gain a strategic advantage by embracing a new technology with substantial risk, or gain a strategic advantage by waiting for superior follow-on technologies. Despite the importance of this decision, academic literature has been unable to provide conclusive empirical evidence to support or refute the existence of first mover or second mover strategic advantage or even of any strategic disadvantage to being a first mover or a second mover (Suarez & Lanzolla, 2007).

This paper is a longitudinal study that examines a set of homogeneous medium-sized information-intensive and information-dependent organizations as they pursue the four possible strategies: adopt (or do not adopt) a new, outward-looking information technology when it is first introduced, or to wait and adopt (or not adopt) the technology after the technology has matured. It addresses the question, is there a first-mover strategic advantage (or disadvantage) or a second mover strategic advantage (or disadvantage)?

BACKGROUND

Credit unions are the cooperative not-for-profit branch of the banking industry. The goal of a credit union is generally not maximizing shareholders' wealth as in the standard theory of the firm, but rather maximizing its members' benefits. The services that credit unions can offer members are limited by federal charter, so credit unions can be easily compared to each other with the vast majority of these services being variations on deposit and loan instruments. In addition, all US credit unions are required by law to report financial results, management actions, and the use of information technology. They are information intensive and are highly dependent on information technology. Their primary operational task is to track the flow and storage of (primarily digital) money to and from its members. With a relatively low level of complexity, highly substitutable business processes, and a high degree of visibility in their usage of IT, credit unions are excellent organizations to examine the of value of information technology.

Hype and the Visible Information System

Information technology has emerged from being an invisible component of organizational infrastructure to being a highly visible service provider as well as a shaper of public opinion about that organization. From early financial and accounting systems to strategic inter-organizational integrated supply chain systems, organizational IT has been invisible to the outside world. While the power of IT and the breadth and depth of information available to the organization has increased exponentially, few outside of the organization's information systems group are excited about these invisible advances. Innovative invisible technology may give an organization a strategic advantage in the long term, but it will not necessarily attract customers.

Today, high-speed telecommunications, personal computers, browsers, the Internet, and the World Wide Web have combined to make an organization's information systems highly visible. The sophistication of an organization's IT is directly reflected in the customer's eye by the sophistication of its website. For better or worse, a slick website implies advanced technology whereas no web presence or a very basic informational website implies a technologically backwards organization.

We propose that information-intensive, information-dependent organizations that adopt a new, visible, and outward-looking technology during a time of hype should experience long-term gains and will experience a strategic advantage over those that do not adopt the technology during the same time. Similar organizations that do not adopt the new technology during more normal times will experience long-term losses and will experience a strategic disadvantage compared to similar organizations that do adopt the same technology. Those adopters may not have a strategic advantage, but they will avoid the strategic disadvantage.

The period from approximately 1998 through 2002 was a time of tremendous excitement about Internet, the World Wide Web, and what being online could do for organizations. Newspapers, magazines, and the popular press drove this excitement with stories of new technologies, new business models, and new capabilities. In this paper, we will refer to the Web period from 1998 through 2002 as the Web *Hype Era*. During the Hype Era it seemed that any company that had anything to do with the Internet experienced tremendous stock growth.

This rapid expansion slowed by the end of 2002 when the Web entered a more measured period. By 2003 it was understood that the Web alone could not bring success, and that a successful Internet strategy included a complete integration of the Web with the organization's backend process. Far from being hype-driven and seeing any company with a Web presence as being highly technologically advanced, the public expected organizations to have at the very least an informational Web presence, and preferred a transactional presence to buy, sell, and transfer goods, services, and finances. In the public's eye, e-commerce changed from being glamorous to being something that is expected. For the purposes of this paper, we will refer to the period from 2003 through 2007 (and continuing to today) as the Web *Normal Era*.

The Visible Technology

We use a four-level classification scheme for this paper: *No-Web* credit unions do not have a Web presence at all. These credit unions may support email or telephone transactions but do not have a website. *Info-Web* credit unions use information-only websites to keep their members close. These sites are primarily used for member convenience and online customer service, giving basic information such as locations and hours of operation. *Trans-Web* credit unions implement the most visible element of e-commerce. These websites allow customers to conduct virtually the same business as they would in a "brick and mortar" organization including electronic bill payment, automated loan applications, electronic funds transfer, online credit applications, and tools for financial and retirement planning.

STRATEGIC ADVANTAGE

With each new technological advance, organizational management must decide whether to adopt the new technology and gain a first mover strategic advantage or to avoid the "bleeding edge" and wait for more advanced follow-on technology. However, empirical research has been unable to unambiguously show whether a first-mover or a second-mover strategic advantage exists (Magnusson, Westjohn, & Boggs, 2009) and has been unable to resolve the conflicting evidence and give managers coherent guidelines for developing their technology strategy.

Suarez and Lanzolla's (2007) first mover advantage theory is based on two environmental enablers of FMA isolating mechanisms: the pace of technology evolution and the pace of market evolution. The pace of technological evolution covers the period of time from the first introduction of the innovative technology into the market to its onset of maturity, identified as the period after commercialization with the emergence of a dominant design and a significant decline in new adoptions of the technology (Agarwal, Sarkar, & Echambadi, 2002). A smooth pace of evolution allows the first mover to establish dominance in a particular area and demonstrate technology leadership. Customers see the advantage and feel safe adopting the technology. Second movers will not have a more advanced technology (as with an abrupt pace of evolution) to use to differentiate their own products that will allow them to capture the advantage.

The pace of market evolution can be measured as number of sales, household penetration, or number of adopters over time from first commercialization of the innovation to an eventual market maturity and decline (Mahajan, Muller, & Bass, 1990). Effects should be most prevalent in slow-growth markets where there is product differentiation based on features and where the number of new customers is relatively limited. Organizations easily enter a fast-paced abrupt market with an abundance of customers, and even with the same technology can successfully compete with the first movers and effectively remove their initial advantage.

When the pace of technological evolution is smooth and the pace of market evolution is smooth, first mover strategic effects are most pronounced. First movers can introduce the technology and capture the market. Later movers will have no new technology and few remaining customers to overcome the first movers' advantage. On the other hand, when the pace of technological evolution is abrupt and the pace of market evolution is abrupt, first mover strategic advantage effects are disabled. Later movers can introduce advances on the technology to a large number of new customers and remove the first movers' advantage or even gain second mover advantage.

It would appear that organizational management has a clear strategy: where technological evolution is smooth and where market evolution is smooth, move first. Where technological evolution is abrupt and where market evolution is abrupt, move second. However, there is a third variable that must be considered: the pace of customer evolution driven by the "hype cycle."

During a time of significant hype, strong positive social influence (such as influential people, the customer's culture, and the "coolness" of the technology) will drive customer evolution to excitedly embrace the new technology. During more normal times the hype and strong social influence will not exist. The technology (for example, having a transactional website) moves from being an exotic technology to something one expects to find in organizations.

By any measure the period between 1997 and 2000 can be characterized as a time of rapidly evolving Internet and World Wide Web technology and as a time of a rapidly evolving Internet marketplace as the technology of the Web and its adoption by organizations moved from virtually nothing to being commonplace. This time should *not* favor first movers as second movers can take advantage of the more advanced technology and a rapidly expanding market. However, we suggest that considerable hype and highly positive social influence will overwhelm the prediction of Suarez and Lanzolla (2007) and will result in a sustainable first mover strategic advantage. During a more normal time of smooth technological and market evolution the lack of hype and the general acceptance of the technology will not necessarily lead to an adopter's strategic advantage, but rather to the non-adopters strategic disadvantage.

H1: Hype Era adopters of visible technology will achieve a strategic advantage.

H2: Normal Era non-adopters will be at a strategic disadvantage.

MEASURES OF STRATEGIC ADVANTAGE

One measure of strategic advantage is the overall efficiency of the organization. Organizations with visible information technology will use their assets in the most efficient way possible to provide the most services and the best services to their customers (Riquelme & Kam, 2007). A more efficient credit union will have lower costs to members, lower interest rates available on loans, and higher interest rates on investments. As information technology in the form of a more advanced website is added to the credit union, the overall efficiency of the conversion of inputs to outputs should increase. Higher-technology CUs in the Hype Era will be more successful and more efficient than the lower-technology CUs. Higher-technology credit unions in the Normal Era should have at their disposal more tools supporting their online operations and better integration between their frontend websites and their backend systems resulting in generally higher efficiencies; lower technology CUs will be at a strategic disadvantage.

H1a: Hype Era adopters with higher levels of visible technology will increase efficiency compared to Hype Era non-adopters.

H2a: Efficiency will be lower for Normal Era non-adopters compared to Normal Era adopters.

A key reason for implementing visible information technology in organizations is to improve customer relations and to attract new customers. Despite the lack of face-to-face contact in what is traditionally a one-on-one service relationship, the excitement of going online during the Hype Era combined with the convenience of round-the-clock banking services from home should result in a strategic advantage for the higher-technology CUs. However, during the Normal Era online banking will have moved from an exotic technology to something that customers expect. Having online banking services will no longer attract new members. However, not having online banking services may significantly discourage new members and may cause existing members to move to another institution. Credit unions without online services will give their customers a strategic disservice.

H1b: Hype Era adopters with higher levels of visible technology will increase membership compared to Hype Era non-adopters.

H2b: Membership will decrease for Normal Era non-adopters compared to Normal Era adopters.

The general "health" of an organization is related to the amount of customer activity in that organization. In a financial institution, customer activity can be determined by the number of deposits and the number of loans per customer. Simply increasing (or even retaining) customers is not enough for an organization to survive and prosper. Transactional websites may not provide any more basic information than an informational website, but they provide higher levels of customer service that are realized as a higher number of deposits and loans per member. Hype Era increased member confidence in high-tech CUs will result in increased deposits allowing the CU to increase the number of loans available. Member activity will increase indicating a healthy and expanding CU. Normal Era low-tech CUs will experience a loss of confidence from their members who reduce their deposits causing the CU to reduce the loans available.

H1c: Hype Era adopters with higher levels of visible technology will have higher customer activity than Hype Era non-adopters.

H2c: Customer activity will be lower for Normal Era non-adopters compared to Normal Era adopters.

It is often assumed that online banking will reduce the number of staff positions needed and will reduce infrastructure costs (Fredriksson, 2005). However, the context in which an organization operates will affect how IT impacts personnel (Zuboff, 1988). There are several theories of the relationship between IT and employees in the banking industry. The first is that increased use of IT will increase overall employee costs due to the need for people with more expensive technical skill sets. The second theory is that increased use of IT will cause lower personnel costs due to "de-skilling" because of either the transfer of knowledge and technical work to the information systems or the replacement of human labor with technology (Winter & Taylor, 1996). An overall reduction in the number of employees may not be seen, and may not even be desirable, in a service-oriented organization (Phil, 1997). Another theory proposes that the effects of IT on employee wages depends on the context of the organization (Zuboff, 1988). More recent studies (Prasad & Harker, 1997) suggest that that there is an interactive effect between IT and bank industry employees, and that increased investment in personnel (and hence higher employee costs) in conjunction with IT investment is related to obtaining higher performance and return from the information system.

The rapid expansion of relatively non-technical new members in the Hype Era will decrease the number of members per employee. In the Normal Era fewer members will be joining and those members will be relatively more technically-literate.

H1d: Hype Era adopters with higher levels of visible technology will decrease the number of customers per employee compared to Hype Era non-adopters.

H2d: The number of customers per employee will increase for Normal Era non-adopters compared to Normal Era adopters.

RESEARCH DESIGN

The NCUA database contains "official" financial data as well as self-reported data. Three months were spent cleaning and verifying the database to ensure that the data was correct. For example, the CUs' website URL addresses were verified, self-reported membership numbers were checked for consistency (membership going from 5,100 to 510 to 5,100 in consecutive reports), numbers of employees were checked (going from 55 to 0 to 54 in consecutive reports), and so on.

The NCUA (National Credit Union Association, an independent federal agency) database contains financial and other data for over 12,000 credit unions. However, many of these CUs had to be excluded from the study in order to achieve a relatively homogeneous population. Hype Era CUs had to be in operation continuously from 1994 through 2002. Normal Era CUs had to be in operation continuously from 1999 through 2007. Then, a CU that merged with another would experience a sharp increase in assets, membership, loans, and other variables that would confound the changes brought about by a CU's technology transition. The NCUA's list of credit union mergers, acquisitions, and conversions was used to exclude merged credit unions.

Finally, CUs with assets under $10 million generally lack the resources to implement sophisticated information systems. Larger credit unions with assets over $100 million have more resources available and will use those resources to implement leading edge technology with extensive online services. This study examines mid-range CUs with assets between $10 million and $100 million. These credit unions have the resources to implement informational or transactional websites (or to remain offline) and are representative of mid-sized information-dependent and information-intensive organizations in general. After filtering the database through these criteria, 3,052 mid-range CUs remained in the Hype Era and 3,116 mid-range CUs remained in the Normal Era.

The study was performed as a retrospective pre-post quasi-experiment (Cook & Campbell, 1979). The design of the study follows that used by Venkatraman and Zaheer (1990). For the Hype Era, selection began with a set of credit unions that had no web presence from 1994 to 1998. This set was then divided into three subsets: those that remained without a web presence (No-Web) through 2002, those that transitioned to an informational website (Info-Web) in 1998 and remained so through 2002, and those that transitioned to a transactional website (Trans-Web, that supported home banking functions such as account transfers, bill and loan payments, merchandise purchases, and electronic cash) in 1998 and remained so through 2002.

Matched Triples, Matched Pairs

One hundred matched triples were randomly selected for the Hype-era study. Each No-Web credit union was matched with an immediately "adjacent" (on assets, members, and employees) Info-Web and Trans-Web credit union. If the No-Web credit union did not have an immediately adjacent Info-Web or Trans-Web credit union, another No-Web was randomly selected.

By 2003 very few credit unions remained that were not online and even fewer remained No-Web by December 2007. Therefore, No-Web credit unions were not considered. One hundred matched pairs of credit unions were created from credit unions that remained Info-Web from 2003 through 2007 and from those credit unions that transitioned to Trans-Web in 2003.

There are two advantages to using matched sets. First, the credit unions all start with nearly identical characteristics and their progress is tracked for three years before they implement the new technologies. This means that any differences in the management of the credit union, use of information technology, membership characteristics, region of the country, or other variables will have three years to emerge before the new information technology is implemented. For example, it can be argued that the higher-technology credit unions had better management than the lower-technology CUs and this better management resulted in their higher performance. However, the effects of the better management will become apparent almost immediately instead of appearing at the point where the new technology is implemented. All credit unions in this study start at the same point, with the matching controlling for influences other than the treatment: the change from No-Web to Info-Web or to Trans-Web in the Hype Era or the change from Info-Web to Trans-Web in the Normal Era.

Second, the economies of scale enjoyed by the very large credit unions are matched in all CU sets. For example, most large credit unions became Trans-Web whereas smaller credit unions remained at No-Web. Matching credit union sizes allows changes in efficiency to be attributed to change in state rather than to the larger credit unions' economy of scale. This process brings IT value into much clearer view.

Efficiency Analysis

This study uses BCC (Banker, Charnes, & Cooper, 1984) input-oriented Data Envelopment Analysis (DEA), a model that uses varying returns to scale that allows different economies of scale to be taken into account in the efficiency calculations. Briefly, DEA is a non-parametric linear programming technique where a set of best practices defines a production frontier where no other observation (called a "decision-making unit," DMU) or combination of observations has as much or more of every output for as little or less of every input (Berger & Humphrey, 1997). The inputs used to generate the outputs are assets and office operations expenses. A credit union's assets include cash, investments, land and building, fixed assets, and "other assets." It is the credit union's total assets less the loans outstanding. The rationale for office expenses as an input variable follows the theory that an increase in information technology will produce a reduction in costs in high-tech companies (Zhu & Kraemer, 2002).

A credit union attempts to maximize the services and benefits to its members (Peterson, 2001). Following Worthington (1999), these benefits are measured as the dollar amount of loans and the dollar amount of deposits generated by its members. These outputs are used as indicators of the overall service to members provided by the credit union.

RESULTS: THE HYPE ERA

The Web Hype Era from 1994 to 2002 is characterized by a great deal of media attention on a new technology followed by a great deal of public excitement and increased expectations about the technology and the organizations that have implemented it. An organization that adopts a new highly visible technology during a Hype Era should gain a strategic advantage over those organizations that do not adopt the technology. The results are shown below in Table 1.

CU Efficiencies

All CU efficiencies increased during the Hype Era as seen in Table 1 (Efficiency). Efficiencies were not statistically significantly different from 1994 where no CUs had any Web presence through 1998 when the CUs selected their online strategies. A statistically significant difference appeared in 1999 as the Trans-Web CUs increased their efficiency over both Info-Web and No-Web CUs. This difference remained and expanded through the end of the period. There was no statistically significant difference in efficiency between the Info-Web and the No-Web CUs. These results support Hypothesis H1a for the highest visible technology CUs with transactional websites but there is no support for Hypothesis H1a for the medium visible technology CUs with only informational websites.

The most efficient Hype Era credit unions (with a DEA efficiency score of 100%) were found in 2002. This indicates that credit unions were relatively less efficient in 1994 compared to the same set of credit unions in 2002. Technology changes such as more efficient and more effective information systems in general "pushed out" the efficiency frontier between 1994 and 2002 for all credit unions during this time period. An examination of the information technology in place (the type of system and system vendor) in the NCUA database indicates a consistent mix and no systematic difference in IT vendor between the three types of CU. The individual CU made the choice of their online presence regardless of their IT vendor. The CUs with the transactional websites had the greatest increase in efficiency indicating that they were strategically better able

Table 1. Web hype era results

Efficiency	1994	1995	1996	1997	1998	1999	2000	2001	2002
No Web	65.70%	64.80%	65.50%	65.70%	66.20%	65.70%	66.10%	67.40%	69.10%
Info Web	66.30%	65.70%	65.90%	66.50%	67.20%	67.90%	68.40%	69.20%	70.70%
Trans Web	67.70%	66.30%	66.80%	67.50%	68.50%	70.30%	71.40%	72.90%	75.10%
no/info	0.891	0.709	0.880	0.798	0.818	0.434	0.424	0.604	0.674
info/trans	0.280	0.662	0.576	0.374	0.283	***0.078**	****0.034**	****0.026**	****0.025**
no/trans	0.260	0.343	0.491	0.277	0.187	****0.012**	*****0.004**	*****0.005**	*****0.003**
Members									
No Web	5,843	6,016	6,064	6,155	6,186	6,248	6,248	6,281	6,326
Info Web	5,901	5,999	6,031	6,293	6,426	6,593	6,742	6,852	6,988
Trans Web	5,872	6,166	6,463	6,657	6,948	7,186	7,478	7,682	7,892
no/info	0.825	0.835	0.738	0.473	0.346	0.187	***0.095**	***0.063**	****0.043**
info/trans	0.883	0.855	0.573	0.786	0.441	0.436	0.316	0.280	0.277
no/trans	0.934	0.716	0.408	0.341	0.116	****0.050**	****0.013**	*****0.007**	*****0.004**
Activity									
No Web	6,347	6,470	6,625	6,644	6,798	6,981	7,247	7,641	7,922
Info Web	6,366	6,469	6,565	6,813	6,973	7,228	7,362	7,810	8,262
Trans Web	6,379	6,702	6,941	7,144	7,567	7,887	8,197	8,724	9,195
no/info	0.858	0.971	0.944	0.703	0.613	0.52	0.736	0.563	0.193
info/trans	0.986	0.505	0.217	0.236	***0.065**	****0.029**	*****0.009**	****0.013**	****0.023**
no/trans	0.841	0.497	0.305	0.124	****0.018**	*****0.005**	*****0.003**	*****0.002**	*****0.001**
Mem/Emp									
No Web	515	518	513	503	500	503	510	505	499
Info Web	514	499	485	476	471	466	463	463	466
Trans Web	515	499	480	466	459	456	448	436	428
no/info	0.902	0.480	0.102	0.204	0.114	0.120	***0.085**	0.111	0.227
info/trans	0.965	0.751	0.720	0.845	0.883	0.706	0.411	***0.092**	****0.042**
no/trans	0.969	0.339	0.101	0.113	***0.068**	***0.064**	****0.014**	*****0.003**	*****0.001**
	Control	Control	Control	Control	Treat	Test	Test	Test	Test

to convert their assets and operations expenses into real services for their customers, resulting in more deposits and more loans.

Credit Union Membership

The Hype Era created a great deal of excitement about online organizations. Nonprofit organizations needing to make their services known can take advantage of this excitement and expand their membership more effectively through their websites than organizations that remain offline. Hypothesis 2 stated that the higher-technology CUs will be able to attract more members than the lower-technology CUs. A one-way ANOVA was performed across the three sets of credit union membership numbers for each year in the Hype Era from 1994 through 2002. A second nonparametric test with two independent samples was performed testing No-Web against Info-Web, Info-Web against Trans-Web, and No-Web against Trans-Web.

There was a statistically significant increase in membership for all three types of Hype Era credit union during the Hype Era. Highly significant increases were found for the Trans-Web CUs and the Info-Web CU, with a marginally significant increase for the No-Web CU. The differences between the strategies became clear in 1999. One year after the online strategy was in place, the Trans-Web CUs had statistically significantly more members than the No-Web CUs. Two years after the online strategy was in place, the Info-Web CUs had significantly more members than the No-Web CUs. There was no statistically significant difference in the number of members between the Info-Web and the Trans-Web CUs during the Hype Era. This indicates that while having a website is effective in recruiting and retaining members, the ability for the member to conduct business with the CU over the Web did not significantly enhance the CU's ability to attract members. A possible cause may be that users during the Hype Era are relatively inexperienced (or they mistrust) online transactions. These results support Hypothesis H1b.

Activity Per Member and CU Health

The success of a CU website is measured not only in the increase in the number of members, but what the members are doing with the credit union through the web. This is "activity," computed as deposits plus loans divided by the number of members. The amount of activity for each member is computed as the dollar amount of deposits and the dollar amount of loans divided by the number of members for each credit union. The results for the Hype Era indicate that activity per member rose each year through 2002 with an overall difference between the three strategies in 1999. Those CUs with transactional websites had significantly more activity than either the No-Web or the Info-Web CUs starting in 1998 and continuing through the end of the Era. There is no significant difference in activity per member between the No-Web and Info-Web CUs. This suggests that the Trans-Web CU not only recruited and retained members (H1b), but that these members performed more higher-value activities in the CU in the form of more loans and more deposits than the No-Web and the Info-Web members. These results support hypothesis H1c.

Members Per Employee

The Number of members per employee is an indicator of the service level that can be provided by the CU to their membership. The lower the number, the more employees are available for each member to handle the non-routine questions. It also indicates that the CU is healthy enough to hire more employees. Theory predicts that the addition of advanced technology can cause the number of employees in an organization to go up or to go down. Routine tasks may be automated allowing the CU to reduce headcount. However, with service rather than profit being the goal of the nonprofit CU, increasing activity may cause the CU to hire more employees to deal with an increasing number of unstructured problems.

Although the number of members increased significantly for all three types of CU during the Hype Era, the number of members per employee remained stable for the No-Web CUs. The number of members per employee decreased significantly for both the Info-Web and the Trans-Web CUs. However, between the three types of CU, the difference in the number of members per employee was statistically significant only for the Trans-Web CUs. Except for a marginally significant difference ($p=0.085$) between the No-Web and the Info-Web CUs in 2000, there was no difference in the number of members per employee for these types of CU. However, in 2000 the Trans-Web CUs had a statistically significantly difference in members per employee from the No-Web CUs and then different from the Info-Web CUs in 2001.

These results support hypothesis H1d and follow the theory (Pinsonneault & Kraemer, 2002) that the Trans-Web CUs would hire additional employees to provide even better service to their members as they deal with more unstructured problems. However, the tasks that the additional employees took on cannot be demonstrated with the data that was collected, so further study is required to determine the actual cause (and the actual effect) of the lower member/employee ratio.

RESULTS: THE NORMAL ERA

The Web Normal Era from 1999 through the present (December 2007 in this study) has none of the hype and excitement about the Internet and Web technology that existed during the Hype Era. During the Normal Era the Web is more or less taken for granted and every organization is expected to have some sort of web presence. By 2007 this is very much the case with very few credit unions being offline, and those that were offline tended to be very small (under $1 mission in assets) or entirely manual in their operation.

One hundred matched pairs of credit unions were studied during the Normal Era. All were online with an informational website in 1999. In 2002 one of the pair chose to implement a transactional website, the other remained with an informational website. The lower-technology (non-adopting) CUs should experience a strategic disadvantage (H2) during the Normal Era as they struggle to provide services to their membership and try to remain a viable organization. The results are shown in Table 2.

Credit Union Efficiency

Data Envelopment Analysis was performed on the 100 matched pairs of CUs. A DMU was created for each CU in each of the 9 years of the Normal Era, so the analysis was performed over 1,800 DMUs. There was no significant difference in efficiencies between the Info-Web and the Trans-Web CUs during the first few years of the Normal Era. However, efficiency changes became evident and statistically significant in 2004, one year following the Trans-Web CUs' conversion and remained significant throughout the rest of the Normal Era. Compared to the efficiency changes found in the Hype Era, the significance did not come from the increased efficiency of the Trans-Web CUs but rather from the decreased efficiencies of the Info-Web CUs. The results support Hypothesis H2a in that there is significant strategic disadvantage for the lower-technology CUs in the Normal Era compared to the higher-technology CUs.

Credit Union Membership

The medium-sized Trans-Web credit unions of the Normal Era modestly increased their membership while the Info-Web CUs lost membership. The difference between the two types of CU became statistically significant in 2007. With the only difference between the two types of credit union being the type of website in use, the results indicate that during the Normal Era the CU members expect online banking services to be available through a transactional website. The expansion of e-commerce during the Hype Era and continuing through the Normal Era has made transactional websites common with a considerable amount of business being transacted through them daily. The Normal Era non-adopting CUs are at a strategic disadvantage, supporting H2b.

Activity Per Member and CU Health

The amount of activity rose for both types of CU during the early part of the Normal Era (See Table 2, Activity). However, by 2005 increases for the Info-Web CUs stopped, leveled out, and became significantly different from the Trans-Web CUs. Activity remained stable for the Info-Web CUs throughout the rest of the period while activity increased steadily for the Trans-Web CUs. While

Table 2. Web normal era results, info web vs. trans-web signficance

Efficiency	1999	2000	2001	2002	2003	2004	2005	2006	2007
Info Web	93.70%	93.00%	92.50%	92.50%	92.70%	92.10%	91.40%	90.20%	89.30%
Trans Web	93.70%	93.20%	93.30%	93.20%	93.40%	93.40%	92.70%	92.70%	92.40%
overall sig	0.995	0.771	0.259	0.347	0.288	****0.045**	*****0.045**	*****0.000**	*****0.000**
Members									
Info Web	5,570	5,670	5,712	5,722	5,739	5,692	5,634	5,457	5,316
Trans Web	5,674	5,800	5,929	5,998	6,103	6,153	6,204	6,294	6,337
sig	0.832	0.680	0.675	0.606	0.511	0.439	0.328	0.156	***0.094**
Activity									
Info Web	6,961	7,074	7,466	7,773	8,071	8,267	8,188	8,135	8,226
Trans Web	7,099	7,267	7,686	7,944	8,292	8,646	8,856	8,951	9,231
sig	0.605	0.468	0.432	0.557	0.467	0.228	****0.034**	****0.012**	*****0.004**
Mem/Emp									
Info Web	484	482	489	483	475	465	458	451	447
Trans Web	488	479	481	473	463	456	445	441	434
sig	0.805	0.868	0.694	0.564	0.544	0.645	0.485	0.609	0.496
	Control	Control	Control	Control	Treat	Test	Test	Test	Test

the Info-Web CUs cannot be considered unhealthy, the lack of growth should be a warning indicator to their management. These results support H2c.

Members Per Employee

The result shown for the Normal Era members per employee analysis (Table 2, Mem/Emp) appears to be straightforward: there is no significant difference between the numbers of members per employee for either the Info-Web or the Trans-Web credit unions. However, put into the context of the actual number of members in the credit union, it tells a very different tale. Normal Era Trans-Web CUs behave much as the Hype Era CUs: Each employee is responsible for fewer members potentially giving the credit union more capability to handle unstructured problems and give more personalized service where needed. The number of members is increasing fairly rapidly, and the number of employees to help those members is increasing even more rapidly. On the other hand, Normal Era Info-Web CUs have a decreasing membership. In order to maintain the same decreasing member to employee ratio as the Trans-Web CUs, the Info-Web CUs must have a workforce that is also decreasing in number. As expected, H2d is not supported in the Normal Era.

DISCUSSION

This paper investigated the effect that "going online" has on medium-sized information-dependent and information-intensive organizations: credit unions during the Web Hype Era and the Web Normal Era. Credit unions are finding themselves in intense competition from commercial banks that have extensive marketing campaigns and who offer many of the same products. Banks often have much greater economies of scale and generally have more resources which allow them to implement the latest information technologies (if they choose to). The primary goal of the credit union is to provide excellent member service and low cost financial products as a non-profit entity.

Rapid customer evolution during the Hype Era overwhelmed the effect of rapid technology and rapid market evolution. Strong positive social influence drove the initial customer evolution and opened a window for first mover credit unions implementing transactional websites to gain a significant advantage over informational websites and non-adopters, and for informational websites to gain a significant advantage over non-adopters. Those credit unions that went online attracted more members and grew larger than those who did not as members "jumped on the bandwagon" of e-commerce hype. The reputation as being technologically advanced persisted and allowed the first movers to continue to grow through 2002.

However, in the Normal Era social influence was not a factor as customers had evolved to being more web-conscious and knowledgeable about e-commerce. Adopters in the Normal Era found that there was an advantage to implementing transactional websites but not so much to attract members and grow, but to avoid disaster as members defected from offline credit unions to financial institutions that could meet their online transactional needs. These later adopters benefitted from rapidly advancing technology and an expanding market, but this could not overcome the first movers' advantage. Adopting the new technology did not create a significant increase in their efficiency, membership, or activity. However, it did allow them to survive. Those credit unions that did not adopt the more advanced technology during the Normal Era found themselves at a considerable strategic disadvantage. Low switching costs made moving easy and customers did so in large numbers, away from offline credit unions.

These results indicate that the level of hype accompanying a new outward-looking technology can determine whether the first mover or the second mover can gain a strategic advantage. In a time of rapid technological evolution and rapid market evolution, a high level of hype favors the first mover. A low level of hype will favor the second mover. During a time of steady technological evolution and steady market evolution as in the Normal Era, the lack of hype allowed the later adopter to survive whereas the non-adopter was at a strategic disadvantage.

As the economy evolves more rapidly to an information economy, information technology advances that directly affect the customer rather than an organization's internal operations will become more important. Each of these will appear with more or less media hype. Organizations must decide to adopt the new technology or wait for the technology to mature. This study may help make this very difficult decision somewhat easier.

REFERENCES

Agarwal, R., Sarkar, M. B., & Echambadi, R. (2002). The Conditioning Effect of Time on Firm Survival: An Industry Life Cycle Approach. *Academy of Management Journal*, *45*, 971–994. doi:10.2307/3069325

Banker, R. D., Charnes, A., & Cooper, W. W. (1984). Some Models for Estimating Technical and Scale Inefficiencies in Data Envelopment Analysis. *Management Science*, *30*(9), 1078–1092. doi:10.1287/mnsc.30.9.1078

Berger, A. N., & Humphrey, D. B. (1997). Efficiency of Financial Institutions: International Survey and Directions for Future Research. *European Journal of Operational Research*, *98*, 175–212. doi:10.1016/S0377-2217(96)00342-6

Clemons, E. K., & Weber, B. W. (1990). Strategic Information Technology Investments: Guidelines for Decision Making. *Journal of Management Information Systems*, *7*(2), 9–28.

Cook, T. D., & Campbell, D. T. (1979). *Quasi-Experimentation: Design and Analysis Issues for Field Settings*. Boston: Houghton-Mifflin.

Fredriksson, O. (2005). *Relationship and Loyalty Attitude Differences Among Swedish Retail Bank Clients: E-banking Versus Branch Office Users*. New York: Free Press.

Hidding, G. J., Wilson, T., Williams, J. R., & Kuncheria, T. (2008). Complementary Resources' Role in First Movers and Followers in I.T. Industries. *Journal of Information Science and Technology*, *5*(3), 3–23.

Karmakar, U. S., & Apte, U. M. (2007). Operations Management in the Information Economy: Information Products, Processes and Chains. *Journal of Operations Management*, *25*(2), 438–453. doi:10.1016/j.jom.2006.11.001

Magnusson, P., Westjohn, S. A., & Boggs, D. J. (2009). Order-of-Entry Effects for Service Firms in Devleoping Markets: An Examination of Multinational Advertising Agencies. *Journal of International Marketing*, *17*(2), 23–41. doi:10.1509/jimk.17.2.23

Mahajan, V., Muller, E., & Bass, F. M. (1990). New Product Diffusion in Marketing: A Review and Directions for Research. *Journal of Marketing*, *54*, 1–26. doi:10.2307/1252170

Nehmzow, C. (1997). The Internet Will Shake Banking's Medieval Foundations. *Journal of Internet Banking and Commerce, 2*.

Peterson, A. H. (2001). Customer Relationship Management. *Credit Union Magazine*, *67*(7), 4a–6a.

Phil, B. (1997). Pennsylvania Professor Touts Personnel Investment. *America's Community Banker, 6*(8).

Pinsonneault, A., & Kraemer, K. L. (2002). Exploring the Role of Information Technology in Organizational Downsizing: A Tale of Two American Cities. *Organization Science*, *13*(2), 191–208. doi:10.1287/orsc.13.2.191.537

Porter, M. E., & Millar, V. E. (1985). How Information Gives You Competitive Advantage. *Harvard Business Review*, 149–174.

Prasad, B., & Harker, P. T. (1997). *Examining the Contribution of Information Technology Toward Productivity and Profitability in U.S. Retail Banking (No. 97-09)*. Philadelphia: The Wharton School, University of Pennsylvania.

Riquelme, H., & Kam, B. H. (2007). Online Converstion Rates Among Australian Financial Institutions: A Qualitative Exploration. *Jouranl of Financial Services Marketing*, *11*(4), 290–300. doi:10.1057/palgrave.fsm.4760047

Suarez, F., & Lanzolla, G. (2007). The Role of Environmental Dynamics in Building a First Mover Advantage Theory. *Academy of Management Review*, *22*(2), 377–392.

Tushman, M., & Anderson, M. L. (1990). Technological Discontinuities and Dominant Designs: A Cyclical Model of Technological Change. *Administrative Science Quarterly*, *35*, 604–633. doi:10.2307/2393511

Venkatraman, N., & Zaheer, A. (1990). Electronic Integration and Strategic Advantage: A Quasi-Experimental Study in the Insurance Industry. *Information Systems Research*, *1*(4), 377–393. doi:10.1287/isre.1.4.377

Winter, S., & Taylor, S. L. (1996). The Role of IT in the Transformation of Work: A Comparison of Post-industrial, Industrial, and Proto-industrial Organization. *Information Systems Research*, *7*(1), 5–22. doi:10.1287/isre.7.1.5

Worthington, A. C. (1999). Measuring Technical Efficiency in Australian Credit Unions. *The Manchester School*, *67*(2), 231–248. doi:10.1111/1467-9957.00144

Zhu, K., & Kraemer, K. L. (2002). E-Commerce Metrics for Net-Enhanced Organizations: Assessing the Value of E-Commerce to Firm Performance in the Manufacturing Sector. *Information Systems Research*, *13*(3), 275–295. doi:10.1287/isre.13.3.275.82

Zuboff, S. (1988). *In the Age of the Smart Machine: The Future of Work and Power*. New York: Basic Books.

This work was previously published in the Information Resources Management Journal, Volume 24, Issue 1, edited by Mehdi Khosrow-Pour, pp. 14-27, copyright 2013 by IGI Publishing (an imprint of IGI Global).

Chapter 3
Governing Information Security: Governance Domains and Decision Rights Allocation Patterns

Yu "Andy" Wu
University of North Texas, USA

Carol Saunders
University of Central Florida, USA

ABSTRACT

Governance of the information security function is critical to effective security. In this paper, the authors present a conceptual model for security governance from the perspective of decision rights allocation. Based on Da Veiga and Eloff's (2007) framework for security governance and two high-level information security documents published by the National Institute of Standards and Technology (NIST), the authors present seven domains of information security governance. For each of the governance domains, they propose a main decision type, using the taxonomy of information technology decisions defined by Weill and Ross (2004). This framework recommends the selection of decision rights allocation patterns that are proper to those decision types to ensure good security decisions. As a result, a balance can be achieved between decisional authority and responsibility for information security.

INTRODUCTION

Increasingly, the advantages of information technology (IT) governance are being recognized. Good IT governance can promote empowerment and control of IT professionals. Decision making authority as an area of IT governance has been examined by some researchers (e.g., Grover, Henry, & Thatcher, 2007; Weill, 2004; Weill & Ross, 2004). However, more scrutiny is needed of the extension of governance concepts to information security. For instance, Grover et al. (2007) do not specifically address security and Weill and Ross (2004) treat "security and risk" simply as a cluster in "IT infrastructure services." This classification reflects the traditional view of information security as a mere technical issue. Fresh considerations of information security call for a more fine-grained treatment of governance of security decisions. In particular, while some decisions have a clear tech-

DOI: 10.4018/978-1-4666-3616-3.ch003

nology orientation, others must address strategic, business-oriented goals. Still others lie somewhere in between. None can be ignored.

To aid the study and practice of information security governance, we propose a conceptual governance framework (Figure 1). It specifically deals with security decision rights and is based on the synthesis of a number of relevant concepts, principles, and taxonomies: (1) The concept of "structures of responsibilities" in information security (Backhouse & Dhillon, 1996); (2) The principle of harmonizing responsibility (accountability) with commensurate decision authority (Grover et al., 2007); (3) The principle of giving decision authority to the organizational unit with the best information for the decision (Galbraith, 1973, 1993; Simon, 1960); (4) A taxonomy of IT decision types (Weill, 2004; Weill & Ross, 2004); (5) A taxonomy of key domains in information security derived from Da Veiga and Eloff (2007) and two high-level information security documents published by the National Institute of Standards and Technology (NIST), SP 800-35 and SP 800-100; and (6) The tested practice of applying patterns to recurrent problems (Schumacher, Fernandez-Buglioni, Hybertson, Buschmann, & Sommerlad, 2006; Weill, 2004; Weill & Ross, 2004).

Figure 1. Information Security Governance Model

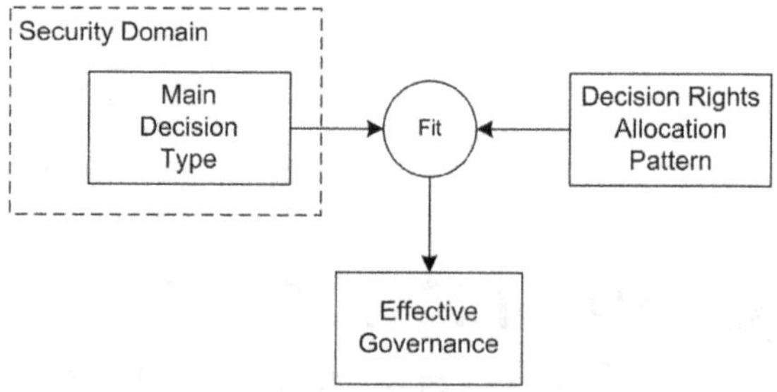

In the following sections, we elaborate on each of these as we build our information security governance framework. Tables 1 and 2 summarize its major components.

Our framework contributes to the IT governance literature by moving from Weill and Ross' (2004) single-facet decision subtype of "security and risk" to a broader range of decision types involved in information security. For the information security literature, our framework connects a now well-established taxonomy of IT decision

Table 1. Weill and Ross (2004) Governance archetypes

Archetype	Decision Rights Allocation Mechanisms	Interaction Pattern Between Business Management and IT Departments
Business monarchy	Senior business executives make IT decisions for the entire enterprise. The IT executive is considered as one voice in the decision making.	Business executives make decisions about IT. The enterprise IT head, the CIO, is an equal partner with other executives.
IT monarchy	IT professionals make the IT decisions.	IT monarchy may be implemented in different flavors, involving IT professionals at enterprise IT function or business unit IT function to variable degrees.
Feudal	Business unit management makes IT decisions.	IT function may implement these decisions at the enterprise or business unit level.
Federal	Both the enterprise and business unit leaders are involved in making IT decisions.	Either enterprise IT function or business unit IT function or both can be involved in decision making.
IT duopoly	Decisions are made by the duo of IT executives and either enterprise business executives or business unit leaders.	This archetype also incarnate in one of these two forms: (a) "Bicycle wheel" with the enterprise IT function sitting at the hub. Sitting at the rim are the business units, each of which forms a spoke together with the hub; or (b) "T" arrangement, with the enterprise IT head having overlapping memberships in an executive committee and an IT committee.
Anarchy	No IT governance.	

Table 2. The domains of information security governance according to Veiga and Eloff (2007), mapped to NIST SP800-35, NIST SP800-100, with recommended governance archetypes from Weill and Ross (2004)

Security Domain	Da Veiga & Eloff (2007) Framework	NIST SP800-35	NIST SP800-100	IT Decision Type	Recommended Weill & Ross (2004) Archetype	Rationale for Recommendation	Major Symptoms of Improper Decision Rights Allocation
Strategy	Strategic	Strategic/ mission	Strategic planning	IT principles	Business Monarchy	Business leaders have knowledge of company's strategies, which security strategy should support. No detailed technical knowledge required.	Security program lacks strategic view and is not aligned with business objectives. Security is afterthought.
Organization	Security management and organization	Organizational	Organizational structure	IT principles	Business Monarchy	Placement of security function requires a holistic and strategic view of the organization.	Security function is improperly situated in the organizational structure, limiting its power and visibility or causing conflict of interests.
Technology	Technology protection and operations	Technical/ architectural	Enterprise architecture, Implementation	IT architecture, IT infrastructure	IT monarchy	Technical know-how is needed for selecting software and hardware security mechanisms and for configuring infrastructural components effectively.	Mis-specification of security and network typologies. Mis-configuration of technologies or infrastructure. Ineffective technical security control.
Policy	Security policies	Policy/ process	Policies and guidance	Business application needs	IT duopoly	Requires ability to analyze technical and security implications of expected behaviors ("how-to") and authority to ensure correct capture of security needs ("why").	Security policies are written based on theory and generic templates. Unenforceable due to misfit with company's business and IT realities.
People	User security management	Personnel	Roles and responsibilities	Business application needs	Federal	Enterprise business leaders set the tone of training. Business unit leaders oversee the accurate capture of training needs. IT professionals also may be needed to develop training programs in house or to assist hired trainers.	Training program does not fit users' needs for security. Users are insufficiently trained, bypass security measures, or do not know how to react properly when security breaches occur.
Monitoring	Security program management		Ongoing monitoring	Business application needs	Business monarchy	Monitoring function's independence is crucial and can be protected by centering monitoring decisions on top executives or board of directors.	Enterprise leaders do not have accurate information about the effectiveness of security program.
Budget	(ROI/metrics under strategic)	Budgetary/ funding		IT investments and prioritization	IT duopoly	Requires financial (quantitative) and qualitative evaluation of business impacts of security investments. Business case has to be presented and debated for rivaling projects.	Under- or over-investment in information security. Waste or insufficiency in human or technical resources for security.

types (Weill, 2004; Weill & Ross, 2004) to the major organizational, human, and technical dimensions of information security. It also extends the concept of matching decision types and authority to the realm of information security.

THE IMPORTANCE OF DECISION RIGHTS ALLOCATION

To truly understand formal and informal behaviors related to information security, organizations must identify their "structures of responsibilities" (Backhouse & Dhillon, 1996). Such structures help to identify the "agents" who can assume responsibility for their actions and take purposive actions to protect information assets. Although Backhouse and Dhillon's (1996) focus is on individuals, the concept of structure of responsibilities can be readily extended to organizational units as agents and used to ensure that all agents' behaviors are in line with secure practices. However, agents should have power commensurate with their responsibilities, including the proper decision rights to search for and take actions that benefit the organization (Aghion & Tirole, 1997; Eldridge, 2007). Proper allocation of decision rights also improves decision quality. Different organizational units are the "natural subdivisions" for different decision types depending on the contexts of the decisions (Simon, 1960). Neither centralized nor decentralized decision making is always a good thing. Instead, "different decisions need to be made in different organizational locations" (Simon, 1960, p. 44) so that decisions are made by the organizational unit that has direct access to the best information for the issue at hand (Galbraith, 1973, 1993). A number of researchers argued that proper allocation of decision rights was the heart of IT governance. For instance, Luftman and Brier (1999) defined IT governance as the degree to which the authority for making IT decisions is defined and shared among management. Sambamurthy and Zmud (2000) were of the view that IT governance defines "the locus of enterprise decision-making authority for IT activities" (p. 105). According to Weill and Vitale (2002), "IT governance describes a firm's overall process for sharing IS decision rights and monitoring the performance of IT investments" (p. 29).

From an organizational perspective, IT governance harmonizes the relationships among four major groups of the organization: top management, business unit, enterprise IT function, and business IT function (Weill & Ross, 2004). The overall goal of governance is to bestow upon each group the decision rights proper to the decision types for which the group is normally expected to shoulder and for which it has the best information. As the result, a balance can be achieved between each group's decisional authority and responsibility.

This balancing act, however, is too complex for a one-size-fits-all solution. Grover et al. (2007) divided the major IT decisions into six categories that were very similar to the Weill-Ross taxonomy. They found that a mismatch between decision authority and responsibility for each decision type contaminated relationships and caused suboptimal outcomes from IT activities (Grover et al., 2007). To achieve a similar level of granularity in our discussion, we deduced seven domains of information security governance from the extant literature and related each of them to one of the IT decision types in the Weill-Ross taxonomy.

IT DECISION TYPES AND DECISION RIGHTS ALLOCATION PATTERNS

Weill and Ross (2004) categorized IT decisions into five major types: IT principles, IT architecture, IT infrastructure, business application needs, and IT investment and prioritization. These five major IT decision types could be identified because they are shared and recurrent organizational decisions. It has become a common practice for organizations to use patterns when they seek effective and efficient solutions to recurrent needs. The concept of patterns arguably has originated in architecture and is widely applied in software development (Schumacher et al., 2006).

In terms of decision-making patterns, Weill and Ross' (2004) study of 256 enterprises showed that high performing companies used an appropriate decision rights allocation pattern for each IT decision type. For instance, duopoly was used by the largest portion (36%) of organizations for decisions related to IT principles; for IT infrastructure decisions, IT monarchy (59%) was the most popular. To draw attention to these decision rights allocation patterns, Weill and Ross (2004) intentionally described them with a set of provocative political archetypes. Table 1 summarizes these archetypes. Business monarchy and feudal archetypes place enterprise executives or business unit heads, respectively, at the helm. With the federal archetype both the business unit and enterprise executives hold decision rights. In contrast, the IT monarchy puts decisions squarely on the shoulders of the IT professionals. In the IT duopoly, decisions are made by both IT executives and business executives, while no IT governance is practiced with anarchy.

The decision rights patterns identified by Weill and Ross (2004) and Grover et al. (2007) were applied to a good variety of IT decisions. In contrast, most security-related patterns have been developed for technical problems. For instance, among the patterns identified by Schumacher et al. (2006), very few were concerned with managerial issues, e.g., the "Enterprise Security and Risk Management" pattern. To the best of our knowledge, no effort has been made to study the effects of decision rights patterns on information security decisions. Therefore, our framework (Figure 1) fills this void by showing the importance of the fit between decision rights allocation patterns and a wide spectrum of key decision types in information security. Later, we will discuss some key typical decision types by relating them to the major domains of security governance.

THE SEVEN DOMAINS OF INFORMATION SECURITY GOVERNANCE

An information security governance framework developed by Da Veiga and Eloff (2007) synthesized a number of information security governance models and proposed six domains of information security. Based on our analyses of two NIST publications, we added one more domain to those six in the Da Veiga and Eloff framework. We also adopted more concise labels for each of the seven domains.

The NIST Special Publications (SP) 800 series contains a number of publications on a variety of topics on information security. Of particular interest are publications that provided a high-level, comprehensive view on information security. We searched the SP series publications that are on the current list at the NIST website (http://csrc.nist.gov/publications/PubsSPs.html) and found four publications that offered a high-level governance perspective: (1) SP 800-100 *Information Security Handbook: A Guide for Managers*; (2) SP 800-35 *Guide to Information Security Services*; (3) SP 800-14 *Generally Accepted Principles and Practices for Security Information Technology Systems*; and (4) SP 800-12 *An Introduction to Computer Security: The NIST Handbook.*

Among these publications, SP 800-35 and SP 800-100 present dimensions of information security at the same abstraction level as Da Veiga and Eloff (2007). SP800-35 suggests that a set of six dimensions should be examined when an organization chooses a provider of information security services. Five of the six dimensions appear as components of the security governance model in SP 800-100. In Table 2, we list the dimensions from SP 800-35 and SP 800-100 alongside those from Da Veiga and Eloff (2007). As the table shows, the dimensions included in the NIST publications and the Da Veiga and Eloff (2007) framework are very similar. The minor differences are easy to resolve:

1. **Security Budget:** NIST SP 800-35 had a distinctive budgetary/funding dimension. Although the Da Veiga-Eloff Framework did not treat it as a stand-alone dimension, it can be found in the ROI/Metrics/Measurement component. Given the mounting costs of protecting information assets, and the increasing practice of applying traditional capital budgeting methodologies to information security (Gordon & Loeb, 2002, 2006), we suggest that this area of security be treated as a distinctive dimension.
2. **Monitoring:** This dimension was present in both the Da Veiga-Eloff Framework and the NIST governance model. It was in fact surprising to see it missing from NIST 800-35 because NIST addressed both internal and external providers of security services. Obviously monitoring is needed to ensure quality work from external service providers. If security services are provided internally, independent monitoring is also a source of assurance (Von Solms, 2005). Therefore, it should be a distinctive dimension as in the Da Veiga-Eloff Framework and the NIST governance model.

Thus, we arrived at seven domains of security governance: Strategy, Organization, Technology, Policy, People, Monitoring, and Budget (for the consideration of succinctness, we adopted the SP 800-35 terminology to a large extent).

MATCHING ARCHETYPES WITH THE GOVERNANCE DOMAINS

In this section, we demonstrate the importance of proper allocation of decision rights in security governance according to the decision type that is dominant within each of the seven governance domains. Specifically, each governance domain tends to relate best to one of the five Weill-Ross decision types. We then propose applying a preferred archetype (decision rights allocation pattern) to decisions in that domain. If an appropriate archetype is generally used for decision-making in that domain, the likelihood is increased that best governance is achieved (See Figure 2 for an overview).

Strategy Domain

The *strategy domain* is the "mission statement" and high-level strategic plan for the organization's information security function (Osborne, 2006). A number of overall goals are possible for an organization's information security efforts, such as protecting customer information confidentiality, complying strictly with regulations, maintaining a security baseline that is above the industry benchmark, preparation for interruption to business activities, etc. (Egan, 2005; Van der Haar & Von Solms, 2003). Organizations differ in their views of the relative importance of each of these goals and how they prioritize the goals (Van der Haar & Von Solms, 2003). In addition, security goals often are at odds with an organization's business goals. Security protection can create diversion of resources from alternative uses that build new capabilities and enhance productivity. They also can introduce new complexities and inflexibilities in resource utilization (Anderson & Choobineh, 2008). Based on its business and technological contexts, an organization determines the level of its commitment to each of the security goals (Van der Haar & Von Solms, 2003). The security goals that receive high levels of commitment signify the organization's utmost concern for security and the strategic aims of its information security program.

For instance, business continuity is an increasingly critical concern as organizations' dependency on IT rises. However, different organizations may assign to it different levels of strategic importance. A lower level may be the result of lower awareness of the risks that disasters may cause to information assets; lack of experience with disasters; resource limitations; and various

Figure 2. Matching governance domain decisions and decision rights allocation patterns

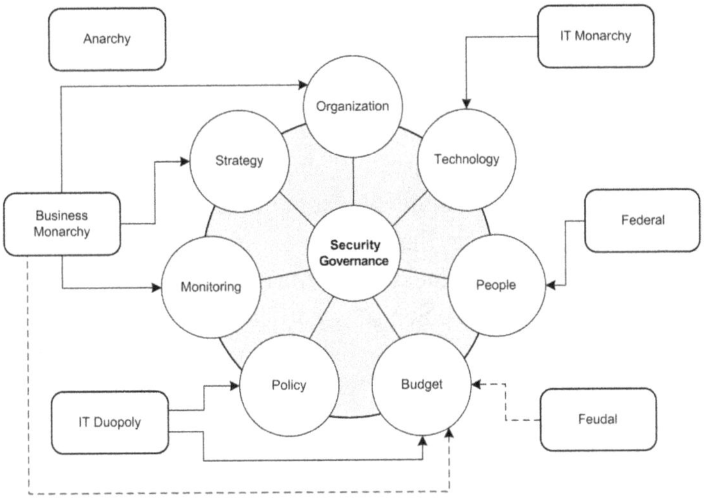

This figure depicts the use of fitting governance archetypes – patterns of allocating decision rights – to domains of information security governance. Because of the nature of decisions in each domain, success is more likely if the organization selects, for the domain, an archetype that optimizes decision quality. The solid arrowed lines demonstrate our recommendations for such match between archetypes and domains. Unique organizational contingencies may necessitate variations. The dashed arrowed lines show two possible alternative archetypes for the budget domain.

other factors. Regardless of the reason, organizations that place lower strategic importance on business continuity become more vulnerable to disasters. When a disaster, such as September 11 or Katrina, does strike, these organizations face more challenges in resuming their business than those who are more strategic with business continuity do (Fonseca & Nobel, 2005; Gibson, 2001, 2006).

Security strategy is hardly a technical decision. It is often defined based on the company's mission, overall strategy, business model, and the demands of its business environment. Johnston and Hale (2009) found that when it is included as part of the organizational planning process, information security can be aligned with other core business assets and processes critical to the success of the firm. Deciding on the security strategy, therefore, requires decision makers who thoroughly understand the company's strategic view and management systems (LeVeque, 2006). Thus, a business monarchy is the best match, in which the top executives set the tone for the company's security. As part of the business monarchy's "ruling class," the CIO directs the reality check of the decided security strategy. If necessary, the IT function can provide the required technical input to support the decision.

Organization Domain

The *organization domain* focuses on information-security related organizational design and reporting structures (Da Veiga & Eloff, 2007). There are a lot of options for the placement of the information security function in the reporting structures and for the title of the person in charge (Fitzgerald, 2007; Kovacich, 2003; Wylder, 2004). To use Weill and Ross' (2004) IT decision type terminology, decisions related to the placement of the security function are "IT Principle" decisions because they serve the purpose of "[c]larifying the business role of IT" (Weill & Ross, 2004, p. 10).

The traditional view on information security is that it is a technical undertaking (Fitzgerald, 2007; Fumy & Sauerbrey, 2006; Maiwald & Sieglein,

2002). Accordingly, in many organizations, the information security function reports to the IT leader such as the CIO. In smaller organizations, the IT staff may even double as the security staff. As IT touches on more and more business processes, organizations' perspectives on information security broaden. The placement possibilities for the information security function are many. A company that sees security in a broader risk-management context may move it outside of the IT function and place it under the risk management chief (Fitzgerald, 2007). Some others have the security function report to the CFO, an arrangement based on the view that the CFO is ultimately responsible for all information assets regardless of how they are processed (Poore, 2007). The security function may be situated under the head for compliance (e.g., general counsel, chief compliance officer) if the organization stresses the legal or regulatory implications of security. Although it is not always possible, the security function may report directly to the CEO – an arrangement bestowing the function the largest scope and highest visibility (Maiwald & Sieglein, 2002). This arrangement may be the result of a strategy that emphasizes the value-adding potential of information security. Regardless of the specific configuration chosen for the reporting relationship, the choice reflects the organization's take on security governance: whether (1) information security is a technology, or (2) information technology is only one arena in which information security plays an important role in the organization (Poore, 2007).

Designing reporting relationships that involve high-level executives is not a trivial issue that business unit or IT leaders can decide alone or even together. High-level executives must be involved. Given the fundamental nature of the placement decisions, business monarchy is the preferred archetype because it fosters a holistic approach to organizational design and paves the path to an arrangement that enables the security function to support, to its fullest capacity, the organization's business strategies.

Technology Domain

The *technology domain* focuses on security-related decisions on IT architecture and infrastructure. *IT architecture* is "the organizing logic for data, applications, and infrastructure, captured in a set of policies, relationships, and technical choices to achieve desired business and technical standardization and integration " (Weill & Ross, 2004, p. 30).

The technical security architecture provides the organizing logic for security infrastructure components and focuses on how an organization's network and security topology is designed. For instance, a widely used security topology is demilitarized zones (DMZs). A DMZ is a buffer between the presumably hostile, public Internet and the organization's internal networks. DMZ design calls for a series of decisions on firewall setup and server configuration. In the larger picture, a DMZ is part of a layered protection architecture whose design involves numerous technical decisions. These decisions require a high level of technical expertise.

Most organizations in the Weill and Ross (2004) study rely on IT monarchy to make decisions on IT architecture. Grover et al. (2007) found that holding top management accountable for IT architecture decisions does not help the relationship between top management and the IT function. IT managers reported that IT architecture decisions are outside top management's expertise or experience. Most of the time, a team of IT professionals from both the headquarters and business units makes architectural decisions.

IT architecture lays down the foundation for building *IT infrastructure*, which is "the shared and reliable services used by multiple applications" (Weill & Ross, 2004, pp. 34-35). Security infrastructure provides protection by arranging security mechanisms according to the security architecture specifications.

The most conspicuous infrastructural components are those directly related to security. Firewalls, intrusion detection systems (IDSs), and encryption devices are the most obvious examples. In addition, many security infrastructure components can be built by hardening existing network infrastructure components and computing platforms. For instance, the primary function of routers and switches is to provide network connectivity. However, they can act as the first line of defense with their security-related configuration such as access lists, virtual local network networks (VLANs), etc. An effective security infrastructure therefore depends on a number of decisions on the selection and configuration of hardware and software technologies. Grover et al. (2007) found that the IT and top managers tended to agree that IT management should be given greater decision rights for IT infrastructure decisions. We suggest that, more specifically, enterprise IT is in the best position for infrastructural decisions. Common objectives for security infrastructure are to achieve consistency in protection, economy of scale, and synergy among the components. For these reasons, the enterprise IT function typically is responsible for managing the dedicated security mechanisms. Also, general IT infrastructure such as enterprise network devices (routers, switches, etc.) is often centrally controlled by the enterprise IT function. Thus, in Simon's terminology, the enterprise IT function is the "natural subdivision" for security infrastructure decisions.

In summary, the preferred archetype for the technology domain is IT monarchy. Having enterprise or business unit leaders make technical architecture decisions would be micromanagement and would not work well because they lack the technical knowledge. IT monarchy fits these decisions well because only IT managers have the technical expertise to design and implement such systems.

Policy Domain

The *policy domain* focuses on security policies, which are statements about management's expectations of the organization's information security program. Security policies range from broad program-wide policies to lower-level policies that control specific security areas (e.g., Internet use, access control, etc.) or individual applications (e.g., payroll systems, telecom systems, etc.) (Peltier, 2004). Supplemented by security standards, guidelines, and procedures, policies encourage standardized employee behaviors where security is concerned (Tudor, 2001). Standardization serves both internal and external goals. Internally, it ensures that behaviors jeopardizing the security of information assets are detected and subjected to disciplinary actions, with a high level of impartiality. Externally, it demonstrates the organization's exercise of due diligence to its stakeholders, thus establishing a basis to avoid litigation (Maiwald & Sieglein, 2002; Tudor, 2001).

A common pitfall in the policy domain is to produce security policies that managers and employees alike ignore. To ensure enforceability, security policies must serve real security needs and be technically viable. They must address not only the "how-to" but also the "why" of the expected behaviors (Hansche, Berti, & Hare, 2004). To establish the "why," a critical first step is to capture correctly users' security requirements. During this process, business users express how they expect the security function to support their business activities. They also provide information about their daily operations so that the risks that those operations may entail can be evaluated.

IT duopoly is a good fit for policy domain decisions because both IT and business leaders' authority and input are needed. IT leaders are needed for the "how-to." With their technical knowledge, they are in a good position to analyze the technical and security implications of user behaviors and business processes. Their judgment can prevent unrealistic business requirements from slipping into the policies. However, the "why" usually comes from the business leaders (Hansche et al., 2004). Enterprise business leaders are needed to maintain a strategic view and to ensure that business units cooperate with security staff in following proper methodologies for requirement extraction, such as the OCTAVE method (Alberts & Dorofee, 2003). In this view, IT duopoly between enterprise IT and business unit leaders is likely the best pattern. It ensures that the resulting policies are flexible enough to cover all essential business requirements and yet are standardized across all business units in terms of how expected behaviors should be carried out.

People Domain

The *people domain* is concerned with user training and awareness to achieve desired user behaviors (Da Veiga & Eloff, 2007). Proper training prevents security risks originating from internal users (Chun, 2007). Also, speedier containment of damage and effective incident response are more likely when users are properly trained (Hansche, 2007).

The people domain typically encompasses decisions with two conflicting objectives – fostering creative solutions and disciplined execution (Weill & Ross, 2004). Information security should foster creative solutions by facing up to the threats and challenges introduced by new business practices and models. On the other hand, organizations must balance enhanced information security against personnel productivity losses and user inconvenience. As security attacks become more sophisticated, obeying security measures to deflect those attacks places increased cognitive demands on users (e.g., long passwords with special characters for system logon) and sacrifices productivity (e.g., the daily chore of scanning emails to spot phishing attempts). The key to striking a delicate balance between security and productivity is the precise capture of business needs for security policies, training, and monitoring.

The preferred decision rights allocation pattern for the people domain is federal because it allows input from top management and business unit managers. For one, a main purpose of awareness and training program is to inform the users throughout the organization of the security policies that are in place (Davis, 2007). To achieve this understanding, enterprise executives' involvement is desirable for executive buy-in and commitment (Hansche, 2007; Tudor, 2001). Top executives may also be involved to prioritize training based on what they perceive as the organization's greatest risks (Hansche, 2007). In addition, business unit leaders are needed to ensure the applicability of training to their units. They are in the best position to describe accurately their units' training needs. Based on these needs, the exact contents and delivery mode of training are determined (Hansche, 2007). A successful training program is one that is customized to fit each type of users and the information systems that support them. It engages users and the training materials are pertinent to the trainees' job duties (Tudor, 2001).

Depending on the degree of technical specificity of the organization's information systems, the federal archetype adopted may or may not include IT professionals in decision making. Organizations with more general-purpose systems may consider outsourcing the training to specialized training providers. Those using internally developed or complex systems, however, may obtain better training results by heavily involving IT professionals inside the organization.

Monitoring Domain

The *monitoring domain* is concerned with assessing the effectiveness of security measures, as well as gathering information about employee compliance with security policies and regulations (Da Veiga & Eloff, 2007; Wylder, 2004). The monitoring information can then be used to improve security measures and internal control processes (Maiwald & Sieglein, 2002). Thus, monitoring is a continuous cycle of testing, reporting, and improvement (Wylder, 2004).

Monitoring usually is performed through security assessments. A security assessment is the process of determining whether the existing information security program adequately addresses the firm's security risks and adapts to business changes (Kairab, 2005; Snedaker, 2006). Depending on the scenario, the scope of assessments can range from focused to comprehensive (Maiwald & Sieglein, 2002): (1) a *vulnerability scan* is a preliminary test of potential vulnerabilities; (2) a *penetration test* takes advantage of vulnerability information discovered in vulnerability scans to penetrate the defense measures; (3) a *risk assessment* is an extensive assessment that evaluates not just technical vulnerabilities but also managerial and operational controls; or (4) an *IT audit* is an intensive assessment that focuses on particular infrastructure components or systems.

Activities in this governance domain also include monitoring employee behaviors for compliance with security policies. This monitoring is achieved by collecting system usage and security compliance information. Information sources can include audit trails from system or application logs, security appliance logs, penetration test results, etc. Management of the information can be assisted by using security information management (SIM) products (Wylder, 2004).

Whereas the policy domain establishes the organization's business needs for information security and the people domain propagates the understanding of those needs throughout the organization, the monitoring domain follows up on how well those needs are fulfilled. Therefore, decisions in this domain are concerned with business application needs. However, the archetypes that Weill and Ross (2004) found typical of business needs decisions, i.e., duopoly or federal archetype, may not work as well as they would with the policy and people domains. Rather, we suggest business monarchy as the best fit for this domain.

In regard to monitoring, one central decision is about who will perform the monitoring activities. Another is how they should report the findings. Other decisions include the staffing level for the monitoring process, the skills of the staff, etc. (Wylder, 2004). When making these decisions, the critical consideration is the independence of the monitoring function, which can be achieved by separating security implementation from compliance checking (Von Solms, 2005). Duopoly is not a proper choice because of the potential conflict of interests, especially in those organizations where the security function also reports to the IT leader such as the CIO. At the very least, a modified version of the duopoly is needed; a security monitoring function may be established independently of the IT function and the modified duopoly is then created between the business executives and the monitoring function.

In the same vein, conflict of interests may also arise if the monitoring function is not independent of business units. Therefore, business monarchy is preferred over the federal archetype, the other archetype Weill and Ross (2004) suggest for business needs decisions. To sum up, top management decisions are crucial for this domain. More specifically, this monarchy can be in the form or an executive committee where the IT, financial, and compliance executives are all members. In fact, most likely, the audit committee of the board of directors is where the decisions are made regarding security monitoring.

Budget Domain

The *budget domain* is concerned with decisions about IT investments in security and the prioritization of security decisions related to risk. The "FUD factor" (fear, uncertainty, and doubt) used to be all that was needed to get top management to invest in security. As information security becomes a routine concern in daily operations, security managers increasingly have to justify their budget requests financially. The CSI Computer Crime and Security Survey (Richardson, 2008) finds that companies are continuing the trend of using financial criteria such as the Net Present Value (NPV) to make decisions about security spending. In 2008, 44% of the respondents used Return on Investment (ROI) analysis; 26% used Net Present Value (NPV); and 23% used Internal Rate of Return (IRR) to evaluate security investments.

Of course, many more evaluation factors are at work. Qualitative cost-benefit assessments often supplement, even substitute for, quantitative financial analytical methods. Organizational units may have competing "wishlists" for security-related purchases that benefit their unique needs. The IT function also should have a significant say in these decisions, as it is in the best position to assess whether and how the investments may fit with the company's current IT infrastructure and application portfolio.

Thus, the preferred governance pattern for investment and prioritization decisions is an IT duopoly. In particular, a good fit is the T-arrangement duopoly pattern, such as an executive committee composed of business executives (the horizontal part of the T) and IT executives and managers (the vertical part of the T). Another possibility involves both the IT steering committee and budget committee, with the CIO having overlapping memberships in both. These committees are the venue where IT and business leaders make their cases for their proposed investments and debate the merits and priorities of the investments. Decisions can then be made in the company's best interest.

In the above subsections, we illustrated the importance of selecting proper decision rights allocation patterns for each domain, based on the primary decision types in the domain. Mismatches can have negative consequences. An example is the state government described by Tudor (2001). The government included 11 agencies and departments and had adopted a feudal archetype for IT infrastructure decisions. This was an obvious mismatch with our framework, which suggests an IT monarchy for infrastructure decisions. Since decisions regarding the infrastructural components were made locally in the 11 departments, duplications abounded; efficiency, cost-effectiveness, and communication suffered; and efficient management of security infrastructure became difficult. Part of Tudor's prescription for this problem called for removing decision rights from inappropriate departments.

IMPLEMENTATION OF ALLOCATION PATTERNS

Above, we discussed the seven domains of information security governance. For each, we suggested a decision rights allocation pattern that fits well with the main decision type in that governance domain. These patterns are not technical solutions. Rather, they are organizational design configurations that tend to produce positive results when applied to the appropriate types of decisions (Weill & Ross, 2004). In view of Weill and Ross' simplistic treatment of security, our aim here is to draw the attention of organizational designers to the multitude of organizational and human domains that information security encompasses in today's complex environments. For organizational designers, each of these patterns is a particular combination of organizational roles and structural arrangements. Also, in the previous section, we singled out and discussed one security domain at a time. However, when implementing a pattern, a designer must consider all germane security and IT domains simultaneously. A pattern may be used for more than one security domain and it may deal with not only security concerns but also other IT areas. An understanding of the information security domains enhances the probability that organizational designers will consciously consider the possible effects that a pattern may have on information security and plan accordingly. This understanding can be formalized by using a language similar to the software pattern lexicon (Coplien, 1998b), which considers the pattern's problem, context, relevant forces, solution, and rationale. Patterns and pattern language have been successfully applied to organizational design (Coplien, 1998a; Janoff, 1998). Below, we provide an example of describing the business monarchy using the pattern lexicon (Figure 3).

Descriptions for other decision rights allocation patterns can be created in a similar fashion. They can serve as guidelines for using decision rights allocation patterns to address security-re-

Figure 3. Decision rights allocation pattern example

PATTERN:
BUSINESS MONARCHY

Problem
How do we maximize the enterprise business leaders' power and influence when they directly make decisions on certain information security matters?

Context
High-level information security issues may have organization-wide impact.

Forces
The enterprise IT department and numerous business units and their IT departments may all vie for limited enterprise resources to address what they believe to be high-priority IT issues, including those related to information security. Their perception of priorities may not fit the enterprise business mission due to any number of reasons, including tunnel vision, parochial interest, etc. Good decisions are what top executives owe their stockholders. Their duty is to maximize the return on assets, including information assets. Failure to do so can cost top executives their jobs. In addition, they may be personally liable for the organization's lack of compliance with governmental regulations.

Solution
As far as information security is concerned, it is recommended that the following areas be considered whenever new arrangements or changes are made to roles of the top-echelon of executives or committees made up of top executives:
1. Ensuring that top executives are aware of their responsibilities for an information security strategy that strongly supports the organizational mission and strategies. If a security strategy is non-existent, they must see to its creation.
2. Any proposed high-level changes that alter the reporting relationships for the information security function must be thoroughly discussed by the top executives. The business impact of such changes, as well as their business and strategic reasons, must be fully analyzed before the changes are approved.
3. The establishment and placement of a security monitoring function must be decided by the top executives collectively. It is also likely that the board will be involved. Top executives should exercise prudence and pay close attention to the integrity of a checks and balances system between the implementers and auditors of information security measures.
4. In general, the value of business monarchy lies in the top executives' bird's eye view of the organization's operations. They should be able to transcend functional tunnel vision and make final calls on priorities and resource allocation.

Rationale
See discussions on the Strategy, Organization, Monitoring, and Budget domains.

lated considerations optimally. Other presentation formats may work equally well, as long as they are put in writing as agreed upon and established before future changes.

DEVIATIONS FROM MATCHING ALLOCATION PATTERNS

The suggested dominant decision type for each governance domain and the proposed matching pattern are not etched in stone. Depending on the organization, the primary decision type for a governance domain may deviate from our suggestions here. Nor is the matching archetype immutable. To take into account each organization's unique context, some deviation is possible from the matching allocation patterns we proposed here. That is, the pattern-domain matching may need to consider various contingencies. Weill and Ross (2004), while linking dominant decision rights allocation patterns to firm performance, admitted that the best arrangement of decision rights depends on factors such as organizational structure, strategic goals, governance experience, size and diversity, and regional and industry differences. Considerable overlap exists between the contingencies identified by Weill and Ross (2004) and by Weber, Otto and Osterle (2009). Based on their study of data governance in six international companies, Weber et al. (2009) proposed the following contingencies for the organizational placement of decision making authority in IT governance: performance strategy, firm size, diversification breadth, organization structure, competitive strategy, and line IT knowledge.

Although Weill and Ross (2004) were focused on contingencies affecting general IT governance, and Weber et al. (2009) on data governance, similar contingencies may impact security decisions as well. For instance, it is easy to imagine that business monarchy governs security investments decisions if an organization's performance strategy emphasizes stringent budget review and control from a purely business or financial perspective. At large enterprises with an organization structure characterized by many relatively independent business units, a federal archetype that involves the corporate center, business unit leaders, and IT leaders may be the proper archetype for business requirement decisions. Alternatively, the corporate culture may render a feudal archetype the only choice. Regardless of the peculiarities of deviations, the key is to stay faithful to the basic tenet of selecting decision rights allocation patterns based on decision types.

LIMITATIONS AND FUTURE RESEARCH

This paper synthesizes a number of sources from security and governance literature to propose a framework for security governance. Our suggestions for allocating decision rights are based on deductions from this literature and findings of previous research. In most cases a mismatch in applying the framework would lead us to hypothesize poorer performance. However, mismatches may be as important to study as cases in which preferred patterns are followed. In some cases contingencies might apply and a company could perform well even though the preferred archetypes were not used. Accordingly, the framework may need to be expanded to take into account critical contingencies. One challenge in doing so is to move from the current approaches of eyeballing fit to one that more systematically tests the multiple aspects of fit that will occur when trying to apply the patterns. Fit models suggested by Venkatraman (1989) and his colleagues could be applied.

A direction for future research related to this framework is to test it empirically. This may take either a qualitative approach such as the action research method in Weber et al. (2009), or a quantitative approach such as a cross-section study using a survey questionnaire. In either case, a decision right matrix (DRM) (Korhonen & Pirttilä, 2003; Weber et al., 2009), also known as a responsibility chart (Galbraith, 1973; McCann & Gilmore, 1983), may be used to measure how decision rights are allocated for each security domain. Participating organizations are asked to gauge the quality of the decisions and effectiveness of information security for each security governance domain. Organizations whose allocation patterns are congruent with our suggestions here and those with deviant patterns can then be compared in terms of decision quality and security effectiveness.

CONCLUSION

Governance patterns have significant implications for organizations when assigning security responsibilities and accountabilities. The taxonomy of decision types lays out a logical way to group key security decisions and to ensure that all important bases are covered. The archetypes define the decision rights allocation patterns of the major players in the organization – enterprise executives, business unit leaders, enterprise IT, business unit IT, etc. By selecting archetypes that are proper to the major decision types in the seven security governance domains, organizational designers put the decisions in the hands of those who are in the best positions to make important security decisions. As the result, a balance can be achieved between decisional authority and responsibility for information security.

REFERENCES

Aghion, P., & Tirole, J. (1997). Formal and real authority in organizations. *The Journal of Political Economy*, *105*(1), 1–29. doi:10.1086/262063

Alberts, C., & Dorofee, A. (2003). *Managing Information Security Risks: The OCTAVE Approach*. Boston: Addison-Wesley.

Anderson, E. E., & Choobineh, J. (2008). Enterprise information security strategies. *Computers & Security*, *27*, 22–29. doi:10.1016/j.cose.2008.03.002

Backhouse, J., & Dhillon, G. (1996). Structures of responsibility and security of information systems. *European Journal of Information Systems*, *5*, 2–9. doi:10.1057/ejis.1996.7

Chun, S. W. (2007). Change that attitude: The ABCs of a persuasive security awareness program. In Tipton, H. F., & Krause, M. (Eds.), *Information Security Management Handbook* (pp. 521–530). Boca Raton, FL: Auerbach Publications. doi:10.1201/9781439833032.ch43

Coplien, J. O. (1998a). A generative development - Process pattern language. In Rising, L. (Ed.), *The Patterns Handbook: Techniques, Strategies, and Applications* (pp. 243–300). Cambridge, UK: Cambridge University Press.

Coplien, J. O. (1998b). Software design patterns: Common questions and answers. In Rising, L. (Ed.), *The Patterns Handbook: Techniques, Strategies, and Applications* (pp. 311–319). Cambridge, UK: Cambridge University Press.

Da Veiga, A., & Eloff, J. H. P. (2007). An information security governance framework. *Information Systems Management, 24*, 361–372. doi:10.1080/10580530701586136

Davis, J. (2007). Overview of an IT corporate security organization. In Tipton, H. F., & Krause, M. (Eds.), *Information Security Management Handbook* (pp. 567–577). Boca Raton, FL: Auerbach Publications. doi:10.1201/9781439833032.ch47

Egan, M. (2005). *The Executive Guide to Information Security: Threats, Challenges, and Solutions*. Indianapolis, IN: Addison-Wesley.

Eldridge, D. (2007). Optimal allocation of decision rights for value-adding in venture capital. *Management Decision, 45*(5), 897–909. doi:10.1108/00251740710753701

Fitzgerald, T. (2007). Information security governance. In Tipton, H. F., & Krause, M. (Eds.), *Information Security Management Handbook* (pp. 15–34). Boca Raton, FL: Auerbach Publications. doi:10.1201/9781439833032.ch2

Fonseca, B., & Nobel, C. (2005, September 19). Katrina's wrath: Gulf coast business take on daunting task of restoring IT operations after storm. *eWeek*, 22-24.

Fumy, W., & Sauerbrey, J. (Eds.). (2006). *Enterprise Security*. Erlangen, Germany: Publicis Corporate Publishing.

Galbraith, J. R. (1973). *Designing Complex Organizations*. Reading, MA: Addison-Wesley.

Galbraith, J. R. (1993). *Competing with Flexible Lateral Organizations* (2nd ed.). Reading, MA: Addison-Wesley.

Gibson, S. (2001, September 17). Terrorism puts nation and human spirit to extreme test. *eWeek*, 1.

Gibson, S. (2006, August 28). Lessaons learned. *eWeek*, 20-23.

Gordon, L. A., & Loeb, M. P. (2002). Return on information security investments: Myths vs. reality. *Strategic Finance, 11*, 26–31.

Gordon, L. A., & Loeb, M. P. (2006). Budgeting process for information security expenditures. *Communications of the ACM, 49*(1), 121–125. doi:10.1145/1107458.1107465

Grover, V., Henry, R. M., & Thatcher, J. B. (2007). Fix IT-business relationships through better decision rights. *Communications of the ACM, 50*(12), 80–86. doi:10.1145/1323688.1323699

Hansche, S. D. (2007). Making security awareness happen. In Tipton, H. F., & Krause, M. (Eds.), *Information Security Management Handbook* (pp. 541–553). Boca Raton, FL: Auerbach Publications. doi:10.1201/9781439833032.ch45

Hansche, S. D., Berti, J., & Hare, C. (2004). *Official (ISC)² Guide to the CISSP Exam*. Boca Raton, FL: Auerbach Publications.

Janoff, N. (1998). Organizational patterns at AG Communication Systems. In Rising, L. (Ed.), *The Patterns Handbook: Techniques, Strategies, and Applications* (pp. 131–140). Cambridge, UK: Cambridge University Press.

Johnston, A. C., & Hale, R. (2009). Improved security through information security governance. *Communications of the ACM, 52*(1), 126–129. doi:10.1145/1435417.1435446

Kairab, S. (2005). *A Practical Guide to Security Assessments*. Boca Raton, FL: Auerbach Publications.

Korhonen, K., & Pirttilä, T. (2003). Cross-functional decision0making in improving inventory management decision procedures. *International Journal of Production Economics, 81*, 195–203. doi:10.1016/S0925-5273(02)00286-4

Kovacich, G. L. (2003). *The Information Systems Security Officer's Guide: Establishing and Managing an Information Protection Program*. Woburn, MA: Butterworth-Heinemann.

LeVeque, V. (2006). *Information Security: A Strategic Approach*. Hoboken, NJ: Wiley-Interscience.

Luftman, J., & Brier, T. (1999). Achieving and sustaining business-IT alignment. *California Management Review, 42*(1), 109–122.

Maiwald, E., & Sieglein, W. (2002). *Security Planning and Disaster Recovery*. Berkeley, CA: McGraw-Hill/Osborne.

McCann, J. E., & Gilmore, T. N. (1983). Diagnosing organizational decision making through responsibility charting. *Sloan Management Review, 24*(2), 3–15.

Osborne, M. (2006). *How to Cheat at Managing Information Security*. Rockland, MA: Syngress Publishing.

Peltier, T. R. (2004). *Information Security Policies and Procedures: A Practitioner's Reference* (2nd ed.). Boca Raton, FL: Auerbach Publications. doi:10.1201/9780203488737

Poore, R. S. (2007). Information security governance. In Tipton, H. F., & Krause, M. (Eds.), *Information Security Management Handbook* (pp. 89–94). Boca Raton, FL: Auerbach Publications. doi:10.1201/9781439833032.ch8

Richardson, R. (2008). *CSI Computer Crime and Security Survey*. San Francisco: Computer Security Institute.

Sambamurthy, V., & Zmud, R. W. (2000). The organizing logic for an enterprise's IT activities in the digital era - A prognosis of practice and a call for research. *Information Systems Research, 11*(2), 105–114. doi:10.1287/isre.11.2.105.11780

Schumacher, M., Fernandez-Buglioni, E., Hybertson, D., Buschmann, F., & Sommerlad, P. (2006). *Security Patterns*. Chichester, UK: John Wiley & Sons.

Simon, H. A. (1960). *The New Science of Management Decision*. New York: Harper & Brothers Publishers.

Snedaker, S. (2006). *IT Security Project Management Handbook*. Rockland, MA: Syngress.

Tudor, J. K. (2001). *Information Security Architecture*. Boca Raton, FL: Auerbach Publications.

Van der Haar, H., & Von Solms, R. (2003). A model for deriving information security control attribute profiles. *Computers & Security, 22*(3), 233–244. doi:10.1016/S0167-4048(03)00311-0

Venkatraman, N. (1989). The concept of fit in strategy research: Toward verbal and statistical correspondence. *Academy of Management Review, 14*(3), 423–444. doi:10.2307/258177

Von Solms, B. (2005). Information security governance - Compliance management vs operational management. *Computers & Security, 21*(4), 356–371.

Weber, K., Otto, B., & Österle, H. (2009). One size does not fit all - A contigency approach to data governance. *ACM Journal of Data and Information Quality, 1*(1), 4:1-4:27.

Weill, P. (2004). Don't jut lead, govern: How top-performing firms govern IT. *MIS Quarterly Executive*, *3*(1), 1–17.

Weill, P., & Ross, J. W. (2004). *IT Governance: How Top Performers Manage IT Decision Rights for Superior Results*. Boston: Harvard Business School Press.

Weill, P., & Vitale, M. (2002). What IT infrastructural capabilities are needed to implement e-business models. *MISQ Executive*, *1*(1), 17–34.

Wylder, J. (2004). *Strategic Information Security*. Boca Raton, FL: Auerbach Publications.

This work was previously published in the Information Resources Management Journal, Volume 24, Issue 1, edited by Mehdi Khosrow-Pour, pp. 28-45, copyright 2013 by IGI Publishing (an imprint of IGI Global).

Chapter 4
Antecedents to Job Success in Business Process Management:
A Comparison of Two Models

Richard J. Goeke
Widener University, USA

Yvonne L. Antonucci
Widener University, USA

ABSTRACT

Business Process Management (BPM) maximizes firm performance by transforming isolated functional activities into streamlined, cross-functional processes. Being a relatively new discipline, disagreement exists regarding the position structure and qualifications required for success. However, certain individual differences have been associated with job performance, both in general and for specific occupations. Because BPM initiatives can be expensive and risky, understanding these individual differences may help practitioners improve their chances for BPM job success. Two models of job performance have dominated organizational research; one argues that personality traits are the chief determinants, while the other argues that intelligence and experience are most important. This paper uses logistic regression to examine the efficacy of each model in predicting job performance among BPM professionals. Results indicate that intelligence, conscientiousness, and openness to experience are the most important differentiators of BPM job performance.

INTRODUCTION

Over the past several years, interest in Business Process Management (BPM) has risen, as nearly 80% of mid- and large-size companies have implemented some type of BPM effort (Towers & Schurter, 2005). Organizations have long recognized the importance of managing and optimizing corporate components such as people, technology, strategy, structure, and tasks. However, prior efforts to optimize business processes focused on functional process automation, using information technology as the catalyst (Davenport & Short, 1990; Hammer, 1990). Such efforts often had

DOI: 10.4018/978-1-4666-3616-3.ch004

little effect on the firm's competitive position, because the end-to-end, cross-functional linkages important to customer satisfaction and retention remained incomplete (Hung, 2006). The focus on BPM, as the key to the coordination, optimization, and predictability of these components, is quickly evolving as the premier 21st century management practice (Hung, 2006).

Since BPM has evolved into a management discipline that treats business processes as assets to be designed, utilized, and valued, BPM initiatives often become complex, expensive, and time-consuming endeavors (Hammer, 2007). A BPM initiative is defined as any effort to improve organizational performance that takes a holistic, cross-functional view of processes, is guided by strategic imperative, and is enabled by information technology (Hung, 2006). For example, one BPM initiative at Wyeth Pharmaceuticals (now Pfizer) sought to improve the process by which products were delivered to customers. Backed by executive management and sponsored by business units, the initiative involved defining, mapping, and standardizing all processes affecting product delivery. Business managers, operations managers, and technologists across multiple departments integrated their enterprise systems with the revised, standardized business processes, which were aligned with business strategies. The initiative spanned several years, and resulted in substantially more effective and efficient product delivery (Antonucci, Boykin, & Donahue, 2009).

BPM initiatives typically require a variety of knowledge sets, including scientific management, Value Chain, Six Sigma and Lean, along with extensive experience and expertise with the firm's own processes, capabilities, and limitations (Paim, Caulliraux, & Cardoso, 2008). Not surprisingly, organizations have expressed difficulty finding individuals qualified to lead and implement their BPM initiatives (Hill, Sinur, Flint, & Melenovsky, 2006). Therefore, staffing BPM positions with the appropriate leaders and professionals is all the more critical.

Industrial and applied psychologists have long studied the individual differences that correlate with job success. In particular, two schools of thought have emerged. The first model concerns the individual's personality, as certain personality traits are thought to lead to or be counter-productive toward job performance (Barrick & Mount, 1991). The second model argues that an individual's intelligence (or GMA – general mental aptitude) and experience are the prime determinants of job performance (Schmidt & Hunter, 1998; Schmidt, Hunter, Outerbridge, & Goff, 1988). However, measuring either model's constructs in field settings has historically been problematic.

From the respondent's perspective, taking personality and intelligence tests can be time consuming. For example, personality tests can exceed 180 items (Cattell, Cattell, & Cattell, 1993), and intelligence tests are nearly as long (Wechsler, 1997). To the extent that survey length has an inverse relationship with response rate and sample size (Sivo, Saunders, Quing, & Jiang, 2006), a survey with over 300 items would be problematic in field settings. Moreover, the mere collection of personality and intelligence data raises privacy and security issues. For example, development of the model describing the effect of intelligence on job performance relied on military datasets, because comparable data from civilian settings was not available (Schmidt, Hunter, & Outerbridge, 1986).

To overcome these problems, researchers have validated the use of personality "markers" (one word descriptors for personality traits, described later), and the perceptions of outsiders. Outsiders, such as coworkers, managers, and direct reports, have been found to provide reliable and valid assessments of an individual's personality traits, especially as it pertains to job performance. For example, supervisor, coworker, and customer perceptions of sales representative personality traits have been shown to be valid predictors of the sales representatives' job performance (Mount, Barrick, & Strauss, 1994). In addition, managerial perceptions of applicant intelligence and personality are valid predictors of subsequent hirability and productivity (Dunn, Mount, Barrick, & Ones, 1995). Both studies support the notion that outside observers have accurate perceptions about what characteristics are and are not related to job performance (Dunn et al., 1995, p. 506; Mount et al., 1994, p. 273).

The present study measures the impact that both models – personality and intelligence and experience – have on job performance in BPM, by considering the perceptions of outsiders such as coworkers, managers, and direct reports (Dunn et al., 1995; Mount et al., 1994). As such, the present study uses terminology consistent with Dunn et al. (1995) and Mount et al. (1994), by referring to personality and knowledge traits without the word "perceived", since the word "perceived" is implied. These results should be of interest to researchers who desire to understand which model is more robust, especially within the context of a newer discipline. For managers, these results should help address this acute problem in BPM staffing, by defining the individual characteristics that lead to BPM job success.

LITERATURE REVIEW

BPM Background

While the concepts of BPM have been in existence for some time, the application and operations of BPM practices have evolved over time. Historically, organizations improved efficiency by managing their various internal functions and specialties (Taylor, 1911). Deming (1986) introduced the notion of quality and continuous improvement, which was especially effective at improving the production and operations functions. This was followed by business process reengineering (BPR), which introduced process orientation in the form of a one-time reengineering initiative (Davenport, 1993; Davenport & Short, 1990; Hammer, 1990; Hammer & Champy, 1993). The mere focus on process automation, without including cross-functional integration and alignment with overall business strategy, invoked a reconsideration of BPR methods (Grover, Jeong, Kettinger, & Teng, 1995; Kettinger, Teng, & Guha, 1997). Today, the emphasis of BPM includes the integration of business and information technology, such that processes are streamlined and coordinated across functions, and are in accord with business strategy (Hung, 2006). In other words, the goal of BPM is to create a process-centric, customer-focused organization that integrates management, people, process, and technology for both operational and strategic improvement (Fingar, 2006; Harmon, 2004; Hill et al., 2006; Melenovsky, 2005; Rosemann, deBruin, & Power, 2006; Smith & Fingar, 2002).

The successful implementation of many BPM initiatives has been challenging, involving many stages and organizational components (Ravesteyn, Batenburg, & deWaal, 2008; Rosemann & deBruin, 2005). Research has addressed the technology needs of BPM success (Spanyi, 2006), and identified new roles and tasks required among those individuals involved in BPM implementations (Melenovsky & Hill, 2006; Paim et al., 2008). Recent research has also proposed that certain employee attributes, competencies, and traits contribute to BPM success (Rosemann & deBruin, 2005). For example, Ravestyn et al. (2008) suggested that employee knowledge, skills, and attitudes lead to BPM success. Eicker et al. (2008) proposed that individual differences in personality (e.g. determination, assertiveness, and leadership) along with intellect lead to BPM success. However, there has been no empirical research into the individual differences that lead to BPM success. Given that people are the most critical component in any BPM initiative, and that BPM has a high failure rate (Hammer, 2007), it is imperative that individual differences be studied and documented. To address this gap in the literature, the present study analyzed the effects that personality and intelligence differences have on BPM job performance.

Job Performance and Personality

Conventional wisdom suggests that personality is an important differentiator of job performance. Indeed, many would argue that personality is *the* differentiator between job success and failure (c.f., Schmidt & Hunter, 2004), as there are many examples in which a personality conflict or lack of motivation have derailed advancement (Spreier, Fontaine, & Malloy, 2006). But conventional wisdom aside, research into the effect of personality on job performance had been hindered by the lack of consistency in defining personality. Starting in the 1980s, however, psychologists found increasing evidence that personality traits converged around five dimensions (Conley, 1985; Goldberg, 1981). This personality taxonomy became known as the Five Factor Model (or "Big Five") (Barrick & Mount, 1991; Goldberg, 1990), and has proven to be one of the most useful models in personality research (Briggs, 1992). The traits commonly associated with the Big Five are conscientiousness, extraversion, emotional stability, agreeableness, and openness to experience. The effect that each trait is expected to have on BPM job performance is discussed in the next section.

Conscientiousness

Conscientiousness refers to an intrinsic motivation to achieve and perform at a high level (Deveraj, Easley, & Crant, 2008). Additional adjectives of conscientiousness include dependability, being careful, thorough, responsible, and organized (Barrick & Mount, 1991). Conscientious individuals are described as being disciplined, diligent, methodical, and purposeful (Barrick, Mount, & Gupta, 2003). With such a natural association to elevated performance, it is not surprising that conscientiousness has had a positive effect on job performance across a wide range of occupational groups, including professionals (engineers, architects, attorneys, accountants, teachers, doctors and ministers), police, managers (ranging from foreman to top executives), and skilled/semi-skilled workers (including clerical, farmers, medical assistants, assemblers, truck drivers, and production workers) (Barrick & Mount, 1991). Indeed, it is difficult to conceive of any job where conscientiousness would not associate with performance and success (Barrick & Mount, 1991; Barrick, Mount, & Judge, 2001).

With regard to BPM, conscientiousness is expected to positively relate to job performance. Conscientiousness has been positively associated with job performance in professional and managerial positions (Barrick & Mount, 1991; Barrick et al., 2001), and thorough research into a problem, assessing available alternatives, being organized, dependable, and seeing a situation through to completion, would all be beneficial for BPM initiatives as well. Therefore, conscientiousness is expected to have a positive association with an individual's BPM performance.

Proposition 1a: Conscientiousness will be positively associated with BPM job performance.

Extraversion

Extraversion, also known as surgency, includes traits such as being sociable, gregarious, assertive, talkative, and active (Barrick & Mount, 1991). Individuals high in extraversion are also outgoing and place high value on interpersonal relationships (Watson & Clark, 1997). Extraversion is positively related to job performance in occupations that involve interacting with others, especially when trying to influence others and obtain status (Barrick et al., 2001), and is positively correlated with job performance in sales and management positions (Barrick & Mount, 1991). Extraversion has also been found to be the most important predictor of leadership (Judge, Bono, Ilies, & Gerhardt, 2002), as individuals emerging as leaders tend to be active, assertive and energetic (Gough, 1988, 1990).

With regard to BPM, extraversion is expected to positively associate with BPM job performance. First, BPM typically involves working effectively in project teams, and with individuals from different functions (Smith & Fingar, 2002). A willingness to talk with and engage co-workers would be helpful in assessing BPM alternatives. Second, a certain amount of leadership may be beneficial in achieving BPM success (Spanyi, 2006). BPM efforts can include many individuals with possibly divergent interests and priorities, and as such, bringing about consensus through vision and inspiration may be especially conducive for BPM success (Hammer, 2007). Therefore, extraversion is expected to be positively associated with an individual's BPM performance.

Proposition 1b: Extraversion will be positively associated with BPM job performance.

Emotional Stability

Emotional Stability refers to an individual's emotional well-being. Emotionally stable people are well-adjusted, not anxious, not self-conscious, not paranoid, and not neurotic (Barrick & Mount, 1991). Emotional stability has been positively correlated with job performance (Barrick & Mount, 2000), although the effect was small[1]. Other traits associated with emotional stability include self-confidence and self-esteem (McCrae & Costa, 1991), which have also been associated with leadership (Bass & Bass, 2008).

With regard to BPM, an emotionally stable individual should have an advantage over an individual with less emotional stability. Having a sense of well-being, calmness, and confidence would be beneficial in most any endeavor. This may be especially true of BPM, because BPM implements solutions that span functional boundaries, and thus may cause angst among functional managers (Hammer, 2007). A calming, confident presence, then, may be conducive to BPM success. Moreover, given that emotional stability is associated with leadership, which in turn is thought to contribute to BPM success (Hammer, 2007), emotional stability is expected to have a positive association with an individual's BPM performance.

Proposition 1c: Emotional stability will be positively associated with BPM job performance.

Agreeableness

Agreeableness includes traits such as courteousness, being flexible, trusting, good-natured, cooperative, forgiving, soft-hearted, and tolerant (Barrick & Mount, 1991). Other adjectives describing agreeable personalities include being likable, kind, considerate, and helpful (Graziano & Eisenberg, 1997). Barrick and Mount (1991) originally found no correlation between agreeableness and job performance, but their follow-up meta-analysis found that agreeableness was important in jobs requiring substantial interpersonal interaction and teamwork (Barrick ct al., 2001). Agreeableness has also been found to be positively correlated with leadership (Judge & Bono, 2000; Judge et al., 2002).

With regard to BPM, agreeableness is expected to have a positive effect on individual performance. First, BPM typically entails interaction with constituents from a variety of backgrounds, which often requires substantial collaboration and teamwork (Hammer, 2007). Therefore, agreeableness may be salient for BPM job success, especially in cross-functional initiatives. Second, BPM is still relatively new in many organizations (Hill et al., 2006; Rosemann & deBruin, 2005). To encourage change management and improve the formal positional power of BPM, being agreeable may result in greater BPM success than being less agreeable. Therefore, agreeableness is expected to have a positive association with individual BPM performance.

Proposition 1d: Agreeableness will be positively associated with BPM job performance.

Openness to Experience

Although openness to experience (or openness) is the least studied of the Big Five traits (Judge & Bono, 2000), there is ample reason to believe that openness will be positively associated with BPM job performance. First, BPM professionals often must challenge existing ways of doing business, by reconfiguring processes to minimize non-value added activities (Smart, Maddern, & Maull, 2009). Barrick and Mount (1991) defined openness to include a willingness to try different things, and open individuals are marked by divergent thinking (McCrae, 1987), and being less likely to accept the status quo (Costa & McCrae, 1988; McCrae, 1996). Therefore, openness would likely be beneficial in BPM environments marked by change. In addition, BPM professionals must be creative, in that the design of new, end-to-end organizational processes often involves fresh and original thinking (Adamides & Karacapilidis, 2006). Openness, which is positively correlated with being imaginative, curious, original, and creative (Barrick & Mount, 1991), would likely be ameliorative to BPM performance. Third, the goal of BPM is to transform functionally-oriented business practices into integrated cross-functional processes (Melenovsky, 2005; Rosemann et al., 2006). Such changes can be disruptive, because they challenge the established workplace culture, customs, and norms (Garvin, 1995; Hammer, 2007). Being open to new ideas and new ways of doing things would likely be advantageous, and not surprisingly, openness has been positively correlated with handling work situations marked by change and unpredictability (Hough & Furnham, 2002; Thoresen, Bradley, Bliese, & Thoresen, 2004). Finally, research has found a positive correlation between openness and training effectiveness (Barrick & Mount, 1991). There is anecdotal evidence suggesting that training is important for BPM success, as BPM professionals often must gain proficiency in a broad spectrum of areas, including internal operations, information technology, and quality management (Paim et al., 2008). Thus, to the extent training is required, then, BPM job success should be positively affected by openness. Therefore, openness to experience is expected to be positively associated with an individual's BPM performance.

Proposition 1e: Openness to Experience will be positively associated with BPM job performance.

Job Performance and Intelligence, Experience

In the world of work, few individual differences have been examined more than intelligence and experience. Intelligence and experience act as important antecedents to the acquisition of expertise (i.e., job knowledge), which in turn positively affects subjective and objective measures of job performance (Schmidt et al., 1986). Having expertise means having a deep knowledge of the skills, techniques, methods, and habits that are required to successfully perform a job (McKeithen, Reitman, Rueter, & Hirtle, 1981; Shanteau, 1992a, 1992b).

The effect of experience on expertise (and hence job performance) is intuitive: those with experience have had more time to gain expertise, and therefore, should have higher performance than those with less experience. Experience has long been used as an important discriminator in applicant assessment, because it is easily obtainable and has robust predictive validity (Cascio, 2006; Levine & Flory, 1975). The research record bears this out, as experience has been found to have a significant positive relationship with expertise (McDaniel, Schmidt, & Hunter, 1988; Schmidt et al., 1986). While experience is important to job performance, intelligence has proven even more salient.

Intelligence (general mental ability or GMA) has had a uniformly positive effect on expertise and performance across all jobs, all job complexity levels, and all experience levels (Hunter, 1980; Hunter & Hunter, 1984; Schmidt & Hunter, 2004). GMA is directly correlated with an individual's ability to learn, and those with higher GMA are able to learn more and learn faster than those with less. McDaniel et al. (1988) found that the correlation between GMA and job knowledge was significant (r=0.46). In addition, scholars suggest that the relationship between experience, intelligence, expertise, and performance may be affected by the job's complexity (McDaniel et al., 1988). Higher complexity jobs, such as those in the professional, scientific, and upper management fields, have a greater number of information processing requirements (Hunter, 1980), which requires outside formal education (McDaniel et al., 1988). Conversely, lower complexity jobs, such as those in the clerical, manual, and some retail fields (Hunter, 1980), have a lower number of information processing requirements. The need for outside formal education in these fields is lower, because job knowledge can usually be obtained only by working on the job (McDaniel et al., 1988).

With regard to BPM, identifying the elements of business processes (e.g., stakeholders, activities, decision gateways, and data), along with potential process improvements, are skills that can take substantial time to master. For example, the BPM success at Wyeth Pharmaceutical's Technical Operations and Products Supply was due in part to the team members' vast business and BP experience (Antonucci et al., 2009). Moreover, to the extent that BPM involves complex activities (Hammer, 2007), intelligence will be beneficial as well. Therefore, intelligence and experience are expected to positively affect BPM job performance.

Proposition 2a: Intelligence will be positively associated with BPM job performance.

Proposition 2b: BPM job experience will be positively associated with BPM job performance.

Relative Importance of Individual Differences

There is substantial research evidence demonstrating that personality traits affect job performance, especially in terms of leadership potential (Judge et al., 2002) and work team performance (Barrick, Stewart, Neubert, & Mount, 1998). Indeed, many practitioners would place greater importance on personality, relegating intelligence to relative unimportance (except perhaps in academic, precareer achievement) (Schmidt & Hunter, 2004). The research evidence, however, clearly indicates that intelligence and experience (especially intelligence) will better predict job performance than personality traits.

A substantial body of research has connected GMA with job performance and career success (Schmidt & Hunter, 2004). Intelligence is positively associated with the occupational level attained (Hunter, 1980; Judge, Higgins, Thoresen, & Barrick, 1999), and performance within the occupation (Schmidt, 2002; Schmidt & Hunter, 2004). In a comprehensive review of work and occupations, Hunter (1980) found that intelligence was the most important predictor of performance in all jobs. Intelligence matters most in jobs of higher complexity (Hunter & Hunter, 1984; Schmidt & Hunter, 2004), but is still a valid predictor of performance for jobs lower in complexity (Pearlman, Schmidt, & Hunter, 1980). In short, it is difficult to think of any job where lower intelligence is preferred over higher intelligence.

Although personality traits (especially conscientiousness) are indicative of job performance across many job categories, they are not uniformly predictive (Barrick & Mount, 1991; Mount & Barrick, 1995). For example, agreeableness positively contributes to team performance (Barrick et al., 1998), but is not a consistent predictor of performance across all jobs (Barrick & Mount, 1991). Likewise, extraversion has been linked to performance in managerial and sales positions, but not in skilled/semi-skilled jobs (Barrick & Mount, 1991). Thus, there is no universal set of personality traits that matters across all jobs and all complexity levels, at least not to the extent that intelligence and experience matters (Schmidt & Hunter, 2004).

Therefore, intelligence and experience (especially intelligence) are expected to matter more than personality when it comes to individual performance in BPM.

Proposition 3: Intelligence and experience will better explain BPM job performance than will personality.

Research Model

The proposed effects of personality, intelligence and experience on BPM job performance are shown in Figure 1.

Figure 1. Research model

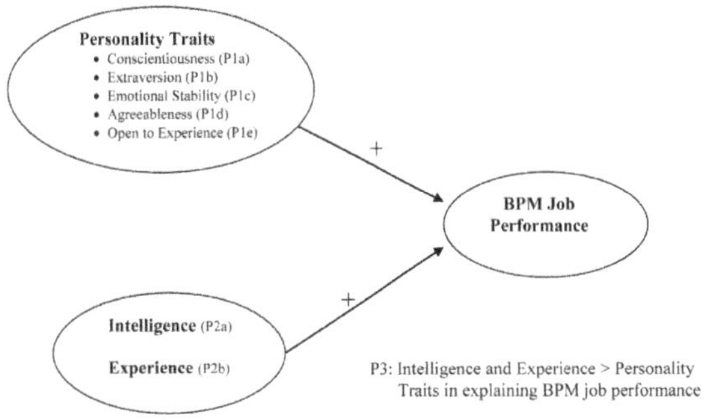

METHODS

Because BPM is a relatively new discipline, professionals knowledgeable of BPM through their membership in the Association of Business Process Management Professionals (ABPMP) were surveyed. ABPMP is a professional society dedicated to the advancement of BPM concepts and practices, and professional societies are often used to obtain respondents, especially when the topic being studied is relatively new (c.f. Watson, Annino, Wixom, Avery, & Rutherford, 2001; Wixom & Watson, 2001). A web-based survey was conducted inquiring about current best practices in BPM, and as part of the study, respondents were asked to consider a BPM professional (e.g. a coworker, supervisor, or direct report) whom they would consider the best performer and another whom they would consider the worst performer. No formal definition of best and worst was provided, given the broad scope and emerging nature of BPM.

Ninety-two respondents provided their perceptions regarding the personality traits for best BPM performers, but six of these respondents did not provide complete data for worst BPM performers. This resulted in a dataset for personality perceptions containing 178 responses (92 best, 86 worst). Likewise, 96 respondents provided their perceptions regarding the intelligence components for best BPM performers, but 18 of these respondents did not provide complete data for worst BPM performers. Therefore, the dataset for intelligence perceptions contained 174 responses (96 best, 78 worst).

Personality perceptions of best and worst BPM performers were measured with "markers", which are one word descriptors previously validated by Goldberg (1992) as accurate measures for each of the Big Five personality traits. The markers used in the present study were taken from those used by Mount et al. (1995) to measure outsider perceptions of sale representatives' personality traits. Two markers were used for each of the Big Five personality traits, making ten markers in total. Respondents indicated their level of agreement that each marker described a best (worst) BPM performer, using a 7-point Likert scale (1=completely disagree, 7=completely agree). The markers for each of the Big Five personality traits are shown in Table 1, Panel A.

Table 1. Measures of personality and intelligence

Panel A: Personality	
Trait	Markers
Conscientiousness	Organized, Systematic
Extraversion	Quiet*, Talkative
Emotional Stability	Moody*, Relaxed
Agreeableness	Rude*, Trustful
Openness to Experience	Unimaginative*, Intellectual
* reverse scored	
Panel B: Intelligence	
Dimension	Measure
Overall intelligence	Rate the best (worst) performer's overall intelligence
Problem-solving	Rate the best (worst) performer's ability to solve problems
Learning	Rate the best (worst) performer's ability to learn new skills

Before proceeding further, convergent and discriminant validity of the markers describing the Big Five personality traits was assessed by administering a confirmatory factor analysis using a varimax rotation. Results of the two factor analyses (one for best performers, one for worst performers) are shown in Table 2.

In both factor analyses, five factors emerged with Eigenvalues > 1.0, the markers converged and discriminated as expected, and the factor patterns were consistent between groups (best performers and worst performers). Therefore, the markers possess adequate validity when describing the Big Five personality traits.

Likewise, intelligence perceptions for best and worst BPM performers were measured using the terminology described by Dunn et al. (1995). Their three measures of intelligence are shown in Table 1, Panel B. Similar to the personality perceptions, respondents expressed their level of agreement using a 7-point Likert scale (1=completely disagree, 7=completely agree) that each intelligence component accurately described the best (worst) BPM performer. Experience was measured on a continuous scale, in which respondents provided the amount of experience (in years) that the best (worst) BPM performer had on the job.

The factor structure of these four measures (three items for intelligence, plus one item for experience) was analyzed with a confirmatory factor analysis using varimax rotation. Results of these factor analyses on the best and worst performers are shown in Table 3.

In both factor analyses, two factors emerged with eigenvalues > 1.0; the measures for intelligence converged and discriminated as expected, and the factor patterns were consistent between groups (best and worst BPM Performers). Experience remained separate as its own factor. Therefore, the items possess adequate validity when describing intelligence and experience.

Because the factor structures for personality and intelligence are consistent between performance groups (i.e. best and worst BPM performers), variable reduction is acceptable in order to simplify statistical analyses (Hair, Anderson, Tatham, & Black, 1998). Summated scales for each of the Big Five personality traits (2 markers for each trait) and intelligence (3 items) were created. Experience was left by itself, and was not included in a summated scale. Descriptive statistics for each summated scale and experience are shown in Table 4.

The results shown in Table 4 indicate that the Big Five personality traits, intelligence, and experience differ significantly between best and worst BPM performers.

Logistic Regression Analysis

Because the dependent variable is dichotomous (best or worst BPM performer), binary logistic regression was chosen as the technique to analyze the propositions. Logistic regression estimates

Table 2. Personality factor pattern

Panel A: Worst BPM Performers					
	Conscientious	Extraversion	Agreeable	Emotional Stability	Open to Experience
Organized	**0.834**	-0.106	0.101	0.166	0.209
Systematic	**0.903**	0.019	0.129	-0.046	0.128
Rude*	0.164	0.003	**0.807**	0.284	0.087
Trustful	0.082	0.109	**0.867**	0.076	0.189
Quiet*	-0.174	**0.898**	-0.033	-0.029	0.003
Talkative	0.105	**0.889**	0.150	-0.095	0.041
Moody*	0.078	0.072	0.244	**0.793**	0.075
Relaxed	0.026	-0.201	0.074	**0.819**	0.045
Intellectual	0.314	0.100	0.151	0.211	**0.650**
Unimaginative*	0.097	-0.031	0.132	-0.029	**0.895**
Panel B: Best BPM Performers					
	Conscientious	Extraversion	Agreeable	Emotional Stability	Open to Experience
Organized	**0.723**	-0.275	0.237	0.018	0.330
Systematic	**0.807**	0.305	-0.107	0.059	-0.118
Rude*	0.089	0.060	**0.692**	0.337	-0.155
Trustful	0.007	-0.125	**0.792**	-0.007	0.070
Quiet*	0.079	**0.613**	0.135	-0.498	-0.017
Talkative	0.034	**0.892**	-0.004	0.07	0.046
Moody*	0.257	-0.032	0.363	**0.635**	-0.083
Relaxed	-0.051	-0.009	0.091	**0.877**	0.123
Intellectual	0.057	0.043	0.08	0.056	**0.949**
Unimaginative*	-0.004	0.171	0.199	0.081	**0.754**
* reverse scored					

Table 3. Intelligence and experience factor pattern

Panel A: Worst BPM Performers		
	Intelligence	Experience
Overall intelligence	**0.870**	0.076
Ability to solve problems	**0.909**	-0.056
Ability to learn new skills	**0.811**	-0.097
Experience	-0.030	**0.995**
Panel B: Best BPM Performers		
	Intelligence	Experience
Overall intelligence	**0.840**	0.025
Ability to solve problems	**0.852**	0.072
Ability to learn new skills	**0.819**	0.049
Experience	0.058	**0.998**

Table 4. Descriptive statistics

	Worst Performer	**Best Performer**	
Construct *(measures)*	Mean (s.d.)	Mean (s.d.)	t (diff)
Conscientious-ness *(2)*	3.680 (1.547)	6.011 (0.852)	12.33***
Agreeableness *(2)*	3.860 (1.569)	5.995 (1.057)	10.57***
Extraversion *(2)*	4.442 (1.417)	4.886 (1.102)	2.32*
Emotional Stability *(2)*	3.517 (1.375)	5.049 (1.262)	7.73***
Open to Experi-ence *(2)*	4.006 (1.401)	5.918 (0.924)	10.67***
Intelligence *(3)*	4.368 (1.169)	6.604 (0.550)	15.55***
Experience *(1)*	3.051 (4.660)	7.375 (6.745)	4.99***

* p < 0.05, *** p < 0.001

the coefficients of a probabilistic model of independent variables that best predict the value of a dependent variable (Ranganathan, Seo, & Babad, 2006). The model is specified as:

$$\Pr(Y=1) = 1 / [1 + e^{(-(\alpha + \Sigma_i \beta_i X_i))}]$$

where $\Pr(Y = 1)$ is the probability that the BPM professional is a best performer. X_i are the independent variables for:

Model 1: Conscientiousness, Agreeableness, Extraversion, Emotional Stability, Openness to Experience
Model 2*:* Intelligence, Experience

β_i are the estimated coefficients, α is a constant, and e is the base of the natural logarithm.

Because the dependent variable is the probability that a respondent is describing a best BPM performer, a positive coefficient of an independent variable implies that for every one unit increase in the independent variable, the probability of a best performer increases by the amount from the above equation. The accompanying odds ratio, then, represents the increase in the odds that a respondent is describing a best performer for each unit increase in the independent variable. The significance of the coefficient is commonly assessed by the Wald statistic (Wald X^2). In addition, an approximation of how well the logistic equation explains the probability of describing a best performer can be obtained by calculating a pseudo-R^2 (Hair et al., 1998, p. 280) as:

$$R^2_{\text{logit}} = \left[-2 \text{ Log } L_{\text{null}} - \left(-2 \text{ Log } L_{\text{model}}\right)\right] / -2 \text{ Log } L_{\text{null}}$$

where -2 Log L_{null} = negative two times the log-likelihood for the model with no predictors, -2 Log L_{model} = negative two times the log-likelihood for the model with predictors,

As in linear regression, the closer the pseudo-R^2 coefficient is to 1, the better the equation explains the dependent variable.

Finally, the efficacy of the logistic equation can be assessed by analyzing how well it places respondents into the correct performance designation. The logistic regression provides probabilities that it would classify individuals as best performers or worst performers; those with probabilities greater than 0.5 are considered best performers, while those with probabilities less than 0.5 are considered worst performers. Subjective assessments of utility are established by comparing how many individuals were correctly placed (either as best performers or worst performers) to those incorrectly placed as "false positives" (those placed as best performers when they were actually worst performers) and "false negatives" (those placed as worst performers when they were actually best performers).

RESULTS

The results of the logistic regressions are shown in Table 5. Model 1 represents the effect that perceived personality traits have on classifying BPM performance, and Model 2 represents the effect that perceived intelligence and experience have on BPM performance.

In Model 1, conscientiousness has the largest and most significant effect on BPM performance. The odds ratio for conscientiousness (0.718) indicates that for every one unit increase in conscientiousness, the odds that the BPM professional is classified as a best performer increases by 71.8%. Openness also is a significant predictor of BPM performance, and acts as a significant differentiator as well, because its odds ratio exceeds 50%. Agreeableness and emotional stability are significant predictors of BPM performance, but their differentiating capabilities are more limited due to their odds ratios being less than 50%. Extraversion is not a significant differentia-

Table 5. Logistic regression analysis for best vs. worst BPM performers

	Model 1: Personality				Model 2: Intelligence and experience			
Variable	*B*	*SE*	Wald χ^2	Odds Ratio	*B*	*SE*	Wald χ^2	Odds Ratio
Conscientiousness	1.264***	0.271	21.813	0.718	-	-	-	-
Extraversion	0.403	0.243	2.752	0.332	-	-	-	-
Emotional Stability	0.450*	0.223	4.068	0.363	-	-	-	-
Agreeableness	0.626**	0.202	9.587	0.465	-	-	-	-
Open to Experience	0.741**	0.249	8.883	0.523	-	-	-	-
Intelligence	-	-	-	-	2.551***	0.391	42.667	0.922
Experience	-	-	-	-	0.130*	0.055	5.604	0.122

* $p < 0.05$, ** $p < 0.01$, *** $p < 0.001$

tor of BPM performance. Therefore, Propositions 1a and 1e have strong support, Propositions 1c and 1d have moderate support, and Proposition 1b is not supported.

In Model 2, perceptions of intelligence have a large and significant impact on BPM performance. Moreover, the odds ratio for intelligence (0.922) is even higher than conscientiousness; for every one unit increase in intelligence, the odds of a BPM professional being classified as a best performer increases 92.2%. Experience also had a significant effect on perceptions of BPM performance, although its odds ratio was below 50%. Therefore, Proposition 2a has strong support, but Proposition 2b has moderate support.

To compare the efficacy of each model in classifying BPM job performance (Proposition 3), the pseudo R^2 was calculated, and each equation's classification accuracy was compared. Results are presented Table 6.

Results in Table 5 indicate that both models possess acceptable pseudo-R^2 measures, and that both models classify BPM performers better than random choice[2]. However, the advantage goes to Model 2, as its R^2 is slightly higher, and Model 2 classifies BPM performers slightly better than Model 1. Therefore, Proposition 3 is accepted as well.

The results of the analyses regarding Propositions 1, 2, and 3 are summarized in Table 7.

DISCUSSION

This study addressed three research questions. First, the extent to which individual personality differences affect BPM job performance was examined. The results indicate that two personality traits – conscientiousness and openness to experience – significantly differentiate between best and worst BPM performance. These findings are not surprising. Conscientiousness has been a consistent predictor of job performance in a broad spectrum of jobs (Barrick & Mount, 1991; Schmidt & Hunter, 1998, 2004), and the fact that conscientiousness is important in BPM only

Table 6. Model comparison

		Actual Classification		Logistic Regression Classification				
	Pseudo R^2	Best	Worst	Best	Worst	Correct	False Pos.	False Neg.
Model 1	0.634	51.7%	48.3%	46.6%	42.7%	89.3%	5.1%	5.6%
Model 2	0.655	55.2%	44.8%	52.3%	39.1%	91.4%	2.9%	5.7%

Table 7: Summary results

Proposition	Outcome
P1a: Conscientiousness will be positively associated with BPM job performance	Supported
P1b: Extraversion will be positively associated with BPM job performance	Not Supported
P1c: Emotional stability will be positively associated with BPM job performance	Moderate Support
P1d: Agreeableness will be positively associated with BPM job performance	Moderate Support
P1e: Openness to experience will be positively associated with BPM job performance	Supported
P2a: Intelligence will be positively associated with BPM job performance	Supported
P2b: Experience will be positively associated with BPM job performance	Moderate Support
P3: Intelligence and experience will better explain BPM job performance than personality	Supported

adds to its robust stature. The findings regarding openness to experience make sense as well. Individuals scoring high in openness are willing to try new and different things, are actively engaged in learning experiences, are comfortable with change, and are unsatisfied with the status quo (Deveraj et al., 2008). These tendencies should be conducive to success in BPM, because BPM incorporates continuous learning, challenging the status quo, and trying to do things new ways (Hammer, 2007). Therefore, the findings regarding conscientiousness and openness are as expected.

Two additional personality traits – agreeableness and emotional stability – proved to be important predictors of BPM performance, but their discriminating power was weaker. These results also make sense. Agreeableness, while important, matters most in jobs that require significant interpersonal interaction, such as work teams (Barrick et al., 1998). However, of the original Big Five personality traits, agreeableness had the lowest correlation with job performance (Barrick & Mount, 1991). Likewise, emotional stability, while important, may have diminished effects as well, due to the aforementioned range restriction that can occur with this trait.

What was surprising was the non-significant effect that extraversion had on BPM performance. Extraversion is an important trait in sales and leadership positions (Barrick & Mount, 1991), and we thought that because BPM may incorporate a certain amount of salesmanship and leadership, that extraversion would be important as well. Perhaps BPM does not need to be "sold" as much as we had thought, but rather, has become a legitimate, recognized practice within the organization. Also, BPM may not require the leadership that is often necessary when new programs are introduced, which only adds to the notion that BPM may have matured as a discipline in the work world. These explanations are only suggestions, however, and thus would make for interesting future research.

The second research question examined the extent to which individual differences in intelligence and experience affect BPM performance. As expected, intelligence has a significant effect in predicting BPM performance ($p<0.001$). Moreover, intelligence is an excellent discriminator as well; the calculated odds ratio for intelligence is so high (0.922), that it is nearly certain that increases in intelligence are associated with higher BPM job performance. In that intelligence has been positively associated with training success (Hunter, 1986; Hunter & Hunter, 1984), solving problems, and learning new skills (Hunter, 1983), it makes sense that intelligence is positively associated with BPM job performance as well.

Experience is also a significant predictor of BPM job performance ($p<0.05$), but its odds ratio is smaller, which indicates less differentiating power. These results are not unexpected either, because experience is thought to become less important (and intelligence become more important) as job complexity increases (McDaniel et al., 1988). BPM can be a very complex undertaking, incorporating a large number of information processing needs (Hammer, 2007). For example, just defining the focal problem in a BPM project can require dozens of interviews with affected stakeholders (Hammer, 2007; Rosemann & deBruin, 2005).

Each of these inputs must be defined, mapped, and understood, so that a workable BPM solution can be proposed (Hammer, 2007). To the extent, then, that BPM is complex, it is reasonable to find that experience had smaller effects on BPM performance than intelligence.

The final research question addressed the question as to which individual difference model – personality traits or intelligence and experience – mattered most in predicting BPM job performance. Both models performed well, but the one incorporating intelligence and experience performed slightly better than personality traits. While the difference between these two models may have little statistical significance (in fact, the difference cannot be calculated due to the use of pseudo-R^2 values), the difference may have greater practical significance. From a practical view, Model 2 not only classifies BPM performers slightly better, but has greater parsimony than Model 1. Model 2 uses just four items to measure two constructs, while Model 1 uses ten items to measure five constructs. Therefore, in terms of practical utility, Model 2 incorporating intelligence and experience as predictors of BPM performance has an advantage over the alternative model incorporating personality traits. These results were expected as well, because intelligence has proven to be a better predictor of job performance than personality (Schmidt & Hunter, 1998, 2004).

It is interesting to note that the two variables having the strongest differentiating effect on BPM job performance – intelligence and conscientiousness – have been reported as important before. Schmidt and Hunter (1998) found that GMA had the highest predictive validity concerning job performance, and conscientiousness added significant incremental validity beyond GMA. In addition, hiring managers reported that GMA and conscientiousness were the two most salient variables regarding applicant hire-ability (Dunn et al., 1995). Thus, these results confirm the importance of intelligence and conscientiousness in job performance.

In addition, the fact that openness to experience matters in BPM job success has practical and theoretical implications. As organizations strive to develop and sustain a process-aware organizational culture, the need for rapid change in diverse situations increases. The broadminded and divergent thinking traits encompassed in openness indicates that the presence of individuals who possess this trait may have an increased ability for understanding and communicating business processes across the organization. From a theoretical standpoint, openness is positively correlated with intelligence (Schmidt & Hunter, 2004), especially aspects related to creativity (McCrae, 1987). Openness is also associated with Holland's (1985) investigative occupations (Barrick et al., 2003), which include being analytical, scientific, and comfortable working with theory and information. Thus, success in BPM positions may require being both creative and analytical.

Limitations, Future Research, and Contributions

Before discussing the contributions of the present study, it is important to review its limitations. The first limitation pertains to the nature of the dataset used. Although the size of the sample was more than adequate for the tests administered, it is important to note that respondents came primarily from membership in ABPMP. Because ABPMP members are knowledgeable in BPM principals and methods, such respondents may have more mature BPM programs. Therefore, these results may not be generalizable to those firms with newer BPM initiatives. However, to the extent that these results reflect the most current and advanced thinking in BPM, the findings should be ameliorative to both newer and more mature BPM programs. Second, no formal definitions for best and worst BPM performer were provided, nor were any specific BPM positions defined. A common tradeoff in research is the need to balance internal validity against sample size (Kerlinger &

Lee, 2000), and the present study was not immune from this conundrum. While providing definitions may have strengthened internal validity, it would likely have come at the expense of sample size. For example, in a small sample of firms (n=4) active in BPM, 38 separate job titles were found to be in use (Melenovsky & Hill, 2006). Moreover, the responsibilities associated with BPM jobs can vary between firms as well (Paim et al., 2008). Given the broad scope and nature of BPM initiatives, it seemed infeasible that any one definition of BPM job titles, responsibilities, and best/worst performance criteria would be universally accepted. Despite this limitation, significant differences between best and worst BPM performers (See Table 4) were observed. Therefore, these results are still useful when comparing the two extremes in job performance, and indicate just how strongly individual differences in personality, intelligence, and experience behave. Third, it is important to keep in mind that the present research measured others' perceptions of individual traits, and did not measure the actual traits themselves. Although this approach is consistent with much prior research (c.f., Dunn et al., 1995; Mount et al., 1994), actual measurement of intelligence and personality may yield results different than those presented here.

A final limitation concerns the potential presence of common method bias, which results from problems within the data collection process itself. Common method bias can arise from many sources (Podsakoff, MacKenzie, Lee, & Podsakoff, 2003), but one in particular - context-induced moods - may have affected results. A context-induced mood refers to the notion that one survey item can set the mood for subsequent items in the survey (Peterson, 2000; Podsakoff et al., 2003). In the present study, respondents were asked to consider a best (worst) BPM performer, and then provide perceptions regarding that best (worst) performer's intelligence and personality traits. This may have inadvertently set the respondent's mood, such that a respondent may feel highly ambivalent about classifying a best performer as low in intelligence. To measure the extent of any common method bias, Harman's single-factor test (Podsakoff et al., 2003) was administered on the best performers, worst performers, and then the combined datasets. In each case, multiple factors emerged, and no single factor accounted for a majority of the covariance. Based on these results, common method bias is not considered a significant study limitation.

Future research may be able to address these limitations, and thus extend our knowledge of the individual differences leading to BPM job success. As discussed previously, leadership is important to BPM success (Hammer, 2007), and certain BPM jobs may incorporate leadership more than others. Therefore, considering personality traits by BPM job level may further explain the personality differences associated with BPM job performance. In addition, future research may consider certain individual difference combinations, such as conscientiousness plus agreeableness (c.f., Witt, Burke, Barrick, & Mount, 2002), or intelligence plus conscientiousness (Schmidt & Hunter, 1998, 2004), which may have better predictive validity than the two models considered here. With regard to experience, it may be more important to have experience with the firm (i.e. gain experience with the firm's processes) rather than having experience with a specific BPM job. Therefore, adding this variable may help us better understand the role that experience plays in explaining BPM job performance.

Despite these limitations, this research makes several important contributions. From a research standpoint, these results are largely confirmatory. The descriptors and markers for intelligence and personality demonstrated substantial construct validity. The Big Five personality traits behaved largely as expected, which confirms the robust research record for the Big Five. In addition, intelligence proved to be the most salient differentiator of BPM performance, as expected. And, intelligence trumped personality in terms of differentiating between superior and inferior

BPM job performance, which also is confirmatory. In addition, these results extend those of prior research, in that the two dominant models of job performance have proven robust when applied to a relatively new discipline.

For practitioners, this research is among the first to tackle a problem being felt in the BPM community, which is the definition of those individual traits that lead to superior (or lackluster) BPM job performance. As suggested by theory, the "tried and true" differentiators of job performance – intelligence and conscientiousness – are valid for BPM as well. In addition, openness to experience proved to be important to BPM job performance. By definition, open individuals are willing to learn new things, try new things, and challenge the status quo. Thus, to the extent that superior BPM job performance depends on the individual performing that job, BPM professionals with higher levels of intelligence, conscientiousness, and openness should have a significant advantage over those with less.

REFERENCES

Adamides, E. D., & Karacapilidis, N. (2006). A knowledge centred framework for collaborative business process modeling. *Business Process Management Journal*, *12*(5), 557–575. doi:10.1108/14637150610690993

Antonucci, Y. L., Boykin, D., & Donahue, K. (2009). Wyeth Pharmaceuticals: In pursuit of process excellence . In Snabe, J. H., Rosenberg, A., Moller, C., & Scavillo, M. (Eds.), *Business process management: The SAP roadmap* (pp. 319–344). Boston: Galileo Press.

Barrick, M. R., & Mount, M. K. (1991). The Big Five personality dimensions and job performance: A meta-analysis. *Personnel Psychology*, *44*(1), 1–26. doi:10.1111/j.1744-6570.1991.tb00688.x

Barrick, M. R., & Mount, M. K. (2000). Select on conscientiousness and emotional stability. In Locke, E. A. (Ed.), *Handbook of principles of organizational behavior*. Malden, MA: Blackwell Publishing.

Barrick, M. R., Mount, M. K., & Gupta, R. (2003). Meta-analysis of the relationship between the five-factor model of personality and Holland's occupational types. *Personnel Psychology*, *56*, 45–74. doi:10.1111/j.1744-6570.2003.tb00143.x

Barrick, M. R., Mount, M. K., & Judge, T. A. (2001). Personality and Performance at the Beginning of the New Millennium: What Do We Know and Where Do We Go Next? *International Journal of Selection and Assessment*, *9*(1-2), 9–30. doi:10.1111/1468-2389.00160

Barrick, M. R., Stewart, G. L., Neubert, M. J., & Mount, M. K. (1998). Relating member ability and personality to work-team process and team effectiveness. *The Journal of Applied Psychology*, *83*(3), 377–391. doi:10.1037/0021-9010.83.3.377

Bass, B. M., & Bass, R. (2008). *Bass & Stogdill's handbook of leadership: Theory, research, and managerial applications* (4th ed.). New York: Free Press.

Briggs, S. R. (1992). Assessing the five-factor model of personality description. *Journal of Personality*, *60*(2), 253–293. doi:10.1111/j.1467-6494.1992.tb00974.x

Cascio, W. F. (2006). *Managing Human Resources: Productivity, Quality of Work Life, Profits* (7th ed.). New York: McGraw-Hill/Irwin.

Cattell, R. B., Cattell, A. K., & Cattell, H. E. P. (1993). *16 Personality Factor Inventory* (5th ed.). Champaign, IL: The Institute for Personality and Ability Testing.

Conley, J. J. (1985). Longitudinal stability of personality traits: A multitrait-multimethod-multioccasion analysis. *Journal of Personality and Social Psychology*, *49*(5), 1266–1282. doi:10.1037/0022-3514.49.5.1266

Costa, P. T., & McCrae, R. R. (1988). Personality in adulthood: A 6-year longitudinal study of self-reports and spouse ratings on the NEO Personality Inventory. *Journal of Personality and Social Psychology*, *54*(5), 853–863. doi:10.1037/0022-3514.54.5.853

Davenport, T. H. (1993). Integrate process reengineering and TQM. *Planning Review*, *21*(3), 6–12.

Davenport, T. H., & Short, J. E. (1990). The new industrial engineering: Information technology and process redesign. *Sloan Management Review*, *31*(4), 11–27.

Demming, W. E. (1986). *Out of the crisis*. Cambridge, MA: MIT Press.

Deveraj, S., Easley, R. F., & Crant, J. M. (2008). How does personality matter? Relating the Five-Factor model to technology acceptance and use. *Information Systems Research*, *19*(1), 93–105. doi:10.1287/isre.1070.0153

Dunn, W. S., Mount, M. K., Barrick, M. R., & Ones, D. S. (1995). Relative importance of personality and general mental ability in manager's judgements of applicant qualifications. *The Journal of Applied Psychology*, *80*(4), 500–509. doi:10.1037/0021-9010.80.4.500

Eicker, S., Kochbeck, J., & Schuler, P. (2008). *Employee competencies for business process management*. Paper presented at the International Conference on Business Information Systems, Innsbruck, Austria.

Fingar, P. (2006). The MBA is dead, long live the MBI. *BPTrends*, *4*(12), 1–7.

Garvin, D. A. (1995). Leveraging processes for strategic advantage. *Harvard Business Review*, *73*(5), 76–90.

Goldberg, L. R. (1981). Language and individual differences: The search for universals in personality lexicons. In Wheeler, L. (Ed.), *Review of personality and social psychology* (*Vol. 2*, pp. 141–166). Beverly Hills, CA: Sage.

Goldberg, L. R. (1990). An alternative "description of personality": The Big Five factor structure. *Journal of Personality and Social Psychology*, *59*(6), 1216–1229. doi:10.1037/0022-3514.59.6.1216

Goldberg, L. R. (1992). The development of markers for the Big-Five factor structure. *Psychological Assessment*, *4*(1), 26–42. doi:10.1037/1040-3590.4.1.26

Gough, H. (1988). *Manual for the California Psychological Inventory*. Palo Alto, CA: Consulting Psychologists Press.

Gough, H. (1990). Testing for leadership with the California Psychological Inventory. In Clark, K. E., & Clark, M. B. (Eds.), *Measures of leadership* (pp. 355–379). West Orange, NJ: Leadership Library of America.

Graziano, W. G., & Eisenberg, N. G. (1997). Agreeableness: A dimension of personality. In Hogan, R., Johnson, J., & Briggs, S. R. (Eds.), *Handbook of Personality Psychology* (pp. 795–824). San Diego, CA: Academic Press. doi:10.1016/B978-012134645-4/50031-7

Grover, V., Jeong, S., Kettinger, W., & Teng, J. (1995). The implementation of business process reengineering. *Journal of Management Information Systems*, *12*(1), 109–144.

Hair, J. F., Anderson, R. E., Tatham, R. L., & Black, W. C. (1998). *Multivariate Data Analysis* (5th ed.). Singapore: Pearson Education.

Hammer, M. (1990). Reengineering work: Don't automate, obliterate. *Harvard Business Review*, *68*(4), 104–112.

Hammer, M. (2007). The process audit. *Harvard Business Review*, *85*(4), 111–123.

Hammer, M., & Champy, J. (1993). *Reengineering the corporation: A manifesto for reengineering business revolution*. New York: Harper.

Harmon, P. (2004). Evaluating an organization's business process maturity. *BP Trends*, *2*(3), 1–11.

Hill, J. B., Sinur, J., Flint, D., & Melenovsky, M. J. (2006). *Gartner's position on business process management (Rep. No. G00136533)*. Stamford, CT: Gartner Research.

Holland, J. L. (1985). *Making vocational choices: A theory of vocational personalities and work environments*. Englewood Cliffs, NJ: Prentice-Hall.

Hough, L. M., & Furnham, A. (2002). Importance and use of personality variables in work settings. In Borman, W. C., Ilgen, D. R., & Klimoski, R. J. (Eds.), *Comprehensive Handbook of Psychology* (pp. 131–169). New York: Wiley.

Hung, R. Y.-Y. (2006). Business process management as competitive advantage: A review and empirical study. *Total Quality Management*, *17*(1), 21–40. doi:10.1080/14783360500249836

Hunter, J. E. (1980). *Test validation for 12,000 jobs: An application of synthetic validity and validity generalization to the General Aptitude Test Battery*. Washington, DC: U.S. Department of Labor.

Hunter, J. E. (1983). A causal analysis of cognitive ability, job knowledge, job performance, and supervisory ratings. In Landy, F., Zedeck, S., & Cleveland, J. (Eds.), *Performance measurement and theory* (pp. 257–266). Hillsdale, NJ: Erlbaum.

Hunter, J. E. (1986). Cognitive ability, cognitive aptitudes, job knowledge and job performance. *Journal of Vocational Behavior*, *29*(3), 340–362. doi:10.1016/0001-8791(86)90013-8

Hunter, J. E., & Hunter, R. F. (1984). Validity and utility of alternative predictors of job performance. *Psychological Bulletin*, *96*(1), 72–98. doi:10.1037/0033-2909.96.1.72

Judge, T. A., & Bono, J. E. (2000). Five-Factor model of personality and transformational leadership. *The Journal of Applied Psychology*, *85*(5), 751–765. doi:10.1037/0021-9010.85.5.751

Judge, T. A., Bono, J. E., Ilies, R., & Gerhardt, M. W. (2002). Personality and leadership: A qualitative and quantitative review. *The Journal of Applied Psychology*, *87*(4), 765–780. doi:10.1037/0021-9010.87.4.765

Judge, T. A., Higgins, C. A., Thoresen, C. J., & Barrick, M. R. (1999). The Big Five personality traits, general mental ability and career success across the life span. *Personnel Psychology*, *52*(3), 621–652. doi:10.1111/j.1744-6570.1999.tb00174.x

Kerlinger, F. N., & Lee, H. B. (2000). *Foundations of Behavioral Research* (4th ed.). Fort Worth, TX: Harcourt College Publishers.

Kettinger, W. J., Teng, J. T. C., & Guha, S. (1997). Business process change: A study of methodologies, techniques, and tools. *Management Information Systems Quarterly*, *21*(1), 55–79. doi:10.2307/249742

Levine, E. L., & Flory, A. (1975). Evaluation of job applicants: A conceptual framework. *Public Personnel Management*, *4*, 378–385.

McCrae, R. R. (1987). Creativity, divergent thinking, and openness to experience. *Journal of Personality and Social Psychology*, *52*(6), 1258–1265. doi:10.1037/0022-3514.52.6.1258

McCrae, R. R. (1996). Social consequences of experiential openness. *Psychological Bulletin, 120*(3), 323–337. doi:10.1037/0033-2909.120.3.323

McCrae, R. R., & Costa, P. T. (1991). Adding liebe und arbeit: The full five-factor model and well-being. *Personality and Social Psychology Bulletin, 17*(2), 227–232. doi:10.1177/0146167291101700217

McDaniel, M. A., Schmidt, F. L., & Hunter, J. E. (1988). Job experience correlates of job performance. *The Journal of Applied Psychology, 73*(2), 327–330. doi:10.1037/0021-9010.73.2.327

McKeithen, K. B., Reitman, J. S., Rueter, H. H., & Hirtle, S. C. (1981). Knowledge organization and skill differences in computer programmers. *Cognitive Psychology, 13*(3), 307–325. doi:10.1016/0010-0285(81)90012-8

Melenovsky, M. J. (2005). *Align roles and responsibilities to make BPM work(Rep. No. G00127680).* Stamford, CT: Gartner Research.

Melenovsky, M. J., & Hill, J. B. (2006). *Role definition and organizational structure: Business Process Improvement (Rep. No. G00141487).* Stamford, CT: Gartner Research.

Mount, M. K., & Barrick, M. R. (1995). The big five personality dimensions: Implications for research and practices in human resource management. In Ferris, G. (Ed.), *Research in personnel and human resources management* (*Vol. 13*, pp. 153–200). Greenwich, CT: JAI Press.

Mount, M. K., Barrick, M. R., & Strauss, J. P. (1994). Validity of observer ratings of the Big Five personality factors. *The Journal of Applied Psychology, 79*(2), 272–280. doi:10.1037/0021-9010.79.2.272

Paim, R., Caulliraux, H. M., & Cardoso, R. (2008). Process management tasks: a conceptual and practical view. *Business Process Management Journal, 14*(5), 694–723. doi:10.1108/14637150810903066

Pearlman, K., Schmidt, F. L., & Hunter, J. E. (1980). Validity generalization results for tests used to predict job proficiency and training criteria in clerical positions. *The Journal of Applied Psychology, 65*(4), 373–407. doi:10.1037/0021-9010.65.4.373

Peterson, R. A. (2000). *Constructing effective questionnaires*. Thousand Oaks, CA: Sage.

Podsakoff, P. M., MacKenzie, S. B., Lee, J. Y., & Podsakoff, N. P. (2003). Common method biases in behavioral research: A critical review of the literature and recommended remedies. *The Journal of Applied Psychology, 88*(5), 879–903. doi:10.1037/0021-9010.88.5.879

Ranganathan, C., Seo, D., & Babad, Y. (2006). Switching behavior of mbile users: do users' relational investments and demographics matter? *European Journal of Information Systems, 15*(3), 269–276. doi:10.1057/palgrave.ejis.3000616

Ravesteyn, P., Batenburg, R., & deWaal, B. (2008). In search of competencies needed in BPM projects. *Communications of the IIMA, 8*(2), 23–30.

Rosemann, M., & deBruin, T. (2005). Application of the holistic model for determining BP maturity. *BP Trends*, 1-21.

Rosemann, M., deBruin, T., & Power, B. (2006). BPM Maturity. In Jeston, J., & Nelis, J. (Eds.), *Business Process Management: Practical guidelines to successful implementation* (pp. 299–315). Amsterdam, The Netherlands: Elsevier.

Schmidt, F. L. (2002). The role of general cognitive ability and job performance: Why there can be no debate. *Human Performance, 15*(1), 187–210. doi:10.1207/S15327043HUP1501&02_12

Schmidt, F. L., & Hunter, J. E. (1998). The validity and utility of selection methods in personnel psychology: Practical and theoretical implications of 85 years of research findings. *Psychological Bulletin, 124*(2), 262–274. doi:10.1037/0033-2909.124.2.262

Schmidt, F. L., & Hunter, J. E. (2004). General mental ability in the world of work: Occupational attainment and job performance. *Journal of Personality and Social Psychology, 86*(1), 162–173. doi:10.1037/0022-3514.86.1.162

Schmidt, F. L., Hunter, J. E., & Outerbridge, A. N. (1986). Impact of job experience and ability on job knowledge, work sample performance, and supervisory ratings of performance. *The Journal of Applied Psychology, 71*(3), 432–439. doi:10.1037/0021-9010.71.3.432

Schmidt, F. L., Hunter, J. E., Outerbridge, A. N., & Goff, S. (1988). Joint relation of experience and ability with job performance: Test of three hypotheses. *The Journal of Applied Psychology, 73*(1), 46–57. doi:10.1037/0021-9010.73.1.46

Shanteau, J. (1992a). Competence in experts: The role of task characteristics. *Organizational Behavior and Human Decision Processes, 53*(2), 252–266. doi:10.1016/0749-5978(92)90064-E

Shanteau, J. (1992b). How much information does an expert use? Is it relevant? *Acta Psychologica, 81*(1), 75–86. doi:10.1016/0001-6918(92)90012-3

Sivo, S. A., Saunders, C., Quing, C., & Jiang, J. (2006). How low should you go? Response rates and the validity of inference in IS questionnaire research. *Journal of the Association for Information Systems, 7*(6), 351–413.

Smart, P. A., Maddern, H., & Maull, R. S. (2009). Understanding business process management: Implications for theory and practice. *British Academy of Management, 20*(4), 491–507.

Smith, H., & Fingar, P. (2002). *Business process management (BPM): The third wave*. Tampa, FL: Meghan-Kiffer Press.

Spanyi, A. (2006). *More for less*. Tampa, FL: Meghan-Kiffer Press.

Spreier, S. W., Fontaine, M. H., & Malloy, R. L. (2006). Leadership run amok: The destructive potential of overachievers. *Harvard Business Review, 84*(6), 72–82.

Taylor, F. W. (1911). *Scientific management*. New York: Harper & Brothers.

Thoresen, C. J., Bradley, J. C., Bliese, P. D., & Thoresen, J. D. (2004). The Big Five personality traits and individual job performance growth trajectories in maintenance and transitional job stages. *The Journal of Applied Psychology, 89*(5), 835–853. doi:10.1037/0021-9010.89.5.835

Towers, S., & Schurter, T. (2005). *Building on experience: An executive report*. Business Process Management Group.

Watson, D. L., & Clark, A. (1997). Extraversion and its positive emotional core. In Hogan, R., Johnson, J., & Briggs, S. R. (Eds.), *Handbook of Personality Psychology* (pp. 767–793). San Diego, CA: Academic Press. doi:10.1016/B978-012134645-4/50030-5

Watson, H. J., Annino, D. A., Wixom, B. H., Avery, K. L., & Rutherford, M. (2001). Current practices in data warehousing. *Information Systems Management, 18*(1), 47–55. doi:10.1201/1078/43194.18.1.20010101/31264.6

Wechsler, D. (1997). *Wechsler Adult Intelligence Scale (WAIS-III)* (3rd ed.). New York: Psychological Corporation.

Witt, L. A., Burke, L. A., Barrick, M. R., & Mount, M. K. (2002). The interactive effects of conscientiousness and agreeableness on job performance. *The Journal of Applied Psychology*, *87*(1), 164–169. doi:10.1037/0021-9010.87.1.164

Wixom, B. H., & Watson, H. J. (2001). An empirical investigation of the factors affecting data warehousing success. *Management Information Systems Quarterly*, *25*(1), 17–41. doi:10.2307/3250957

ENDNOTES

1. In their original meta-analysis, Barrick and Mount (1991) found no correlation between emotional stability and job performance. They attributed their findings to range restriction, because most emotionally unstable individuals have been removed from the workplace.
2. If one were to classify Best and Worst BPM performers by personality traits, guessing would have a 50.05% accuracy ($(92/178)^2 + (1-92/178)^2 = 0.5005$). Using intelligence and experience, guessing would have a 50.54% accuracy ($(96/174)^2 + (1-96/174)^2 = 0.5054$).

This work was previously published in the Information Resources Management Journal, Volume 24, Issue 1, edited by Mehdi Khosrow-Pour, pp. 46-65, copyright 2013 by IGI Publishing (an imprint of IGI Global).

Chapter 5
An Integrated Strategic Framework for E-Government Initiatives

Fatemeh Saghafi
Iran Telecommunication Research Center, Iran

Akbar Kary Dolat Abadi
Shahid Sattari University, Iran

Behrouz Zarei
Tehran University, Iran

Kolsoom Abbasi Shahkooh
Iran Telecommunication Research Center, Iran

ABSTRACT

The widespread applications of information and communication technologies have attracted many countries to e-government. Nonetheless, setting appropriate goals for e-government initiatives is an important factor for the success of these projects. This study provides a context-based framework for understanding e-government initiatives in different countries, including degree of e-government readiness, degree of transparency, and level of democratization. According to these determinants, 141 countries are categorized using Parson's generic strategy of IT. Classification of countries in this framework shows significant correlations between these determinants and GDP index, which is an important outcome for country performance. This framework provides a roadmap for policymakers to formulate goals for their e-government initiatives commensurate with their respective environments.

INTRODUCTION

E-government is becoming an important public service concept for many countries in order to adapt with the modern environment. E-government has contributed to a great number of opportunities enhancing the government performance. It affects all of the government functions and private sectors and leads to new ways of interaction between citizens and government (Zarei, Ghapanchi, & Sattary, 2008). Numerous advantages have been reported for the e-government. For instance, it contributes to a more intelligent and agile government, with improved provision of services and a new instrument for the interaction between citizens and government (Sarantis, Charalabidis, & Askounis,

DOI: 10.4018/978-1-4666-3616-3.ch005

2011). Greater transparency, equality of access and confidence are some additional advantages of the e-government (Abbasi Shahkooh, Abbasi Shahkooh, & Abdollahi, 2008; Turban, King, Lee, Warkentin, & Chang, 2002).

E-government can be considered as a revolution based on the communion and partnership among all government stakeholders (Rowley, 2011) in which information and communications flow in a cyber space and increase the networking opportunities and organizational performance (Lowry, Albrecht, & Nunamaker, 2003). In fact, information technology based networks, transform the relations between people and government. Deployment of e-government enables the citizens, businesses, employees and other government agencies to access the government services and networks through a single portal and exchange information without time and space limitations (Institute for Trade Studies and Research, 2004). Governments all around the world, continuously put efforts to improve the customer services. Each country implements e-government for specific reasons which are different from other countries (Strejcek & Theil, 2004). Nevertheless, most governments face problems and difficulties in their legacy systems such as bureaucracy tendencies in administration and governance systems, centralized decision making schemes, complexity of reworks in public sector, lack of information sharing among the public agencies, and lack of efficient information and communications technology infrastructures (Altameem, Zairi, & Alshawi, 2006). With the huge investigations in e-government initiatives (Peters, Jansen, & Engers, 2004) governments are trying to attain this goal.

Governments all around the world compete to deploy and implement the e-government concept (theory) in their countries, however, studies show a great number of failures (Braa & Hedberg, 2000; Kitiyadisai, 2000). According to Heeks (2004), in developed countries, 35% of the e-government initiatives have completely failed, 50% have partially failed and only 15% were successful. The main reasons for these failures are the lack of an explicit strategy and inconsistency among the selected strategies.

One strand deals with the values to be achieved through the e-government initiatives. In the values strand context, e-government could be considered as an instrument that enhances the ability and capacity of the government in order to achieve the established values that constitute the fundamental and principal goals of the government. For instance, a goal of an e-government project is to realize a Web-enabled policy discourse. We would not expect this initiative to succeed in an environment where both the technology infrastructure and democratization levels are low. By the same token, an initiative that aims to achieve transactional transparency may not be successful in an environment with a low level of e-government readiness. Those values encompass, interalignment, efficiency (Holliday & Kwok, 2004), economy, accountability, effectiveness, transparency, service quality (Hazlett & Hill, 2003), integrity, democratic responsiveness (Kossick, 2002), continuous change in democratic paradigms (Ho & Ni, 2002), rule of law, citizen participation (Netchaeva, 2002) and empowerment (Wong & Welch, 2004). Principal goals for every e-government project must be related to the value system. Notable issues identified in this strand are related to the unintended results and outcomes of e-government project, enablers or obstacles in adopting the e-government and its technical dimensions. These issues are interrelated and should be considered holistically. The effectiveness of e-government initiatives achieving their goals (economic or political) may hinge crucially on the congruence among the goals these initiatives seek to achieve and the underlying contextual environment (setting) within which these initiatives are undertaken.

A FRAMEWORK FOR CONTEXT-BASED STRATEGY OF E-GOVERNMENT

Our proposed framework is structurally similar to Bozeman's multidimensional framework (Bozeman, 1987). However, the two frameworks are substantively different in terms of purpose, dimensions, and implications of the various blends of the dimensions. While Bozeman's model intends to explain the degree of openness of an organization and its impact on organizational behavior, our framework aims to explain the relationship between the goals of e-government initiatives and their contexts at national and macro-level. Furthermore, Bozeman's model is pitched at a micro-organizational level and has economic and political authority dimensions. In contrast, our model's focus is on the macro-level environment and has got three macro-dimensions including e-government readiness, democratization, and transparency.

Generally speaking, e-government initiatives embrace two kinds of values: (1) political values and (2) resource and infrastructure efficiency-related values. Efficiency-related values are common to all initiatives and are common dominators in all countries and government systems (a country is whether democratic or not, or whether is rich or poor). Political goals of an e-government initiative are contingent on two major dimensions: democratization and e-government transparency. On the other hand, e-government transparency also affects the efficiency of the two other indices. Therefore, these three factors are considered as core values of e-government concept.

E-government readiness index is a weighted average (composite) measure which is measured based on a number of sub-indices: e-government website assessment index, telecommunication infrastructure index, and human capital (United Nations, 2004). The democratization index is a measure of political development and it is composed of seven sub-indices: electoral process; civil society; independent media; governance and public administration; Judicial Framework and Independence; and corruption (Transparency International, 2008). Countries high on this index generally have democratic form of government whereas those low on this index have generally authoritarian form of government.

Transparency is one of the most important issues in order to enhance the relationship between the public and the government. An activity is transparent if (Pope, 2000) all the related information for that activity is accessible for public without any limitation. Also, transparency has been defined (Heeks, 2004a) as open course of information relevant to decisions and activities from the source to the recipients. Richard defines the electronic transparency as use of the information and communication technologies to utilize all the information relevant to the transparency (Heeks, 2004b).

In Figure 1, an integrative value strategy framework for e-government initiatives is illustrated in 8 individual quadrants. The three principal axes in Figure 1 determine the contextual situation of the countries. These 8 quadrants are shown in Figure 1 and Table 1. The negative sign in Table 1 indicates that the value of a dimension is lower than the average, and the positive sign indicates that the value is higher than the average. Since the

Figure 1. An integrative value strategy framework for e-government initiatives based on three perpendicular axes (indices)

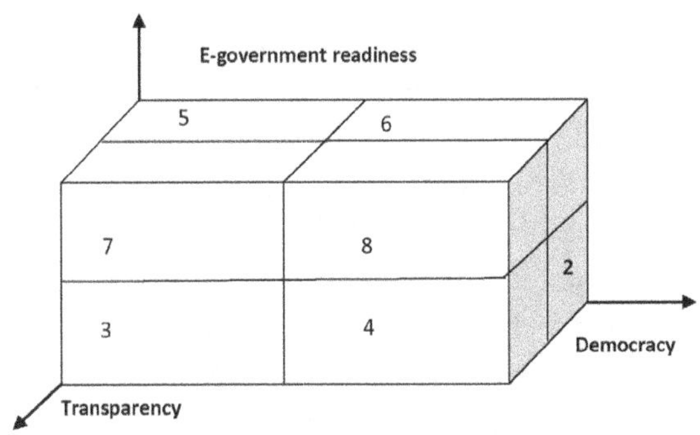

Table 1. Value-based strategic integrative e-government framework

Row	E-government readiness	Transparency	Democracy	E-government application	Adopted strategy
1	-	-	-	Only for international government relations (expository e-government)	Scarce resources/free market/ monopoly/necessary evil
2	-	-	+	Participational and non-transparent e-government	Scarce resources/monopoly
3	-	+	-	Transparent e-government (at citizen level but not government)	Scarce resources/monopoly
4	-	+	+	Open consultational e-government	Scarce resources/monopoly/ free market
5	+	-	-	Transactional e-government	Centrally planned/free market
6	+	-	+	Non-transparent participational e-government	Centrally planned/monopoly
7	+	+	-	Open transactional e-government	Centrally planned/monopoly
8	+	+	+	Transparent participational e-government	Leading edge/centrally planned

e-government initiatives of every country must be aligned with its government context and policy, the fifth column of the Table 1 is dedicated to the relevant application of e-government in that category. In the last column, adoptable strategies for successful e-government initiatives are deducted by using Parson's general information technology strategies (Parsons, 1983a, 1983b). These strategies are described as follows (Parsons, 1983a, 1983b).

- **Centrally Planned:** In centrally planned, IT strategy firms attempt to integrate their corporate strategy and their information systems strategy. The firm will focus on integrated systems so that maximum utilization is made of computer processing power. A centralized IT department will use a top down planning approach.
- **Leading Edge:** This strategy implies that the firm continuously updates its hardware and software with the latest developments available in the market. In such a strategy, state-of-the-art-technology is continually acquired. Experimentation is encouraged in the hope that discoveries will lead to superior performance and the sustainable competitive advantage.
- **Free Market:** This IT strategy assumes that the user is best qualified to determine his or her needs. In such circumstances, the user is entitled to acquire hardware, software and services either from IT department or from any outside vendor. The only rule which is strictly applied is that the user obtains his IS services at a reasonable price.
- **Monopoly:** The monopoly IT strategy rests on the premise that there should be one single source of computer services in the organization. The primary criterion for the success of monopoly strategy is the satisfaction of the user. In order to ensure this, there should be considerable excess capacity in the IT department to cope with the peaks in demand. One of the major difficulties facing the firm in implementing the strategy is the measurement of user satisfaction.
- **Scarce Resource:** The scarce resource IT strategy relies on the intensive control of money being spent on the IT department. Very strict budgets are set and the IT department is often simply not permitted under any circumstances to exceed the amounts laid down. A scarce resource

strategy is based on the concept that administration is an unproductive cost and thus management must minimize all expenditure in this direction.

- **Necessary Evil:** The necessary evil IT strategy is based on the belief that the use of computers should be curtailed as much as possible. Only applications that cannot be performed without the use of a computer and which are very well cost-justified are entertained. A minimum amount is spent on hardware, software and people. As a result firms pursuing this strategy often encounter a high turnover of their programmers, analysts and operator.

Parson's six strategies are modified to fit the e-government as follows.

If countries attempt to integrate and align their e-government strategy with their environment, their strategy is named "centrally planned" and intends to create a competitive advantage for the country. If the country links the existing condition of the e-government to their contextual requirements, this strategy is named "leading edge" and requires an extensive investment in R&D activities to create a long-term competitive advantage. If a country assumes that the users are qualified to determine their needs. The only rule which is strictly applied is that the user obtains e-government services at a reasonable price and this strategy is named "free market". A "monopoly" e-government strategy is applicable either through the direct policies or informal agreements. Countries that employ this strategy must ensure the linkage between current conditions of e-government and contextual requirements. "Scarce resource" strategy is used when e-government is considered as a scarce resource in a country and tries to limit its usage. If a country, because of the past experiences and undesirable outcomes, sees the e-government as a necessary or imperative evil, it's strategy is named "necessary evil". In this case, e-government initiatives are implemented, if countries are absolutely confident that they will lead to the determined goals.

DATA ANALYSIS

In this section, 141 countries are distributed into 8 quadrants according to our framework in Figure 2. We used the transparency score (CPI) provided by TI (Transparency International, 2008), rank of democratization (Goehring, 2007), and e-government readiness score provided by the United Nations (United Nations, 2008). Figure 2 shows a three dimensional scatter plot of the data. This figure shows that the data are scattered on diameter, and there is limited data in other quadrants. Countries in each quadrant, average and standard deviation of scores are provided in Table 2.

Table 2 shows that, countries in group 8 have a significant average values in all the three indices. The values of these indices reduce by moving toward countries in group 1. In Figure 2 and Table 2 there are no countries with significant transparency and democracy indices and poor e-government readiness. So it can be concluded that success in transparency and democracy is based on success in e-government readiness.

Figure 2. A three dimensional Scatter plot of E-government, Democracy and CPI indices for 141 countries

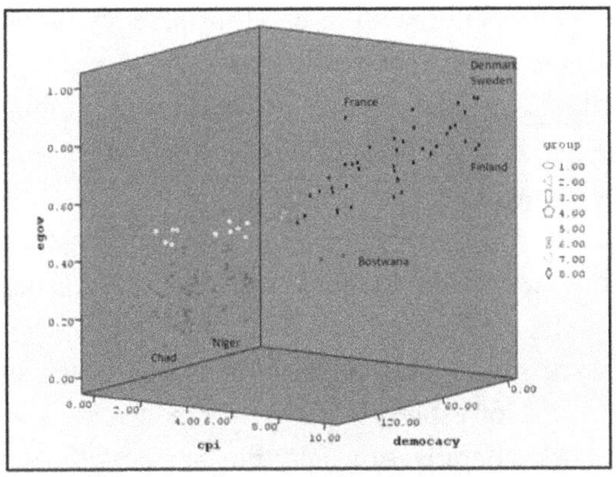

Table 2. Classification of countries in the integrative strategic e-government framework

Group No.	Countries	Average of quadrant	S.D. of quadrant
1	Morocco, Gabon, Madagascar, Sri Lanka, Tanzania, Algeria, Armenia, Burkina Faso, Guatemala, Moldova, Uganda, Malawi, Mauritania, Niger, Zambia, Nepal, Cameroon, Angola, Guinea-Bissau, Nigeria, Kenya, Cambodia, Central African Republic, Haiti, Eritrea, Rwanda, Solomon Islands, Viet Nam, Burundi, Libya, Yemen, Ethiopia, Pakistan, Syria, Gambia, Togo, Cote d'Ivoire, Kyrgyzstan, Liberia, Tajikistan, Zimbabwe, Bangladesh, Turkmenistan, Guinea, Laos, Afghanistan, Chad, Sudan, Uzbekistan, Iraq, Myanmar	2008 CPI= 2.39 E-gov. Score08=0.27 Democ-Rank08=116.4	2008 CPI= 0.485 E-gov. Score08=0.90 Democ-Rank08=19.62
2	Ghana, Senegal, India, Mozambique, Benín, Mali, Nicaragua, Honduras, Indonesia, Sierra Leone, Iran	2008 CPI= 2.85 E-gov. Score08=0.286 Democ-Rank08=57.2	2008 CPI= 0.558 E-gov. Score08=0.101 Democ-Rank08=12.68
3	Tunisia, Cuba	2008 CPI= 4.2 E-gov. Score08=0.376 Democ-Rank08=115.5	2008 CPI= 0.00 E-gov. Score08=0.037 Democ-Rank08=12.02
4	Botswana, Namibia	2008 CPI= 4.95 E-gov. Score08=0.354 Democ-Rank08=42	2008 CPI= 0.636 E-gov. Score08=0.014 Democ-Rank08=1.41
5	Georgia, Thailand, Lebanon, Egypt, Philippines, China, Saudi Arabia, Russia, Azerbaijan, Belarus, Kazakhstan, Venezuela	2008 CPI= 2.717 E-gov. Score08=0.491 Democ-Rank08=112.5	2008 CPI= 0.593 E-gov. Score08=0.030 Democ-Rank08=22.62
6	Colombia, Romania, Brasil, México, Perú, Serbia, Jamaica, Lesoto, Panamá, Dominican Republic, Mongolia, Albania, Argentina, Bolivia, Ukraine, Paraguay, Ecuador	2008 CPI=3.123 E-gov. Score08=0.505 Democ-Rank08=57.55	2008 CPI= 0.453 E-gov. Score08=0.054 Democ-Rank08=9.85
7	United Arab Emirates, Malaysia, Bhutan, Jordan, Oman, Kuwait	2008 CPI= 4.916 E-gov. Score08=0.513 Democ-Rank08=79.67	2008 CPI= 0.475 E-gov. Score08=0.116 Democ-Rank08=4.501
8	Denmark, Finland, New Zealand, Sweden, Netherlands, Switzerland, Canada, Norway, Australia, United Kingdom, Austria, Germany, Ireland, Japan, France, USA, Belgium, Chile, Spain, Uruguay, Slovenia, Estonia, Portugal, Hungary, Czech Republic, Italy, South Korea, Costa Rica, Slovakia, Lithuania, Mauritius, Greece, Poland, Bulgaria, Singapore, South Africa, Latvia, Croatia, Turkey, El Salvador	2008 CPI= 6.672 E-gov. Score08=0.692 Democ-Rank08=22.37	2008 CPI= 1.846 E-gov. Score08=0.122 Democ-Rank08=15.97

The relationships between the determinants of e-government are specified through the correlation coefficient shown in Table 3. According to Table 3, there is a significant correlation between e-government readiness and transparency (about 83%), e-transparency and democracy (about 80%), and e-government readiness and democracy (about 70%). So, these reciprocal relations between all the elements are considerable.

According to the above definitions and results, strategies related to each quadrant (Figure 1) are:

Quadrant 1*:* This disposition is delineated by the lowest levels of e-government readiness, democratization, and transparency. In such an environment, e-government is just used for the government's international relations but not the people. Since there is no sufficient infrastructure, and intention for openness of information, scarce resources must be used to help the government goals. In other words, the realistically achievable e-government goal is to provide access to government information. Countries which fall in this quadrant e.g. (mostly African countries) are likely to be characterized by extreme scarcity of resources which dictates a paramount focus on efficiency. Political goals (e.g. democratic responsiveness, public accountability, transparency, etc) are virtually luxury for countries in this quadrant. A principal concern here is that e-government

Table 3. Reciprocal correlations for e-government readiness; transparency scores and democracy rank

	2008 CPI	Democ-Rank08	E-gover Score08
2008 CPI	1	-.798	.827
Democ-Rank08	-.798	1	-.731
E-goverScore08	.827	-.731	1

may be used as an instrument of control and manipulation. For example, in a dictatorship regime, the government may provide a kind of information that will serve its hidden goals. Thus, the strategic disposition of e-government initiatives undertaken by countries in this quadrant, are informational and mainly emphasize on access to government information. Therefore, strategies such as scarce resources, free market, monopoly and necessary evil are suggested for these initiatives.

Quadrant 2: This disposition is represented by high level of democratization and low level of e-government readiness and transparency. It suggests a consultational disposition, where values do not require policy dialogue between the government and citizens. Here, citizens are considered as human capital and thus, scarce resources and monopoly strategies are suggested. E-government Adaption model (GAM) are proposed for adoption the technology in these countries (Akhter Shareef, Kumar, & Dwivedi 2011).

Quadrant 3: This quadrant is represented by high transparency and low levels of e-government readiness and democratization. However, e-government initiatives can use information systems to serve their goals of transaction and relation transparencies between citizens and government agencies. Scarce resources and monopoly strategies are suggested.

Quadrant 4: This quadrant is represented by high levels of transparency and democratization and low level of e-government readiness. Political values are more likely to be paramount tough, the limited e-government infrastructure here poses a real constraint on the realization of these values. Nevertheless, democratic values (e.g. transparency and integrity) that do not require policy dialogue between the government and the citizens, are still achievable under this context. In contrast, values such as democratic participation and responsiveness presume citizen-government dialogue or interactivity. However, values may not be fully supported by the technological and educational levels in this quadrant. In this context, lack of e-government infrastructure capabilities and capacities are barriers for effective citizen participation. In other words, here interactions are rather G2C than C2G. Thus, the strategic disposition of e-government initiatives undertaken by countries in this quadrant, are based on the consultational, scarce resources, monopoly and free market strategies.

Quadrant 5: This quadrant is delineated by high level of e-government readiness and low levels of transparency and democratization. Three values are likely to be dominant in this quadrant: transactional efficiency, effectiveness/quality of service, and integrity in the delivery of public services. Countries in this quadrant (e.g. Malaysia and Singapore) seek to provide not only efficient access to information but also efficient and effective delivery of public services and integrity in the provision of those services. Here the focus is on the efficiency, effectiveness, and expectation of citizens in an environment of high e-government readiness – an environment characterized by high literacy and diffusion of computer and Internet usage in the society (Figure 2). Focus on effective service delivery may be a pragmatic policy option in an environment where a higher democratization is not viable for one reason or another. Thus, interactions are mostly G2C and G2B and e-government usage is mainly transactional. Centrally planned and free market strategies are suggested.

Quadrant 6: This quadrant is characterized by high levels of e-government readiness and democratization and low level of transparency. The strategic disposition of e-government initiatives undertaken by countries in this quadrant, should be transactional i.e. transactions and interactions between citizens and business activities. Here, centrally planned and monopoly strategies are suggested.

Quadrant 7: This quadrant is represented by high level of transparency and e-government readiness and low level of democratization. This disposition proposes a participational but non-transparent e-government, i.e., there are interactions and transactions among citizens and surveys are conducted but there's non-transparency to some extent in government policies. Here, centrally planned and monopoly strategies are suggested.

Quadrant 8: In this quadrant, all three indices are on high levels. What sets this quadrant apart from the previous 7 quadrants is that it represents a setting in which the realization of all the goals (both political and efficiency related) of e-government is feasible. Although political goals are paramount here, efficiency-related goals are also important, especially in the context of prolonged economic stagnation and concomitant chronic fiscal deficits. In addition, public accountability, which is expectedly the outcome of high democratization, dictates not only the efficient and effective use of public resources but also integrity in the use of this aspect of public trust. A high level of e-government readiness allows a higher level of web-enabled citizen participation in public policy discourse or dialogue in the broadest sense in comparison to the previous dispositions. Thus, we have a participational and transparent e-government. Here, centrally planned and leading edge strategies are suggested. Spain (Muñoz-Cañavate & Hípola, 2011) is a sample of these countries.

The proposed framework in this paper can lead us to good information about the outcomes of countries. For this purpose we identified the relationship between classification of countries in this framework and GDP index (United Nations Development Programme, 2007). It is based on gross domestic product per capita in purchasing power parity terms in US dollars (United Nations Development Programme, 2007): GDP index(i) = [log(GDP(Country(i) per Capita in US$)-log(100)]/[(log(GDP(maximum)-log(100)]

Figure 3 shows a two dimensional Scatter plot of GDP index versus 8 groups (quadrants). It seems that there is a significant relationship between the groups and GDP index. So we will examine the relation between GDP indexes with e-government readiness; transparency scores, democracy rank and groups with reciprocal correlation, ANOVA analysis and linear regression.

Figure 3. A two dimensional Scatter plot of GDP index versus 8 Groups(quadrants) for 141 countries

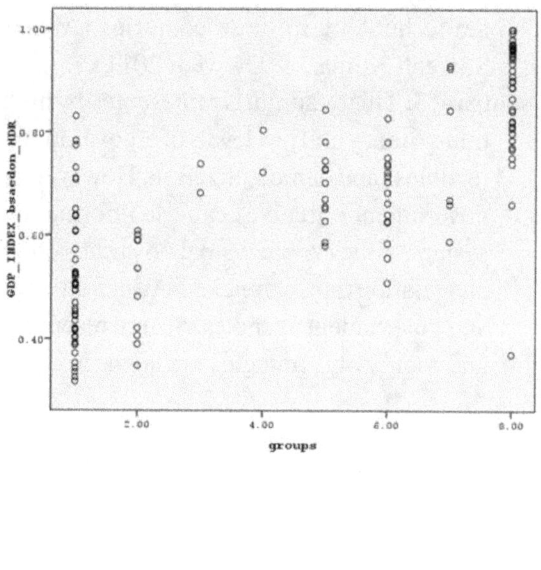

According to Table 4, there is a significant correlation between 8 identified groups with CPI, e-government readiness, transparency and GDP index(.75, .86, -.79 and .73 respectively as shown in the first row of Table 4), between GDP index and groups, e-transparency, e-government readiness, democracy (.79, .77, .86, and -.64 respectively as shown in forth row of Table 4). Thus, these reciprocal relations between all elements are significant at the 0.01 level.

Linear Regression estimates the coefficiencies of the linear equation, involving one or more independent variables, which best predict the value of the dependent variable. Table 5 shows the result of linear regression estimation between GDP index with democracy rank, transparency, e-government score and groups of countries. As Table 5 shows, the coefficient of determination (R square) is .769 which means that these variables can predict about 80% of GDP index changes. Table 6 shows the result of ANOVA analysis and Table 7 shows the coefficiency of the linear model significant at the 0.01 level.

DISCUSSION AND CONCLUSION

The proposed framework underscores the importance of context in e-government initiatives. The goals or values that such initiatives seek depend to the settings under which those initiatives are undertaken. The fact that national e-government initiatives differ, in terms of the goals they are designed to achieve, is a reflection of the influence of the contexts. Among the myriad of contextual factors influencing the goals of e-government initiatives, technical and political factors appear to be the most important. The level of e-government readiness, the technical or infrastructural factor, indicates the degree of computer and Internet

Table 4. Reciprocal correlation calculations for e-government readiness; transparency scores, GDP index, democracy rank and proposed Gropups

		groups	2008 CPI	E-gover Score08	Democ-Rank08	GDP_index 2007
Groups	Pearson Correlation	1	.756(**)	.866(**)	-.795(**)	.793(**)
	Sig. (2-tailed)		.000	.000	.000	.000
	N	141	141	141	141	137
2008 CPI	Pearson Correlation	.756(**)	1	.827(**)	-.798(**)	.779(**)
	Sig. (2-tailed)	.000		.000	.000	.000
	N	141	141	141	141	137
E-goverScore08	Pearson Correlation	.866(**)	.827(**)	1	-.731(**)	.860(**)
	Sig. (2-tailed)	.000	.000		.000	.000
	N	141	141	141	141	137
Democ-Rank08	Pearson Correlation	-.795(**)	-.798(**)	-.731(**)	1	-.644(**)
	Sig. (2-tailed)	.000	.000	.000		.000
	N	141	141	141	141	137
GDP_index 2007	Pearson Correlation	.793(**)	.779(**)	.860(**)	-.644(**)	1
	Sig. (2-tailed)	.000	.000	.000	.000	
	N	137	137	137	137	137

** Correlation is significant at the 0.01 level (2-tailed).

Table 5. Linear Regression estimation (Model Summary) of GDP index with democracy rank, Transparency, e-government score and groups

Model	R	R Square	Adjusted R Square	Std. Error of the Estimate
1	.877(a)	.769	.762	.09465

a Predictors: (Constant), Democ-Rank08, 2008 CPI, E-goverScore08,groups

penetration in the society and, concomitantly, the feasibility of using these digital technologies to realize public policy goals. Thus, a low level of e-government readiness may substantially constrain what a government can seek to achieve through the Internet.

The political environment in which e-government initiatives are undertaken is of paramount importance. The primacy of politics here stems from the view that politics represents the authoritative allocation of values or goals for the society. Such values comprise public accountability, citizen participation, efficiency, effectiveness, economy, democratic, responsiveness, integrity in public service, service quality, security, decrease of digital divide (Brandtzeg, Heim, & Karahasanovic, 2011), public health, and public safety. These values are likely to receive different degree of emphasis as public policy goals. In a setting where a high level of democratization exists, one would expect a greater emphasis on democratic values: political accountability, democratic responsiveness, transparency and integrity in public service, citizen participation, etc. On the other hand, such values are unlikely to be emphasized in an environment of low level of democratization. From this perspective, the level of democratization appears to be an important contextual factor influencing the relative emphasis on democracy-related values. Thus, in a context of a high level of democratization and a high level of e-government readiness, one would expect democracy-related values to be dominant values in e-government initiatives, as are issues like

Table 6. ANOVA model

Model		Sum of Squares	df	Mean Square	F	Sig.
1	Regression	3.947	4	.987	110.125	.000(a)
	Residual	1.183	132	.009		
	Total	5.129	136			

a Predictors: (Constant), Democ-Rank08, 2008 CPI, E-goverScore08, groups
b Dependent Variable: GDP index 2007

Table 7. Coefficients of linear Regression estimation model

		Unstandardized Coefficients		Standardized Coefficients	t	Sig.
Model		B	Std. Error	Beta	B	Std. Error
1	(Constant)	.205	.052		3.934	.000
	groups	.016	.006	.254	2.689	.008
	2008 CPI	.026	.008	.286	3.312	.001
	E-goverScore08	.515	.097	.523	5.313	.000
	Democ-Rank08	.001	.000	.162	2.034	.044

a Dependent Variable: GDP index 2007

privacy, security, and confidentiality. In such an environment, the mode of interactions between two of the principal stakeholders (namely, government and citizens) is discursive or interactive. In terms of e-government terminology, the interactions are not only G2C but also C2G. More specifically, citizens are not passive recipients of government proposals or actions; they actively seek to influence government policy outputs. When the third influential factor i.e. transparency is added to the other factors, leads to a complex but more logical decision making. Transparency contributes to the application of e-government initiatives for open and free information exchange and transactions tracking that contribute to citizenship enhancement and promotion.

As a concluding remark, the contemporary interaction of these three dimensions results in a comprehensive and integrated perspective that determines 8 distinctive context-based e-government initiatives. Results of correlation and ANOVA analysis shows GDP index of these 141 countries have a significant relation with e-government score, democracy, and transparency in 8 quadrants of them. These strategies help the policymakers to align and match their e-government goals and strategies with their context. This framework provides a mixture of perspectives dealing with its various facets along with three principal dimensions. Furthermore, difference among e-government initiatives undertaken in countries worldwide (e.g. technological, cultural, political and economical) have been verified and interpreted and a conceptual roadmap has been proposed for e-government initiative's planning and evaluation. This framework can be used to explain existing e-government efforts and initiatives. It can also provide insights about reasons a government has pursued specific goals through a particular e-government initiative. Second, it may be used as a normative model for guiding e-government initiatives.

The framework serves as a heuristic to help researchers and practitioners who are interested in:

1. Determining and appreciating the importance of the goal-context compatibility for the success or failure of e-government initiatives;
2. Evaluating e-government initiatives in terms of the congruence, or lack thereof, of the stated goals with the given environment or context; and
3. Formulating empirically testable hypothesis relating e-government initiatives to their environments.

REFERENCES

Abbasi Shahkooh, K., Abbasi Shahkooh, S., & Abdollahi, A. (2008). Corruption Reduction in Developing Countries Based on E-government. *World Applied Science Journal*, *4*(2), 1–7.

Akhter Shareef, M., Kumar, V., & Kumar, U. (2011). e-Government Adoption Model (GAM): Differing service maturity levels Original Research Article. *Government Information Quarterly*, *28*(1), 17–35. doi:10.1016/j.giq.2010.05.006

Altameem, T., Zairi, M., & Alshawi, S. (2006). Critical Success Factors of E-Government: A Proposed Model for E-Government Implementation. In *Proceedings of the Innovations in Information Technology Conference* (pp. 1-5).

Antonio Muñoz-Cañavate, A., & Hípola, P. (2011). Electronic administration in Spain: From its beginnings to the present Original Research Article. *Government Information Quarterly*, *28*(1), 74–90. doi:10.1016/j.giq.2010.05.008

Bozeman, B. (1987). *All organizations are public: Bridging public and private organizational theories*. San Francisco, CA: Jossey-Bass.

Braa, J., & Hedberg, C. (2000). *Developing district-based health care information systems, Information Flows, Local Improvisations and Work Practices*. Paper presented at the IFIPWG9.4 Conference, Cape Town, South Africa.

Brandtzeg, P. B., Heim, J., & Karahasanovic, A. (2011). Understanding the new digital divide—A typology of Internet users in Europe Original Research Article. *International Journal of Human-Computer Studies*, *69*(3), 123–138. doi:10.1016/j.ijhcs.2010.11.004

Goehring, J. (2007). *Nations in Transit 2007. Democratization from Central Europe to Eurasia*. New York, NY: Freedom House.

Hazlett, S. A., & Hill, F. M. (2003). E-government: The realities of using IT to transform the public sector. *Managing Service Quality*, *13*(6), 445–452. doi:10.1108/09604520310506504

Heeks, R. (2004a). *E-government as a Carrier of Context*. Manchester, UK: Institute for Development Policy and Management, University of Manchester.

Heeks, R. (2004b). *E-government for development, transparency definition*. Manchester, UK: Institute for Development Policy and Management, University of Manchester.

Ho, A. T., & Ni, A. Y. (2004). Explaining the adoption of e-government features: A case study of Iowa county treasurers' offices. *American Review of Public Administration*, *34*(2), 164–180. doi:10.1177/0275074004264355

Holliday, I., & Kwok, R. C. W. (2004). Governance in the information age: Building e-government in Hong Kong. *New Media & Society*, *6*, 549–570. doi:10.1177/146144804044334

Institute for Trade Studies and Research (ITSR). (2004). *Electronic commerce, concepts and applications*. Tehran, Iran: Author.

Kitiyadisai, K. (2000). *The implementation of IT in reengineering the Thai Revenue Department, Information Flows, Local Improvisations and Work Practices*. Paper presented at the IFIPWG9.4 Conference, Cape Town, South Africa.

Kossick, R. M. (2002). Mexico's emerging E-government program: The role of the Internet in promoting economic development, democratic governance and the Rule of the Law. *Law and Business Review of the Americas*, 141-187.

Lowry, P. B., Albrecht, C. C., & Nunamaker, J. F. (2003). Evolutionary development and research on Internet-based collaborative writing tools and processes to enhance e-Writing in an e-Government setting. *Decision Support Systems*, *34*, 229–252. doi:10.1016/S0167-9236(02)00119-7

Netchaeva, I. (2002). E-government and e-democracy: A comparison of opportunities in the North and South. *Gazette*, *64*(5), 467–477. doi:10.1177/17480485020640050601

Parsons, G. L. (1983a). *Fitting Information Systems Technology to the Corporate Needs: The Linking Strategy*. Boston, MA: HBS Case Services.

Parsons, G. L. (1983b). Information technology: a new competitive weapon. *Sloan Management Review*, *25*(1), 3–14.

Peters, R., Jansen, M., & Engers, T. (2004). Measuring e-government impact: existing practices. In *Proceedings of the Sixth International Conference on Electronic Commerce*, Delft, The Netherlands (pp. 480-488).

Pope, J. (2000). *Transparency International Sourcebook 2000: Confronting Corruption, The Elements of a National Integrity System* (3rd ed.). Berlin, Germany: Transparency International.

Rowley, J. (2011). e-Government stakeholders—Who are they and what do they want? *International Journal of Information Management*, *31*(1), 53–62. doi:10.1016/j.ijinfomgt.2010.05.005

Sarantis, D., Charalabidis, Y., & Askounis, D. (2011). A goal-driven management framework for electronic government transformation projects implementation. *Government Information Quarterly*, *28*(1), 117–128. doi:10.1016/j.giq.2009.10.006

Strejcek, G., & Theil, M. (2004). Technology push, legislation pull? E-government in the European Union. *Decision Support Systems*, *34*(1), 305–313.

Transparency International. (2008). *Global Corruption Report 2008, Corruption in the water sector*. Cambridge, UK: Cambridge University Press.

Turban, E., King, D., Lee, J., Warkentin, M., & Chang, H. M. (2002). *Electronic commerce 2002, a managerial perspective* (2nd ed.). Upper Saddle River, NJ: Prentice Hall.

United Nations. (2004). *Global E-Government Readiness Report*. New York, NY: Department of Economic and Social Affairs, United Nations.

United Nations. (2008). *UN E-Government Survey 2008 form e-government to connected governance*. New York, NY: Department of Economic and Social Affairs, Division for Public Administration and Development Management, United Nations.

United Nations Development Programme (UNDP). (2007). *Human Development Report 2007/2008*. New York, NY: Author.

Wong, W., & Welch, E. (2004). Does e-government promote accountability? A comparative analysis of Website openness and government accountability. *Governance: An International Journal of Policy/ Administration and Institutions*, *17*(2), 275–297.

Zarei, B., Ghapanchi, A., & Sattary, B. (2008). Toward national e-government development models for developing countries: A nine-stage model. *The International Information & Library Review*, *40*(3), 199–208. doi:10.1016/j.iilr.2008.04.001

This work was previously published in the Information Resources Management Journal, Volume 24, Issue 2, edited by Mehdi Khosrow-Pour, pp. 1-15, copyright 2013 by IGI Publishing (an imprint of IGI Global).

Chapter 6
What Drives Malaysian E-Government Adoption?
An Empirical Analysis

Alain Yee-Loong Chong
The Hong Kong Polytechnic University, Hong Kong

ABSTRACT

In this paper, the author investigates the factors that affect the adoption of e-government in Malaysia. Variables like perceived usefulness, perceived ease of use, compatibility, trust and demographic profiles of users are included in this research. Data was collected from 418 respondents, and multiple regression analysis is employed to test the research model. The results show that perceived usefulness, perceived ease of use, compatibility, trust and age have significant relationships with e-government adoption. The results from this study are useful for Malaysian government in formulating appropriate strategies to improve the adoption of e-government applications in Malaysia.

1.0 INTRODUCTION

The growth of internet has transformed businesses and industries. Many businesses today have incorporated e-business as part of their business models and strategies. The transformation in the business models is not only in the private sector, but also in the public sector. Increasingly, government are beginning to make use of the internet to interact with its citizens. The application of internet in government operations is known as e-government (Lean et al., 2009). E-government can be in the form of digital interactions between government and its citizen, government to businesses, and between government agencies.

Like many developing countries, the Malaysian government has been investing in e-government (Lean et al., 2009). One reason why the government invested in e-government is to increase the transparency in its administrative procedures and decision makings, as well as being able to deliver its services to its citizens and businesses efficiently

DOI: 10.4018/978-1-4666-3616-3.ch006

(Arduini et al., 2010). Although Malaysia is still a developing country, it has placed a lot of emphasis on the developments of information technologies (Chong & Ooi, 2008). One of the key aims of the Malaysian government is to achieve developed nation status by the year 2020, and information technologies and multimedia are part of the nation's strategy to achieve the plan. In order to realize the aim, the Malaysian government has driven the information technologies sector by implementing the Multimedia Super Corridor (MSC) initiative. The idea of the MSC is similar to the Silicon Valley in the United States, whereby the Malaysia government has designated areas that focused on the development of information technologies. There are several "flagship applications" that are part of the overall MSC strategic plans. One of the flagship applications is e-government. The e-government initiative was started by the Malaysian government in 2004 (Lean et al., 2009). Some of the Malaysian e-government applications include allowing users to submit their taxes online, checking and paying their traffic offenses fines, and paying electricity and water bills. Although e-government applications from the Malaysian government have started in 2004, its adoption by the Malaysian citizens remains low (Lean et al., 2009). Malaysia's e-government adoptions remained behind countries such as Singapore, Taiwan, and Hong Kong (Lean et al., 2009).

Like many developing countries, Malaysia is a country that is in transitions from being a developing nation to a developed nation. However, in order to achieve efficiencies in the government, one way to do so is through e-government. The information technologies infrastructure in Malaysia is well developed, and many of its citizens have access to the Internet and many are even using mobile devices to access the internet (Wei et al., 2009). Although existing literature have being conducted to study on the adoptions of e-government (Arduini et al., 2010; Bélanger & Carter, 2008; Gilbert et al., 2004), most of these studies have been conducted in western countries or in developed nations. There has been few studies which have focused on fast growing, developing nations such as Malaysia. In order to bridge the gap in existing research in e-government studies, this research aims to investigate the factors that affect the adoptions of e-government in Malaysia.

2.0 LITERATURE REVIEW

2.1 E-Government

Although e-government is no longer a new concept, and governments in many parts of the world are using the internet to provide services to its citizens, there is still no universally accepted definition of e-government (Yildiz, 2007). According to the United Nations and American Society for Public Administration (2002), e-government is the usage of the internet and the World Wide Web to deliver government information and services to its citizens. Yildiz (2007) further stated that other than the internet, other technologies that can use to support the delivery of e-government including databases, networking, multimedia, personal identification technologies, etc. Fang (2002) stated that e-government include government activities such as acquiring and providing products and services, placing and receiving orders, providing and obtaining information, and financial transactions that are conducted over electronic communications.

Although the definitions of e-government extend beyond the use of internet technologies, Criado and Ramilo (2003) in their study on e-government practices in Spain, specifically narrowed down their study of e-government to government websites. E-government is defined by Layne and Lee (2001) as the government's use of web-based internet technology to provide access and delivery of government information and services to its citizens, business partners, employees, and government entities (Layne & Lee, 2001). The models of e-government have often been categorized as government to citizen, government to business, government to government (Brown & Brudney, 2001).

For this research, we have adopted the definition of e-government from Layne and Lee (2001), as is consistent with other definitions of e-government, as well as including the main models of e-governments as stated by Brown and Brudney (2001). However, instead of just looking at web-based internet technology, this study defines e-government as government's use of electronic communications to provide access and delivery of government information and services to its citizens, business partners, employees, and government entities.

2.2 Factors Affecting the Adoptions of E-Government

Past studies on information technologies adoptions have focused on deriving their models from Technology Acceptance Model (TAM) (Davis, 1989) as well as Diffusion of Innovation (DOI) model (Rogers, 1995).

According to TAM, two factors that can predict an individual's attitudes towards using a new technology are perceived usefulness and perceived ease of use (Davis, 1989; Chong et al., 2010). Perceived usefulness is the degree which an individual believes using the particular system would improve his or her job performance (Davis, 1989). Therefore from the perspective of e-government, it could include benefits for citizens such as reducing time spent on going to the government office, and therefore improve efficiency. Perceived ease of use is defined as whether the technology is perceived as being free of efforts to use. Jeyaraj et al. (2006) in their meta-analysis of predictors of technology adoptions by both organizations and individuals found that TAM is one of the most wide cited and used technology adoption models.

Rogers (1995) in his DOI model stated that the rate of adoption of an innovation can be determined by the attributes of the particular innovation, and they are: relative advantage, compatibility, complexity, trialability, and observability. Relative advantage is the "degree which the innovation is perceived as being better than the idea it supersedes". Compatibility is the degree which the innovation is perceived as being "consistent with existing values, past experience, and needs of potential adopters". Complexity is similar to ease of use in TAM, whereby it is defined as the degree which an innovation is perceived as being "difficult and understand and use". Trialability is the degree which an innovation may be given "experimental with on a limited basis". Lastly, Observability is the degree which the results of the innovation is "visible to others" (Chong & Ooi, 2008).

Both TAM and DOI have been applied in various technologies such as online banking (Chong et al., 2010), mobile commerce (Wei et al., 2009), e-business (Chong et al., 2009), e-government (Carter & Bélanger, 2005). Although both TAM and DOI are common technology adoption models, many recent technology adoption studies have now extended these models by including additional variables. These studies tend to be on technologies that have specific unique attributes, and therefore traditional variables in TAM and DOI are not sufficient to predict the adoptions by users (Chong & Ooi, 2008). Wei et al. (2009) for example, extended the TAM model by including additional variables such as social influence and security perceptions in their study of m-commerce adoption. As e-government often involves using data from its citizens, many e-government adoption studies have often included variables such as trust and securities (Al-Busaidy & Weerakkody, 2009; Bélanger & Carter, 2008).

Many of these studies have also neglected the effects of users' demographic profiles (Yang, 2005). It is important to know the demographic profiles of e-government users, as this will allow the government to formulate strategies to increase the adoption of e-government based on users' demographic profiles. Existing studies on technology adoptions that have revealed that user's demographic profiles are able to differentiate between their internet usages patterns (Teo, 2001). Therefore this study extends the traditional TAM and DOI model in the study of e-government adoption by including additional variables of trust, and demographic profiles of users.

3.0 HYPOTHESES DEVELOPMENT AND RESEARCH MODEL

3.1 Perceived Usefulness

Perceived usefulness is similar with relative advantage, in that the individuals who use e-government believe that the system will improve his or her job performance when compared to the previous methods. Perceived usefulness is one of the most widely used variables in the study of technology adoption (Jeyaraj et al., 2006). In the study of e-government, perceived usefulness is also found to a consistent variable to predict citizens' intention to adopt e-government. For example, Horst et al. (2007) in their study of e-government services in the Netherlands, found that perceived usefulness is one of the most significant influence on users' e-government adoption decision. Lean et al. (2009) in their study of e-government in Malaysia have similar results to support those from Horst et al. (2007). However, not all studies on e-government adoption have found the significant and positive relationships between perceived usefulness and adoption of e-government. Carter and Bélanger (2005) found that perceived usefulness was not significant in their study of e-government adoption. Given the contradictory results, this study hypothesizes that:

H1: Perceived usefulness has a significant and positive relationship with the adoption of e-government.

3.2 Perceived Ease of Use

Similar to perceived usefulness, perceived ease of use is also one of the variable derived from TAM. It is very similar to the complexity variable used in DOI. Although a user might find e-government as being useful, he or she might also find that the e-government is difficult to use, and therefore hinder his or her adoption of e-government. Perceived ease of use has also been examined in previous e-government adoption studies (Lean et al., 2009; Carter & Bélanger, 2005), and have found to have a significant influence on users' decisions to adopt e-government. Using e-government systems might be difficult for users who are not familiar with computers or the internet. For example, in order to file for tax returns online in Malaysia, users need to register online, as well as obtaining a security code during the first time registration. This might be considered as being too complicated to users, and therefore unwilling to proceed with the e-government adoption. This study therefore hypothesizes that:

H2: Perceived ease of use has a significant and positive relationship with the adoption of e-government.

3.3 Compatibility

Compatibility is the degree to which e-government is perceived as being compatible with existing values, beliefs, experiences, and needs of the users (Van Slyke et al., 2004). Lean et al. (2009) for example, found that compatibility is able to predict citizen's decisions to adopt e-government. However, not all studies supported this. Phang et al. (2005) for example, found that compatibility has insignificant relationship with senior citizens' intentions to adopt e-government. Users who have not adopted e-government might be conducting certain services such as filing for tax returns, paying their fines etc. through offline, manual processes. To move from this offline, traditional procedure and use e-government services involve a change of mindsets, and experiencing something new. This might not be compatible with the users' existing ways of doing things. In Malaysia in particular, the users have high uncertainty avoidance and might be unwilling to take risks. They are comfortable with using the previous methods of interacting with government, and therefore might feel uncomfortable when using e-government. This study therefore hypothesizes that:

H3: Compatibility has a significant and positive relationship with the adoption of e-government.

3.4 Trust

In this research, trust is defined as the extent that an individual believes that using e-government is secure and has no privacy threats (Wei et al., 2009). When conducting transactions through e-government, users might involve conducting transactions online, or providing sensitive, personal data. For example, users will pay fines online might involve transferring funds from their bank accounts to the e-government website. Filing tax returns online will involve providing confidential information such as salary, household details online. Therefore in order for users to provide such sensitive and personal information online, they must trust that the e-government website is secure. Past studies on e-government have revealed that trust is one of the significant factors that affects users' decisions to adopt e-government (Bélanger & Carter, 2008; Lean et al., 2009). As such, this study hypothesizes that:

H4: Trust has a significant and positive relationship with the adoption of e-government.

3.5 Demographic Variables

In many past studies on e-government adoptions, demographic profiles of users have not being taken into considerations (Phang et al., 2005; Lean et al., 2009; Bélanger & Carter, 2008). However, it is often found that users with different demographic profiles such as educational level and age for example, have different internet usage patterns (Teo, 2001). Liebermann and Stashevsky (2002) for example, found that people who are older will tend to perceive Internet as being higher risks when compared to the younger users. Similarly, Morris and Venkatest (2000) found that age have a direct and significant effect on users' perception on the usefulness of technologies. In terms of educational level, Rhee and Kim (2004) found that those with higher level of education are far more likely to use the Internet. One possible explanation was that those who have higher educational level will have more knowledge on computers and the Internet, and is therefore more likely to use it. Based on these findings, the following hypotheses are developed:

H5: Age has a significant and negative relationship with the adoption of e-government.

H6: Educational level has a significant and positive relationship with the adoption of e-government.

3.6 Research Model

Based on the literature review and hypotheses development, a research model is developed (See Figure 1). The research model shows that perceived usefulness, perceived ease of use, compatibility, trust and educational level are positively related to e-government adoption, while age is negatively related to e-government adoption.

4.0 METHODOLOGY

4.1 Sample and Procedure

Survey questionnaires were developed to test this research's hypotheses. The surveys were distributed to several government offices in Putrajaya,

Figure 1. Research model

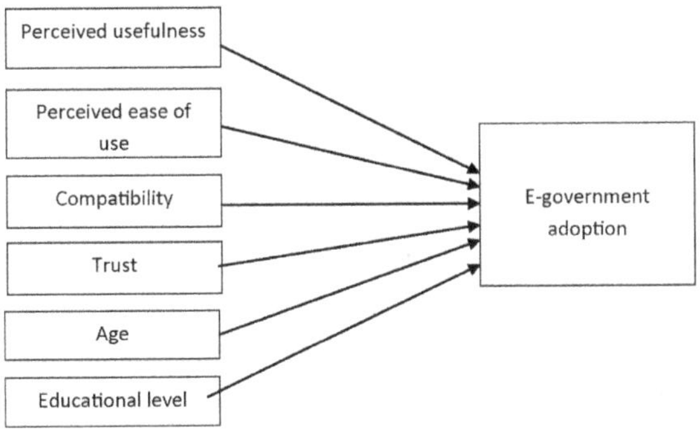

Malaysia. Putrajaya was selected to distribute the survey as it is federal administrative centre of Malaysia where many government offices and departments are located. The surveys were distributed to various Malaysian citizens who enter the selected government offices. A total of 418 usable surveys were collected. Table 1 summarizes the demographic profile of the respondents.

Table 1. Demographic profiles

Demographic Profile	Number	Percentages
Gender		
Male	213	51.0
Female	205	49.0
Age		
16-20	10	2.4
21-25	133	31.8
26-30	105	25.1
31-35	85	20.3
36-40	55	13.2
>40	30	7.2
Highest Educational Level		
Primary	12	2.9
Secondary	64	15.3
Diploma/Polytechnic	144	34.4
Bachelor degree	171	40.9
Postgraduate degree	27	6.5

4.2 Variable Measurement

The independent and dependent variables used in this study are adapted from Wei et al. (2009), Van Slyke et al. (2004), and Teo (2001). The demographic variables were measured in terms of age and educational level. The other four independent variables were measured on a 5 point Likert Scale ranging from 1 (strongly disagree) to 5 (strongly agree). A total of 14 items were used to measure the four independent variables of perceived usefulness, perceived ease of use, compatibility and trust. E-government adoption is measured based on 3 items using a 5 point Likert Scale (See the Appendix for survey questionnaire used in this research).

4.3 Scale Reliability and Construct Validity

In order to access the reliability of the questionnaire items, Cronbach's alpha was applied. As shown on Table 2, all the items' Cronbach's alpha values are greater than 0.70, thus confirming that the item measurements of the constructs are reliable (Nunnally, 1978).

Table 2. Reliability analysis

Variables	Cronbach alpha
Perceived usefulness	0.979
Perceived ease of use	0.945
Compatibility	0.981
Trust	0.974
e-government adoption.	0.970

In order to evaluate the validity of constructs used in this research, factor analysis is conducted. Principle component analysis is selected as the aim of the factor analysis is to determine how and to what extent the items are linked to their underlying factors (Chong & Ooi, 2008). Factor loadings of 0.50 are used as the cut-off point (Hair et al., 2006). Factors that have eigenvalues of more than 1 are considered significant, while those below 1 are considered insignificant and therefore were disregard (Chong & Ooi, 2008). Based on Table 3, all items had loading factors of more than 0.50, thus confirming that each construct used in this study is valid.

4.4 Multiple Regression Analysis and Results

Table 4 shows the result of the multiple regression analysis.

The table shows that the values for Tolerance are all greater than 0.1, and variation inflation factors (VIF) are less than 10. Therefore the data this research did not have multicollinearity problems. The *F*-statistics produced (F=508.32) were significant at 1 percent level (Sig. F<0.01), thus confirming the fitness for the research model. Thus there is a statistically significant relationship between the adoption factors and the e-government adoption. The adjusted R^2 value is was 0.881. Thus the adoption factors in the model can significantly account for 88.1 percent in the adoption of e-government.

The results show that age, perceived usefulness, perceived ease of use, compatibility and trust all have p value of less than 0.001. Therefore H1, H2, H3, H4, and H5 are supported. As educational level has a p-value of more than 0.05, H6 is therefore rejected. Based on the Beta values, the most important factors that affect the adoption of e-government are trust, perceived ease of use, perceived usefulness, age, and compatibility.

Table 3. Factor analysis

Constructs	No of Items	Factor Loadings	Eigenvalues	Percentage of variance
Perceived usefulness	4	0.947 0.972	3.766	94.161
Perceived ease of use	4	0.848 – 0.973	3.521	88.018
Compat-ibility	3	0.984 – 0.987	2.855	95.157
Trust	3	0.969 – 0.990	2.892	96.386
e-gov-ernment adoption	3	0.940 – 0.945	2.828	94.280

Table 4. Multiple regression analysis

Predictor variables	Beta	Sig	Tolerance	VIF
Perceived usefulness	0.177	0.000	0.349	2.865
Perceived ease of use	0.214	0.000	0.531	1.882
Compatibility	0.061	0.007	0.563	1.774
Trust	0.553	0.000	0.325	3.078
Age	-0.12	0.000	0.542	1.845
Educational level	-0.023	0.343	0.474	2.104

Notes: Overall model F = 508.325, $p < 0.01$; R^2 =0.881, adjusted R^2 =0.879

5.0 DISCUSSION

Perceived usefulness, perceived ease of use, and compatibility are variables derived from TAM and DOI. The result shows that they have a positive and significant influence on users' decisions to adopt e-government. For users, it is important for them to find e-government applications useful before they adopt it. This is consistent with past adoption studies from Horst et al. (2007) and Lean et al. (2009). Therefore governments need to put in efforts to ensure that the e-government applications are useful to the users. However, it should be noted that the users are more concern with the perceived ease of use of e-government applications than its perceived usefulness. Therefore if the e-government applications is useful but is deemed complicated by the users, the applications will not be adopted by the users. In designing e-government applications, sometimes there is a trade-offs between the applications' usefulness and their ease of use. Careful considerations are needed by the application developers to find a balance between these two.

Compatibility also has a significant influence on users' decision to adopt e-government. This shows that users need to ensure that using e-government fits well with their current style of doing things. As most users in Malaysia are used to using offline methods when dealing with government processes (e.g. paying fines, submitting tax returns), it is important to ensure that the users are comfortable with using e-government applications.

The most significant variable affecting the adoption of e-government in this study is trust. This is understandable as users will often need to submit private information online in their dealings with e-government applications. The Malaysian government needs to ensure that confidence in their applications' securities and privacies remain high. This is consistent with past studies on e-government adoptions by Bélanger and Carter (2008) and Lean et al. (2009).

In terms of demographic variables, our research shows that educational level has no influence on users' decisions to adopt e-government. This contradicts with past studies such as Rhee and Kim (2004). This could mean that in general, regardless of users' educational level, they are quite aware of e-government applications. Unlike studies by Rhee and Kim (2004), users with lower educational level will also engage with e-government applications. However, result reveals that younger users are more likely to use e-government applications when compared to older people. This could be that older people are used to interacting with the government via offline methods. For examples, they might have been submitting their tax returns via mail postage for many years, and to change to online submission might not be compatible with their previous practices. Young people on the other hand, are usually more aware of internet technologies, are therefore are more likely to adopt e-government when compared to older users. They might also spend more time using the Internet (Teo, 2001), and therefore feel that e-government is compatible with their current practices.

6.0 CONCLUSION AND IMPLICATIONS

This study investigates the factors affecting Malaysian users' intention to adopt e-government. This study has extended previous studies on e-government by including variables from the traditional TAM and DOI model, and includes additional variables such as trust and demographic profiles. There are several implications for this study.

This is one of the first few studies that have included demographic variables in the study of e-government adoption in Malaysia. Based on this result, government can formulate strategies to improve the adoptions of e-government by older users. In order to attract the older users to adopt e-government, the applications should be secure, easy to use, useful, and compatible with the users' values and practices. The Malaysian government can apply several strategies to improve trust in e-government applications. Firstly, the current e-government applications' security and privacy features should be improved. Government should also change the perceptions of the users by emphasizing on the safety features offered by the e-government applications. The government can have marketing campaigns to educate consumers, or create awareness among them. This practise has been done by the Malaysian government whereby television advertisements are being used to promote several e-government applications. For e-government applications involving financial transactions or submission of sensitive and private information, the e-government applications should pass the message to users that the web security facilities such as encryptions and firewalls are able to eliminate third party intrusions.

The result also shows that traditional variables found in TAM and DOI are not sufficient to predict e-commerce adoption. Instead, government should focus on trust as well as younger users when planning for improving current e-government adoption in Malaysia.

7.0 LIMITATIONS AND FUTURE STUDIES

This study has several limitations. Firstly, the study is conducted in Malaysia. Future studies can extend this study by conducting a similar study in other countries. Secondly, there is a risk that additional adoption factors have not been included in this model. Constructs such as self efficacy, perceived enjoyment, and national culture for example, can be included in future research models.

REFERENCES

Al-Busaidy, M., & Weerakkody, V. (2009). E-government diffusion in Oman: a public sector employees' perspective. *Transforming Government: People. Process and Policy, 3*(4), 375–393.

Arduini, D., Belotti, F., Denni, M., Giungato, G., & Zanfei, A. (2010). Technology adoption and innovation in public services the case of e-government in Italy. *Information Economics and Policy, 22*(3), 257–275. doi:10.1016/j.infoecopol.2009.12.007

Bélanger, F., & Carter, L. (2008). Trust and risk in e-government adoption. *The Journal of Strategic Information Systems, 17*(2), 165–176. doi:10.1016/j.jsis.2007.12.002

Brown, M. M., & Brudney, J. L. (2001). *Achieving advanced electronic government services: An examination of obstacles and implications from an international perspective*. Paper presented at the National Public Management Research Conference, Bloomington, IN.

Carter, L., & Bélanger, F. (2005). The utilization of e-government services: citizen trust, innovation and acceptance factors. *Information Systems Journal, 15*(1), 5–25. doi:10.1111/j.1365-2575.2005.00183.x

Chong, A. Y. L., & Ooi, K. B. (2008). Adoption of interorganizational system standards in supply chains: an empirical analysis of RosettaNet standards. *Industrial Management & Data Systems, 108*(4), 529–547. doi:10.1108/02635570810868371

Chong, A. Y. L., Ooi, K. B., Lin, B., & Tan, B. I. (2010). Online banking adoption: an empirical analysis. *International Journal of Bank Marketing, 28*(4), 267–287. doi:10.1108/02652321011054963

Chong, A. Y. L., Ooi, K. B., & Sohal, A. (2009). The relationship between supply chain factors and adoption of e-Collaboration tools: An empirical examination. *International Journal of Production Economics, 122*(1), 150–160. doi:10.1016/j.ijpe.2009.05.012

Criado, J. I., & Ramilo, M. C. (2003). E-government in practice: An analysis of Web site orientation to the citizens in Spanish municipalities. *International Journal of Public Sector Management, 16*(3), 191–218. doi:10.1108/09513550310472320

Davis, F. D. (1989). Perceived usefulness, perceived ease of use, and user acceptance of information technology. *Management Information Systems Quarterly, 13*(3), 319–340. doi:10.2307/249008

Fang, Z. (2002). E-government in digital era: concept, practice, and development. *International Journal of the Computer, the Internet and Management, 10*(2), 1-22.

Gilbert, D., Balestrini, P., & Littleboy, D. (2004). Barriers and benefits in the adoption of e-government. *International Journal of Public Sector Management, 17*(4), 286–301. doi:10.1108/09513550410539794

Hair, J. F., Black, W. C., Babin, B. J., Anderson, R. E., & Tatham, R. L. (2006). *Multivariate Data Analysis*. Upper Saddle River, NJ: Pearson Prentice Hall.

Horst, M., Kuttschreuter, M., & Gutteling, J. M. (2007). Perceived usefulness, personal experiences, risk perception and trust as determinants of adoption of e-government services in The Netherlands. *Computers in Human Behavior, 23*(4), 1838–1852. doi:10.1016/j.chb.2005.11.003

Jeyaraj, A., Rottman, J. W., & Lacity, M. C. (2006). A review of the predictors, linkages, and biases in IT innovation adoption research. *Journal of Information Technology, 21*(1), 1–23. doi:10.1057/palgrave.jit.2000056

Layne, K., & Lee, J. (2001). Developing fully functional E-government: A four stage model. *Government Information Quarterly, 18*(2), 122–136. doi:10.1016/S0740-624X(01)00066-1

Liebermann, Y., & Stashevsky, S. (2002). Perceived risks as barriers to Internet and e-commerce usage. *Qualitative Market Research: An International Journal, 5*(4), 291–300. doi:10.1108/13522750210443245

Morris, M. G., & Venkatesh, V. (2000). Age differences in technology adoption decisions: Implications for a changing work force. *Personnel Psychology, 53*(2), 375–403. doi:10.1111/j.1744-6570.2000.tb00206.x

Nunnally, J. (1978). *Psychometric Theory*. New York, NY: McGraw-Hill.

Phang, C. W., Li, Y., Sutanto, J., & Kankanhalli, A. (2005). Senior citizens' adoption of Egovernment: In quest of the antecedents of perceived usefulness. In *Proceedings of the 38th Hawaii International Conference on System Science* (pp. 1-8).

Rhee, K. Y., & Kim, W. B. (2004). The adoption and use of the Internet in South Korea. *Journal of Computer-Mediated Communication, 9*(4). Retrieved December 2, 2010, from http://jcmc.indiana.edu/vol9/issue4/rhee.html

Rogers, E. M. (1995). *Diffusion of innovations*. New York, NY: Free Press.

Teo, T. S. H. (2001). Demographic and motivation variables associated with Internet usage activities. *Internet Research, 11*(2), 125–137. doi:10.1108/10662240110695089

United Nations and American Society for Public Administration (ASPA). (2002). *Benchmarking e-government: A global perspective*. New York, NY: UN Publications.

Van Slyke, C., Belanger, F., & Comunale, C. L. (2004). Factors influencing the adoption of web-based shopping: The impact of trust. *The Data Base for Advances in Information Systems, 35*(2), 32–49.

Wei, T. T., Marthandan, G., Chong, A. Y. L., Ooi, K. B., & Arumugam, S. (2009). What drives Malaysian m-commerce adoption? An empirical analysis. *Industrial Management & Data Systems, 109*(3), 370–388. doi:10.1108/02635570910939399

Yang, K. C. C. (2005). Exploring factors affecting the adoption of mobile commerce in Singapore. *Telematics and Informatics, 22*(3), 257–277. doi:10.1016/j.tele.2004.11.003

Yildiz, M. (2007). E-government research: Reviewing the literature, limitations, and ways forward. *Government Information Quarterly, 24*(3), 646–665. doi:10.1016/j.giq.2007.01.002

APPENDIX: QUESTIONNAIRE

Please indicate your agreement or disagreement with the following statements (1 = strong disagree, 2 = disagree, 3 = neutral, 4= agree, 5 = strongly agree).

Perceived ease of use:

1. Learning e-government would be easy for me.
2. I would find it easy to use e-government to do what I wanted to do.
3. It would be easy for me to become skillful at using e-government.
4. I find e-government easy to use.

Perceived usefulness:

5. Using e-government improves my work performance.
6. Using e-government improves my productivity.
7. I find that e-government is more convenient than previous offline methods.
8. Using e-government enhances my effectiveness in my work

Compatibility:

9. I think that using the e-government fits well with the way I like to interact with government services.
10. Using e-government fits into my style.
11. Using e-government is compatible with how I like to do things.

Trust:

12. In my opinion, e-government applications are trustworthy.
13. I believe transactions made through e-government applications will be processed securely
14. I believe my personal information will be kept confidential while using e-government applications.

Intentions to use:

15. I believe I will use e-government applications in the future.
16. Assume I have access to the Internet, I will use g-government applications.
17. I will my interests towards e-government applications will increase in the future.

This work was previously published in the Information Resources Management Journal, Volume 24, Issue 2, edited by Mehdi Khosrow-Pour, pp. 16-27, copyright 2013 by IGI Publishing (an imprint of IGI Global).

Chapter 7
Bundling Processes between Private and Public Organizations:
A Qualitative Study

Armin Sharafi
Technische Universität München, Germany

Christian Ikas
Technische Universität München, Germany

Marlen Jurisch
Technische Universität München, Germany

Petra Wolf
Technische Universität München, Germany

Helmut Krcmar
Technische Universität München, Germany

ABSTRACT

Businesses are aching under the burdens entailed by public reporting duties while public administrations are faced with rising cost pressures. Fostered by the diffusion and maturation of information technology, businesses put forth growing demands in regard to the quality, integration and usability of public services. An effective means of meeting these challenges is through the identification and bundling of processes caused by reporting duties. Incorporating corresponding concepts from the business sector, to the authors develop an approach for process bundling tailored to public organizations. The authors demonstrate the approach on waste management reporting duties. This paper provides guidance for practitioners striving to optimize information flows and reduce redundancies within B2G contacts. As a result, both public administrations and businesses benefit from a more straightforward and cost-efficient provision of public services.

DOI: 10.4018/978-1-4666-3616-3.ch007

1 INTRODUCTION

E-Government aims at improving the relationships that public administrations hold with their customers by providing more efficient and effective services (Hughes, 2003). Many E-Government efforts are enabled by information technology, which provides the possibility to automate public service processes. It allows for the uninterrupted execution of public services and processes, accompanied by a simultaneous increase in customer orientation.

As citizens and businesses are demanding greater customer orientation and an integration of their needs, public administrations are forced to adjust their ways of providing services and processes. Concurrently, public institutions are faced with constant cost and performance pressures, which render swift action even more imperative. On the other hand, businesses are heavily burdened by administrative duties entailing significant expenses. Specifically, in 2008, the Federal Statistical Office in Germany identified 9,324 reporting duties between businesses and governmental institutions in Germany. Bureaucratic expenses for reporting duties on part of the German economy total approximately 47.6 billion Euros annually (Sharafi, Wolf, & Krcmar, 2010). While 22.5 billion Euros are accounted for by national legislation, 25.1 billion Euros are spent to fulfill EU- and international regulations. Consequently, businesses are growing dissatisfied, accusing their local and national governments of practicing insufficient transparency and following antiquated structures (Rodenhagen, Diekhans, & Rieckmann, 2009). These developments call for a change in how public administrations deliver value to their customers. Analyzing and optimizing the processes underlying public services can present a first step towards more customer orientation.

In the business sector, there has been significant research into process improvement, process modeling, and process-oriented reorganization (Becker, Algermissen, & Niehaves, 2006). This is reflected in an extensive base of knowledge and experience concerning business process reengineering (BPR) and similar measures. In contrast to the business domain, public administrations do not have a comprehensive array of methodologies for process change at its disposal (Becker et al., 2006; Scheer, Nüttgens, & Zimmermann, 1996). Consequently, it seems reasonable to turn to the business sector for guidance on this issue. It becomes apparent, however, that BPR-related approaches do not necessarily lend themselves easily to corresponding applications in the public sector (Jurisch et al., 2010). In particular, bureaucratic principles impose unique requirements and restrictions on any potential process changes, as does the concept of federalism. Since public administrations are inherently characterized by regulations, differing jurisdictions, and multiple levels of administration, it demands for a dedicated approach to process improvement. In order to accommodate the unique needs of the public sector, we set out to derive a more targeted approach named process bundling. This leads us to our first research question: *(1) How should a purposeful approach for improving processes between public administrations and companies be structured?*

Prompted by aforementioned practical issues observed in the field of public administration, our research aims to enable practitioners to improve upon these conditions. In order to ensure the feasibility of our recommendations for practice, we complete our analysis by examining the question: *(2) How should this approach be applied to a concrete domain setting and what benefits may be expected as a result?*

We will begin by introducing and defining the term *process bundling* as well as the underlying motivations for process bundling in public administrations. Subsequently, we will provide theoretical background on the issue of identifying suitable processes as candidates for bundling. This step will comprise an analysis of current criteria as well as the introduction of an additional set of identification principles. Incorporating these results, an approach to process bundling in the domain of public services will be proposed and subsequently applied in the field of industrial waste disposal in Germany. We will conclude with a discussion of our findings and implications for both practice and future research.

2 PROCESS BUNDLING

2.1 What is Process Bundling

Traditional public administrations exhibit a variety of common principles, including bureaucracy, hierarchical organization, bureaucratic delivery and the dichotomy of politics and administration (Hughes, 2003). These features result in an occasionally excessive number of functions and departments within those entities. This results in a myriad of information flows and data transactions within these institutions as well as in cooperation with business actors. Reportedly, tasks related to information-processing comprise over 90% of administrative processes.

Common business concepts such as value creation, competitive edge, or profit maximization are typically not the foci of public administrations. Legal regulations form the basis of public institutions' actions, mandating them with the delivery of public services to citizens, businesses, and other governmental institutions. Hence, public administrations create processes which aim to implement public services and monitor compliance to legal regulations. Public service processes entail a plethora of recurring activities (Scheer et al., 1996; Wolf, Jurisch, & Krcmar, 2010), substantial user integration as well as a variety of contact points (Becker et al., 2006). As such, they feature significant potential for improvements enabled by process bundling.

Within the context of public administrations, process bundles serve to align distinct activities and their resulting processes along a well-defined value chain. Hence, process bundling aims to integrate cross-functional or cross-organizational processes by instituting a common data base, linking processes organizationally or technically. As an example, we may regard the process of awarding a loan. Over the course of this transaction, the bank in charge communicates with several public institutions. These institutions often lack technically supported infrastructure, consequently depending on manual labor (i.e. fiscal authorities, notary, land registry, bankruptcy court, etc.) (Sharafi et al., 2010). The integration or interlinking of these processes by means of a process bundle would alter or redirect information flows without changing any of their actual content. This would facilitate a smoother and more efficient handling of the loan award process.

2.2 Reasons for Bundling

The concept of bundling processes or services is neither new nor revolutionary. Particularly in the service domain, bundling has been on the research agenda for over a decade. Our review of the literature on the service domain disclosed that the rationale behind bundling varies in complexity. Nevertheless, two reasons prevail – increasing profits and saving costs (Jurisch, Wolf, & Krcmar, 2010). As they are mostly non-profit oriented, public administrations typically focus on the latter and strive to align their operations in a cost-efficient and user-oriented manner. Limited yearly budgets are presumably the most intrinsic constraint faced by public institutions. The German government puts high hopes in the effects of process bundling, expecting to cut bureaucracy costs by over 15%. It is contended that the joined transaction of bundle components as well as their joined distribution may result in cost savings (Geng, Stinchcombe, & Whinston, 2006). Moreover, it is desired to decrease through-put times by streamlining administrative processes.

Further, process bundling may facilitate the interaction of business and public authorities by integrating and aligning processes and corresponding IT systems. This requires a purposeful overhaul of legal regulations and public service processes in order to achieve an IT-supported and continuous execution of these processes. The revision of current bureaucratic structures and the subsequent bundling of processes may increase organizations' effectiveness and flexibility.

3 AN APPROACH FOR PUBLIC SERVICE PROCESS BUNDLING

In order to provide valuable guidance for process bundling in the field public administration, we developed an approach to support the bundling of public service processes. The approach consists of four main phases, each comprising a varying number of steps: *Domain Analysis*, *Process Analysis*, *Process Bundling* and *Multidimensional Cost-Benefit Analysis* (See Figure 1). Further, it is designed to serve as a model for systematically bundling processes in order to increase their integration within the respective institution or across external value chains. Before demonstrating the approach by means of a qualitative study in the next section, we will elaborate on each of the phases.

3.1 Domain Analysis

Process bundling aims to change or redirect information flows between activities in order to increase their efficiency without changing the actual content of the information. In order to detect inefficiencies, researchers need to study the corresponding information flows (Klischewski, 2004). Obtaining a comprehensive knowledge of the interacting information flows demands for the screening of a large number of processes. The bottom-up process analysis employed by many BPR-related approaches (O'Neill & Sohal, 1999) is very expensive and time-consuming. Hence, we posit that a top-down approach (Chourabi, Mellouli, & Bouslama, 2009) is needed in order to account for the special needs of the domain of public administration. By allowing for a bird's eye view, it enables researchers to preselect processes based on a set of primary bundling principles.

In the following, we will introduce the primary principles of content-, context- and event-based bundling. The application of these superordinate principles makes for an early structuring of the considered field. Instead of delving into detailed analysis right off the bat, researchers may save resources by delimiting the field early on and highlighting processes which warrant in-depth analysis. An essential trait of this approach is that one is limited to the use of a single primary principle, i.e., processes cannot be structured by their context- and their content-related similarities at the same time (Jurisch et al., 2010).

We will focus on the identification of business-to-government (B2G) contacts, as they generally occur with higher frequency and repetition than citizen-to-government (C2G) contacts. Significant savings in regard to bureaucracy costs may be induced by B2G process changes, for these contacts constitute a rather time- and resource-consuming task on part of the affected companies.

Context-Based Bundling

One way of identifying suitable bundling candidates is to analyze B2G contacts according to their affiliation with a certain business process. As value adding and support processes frequently feature several points of contact with public administration, it is expedient to bundle these contacts along the process flow. When applying for a loan, for instance, a business is bound to contact several entities of public administration: the local tax office, the notary, the land registry

Figure 1. The four phases composing the proposed approach for public service process bundling

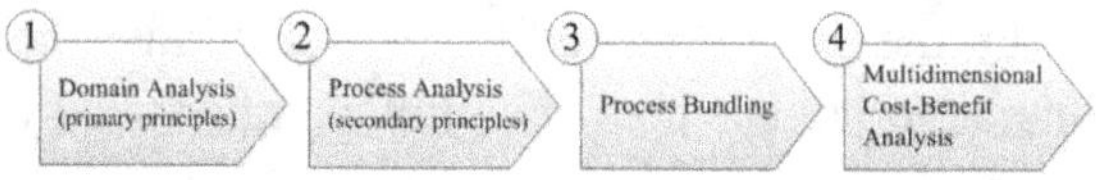

office, and the bankruptcy court. By associating B2G contacts with the respective encompassing process – in this case the loan award process – it is possible to structure them in a way that is more congruent with their business context. As an example of this method, Jurisch et al. (2010) use an industry specific process landscape in order to analyze B2G contacts of financial service providers. By identifying contacts which belong to the same process cluster, they obtain a basic structure for identifying processes as bundling candidates.

In summary, the identification of bundling candidates from a context-based view is guided by their affiliation to business processes or process clusters, e.g. their value-adding context. Consequently, employing this principle entails the mapping of B2G contacts to affiliated processes.

Content-Based Bundling

The content-based bundling approach aims to bundle processes which are similar in regard to their content. Due to the large number of B2G reporting duties in Germany, many reports overlap in regard to the information they provide, exhibiting potential for the integration of information flows. By bundling processes containing similar information, it is possible to remove redundancies among these information flows (Katzenstein & Lerch, 2000). This enables businesses to lower their expenses incurred by bureaucracy. Simultaneously, the consolidated set of processes is less prone to produce incorrect information or data inconsistencies, thereby increasing information quality (Lee, 2004). In order to ensure the suitability of the bundling set, three conditions need to be met: (1) the contents of the processes exhibit a certain degree of similarity or redundancy, (2) the same user group, or companies respectively, have to be affected by the B2G contacts, (3) the direction of the information flow has to be congruent (e.g. in all cases directed from businesses to public administrations).

Event-Based Bundling

The selection of processes from an event-based point of view aims to structure public services according to typical and recurring business events. Such events may include the acquisition of a subsidiary or the application for a building permit. The occurrence and frequency of such events determine when businesses need to contact public administration (von Lucke, 2008), which often entails dealing with various functional departments or agencies. The aim is to enable public administration to provide a single point of contact by restructuring information flows. This reduces expenses on part of the company and may increase information quality by removing any potential for redundancies and duplicate data.

Concluding the *Domain Analysis*, the categorized B2G contacts are filtered and selected based on the applied primary bundling principle. Thus, the *selection of candidates for detailed analysis* finalizes the results of the *Domain Analysis* phase, yielding the input for the *Process Analysis* phase. The B2G contacts identified by means of the process library mark a starting point for the creation of consolidated process chains.

3.2 Process Analysis

Having delineated the field of potential bundling candidates in the preceding phase, researchers may now analyze the remaining processes in more detail from a bottom-up perspective. In contrast to the top-down criteria, the three criteria *performance*, *integration* and *complexity* may be evaluated side by side for each process.

The purpose of the *Process Analysis* is to collect detailed information on the considered B2G contacts in order to identify conditions and requirements pertaining to their bundling. Subsequently, it is possible to narrow down and further structure the field of contacts by employing process evaluation criteria. This phase is split into two steps of information collection, *(1) functional analysis* (Chourabi et al., 2009; Lacerda, Cassel, & Rodrigues, 2010) and *(2) technological analysis* (Kettinger, Teng, & Guha, 1997), and one step of information utilization, *(3) selection of candidates for bundling* (Schwabe & Krcmar, 1996). While the former aspect calls for analysis on the functional level, the latter deals with technological conditions and requirements, which further qualify and restrict bundling potentials. These two steps of information collection yield one *as-is profile* for each considered process, enabling the researchers to purposefully select a final array of processes for bundling. In the following, we will describe the three steps of this phase in more detail.

The *functional analysis* breaks down information flows between businesses and public administrative entities, producing a detailed description of each process. Information is collected through legal regulations and forms. Further, in order to provide a basis for the selection of processes, it is essential to collect several attributes relating to conceptual, legal and cost perspectives. In addition, process dependencies, bureaucracy costs according to the Standard Cost Model (for additional information visit http://www.administrative-burdens.com by the SCM network), the number of businesses impacted by the process and further properties are recorded. In order to refine our search for suitable bundling candidates, we utilize process evaluation criteria as secondary bundling principles. These principles include the criteria *performance*, *complexity* and *integration*. Indicators evaluating a process' *performance* are frequently employed by process reorganization and optimization approaches. Opportunities for optimization may be uncovered by analyzing parameters such as through-put time, costs, and quality. Frequently, customer satisfaction is considerably correlated to process quality, representing another key indicator for process performance (Davenport & Beers, 1995). The concept of process *integration* may be used as another principle for prioritizing the identified bundling candidates. This approach entails the examination of information flows associated with the respective processes, highlighting criteria such as information integration, timeliness, accessibility, granularity and transparency (Berente, Vandenbosch, & Aubert, 2009). *Complexity* indicators serve to highlight bundling candidates by considering the number of cases, variants, and actors involved in a process. When identifying process bundles in public administration, it is desirable to select processes featuring high case volumes and the same group of users. Criteria of these three groups may be employed side-by-side and are thus not mutually exclusive.

The *technological analysis* serves to examine the extent to which the B2G contacts in question are currently supported by IT infrastructure, enabling researchers to deduce restrictions and possibilities for future process bundles. This includes an analysis of information systems on both the business and the government side and their interoperability (Klischewski, 2004), including interfaces for data exchange, transport protocols and data formats. The required information may be gathered by working through, among others, legal regulations, public documents, product and system descriptions, interface specifications as well as by conducting interviews.

Having compiled an as-is profile for each of the processes, the researchers may now proceed to the *selection of candidates for bundling*. In this step, one or multiple final sets of suitable bundling candidates are selected. Each process comprising these sets will be assigned it's as-is profile, which is to be merged and transformed into a common, overarching to-be profile in the next phase. The selection of candidates is based on the secondary bundling principles introduced above. In contrast to the primary bundling principles, the secondary principles are not mutually exclusive but may be regarded side by side within a single analysis. Employing the information contained in the as-is profiles, it is now possible to assess each B2G contact in terms of performance, process integration and complexity. For instance, in order to elicit suitable sets of bundling candidates, it is advisable to select processes with a high degree of routine, a large number of affected businesses and a significant cost value as assessed by the SCM. Moreover, it should be assured that there are no other concerns prohibiting a successful bundling activity, for instance in regard to the IT infrastructure (Al-Mashari & Zairi, 1999). The bundling sets serve as input for the subsequent phase of *Process Bundling*.

Concluding, the *Process Analysis* provides a final list of bundling candidates selected by means of the secondary bundling principles as well as an as-is profile illustrating further details about each of the candidates' properties, inner workings and implications.

3.3 Process Bundling

The *Process Bundling* phase is concerned with combining the selected bundling candidates into appropriately structured process bundles. These bundles need to fulfill all functionalities encompassed by the present process landscape. The phase comprises the three steps of *requirements specification*, *functional conception* and *technological conception*.

This phase is inspired by the DeMarco's (1978) "Structured Analysis". Similar approaches have been introduced by Ross and Schomann (1977) and Mac Menamin (1988). According to their propositions, a system is to be assessed first by an analysis of its processes. Subsequently, changes are proposed and integrated into the target model (DeMarco, 1978).

Especially from a functional point of view, the as-is profiles created in the previous phase serve as a basis for the step of *requirements specification*. It is advisable for the researchers to enhance this foundation by incorporating additional expert opinions (e.g. through interviews), thereby acquiring supplemental insight. Also, data security and data protection issues require thorough consideration (Garcia, Maciel, & Pinto, 2005). *Requirements specification* occurs on several levels, setting demands for the to-be profile by incorporating process-related, technology-related, legal and actor-related aspects. Finally, it is crucial to involve representatives of all affected processes in order to obtain an aligned set of requirements as well as to ensure actor commitment (Janssen & Cresswell, 2005). Based on this information, it is possible to create a first draft for the to-be profile of the emerging process bundle. This to-be profile may be presented to the previously consulted experts in order to obtain their judgment and possibly initiate any necessary adjustments.

Oftentimes, a process bundle comprises one or multiple processes which serve to accumulate data and one or multiple other processes which combine, filter or aggregate these data. The *functional conception* aims to coordinate and align these data flows while adhering to legal regulations and time dependencies. Thus, it is possible to obtain a process chain illustrating all requirements collected up to this point.

The technological conception strives to create an additional perspective by describing the technological workings and implications of the proposed process bundle. This description is based on the data collected in the second phase, *Process Analysis*. In order to automate any points of contact between the processes, it is necessary to integrate the respective information systems, aligning any relevant interfaces and data formats (Lam & Shankararaman, 2004; Vernadat, 2002). Within this step, an assessment can be made about the current situation pertaining to systems integration, possibly highlighting issues which need to be addressed on either side in order to implement such integration. Further, the *technological conception* acts as a valuable tool of visualizing information flows by representing message and information transfers between different actors and systems, for instance by means of the Business Process Modeling Notation (BPMN). These efforts yield a comprehensive specification of the to-be profile, providing a foundation for the *Multidimensional Cost-Benefit Analysis* in the last phase.

3.4 Multidimensional Cost-Benefit Analysis

Our original intent for creating a structured approach for process bundling was rooted in the aim of cutting costs and reducing redundancies in the public sector. In order to assess the degree to which the proposed to-be profile will presumably be able to meet these and other notable criteria, it is advisable to examine its potential by means of a *Multidimensional Cost-Benefit Analysis* (Wolf & Krcmar, 2005). The purpose of this analysis is to evaluate and prioritize any proposed bundling scenarios in regard to their potential benefit. Benefits as well as restrictions may be derived in several areas, including economic, organizational and process-related, technological and legal aspects.

As our efforts were initiated with the focus on reducing bureaucracy costs, we will heavily emphasize economic aspects when assessing a proposed process bundle. Hence, prospective cost savings play a crucial role in rating and prioritizing bundling endeavors. It is feasible to deduce the savings potential by identifying the relevant processes in an SCM database and cumulating the corresponding costs of dispensable processes. Yet, estimates collected in this manner will likely represent an approximation rather than a precise measurement (Nijsen, 2009) and may not be accurate in some cases (den Butter, de Graaf, & Nijsen, 2009). If such numbers are not available, they may be obtained by interviews with affected companies or similar techniques.

From the organizational and process-related point of view it is relevant to evaluate the degree to which processes are covered by IT as well as to assess the extent of data reuse. Other points of evaluation are the reduction of errors, the increase in interconnectedness, and the quality of the data (Andersen, 2004) on part of the public service provider. Further important benefits from this perspective include more transparent information flows and a quicker handling of transactions (Andersen, 2004) and decisions by the public institution.

The last two perspectives mainly deal with potential restrictions rather than benefits. These restrictions need to be evaluated as to whether they conflict with the proposed process bundle. From a technological perspective, it is necessary to analyze whether the to-be profile may be realistically created from the current IT situation, regarding both cost and time issues. Finally, legal restrictions may hinder the implementation of the to-be profile (Alpar & Olbrich, 2005). For instance, privacy and data security concerns may prohibit the sharing and reuse of certain information across different public institutions.

Generally, the criteria evaluated in the benefit analysis should be kept on a medium level of detail since in-depth data is often not obtainable in the planning phase. The benefit analysis does not synthesize all evaluation perspectives into one final rating, enabling the participating actors to weigh each dimension according to the demands of the specific environment. Concluding, the benefit analysis serves as a final assessment of the to-be profile. As a result, non-lucrative bundling scenarios may be abandoned, whereas a suitable order of implementation may be determined for the ones remaining.

4 APPLICATION – PROCESS BUNDLING IN INDUSTRIAL WASTE DISPOSAL

In order to illustrate the preceding theoretical observations and the proposed process model, we conducted a case study on environmental reporting duties of businesses in Germany. The specific aim in this case study is to design a more efficient way of reporting a specific type of environmental data to governmental institutions.

4.1 Research Design

Glaser and Strauss (1967) encourage researchers to incorporate multiple data collection techniques to ensure for data triangulation. More so, multiple sources allow for the consideration of multiple viewpoints from which a phenomena can be analyzed, substantiated, and its properties be developed (Glaser & Strauss, 1967). Our data collection strategy encompassed semi-structured interviews, process modeling, and document analysis.

We conducted a series of 18 semi-structured interviews with 15 experts over 24 months. Here, qualitative expert interviews allowed for the gathering of rich data and the construction of a deeper understanding of the phenomenon under investigation. The participating experts were identified through a convenience sampling procedure. The European Pollutant Release and Transfer Register formed the basis for our sampling selection. It enabled us to narrow down the population to a total of 36 companies, all involved in the industrial disposal of hazardous and non-hazardous waste. We contacted senior-management and other personal responsible for issuing reporting duties in each company. Out of the initial set of 36 companies, we were able to conduct semi-structured telephone interviews with 11 of them. In addition to private companies we also held 6 interviews with 3 public administrations on the national and state level. Furthermore, we conducted 1 interview with a state-level Chamber of Commerce. Each interview lasted approximately 45 minutes. The interviews began by asking broad questions about the required waste disposal reporting duties, before proceeding to ask more specific questions about the time and resources needed to administer them. Based on the specialization of the expert the interview focused on a certain aspect of the process bundling approach (See Table 1). All interviews were tape-recorded and transcribed. The transcripts were then analyzed and coded.

Table 1. Summary details of the sample interviewed

Expert ID	Affiliation	Interview Background	Interview Rounds	Primary Interview Content
Expert 1	Private Company	Telephone	1	Process Analysis
Expert 2	Private Company	Telephone	1	Process Analysis
Expert 3	Private Company	Telephone	1	Process Analysis
Expert 4	Public Administration	Face-to-face	2	Domain Analysis Process Bundling
Expert 5	Public Administration	Face-to-face	2	Domain Analysis Process Bundling
Expert 6	Public Administration	Face-to-face	2	Domain Analysis Process Bundling
Expert 7	Private Company	Telephone	1	Process Bundling
Expert 8	Chamber of Commerce	Face-to-face	1	Domain Analysis
Expert 9	Private Company	Telephone	1	Benefit Analysis
Expert 10	Private Company	Telephone	1	Process Analysis Benefit Analysis
Expert 11	Private Company	Telephone	1	Benefit Analysis
Expert 12	Private Company	Telephone	1	Benefit Analysis
Expert 13	Private Company	Telephone	1	Process Analysis Benefit Analysis
Expert 14	Private Company	Telephone	1	Benefit Analysis
Expert 15	Private Company	Telephone	1	Benefit Analysis

4.2 Application Domain Environment

Today, the waste disposal sector in Germany comprises more than 160,000 employees as well as a turnover of about 40 billion Euro (Sharafi et al., 2010). Since the year 2000, the quantity of dangerous waste has risen from 15 to 20 million tons a year. Therefore, 250,000 companies and 320 authorities create and deal with approximately 10,000 records of proper waste management, 3 million data sheets and 14 million dock receipts concerning the waste notification system (Schwarz & Hoffmann, 2009). According to the German Federal Statistical Office, 214 reporting duties were identified concerning the industrial sector wastewater, waste and miscellaneous waste disposal. Through a detailed consideration of each duty regarding corresponding bureaucracy, it is possible to allocate specific costs to 177 reporting duties. In total, these processes cause bureaucracy costs of 176.9 million Euro (Sharafi et al., 2010), demonstrating the relevance of achieving and measuring cost reductions. After a brief explanation of 3 processes analyzed in our case study, the applied *Process Analysis* explores the listed processes in more detail. The goal is to identify concrete links between these processes which enable the creation of integrated process bundles.

4.3 Application Of The Analysis Approach

Having established the conceptual groundwork, we will now move on to apply our analysis approach in the industry sector of waste disposal in Germany. For our concrete domain, this will entail a domain analysis in the field of environment and the creation of three as-is profiles, one for each of the processes selected for the proposed process bundle. This is followed by the creation of one to-be profile for the process bundle and a concluding benefit analysis (See Figure 2).

Figure 2. The proposed approach as applied to the domain of waste disposal in Germany

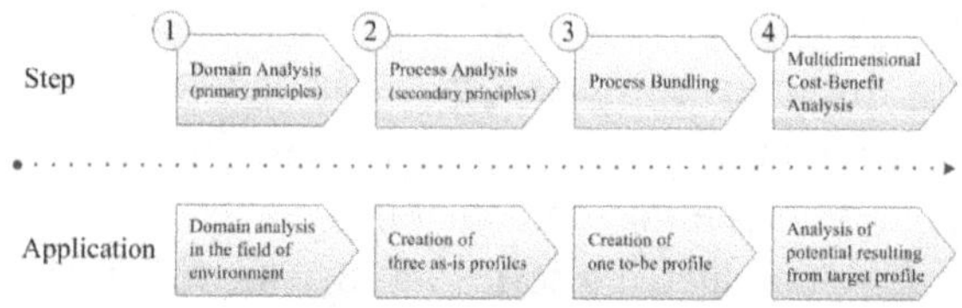

Domain Analysis

As elaborated above, the concept of primary bundling principles requires us to regard the respective processes from a content-related, a context-related, or an event-related perspective. Assuming many of the considered environmental reporting duties to be similar, we decided in favor of the content-related perspective in order to select bundling candidates most effectively. Thus, by measuring similarity of reporting duties, including their structure and data content, we were able to uncover redundancies and other inadequacies. This provided us with the opportunity to create a more efficient design for these reporting duties.

Marking the start of our investigation, the *task analysis* served to delineate the scope and type of tasks to be considered. As part of our information search we examined legislative specifications and statutes in the field of environmental protection and environmental agencies. We used various types of documents as sources for our document analysis, among them process descriptions, legal documents and regulations, organization and task plans, workflow diagrams, descriptions of the IT architecture, and reports concerning the fulfillment of the designated reporting duties. Based on this analysis, we identified typical mandatory reporting duties relating to waste disposal and environmental concerns, which resulted in a list of B2G processes.

During the *general work process analysis*, we discerned between different types of reporting duties, such as reports, applications and notices.

Further, we considered content-related similarities of the processes, employing content as the primary bundling principle. Based on a domain model for environment compliance (Krcmar, Dold, Fischer, Strobel, & Seifert, 2000), we first categorized processes by the type of substance they reported on (e.g. waste, wastewater) and subsequently by their object of reporting (e.g. quantity, pollutants). As a result, we received a table with all remaining relevant processes as well as additional information for each process (such as type of report, type of substance, legal basis etc.).

We completed the *Domain Analysis* phase by assigning relevant actors to each analyzed B2G contact in the step of *interaction analysis*. The interaction analysis was mainly based on knowledge gathered during document analysis, especially from legislative specifications and forms used in the domain.

Throughout the course of the *Domain Analysis*, we managed to identify 339 processes between businesses and public entities. We collected these processes in a data library, enabling us to analyze and select processes based on certain attributes (e.g. common legislative basis, involved actors). Part of the library is shown in Figure 3.

The resulting compilation of processes formed a basis for the subsequent *selection of candidates for detailed analysis*. By applying filters to our process library created in the previous steps, we were able to cluster processes with a similar structure and content (e.g. type of concerned substance, involved actors, and reporting period). In regard to the type of substance to be reported on, we encountered the largest grouping within the field of reporting duties concerning the waste disposal management sector. Three of them were strikingly similar in their content, for they all dealt with type and quantity of waste. These three reporting duties included *eANV*, *PRTR* and the *environmental statistic report*, which we introduce in the following.

German Electronic Waste Notification System (eANV)

All involved actors (producer and transporter of waste, waste disposal contractor, public authority) are obliged to complete a so-called "waste data sheet". Besides information about type and quantity of waste, it also contains information about the participating waste disposal partners and the actual transaction. Hence, every involved actor

Figure 3. Process data library – part of the resulting list through the Domain Analysis

No.	Processes domain environment	Classification			Involved actors (business)			Involved actors (government)			Legislative basis
	name of process/ reporting duty	type (request/re-port/no-tification)	type of substance	object	producer	transporter	waste disposal contractor	Licensing authority waste	Licensing authority for facility	State Office for Statistics	
34	waste report to PRTR (Pollutant Release and Transfer Register)	report	waste	quantity, type of waste	x		x		x		European PRTR Regulation (E-PRTR-VO VO 166/2006 EU)
89	environmental statistic report waste disposal	report	waste	quantity, type of waste			x			x	German Environmental Statistical Law(UStatG)
239	verification about the disposal of (dangerous) waste	notifiation	waste	quantity, type of waste	x	x	x	x			Ordinance on Waste Recovery and Disposal Records (Nachweisverordnung - NachwV)

is bound to adhere to certain regulations which mandate the creation, completion, or storage of corresponding waste data sheets. Consequently, many procedures with almost identical task structures seem to appear regularly. While the content of the forms is quite similar, there are different formats (paper based forms etc.), varying levels of detail and partially different addressees. The electronic waste notification system (eANV) was introduced in Germany in April 2010 (legislative basis § 45 Abs. 2 KrW-/AbfG). The previous non-automated waste notification system frequently caused redundancies as well as inconsistencies concerning the data collection, resulting in avoidable administrative costs.

E-PRTR

The aim of the introduction of the European Pollutant Release and Transfer Register (E-PRTR) was to contribute to transparency and public participation in environmental decision-making. The E-PRTR contains important environmental data about industrial facilities within the EU. It replaces and improves upon the previous European Pollutant Emission Register (EPER). The new register contains data, annually reported by some 24,000 industrial facilities covering 65 economic activities across Europe, including several industry sectors like waste and waste water management. Each facility which fulfils certain criteria has to report to E-PRTR including data about the amounts of pollutant released to air, water and land as well as off-site transfers of waste and of pollutants in waste water from a list of 91 key pollutants. Data are mostly reported annually by the respective facility to responsible authorities. The technical support is provided by national data acquisition software (BUBE), which is used by the operator to transfer reportable data online to PRTR, followed by an automated transmission. This reporting duty is important for our considerations as waste producers and waste disposal contractors have to transmit data regarding the type and amount of waste.

Environmental Statistic Report Waste Disposal

According to the German environmental law (UStatG § 1), statistics have to be collected for purposes of environmental policies and fulfilling European and international reporting duties. UStatG § 2 demands for statistics which include inquiries about waste disposal, waste which has to be proved for disposal and disposal of special waste (UStatG § 5). Especially concerning waste disposal, § 3 paragraph 1 (UStatG) registers data from involved facilities requiring admissions for disposing waste. As a result, among other information, type, amount, nature and origin of the handled waste have to be reported every year. Number, type and location of the respective facility have to be reported every two years to the responsible authority by the same companies (waste producers and waste disposal contractors). This is only a small excerpt of the UStatG to display the content of the considered law and its resulting reporting duties. In order to enable electronic processing of reporting duties, the need for an online-available reporting system arose.

Process Analysis

During *Process Analysis*, we investigated the processes further in order to reveal their suitability for bundling. Our main goal was to further limit as well as to structure the field of potential bundling candidates by considering secondary bundling principles. This perspective was amended by technical aspects, yielding one as-is profile for each process. The results of this analysis determined which processes were chosen to enter the phase of *Process Bundling*.

As elaborated on in previous sections, all secondary bundling principles may be regarded side by side within a single analysis. For practical reasons, we mainly focused on the *complexity* principle but also considered bureaucracy costs as included in the *performance* principle. In regard to complexity, we put emphasis on the degree of routine of a process, favoring processes which occur with high frequency. Further, we investigated possible variants of the respective processes and their duration. In order to identify the bundling candidates most promising in regard to cost reductions, we also analyzed the costs associated with them by means of the SCM model.

During the *analysis of used tools*, we examined how the B2G contacts in question were currently supported by IT infrastructure, deducing restrictions and possibilities for future process bundles. This included an analysis of information systems on both the business and the government side, interfaces for data exchange, transport protocols, and data formats. We gathered this information by working through legal regulations, public documents, product and system descriptions, interface specifications, and by conducting interviews.

The detailed process left us with three as-is profiles, describing each of the processes in detail. These profiles comprise the joint output of the *Domain Analysis* and the *Process Analysis* and serve as input for the next phase: *Process Bundling*.

Process Bundling

In the *Process Bundling* phase, we developed a functional concept in order to integrate the selected bundling candidates based on the information gathered in the preceding phases, and subsequently designed a to-be profile. This target profile was based on the as-is profiles of the respective processes which were chosen to be bundled and was designed in order to increase their efficiency and possibly enhance their quality. However, we applied no actual changes to the nature of these processes, such as their actors, purpose and function, or outputs. Any changes solely result from removing redundancies, uniting related information flows, and similar measures.

Figure 4 illustrates the reporting duties of industrial waste disposal contractors pertaining to *eANV*, *PRTR* and the *environmental statistic report waste disposal*, respectively. Regarded from a functional perspective, we aimed to purposefully bundle these processes by aggregating and reusing data between these processes. Specifically, in our proposed process bundle we used the data collected within the context of *eANV* to cover the reporting duties incurred by *PRTR*. Simultaneously, the same data also suffices to meet the information needs put forth by the *environmental statistic report waste disposal*. All three processes feature the same involved actors on the business side, the same direction of information flow and a significant overlap in the information content. These conditions allowed for the described bundling of these B2G contacts.

In order to demonstrate the concrete workings of the integrated process bundle, we created a BPMN model, depicting the involved documents and actors as well as communication flows between these actors (See Figure 5).

Firstly, relevant data is gathered for the *eANV* report by the involved actors on the business side: waste producer, waste transporter and waste disposal contractor. Once the respective reports are verified, they can be aggregated for future reuse in the context of *PRTR* and the *environmental*

Figure 4. Three reporting duties of companies

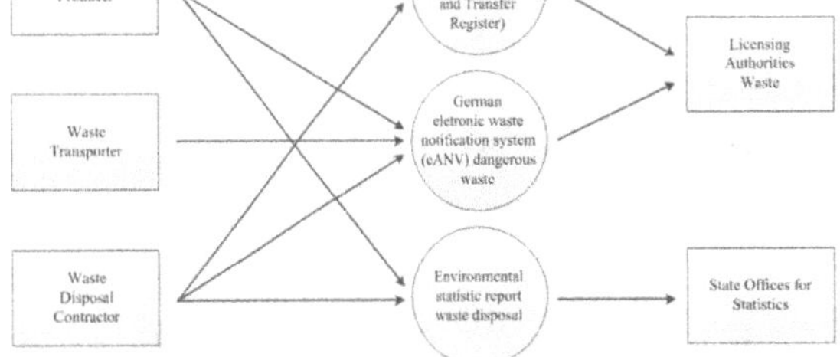

Figure 5. Target process bundle PRTR – eANV – environmental statistic report

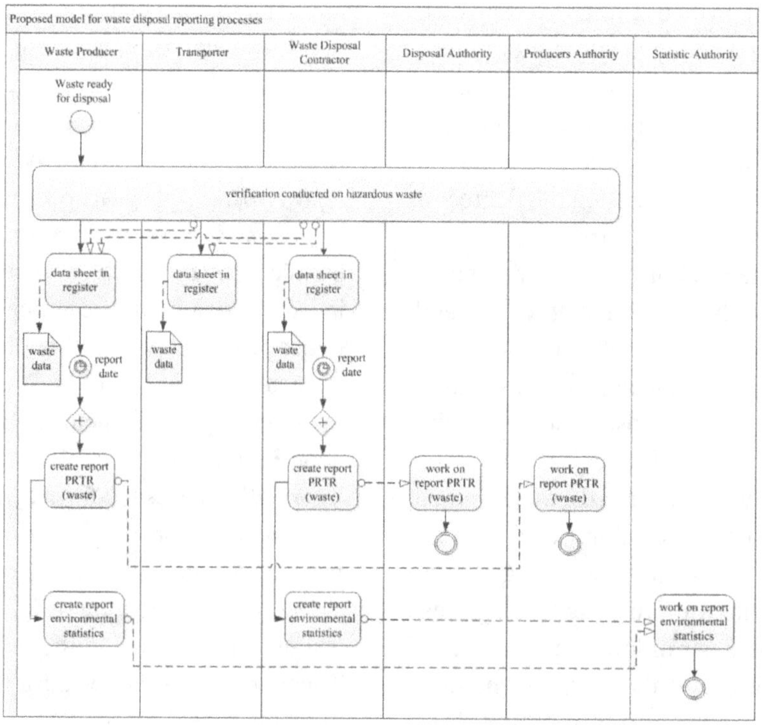

statistic report. The interaction is closed for the waste transporter, for it is not subject to these obligations. Once the reporting dates approach, the stored data will be used to automatically create the *PRTR* and *environmental statistic reports* of both the waste producer and the waste disposal contractor. Finally, the information is to be transmitted and checked by the respective authorities on the government side: disposal authority, producers' authority and statistic authority.

By purposefully reusing information as well as linking relevant information flows, this process model aims to provide a more efficient way for businesses to fulfil their reporting duties to government entities.

Multidimensional Cost-Benefit Analysis

In order to identify the benefits of the proposed bundling activity, we determined the bureaucracy costs entailed by both the *E-PRTR* and the *environmental statistic* reporting duties. The exclusive focus on monetary benefits was assumed for practical reasons.

According to the Federal Statistical Office of Germany, the costs incurred for businesses by the environmental statistic report total 479,000 Euro each year. Since no information was available on the bureaucratic efforts induced by reporting duties relating to PRTR, we conducted qualitative interviews among German waste disposal companies. We asked each company to provide information about their yearly effort required to fulfill the PRTR reporting duties. In order to ensure consistency, we calculated the resulting costs according to the Standard Cost Model. Consequently, we gathered information on the frequency and the duration of these activities as well as the corresponding hourly rate. The average yearly cost incurred by the PRTR reporting duties across all companies amounted to approximately 400 Euro each year. In 2008, 4,590 businesses reported PRTR data. Due to several limitations which apply to our interview series, an extrapolation of our results is not possible. These limitations include the limited number of surveyed businesses as well as the fact that no distinction between hazardous and non-hazardous waste was made. Yet, it is apparent that the costs incurred by the regarded reporting duties are significant. In light of other benefits not included in our analysis, for instance data quality and increased transparency, we posit that there is considerable potential in implementing the proposed process bundle.

5 DISCUSSION AND CONCLUSION

As a response to the current cost and performance pressures in the sector of public administration, we established the potential of process bundling in public services. We set out to derive an approach specifically tailored to the distinct characteristics exhibited by the domain of public administration. In particular, this was motivated by the goal of achieving cost savings as well as facilitating the interaction between businesses and public administration.

These introduced an approach for public service process bundling, consisting of the four phases of *Domain Analysis*, *Process Analysis*, *Process Bundling* and *Multidimensional Cost-Benefit Analysis*. The aim of this approach is to design and evaluate process bundles in the domain of B2G contacts. This is achieved by a thorough top-down study of the respective domain and a subsequent selection of relevant processes. After undergoing further analysis from a bottom-down perspective, each of these processes is depicted in an as-is profile and potentially assigned to a process bundle before being merged into a to-be profile. Finally, a multidimensional benefit analysis assesses the proposals' potential as well as its feasibility, providing assistance in selecting and prioritizing process bundles for final implementation.

We demonstrated our approach by applying it in the domain of waste disposal reporting duties in Germany. The field of processes to be considered was delineated from a content-related perspective. After identifying three processes as candidates for bundling, we created a to-be profile for the proposed bundle. By reusing previously recorded information in a purposeful manner, this proposed process bundle removes redundancies in the information flow and reduces the administrative burden on part of the affected companies. We concluded by establishing that the bundling activity features significant potential benefit.

The proposed approach for public service process bundling is to serve as a guideline for practitioners, aimed at reducing costs and improving process quality. By means of the derived approach, actors in public institutions will be able to analyze their processes in regard to overlapping content, recurring information and related redundancies. Further, the integration of processes with similar structure, for instance in terms of identical actors or overlapping flows of information, will be facilitated. As a result of these measures, we expect significant cost savings for the sector of public administration, taking the pressure off of heavily strained public budgets. In addition, process quality may rise and error rates decrease as redundancies and duplicate data are removed. This will aid public administrations in their quest to provide effective, well-structured and user friendly services. By offering single points of contact for frequently recurring concerns and requests, public service providers will be able to significantly enhance their E-Government capabilities. This is crucial for meeting the demands posed by the evolving information society. The affected businesses will encounter more streamlined public administrative processes, enabling them to save significant costs. Businesses would also benefit from shorter response times on part of administrative entities.

In spite of these contributions, our research is subject to significant limitations. Firstly, we applied the proposed approach only in one domain as well as with a limited set of processes. Further, the sample size used for the benefit analysis is not representative for the potentially affected population.

There are various opportunities for future research to build on these findings. In particular, it is indispensable to systematically examine the suitability of the proposed bundling principles. In addition to their validation for the application at hand, it would be advisable to investigate their transferability to the analysis of C2G contacts. Furthermore, the applicability of the approach in other domains as well as the feasibility of the resulting process bundles should be analyzed.

REFERENCES

Al-Mashari, M., & Zairi, M. (1999). BPR implementation process: an analysis of key success and failure factors. *Business Process Management Journal*, *5*(1), 87–112. doi:10.1108/14637159910249108

Alpar, P., & Olbrich, S. (2005). Legal requirements and Modelling of Processes in e-Government. *Electronic. Journal of E-Government*, *3*(3), 139–148.

Andersen, K. (2004). *E-government and public sector process rebuilding: dilettantes, wheel barrows, and diamonds*. Dordrecht, The Netherlands: Kluwer Academic Publishers.

Becker, J., Algermissen, L., & Niehaves, B. (2006). A procedure model for process oriented e-government projects. *Business Process Management Journal*, *12*(1), 61–75. doi:10.1108/14637150610643760

Berente, N., Vandenbosch, B., & Aubert, B. (2009). Information flows and business process integration. *Business Process Management Journal*, *15*(1), 119–141. doi:10.1108/14637150910931505

Chourabi, H., Mellouli, S., & Bouslama, F. (2009). Modeling e-government business processes: New approaches to transparent and efficient performance. *Information Polity*, *14*(1), 91–109.

Davenport, T. H., & Beers, M. C. (1995). Managing information about processes. *Journal of Management Information Systems*, *12*(1), 57–80.

DeMarco, T. (1978). *Structured Analysis and System Specification*. New York, NY: Yourdon Press.

den Butter, F. A. G., de Graaf, M., & Nijsen, A. (2009). *The Transaction Costs Perspective on Costs and Benefits of Government Regulation*. Rotterdam, The Netherlands: Tinbergen Institute.

Garcia, A. C. B., Maciel, C., & Pinto, F. B. (2005). A Quality Inspection Method to Evaluate E-Government Sites. In M. Wimmer, R. Traunmüller, Å. Grönlund, & K. Andersen (Eds.), *Electronic Government* (LNCS 3591, pp. 198-209).

Geng, X., Stinchcombe, M. B., & Whinston, A. B. (2006). Product Bundling. In Hendershott, T. (Ed.), *Handbook of Economics and Information Systems* (pp. 499–525). Amsterdam, The Netherlands: Elsevier.

Glaser, B. G., & Strauss, A. L. (1967). *The Discovery of Grounded Theory: Strategies for Qualitative Research*. Chicago, IL: Aldine Publishing Company.

Hughes, O. E. (2003). *Public Management and Administration* (3rd ed.). New York, NY: Palgrave Macmillan.

Janssen, M., & Cresswell, A. M. (2005). An enterprise application integration methodology for e-government. *The Journal of Enterprise Information Management*, *18*(5), 531–547. doi:10.1108/17410390510623990

Jurisch, M., Wolf, P., & Krcmar, H. (2010). Toward a Formal Approach to Process Bundling in Public Administrations. In M. Wimmer, J.-L. Chappelet, M. Janssen, & H. Scholl (Eds.), *Electronic Government* (LNCS 6228, pp. 412-423).

Katzenstein, G., & Lerch, F. J. (2000). Beneath the Surface of Organizational Processes: A Social Representation Framework for Business Process Redesign. *ACM Transactions on Information Systems*, *18*(4), 383–422. doi:10.1145/358108.358111

Kettinger, W. J., Teng, J. T. C., & Guha, S. (1997). Business Process Change: A Study of Methodologies, Techniques, and Tools. *Management Information Systems Quarterly*, *21*(1), 55–80. doi:10.2307/249742

Klischewski, R. (2004). Information Integration or Process Integration? How to Achieve Interoperability in Administration. In R. Traunmüller (Ed.), *Electronic Government* (LNCS 3183, pp. 57-65).

Krcmar, H., Dold, G., Fischer, H., Strobel, M., & Seifert, E. (2000). *Informationssysteme für das Umweltmanagement - Das Referenzmodell ECO-Integral*. Munich, Germany: R. Oldenbourg Verlag.

Lacerda, D. P., Cassel, R. A., & Rodrigues, L. H. (2010). Service process analysis using process engineering and the theory of constraints thinking process. *Business Process Management Journal*, *16*(2), 264–281. doi:10.1108/14637151011035598

Lam, W., & Shankararaman, V. (2004). An Enterprise Integration Methodology. *IT Professional*, *6*(2), 40–48. doi:10.1109/MITP.2004.1278864

Lee, I. (2004). Evaluating business process-integrated information technology investment. *Business Process Management Journal*, *10*(2), 214–233. doi:10.1108/14637150410530271

MacMenamin, S. M., & Palmer, J. F. (1988). *Strukturierte Systemanalyse*. Munich, Germany: Hanser.

Nijsen, A. (2009). SCM to Measure Compliance Costs. In *Business Regulation and Public Policy* (*Vol. 20*, pp. 1–22). New York, NY: Springer. doi:10.1007/978-0-387-77678-1_5

O'Neill, P., & Sohal, A. S. (1999). Business Process Reengineering. A review of recent literature. *Technovation*, *19*(9), 571–581. doi:10.1016/S0166-4972(99)00059-0

Rodenhagen, J., Diekhans, B., & Rieckmann, P. (2009). Prozessmanagement im Kontext des E-Government 2.0 - Einsatzfelder, Rahmenbedingungen, und aktuelle Maßnahmen. *Praxis der Wirtschaftsinformatik*, *265*(265), 36–50.

Ross, D. T., & Schoman, K. E. Jr. (1977). Structured analysis for requirements definition. *IEEE Transactions on Software Engineering*, *3*(1), 6–15. doi:10.1109/TSE.1977.229899

Scheer, A.-W., Nüttgens, M., & Zimmermann, V. (Eds.). (1996). *Business Process Reengineering in der Verwaltung*. Wiesbaden, Germany: Gabler.

Schwabe, G., & Krcmar, H. (1996). Der Needs Driven Approach - eine Methode zur Gestaltung von Telekooperation. In Schwabe, G., Krcmar, H., & Lewe, H. (Eds.), *Herausforderung Telekooperation*. Berlin, Germany: Springer.

Schwarz, J. P., & Hoffmann, S. (2009). *Behörden und Unternehmen entlasten - Bürokratiekosten senken.* Retrieved February 11, 2010, from http://www.egovernment-computing.de/index.cfm?pid=7476&pk=202981&print=true&printtype=article

Sharafi, A., Wolf, P., & Krcmar, H. (2010). Process and Data-Oriented Approach for Bundling Corporate Reporting Duties to Public Authorities – A Case Study on the Example of Waste Management Reporting. In M. Wimmer, J.-L. Chappelet, M. Janssen, & H. Scholl (Eds.), *Electronic Government* (LNCS 6228, pp. 400-411).

Vernadat, F. B. (2002). Enterprise modeling and integration (EMI): Current status and research perspectives. *Annual Reviews in Control*, *26*(1), 15–25. doi:10.1016/S1367-5788(02)80006-2

von Lucke, J. (2008). *Hochleistungsportale für die öffentliche Verwaltung*. Cologne, Germany: Joseph Eul Verlag GmbH.

Wolf, P., Jurisch, M., & Krcmar, H. (2010). *Analyse und Design von Prozessketten*. Paper presented at the Fachtagung Verwaltungsinformatik (FTVI) Conference.

Wolf, P., & Krcmar, H. (2005). Prozessorientierte Wirtschaftlichkeitsuntersuchung für E-Government. *Wirtschaftsinformatik*, *47*(5), 337–346.

This work was previously published in the Information Resources Management Journal, Volume 24, Issue 2, edited by Mehdi Khosrow-Pour, pp. 28-45, copyright 2013 by IGI Publishing (an imprint of IGI Global).

Chapter 8
Impact of e-CRM on Website Loyalty of a Public Organization's Customers

Wen-Jang Jih
Middle Tennessee State University, USA

ABSTRACT

Web-enabled customer relationship management, or e-CRM, is able to simultaneously achieve the conflicting goals of strategic flexibility and operational efficiency in developing and executing innovative e-commerce marketing strategies. A multi-disciplinary field, involving such areas as marketing, economics, business strategy, information systems, social psychology and consumer behavior, e-CRM strengthens customer relationships via a portfolio of trust-building practices with the support of powerful information technologies. While most literature in e-CRM has examined how firms formulate and implement e-CRM initiatives, there is little information on the overall quality of an e-commerce firm's e-CRM practices from the consumer point of view. This research proposes such a consumer-oriented concept, e-CRM value, based on existing e-CRM research, and examines the effect of e-CRM value on website loyalty. An empirical study is conducted to validate the theoretical model. Customers' perceptions of e-CRM value have positive causal effects on their website loyalty. Valuable implications can be derived from this finding for public organizations in managing their customer relationships.

INTRODUCTION

An integral component of information infrastructure for business operations and managerial decision making, Internet technologies are playing a strategic role in all major business activities. The World-Wide Web (or simply the Web), by far the most visible aspect of the Internet, now contains information and knowledge about virtually any domain one can practically think of. Its global connectivity and interactive features are even more valuable and influential for all management and business purposes. These two mutually reinforcing forces provided by the Web, content and com-

DOI: 10.4018/978-1-4666-3616-3.ch008

munication, are helping to reshape the business landscape in the era that is driven primarily by knowledge and innovation. Marketing activities, especially, are increasingly incorporating the Web in the strategic initiatives and rely on the website as the primary platform of interaction with existing and prospective customers that are otherwise difficult to reach for technical or financial reasons. In some information and knowledge-intensive industries (information technology, insurance, and banking, for example), the website is becoming an ever more important source of impact upon customers' purchasing decisions. Leveraging the great power of information and knowledge in the knowledge economy, both companies and customers are looking to website tools as strategic vehicles for obtaining maximum value in the e-commerce market.

In light of the strategic value of the Internet as a crucial enabling technology, companies are increasingly placing their emphasis on managing customer relationship (CRM) through effective website design and management. Technological advances in such areas as search engines, blogs, Really Simple Syndication (RSS 2.0), social networking services, highly distributed databases, multimedia, personalization, localization, and computer-telephone integration (i.e., voice-over-IP technology) have provided a rich set of system capabilities and are prompting for implementation of innovative and highly interactive mechanisms to serve prospective as well as existing customers (Chen et al., 2007). Given the growing popularity of Web-enabled CRM (or e-CRM), it is clear that business researchers and management of all sectors must possess a systematic understanding of important aspects of this important business movement.

Due to the multidisciplinary nature of the field, a variety of issues surrounding e-CRM have been investigated from different points of view. In particular, research in information systems has identified the importance of evaluation technology applications from the user perspective (Gefen & Straub, 2000). Whereas information system specialists often speak technological languages with each other, users are mainly concerned about functional capabilities associated with business operations and decisions. Looking at the applications from the user's point of view increases the probability that technological investment and business imperatives are properly aligned from the early stage of decision cycle. Tung (2007) viewed e-CRM as a major business innovation and studied the process and pattern of organizations adopting e-CRM. The study re-confirmed and therefore increased the validity of the well-recognized conceptual framework in technology innovation management. For the early adopters, e-CRM has indeed become an integral component of their major business processes. Both the scope and the depth of e-CRM applications are increasing in many of those organizations.

Chen and Chen (2004) investigated the success factors of e-CRM strategies in practice. Min et al. (2002) examined Internet applications in marketing in terms of generation, distribution, and application of market information. Both studies revealed the importance of collecting, processing, and communicating customer and market information both within the organization and across the organizational boundaries. Although these two and several other studies investigated e-CRM from the organization's perspective, the crucial role of users was evident and was emphasized throughout their discussions. To stay competitive, organizations must work hard to engage customers in major business processes, such as developing innovative new product/service and customer support. Information management is indeed ubiquitous in these processes, for both the organization and the customer. Operationally, one would increasingly find it difficult to identify a product or service, physical or logical, that does not significantly depend on information gathering, processing and dissemination in most, if not all, stages of marketing activities.

A number of studies in consumer behavior also have confirmed the value of examining e-CRM issues from customer/user point of view (Lee et al., 2006; Scullin et al., 2004). These studies suggested that, in order to obtain a systematic understanding of the highly composite nature of e-CRM, more research must be conducted along a variety of distinctive behavioral dimensions and at deeper levels of customer profiles. Customer knowledge is a vital strategic asset. Every major aspect of organization operations and decisions must be backed by adequate customer knowledge. This paper is a response to that calling. Specifically, the paper proposes a customer-based framework for a systematic inquiry of the impact of an organization's CRM practices, as implemented through websites, on website loyalty. The research framework seeks to answer the following two questions:

1. What are the significant components of website users' perceived value of e-commerce firms' CRM activities, or e-CRM value?
2. Does website users' perceived e-CRM value significantly affect their loyalty to the websites?

Answering these questions would shed some light on the value perception of e-CRM value from the e-commerce customer's point of view, and thus contribute to systematic accumulation of knowledge and insight regarding this important business concept.

In the rest of the paper, we describe the concept of CRM and e-CRM. We also address measurement issues of e-CRM as proposed in the existing literature. The concept of customer loyalty is described in the same section. The third section of the paper discusses key research issues including constructs definition and measurement, survey instrument design and data analysis. The concluding section suggests directions for further research and managerial consideration.

FROM CRM TO E-CRM

A manifestation of an organization's customer and market orientation, CRM is a concept that influences business and organizational management at operational, tactical, and strategic levels by focusing on consumer characteristics and looking at organizational operations and decision from outside in. Although the importance of customer orientation has never been neglected in the past decades, it is becoming an even more critical issue in today's knowledge-driven market. With the great wealth of knowledge content both readily available and easily accessible to customers on the Web, the expectation for service and product quality and more pleasant consuming experience also has escalated. In seeking viable ways to enhance competitive advantage in a business environment characterized by globalization, fierce competition, environmental sustainability and other challenges, organizations are not only looking to customer as a major source of market information and knowledge, they are also linking customers with vital aspects of their product value chains. As a result, many important business processes such as new product/service design and customer service in these customer-centric organizations are now even more driven by customer-oriented thinking than ever before.

The concept of CRM can be traced back to a traditional wisdom for good business practice, relationship management (Parvatiyar & Sheth, 2001). Defined as an integrated effort of a business to identify, maintain, and build up a human network with individual customers, relationship management activities seek to strengthen the network for the mutual benefit of both sides through interaction, individualized and value-added contacts over a long period of time (Shani & Chalasani, 1992). The desire of customers for pleasant experience throughout the entire cycle of product/service acquisition and consumption has never diminished. The broadened choices presented to the customer actually even make it harder for organizations to ensure expected customer satisfaction for an extended period of time. Further, the vastly improved information flow enabled by recent advancements of computing and networking technologies has significantly increased the importance and elevated the business value of a systematic management of customer relationship (Parvatiyar & Sheth, 2001).

Multiple definitions of CRM exist in the literature, but no universally accepted one has been agreed upon (Ngai, 2005). This is partly due to the young stage of the field, and partly a reflection of the multidisciplinary nature of the endeavor. For example, defining CRM from customer communications point of view, Swift (2001) viewed CRM as an "enterprise approach to understanding and influencing customer behavior through meaningful communications in order to improve customer acquisition, customer retention, customer loyalty, and customer profitability" (p. 12). Emphasizing the strategic role in resource integration, Kincaid (2003) considered CRM as "the strategic use of information, processes, technology, and people to manage the customer's relationship with your company (marketing, sales, services, and support) across the whole customer life cycle" (p. 41). Kennedy (2006) views CRM as a business philosophy that is "about identifying a company's best customers and maximizing the value from them by satisfying and retaining them" (p. 58). In information management, CRM is an amalgamation of information technology application and relationship marketing. With relationship marketing serving as the strategic foundation for the design of system architecture and functional capabilities, a CRM may incorporate a variety of information technologies to automate and integrate such enterprise-wide processes as sales, customer service, and product configuration (Scullin et al., 2004; Turban et al., 2004). The rapid advancement and universal adoption of Internet technologies have made information and knowledge exchange technologies, especially Internet-based technologies (e-mail, world wide web, chat room, e-forums, etc.), a core component of CRM systems (Ad Hamid, 2005). With Internet programs serving primarily as user interface and back office applications providing database processing capabilities, today's CRM systems are increasingly being implemented using Internet technologies, called e-CRM systems, and are making customer relationship management as easy and convenient as never before (Jih et al., 2006). The focus of business thinking, as a result, is now more on the design and delivery of product or service and less on technical concerns.

A relatively recent development, e-CRM has extended not only in the scope of business functions and processes that are covered, but also in the underlying technologies that enable the applications integration. In its early stage, automatic tools separately support such marketing functions as identifying potential customer, keeping track of customer contacts, customizing product configurations for unique customer requirements, and providing other value-added customer services. Currently converging information technologies prompt use of an integrated approach to managing customer relationship as an enterprise-wide effort. The e-CRM for Enterprise CRM (Peppard, 2000) and the e-CRM for electronic CRM (Kennedy, 2006) are mutually reinforcing each other. On the business and customer side, organizations are engaging customers in major decisions from the very early stage. A recent example involves a residential community in metropolitan suburban city in Tennessee. In order to lure an up-end grocery store chain to add a location in the region, they created a website to collect community members' signatures as a voice of welcome. The company has added several successful locations elsewhere using the same strategy. Enabled by the Internet-based technological capabilities, customers can act proactively to bring about significant customer value provided by the organizations.

E-CRM VALUE

E-CRM implementations can be expected to produce significant value for companies and customers in today's highly connected society. From the business point of view, the value propositions of e-CRM implementations at the operational level include such benefits as reduction of the cost of communicating with customers, reduction of administrative and operational costs, streamlined workflows, improved sales through better segmentation, and enhanced overall customer interactions (Ad Hamid, 2005). Coupled with significant time-saving and productivity increase due to morale boost, these operational benefits often contribute to even more encompassing business benefits at the strategic level. Numerous studies have reported major strategic benefits. Scullin et al. (2004), for example, specifically emphasized benefits in three areas associated with marketing strategy: strategic alliance, customer strategy, and product differentiation. Both strategic and operational benefits are realized via viewing customers as an essential component of major business processes. Customer interactions are embedded in the decision making process, with communication channels designed to encourage free flow of customer opinions and company responses.

From the e-marketer's point of view, quality interaction allows for collection of meaningful customer information that is often required to design customized or even personalized products or services. This personalized marketing approach is characterized by "the capability of the companies to present their goods and services customized to fit the distinct personal interests and needs of the customer" (Ross, 2005, p. 40). Enabled by customer knowledge, product/service personalization generally leads to better customer satisfaction, which may in turn result in greater customer loyalty (Anderson & Srinivasan, 2003). The concept of customer value as an essential deliverable is widely discussed in CRM literature (Day, 1994; Slater, 1997). Personalized interactivity of e-CRM provides even more welcomed features in strengthening companies' capability to reach and serve their customers.

Several researchers have proposed specific aspects of customer value in the e-commerce environment. Szymanski and Hise (2000) suggested that e-satisfaction is a function of shopping convenience, product and service offerings, and financial security. Extending the traditional concept of market orientation, Min et al. (2002) coined the term "Internet-mediated Market Orientation" to attribute the benefit of e-commerce to marketers' capability to generate market information, distribute market information, and act on the collected market information. The notion is validated by Lee et al. (2006) in an empirical study, using Taiwanese consumer data, to determine the positive effect of the three aspects of internet-mediated market orientation on customer website satisfaction.

Srinivasan et al. (2002) conducted a study to investigate the factors affecting customer loyalty in an online business-to-consumer context. The model identified eight factors influencing customer loyalty: customization, contact interaction, cultivation, care, community, choice, convenience, character. The result of regression analysis showed that all eight factors significantly influenced customer loyalty. The study suggested the importance of these eight antecedents in forming customers' perceived value of e-commerce firms' CRM activities. In a separate study, Szymanski and Hise (2000) found that e-satisfaction was significantly affected by shopping convenience, product information provision, website design, and financial security. The website design in the latter model may be reconciled with the Character factor in the model developed by Srinivasan et al. In addition, financial security has been found to be an important factor in the e-CRM studies that investigate more security-sensitive industries such as banking (Jih et al., 2004). An integration of the previous research findings and suggestions prompted us to define the e-CRM value from the customer perspective in terms of these nine components: customization, contact interactivity, cultivation, care, community, choice, convenience, security, and market response.

WEBSITE LOYALTY

Customer loyalty is often associated with repeat purchasing. However, as pointed out by Jacoby and Kyner (1973), although loyal customers tend to purchase repetitively, those who purchase repetitively do not necessarily do so out of loyalty, such as what might happen in the scenario of lacking an alternative offering. Customer loyalty usually is strengthened as a result of satisfaction with the product or service received from the seller. This is applicable in the physical economy and even more so in the Internet-enabled, online commerce. In light of the importance of the customer loyalty in the company's marketing strategy, a number of researchers have examined the nature of as well as factors affecting customer loyalty. Early views of brand loyalty almost exclusively emphasized the customer behavior of repeat purchase over a period of time (Brown, 1952; Cunningham, 1956; Lipstein, 1959; Kuehn, 1962; Day, 1969; Newman & Werbel, 1973; Reynolds & Darden, 1974; Monroe & Guiltinan, 1975). More recent research, however, contended that customer loyalty and repeat purchase do not equal (Dick & Basu, 1994). This latter view suggests that, when examining the impact of customer loyalty on the company's marketing performance, a distinction ought to be made between behavioral and attitudinal aspects of the concept (Chaudhuri & Holbrook, 2001; Jacoby & Kyner, 1973; Lim & Razzaque, 1997; Dick & Basu, 1994). Our research investigated the effect of e-CRM value as perceived by online shoppers on their loyalty to their chosen e-commerce website. Further, the customer-perceived e-CRM value is viewed as a composite variable with multiple features in this research. No distinction, however, is made between different types of loyalty. The effect of e-CRM value as perceived by the customer on the overall customer loyalty is investigated.

High customer loyalty is important for a seller's profitability. Acquiring a new customer generally costs many times that of selling to an existing customer. The cost of serving a customer throughout the customer service life cycle is higher during the early transactions than when the loyal customer returns for repeat purchase (Reichheld & Sasser, 1990). Customer loyalty to a business that sells online, or e-loyalty, is especially hard to come by since the Internet is a nearly perfect market due to convenient access to product and service information. The dramatic reduction of information asymmetry can result in fierce price competition and low brand loyalty. Enhancing customer loyalty through a superb website is, therefore, an important strategic goal of public organizations as service providers (Kumar & Shah, 2004).

Customer loyalty is a compound concept. Early views of brand loyalty almost exclusively emphasized the customer behavior of repeat purchase over a period of time (Cunningham, 1956; Day, 1969; Newman & Werbel, 1973; Reynolds & Darden, 1974; Monroe & Guiltinan, 1975). More recent research, however, contended that customer loyalty and repeat purchase do not equal (Dick & Basu, 1994; Dekimpe, et al., 1997). Jacoby and Kyner (1973), for example, have indicated loyal customers tend to purchase repetitively but those who purchase repetitively do not necessarily do so out of loyalty, such as the scenario of lacking an alternative offering. Blattberg and Neslin (1990) also pointed out in their theory of repeat purchase that customers may purchase repetitively out of loyalty or as a result of promotion campaign. If motivated primarily by promotional offering, they would stop purchasing once the promotion ends. Strictly speaking, there is no customer loyalty involved in this scenario. True customer loyalty is driven by internal factors. A meaningful measurement of brand loyalty is considered to encompass both behavioral and attitudinal aspects of the concept (Chaudhuri & Holbrook, 2001; Jacoby & Kyner, 1973; Lim & Razzaque, 1997; Dick & Basu, 1994; Gommans et al., 2001). Although behavioral loyalty and attitudinal loyalty are two conceptually distinctive concepts, they often mutually reinforce each other in strengthening overall customer loyalty (Rowley, 2000).

Based on the literature review, we propose a research framework that represents customer-perceived e-CRM value in terms of nine components of website features: customization, contact interactivity, cultivation, care, community, choice, convenience, security, and market response. The literature on CRM and e-CRM reviewed above more specifically suggest the general hypothesis that customer-perceived e-CRM value positively affects the level of loyalty to their chosen websites. This general hypothesis can be broken down to the following two research hypotheses:

H1: e-CRM value can be adequately measured in terms of customization, contact interactivity, cultivation, care, community, choice, convenience, security, and market response.
H2: e-CRM value positively affects e-loyalty.

The research framework and the hypotheses are graphically depicted in Figure 1.

Figure 1. Conceptual framework

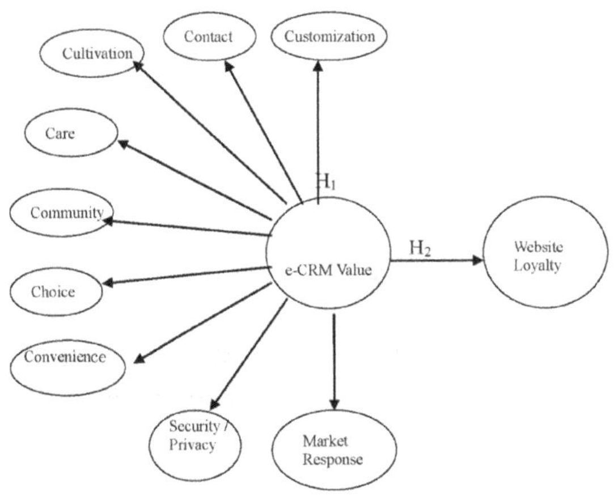

DEFINITIONS AND MEASUREMENT

The composite variable in the first hypothesis, e-loyalty, is conceptually defined as "the customer's favorable attitude toward an electronic business resulting in repeat buying behavior" (Anderson & Srinivasan, 2003, p. 125). It is operationally defined as customer-perceived importance of multiple features of a website. The hypothesized construct of e-CRM value consisting of nine components is validated by a variety of reliability and validity tests. The hypothesized causal effect of e-CRM value on e-loyalty is validated by the structural equation modeling technique. A number of index values are obtained to evaluate the fitness of the theoretical models with regards to both hypotheses. The definitions of the first seven factors in the measurement of the e-CRM value as presented in Srinivasan et al. (2002) are adopted in this research. The definitions of these seven factors and the remaining two are described as follows.

In the Srinivasan et al.'s e-loyalty model, customization was defined as the customer's perception of an e-tailer's website feature to tailor products, services, and user interface to individual customers. Contact interactivity was operationally defined as "the availability and effectiveness of customer support tools on a website, and the degree to which two-way communication with customers is facilitated" (p. 42). Cultivation was defined as the effort of the e-tailer in providing desired information and cross-selling offers to customers. Care referred to "the extent to which a customer is kept informed about the availability of preferred products and status of orders, and the level of efforts expended to minimize disruptions in providing desired services" (p. 43). Community was measured in terms of "the extent to which customers are provided with the opportunity and ability to share opinions among themselves through comment links, buying circles, and chat rooms sponsored by the e-retailer" (p. 43). The number of product or service alternatives made available either on the website or through external links characterizes the choice factor of an e-tailer's website. Security was measured by the customer's trust in the e-tailer's protection of customer privacy and security mechanism. Finally, market response was measured in this research by three question items: e-tailer's responsiveness to the change of the customer's product or service requirement, e-tailer's responsiveness to market change, and the e-tailer's responsiveness to customers' opinion and suggestion. Each of these nine independent variable factors and the dependent variable, website-loyalty, is represented by three question items, resulting in a total of 30 questions in the survey questionnaire. This is in contrast with Srinivasan et al.'s research in which five questions were used for each factor. Our choice of three questions was the result of our analysis of the questions' reliability measures (i.e., Cronbach's α values). To demonstrate the adequacy of this research framework, a study was conducted with primary data collected to test the model empirically. The following two sections present the testing approach.

DATA ANALYSIS

In determining the adequacy of e-CRM value measurement, the reliability of each of the nine aspects of e-CRM value and that of the website loyalty was assessed using Cronbach's α value. First-order confirmatory factor analysis was then employed to evaluate the discriminant validity and convergent validity (two essential aspects of construct validity) of the measurement instrument. Finally, second-order confirmatory factor analysis was used to establish the adequacy of the e-CRM value measurement. Overall, our analysis revealed that the instrument we used to measure e-CRM value passed reliability test, validity test, and also satisfied the adequacy criteria.

The reliability test of the measurement was done via Cronbach's α value. As shown in Table 1, the Cronbach's α value of each of the nine aspects of e-CRM value was 0.714, 0.702, 0.761, 0.843, 0.833, 0.829, p.849, 0.876, and 0.802, respectively. According to Cuieford (1965), in measuring a variable such as what's investigated in this research, a Cronbach's α value that is greater than 0.7 indicates high reliability and a measurement scale with Cronbach's α value less than 0.35 represents unacceptable reliability. A Cronbach's α value between 0.35 and 0.7 has fair but acceptable reliability. Since all aspects of our e-CRM measurement have Cronbach's α values greater than 0.7, a high reliability of the measurement instrument is evident. In addition, the Cronbach's α value of website loyalty measurement, 0.917, also shows high reliability.

The convergent validity expresses the degree to which measures of construct that are related to each other in theory are observed to be related to each other. In this study, the convergent validities of e-CRM value measurement were indicated by the squared multiple correlations (SMC), construct composite reliabilities, and the average variance extracted values. The fact that all SMC values are greater than 0.5, all construct composite reliability values are greater than 0.7, and average variances extracted are all greater than 0.5, suggests acceptable convergent validity of the e-CRM value constructs measurement (Table 1). Another important aspect of construct validity, discriminant validity, indicates the extent to which measures of constructs that are not related to each other in theory are observed to not be related to each other. Fornell and Larcker (1981) contended that acceptable discriminant validity can be demonstrated by the average variance extracted of a construct exceeding the squared correlation between this construct and each of other constructs. Table 2 presents these average variance extracted values and squared correlation coefficients. The

Table 1. Reliability and convergent validity of research constructs

Constructs	Items	Standardized Regression Weights	Cronbach's α	Squared Multiple Correlations	Average Variance Extracted	Composite Reliabilities
Customization	1	0.724	0.714	.0524	0.517	0.762
	2	0.713		0.509		
	3	0.719		0.517		
Contact/Interaction	4	0.722	0.702	0.521	0.513	0.759
	5	0.716		0.513		
	6	0.710		0.504		
Cultivation	7	0.720	0.761	0.518	0.547	0.784
	8	0.728		0.530		
	9	0.770		0.593		
Care	10	0.920	0.843	0.547	0.649	0.864
	11	0.865		0.749		
	12	0.806		0.650		
Community	13	0.778	0.833	0.605	0.660	0.852
	14	0.925		0.856		
	15	0.721		0.520		
Choice	16	0.789	0.829	0.623	0.631	0.836
	17	0.877		0.769		
	18	0.707		0.500		
Convenience	19	0.756	0.849	0.571	0.656	0.814
	20	0.863		0.744		
	21	0.807		0.652		
Security	22	0.832	0.878	0.692	0.716	0.883
	23	0.938		0.879		
	24	0.760		0.577		
Market Responsiveness	25	0.784	0.802	0.614	0.598	0.817
	26	0.807		0.652		
	27	0.730		0.527		
Website Loyalty	28	0.804	0.917	0.646	0.548	0.916
	29	0.947		0.897		
	30	0.900		0.810		

average variance extracted of customization, for example, is 0.517, with its squared correlations with other constructs being 0.354 (Contact Interactivity), 0.403 (Cultivation), 0.345 (Care), 0.186 (Community), 0.297 (Choice), 0.319 (Convenience), 0.294 (Security), 0.362 (Market Response), and 0.325 (Website Loyalty), respectively. Table 2, therefore, provides evidence of acceptable discriminant validity of our measurement. With both convergent validity and dis-

Table 2. Discriminant validity evaluation of research constructs

Constructs	Customization	Contact/ Interaction	Cultivation	Care	Community	Choice	Convenience	Security	Market Responsiveness	Website Loyalty
Customization	0.517									
Contact/Interaction	0.354	0.513								
Cultivation	0.403	0.329	0.547							
Care	0.345	0.324	0.475	0.649						
Community	0.186	0.262	0.207	0.250	0.660					
Choice	0.297	0.319	0.247	0.244	0.244	0.631				
Convenience	0.319	0.286	0.262	0.259	0.211	0.465	0.656			
Security	0.294	0.178	0.300	0.272	0.141	0.256	0.348	0.716		
Market Responsive-ness	0.362	0.342	0.404	0.494	0.266	0.275	0.291	0.339	0.598	
Website Loyalty	0.325	0.278	0.362	0.331	0.166	0.270	0.317	0.287	0.304	0.548

Note: Measures on the diagonal are extracted variance percentages. The rest are squared correlation coefficients.

criminant validity being acceptable, the construct validity of our measurement is, therefore, deemed acceptable.

The adequacy of the e-CRM value measurement was further evaluated through a second-order confirmatory factory analysis. A set of fitness indices produced by the analysis provides the basis of the evaluation, including goodness-of-fit (GFI), adjusted goodness-of-fit (AGFI), normed fit index (NFI), comparative fitness index (CFI), and root mean square error of approximation (RMSEA). According to the analyses of Bollen (1989), Hair et al. (1998), and Bentler (1995), a valid theoretical model is characterized by the values of GFI, AGFI, and NFI greater than 0.9, GFI value greater than 0.95, and RMSEA less than 0.08. The values of these indices produced by the second-order confirmatory factor analysis were GFI = 0.937, AGFI = 0.900, NFI = 0.931, CFI = 0.941, and RMSEA = 0.077, all passing the evaluation criteria stated above. Furthermore, Table 3 also shows that the t-values of all standard structure coefficients are significant. The validity of the e-CRM value measurement model adopted by this research is confirmed. Hypothesis 1 is accepted.

Hypothesis 2 was tested using structural equation modeling. All model fit indices, as shown in Table 4, pass the evaluation criteria: GFI = 0.923 (> 0.9), AGFI = 0.910 (> 0.9), NFI = 0.962 (> 0.9), CFI = 0.951 (> 0.9) and RMSEA = 0.065 (, 0.08). The standardized structure coefficient value is 0.754 (t-value = 11.055, significant at 0.01 level). These results lead to acceptance of the hypothesis, i.e., E-CRM value positively affects website loyalty.

CONCLUSION AND SUGGESTIONS

Innovative implementation of customer-centric CRM program is crucial to a public organization's strategy. Measuring customers' perception of how well the organization's e-CRM practice goes, however, often is challenging due to the complex and dynamic nature of the interactions

Table 3. Second-order confirmatory factor analysis of e-CRM value

Construct	Question Item	Confirmatory Factor Analysis			
		First-Order		Second-Order	
		Standardized Coefficient	t value	Standardized Coefficient	t value
Customiza-tion	1. The advertisement and promotion from this website fit me perfectly.			0.653	---
	2. I can find products and services that satisfy my personal require-ments from this website.	0.913	---a	0.699	13.01
	3. This website makes me feel like a VIP.			0.647	13.33
Interactivity	4. The website allows me to browse products from different points of view.			0.662	10.68
	5. The search feature of the website makes it very easy to find the products I look for.	0.880	11.02	0.650	10.53
	6. The website is very responsive and effective in answering my questions.			0.660	---
Cultivation	7. The website's various campaigns really appeal to me.			0.649	12.04
	8. I feel this website acts aggressively to cultivate customer rela-tionship.	0.897	12.68	0.747	13.86
	9. This website sends me information to save my effort and time in information search.			0.751	---
Care	10. This website is sensitive in responding to my problems.			0.765	16.22
	11. This website is hospitable and friendly to its visitors.	0.854	13.29	0.830	17.86
	12. I trust this website does its very best to serve customers.			0.820	---
Community	13. This website provides a forum in support of customer sharing of shopping experience.			0.778	13.98
	14. This website encourages me to express my own opinions and comments.	0.656	9.80	0.895	14.94
	15. The customers of this website actively participate in the discus-sions on its forum.			0.709	---
Choice	16. This website facilitates one-stop shopping due to its wide vari-ety of product/services.	0.774	11.15	0.790	14.37
	17. I am satisfied with the choices that are available on this website.			0.866	15.304
	18. I don't feel constrained by the choices available on this website.			0.721	---
Conve-nience	19. I easily completed my purchasing the first time I logged onto the website			0.789	16.39
	20. It's very convenient to shop on this website.	0.789	12.33	0.828	17.24
	21. Shopping on this website saves me lots of time.			0.811	---
Security	22. I trust this website in protecting user privacy.			0.865	17.72
	23. I don't worry about this website's security mechanisms.	0.733	11.37	0.903	18.33
	24. I feel comfortable to provide my private information to this website.			0.764	---
Market Response	25. This website is serious about changes of customer requirements and their demand s for products.			0.768	14.58
	26. This website is very responsive to competition's actions in the marketplace.	0.900	12.78	0.753	14.30
	27. This website quickly responds to customer comments and sug-gestions.			0.751	---

a: Loading fixed

Table 4. Validation of research model

Causal Effect Path	Expected Result	Standardized Coefficient	t-value
e-CRM Value -> Website Loyalty	+	0.754	11.055*
Fitness Indices	**Criteria**		**Fitness Assessment**
GFI	> 0.9	0.923	Good
AGFI	> 0.9	0.910	Good
NFI	> 0.9	0.962	Good
CFI	> 0.95	0.951	Good
RMSEA	< 0.08	0.065	Good

*p< 0.01

between the website and the customer. This research explores the concept of e-CRM value as a measure of consumer-perceived value of CRM practices conducted by e-commerce firms by integrating and extending the works found in the existing literature. Specifically, the eight-factor antecedents model of Srinivasan et al. (2002) was slightly modified and adapted to come up with a nine-component framework for e-CRM value. A measurement instrument is developed to operationalize the proposed framework. Using both first- and second-order confirmatory factor analyses, the conceptual framework and the measurement instrument are empirically validated with the primary data collected in a pilot study. It was found that the framework formed by the proposed nine dimensions – customization, contact interactivity, cultivation, care, community, choice, convenience, security, and market response – does adequately measure customer-perceived value delivered by the e-commerce company through its e-CRM implementation. Using structural equations modeling analysis, the study also reveals the positive causal effect of e-CRM value on customers' website loyalty.

The research findings have important implications for managers of public organizations. Most of the factors that determine customers' perceived e-CRM value are closely related to the information and knowledge flow between product/service providers and customers. Simply providing basic product or service information to facilitate consumers' purchasing decision making is not enough for development of long-term customer loyalty. Today's online customers demand in-depth information and even proprietary knowledge in their purchasing decision-making process. Public organizations empowered by Internet technologies must act innovatively and aggressively to engage customers in two-way and open communications, using Web 2.0 tools such as blogs or social networking services to strengthen mutual trust.

For e-commerce and e-service researchers, this study tests an efficient measurement instrument to assess e-CRM value perception, with each factor only consisting of three question items. The external validity of the instrument is subject to validation in different contextual settings, especially different cultural environments. Another promising research direction involves how various categories of information technologies, such as Web 2.0 tools, can be used to enhance e-CRM value perception. To be fruitful, research addressing these issues must consider industrial, organizational, and individual (website visitor) characteristics in the research design. Websites promoted social welfare, for example, may be perceived differently from the websites that represent governmental regulatory agencies. Consumers may have different expectations for and thus exhibit different attitudes toward large websites and much smaller websites. As another example, regular website visitors may perceive differently from their ad hoc counterparts of the same website. Including data of finer granularity in the analysis would shed light on how the effect of e-CRM value on consumers' website loyalty is mediated by institutional and individual characteristics.

REFERENCES

Ad Hamid, N. R. (2005). E-CRM: Are we there yet? *Journal of American Academy of Business*, *6*(1), 51–57.

Anderson, R. E., & Srinivasan, S. (2003). E-satisfaction and e-loyalty: A contingency framework. *Psychology and Marketing*, *20*(3), 123–138. doi:10.1002/mar.10063

Bentler, P. M., & Hu, L. T. (1995). Evaluating model fit. In Hoyle, R. H. (Ed.), *Structural Equation Modeling* (pp. 76–99). Thousand Oaks, CA: Sage.

Bollen, K. A. (1989). *Structural Equations with Latent Variables*. New York, NY: Wiley.

Brown, G. H. (1952). Brand loyalty – fact or fiction? *Advertising Age*, *23*, 53–55.

Chaudhuri, A., & Holbrook, M. B. (2001). The chain of effects from brand trust and brand affect to brand performance: the role of brand loyalty. *Journal of Marketing*, *65*(2), 81–93. doi:10.1509/jmkg.65.2.81.18255

Chen, H. M., Chen, Q., & Kazman, R. (2007). The affective and cognitive impacts of perceived touch on online customers' intention to return in the Web-based eCRM environment. *Journal of Electronic Commerce in Organizations*, *5*(1), 69–91. doi:10.4018/jeco.2007010104

Chen, Q., & Chen, H. M. (2004). Exploring the success factors of eCRM strategies in practice. *Journal of Database Marketing & Customer Strategy Management*, *11*(4), 333–343. doi:10.1057/palgrave.dbm.3240232

Cuieford, J. P. (1965). *Fundamental Statistics in Psychology and Education* (4th ed.). New York, NY: McGraw Hill.

Cunningham, R. M. (1956). Brand-Loyalty-What, where, how much. *Harvard Business Review*, *34*(1), 116–128.

Day, G. S. (1969). A two-dimensional concept of brand loyalty. *JMR, Journal of Marketing Research*, *9*, 29–36.

Day, G. S. (1994). The capabilities of market-driven organizations. *Journal of Marketing*, *58*(4), 37–52. doi:10.2307/1251915

Dekimpe, M. G., Pierre, F., Srinath, G., Gary, L. L., & Christophe, V. B. (1997). Generalizing about trade show effectiveness: A cross-national comparison. *Journal of Marketing*, *61*(4), 55–64. doi:10.2307/1252086

Dick, A. S., & Basu, K. (1994). Customer loyalty: Toward an integrated conceptual framework. *Journal of the Academy of Marketing Science*, *22*, 99–113. doi:10.1177/0092070394222001

Fornell, C., & Larcker, D. F. (1981). Evaluating structural equations models with unobservable variables and measurement error. *JMR, Journal of Marketing Research*, *18*, 39–50. doi:10.2307/3151312

Gefen, D., & Straub, D. (2000). The relative importance of perceived ease of use in IS adoption: A study of e-commerce adoption. *Journal of the Association for Information Systems*. Retrieved from http://jais.isworld.org?articles/1-8/article.htm

Hair, J. F., Anderson, R. E., Tatam, R. L., & Black, W. C. (1998). *Multivariate Data Analysis* (5th ed.). Upper Saddle River, NJ: Prentice-Hall.

Jacoby, J., & Kyner, D. B. (1973). Brand loyalty vs. repeat purchasing behavior. *JMR, Journal of Marketing Research*, *10*(1), 1–9. doi:10.2307/3149402

Jih, W. J., Lee, S. F., & Fang, S. R. (2006). Investigating the impact of customer relationship management practices of e-commerce on online customers' website satisfaction: A model-building approach. *International Journal of E-Business Research*, *2*(4), 61–77. doi:10.4018/jebr.2006100104

Jih, W. J., Wong, S., & Chang, C. B. (2004). Effect of perceived risk on adoption of internet banking: An empirical investigation. *International Journal of Electronic Business Research*, *1*(1), 91–105.

Kennedy, A. (2006). Electronic customer relationship management (eCRM): Opportunities and challenges in a digital world. *Irish Marketing Review*, *18*(1-2), 58–68.

Kincad, J. W. (2003). *Customer Relationship Management: Getting It Right!* Upper Saddle River, NJ: Prentice-Hall PTR.

Kuehn, A. (1962). Consumer brand choice as a learning process. *Journal of Advertising Research*, *2*, 10–17.

Lee, S. F., Jih, W. J., & Fang, S. R. (2006). Investigating the impact of customer relationship management practices of e-commerce on online customers' website satisfaction: A model-building approach. *International Journal of E-Business Research*, *2*(4), 61–77. doi:10.4018/jebr.2006100104

Lim, K. S., & Razzaque, M. A. (1997). Brand loyalty and situational effects: An interactionist perspective. *Journal of International Consumer Marketing*, *9*(4), 95–115. doi:10.1300/J046v09n04_06

Lipstein, B. (1959). The dynamics of brand loyalty and brand switching. In *Proceedings of the Fifth Annual Conference of the Advertising Research Foundation* (pp. 101-108). New York, NY: Advertising Research Foundation.

Min, S., Song, S., & Keebler, J. S. (2002). An Internet-mediated market orientation (IMO): Building a theory. *Journal of Marketing Theory and Practice*, *10*(2), 1–11.

Monroe, K. B., & Guiltinan, J. P. (1975). A path-analytic exploration of retail patronage influences. *The Journal of Consumer Research*, *2*, 19–28. doi:10.1086/208612

Newman, J. W., & Werbel, R. A. (1973). Multivariate analysis of brand loyalty for major household appliances. *JMR, Journal of Marketing Research*, *10*(4), 404–409. doi:10.2307/3149388

Ngai, E. W. T. (2005). Customer relationship management research (1992-2002): An academic literature and classification. *Marketing Intelligence & Planning*, *23*(6-7), 582–605. doi:10.1108/02634500510624147

Parvatiyar, A., & Sheth, J. N. (2001). Customer relationship management: Emerging practice, process, and discipline. *Journal of Economic & Social Research*, *3*(2), 1–34.

Peppard, J. (2000). Customer Relationship Management (CRM) in financial services. *European Management Journal*, *18*(3), 312–326. doi:10.1016/S0263-2373(00)00013-X

Reynolds, F. D., & Darden, W. R. (1974). *Constructing Life Style and Psychograghics*. Chicago, IL: AMA.

Reynolds, F. D., Darden, W. R., & Martin, W. (1974). Developing an image of the store-loyal customer. *Journal of Retailing*, *50*(4), 73–84.

Ross, D. (2005). E-CRM from a study chain management perspective. *Information Systems Management*, *22*(1), 37–44. doi:10.1201/1078/44912.22.1.20051201/85737.5

Scullin, S. S., Fjermestad, J., & Romano, N. C. Jr. (2004). E-relationship marketing: changes in traditional marketing as an outcome of electronic customer relationship management. *Journal of Enterprise Information Systems*, *17*(6), 410–415.

Shani, D., & Chalasani, S. (1992). Exploiting niches using relationship marketing. *Journal of Consumer Marketing*, *9*(3), 33–42. doi:10.1108/07363769210035215

Slater, S. F. (1997). Developing a customer value-based theory of the firm. *Journal of the Academy of Marketing Science*, *25*(2), 162–167. doi:10.1007/BF02894352

Srinivasan, S. S., Anderson, R., & Ponnavolu, K. (2002). Customer loyalty in E-commerce: An exploration of its antecedents and consequences. *Journal of Retailing*, *78*(1), 41–50. doi:10.1016/S0022-4359(01)00065-3

Swift, R. S. (2001). *Accelerating Customer Relationships Using CRM and Relationship Technologies*. Upper Saddle River, NJ: Prentice-Hall PTR.

Szymanski, D. M., & Hise, R. T. (2000). E-satisfaction: An initial examination. *Journal of Retailing*, *76*(3), 309–322. doi:10.1016/S0022-4359(00)00035-X

Tung, F. C. (2007). Using the e-CRM information system in the hi-tech industry: Predicting salesperson intentions. *Journal of American Academy of Business*, *11*(2), 131–136.

Turban, E., King, D., Lee, J., & Viehland, D. (2004). *Electronic Commerce: A Managerial Perspective*. Upper Saddle River, NJ: Prentice-Hall.

This work was previously published in the Information Resources Management Journal, Volume 24, Issue 2, edited by Mehdi Khosrow-Pour, pp. 46-60, copyright 2013 by IGI Publishing (an imprint of IGI Global).

Chapter 9
Success of Public Knowledge Management in the Light of the Rossian Ethics

Mehdi Shami Zanjani
University of Tehran, Iran

Hossein Dabbagh
Shahid Beheshti University, Iran

Roshanak Rouzbehani
University of Tehran, Iran

ABSTRACT

Researchers have attempted to integrate the fields of management and ethics for the past 50 years. Although the moral aspects of knowledge management have been studied, its philosophical attitude has been overshadowed. This work designs a philosophical background—in moral philosophy—for public knowledge management. To achieve the research goal, the relationships between human critical success factors of knowledge management and moral duties are discussed. These moral duties are based on the Rossian ethical framework. The authors recommend moral duties to public organizations that try to manage knowledge successfully. The results show that "beneficence" is the most significant to knowledge management success in the public sector. In this paper, the authors integrate knowledge management with the Rossian ethical framework to increase successful knowledge management in public organizations.

INTRODUCTION

It is said that the economics of new age is shaped on the basis of knowledge and network (Kelly, 1999; Lester, 2000). We can consider the intellectual property movement in the third industrial revolution as the most important characteristics of novel business (Thurow, 2003). Based on this fact, the nature of organizations is changed in a way that intangible assets such as knowledge and human resources rather than tangible and physical assets determine the value of organizations

DOI: 10.4018/978-1-4666-3616-3.ch009

(Stewart, 1997). Therefore, the importance of knowledge management, increasingly, is taken into account (Alavi, 2000).

It is near a half of century that management scholars and philosophers attempt to set up relations between the two sciences: management and philosophy. The issue is about how we can have an effective knowledge management incorporating ethics? Is this possible?

Researchers who work on knowledge management, commonly consider that knowledge and its processes (process of acquire, refine, maintenance, and disseminate of knowledge) should be ethical. In other words, they believe in morality of knowledge and ethical information (Geva, 2006; Blanchard, 1987; Land et al., 2007; Mason et al., 1986; Carroll & Scherer, 1999).

The main point in these articles is in regards to the subject of some moral advice or recommendations to knowledge managers and workers. In fact, these ideas help public organizations to move towards ethical knowledge management. Nevertheless, two issues have been over looked. First, a philosophical understanding for these moral advice and suggestions has been neglected. Whereas, we need some background in moral philosophy in order to achieve successful knowledge management, because without a firm philosophical foundation, any advice would be arbitrary. Second, the effect of declared moral advice is not clear in knowledge management success. Namely; it is vague that how moral advice helps us to have successful knowledge management. It follows from this that without considering moral philosophy (especially Meta ethics) and obvious linkage between moral duties and knowledge management, we could not have successful knowledge-based organizations.

In contrast, the viewpoint of this paper is totally different. Since moral philosophy, normatively, suggests some moral duties for being successful in knowledge management, we can put forward the tabloid of this work in this way: ethics is used as a context or nexus for knowledge management success.

By the way, the relations between knowledge management human critical success factors and some moral duties are investigated. These moral duties are taken from the ethics of prima facie duties of Ross; one of the controversial moral philosophers in twentieth century.

This paper is organized as follows: after an introduction, the next section deals with the literature, especially our points of view about ethics, knowledge management and knowledge management success factors. Thereafter, the framework is discussed. This framework examines moral duties of Rossian ethics and human critical success factors. Suitable moral duties are also proposed for public organizations which try to manage knowledge flawlessly. Furthermore, corresponding moral duties to knowledge management success factors will be illustrated.

This paper has important implications for public organizations seeking to improve their knowledge management through morality.

THEORETICAL BACKGROUND

Ethics

According to some philosophers, animals and humans can be distinguished from each other by reason of morality. In other words, humans can be labeled as moral animals. Thus, morality and its branches speak about human and humanity in every debate.

At this point, let us have a look at ethics and its different branches in general. Moral philosophy, according to some categorizations, consists of meta-ethics, normative ethics and applied ethics (LaFollette, 1997). Normative ethics take care of ethical theories which say that what ought and ought not to be done in different circumstances. To do this, these theories have to give their explanation of the concepts 'goodness' and 'badness' in the first place. For instance, consequentialism, as an ethical theory holds that goodness and moral obligation are associated with the total amount of pleasure and pain in each moral situation. Morally speaking, the more the total pleasure is, the better the situation with which we are faced will be. Deontologism, virtue ethics and intuitionism are other theories which are discussed in normative ethics (Baron et al., 1997).

Applied ethics, on the other hand, deals with practical and realistic issues in different field such as: medicine, business[1], environment, engineering and information technology (IT) with which we are confronted in everyday life. An applied ethicist attempts to concretize the mentioned ethical theories in order to give an account of how the issues can be resolved.

Moreover, meta-ethics which is the most philosophical part of moral philosophy, takes into account ethical concepts and propositions from metaphysical, epistemological and semantic point of view. Whether or not, the very idea of 'goodness', for instance, can be defined by employing other concepts is discussed in meta-ethics. Whether or not there are some moral rules and principles, by the aid of which, we can arrive at justified moral judgment in different occasions, again, is disputed in meta-ethics. Also, the Rossian framework which is concerned in this article is discussed in meta-ethics.

Having applied Rossian moral philosophy in this article, let us give an outline of Kantian ethics and his follower, Ross. For the sake of that we should begin with Kantian ethics, and then we go on Rossian ethics.

Kantian ethics consists of a substantive aspect and a formal one. According to substantive characteristic, each human being, on its own, is an end, normatively speaking. We are not authorized to behave in a way with others that they are regarded as property or thing. This notion can be dubbed 'principle of ends' is absolute and categorical in the Kantian story. Moreover, formal aspect of Kantian ethics holds that each ethical principle has to be categorized in a way that it can be utilized universally. Whether or not a principle is universalizable can guarantee that it is moral. Morality is associated with universalizability (Kant, 1997).

Kant (1963) posited that a person's ultimate goal is virtue and other goals are less important or should be contributory to this primary goal. Also Kant (1963) identified a categorical imperative that could provide the standard by which to guide one's conduct. This is also known as the golden rule: Do unto others, as you would have them do unto you. Kant believes this to be valid universally, applicable to all people, in every country, at all times.

After Kant, many philosophers criticize Kant's Moral philosophy. Among these critics Ross gaze at Kant's ethics optimistically and brightly. In twentieth century, Ross put pen to paper two famous books. By 1920, he published *The Right and the Good*, and in 1939 he wrote *The Foundations of Ethics*. In fact, Ross by these books intends to rehabilitate Kant's Deontologism. He does not believe in universalizability principle of Kant. In support of that, he establishes ethics of prima facie duties. He introduces seven duties to set up his framework: fidelity, reparation, gratitude, justice, beneficence, self-improvement and non-malfeasance. Ross believes that by employing these duties in our life we could obtain morality. Consider the following quote by Ross:

I suggest 'prima facie duty' or 'conditional duty' as a brief way of referring to the characteristic (quite distinct from that of being a duty proper) which an act has, in virtue of being of a certain kind (e.g. the keeping of promise), of being an act which would be a duty proper if it were not at the same time of another kind which is morally significant[2].

He after reviewing and revising his list of basic duties writes:

These seem to be, in principle, all the ways in which prima facia duties arise. In actual experience they are compounded together in highly complex ways[3].

Knowledge Management

Authors such as Drucker (1993) and Toffler (1990) had anticipated knowledge to become the most important resource in the "knowledge society". Knowledge can be defined as a combination of experience; values, contextual information and expert insight that help evaluate and incorporate new experience and information (Gammelgaard & Ritter, 2000). Iske and Boersma (2005) expressed that knowledge results from the interaction of someone's insights (past experience, intuition and attitude), information and imagination (generating ideas and visualizing futures).

Knowledge if properly utilized and leveraged can drive organizations to become more innovative, competitive, and sustainable. Knowledge management is the active management of creating, disseminating, and applying knowledge to strategic ends (Berdrow & Lane, 2003). The function of knowledge management is to allow an organization to leverage its information resources and knowledge assets by remembering and applying experience (Boh, 2007)

In general, KM must be seen as a strategy to manage organizational knowledge assets to support management decision making, to enhance competitiveness, and to increase capacity for creativity and innovation (Nunes et al., 2006). Based upon that, APQC defines KM as an emerging set of strategies and approaches to create, safeguard, and use knowledge assets (including people and information), which allow knowledge to flow to the right people at the right time so they can apply these assets to create more value for the enterprise (Hasanali, 2002). Hence, Knowledge, and consequently its management, is currently being touted as the basis of future economic competitiveness.

If KM is a vital determinant to an organization's success and competitiveness, then it is important to know how it can be done successfully. Quinn and colleagues assert that the analysis of critical success factors provide an important meaning to KM through the identification of core processes that are critical to successful KM implementation (Quinn et al., 1996). As Choi (2000) supports, a KM programme needs to identify critical success factors to gauge its performance.

Critical Success Factors (CSFs) can be defined as "areas in which results, if they are satisfactory, will ensure successful competitive performance for the organization" (Rockart, 1979). Saraph et al., (1989) viewed them as those critical areas of managerial planning and action that must be practiced in order to achieve effectiveness. Mathi (2004) defines key success factor as a performance area of critical importance in achieving consistently high productivity. In terms of KM, they can be viewed as those activities and practices that should be addressed in order to ensure its successful implementation. These practices would either need to be nurtured if they already existed or be developed if they were still not in place. Based on the above definition, critical success factors are treated as those internal factors which are controllable by an organization. External factors such as environmental influences are not taken into account since organizations have little control over them when implementing KM (Wong, 2005).

Several investigations have been done on this issue and a range of KM critical success factors have been identified. For the purpose of this paper, many related researches and papers have been broadly reviewed so that an inclusive list of KM CSF can be recognized. Amongst the investigations done on identifying KM CSFs, Chong and Choi (2005) and Jennex and Olfman (2005) have presented more comprehensive list of success factors.

Chong and Choi (2005) state that there are 11 key KM components to successful KM implementation.

Jennex and Olfman (2005) have presented a success factor framework for Knowledge Management Systems (KMS) that is constructed by reviewing the literature. They analyzed recognized CSF for similar concepts and combined them into composite success factors.

Bear in mind that Jennex and Olfman (2005) work on KMS success factors thus some of these factors are more related to KM systems than KM itself.

Taking into account the strength of these two models, in this study we combine the identified factors and also others studies to achieve a comprehensive list of KM CSFs.

In literature KM CSFs are classified with different approaches Ruggles (1998) points out that the success factors are people, process and technology that are needs to be balanced in a 50/25/25 relation. People need to be the major focus with 50% of the time and budget of a KM implementation project while process and technology only need 25% each. Yu et al identified three main dimensions: organizational characteristics, IT and managerial support. Mathi (2004) categorized them into business processes and human processes. Whereas some KM success factors are human-oriented; means that human being has a key role in them, and others are non-human-oriented, i.e. technology plays more important role in them, in this paper we investigate success factors into two dimensions: technical and human. What's more ethics is related to matters that human beings are their subjects. So with this classification a logical relationship between ethics and KM success is formed. Technical enablers or success factors are like technology or information systems infrastructure, knowledge structure and performance measurement. These factors are more related to organization technology level and IT support and people role is not considered in them. A further dimension that is as significant as technical factors in KM success, even more important, is human enablers or success factors. Human CSFs are related to people in organization and their social interrelations (See Figure 1).

Ethics in KM

Based on Carrol's view (1999), we have three models of management morality for the new century: Moral management, Immoral management and Amoral management. In his article, he puts emphasis on the lack of consideration to moral management, "little attention has been given to… moral or ethical management". Following from this the significance of moral management more and more is being considered. There are many other researchers that reflect on morality in

Figure 1. The two dimensions of KM critical success factors (human and technical) and researchers who have identified these success factors in details

CSfs	No.	Success factors	Researchers
Human CSFs	1	Motivation and commitment	Alavi and leidner (1999), Barna (2002), Cross and Baird (2000), Davenport et al (1998), Ginsberg and Kambil (1999), Housechild et al (2001), Jennex and Olfman (2000), Malhotra and Galletta (2003), Wong and spinwall (2005), Yahya and Goh (2002), Yu et al (2004)
	2	Training and empowerment	Choi (2000), Mondy et al (2002), Garavan et al (2000), Hung et al (2005), Hwang (2003), Moffett et al (2003), Salleh and Goh (2002), Anahotu (1998), Bhatt (2002), Choi (2000), Matinez (1998), Senge (1991), Verespej (1999), Greenground (1998), Cohen and Backer (1999), Yahya and Goh (2002)
	3	Communication	Burger (2004), Holsapple and joshi (2000), Egbu (2004), Sarker et al (2005), Tobin (2003), Yu et al (2004)
	4	Knowledge-friendly culture	Alavi and leidner (1999), APQC (1999), Barna (2002), Buckman (1999), Choi (2000), Davenport et al (1998), Greengard (1998), Gupta et al (2000), Jennex and Olfman (2000), Jager (1999), Hasanali (2002), Lang (2004), McDermott and O'Dell (2001), Ribiere (2001), Ryan and Prybutok (2001), Skyrme and Amidon (1997), Wild et al (2002), Wong (2005), Yu et al (2004)
	5	Teamwork	Choi (2000), Civi (2000), Geraint (1998), Haas (2002), Mohrman et al (1995), Martinez (1998), Ulrich (1998), Phillips (1994), Ryan and Prybutok (2001), verespej (1999)
	6	Protection of knowledge	Jennex and Olfman (2000), Sage and Rouse (1999)
	7	Learning organization (continuous learning)	Barna (2002), Bixler (2002), Cross and Baird (2000), Sage and Rouse (1999), Skyrme and Amidon (1997), Yu et al (2004)
	8	Top management support	Abell and Oxbrow (1999), APQC (1999), Choi (2000), Civi (2000), Davenport et al (1998), Holsapple and joshi (2000), Hasanali (2002), Kalling (2003), Moffett et al (2003), Pemberton et al (2002), Ryan and Prybutok (2001), Salleh and Goh (2002), Skyrme and Amidon (1997), Liebowitz (1999), Lee and Choi (2003), Hriharan (2005), Koh et al (2005), Wong (2005),
Technical CSFs	9	Knowledge strategy	Barna (2002), Davenport et al (1998), Ginsberg and Kambil (1999), Holsapple and joshi (2000), Jenexx et al (2003), Koskinen (2001), Mandviwalla et al (1998), Sage and Rouse (1999), Skyrme and Samidon (1997), Wong and Aspinwall (2005),Yu et al (2004)
	10	Work processes	Barna (2002), Cross and Baird (2000), Elliott and O'Dell (1999), Hariharan (2005), Jennex and Olfman (2000)
	11	Knowledge structure	Hasanali (2002), Choi (2000), Davenport and Klahr (1998), Greco (1999), Hsieh et al (2002), Ulrich (1998), Wenger and Snyder (2000)
	12	Benchmarking	Choi (2000), Davis (1996), Day and Wendler (1998), O'Dell and Grayson (1998), Moffett et al (2003)
	13	Performance measurement	Alavi and Leidner (1999), APQC (1999), Choi (2000), Bassi and Van Buren (1999), Beijerse (2000), Caneiro (2001), Elliott and O'Dell(1999), Harharan (2005), Gooijer (2000), Matinez (1998), Moffett et al (2003), Pearson (1999), Koh et al (2005), Wong and Aspinwall (2005), Wong (2005),
	14	Elimination of organizational constraints	Bonaventura (1997), Choi (2000), Clarke and rollo (2001), Demarest (1997), McCune (1999), McDermott and O'Dell (2001)
	15	Technology (Information systems) infrastructure	Alavi and leidner (1999), APQC (1999), Barna (2002), Bhatt (2002), Bontis et al (2000), Choi (2000), Cross and Baird (2000), Davenport et al (1998), Ginsberg and Kambil (1999), Jennex and Olfman (2000), Mandviwalla et al (1998), Sage and Rouse (1999), Kotorov and Hsu (2001), McCampbell et al (1999), Moffett et al (2003), Ryan and Prybutok (2001), Wong (2005), Yu et al (2004)

management. For example Blanchard (1987) in his work about "Ethical Management" introduces five "P" principles to manage ethically. These are Purpose, Pride, Patience, Persistence, and Perspective. Along with, Josephson (2001) believes that ethics is the capability to distinguish right from wrong and engage a duty to do what is good and right. Mckerow (1997) also mentioned:

Ethics goes far beyond legal issues (which are often the major concern for administrators) and poses the questions: What is good? What is right? What ought one to do?

Moreover, Lichtman (1998) identified eight core ethical values: (1) loyalty, (2) honesty, (3) fairness, (4) caring, (5) respect, (6) tolerance, (7) duty, and (8) moral courage. Moorhouse's (2002) research resulted in consistent findings. However, Moorhouse went a step further in the research with a result that ranked the important characteristics of an ethical leader. The top five characteristics were identified as: (1) integrity, (2) following Biblical principle of behavior, (3) honest/truthful, (4) high moral standard/firm conviction, and (5) being fair/unbiased.

To this point, all mentioned researchers have studied the overall relationship between ethics and management. Nevertheless the numbers of academics who work on ethics of KM or ethical KM are not many. Just few researchers in information management, for instance, Mason and Collins (1986) spend their time on "ethical issues of the information age". They found four categories: Privacy, Accuracy, Property and Accessibility (PAPA).

What is more, Land and et al (2007) have a discussion about "The Ethics of Knowledge Management" to illustrate why KM research requires an ethical aspect. In addition, they set up a classification of disciplines contributing to current notions of KM. Along with, Baskervile and Dulopovici (2006) discuss about "The ethics of knowledge transfer and conversation: property or privacy right?". Hosein (2005) also has a word about "Researching the ethics of knowledge management: The case of data-mining".

Taverekere (Kanti) Srikantaiah talks about "The Importance of Ethics in KM" and proposes four stages for KM and some questions about ethics in these stages. At the end he concludes that "Ethics is incorporated in KM studies and applications". Also, Ritter in her speech entitled "Information Ethics and Knowledge Professionals" puts forward several questions about the relationships of ethics and KM. Her main inquiry, which is exactly our concern too, is about existence of ethical and philosophical foundations of knowledge management concepts, frameworks, and principles (ICKM, 2008).

As discussed above, in the course of literature on ethics and KM, researchers didn't consider philosophical background for moral issues and didn't try to set up a framework for morality in KM. However, we believe that without considering moral philosophy, the connection between ethics and KM is not evident.

Below we talk about CSF and Rossian framework to a greater extent, and then our framework for morality of KM is discussed.

RESEARCH APPROACH

The Delphi method was conceived as a group technique whose aim was to obtain the most reliable consensus of opinion of a group of public experts by means of a series of questionnaires with controlled opinion feedback (Dalkey, 1963). It is a method of structuring communication between groups of people who can provide valuable contributions in order to resolve a complex problem (Linstone, 1975). The method has proven a popular tool in information systems research (Brancheau, 1996; Cegielski, 2001; Hayne, 2000; Holsapple, 2002). One of the contributions of the Delphi study by Holsapple and Joshi, for example, is that it provides a common language for discourse about knowledge management (Okoli, 2004). Since the theory about knowledge management still represents an emergent and sometimes confusing field, the Delphi method seems to be one of the most suitable research strategies in this area. The other reasons for selecting the Delphi method for this research are:

1. Delphi researchers employ this method primarily in cases where judgmental information is indispensable.
2. A panel study most appropriately answers the research questions, rather than any individual expert's responses. Delphi is desirable in that it does not require the experts to meet physically, which could be impractical for busy experts.
3. Although there may be a relatively limited number of experts with knowledge about the research questions, the Delphi panel size requirements are modest (Paliwoda, 1983). A Delphi study does not depend on a statistical sample that attempts to be representative of any population. It is a group decision mechanism requiring qualified experts who have deep understanding of the issues. Thus, the literature recommends 10–18 experts on a Delphi panel (Okoli, 2004).
4. Test-retest reliability is not relevant in the method, since researchers expect respondents to revise their responses (Okoli, 2004).
5. The Delphi study is flexible in its design, and amenable to follow-up interviews. This permits the collection of richer data leading to a deeper understanding of the fundamental research questions.

In this research, a panel which consists of 10 skilled IT managers and moral philosophy scholars with a perfect understanding of the public sector but also with a very good knowledge of the area was set up. Consensus of experts on definition and description of the CSFs and moral duties of Rossian framework was reached. Then, through questionnaires, experts tried to indicate whether there is any link between each moral duty and each CFS or not. Due to this, they answered this question: "is the given moral duty has an effect on the given KM human CSF?" The Delphi questionnaires were administered using e-mail and fax. This process was lasted two months. The panelists were free to use whichever of these media was most convenient. The experts were consulted twice on the same question, so that they could reconsider their answer, aided by the feedbacks they received from the rest of the experts. The follow-up interviews were administrated in some cases. The exchange of information between the experts was not free but was carried out by means of a study group coordinator, so that all irrelevant information is eliminated. The experts were asked to justify their reasoning because of its valuable aid to understanding the causal relationships between factors and moral duties, an understanding that was necessary to build the framework.

FRAMEWORK

As discussed above, without considering moral philosophy and a clear linkage between moral duties and KM, having successful ethical KM is hardly achievable. Hence, in the framework illustrated below, relations between KM human critical success factors and moral duties taken from the Rossian ethics will be examined in public sector. The interaction between these two aspects (KM human CSFs and Rossian moral duties) helps public organizations to apply ethics to be more efficient in KM.

Below, we start by presenting our definitions of KM human CSF as discussed above. Then, moral duties of Rossian ethical framework are introduced. Finally, the framework composed of these two aspects is demonstrated.

Human Critical Success Factors

In the literature more emphasis is on the technical factors for having successful KM. Mathi (2004) thinks that the key to successful KM projects is focusing on people first, not cutting-edge technology. Also, Reyes believes that in KM there is a principle called "85-15 principle". He cites that 85% regarding the human factors and 15% are the tools and technology. In his opinion "everything stored on computers are data bits and bytes, real knowledge will always reside in the being of the human factor-the human being". He considers the importance of human factors from several perspectives. First, knowledge is created by a human and machines merely store data that signifies this knowledge. Next, the rate at which knowledge can be produced depends on the human factor. Third, if you disregard the human factor, all that is remained is a software system and "a black box-nothing more-a mere business vanity" (IT toolbox.com).

In view of Thomas et al. (2001) in their article "The knowledge management puzzle: Human and social factors in knowledge management" indicate that human and social factors are missing pieces of KM puzzle. Therefore, they argue that knowledge management systems must take both human and social factors into account.

Following from this, human factors have a more important role in KM success, and in view of the fact that moral duties have strong relations with human beings, in this work we focused on the second dimension of KM CSF, human CSF. These factors are showing in Figure 2.

Figure 2. Human CSF

No.	Human CSFs	Description
1	Motivation and commitment	Being effected from internal or external forces to achieve certain goals and Being bound emotionally/intellectually to a course of action or to another person/other persons.
2	Training and empowerment	Leading to skilled behavior and increasing the strength of individuals.
3	Knowledge-friendly culture	Environment where no individual considers that they will be threatened by knowledge sharing, or that it will destabilize their position within the company.
4	Team working	Cooperative effort and joint actions by a group of people for a common end.
5	Top management support	The process of giving morals, materials, financial aid or courage to develop KM successfully.
6	Learning organization (continuous learning)	A group of people who are continually enhancing their capabilities. People who are "fully awakened" and are engaged in their work, striving to reach their potential.
7	Protection of knowledge	The process of preserving from knowledge loss.
8	Communication (Existence of several communication channels)	The process of exchanging information, ideas, and feelings through written or spoken words, symbols or actions.

The Rossian Ethical Framework

In this article we choose Ross among many philosophers in moral philosophy such as Kant, Moore, Dancy. The argument of this preference is: (1) we prefer to apply philosophy of philosophers that are contemporary i.e. they lived in 20th century. (2) Ross has classification and categorization in ethics which other moral philosophers do not have. Explicitly, he has methodic ethical framework with seven duties. After Ross, interpreters of his philosophy, like McNaughton, develop his framework. McNaughton proposes some features for each duty that make the framework applicable.

According to Ross, we have several prima facie duties; i.e. we are required to pick out different forms of behavior that respond to different morally relevant non-moral properties which are general, underived and have invariant deontic valences.[4] These Rossian duties are: fidelity, reparation, gratitude, justice, beneficience, self-improvement and non-malfeasance. In cases in which we deal with only one morally relevant feature, that feature determines the ultimate metaphysical status of the case. In cases in which more than one prima facie duty are combined together and come into conflict, each morally relevant non-moral property exercises its deontic valence and contributes to the moral evaluation of the case. The ultimate outcome depends on the way in which these morally relevant features are combined together. In order to find out and pick out the ultimate outcome of the combination of these prima facie duties which makes our actual duty and arrive at justified moral judgments, we have to use our moral intuition.

In Ross's view, the list of prima facie duties is not complete; it is an open-ended list because there is no guarantee that we have discovered all prima facie duties (i.e., all morally relevant non-moral properties).

We can distinguish five different claims in the Rossian ethical system: four metaphysical claims and an epistemological one. According to the first metaphysical claim, there are several prima facie duties which are general. In other words, these are duties to respond to morally relevant features that contribute to the moral evaluation of concrete ethical situations in a regular way, i.e. they make the same contribution to each situation. The second metaphysical claim is that the list of prima facie duties is open-ended which means that, in principle, the list can be bigger or smaller. The third claim is that these prima facie duties are underived and fundamental in the sense that they cannot be reduced to more basic duties. According to the fourth metaphysical claim, there is no such thing as a lexical order and hierarchy for these prima facie duties. They can combine together and contribute to the moral evaluation of different cases in different ways to the extent that we cannot determine what would constitute the ultimate outcome (actual duty) in advance. In other words, as there is no lexical order between prima facie duties, actual duties cannot be subsumed under a general rule. Actual duties in different concrete situations are formulated in different ways.

According to the epistemological claim, in order to arrive at a justified moral judgment or an actual duty in a concrete ethical situation, we have to use a faculty of intuition. By intuition, Ross refers to a source of knowledge which is perceptual and non-inferential. In other words, as there is no lexical order between prima facie duties, we cannot arrive at justified moral judgments through rules governing prima facie duties and their combinations (as in `Kantianism and Utilitarianism).[5] Ross does not believe that we can arrive at moral judgments by the mediation of a moral rule. There is no such thing as a theoretical procedure in this relation. Rather, according to Ross, we arrive at moral judgments perceptually and non-inferentially. We pick up the ultimate outcome of the combination of morally relevant features directly by looking at the case in more detail in order to arrive at a moral judgment. Ross claims that there is no such thing as a set of moral rules which can guide us to arrive at moral judgment. Direct experience is the point of departure.

To end with, according to McNaughton:

Here is summery of the items on Ross's original list:

1. Duties resting on a previous of my own. These in turn divide into two main categories:
    a. Duties of fidelity, these result from my having made a promise or something like a promise,
    b. Duties of reparation, these stem from my having done something wrong so that I am now required to make amends.
2. Duties resting on pervious acts of others, these are duties of gratitude, which I owe to those who have helped me.
3. Duties to prevent (or overturn) a distribution of benefits and burdens which is not in accordance whit the merit of the persons concerned, these are duties of justice.
4. Duties which rest on the fact that there are other people in the world whose condition we could make better, these are duties of beneficence.
5. Duties which rest on the fact that I could better myself, these are duties of self-improvement.
6. Duties of not injuring others, these are duties on non- malfeasance." [6]

Also, Dancy describes Rossian ethics in this way:

For him [Ross], respectable agents are ones who are sensitive to the morally relevant features of the situations they find themselves in, not in a general way but just case by case. There is a stress on perception here; moral agents see as relevant the features that are relevant, and see as most relevant the ones that in fact are most relevant.[7]

Interacting Two Dimensions

Interacting between the two dimensions –KM human CSFs versus Rossian moral duties- create a framework illustrates that which moral duty has an impact on which human CSF (Figure 3). For example education and empowerment as a CSF is influenced by three moral duties, beneficence, self-improvement and justice. It means that for achieving this success factor in an organization, we need to educate employees of these moral duties.

As an important outcome of this framework, we sum up indicated relations of each moral duty with CSFs. The result number shows that how many CSFs are affected by given specific duty. As it is shown in the framework above, the duty of beneficence that has maximum relations with CSFs seems to be the most significant duty (as shown below, Commitment & Motivation of Knowledge Workers, Education & Empowerment, Knowledge Friendly Culture, Teamwork, Senior Management Support and Channels for Knowledge Transfer are the CSFs affected by beneficence). In other words, organizations which want to be successful in KM must take care of beneficence as a critical moral duty. After beneficence, fidelity and self-improvement are other moral duties that are more needed for organizations which desire successful KM. it's important to note that other duties are also significant for supporting successful KM. public organizations should notice the relationship between each duty and human CSFs to utilize these duties in a proper way. For example, fidelity and non-malfeasance are duties that facilitate security of knowledge as a human CSF for KM.

Figure 3. Moral duty and its impact on human CSF

		Fidelity	Gratitude	Reparation	Beneficence	Self-Improvement	Justice	Non-Malfeasance
1	Commitment & Motivation of Knowledge Workers	■	■	■	■	■	■	■
2	Education & Empowerment				■	■	■	
3	Knowledge Friendly Culture				■	■		■
4	Teamwork	■	■	■	■		■	
5	Senior Management Support	■	■		■			
6	Learning Organization			■		■		
7	Security/Protection of Knowledge	■						■
8	Channels for Knowledge Transfer	■	■	■	■	■		
	Total	5	4	4	6	5	3	3

EVALUATION AND DISCUSSION

We should bear in mind that humanities are divided into two disciplines: empirical and non-empirical. For example, consider disciplines like management, sociology and psychology. In these disciplines experience helps us to justify scientific theories. In other words, in these disciplines for accepting a theory, we make use of experience. In contrary, non-empirical disciplines such as philosophy, ethics and history do not rely on experience. In fact, experience has no role in proving or refuting a theory. In these disciplines reason itself play a key role in justification. Since this article is interdisciplinary and tries to make a relationship between an empirical discipline (management) and non-empirical discipline (ethics), validation of proposed framework does not necessarily depend on experience. What's more, practical testing is not the charge of this article however we just theorized the relationship between ethics and KM. Also we must consider the point which philosophers (in philosophy of science) have proposed; the difference between context of discovery and context of justification. In context of discovery we do not need experience; rather we theorize a theory by reason. In context of justification we utilize experience to validate a theory. This article belongs to context of discovery; namely, doing practical investigation or implication is not the task of this article. Of course in further researches doing practical examination is needed.

CONCLUSION

Although KM ethics has been discussed in various circles we still face considerable questions that are yet to be answered, or enough attention has not been paid in the literature regarding some fundamental issues. For instance we may still be asking: "Shall we propose some moral advices and duties to knowledge managers in public organizations? What is our philosophical background of these moral duties? How do moral duties help us to foster successful KM in organizations?" We tried to answer the aforementioned critical questions in our study by highlighting the relationship between two important dimensions: KM human critical success factors and moral duties based on the Rossian ethics. A framework is presented to show how the two dimensions interact. We sum up indicated relations of each moral duty with CSFs. The result number shows that how many CSFs are affected by a given duty. As an important outcome of this framework, organizations which want to be successful in KM must acknowledge the importance of beneficence as a moral duty.

The paper has important implications for public organizations seeking to improve their KM success by applying moral duties. It will remain for future researches to scrutinize other ethical frameworks and do practical testing to examine the proposed framework. The framework could be implemented in various public organizations. Researches may make hypothesis based on our results and test them in their organizations or may study the relationship between Rossian moral duties and KM CSFs without considering our results. Scholars, also, can make an enquiry that in fact is there a strong relation between successful KM and ethical KM? Namely, could a successful KM be unethical?

REFERENCES

Alavi, M. (2000). Managing Organizational Knowledge. In Zmud, R. (Ed.), *Framing the Domains of IT Management*. Cincinnati, OH: Pinnaflex Educational Resources.

Baron, M., Pettit, P., & Slote, M. (1997). *Three Methods of Ethics: A Debate*. Oxford, UK: Blackwell.

Berdrow, I., & Lane, H. W. (2003). International joint ventures: Creating value through successful Knowledge Management. *Journal of World Business*, *38*, 15–30. doi:10.1016/S1090-9516(02)00106-2

Blanchard, K. (1987). Ethical Management. *Executive Excellence*, *11*(4), 3–4.

Boh, W. F. (2007). Mechanisms for sharing knowledge in project-based organizations. *Information and Organization*, *17*, 27–58. doi:10.1016/j.infoandorg.2006.10.001

Brancheau, J. C., Janz, B. D., & Wetherbe, J. C. (1996). Key issues in information systems management: 1994–95 SIM Delphi results. *Management Information Systems Quarterly*, *20*(2), 225–242. doi:10.2307/249479

Carroll, A., & Scherer, R. (1999). Models of management morality for new millennium. *Business Ethics Quarterly*, *11*(2), 365–371. doi:10.2307/3857754

Cegielski, C. G. (2001). *A Model of the Factors that Affect the Integration of Emerging Information Technology into Corporate Strategy*. Unpublished doctoral dissertation, University of Mississippi.

Chong, S. (2006). KM critical success factors: A comparison of perceived importance versus implementation in Malaysian ICT companies. *The Learning Organization*, *13*(3), 230–256. doi:10.1108/09696470610661108

Chong, S.C., & Choi, Y.S. (2005). Critical factors in the successful implementation of knowledge management. *Journal of Knowledge Management Practice, 6*.

Dalkey, N., & Helmer, O. (1963). An experimental application of the Delphi method to the use of experts. *Management Science*, *9*(3), 458–467. doi:10.1287/mnsc.9.3.458

Dancy, J. (1991). An Ethics of Prima Facie Duties. In Singer, P. (Ed.), *A Companion to Ethics* (pp. 225–226). Oxford, UK: Blackwell.

Drucker, P. F. (1993). *Post-Capitalist Society*. Oxford, UK: Butterworth Heinemann.

Gammelgaard, J., & Ritter, T. (2000). *Knowledge retrieval process in multinational consulting firms*. Frederiksberg, Denmark: Danish Social Sciences Research Council. Retrieved from http://web.cbs.dk/departments/int/seminarpapers/JG-Knowledge.pdf

Geva, A. (2006). A typology of moral problems in business: A framework for ethical management. *Journal of Business Ethics*, *69*, 134–147. doi:10.1007/s10551-006-9072-y

Hasanali, F. (2002). *Critical Success Factors of Knowledge Management*. Houston, TX: APQC.

Hayne, S., & Pollard, C. (2000). A comparative analysis of critical issues facing Canadian information systems personnel: a national and global perspective. *Information & Management*, *38*(2), 73–86. doi:10.1016/S0378-7206(00)00056-2

Holsapple, P., & Josh, I, K. (2002). Knowledge manipulation activities: results of a Delphi study. *Information & Management*, *39*(6), 477–490. doi:10.1016/S0378-7206(01)00109-4

Hosein, I. (2005). *Researching the ethics of Knowledge Management: the case of Data-mining*.

Iske, P., & Boersma, W. (2005). Connected brains-question and answer systems for knowledge sharing: concepts, implementation and return on investment. *Journal of Knowledge Management*, *9*(1), 126–145. doi:10.1108/13673270510583018

Jennex, M., & Olfman, L. (2005). Assessing Knowledge Management success. *International Journal of Knowledge Management*, *1*(2), 33–49. doi:10.4018/jkm.2005040104

Josephson, M. (2001). *Making ethical decisions*. Retrieved from http://www.josephsoninstitute.org/MED/medtoc.htm

Kant, I. (1997). *Critique of Practical Reason* (Gregor, M., Trans.). Cambridge, UK: Cambridge University Press.

Kelly, K. (1999). *New rules for the new economy: 10 radical strategies for a connected world*. New York, NY: Penguin Books.

LaFollette, H. (1997). Theorizing about Morality. In LaFollette, H. (Ed.), *Ethics in Practice: an Anthology* (pp. 3–10). Oxford, UK: Blackwell.

Land, F., Amjad, U., & Nolas, S. (2004). *Knowledge management: The dark side of KM*. Paper presented at the ETHICOMP Conference.

Land, F., Amjad, U., & Nolas, S. (2007). The ethics of Knowledge Management. *Journal of Knowledge Management*, *3*(1), 1–9. doi:10.4018/jkm.2007010101

Lester, C. (2000). *Building Wealth: The New Rules for Individuals, Companies, and Nations in a Knowledge-Based Economy*. New York, NY: Harper Business.

Lichtman, J. (1998). Invoke employee loyalty. *Workforce*, *77*, 121–122.

Linstone, H., & Turoff, M. (1975). *The Delphi Method. Techniques and Applications*. Reading, MA: Addison-Wesley.

Mason, R., Collins, C., & Cox, E. (1986). Four ethical issues of the Information Age. *Management Information Systems Quarterly*, 5–12. doi:10.2307/248873

Mathi, K. (2004). *Key Success Factors for Knowledge Management.* Unpublished master's thesis, University of Applied Sciences/FH Kempten.

McNaughton, D. (2002). An Unconnected Heap of Duties? In Stratton-Lake, P. (Ed.), *Ethical Intuitionism: Re-evaluations* (pp. 76–91). Oxford, UK: Clarendon Press.

Moorhouse, J. R. (2002). *Desired characteristics of ethical leaders in business, educational, political, and religious organizations from East Tennessee: A Delphi investigation.* Johnson City, TN: East Tennessee State University.

Nunes, M. B., Annansingh, F., Eaglestone, B., & Wakefield, R. (2006). Knowledge management issues in knowledge-intensive SMEs. *The Journal of Documentation*, *62*(1), 101–119. doi:10.1108/00220410610642075

Okoli, C., & Pawlowski, S. D. (2004). The Delphi method as a research tool: an example, design considerations and applications. *Journal of International Management*, *42*, 15–29.

Paliwoda, S. J. (1983). Predicting the future using Delphi. *Management Decision*, *21*(1), 31–38. doi:10.1108/eb001309

Quin, J., Anderson, P., & Finkelstien, S. (1996). Managing professional intellect: Making the most of the best. *Harvard Business Review*, 71–80.

Rockart, J. (1979). Chief executives define their own information needs. *Harvard Business Review*, 81–92.

Ruggles, R. (1998). The state of the notion: knowledge management in practice. *California Management Review*, *40*(3), 80–89.

Saraph, J. V., Benson, P. G., & Schroeder, R. G. (1989). An instrument for measuring the critical factors of quality management. *Decision Sciences*, *20*, 810–829. doi:10.1111/j.1540-5915.1989.tb01421.x

Schwartz, M. (2007). The Business ethics of management theory. *Journal of Management History*, *13*(1), 43–54. doi:10.1108/17511340710715160

Stewart, T. A. (1997). *Intellectual Capital: The new Wealth of Organizations.* New York, NY: Doubleday.

Thomas, J. C., Kellogg, W. A., & Erickson, T. (2001). The Knowledge Management puzzle: Human and social factors in knowledge management. *IBM Systems Journal*, *40*(4), 863–884. doi:10.1147/sj.404.0863

Toffler, A. (1990). *The Third Wave.* New York, NY: Morrow.

Werhane, P., & Freeman, E. (2003). Business Ethics. In Frey, R. G., & Wellman, C. (Eds.), *A Companion to Applied Ethics* (pp. 537–552). London, UK: Blackwell.

Wong, K. Y. (2005). Critical success factors for implementing knowledge management in small and medium enterprises. *Industrial Management & Data Systems*, *105*(3), 261–279. doi:10.1108/02635570510590101

Yu, S., Kim, Y., & Kim, M. (2004). Linking Organizational Knowledge Management Drivers to Knowledge Management Performance: An Exploratory Study. In *Proceedings of HICSS37*. Washington, DC: IEEE Computer Society.

ENDNOTES

1 Talking about Business Ethics is not the charge of this article. For more information you can see: Geva, A. (2006). A Typology of Moral Problems in Business: A Framework for Ethical Management. *Journal of Business Ethics, 69*, 134-147. Schwartz, M. (2007). The Business ethics of management theory. *Journal of Management History, 13*(1), 43-54. Werhane, P., & Freeman, E. (2003). Business Ethics. In R. G. Frey & C. Wellman (Eds.), *A Companion to Applied Ethics* (pp. 537-552). London, UK: Blackwell.

2 Ross, W. (1930). *The Right and the Good*, pp. 19, 20 and 33.

3 Ross, W. (1930). *The Right and the Good*, p. 27.

4 The way in which we utilize the idea of 'prima facie duty' and 'actual duty' deals with the point that prima facie duties have an invariant contribution to the moral evaluation of different cases while the metaphysical status of actual duties entirely depends on the way in which several prima facie duties are combined together in different contexts.

5 According to Kantian ethics, we arrive at justified moral judgment by utilizing the Categorical Imperative. We cannot arrive at tenable moral judgments perceptually. By perception, I mean something which is grasped directly and non-theoretically. Likewise, according to Utilitarian ethics, we arrive at justified moral judgments through the principle of utility. We cannot do so non-theoretically.

6 McNaughton, D. (2006). An Unconnected Heap of Duties? In P. Stratton-Lake (Ed.), *Ethical Intuitionism* (p. 79). Oxford, UK: Oxford University Press.

7 Dancy, J. (1991). An Ethics of Prima Facie Duties. In P. Singer (Ed.), *A Companion to Ethics* (pp. 225-226). Oxford, UK: Blackwell.

This work was previously published in the Information Resources Management Journal, Volume 24, Issue 2, edited by Mehdi Khosrow-Pour, pp. 61-75, copyright 2013 by IGI Publishing (an imprint of IGI Global).

Chapter 10
Challenges Faced by Megacities in the Future

Ali Assadian
University of California, San Diego, USA

Mostafa Nejati
Universiti Sains Malaysia, Malaysia

ABSTRACT

The advancement of science, industry, and digital technologies has shaped the lives of many people and has encouraged more people to live in cities. Since 2007, the urban population has exceeded the rural, and this amount is estimated to increase up to 60% of world habitants by 2030, according to the United Nations. Considering that these changes in people's lifestyle can create various challenges to society, identifying and managing the potential future challenges is a vital step to ensure a dignified living without conflicts. This paper studies the challenges that cities and megacities may face in the future and provides solutions to manage and handle them. Reports and statistics from international organizations and the authors' critical analysis have been applied to collect the necessary data. The research findings emphasize the importance of enhanced competitiveness and the quality of life and environment on the development of the city. Moreover, the major infrastructural problems facing cities in the digital world are discussed and the importance of strategic planning and sustainable approach toward resolving urban issues are emphasized.

INTRODUCTION

Overpopulation of cities and excessive emigration of people from the countryside to urban areas has caused growing problems to the cities, which if not managed properly can even cause disasters as cities continue to expand and over-populate. In their essence, cities are places for commercial, cultural, scientific, industrial and social activities. They are also considered as the driving engine of a country toward economic development. Yet, despite their rapid improvement and faster

DOI: 10.4018/978-1-4666-3616-3.ch010

growth rate than rural areas, cities face special economic, social, political, and environmental problems. The first step to tackle these problems is to identify the challenges of the cities of today and the megacities of tomorrow. These cities cannot reach a desired development status unless they can first recognize their current potentials and issues well. Thus, cities need to strategically point out their strengths and weaknesses, and identify their current strategic level. Only then, they can make the right decision on their future targets and pathway to a higher standard of living (PricewaterhouseCoopers, 2005).

Based on the studies and discussions with world's urban experts from different cities throughout the globe, cities' capital and assets can be categorized into six types, including intellectual and social capital, democratic capital, cultural and leisure capital, environmental capital, technical capital, and financial capital (PricewaterhouseCoopers, 2005). Effective use of these assets can result in the successful transition of cities from current levels to their desired strategic level in the future and help overcoming challenges they face.

In the 21st century, cities are faced with numerous challenges. On one hand, they are in danger from the harmful effects of global warming. On the other hand, problems such as discrimination, inequality, and pollution have affected the quality of life of the citizens (UN-HABITAT, 2006). Nonetheless, the main challenge that remains for the cities is the "need for sustainable development".

In recent years, the debate on sustainability and the necessity for development without harming the environment and endangering future generations has been re-emphasized (Blackburn, 2007; Cernea, 1994; Nejati, Md Shahbudin, & Amran, 2010; Robinson et al., 2006) Although there is no unique definition for sustainable development, the most widely accepted definition is the one by World Commission on Environment and Development (1987) whereby sustainable development is defined as the "development that meets the needs of the present without compromising the ability of future generations to meet their own needs". From this definition, concepts such as equality and social justice among nations can be considered as some of the objectives of sustainable development (Ardakani, 2006).

Sustainable development is usually considered to be composed of three main building blocks: environment, society, and economy as shown in Figure 1 (Giddings, Hopwood, & O'Brien, 2002). These three building blocks must be strengthened hand in hand in order to have a sustainable society.

Despite the key roles that cities play in the development of the society, ignoring the negative aspects that might be caused as a result of modernizing and developing cities can be harmful in the long run. Thus, planning and managing strategies for a sustainable and balanced city is vital. According to UN Habitat's World Urban Forum III, there should be a dynamic balance among the objectives of economic, environmental, and socio-cultural development within the framework of a local government whereby the citizens proactively participate in the development process (UN-HABITAT, 2006).

Figure 1. Building-blocks of sustainable development

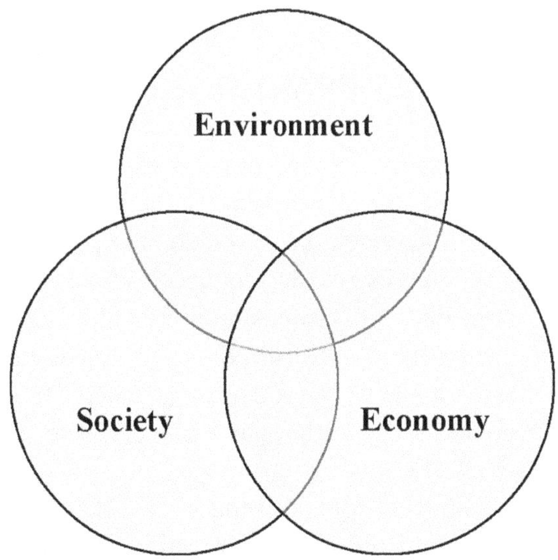

Another point of consideration is the difference between public and private sectors' approach to development. Though organizations regardless of their sector use a wide range of resources (money, equipment, time, infrastructure, people, and knowledge and intellectual capitals, etc.) and have an impact on the society (Nejati, 2010), the public sector is more concerned about the society and the quality of services to the community; whereas the private sector seeks to increase its profit and earn more money. Nonetheless, private companies are gradually, taking a more active role towards practicing their social responsibilities.

As for generating income, the private sector organizations try to compete with their rivals to provide better services and products in order to earn more, whereas the public sector depends on taxes to cover the costs of its services and administrative affairs (PricewaterhouseCoopers, 2005). Although, this different approach in public and private sectors might seem problematic at first, it can indeed be beneficiary to the citizens, because the expectation of public sector in providing better quality services can encourage the private sector to come up with appropriate solutions and alternatives to better meet those expectations. Therefore, the private sector can play a major role in the sustainable development of cities and help to handle cities' prospective challenges.

PRINCIPLE URBAN CONCERNS

Building and maintaining the complex infrastructures of the future megacities has a high priority.. Besides, satisfying the needs of the ever-growing urban population would require city managers to act in line with citizens' expectations. Thus, city managers must balance the three overriding concerns, namely competitiveness, quality of life, and environment, as shown in Figure 2 (Miller & Hazel, 2007).

It should be noted that these three concerns are in line with the three major sustainable development goals, that are social, economical, and environmental goals. Through good governance, a balance between these concerns can be made and the city can get ready for confronting probable challenges in the future.

Figure 2. Three principle urban concerns

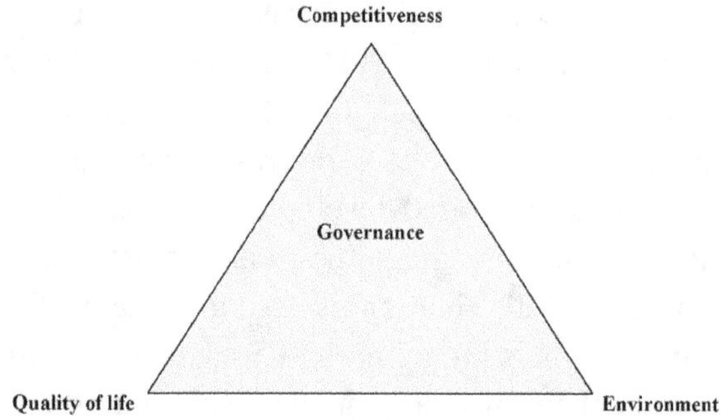

Considering the impacts of megacities' economy on the growth of national economy, the significant role of economical competitiveness can be better understood. According to some recent studies, the city of Tokyo is responsible for 40% of Japan's GDP, while having only 28% of the country's population. Similarly, Paris shapes 30% of France GDP, with only 16% of the French population living there. Even among developing countries, similar examples can be found. The Nigerian capital, Lagos, forms 30% of the country's output, while only 8% of the country's population inhabit there. The same pattern applies to the metropolitan regions of OECD countries (Organisation for Economic Co-operation and Development), as they mostly tend to have higher GDP per capita, higher labor productivity levels, and even faster growth rates than the national level (Miller & Hazel, 2007). These significant impacts of megacities on the development of their respective countries highlight their considerable role in the globalization process.

Thus, possessing proper communication infrastructures and transportation facilities, as well as qualified workforce and experienced managers can encourage new investments and facilitate contribution of megacities to the development of the country. According to the Economist Journal, the existence of transparent business rules and regulations are among one of the most important economical motivations in attracting new investments (Economist Intelligence Unit, 2004).

Also, the standard and quality of life is another important indicator of a city's future. In a sustainable city, the inequalities and injustices are minimized and fair access to the resources and opportunities are provided for all the citizens (Pourezzat, Nejati, & Nejati, 2008).

However, at the time being, the difference between rich and poor is very significant in most cities, while the rich have access to all resources; the poor are deprived from meeting their basic needs.

Poverty, hunger, and sanitation problems are some of the most common social problems today which negatively affect the lives of billions of people worldwide. Therefore, tackling these problems in order to alleviate poverty and narrow the gap between the rich and poor, fight global hunger, and last but not least, provide drinkable water and proper sanitation facilities are among the key goals of sustainability related campaigns and projects (United Nations, 2010). Despite significant progresses made toward achieving the millennium development goals, still there are many gaps to overcome. For instance, the number of people who are undernourished has continued to grow. Today, more than 800 million people, who form almost 19 per cent of the developing world's population, live in absolute poverty, with an income of less than one dollar a day (United Nations, 2007).

Poverty is one of the most challenging and lasting problems of the world that is broadly defined as a system of exclusion from society and social systems (Mwenda & Muuka, 2004). It causes economic, social and psychological deprivation among people who fail to possess essential resources to satisfy the minimal living standards (Jimba, 2000; Ullah & Routray, 2007). As a multi-dimensional problem, poverty needs practical and multidimensional strategies to be reduced and resolved. Such strategies can assist in assessing the causes of poverty and provide practical steps to resolve the problem (Curtis, 2006). Of course, people's empowerment and educating them to enhance their skills are prerequisites to ensure that poverty eradication projects can succeed (Amiri & Nejati Ajibisheh, 2008). Without nurturing people's minds and equipping them with necessary skills and competencies, we cannot expect their o-active participation in the societal activities, hence resulting in the failure of development projects. Therefore, raising awareness and capacity-building are needed to help people transform their lives and ultimately contribute to a more sustainable world. But importantly, whatever strategy is undertaken by the policy-makers, this unjust situation needs to be changed and the social problems (such as poverty, hunger, etc.) should fade away, because only then a sustainable lifestyle can be realized for everyone.

Moreover, protecting the environment is vital to achieve a sustainable lifestyle and provide better standard of living in cities. Unfortunately, problems such as congestion, air and water pollution, waste management and degradation of green areas are already some of the most familiar environmental issues of large cities around the world, especially in the developing countries, which need extra attention to be resolved (Miller & Hazel, 2007).

Although, cities are the sources of environmental problems, they can also be part of the solution (State of the World population, 2007), through strategic and forward-looking management, and implementing the necessary urban systems to facilitate the social and urban lives of citizens in line with environmental considerations. Of course, the people are also aware of the impacts of environment on the quality of life (PricewaterhouseCoopers, 2005); therefore, the urban policymakers should stress on environmental issues in the urban planning and raise more awareness on how everyone can contribute to a more environmental-friendly city. Unfortunately, in many urban development plans, the environmental aspects are ignored or considered less important than other. For instance, the city's focus on generating income and wealth resources has resulted in negligence toward the environmental considerations in many cities in the developing world. They are on the same wrong track that most cities in the developed countries took before; that is the strategy of focusing on generating revenue at first and coming up with solutions and plans to correct their misbehavior toward the environment, later on. Consider the significance of climate change and the environmental problems that exist nowadays compared to before, the continuation of such strategies by cities can be problematic and dangerous to the world's future. Therefore, the developed nations, as well as international organizations should help cities in the developing world to pass the development phase at lower costs and with less harm to the environment and natural resources, because at the end of the day, everyone is living on the same planet and using the same limited resources.

Apart from environmental degradation a higher pollution rate can be seen among the developing cities than the ones in the developed countries, as shown in Figure 3 based on World Bank data. The figure compares the rate of population to the air pollution in different cities, where a city like Tokyo with an approximate population of 35 million people is much less polluted than Delhi with an approximate population of 16 million people. In other words, the pollution rate in Tokyo is 4.3 times less than Delhi, despite being two times more populated than the Indian capital. These figures highlight the importance of considering environmental aspects in the urban planning and decision makings.

Figure 3. Pollution rate compared to the population in different cities (adapted from Miller & Hazel, 2007)

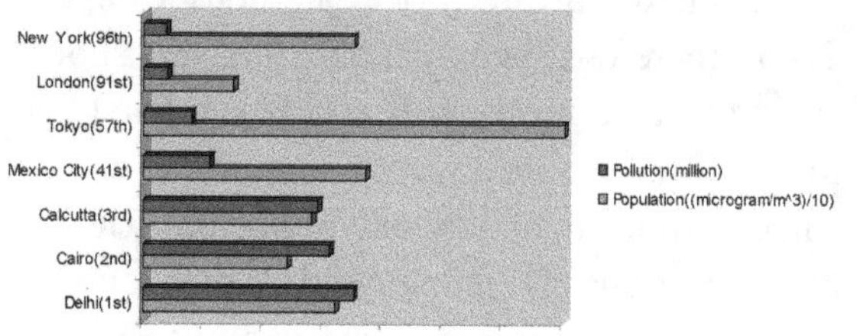

The question that is raised here is whether there is a positive relationship between the concepts of competitiveness, quality of life, and environment. In other words, can cities develop, while protecting the environment and improving the quality of life for their citizens? It is believed that the development of cities depends on the inter-relationship of these concerns as displayed in Figure 4.

Competitive cities can better provide necessary investments and resources to build the required urban infrastructures, improve quality of services, and create economic and social opportunities for their citizens. Besides, developed cities with a clean and healthy environment can attract a wider range of business. Similarly, cities with educated and healthy citizen can better attract investments. All of these show that ignoring even one of the main principle concerns will result in failure to city management (Miller & Hazel, 2007).

Another question to answer is finding the factors which can help to fade away these urban concerns. As discussed, there should be a dynamic balance between economic, environmental and socio-cultural factors of a city. Yet, reaching such a balance requires an effective governance system in which the citizens can pro-actively participate and take actions.

In a study conducted by MRC Mclean Hazel and GlobeScan for Siemens on the priorities of urban stakeholders in 25 megacities worldwide,

Figure 4. The impacts of principle urban concerns on the city development

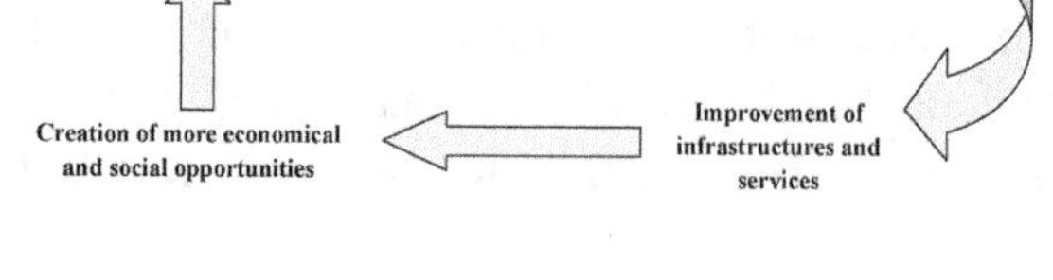

the following five priorities were found to be the major concerns for the decision makers: economical, environmental, social, infrastructural, and investment priorities.

For each of these priorities cities will come across with several challenges now or in the future. Considering the importance of providing the infrastructures as prerequisites of urban development, the authors will look into it more deeply.

URBAN INFRASTRUCTURE

All cities need high-quality infrastructure to facilitate the movement of people and goods and deliver basic services to their population (Miller & Hazel, 2007). A suitable infrastructure provides services in a hidden and unnoticeable way. Depending on the city's growth stage (emerging, transitional, mature), it will have different challenges ahead; thus, each city will deal with these challenges differently than others. Siemens' report on Megacities divided infrastructures problems into five main categories, including: transportation, energy, water and waste water, healthcare, and safety and security; from which, transportation is and will continue to be the biggest problem that any metropolitan area faces (Miller & Hazel, 2007).

The researchers find these divisions suitable for their cause and used them with a slight modification.

TRANSPORTATION

Traffic, congestion and inefficiency of public transportation systems are noticeable issues in big cities, as they reduce urban productivity particularly in megacities (Transportation Research Board, 1996). The importance of transportation systems is to a great extend, as it plays a major role in defining the quality of life in a metropolitan area. Moreover, a sustainable transportation system will have an unprecedented affect on the economic growth and contributes to equitable access in meeting people's basic needs. A well developed transportation system provides to older people and young children a safer and cheaper way to access social services such as healthcare and schools, respectively (UN-HABITAT, 2006). For example, in Delhi, 75% of available road space is occupied by cars which only contribute to the displacement of 20% of the population (InWEnt, 2007). Thus, this data shows the importance of transportation infrastructure and provides an insight on how disastrous the situation is in developing countries. The importance of addressing transportation issue is so significant that "Canadian Mayor's Caucus" report in 2006 emphasized the joint effort of Municipal, Provincial, and Federal governments for tackling the problem.

The report prepared by MRC McLean Hazel and GlobeScan for Siemens (Miller & Hazel, 2007), questioning stakeholders' opinion of 25 megacities on addressing transportation problems, show different opinions exist and no single solution comes out as the best solution; while some prefer investing on new transportation capacity as the primary solution (12%), others believe in increasing efficiency of the existing infrastructure (33%). Although, in recent years demand management solutions which promote sustainable transportation systems through "push" and "pull" techniques have gain momentum, however, based on the mentioned research, only 9% of respondent believed in their usefulness.

No matter what kind of the solution city officials employ the success of their strategies and policies depend highly on a well thought intelligent system, which uses information and communication technologies to execute their plans efficiently; thus, leading to an intelligent mobility and transportation system. Intelligent Transportation Systems (ITS) have been around for many years, however, a new generation of ITS are being put into practice where traffics are predicted, variable parking prices are used, real-time travelling advices are provided, and traffic management is improved (Intelligent Transport, 2009). All these new achievement could not have been reached unless the communication infrastructures are well developed to their current levels in many countries, where a lot of information can be carried from one place to another through different communication means.

ENERGY

Humans' life is dependent on Energy. More importantly, our dependency on energy increases on a daily basis. From heating, cooling, or lighting our houses and working environments, to cooking and moving from one place to another, some sort of energy is required. As cities grow, so does their dependency on energy. As explained by UN Habitat report, "energy is at the base of an effective city life. When power supply fails, cities stop working. Power is essential condition, for our schools and hospitals, for industry and commerce, for food supply and transportation" (UN-HABITAT, 2006), thus, it is important to build and maintain a solid plan that not only focus on conservation of energy, but also considers how to respond to the ever increasing energy demand. It is worth mentioning that in order to address the increase in energy demand on one hand, and to lower our carbon footprint produced by energy consumption on the other hand, it is important to focus more on renewable sources of energy.

Besides, no matter in what country people live, it is important to consider a plan fighting against "fuel poverty" to ensure a higher standard of living for citizens, because even in a developed city like Newcastle in England, it is estimated that over one fourth of the households live in fuel poverty (Newcastle City Council, 2006). To do so and in order to conserve energy and minimize the harmful impacts of energy usage on the environment, the energy efficiency needs to improve.

There is no doubt that transportation and energy have a direct relationship. Reducing the time spent in traffic jams will help reduce energy usage simply because the vehicles will spend less time traveling a certain distance. Moreover, in most parts of the world, especially in the developing countries, transportation is the fastest growing consumer of energy, and is expected to grow in the years to come. For instance, in the next 30 years it is expected that in China and India motorization will increase by 360% and 660% respectively (InWEnt, 2007).

It is important to change people's attitude and behavior towards using public transportation systems, thus, minimizing individual displacement and saving more energy. Furthermore, no matter if the launch of electric vehicles is successful or not (Ramsey, 2010), electricity will continue to remain the biggest form of energy in use. As the driving force behind commerce and industry, electricity has the following features:

- It can be easily transformed into other forms of energy,
- It is easier and safer to transmit from one point to another,
- And, most important of all, electricity is emission free at the point of consumption.

Thus, because of these features electricity has become the single most important form of energy consumed throughout the world. Interestingly, while from 1972 until 2002, the world GDP grew at 3.3%, electricity consumption grew at 3.6%. Furthermore, the International Energy Agency (2006) reports that one additional dollar investment in more efficient electrical equipment and building would avoid two dollars investment in electricity supply. Not to mention that the electrical energy can be responsible for harming the environment; for instance, in the city of Munich alone in 2008, the total electricity consumed by households, trade, industry, commerce, services, and transport was responsible for about 39% of all CO2 emissions in the city (Siemens, 2009).

However, beside the inefficiency of the system as a whole, one of the most important problems in tackling demand increase for electricity is the existence of old infrastructures in generating, transmitting and distributing of electricity. Thus, new investments are needed to build infrastructures, however, this can be seen as an opportunity to prioritize the use of renewable sources of energy and distributed generation systems because these types of energies not only can meet new demand with less pollution, but as sustainable solutions, they will also have positive impacts on maintaining a sustainable global weather condition. Furthermore, distributed generation systems produce electricity close to the consuming point; therefore, they can significantly increase the efficiency of electric systems. In order to take advantage of sustainable energy systems it is necessary to develop a competitive energy market, where private sector companies can have a dominant role in securing cheap and clean energy and help increase the efficiency of the electricity systems in a shorter period of time. Additionally, the establishment of electricity market will ensure a secure operation and facilitate the economic operation (Shahidehpour, Yamin, & Li, 2002). But increasing the production from renewable sources cannot be met unless a highly integrated information system is used, where different kinds of renewable energy sources work in conjunction with one another to meet the online demand with the cheapest rate of producing electricity.

WATER AND WASTEWATER

Managing water and waste water networks is one the most important steps for building a healthy city. Access to safe drinking water has a dramatic effect on increasing public health. However, access to clean and sanitized water is more expensive and difficult for poorer people, thus, more health problems and risks develop in such areas. UN reports suggest that 1.7 million deaths can be avoided each year by providing access to safe drinking water, sanitation, and hygiene (World Water Assessment Programme, 2006).

The contamination of surface water will have a significant impact on the safety of drinking water; as a result, it is important to develop a healthy environment in order to prevent any contamination of rivers and springs. A well designed sewage system will significantly minimize the pollution of surface water and thus increase water supply. However, the most important step to overcome problems arising from water shortage is to reduce water consumption, especially in different industries through developing new techniques. Moreover, using appropriate irrigation systems in horticulture and agriculture fields would have a significant impact on conserving drinking water. For instance, as part of their Net Zero Emission plan, city of Melbourne wants to reduce water consumption by 12% through sustainable water policies, guidelines, and training across the city by 2020 (PricewaterhouseCoopers, 2005). Melbourne's effort in conserving water to build a better life for its citizens reflects the importance of water and a well developed water system in our daily lives. A city needs to have a suitable water and sewage system to address the daily needs of its citizens. Unfortunately, most city officials in developing countries look at developing such infrastructures as expenses. They simply forget how building proper water infrastructures can help reduce the spread of disease and increase public health and thus help the overall economy of the city.

Based on World Health Organization research (2005), in 2002 alone, 1.1 billion people which represent 17% of the population lacked access to improved water sources such as tap water in the house, protected wells and springs, and rain water collection, two third of these people lived in Asia. Moreover, 42% of the world population (2.6 billion people) lacked access to sanitation. Although, 80% of the population who do not have access to drinking water live in villages and rural areas, as migration from these areas to urban parts grow, the problem tends to shift from rural areas to the cities, making it one of the most important challenges that cities have to face, especially in the developing countries. Problems associated with water and sewage systems differ from one country to another. Both developed and developing countries face the problem of corrosion within their current network. However, cities in developing countries have an additional problem: Lack of appropriate water and sewage network at first place.

In general, to overcome water shortages in urban areas, it is necessary to not only reduce water consumption, but also develop wastewater treatment facilities to treat and reuse water.

HEALTHCARE

Like other infrastructure problems, sanitation problems will differ from one country to another based on the degree of development in that society. For instance, in the developed countries the number of aging people is increasing which will lead to an increase in public medical costs. As a result, it is recommended to hedge such increase in healthcare expenses through developing preventive healthcare systems. However, in the developing countries the inadequacy of health and hygienic infrastructure along with financial difficulties are the main concerns. World Bank (2006) reports that developing countries account for 90% of the global disease burden while possessing only 84% of the global population. They also produce 20% of the global gross domestic product (GDP) while 12% of all healthcare spending, moreover, high-income countries spend nearly hundred times more on healthcare costs per capita than low-income countries; and approximately 30 times more on health if adjusted for cost of living differences. This is an indication on how under-financed the healthcare system in the developing countries is. Nevertheless, this does not mean that the developed countries have no financial issues. Based on "Families USA" report published in 2008, the American cities are at the front lines of health care crisis because of the rising number of uninsured Americans, thus lacking sufficient fund to maintain their free services to lower income people (Families USA, 2008).

Another important factor that should be considered is how information system technologies can help improve healthcare systems. Overall, these systems help reduce cost through organizing medical records in better format. Also, these systems can be used to increase chances of saving lives and/or reducing mortality rate by providing the required information to medical centers other areas faster than ever and enabling geographically dispersed team to collaborate with one another.

SAFETY AND SECURITY

There is no doubt that Safety and Security are of the most important issues that any society faces. Problems such as poverty, economic crisis, war, revolutions, and natural disasters have negative effect on safety and security. As the United Nations Human Settlement Programme's report (2007) indicates, "in the last decade or so, the world has witnessed increasing numbers of threats to urban safety and security. While some of these threats have taken the form of dramatic events, many have been manifestations of the nexus of urban poverty and inequality with the physical, economic, social and institutional conditions of slums".

Another important factor on Safety and Security is people's perception. No matter how safe a city is, people's perception on safety has an important impact on what they do and what they think they can achieve. This qualitative factor differentiates this kind of challenge from the others; because, "the ultimate goal of safety [and security] efforts is to create a subjective state of mind. Statistical success is not enough. In 2005, the FBI reported that violent crime has been decreasing in America for a decade, but a Gallup poll showed that two thirds of the population believed the complete opposite" (Miller & Hazel,

2007). Also, media and the flow of information play a substantial role on people's perception on safety. Moreover, the content and type of media will affect people's perception (United Nations Human Settlement Programme, 2007).

Violence can lead to lack of security in a city, thus, affecting people's interest in an area. Furthermore, insecurity can lead to loss of confidence in the local government which plays a pivotal role in developing a better governance system within a country. Numbers and statistics are a small part of a safety and security pack. The most important part is using internet based solutions to raise public awareness and their participation in overcoming security issues. Overall, the intangible aspect of safety and security, media's role, and people's perception differentiates this challenge from the other ones, which requires a more dynamic involvement from individuals. Smarter intelligent services can play a vital role in developing this perception through anticipating crimes and helping preventing them. These systems use real time information to show crime patterns as they are forming. New York's *Real Time Crime Center* system has helped improve public safety with a 27% drop in crime since 2001, making New York the safest largest city in US (IBM, 2009).

CONCLUSION

In a big picture, cities face three major challenges, that are similar to the ones faced in designing sustainable development plans, namely Economic, Social, and Environmental challenges. In order to overcome these challenges, they need to be taken into consideration simultaneously, without sacrificing one aspect for the other. In other words, there should be a balance between them. Moreover, to address these faceted challenges, the following five priorities need to be developed: economic, environmental, social, infrastructure, and investment priorities. The infrastructure priority in itself encompasses other issues. Thus, the infrastructural challenges faced by cities were further looked into. Based on MRC Mclean Hazel and GlobeScan report infrastructure problems can be divided into transportation, electricity (energy), water and wastewater, healthcare, and safety and security challenges. Of the five, transportation is the most important one, for which different solutions have been developed to address the related problems arising in this sector such as push and pull techniques, expansion of public transportation system, and increase the efficiency of current systems.

In terms of energy usage, there is an essential need for improving the energy efficiency and investing on renewable types of energy to overcome the challenge of energies' scarcity and negative environmental impacts of current energy sources. Trends show that the electricity consumption will be almost doubled by 2030. Similarly, the current increasing trend in water consumption will lead to lack of fresh water in the future, necessitating the development of intelligent water and wastewater networks and efficient water treatment systems in the cities.

In the healthcare system both developing and developed countries lack sufficient funding but for different reasons. Cities, as the place that people live tend to carry the most burdens from any inefficiency and lack of funds in this sector.

It is noteworthy to mention that safety and security sector differ from other problems because of the intangible dimension which relates to them: perception of people. Therefore, in order to address any issue, it is recommended to increase people's participation to help enhance safety.

In summary, the officials and decision makers in the cities should concentrate on social, economical and environmental aspects of urban development and at the same time, apply strategic planning approach to visualize and develop a sustainable city for current and future generations. Achieving the mission of sustainable development highly depends on the active participation of all citizens and stakeholders in the society, and is enforced by increasing the awareness of the public and by mobilizing their power to contribute to sustainability. Because no matter how small a contribution by an individual can be, it would play a big role once all those little steps are put together and guided towards the right direction. To achieve such a goal, it is imperative to develop powerful NGOs and local organizations, making people and their organization active participants in issues surrounding their immediate concerns. It is also essential to work on the development of city through strategic planning and identifying the strengths, weaknesses, opportunities and threats confronting the city, and visioning for "smart cities"; in which leading industries such as information and communication technologies (ICT) are extensively applied and a digital nature of the city is formulate where a wide range of services are provided to the citizens through electronic media and e-government portals, resulting in saving time and energy and improving the service quality. The smart city also provides quality education for its citizens and fosters the relation between inhabitants and city officials through good governance.

In addition, improved logistics and effective transport systems add to the standards of living and contribute to sustainable development of the city (Smart Cities, 2007). Above all, sustainable and comprehensive solutions should be sought to resolve the major problems of cities and enable them to reach sustainable development with an emphasis on its competitive advantages.

ACKNOWLEDGMENT

The second author (Mostafa Nejati) would like to acknowledge Universiti Sains Malaysia (USM) for supporting toward the publication of this paper through USM Fellowship.

REFERENCES

Amiri, M., & Nejati Ajibisheh, M. (2008). Role of empowerment and youth involvement in poverty eradication. *Annals of University of Bucharest. Economic and Administrative Series*, *2*, 163–167.

Ardakani, M. H. (2006). *Economic development & planning*. Tehran, Iran: Avaye Noor Publications.

Blackburn, W. R. (2007). *The Sustainability Handbook: The Complete Management Guide to Achieving Social, Economic and Environmental Responsibility*. Washington, DC: Environmental Law Institute.

Cernea, M. M. (1994). Making development sustainable. In Serageldin, I., & Steer, A. (Eds.), *Making development sustainable: form concepts to action* (pp. 7–10). Washington, DC: World Bank.

Curtis, D. (2006). Mind sets and methods: poverty strategies and the awkward potential of the enabling state. *International Journal of Public Sector Management*, *19*(2), 150–164. doi:10.1108/09513550610650419

Economist Intelligence Unit. (2004). *World investment prospects: The revival of globalisation?* Retrieved November 21, 2010, from http://graphics.eiu.com/files/ad_pdfs/WIP_2004.pdf

Families, U. S. A. (2008). *America's Health Care Crisis: Cities on the front lines*. Retrieved November 21, 2010, from http://www.familiesusa.org/assets/pdfs/cities-on-the-front-lines.pdf

Giddings, B., Hopwood, B., & O'Brien, G. (2002). Environment, economy and society: fitting them together into sustainable development. *Sustainable Development*, *10*(4), 187–196. doi:10.1002/sd.199

IBM. (2009). *Safer citizens of a smarter planet.* Retrieved December 5, 2010, from http://www.ibm.com/smarterplanet/us/en/public_safety/visions/index.html

International Energy Agency. (2006). *World Energy outlook 2006.* Retrieved November 21, 2010, from http://www.iea.org/textbase/nppdf/free/2006/weo2006.pdf

InWEnt. (2007). *Governing Emerging Megacities - Challenges and Perspectives.* Retrieved November 21, 2010, from http://www.germany-wuf4.de/dokumente/06_inwent/06.02_en_inwent_governing_emerging_megacities.pdf

Jimba, S. W. (2000). Information technology and the dialectics of poverty in Africa. *New Library World, 101*(1158), 253–262. doi:10.1108/03074800010348714

Miller, D., & Hazel, G. (2007). *Megacity Challenges: A stakeholder perspective.* Retrieved November 21, 2010, from http://www.siemens.com/press/pool/en/events/megacities/media_mrc_globe_170107_d_1431329.pdf

Mwenda, K. K., & Muuka, G. N. (2004). Towards best practices for micro finance institutional engagement in African rural areas; selected cases and agenda for action. *International Journal of Social Economics, 31*(1-2), 143–158. doi:10.1108/03068290410515475

Nejati, M. (2010). Knowledge Management Performance Evaluation: Challenges and Requirements for Organizations. *Technics Technologies Education Management, 5*(1), 251–254.

Nejati, M., Md Shahbudin, A. S., & Amran, A. (2010). Sustainable development: a competitive advantage or a threat? *Business Strategy Series, 11*(2), 84–89. doi:10.1108/17515631011026407

Newcastle City Council. (2006). *Newcastle in 2021- A Regeneration Strategy for Newcastle.* Retrieved November 21, 2010, from http://www.newcastle.gov.uk/wwwfileroot/regen/ppi/RegenStrategyFinalDoc.pdf

Pourezzat, A. A., Nejati, M., & Nejati, M. (2008). E-Government and Empowerment: Impacts on Equal Access to Information and Developing Public Language. *Lex et Scientia, 15*(1), 123–127.

PricewaterhouseCoopers. (2005). *Cities of the Future.* Retrieved November 21, 2010, from http://www.pwc.com/en_GX/gx/government-public-sector-research/pdf/cities-final.pdf

Ramsey, M. (2010, October 17). Bumpy Road for Electrics. *The Wall Street Journal.* Retrieved November 21, 2010, from http://online.wsj.com/article/SB10001424052748704654004575517891616896222.html

Robinson, H. S., Anumba, C. J., Carrillo, P. M., & Al-Ghassani, A. M. (2006). STEPS: a knowledge management maturity roadmap for corporate sustainability. *Business Process Management Journal, 12*(6), 793–808. doi:10.1108/14637150610710936

Shahidehpour, M., Yamin, H., & Li, Z. (2002). *Market Operations in Electric Power Systems.* New York, NY: John Wiley & Sons. doi:10.1002/047122412X

Siemens. (2009). *Sustainable Urban Infrastructure; Munich Edition – paths toward a carbon-free future.* Retrieved November 30, 2010, from http://www.mobility.siemens.com/shared/data/pdf/www/corporate/sustainable_munich_2009_e.pdf

Smart Cities. (2007). *Smart cities: Ranking of European medium-sized cities.* Retrieved November 30, 2010, from http://www.smart-cities.eu/download/smart_cities_final_report.pdf

Transportation Research Board. (1996). *Transportation Options for Megacities in the Developing World*. Retrieved November 30, 2010, from http://trb.org/publications/admin/megacities.pdf

Ullah, A., & Routray, J. K. (2007). Rural poverty alleviation through NGO interventions in Bangladesh: how far is the achievement? *International Journal of Social Economics*, *34*(4), 237–248. doi:10.1108/03068290710734208

UN-HABITAT. (2006). *Our Future: Sustainable Cities – Turning Ideas into Action*. Retrieved November 21, 2010, from http://www.unhabitat.org/downloads/docs/3040_94379_background-final.pdf

United Nations. (2007). *The Millennium Development Goals Report*. New York, NY: Author.

United Nations. (2010). *The Millennium Development Goals Report*. New York, NY: Author.

United Nations Human Settlement Programme (UNHSP). (2007). *United Nations Human Settlement Programme Report*. New York, NY: Author.

World Bank. (2006). *A practitioner's guide - Health Financing Revisited*. Washington, DC: Author.

World Commission on Environment and Development (WCED). (1987). *Our Common Future*. Oxford, UK: Oxford University Press.

World Health Organization. (2005). *Celebrating Water for Life – The International Decade for Action 2005 – 2015*. Washington, DC: Author.

World Water Assessment Programme. (2006). *Water: a shared responsibility – The United Nations World Water Development Report 2*. Retrieved November 21, 2010, from http://unesdoc.unesco.org/images/0014/001444/144409e.pdf

This work was previously published in the Information Resources Management Journal, Volume 24, Issue 2, edited by Mehdi Khosrow-Pour, pp. 76-88, copyright 2013 by IGI Publishing (an imprint of IGI Global).

Chapter 11
Social Engineering:
The Neglected Human Factor for Information Security Management

Xin (Robert) Luo
The University of New Mexico, USA

Alessandro Seazzu
The University of New Mexico, USA

Richard Brody
The University of New Mexico, USA

Stephen Burd
The University of New Mexico, USA

ABSTRACT

Effective information systems security management combines technological measures and managerial efforts. Although various technical means have been employed to cope with security threats, human factors have been comparatively neglected. This article examines human factors that can lead to social engineering intrusions. Social engineering is a technique used by malicious attackers to gain access to desired information by exploiting the flaws in human logic known as cognitive biases. Social engineering is a potential threat to information security and should be considered equally important to its technological counterparts. This article unveils various social engineering attacks and their leading human factors, and discusses several ways to defend against social engineering: education, training, procedure, and policy. The authors further introduce possible countermeasures for social engineering attacks. Future analysis is also presented.

INTRODUCTION

Information systems (IS) security management depends not only on technological measures but also on managerial endeavors. A plethora of technological methods have been developed to address various security issues but human factors that contribute to significant security breaches have been comparatively neglected. The salient key to derailing potential aggressors is a combination of technical, behavioral, and procedural countermeasures. Imagine receiving a phone call in which someone claiming to work for an official agency suggests that you reveal certain information to help repair an urgent system problem. You willingly help the caller who is, in reality, a fraudster seek-

DOI: 10.4018/978-1-4666-3616-3.ch011

ing access to private information. The success of this social engineering attack relies on the natural helpfulness of human users, their psychological weaknesses, and their tendencies to be unaware of the value of the information they possess and to be sloppy about shielding their information.

Within the context of computer and information security, social engineering (SE) is a combination of techniques used to manipulate victims into divulging confidential information or performing actions that compromise security (Mitnick & Simon, 2002). SE attackers, in general, tend to exploit human cognitive biases. SE attacks are non-technical intrusions that rely on human interactions, potentially bypassing technological security mechanisms. Workman (2007) explained that the emotional aspect of the interaction distracts human users and serves to interfere with the potential victim's ability to carefully analyze the content of the message delivered by social engineers (p. 316). He further indicated that, due to human factors, *knowing better but not doing better* is one of the key scholarly and practical issues that has not been fully addressed, particularly in the IS security management paradigm (Workman, 2008). SE is undoubtedly one of the weakest links in the domain of IS security management, because it is beyond the technological control and subject to human nature.

Prior studies on SE generally tended to focus on technological cues triggering the attacks. Behavioral factors for the SE attacks are not usually described and systematically analyzed. As such, this paper contributes to the literature of IS security by holistically analyzing the human behavioral factors that are associated with SE attacks. In addition to extending previous research on SE, we specifically study behaviors and personality traits that are rooted in social psychology and criminology. We believe that this study can theoretically advance behavioral IS security research in the domain of SE management and control, and could also pragmatically inform organizational decision-makers of how individual employees can deal with the ever increasingly sophisticated SE attacks. It is hoped that this study can offer instrumental insights to the often neglected human aspects for information systems security management.

The remainder of this paper is organized as follows. We first revisit the theoretical bases in social psychology in order to analyze three key aspects related to SE. Then we further draw on criminology and social psychology to discuss the personality traits versus SE attack vulnerabilities. The technical and non-technical means that SE attackers can employ are presented next, followed by a proposed multi-dimensional approach including policies, procedures, standards, employee training and awareness programs, and incident response for more effective and efficient IS security management. The paper concludes with a discussion of future SE analysis and suggestions for future research.

PSYCHOLOGICAL ASPECTS

Recent research has discovered that there are certain terms and techniques that are associated with SE and go perhaps far beyond technology and more so into human error and social psychology (Peltier, 2006). Three key aspects of social psychology, *alternative routes to persuasion* (i.e., central route and peripheral route), *attitudes and beliefs that affect human interactions*, and *techniques for persuasion and influence*, could help explain the emotional cues for manipulated SE attacks (Peltier, 2006).

In a central route to persuasion, SE attackers persuade victims to provide desired information without fabricating unreal scenarios. Thus, this comparatively direct route, which depends on the responder's logical thinking toward the marshaled information from the attacker, does not normally succeed. The other route, *peripheral route to persuasion*, can be leveraged by SE attackers to bypass logical argument and counterargument and seek to trigger intrusion. In the peripheral route to persuasion, the attacker tends to make the intended victim more susceptible to persuasion by triggering strong emotions such as fear or excitement in order to interfere with the victim's ability to respond.

Attitudes and beliefs refer to the differences between the victim's attitude and beliefs about the SE attacker and SE attacker's attitudes and beliefs about his anticipated or definite victims. Rooted in social psychology, *persuasion and influence techniques* rely on peripheral routes to persuasion that are effective to influence others. Six factors can constitute effectual persuasions: authority, scarcity, liking and similarity, reciprocation, commitment and consistency, and social proof (Rusch, 1999).

Furthermore, SE attacks are categorized into human-based and technology-based intrusions. Human-based attacks are interactions between the attacker and the victim who possesses valuable information. In contrast, technology-based attacks access confidential information by employing computer software programs such as pop-up windows, e-mail attachments, and websites, etc. While maliciously generated e-mail attachments and websites seek the victim's natural tendency to trust others to divulge information or perform actions, a vicious script-embedded pop-up window manipulates the victim's psychological fear of getting into trouble by repeatedly prompting the victim to re-enter his/her user username and password because the network connection was interrupted and the window will surreptitiously deliver the information entered to the attackers.

According to Allen (2006), and as shown in Figure 1, a typical SE attack is composed of four steps: information gathering, relationship development, exploitation, and execution. An SE attacker initially gathers information about the target(s) such names, phone numbers, birth dates from publicly-accessible information such as directories and organizational charts. Applying this information, he then can try to build rapport with the intended victim to gain his/her trust.

Figure 1. Four-step social engineering attack (adapted from Allen, 2006)

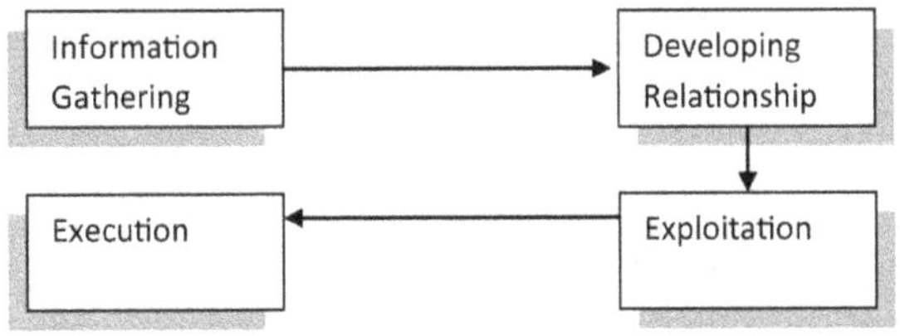

Exploiting the established trust, the SE attacker can then persuade the victim to perform desired actions (i.e., revealing confidential information) which would not normally occur otherwise. In the last stage, the attacker uses the information collected from the victim to carry out attacks.

PERSONALITY TRAITS

This section discusses how SE attackers can exploit different psychological phenomena to specifically recognize the psychological and/or behavioral vulnerabilities of the potential victim in a bid to obtain desired information. These leading psychology-driven personality traits for possible SE attacks include *diffusion of responsibility*, *chance for ingratiation*, *trust relationship*, and *guilt* (Peltier, 2006).

Originating from social psychology and criminology, diffusion of responsibility explains that an individual (i.e., criminal) acting alone, compared with an individual group member, would be held more responsible for behavior leading to a negative consequence. Relating this psychological trigger to SE, researchers have found that targeted victims are made to believe that they are not solely responsible for their actions and this trait works well with *moral duty* when the individual victim conceives that what he/she responds to is of vital importance to the company or its employees (Gragg, 2003; Peltier, 2006). As such, the victim surmises that his/her actions could make the difference between success and failure of the company or the so-called *employee* (the actual SE attacker). Thus, the victim tends to comply with the request to avoid the feeling of guilt.

According to Peltier (2006), chance for ingratiation is when victims are led to believe that compliance with request will enhance their chances of receiving some benefit. This process includes such psychological motives as gaining advantage over a competitor and getting in good with management. *Authority* plays a vital role since people are conditioned to respond to authority figures without painstakingly verifying their legitimacy (Gragg, 2003). Peltier (2006) also found that gender issue, normally opposite sex, can trigger effective and positive persuasions resulting in successful SE intrusions. This perspective is in line with such research as Guadagno and Cialdini (2002) in that a charming or sweet voice of the opposite sex can generally lead to more effective and successful persuasions or interpersonal influences.

SE attackers also tend to establish trust relationships with their intended victims through seemingly innocent conversations or email communications. Human nature is to trust others until they prove they are not trustworthy (Peltier, 2006). Many people, especially customer service agents, help desk receptionists, and business assistants or secretaries who are trained to assist people and not to question the validity of each request, tend to trust others and are naturally helpful. Trust can be built through a number of small interactions which SE attackers try to maintain with the victims. A sign of positive trust is when the victims can recognize the attacker's voice and are willing to converse with and assist the attacker. Some seemingly *mundane* information, such as knowing someone is on vacation and names of children, spouse and pets, can be effortlessly revealed by these victims through a series of slow and casual yet deceitful correspondence and are of vital value to SE attackers, who then can implement a fraudulent plan.

Successful SE attacks can also be triggered by feelings such as guilt and sympathy. Human users have a tendency to believe other's expressed attitudes (i.e., sad voice), behaviors (i.e., facial signs), and statements (i.e., poor performance) are true, and these individuals may attempt to avoid guilt. SE attackers may exploit this weakness by confiding with the intended victims that they have failed to accomplish things and their survival solely depends on the victims' assistance, otherwise significant consequence (normally sad or negative) may occur.

SOCIAL ENGINEERING TECHNIQUES

There are various technical and non-technical means that SE attackers can employ, such as pretexting, phishing, online social engineering, shoulder surfing, and dumpster diving, in order to collect data which can be processed for the attackers to access privileged information. Since users are not aware of the value of the information they possess and are thus careless about protecting it, they tend to reveal weaknesses which may result in unnoticeable (for users themselves) mistakes that potential SE attackers can manipulate.

As the most commonly used SE technique, pretexting is the act of creating and using a contrived scenario to persuade a potential victim to voluntarily reveal information or perform actions. In the business domain, pretexting can be used to manipulate such victims as junior company service representatives into disclosing sensitive information such as customer information, account details, and telephone records through a telephone conversation. Alternatively, the SE attacker might pretend to be a senior member of an organization, pressuring junior members into disclosing useful information which he can leverage to set up remote access to the organization's resources. This simple yet effective attack focuses on the vulnerable psychological aspect of human user who tends to be helpful to satisfy *customers or important users* of the organization.

Phishing, by contrast, is a two-time scam technique of fraudulently obtaining private information. Typically the attacker sends a masqueraded e-mail that appears to originate from a legitimate business, such as a bank or credit card company, requesting "verification" of information and warning of some significant consequences if it is not in accordance with the request. A variant is use of a counterfeit interactive voice response system to harvest personal information such as pin numbers, social security numbers, and account numbers. Phishing attackers may pretend to be a customer service or help desk agent who might be able to deceive victims, who seek for assistance, to divulge private information.

Two additional human-behavioral SE approaches are shoulder surfing and dumpster diving, which might be the oldest forms of SE attack. Shoulder surfing is when someone peeks over victim's shoulder to obtain his/her private information such as access codes and passwords which the victim types on a keypad (i.e., to enter the office or corporate building). The process of engaging in shoulder surfing assumes that the attacker can memorize the victim's confidential information entered and reproduce it for malicious use subsequently. To obtain potentially useful information, attackers may also resort to seemingly useless garbage. Dumpster diving is the practice of sifting through commercial or residential trash to find items that have been discarded for being unusable by their owners. Some SE attackers presuppose that sensitive information, such as manuals, phone books, checks, credit card and bank statements or other corporate commercial records, might be carelessly thrown away. They can use discarded information to obtain private information and to launch SE attacks subsequently.

EFFECTIVE DEFENSES AGAINST SOCIAL ENGINEERING

Because of the sophisticated personality traits that different individuals posses, it is almost impossible to fully protect organizations against SE attacks. As the weakest link of the security management frontline, SE intrusions that are triggered by human factors cannot be simply deferred or mitigated through a technical route which is relatively straightforward against software or hardware malfunctions. As such, technology (i.e., firewall, biometric authentication, and data encryption) alone cannot be the panacea. Instead, a multi-dimensional approach including technology, policies, procedures, standards, employee training and awareness programs, and incident response should be employed to more effectively and efficiently cope with the ever-present threat to the IS security management.

A policy conveys instructions from an organization's senior-most management to those who make decisions, take actions, and perform other duties (Whitman & Mattord, 2009). According to Peltier (2006), organizations should (1) develop clear, concise security policies that are enforced consistently throughout the organization; (2) develop simple rules defining what information is sensitive and develop a data classification policy (i.e., use internal website to answer questions and give advice); and (3) require the requestors identity when restricted actions are required. Despite the inherent personality traits that employees posses across departments, an information security policy can ensure a clear direction on what is expected of employees within the organization (Gragg, 2003). Pragmatically, with strong support from senior management, employees who comply with and have paid attention to such policy may more effectively respond to questionable requests and resist the intruder's pleas. The policy can also guide employees to think seriously about the information's value and further strengthen their confident resistance to persuasion. From a theoretical perspective, Petty et al. (2002) employed persuasion theory and found that increasing employee confidence by laying out clear policies decreases the chance that the persuader will have undue influence on an employee.

A procedure is series of actions that are always carried out by the same method and in the same order to achieve the same result. Policy dictates the circumstances that trigger the procedure and the same procedure might be triggered by multiple policies. This relationship between policy and procedure must be ongoing and consistently reinforced to employees. Based on the recommendations offered by Mitnick and Simon (2002) and Thornburgh (2004), organizations should facilitate prompt recognition of and appropriate reaction to SE attacks by training employees to recognize and properly respond to requestors who: (1) refuse to give a callback number; (2) make out-of-the ordinary requests; (3) claim senior authority; (4) stress urgency; (5) threaten negative consequences of noncompliancc; (6) show discomfort when questioned by employees; and (7) use the name dropping technique. Along with these practical procedures, it is essential that proper procedures be emphasized, reinforced, and implemented throughout organizations, as suggested by (Peltier, 2006). For instance, employees who work in the business service areas (i.e., front desk) must require proper identification confirmation from anyone to perform a service.

A standard should also fortify the process of identification validation (e.g., business badge and phone number or caller-ID cross-examination with the relevant department) as well as the management of password (e.g., no Post-it notes entailing passwords left in the office). In addition, password procedure and standard such as the frequency of password change and sophistication of password setup must be bolstered and maintained by both IT department and management so as to avoid password change/reset request over the phone or email. To thwart dumpster driver, organizations should also more securely manage the disposed commercial materials by utilizing business shredders on a regular (preferably daily) basis.

Mitigation measures should also shed light on human behavioral aspects through employee security education, training, and awareness (SETA) programs in organizations. To tackle acts of human error or failure, SETA can benefit organizations in terms of improving employee behavior, informing members of the organization about where to report violations of policy, and enabling the organization to hold employees accountable for their actions (Whitman & Mattord, 2008). A consistent SETA implementation enables employees to understand the value of the organization's information and to understand their role in overall SE protection strategy (i.e., better resistance to persuasion). To more effectively facilitate the implementation of SETA endeavors, it has been suggested by Peltier (2006), Gragg (2003), and Whitman and Mattord (2008) that such concrete intra-organizational initiatives as distributing newsletters, bulletins, posters, or internet WebPages to disseminate up-to-date security news, recognizing employees for their proper reactions and responses to security threats, circulating regular and creative reminders for the potential dangers, and developing "information security awareness days", etc., shall have a positive impact on the behavioral responses and reactions of employees with regard to potential SE attack recognition and discrimination.

FUTURE RESEARCH

SE attacks are unpredictable because they can surface from external and internal sources. However, we believe that the likelihood of such attacks can be mitigated if employees, at all levels of the organization, perceive their importance to the overall SE protection strategy and thereby exert concerted efforts to lessen the impact of SE attacks. Nonetheless, we must recognize the dilemma that, due to the inevitable exposure to SE attacks, organizations and their employees are at a manifest disadvantage facing infrequent SE intrusions and yet need to be on constant vigilance whereas the SE aggressors can practice SE attacks willingly.

With the mushrooming emergence of social network websites including Classroom.com, MySpace.com, Facebook.com and YouTube.com where inexperienced college students look to keep in touch with their friends and expand social connections, SE aggressors might easily exploit the illogical social reactions of these potential victims to aggravate our campaign against SE attacks. It is hoped that proper security tactics and defends, along with education efforts, shall also be rendered to expanded population segments in a bid to minimize the danger toward SE in our everyday's life. Future research is therefore encouraged to gauge and analyze how SE can be conducted through these social networks and further into organization's networks.

CONCLUSION

Albeit a low-tech level attack, SE can manipulate victims to divulge confidential information due to our illogical understanding or misconception triggered by inherent personality traits. Therefore, in addition to advanced technologies counterattacking various security intrusions, human factors must be equally accounted for effective IS security management. Exploiting the cognitive biases of humans and corporate policies to obtain access to desired resources, SE aggressors can circumvent organization's network infrastructure which however is vulnerable to this seemingly old-fashioned manipulation. To be able to defend themselves from being victimized, employees must withhold commitments from potential SE threats through the consistent implementation of SETA which organizations must continuously instigate with vigilance.

REFERENCES

Allen, M. (2006). *Social Engineering: A Means to Violate a Computer System*. Bethesda, MD: SANS Institute.

Gragg, D. (2003). *A Multi-Level Defense Against Social Engineering*. Bethesda, MD: SANS Institute.

Guadagno, R. E., & Cialdini, R. B. (2002). Online Persuasion: An Examination of Gender Differences in Computer-Mediated Interpersonal Influence. *Group Dynamics*, *6*(1), 38–51. doi:10.1037/1089-2699.6.1.38

Mitnick, K., & Simon, W. (2002). *The Art of Deception: Controlling the Human Element of Security*. New York, NY: John Wiley & Sons.

Peltier, T. (2006). Social Engineering: Concepts and Solutions. *Information System Security*, *15*(5), 13–21. doi:10.1201/1086.1065898X/46353.15.4.20060901/95427.3

Petty, R. E., Brinol, P., & Tormala, Z. L. (2002). Thought Confidence as a Determinant of Persuasion: The Self-Validation Hypothesis. *Journal of Personality and Social Psychology*, *82*(5), 722–741. doi:10.1037/0022-3514.82.5.722

Rusch, J. (1999). *The Social Engineering of Internet Fraud*. Paper presented at the INET'99 Conference, San Jose, CA.

Thornburgh, T. (2004). *Social Engineering: the "dark art"*. Paper presented at the 1st Annual Conference on Information Security Curriculum Development, Kennesaw, GA.

Whitman, M. E., & Mattord, H. J. (2008). *Management of Information Security* (2nd ed.). Florence, KY: Course Technology.

Whitman, M. E., & Mattord, H. J. (2009). *Principles of Information Security* (3rd ed.). Florence, KY: Course Technology.

Workman, M. (2007). Gaining Access with Social Engineering: An Empirical Study of the Threat. *Information System Security*, *16*(6), 315–331. doi:10.1080/10658980701788165

Workman, M. (2008). Wisecrackers: A theory-grounded investigation of phishing and pretext social engineering threats to information security. *Journal of the American Society for Information Science and Technology*, *59*(4), 662–674. doi:10.1002/asi.20779

This work was previously published in the Information Resources Management Journal, Volume 24, Issue 3, edited by Mehdi Khosrow-Pour, pp. 1-8, copyright 2013 by IGI Publishing (an imprint of IGI Global).

Chapter 12
A Decision Table for the Cloud Computing Decision in Small Business

Sathiadev Mahesh
University of New Orleans, USA

Brett J. L. Landry
University of Dallas, USA

T. Sridhar
LeitNet, USA

Kenneth R. Walsh
University of New Orleans, USA

ABSTRACT

An issue facing the manager of a small business is the use of cloud computing to meet the information technology (IT) needs of the firm. These businesses typically have limited in-house IT capabilities and often outsource much of their IT. This paper discusses this rapidly evolving technology and provides a framework for businesses to decide on harnessing the power of cloud computing. It recommends the appropriate decision based on the way in which IT is currently used in the enterprise and future needs to meet competitive challenges. The potential cost savings, technology insurance from cloud computing, and security risks are discussed and factored into the decision.

INTRODUCTION

Small businesses face challenges in owning and managing their IT infrastructure. The advent of e-business models that require 24 by 7 operations has made it even more difficult for these businesses to acquire and maintain the skill-set necessary to host and operate reliable data centers and systems to support the business. Cloud computing, a framework in which the business 'leases' the necessary resource offers these companies the opportunity to obtain a high quality information system without the expense of building a top notch IT team and facility. In this paper, we will look at the cloud computing model and develop a decision table that can be used by managers in determining the best cloud computing strategy for the organization.

In the cloud computing model computing services are located at a well managed data center and delivered to the organization over the Internet. Carr (2008) described a utility computing model where

DOI: 10.4018/978-1-4666-3616-3.ch012

computing would be purchased in a manner similar to electricity or natural gas and business would no longer own and operate a data center or software than they would own and operate their own utility. For small and medium sized businesses, this is an obvious choice since they lack the economies of scale to be able to operate a computing center effectively and efficiently (Cheng, 2010). Counter arguments to this line of reasoning have focused on the fact that electricity is a simple product which is fungible and there is not much difference between the services available or much choice in the matter, whereas computing services have many variables and are not easily comparable. We will work through each argument in this paper and consider its impact on the manager's decision. It must be noted that rapid change in IT has resulted in challenges for managers, and the widespread use of coping mechanisms to handle this complexity (Benamati & Lederer, 2010). Our decision table will provide a framework to support the decision making process.

Most published research on cloud computing has focused on the technology during the past three years, and while the term first appears in 1960, the earliest peer reviewed publications are in 2007. However, the Application Service Provider (ASP) model has been around for much longer. Smith and Kumar present a model for ASP and develop a theory of ASP use (Smith & Kumar, 2004). They review the literature in the field, and highlight service delivery over the internet as a key difference between other outsourcing models and the ASP model. In their theory, there are three sub-contexts for the ASP decision; environmental, organizational, and IS management. The environmental context deals with cost pressures of IT and IT problems. The organizational context deals with the attitude towards risk and ASPs. The IT management context deals with the client's ability to deal with the other two contexts. Smith and Kumar point to the change in software at that time from a local, workstation based interface to a web interface with an "access from anywhere" capability. A taxonomy is developed for ASPs based on the type of service offered (Maleki & Anand, 2008). Another survey of small and medium sized business analyzes the ratings on six factors related to ASPs and the intention to adopt the model (Altaf & Schuff, 2010). Based on an analysis of the survey responses they recommend that ASPs offer flexibility in their offerings since many owner believe that ASP offerings are inflexible while in-house systems are more flexible. In addition they recommend that ASPs be financially stable, and provide clearly Service Level Agreements (SLA). The interesting aspect of this survey of 113 business owners is the degree of knowledge about software offerings through the ASP model.

Cloud computing is relatively new technology, and depends on a robust net infrastructure An ontology for cloud computing proposes five layers, with the top three being Software as a Service (SaaS) offering an application over the internet, the second being the software development environment or platform delivered over the internet (PaaS), and the third being the Infrastructure delivered over the internet (IaaS) (Youseff, Butrico, & DaSilva, 2008). The Infrastructure provided can be computational resources, storage, and communication. In addition they add two lower level layers for the Software kernel and the hardware/firmware. The NIST defines cloud computing as "a model for enabling convenient, on-demand network access to a shared pool of configurable computing resources that can be rapidly provisioned and released with minimal management effort or service provider interaction" (Mell & Grance, 2009). A study of cloud computing growth presents a chart the growth of actual business use of cloud computing (Rosen, 2010). This chart shows rapid growth in the adoption of cloud infrastructure among public web sites in 2009. Many other publications have discussed the business value of cloud computing, identifying applications for public and private clouds (Nolle, 2009; Hand, 2007).

Cloud Computing Models

Software as a service (Saas) delivers the application to the business online, rather than providing the software to be installed and operated by the business. The SaaS model has been through a boom-bust-renewal cycle. During the dot-com boom, the industry started out as ASPs offering to host the applications, and alleviate the hassles of running a complex data center and securing/updating the application. One of the first businesses to use the SaaS approach effectively was the security company F-Secure, that provided workstation anti-virus security through the internet. While the service required the users to connect to and install the software on their machines, billing was managed through the ISP, and was provided through a monthly subscription fee rather than a fixed initial payment for shrink wrapped software. Salesforce.com successfully provided an enterprise class application as a service and change the model by which a business could obtain a Customer Relationship Management (CRM) system and pay for it on a per-user basis (Schwartz, 2007). This revenue model opened up the market for smaller businesses, enabling them to afford enterprise class applications. In addition to eliminating the installation costs which include hardware, software configuration, and staffing, the approach allowed a small business to pay for only the service used, since billing is on service per user approach. If the business has experience using SaaS for certain applications, it has already taken a first step to cloud computing, and is better positioned to make the complete switch.

The number of applications in use in the business is the next issue to be considered. If there is a dominant enterprise system used by the business, it is necessary to determine if cloud computing is an effective alternative for the company. The explosion of cloud computing services has resulted in most enterprise systems being available in the SaaS format. Chau surveyed managers and owners of small businesses to determine the criteria by which they selected packaged software (Chau, 1995). His questionnaire looked at the technical and non-technical ratings of the software and its necessary hardware, as well as the technical and non-technical ratings of the vendor, and opinions of in-house and external consultants. He concludes that owners tend to take a more strategic view considering technical issues and vendor reliability than managers. He recommends that owners take charge of this decision rather than delegating it to professional managers. The cloud computing decision is further complicated by the tendency toward empire building that will impact managerial choice. In-house IT with a staff and budget provide managers with greater control and accomplishment than an outsourced cloud service over which they have no day to day control.

Businesses that have acquired best of breed or custom built applications link them with the enterprise system and one another using systems integration tools. In many cases custom applications have been developed that extract and transfer data between applications. This integration process may use batch jobs run periodically or event trigger operations. One example is a scenario where an organization extracts transaction data from an ERP and places it in a CRM application at the end of each shift. These custom applications are typically linked to custom code built configured into the enterprise system. If the business has either built these in house or through external consultants, it is necessary to determine the effort required to reconstruct these linkages in a cloud environment. SaaS offerings typically provide data in a format, often XML, suitable for transfer to other applications. The SaaS vendor must enable and support features to link applications. The business should also consider the question: Is there a competitive advantage from building unique applications for the business?

The strategic IT model for the enterprise needs to be considered. If the business uses established IT systems to support operations, i.e., if it is in the Support or Factory quadrants of the IT Strategic

Grid (Nolan & McFarlan, 2005; McFarlan, 1984), SaaS models should provide adequate computing support. IT applications for most of the established business models are available in the marketplace. In fact even the established products, such as ERP systems, can provide strategic advantages if businesses use them effectively (Ragowsky & Geffen, 2008). This means that even for small and medium sized businesses in strategic markets, it makes sense to use established software, as long as it is done effectively. The SaaS model offers small and medium sized business managers the opportunity to acquire these systems at a reasonable price due the subscription model and without the challenges of implementing them in house. In the case of leading edge software, small businesses face the problem of learning to use the innovative software and the challenge of hosting the software at their in-house data centers. Studies have shown that most small businesses do not adopt innovative software such as e-learning (Admiraal & Lockhorst, 2009) or CRM unless the small business owners possess a higher product knowledge and see a competitive advantage from the software (Peltier, Schibrowsky, & Zhao, 2009). A study on e-business adoption in the UK showed that strategic intent drives investments in e-business by SMEs (Levy, Powell, & Worrall, 2005). While e-business impacts the market position and allows for new innovations, SaaS focuses more on cost and complexity reduction for the small business manager. SaaS eliminates the need to handle the complexity of hosting software, and will reduce the burden on a small business that intends to implement the software, driving increased adoption of this model.

Platform as a Service (PaaS) If the business model of a start-up is so unique that there is no commercially available system, the business can look into the use of PaaS, or Platform as a Service option in cloud computing to build unique, complex models. The platform offers a collection of software subsystems, termed a solution stack, that works together to create an enterprise application. An example is a business web application built using the dot Net platform that requires the underlying operating system, Windows, along with the web server, IIS, the application server, and a database. A PaaS provides all of these in a single package over the internet, allowing the business to develop its own application without setting up the networks, hardware, software, and configuring the linkages between the systems.

Systems developed using PaaS have to be maintained by the business and may need to be updated when the underlying platform undergoes updates. In addition, the application is locked to the development platform and while there may be many vendors providing hosting services for common platforms, many of the platforms are created and supported by the hosting vendor. This can lead to a situation where the business is locked into the platform, much like the case of SaaS where an enterprise system is used in the business and it is very expensive to make the move to a different system.

PaaS models can be extended to provide a virtual appliance model that supports building blocks which can be assembled to create a composite solution. This will support software life-cycle management and go beyond merely optimizing the use hardware resources or forcing the organization to choose one suite of software products for implementation. This is termed "Composition as a Service" and the model lies between the Infrastructure as a Service and PaaS offerings (Konstantinou, Eilam, Kalantar, Totok, Arnold, & Snible, 2009). It is designed to provide greater flexibility and simpler software development for the cloud environment. Another approach is where a software module is turned into an entity that can be autonomously managed by the cloud management software (Rellermeyer, Duller, & Alonso, 2009). This is an extension of the Open System Group model for distributed systems and shelters the programmer from the complexity of cloud compatible distributed application development.

Infrastructure as a Service (IaaS). At the lowest level of cloud computing, the business may choose to rent infrastructure and eliminate the need to manage in house data centers. The IaaS, option can use proprietary models popularized by Amazon's Web Services which offers storage, databases, monitoring, and other infrastructure in a scalable format. Much of the focus in IaaS has been the scalability offered by the providers, an issue that is important for e-business models that face highly scalable market demand. Many innovative models are inherently risky and it makes sense to rent limited resources to start-up the operation, while the business needs increased computing resources at short notice, if market demand picks up rapidly. The IaaS model typically offers additional capacity on demand from large data centers, where demand from multiple customers is pooled. This enables IaaS providers to be cost effective in providing additional resources as required. This supports an exit strategy for risky business models since there is no long term capital investment in the system. In this model, the business administers IT requirements by calling for more or less services as needed, in addition to managing the development of the system. It is also possible to host an acquired application using IaaS and merely administering the capacity purchased from an IaaS provider. A PaaS provider can offer its platform on an infrastructure cobbled together from a IaaS provider. An example is Appian Anywhere, a Business Process Modeling suite that is offered as a platform and runs on infrastructure provided by Amazon's EC2 infrastructure cloud (North, 2009).

While IaaS offers full control over system capacity management, PaaS and SaaS models can also be configured to include system capacity management. The three models differ largely in the primary focus on business managers. In a purely SaaS model, the contract is based on the number of users and a SLA (service level agreement) and the hardware platform is configured and managed by the provider to meet the SLA. In the PaaS model, the platform is selected by the business, and developers assigned to build a custom system. The business pays for usage based on the selected billing model. The Google platform for example charges for usage based on CPU, bandwidth, storage, and emails. In the IaaS model, the underlying infrastructure components are sized and requested by the business from the provider. The platform is selected from a wide range of available options and custom designed for the business.

This paper is concerned with the decision making process to move business computing to an external cloud. Internal clouds that are designed within the enterprise are not the focus of this paper. We are do not consider grid computing systems composed of multiple machines that are interconnected in a fault tolerant and resilient manner. Applications that are grid aware have the ability to access large scale resources by cumulating the power of many different interconnected machines. Grid computing is used to access surplus resources from distributed machines such as SETI (Delic & Walker, 2008) and in other academic environments (Deelman, Singh, Livny, Berriman, & Good, 2008). While grid computing's primary goal is the marshalling of vast amounts of shared computing power for a single problem, often for leading edge academic research, cloud computing is used with a business focus on streamlining data center operations (Hill & Humphrey, 2009).

CLOUD COMPUTING DECISION PARAMETERS

Business IT Experience

The skill set and facilities available to the business are the starting point for a cloud computing decision. Yap, Soh, and Raman found that consultant effectiveness, vendor support, length of IT experience for the small business, top management support and user participation were positively correlated with IT success in small business (Yap, Soh, & Raman, 1992). Magal and Lewis found that small business owners' awareness and attitude toward IT to be critical to technology implementation in business (Magal & Lewis, 1995). Research in small business IT adoption has shown than CEO and organizational information systems knowledge and innovation characteristics have a positive impact on adoption of information technology (Thong, 1999). In addition, small businesses have understood the need to stay current with changing IT even a decade ago (Riemenschneider & Mykytyn, 2000). Top management support, perceived competitive advantage have been shown to be important factors in the adoption of new IT technologies in small businesses (Premkumar, 2003). The Small Business User Satisfaction with Information Technology (SBUSIT) model argues that software adequacy, system security and integrity, system documentation, vendor support, training and education, and productivity enhancement are the major factors leading to user satisfaction in small businesses with IT (Palvia, 1996). Another study, conducted a decade later, added the internal and external business and technological environment, organizational readiness, trading partners support, financial impact and workflow productivity to the factors that must be critically assessed to determine if a small business is a candidate for IT implementation (Khazanchi, 2005). Based on this research we can conclude that cloud computing will be selected by small businesses only when they are aware of the technology, and reliable vendors are available to offer this service. Since the small businesses we are considering in this paper already have an in-house IT system, they are familiar with the technology and merely need to take a decision on whether to continue with in-house IT or use a different approach offered by cloud computing. Obviously, technological familiarity with cloud computing is essential and the paper introduces the technology, and its benefits and pitfalls.

The first question is whether the business has a data center. If the business currently operates a data center that meets current and future needs, the cost of operating the data center needs to be determined. This should include the cost of hardware, networking, software licensing and software development, data storage and retrieval, and staff to run the operation to determine if IT expenses in control? In addition this cost analysis should take into account any system failures and the business cost associated with the system failures. In addition to current needs, the study should look into the future needs with any expansion into e-business that will require a higher standard of operation with fewer infrastructure failures. Cloud computing essentially involves outsourcing the data center operation. As with any IT outsourcing contract there is the need for a strategic match between client and provider of this service. A metastudy of outsourcing literature during the period 1988-2005 illustrates the development of a strategic partnership between the client and provider (Gonzalez & Llopis, 2006).

A business that has its employees in a single facility, the common operations model for small businesses may prefer to keep its data in-house since the approach ties into the operational model. However, it has become increasingly common for employees to access business systems from remote locations, and even if the business does not have a telecommuting program in place, it makes sense to support remote access for operational efficiency. In addition, many B2B transactions are conducted online and this means the business IT system needs to connect to other systems over the internet. If the business operations are geographically dispersed, even over a single metropolitan area, a cloud computing solution with reliable service guarantees will match and often exceed the operational quality of an in-house operation.

Cloud Application Performance

One of the issues to be considered by the business in a move to cloud computing is the performance of the application. The latency inherent in net applications and the difficulty of providing Quality of Service (QoS) guarantees for net access have been barriers for the adoption of cloud services. The increase in Wide Area Network (WAN) bandwidth and the availability of Virtual Private Network (VPN) technology have reduced the QoS problem while the development of applications for the internet rather than porting "chatty" local workstation based applications has improved performance. Early attempts at delivering desktops over the WAN failed because they attempted to replicate the rich GUI interface of a desktop and deliver over the internet (Festa, 1999). In contrast, with a well designed web application, the traffic is largely between the web server, application engine, and database, all of which are located within the cloud center, and do not face net latency issues. Another technology that enhances cloud computing performance is edge computing, where cache servers located close to the users perform many tasks (Akamai, 2009). Two studies on the performance of cloud computing test Amazon's EC2 and S3 offerings to compare published SLAs with actual performance (Garfinkel, 2007; Palankar, Iamnitchi, Ripeanu, & Garfinkel, 2008). They find satisfactory performance and availability in the 2007-2008 time frame, when the system was in its early phase. Benefits from building an application to use cloud services from the same provider have been demonstrated in this study and others (Costa, Zahn, Rowston, O'Shea, & Schubert, 2009). Many other studies have presented approaches to improving resource efficiency in virtualized environments (Ardagna, Mirandola, Trubian, & Zhang, 2009; Assuncao, Costanzo, & Buyya, 2009), with emphasis on the mobile commerce market (Chun & Maniatis, 2009). Specialized protocols using flexible, customizable headers focusing on reduced overhead to save power and bandwidth have been proposed for cloud networks (Solis & Obraczka, 2004). Various network virtualization approaches are implemented within cloud data centers to speed up transactions and improve the performance of hosted systems (Edwards, Fischer, & Lain, 2009; Albert, 2009; Greenberg et al., 2009; Matthews, Garfinkel, Hoff, & Wheeler, 2009).

Savings from Cloud Computing

Software as a Service has seen a revival with cloud computing by combining the efficiencies of cloud data centers with the cost effectiveness of hosted applications. While investment in infrastructure is minimal for SaaS, the cost is often higher than for internally hosted applications unless the in-house operation is highly inefficient. As software follows hardware to become a commodity, and face even greater cost pressures from increased competition and open source systems, the primary benefit of cloud computing will be the highly efficient operation of cloud data centers. An interesting study is presented by Campbell-Kelly and shows how timesharing of computer services on mainframes was a thriving business model until the early 1980s when Moore's law delivered much cheaper computing power in desktops and local servers (Campbell-Kelly, 2009). Similar technological changes could disrupt the cloud computing economic model. A marked improvement in thermal waste from under-utilized servers could reduce the cooling cost of data centers that typically amount to 40% of overall energy use with servers taking up about 50% of the power (Data Center Energy). A marked improvement in server efficiency (processors and drives) will significantly reduce the cost of data center operation, making the efficiency offered by virtualized server based data centers far less valuable. Servers have typically been designed with the most powerful processors since they have been general purpose devices, designed for 24 by 7 use in a demanding environment. New server designs based on highly efficient, lower powered chips such as cellphone processors have been developed, with a focus on net applications that serve many users but do little complex processing. Two companies, Sea Micro and Smoothstone have planned servers with multiple high efficiency chips that will use far less power than current servers. This is a disruptive technology for cloud computing data centers that focus on energy savings from high server utilization.

Archiving Data and Auditing Site

Business archival needs have expanded with legal needs of the SEC (SEC 17a-3),(SEC 17a-4), meeting the discovery needs outlined in Rule 26(a)(1)(A)(ii) of the Federal Rules of Civil Procedure regarding the location of required documents, and the identifier for the documents. In addition Sarbanes Oxley (SOX-2002) and HIPAA (1996) regulations mandate not only archival but also easy recoverability of corporate data and documents. Hosted solutions from reliable providers meet the required guidelines for the industry more effectively than most small and medium sized businesses. For example, e-mail archiving is one value offered by hosted e-mail solutions. Cloud service providers should be verified based on their adherence to suitable guidelines. This should include a review of the controls in place at the cloud site, document retention and secure destruction process, as well as audits of the facility to meet accepted standards (Gatewood, 2009). The service level agreement with the cloud service provider must be realistic and enforceable with appropriate penalties for service failure (Cunningham & Wilkins, 2009).

One model that can be used for a small business that already has an in-house data center is to use cloud computing for data backup or for business continuity. In the business continuity model, the cloud is used to build a data center with similar infrastructure and will support operations in the event of a disaster. In this case, the infrastructure needs to match that in the in-house data center. Many of the IaaS providers have a proprietary architecture that may not be similar to that used in-house. A distinction should be made between IaaS using proprietary standards and data centers offering space for collocating servers or hosted servers matching your business needs (Bias, 2009).

Audit requirements should be imposed on documents and privacy, especially if personally identifiable information must be ensured. Cloud computing's impact on privacy is impacted by the shared infrastructure between different organizations (Pearson, 2009). While individual applications may be run on separate servers, the process and its data are moved between servers based on demand and it is difficult to pinpoint the specific machines on which an application operates or data resides at any particular time. In addition to security being compromised by malicious operations, the fact that interactions take place on a shared environment enables the cloud service to track transactions. This may reveal internal operations to the cloud service provider. Cloud computing providers focus on operational efficiency and rapid re-provisioning of resources as their competitive advantage, and they may compromise system security in the rush to use the latest technology (Pearson, 2009). Cloud environments need to reduce the amount of personally identifiable information transmitted to and from the cloud and stored on the site. This is achieved using privacy enhancing technologies such as encryption and pseudo anonymization. In addition, data usage in applications sharing resources is clearly specified and limited to the needs of the application. However, processes running in the cloud are susceptible to cross virtual machine attacks (Ristenpart, Tromer, Shacham, & Savage, 2009). Managers need to review the threats from cloud computing, such as threats from security protocols used in cloud computing centers, the potential for business disruption from net connectivity disruptions, and lack of control over physical location (Schwartz, 2008).

An added wrinkle in this decision is the physical location of the service. Transborder dataflow issues, especially differences over data security and privacy have been a challenge for global companies over the past two decades (Regan, 2003). Some regulation of the industry is necessary to provide users with performance standards, leading to further adoption of cloud computing (Nelson, 2009). Public policy issues in cloud computing deal with the need for increased privacy in a cloud environment where data is subject to trans-border data flows and storage and/or archival in other jurisdictions. Another policy issue is the protection of consumers in case of the failure of cloud services as we become more dependent on them. Companies using cloud computing need to be aware of the physical location of their data and may seek to ensure that it lies within legal jurisdiction. Google for example allows commercial and government cloud users to specify location of data and where Google Apps data is stored and meet Federal Information Security Management Act requirements (Google, 2009).

Cloud Security

One of the selling points for cloud computing is the enhanced security offered by a service that has the economies of scale to provide security expertise. One argument that has been made regarding public clouds is the value of storing client information encrypted on server in the cloud with clients' private keys, and sharing that information as needed with multiple vendors, while maintaining privacy (France, 2010). The well publicized outages of cloud services (Brodkin, 2009; Hoover, 2008) security failures (Arrington, 2009), and data outages (Williams, 2009) at cloud centers need to studied carefully. A survey of cryptographic tools to support integrity and reliability of data stored in clouds lists problems such as a loss of availability and integrity at major cloud providers such as Google Docs, and Amazon's S3 (Cachin, Keidar, & Shraer, 2009). Users should have the tools to verify the integrity of cloud stored data, requiring digital signatures for multiple users altering data. A mathematical model for cloud computing data security is presented by Yuefa, Bo, Yaquiang, Quan, and Chaojin (2009). The Federal Trade Commission has conducted conferences (FCC, 2009) on the issue of cloud computing security and the Cloud Security Alliance has suggested guidelines for cloud security (Cloud Security Alliance, 2009) due to the rapid proliferation of these services and the potential for a catastrophic failure if business becomes dependent on these services before they can guarantee reliability.

Cloud Interoperability

One important issue for businesses developing applications using PaaS or IaaS is whether the application can be ported to other clouds or if the business is locked into a particular vendor. The open cloud manifesto lists a set of principles for cloud computing to support interoperability and limit the lock-in to a particular cloud provider (Open Cloud, 2010). Significantly the list of supporters who have signed on does not include powerhouses such as Amazon, Apple, Google, Microsoft, Oracle, or Salesforce. At present there has been little progress on this front and the systems gaining ground have remained locked into separate ecosystems (DMTF, 2009).

Many other standards bodies are involved in cloud computing. These include the Desktop Management Task Force that has specified a format for packaging the software to run as a virtual machine and a group named the Open Cloud Standards Incubator to standardize interactions between cloud environments, the Cloud Security Alliance focusing on security aspects of cloud operations, the organization for advancement of structured information standards that seeks to extend SOA standards to cloud computing, and the storage network industries association which has developed a standard interface for cloud data management (Sridhar, 2009).

Cloud Computing Strategy for Small Business

We will illustrate the decision table (Table 1), its parameters, moderating factors, and alternatives using a case study at a small business in Louisiana, which we will refer to with the pseudonym, NL Networks. The business is a technology company that specializes in setup and support for business computer networks. The technologies implemented by the company are VoIP, SCADA and PCI compliant information systems. The tasks are typically organized around projects, significant

Table 1. Decision table for cloud computing decision

Decision Parameter	**Relevant Level of Decision Parameter**											
IT Application Portfolio	Many Applications										Dominant Application	
Customization	Low			Moderate and limited Application Integration			High level of Customization and Systems Integration			Unique Business Model	Low	High
Demand	S	P	WR	S	P	WR	S	P	WR	WR		
Cloud Computing Alternative	**Strength of Cloud Computing Alternative**											
Current System		-	=			-	+					
SaaS		+			+	++					+++	++
PaaS			++					+	++	+		
IaaS		++								+++		
Cloud Data Center - Colocation	++											
Moderating Factors across all options												
In-house IT Competence	If low then the decision moves towards cloud computing. If high, a TCO analysis of in-house operations should be conducted.											
Business Continuity	Cloud computing should be used for business continuity purposes. If the current data center has a unique configuration, co-location will provide a better match than IaaS											

Demand Codes: Steady (S), Predictable – Will change widely over time, but predictable (P), Wide Range, difficult to predict (WR)
+ evidence for move, ++ strong evidence for move, +++ very strong evidence
- evidence against policy = strong evidence against policy

communication between employees at customer sites and the home office where most of the design and development are completed.

In the decision process for cloud computing use in a small business, the first decision parameter is the IT application portfolio of the organization. If the business uses a single dominant application such as an accounting application, an industry specific business application, cloud hosted versions of the application offer many advantages. In many cases the application is hosted and offered as a service either by the vendor or by authorized providers. If the business uses multiple applications and has hosted them mostly in-house then cloud computing is a new technology with which the organization has limited knowledge. Since local IT expertise will typically be called in to evaluate new IT proposals, cloud computing will be evaluated, not by business owner-managers but by in-house IT talent, that will naturally perceive this as a technology that reduces their size and importance. A study on the determinants of website adoption by small businesses in the UK suggests that pressure from marketing would pressure in house IT to adopt a new technology that would benefit the enterprise, when in-house IT lacks the mastery required to implement the new technology (Simmons, Armstrong, & Durkin, 2008). A similar argument can be applied here to demonstrate the need for small business owners need to drive the adoption of cloud technologies within the business.

In the NL Networks case, the business has four major externally developed applications, MS-Exchange for e-mail and voicemail, QuickBooks for accounting, Microsoft Dynamics for customer relationship management, and FogBugz for software project management and ticketing, where customer help requests are prioritized and processed. NL Networks develops custom software solutions for other companies and one of their products is an internally developed content management system that they sell to clients. Based on the first parameter in the decision table, the IT Application portfolio, they have many applications, ranging from e-mail, to accounting, CRM, and project management and ticketing.

The second decision parameter is the level of customization of the application. This parameter needs to be considered in greater depth when the business has many IS applications. The customization decision parameter needs to be analyzed not only in terms of the degree of customization but also in terms of the level of integration between applications (Nolle, 2009). In cases where the application implementation has followed the "vanilla" approach and there has been little customization, hosted services become even more attractive. They reduce the need for in-house IT and can provide far more reliable data centers with business continuity support. There is strong support for the SaaS model in such cases. In businesses where there has been significant customization of the application, there is still support for the SaaS model, since customization can be performed and continued through the API whether the application is hosted locally or at a remote site. Note that if there is only a single, integrated application that is widely used in the business the SaaS approach is recommended regardless of the level of customization or demand variation in the business.

In many cases customization requires additional hardware resources to support effective operation, since customization of enterprise applications reduces performance. It is possible that the small business has well sized servers that support the customized application effectively and the SaaS service may not provide similar features at the same cost. Most SaaS services offer standard hosting for applications, and achieve economies of scale by offering the same service to many customers. While server virtualization offers customers the ability to resize capacity and acquire it as needed, this adds an additional layer of complexity in the operation. In addition, customized applications face major challenges when the underlying system is upgraded to a new version. Much of the customization needs to be re-worked to function effectively on the upgraded system. The SaaS operation may force upgrades at a schedule that is not the same as the preferred schedule for the small business. Many small businesses operate on application versions long after formal support is terminated for the version. In these cases, the manager should investigate whether the SaaS facility offers support for customized applications and whether it will support the version in use for the planned life cycle.

NL Networks has not customized the applications used to support in-house operations. This brings up an interesting issue. While NL networks would be classified as a technology company with excellent IT skills, their specialization is in network security and custom development in highly specialized areas. They do not have mush in-house expertise in data center management or in customizing e-mail or CRM applications. Management has wisely recognized that they need to concentrate their IT expertise in the fast evolving area of network security and use vanilla applications where possible. They do face the need for application integration and much of that has been met by choosing applications from one vendor, or from vendors that work closely with their primary products. In the second parameter of the decision table, customization, NL Networks falls in the Moderate and Limited Application Integration category.

The third decision parameter is the nature of application demand. The business may operate in a highly dynamic e-commerce field where there is a wide range of demand or operate in a more traditional environment with predictable and relatively stable demand. If the levels of customization and integration are low, and the demand is stable, the small business should move its servers to a cloud data center. Existing servers should be moved to a datacenter offering collocation services that offer a reliable, cost effective data center that can support business continuity as well.

If the demand varies but follows a predictable pattern, the in-house operation needs to continually plan for and acquire new hardware. The IaaS model offers the basic components in a scalable fashion. The business systems are collocated at the IaaS site, and new resources are added based on market demand predictions. It is also possible to host the applications at SaaS sites and match market demand. However, since there is a need for data sharing and some customization, it may be more difficult to get the SaaS model working with multiple providers. There is evidence against keeping an in-house system with demand changes since continual upgrades to hardware in small businesses typically result in widely different devices. This results in a serious maintenance problem over time. The IaaS approach allows the business to choose consistent systems across its scaling requirements. However, since IaaS is often based on proprietary architecture, it may actually result in introducing additional variety in the hardware mix within the enterprise.

In situations where demand varies widely, as in the case in a small business that adds an e-business operation, it is advisable to build the new applications on a common platform to allow easy interoperability. The individual components can be scaled in a hosted center based on demand. A PaaS service will provide a development platform for the new application, while also supporting demand management. This argument is for a scenario where application integration is limited to intra-organizational systems. When application integration is designed to link up with business partners, and in the case of small businesses where the partners are typically larger firms, it is necessary to verify whether the selected cloud model will support integration with the system used by the large business. The small business needs to ensure that its system will work with the partner organization. If there is an "approved" B2B platform, the selected system must work with that platform.

In the case of a unique business model where there are no existing applications that do the job, and the business custom builds the IT system, the IaaS approach is strongly supported. It provides the infrastructure to build the custom system, and highly scalable support for the operation. Demand is bound to vary in a wide range since this is a unique business model. There is some support for the PaaS model if the entire operation can be supported by the toolset available on a single platform. In most cases however, unique models are supported by a modular design with components running on different platforms that work together to provide a unique service. The prototyping approach is used for systems development and the new model may be completely built on one platform from the ground up only if it succeeds. Rosen demonstrates the economic value of cloud computing to start-ups that face difficult to predict and wide load variation in demand, using the case of Animoto, a web based service that generates animated videos based on user provided photos (Rosen, 2010). This start-up with a unique business model scaled usage from 50 to 3500 servers on Amazon's cloud. Other startups that have used cloud computing on an IaaS platform to provide customized services to customers with the convenience of quickly and painlessly ramping up capability to meet customer demand include Spiral Genetics, Melodeo, and SEOmoz (Gohring, 2010).

Higher levels of systems integration lead to a greater need to write custom code and this works more effectively on a common platform, leading to stronger support for the PaaS model over the SaaS when the level of integration between applications increases. In both cases, an increase in demand variation leads to a stronger support for a cloud computing model that can more easily provide increased hardware when necessary, without having to go through an expensive acquisition process for an in-house operation.

The market for network security services is growing overall, and management at NL Networks expects a demand for in-house IT to grow at a moderate pace. They need to hire more engineers to design and implement systems as demand grows and they expect growth, but at a manageable pace. In the decision table, this points to evidence for a move to SaaS, where the core IT applications are hosted in the cloud, by vendors licensed by the application provider.

One interesting fact that we discovered in this case study was that the company had developed a content management system in-house for their own use and offered it to clients for web site hosting. Rather than host client web sites in-house, they used a cloud service to host their CMS which they then provided to their clients. They ended up using the cloud provider to host the system for their own website. After working through the decision table they have begun looking at hosting their common IT applications.

In all cases there are moderating factors of in-house IT competence and business continuity requirements. Cloud computing requires effective and efficient management of operations (Lim, Babu, Chase, & Parekh, 2008), and out-sourced facilities have the economies of scale to offer this support. If in-house IT has a low reputation either because of past failures or because of the small size of the unit, cloud computing offers higher skill levels and economies of scale. This is especially true for small business with a single person who is IT savvy and becomes a single critical point of failure. Employee risk has been shown to be a significant factor in influencing mangers to choose application development outsourcing (Benamati & Rajkumar, 2008). If in-house IT is trusted and believed to be reliable a thorough audit of operation needs to be performed to find any security and business continuity lapses. In addition, this audit should reveal the true total cost of operations for in-house IT taking into account the cost of hardware, software, database, networking, staff, consultants, employee time allocated to IT and other costs.

NL Networks has not had any problems with in-house IT that would move them any further toward cloud computing. They are conducting a detailed analysis of the cost of in-house operations to determine whether to move to cloud computing.

Business continuity is supported by a well-managed cloud operation, first because well managed data centers are robust, located in safe facilities, and connected to multiple net backbones. If the in-house data center has a unique configuration due the customization of applications and home-built systems integration, a data center collocation approach would support continuity without changing other features of the operation. The security issue is related to continuity since a security failure can impact operations in a manner similar to a natural or man-made disaster. As long as the cloud operation meets higher physical and network security standards than an in-house operation, cloud computing is a good strategy for security.

NL Networks does not have any unique configuration that would support the move to co-location. Hence they could move each application to a SaaS service and integrate systems the way the accomplish integration at present. While NL Networks specializes in network security and their primary service is developing customized security projects for business customers, they have limited data center expertise. In addition, NL Networks employees access the system frequently from remote customer locations. Hence, a SaaS provider can provide security matching an in-house facility, since a significant proportion of the data traffic is going to be over the public net through VPNs.

SUMMARY

Cloud computing is a rapidly growing approach to managing IT in the enterprise. This paper reviews the technology, considers the different cloud computing alternatives, and related cost savings and risks. Based on this analysis, the paper presents a decision table to help small business managers in taking a decision on the use of cloud computing and selecting an appropriate strategy. The relevant decision parameters and moderating factors are discussed, and the strengths and weaknesses of various cloud computing alternatives are described in the decision table. Using this information, managers can have a structured approach to navigating the decision on whether or not to migrate towards cloud computing and if so, which approach to use.

The NL Networks case study demonstrates how a small business can use the decision table to get a suitable recommendation for the preferred cloud computing strategy.

REFERENCES

Admiraal, E., & Lockhorst, D. (2009). E-Learning in Small and Medium-sized Enterprises across Europe. *International Small Business Journal*, *27*(6), 743–767. doi:10.1177/0266242609344244

Akamai. (2009). *Contest Data processing from the Edge*. Retrieved April 12, 2010, from http://www.akamai.com/dl/brochures/contest_brochure.pdf

Albert, G. (2009). Enhancing Dynamic Cloud-based Services using Network Virtualization. In *Proceedings of the 1st ACM Workshop on Virtualized Infrastructure and Systems and Architectures,* Barcelona, Spain (pp. 37-44). New York, NY: ACM.

Altaf, F., & Schuff, D. (2010). Taking a Flexible Approach to ASPs. *Communications of the ACM*, *53*(2), 141–143. doi:10.1145/1646353.1646389

Ardagna, D., Mirandola, R., Trubian, M., & Zhang, L. (2009). Run-time resource management in SOA virtualized environments. In *Proceedings of the 1st International Workshop on Quality of Service-Oriented Software Systems,* Amsterdam, The Netherlands.

Arrington, M. (2009). *In Our Inbox: Hundreds of Confidential Twitter Documents*. Retrieved April 12, 2010, from http://techcrunch.com/2009/07/14/in-our-inbox-hundreds-of-confidential-twitter-documents/

Assuncao, D. D., Costanzo, A., & Buyya, R. (2009). Evaluating the Cost-Benefit of Using Cloud Computing to Extend the Capacity of Clouds. In *Proceedings of the HPDC'09 Conference,* Munich, Germany (pp. 141-150).

Benamati, J., & Lederer, A. (2010). Managing the Impact of Rapid IT Change. *Information Resources Management Journal*, *23*(1), 1–16. doi:10.4018/irmj.2010102601

Benamati, J., & Rajkumar, T. (2008). An Outsourcing Acceptance Model: An Application of TAM to Application Development Outsourcing Decisions. *Information Resources Management Journal*, *21*(2), 80–102. doi:10.4018/irmj.2008040105

Bias, R. (2009). *Cloudcenters are Datacenters in the Sky*. Retrieved April 12, 2010, from http://blog.gogrid.com/2009/01/08/cloudcenters are datacenters-in-the-sky/

Brodkin, J. (2009). *Cloud computing outages: Amazon customers the latest to suffer downtime*. Retrieved from http://www.networkworld.com/community/node/48961

Cachin, C., Keidar, I., & Shraer, A. (2009). Trusting the Cloud. *SIGACT News*, *40*(2), 81–87. doi:10.1145/1556154.1556173

Campbell-Kelly, M. (2009). The Rise, Fall, and Resurrection of Software as A Service. *Communications of the ACM*, *52*(5), 28–30. doi:10.1145/1506409.1506419

Carr, N. (2008). *The Big Switch*. New York, NY: Norton.

Chau, P. (1995). Factors used in the selection of packaged software in small businesses: Views of owners and managers. *Information & Management*, *29*, 71–78. doi:10.1016/0378-7206(95)00016-P

Cheng, R. (2010, February 8). *'Cloud Computing': What Exactly is it, Anyway?* Retrieved May 5, 2010, from http://online.wsj.com/article/SB1000142405274870358090457463839131808515 8.html

Chun, B., & Maniatis, P. (2009). Augmented Smartphone Applications Through Clone Cloud Execution. In *Proceedings of the HotOS 2009 Conference,* Monte Verita, Switzerland.

Cloud Security Alliance. (2009). *Security Guidance for Critical Areas of Focus in Cloud Computing.* Retrieved April 12, 2010, from http://www.cloudsecurityalliance.org/csaguide.pdf

Costa, P., Zahn, T., Rowston, A., O'Shea, G., & Schubert, S. (2009). Why should we integrate services, servers, and networking in a data center? In *Proceedings of the 1st ACM Workshop on Research on Enterprise Networking,* Barcelona, Spain (pp. 111-118).

Cunningham, P., & Wilkins, J. (2009). A Walk in the Cloud. *Information Management Journal*, *43*(1), 22–30.

Deelman, E., Singh, G., Livny, M., Berriman, B., & Good, J. (2008). The cost of doing science on the Cloud: The Montage Example. In *Proceedings of the ACM/IEEE Conference on Supercomputing,* Piscatawy, NJ (pp. 1-12).

Delic, K., & Walker, M. (2008). Emergence of the Academic Computing Clouds. *ACM Ubiquity, 9*(31).

DMTF. (2009). *Open Virtualization Format Specification.* Retrieved April 13, 2010, from http://www.dmtf.org/standards/published_documents/DSP0243_1.0.0.pdf

Edwards, A., Fischer, A., & Lain, A. (2009). Diverter: a new approach to networking within virtualized infrastructures. In *Proceedings of the ACM Workshop on Research on Enterprise Networking,* Barcelona, Spain (pp. 103-110).

FCC. (2009). *FCC Public Notice.* Retrieved April 14, 2010, http://hraunfoss.fcc.gov/edocs_public/attachmatch/DA-09-2433A1.pdf

Festa, P. (1999, June 30). Destop.com joining Web-based applications market. *Cnet News.* Retrieved from http://news.cnet.com/Desktop.com-joining-Web-based-applications-market/2100-1023_3-227919.html

France, C. (2010). *Business Information Modeling and the Cloud.* Retrieved April 14, 2010, from http://www.aecbytes.com/feature/2010/BIM_Cloud.html

Garfinkel, S. (2007). *An evaluation for Amazon's Grid Computing Services: EC2,S3,SQS.* Retrieved April 14, 2010, from http://simson.net/clips/academic/2007.harvard.s3.pdf

Gatewood, B. (2009). Clouds on the Information Horizon: How to Avoid the Storm. *Information & Management*, 32–36.

Gohring, N. (2010, September 28). Cloud Services Empower Startups. *New York Times.* Retrieved September 28, 2010, from http://www.nytimes.com

Gonzalez, R. G., & Llopis, J. (2006). Information systems outsourcing: A literature analysis. *Information & Management*, *43*, 821–834. doi:10.1016/j.im.2006.07.002

Google. (2009). *Google apps and government.* Retrieved April 14, 2010, from http://googleenterprise.blogspot.com/2009/09/google-apps-and-government.html

Greenberg, A., Hamilton, J., Jain, N., Kandula, S., Kim, C., & Lahiri, P. (2009). VL2: A scalable and Flexible Data Center Network. *ACM SIGCOMM Computer Communication Review*, *39*(4), 51–62. doi:10.1145/1594977.1592576

Hand, E. (2007). Head in the Clouds. *Nature*, *449*(7165), 963–963. doi:10.1038/449963a

Hill, Z., & Humphrey, M. (2009). Applicability of the Willow Architecture for Cloud Management. In *Proceedings of the 1st Workshop on Automated Control for Datacenters and Clouds (ACDC'09)*, Barcelona, Spain (pp. 31-36).

Hoover, J. (2008). *Outages force Cloud Computing Users to Rethink Tactics.* Retrieved from http://www.informationweek.com/news/services/saas/showArticle.jhtml?articleID=210004236

Khazanchi, D. (2005). Information Technology (IT) Appropriateness: The Contingency Theory of "FIT" and IT implementation in Small and Medium Enterprises. *Journal of CIS*, *45*(3), 88–94.

Konstantinou, A., Eilam, T., Kalantar, M., Totok, A., Arnold, W., & Snible, E. (2009). An architecture for virtual solution composition and deployment in infrastructure clouds. In *Proceedings of the 3rd International Workshop on Virtualization Technologies in Distributed Computing (VTDC'09)*, Barcelona, Spain (pp. 9-18).

Levy, M., Powell, P., & Worrall, L. (2005). Strategic Intent and E-Business in SMEs: Enablers and Inhibitors. *Information Resources Management Journal*, *18*(4), 1–20. doi:10.4018/irmj.2005100101

Lim, H., Babu, S., Chase, J., & Parekh, S. (2008). Automated Control in Cloud Computing: Challenges and Opportunities. In *Proceedings of the 1st Workshop on Automated Control Datacenters and Clouds (ACSC'09)*, Barcelona, Spain (pp. 13-18).

Magal, S., & Lewis, C. (1995). Determinants of Information Technology Success in Small Business. *Journal of CIS*, *35*(3), 75–83.

Maleki, M., & Anand, D. (2008). Service Outsourcing: Information Technology. *SCMS Journal of Indian Management*, *5*(3), 42–52.

Matthews, J., Garfinkel, T., Hoff, C., & Wheeler, J. (2009). Virtual machine Contracts for Datacenter and Cloud Computing Environments. In *Proceedings of the 1st Workshop on Automated Control for Datacenters and Clouds (ACDC'09)*, Barcelona, Spain (pp. 23-30).

McFarlan, F. (1984). Information Technology Changes the Way You Compete. *Harvard Business Review*, *62*(3), 98–103.

Mell, P., & Grance, T. (2009). *The NIST Definition of Cloud Computing.* Retrieved April 12, 2010, from http://csrc.nist.gov/groups/SNS/cloud-computing/cloud-def-v15.doc

Nelson, M. (2009). The Cloud, The Crowd, and Public Policy. *Issues in Science and Technology*, *25*(4), 96–106.

Nolan, R., & McFarlan, F. (2005). Information Technology and the Board of Directors. *Harvard Business Review*, *83*(10), 96–106.

Nolle, T. (2009). *Identifying Applications for Public and Private Clouds.* Retrieved April 14, 2010, from http://searchcloudcomputing.techtarget.com/tip/0,289483,sid201_gci1358701,00.html?track=NL-1329&ad=710605&asrc=EM_NLT_7835341&uid=8788654

North, K. (2009). *The Many Flavors of Platform Services for Cloud Computing*. Retrieved April 14, 2010, from http://www.drdobbs.com/windows/220300737

Open Cloud. (2010). *Open Cloud Manifesto*. Retrieved April 12, 2010, from http://opencloudmanifesto.org/Cloud_Computing_Use_Cases_Whitepaper-3_0.pdf

Palankar, M., Iamnitchi, A., Ripeanu, M., & Garfinkel, S. (2008). Amazon S3 for science Grids: A viable soulution? In *Proceedings of the International Workshop on Data-aware Distributed Computing (DADC'08),* New York, NY (pp. 55-64).

Palvia, P. (1996). A model and instrument for measuring small business user satisfaction with information technology. *Information & Management, 31*(3), 151–163. doi:10.1016/S0378-7206(96)01069-5

Pearson, S. (2009). Taking account of privacy when designing cloud computing services. In *Proceedings of the 2009 ICSE Workshop on Software Engineering Challenges of Cloud Computing,* Vancouver, BC (pp. 44-52).

Peltier, J., Schibrowsky, J., & Zhao, Y. (2009). Understanding the Antecedents to the Adoption of CRM Technology by Small Retailers. *International Small Business Journal, 27*(3), 307–336. doi:10.1177/0266242609102276

Premkumar, G. (2003). A Meta-Analysis of Research on Information Technology Implementation in Small Business. *Journal of Organizational Computing and Electronic Commerce, 13*(2), 91–121. doi:10.1207/S15327744JOCE1302_2

Ragowsky, A., & Geffen, D. (2008). What makes the competitive contribution of ERP strategic. *Database, 39*(2), 33–49.

Regan, P. (2003). Safe Harbors or Free Frontiers? Privacy and Transborder Data Flows. *The Journal of Social Issues, 59*(2), 263–282. doi:10.1111/1540-4560.00064

Rellermeyer, J., Duller, M., & Alonso, G. (2009). Engineering the cloud from software modules. In *Proceedings of the 2009 ICSE Workshop on Software Engineering Challenges of Cloud Computing*, Vancouver, BC.

Riemenschneider, C., & Mykytyn, P. (2000). What small business executives have learned about managing information technology. *Information & Management, 37*(5), 257–269. doi:10.1016/S0378-7206(99)00052-X

Ristenpart, T., Tromer, E., Shacham, H., & Savage, S. (2009). Exploring Information Leakage in Third Party Clouds. In *Proceedings of the CCS '09 Conference,* Chicago, IL.

Rosen, G. (2010). The business of Clouds. *Crossroads, 16*(3), 26–28. doi:10.1145/1734160.1734169

Schwartz, E. (2007). *Salesforce.com launches SaaS platform*. Retrieved from http://www.infoworld.com/t/architecture/salesforcecom-launches-saas-platform-724

Schwartz, E. (2008). The dangers of cloud computing. *Network World Asia, 4*(7), 10–12.

Simmons, G., Armstrong, G., & Durkin, M. (2008). A Conceptualization of the Determinants of Small Business Website Adoption. *International Small Business Journal, 26*(3), 351–389. doi:10.1177/0266242608088743

Smith, M., & Kumar, R. (2004). A theory of Application Service Provider (ASP) use from a client perspective. *Information & Management, 41*(8), 977–1002. doi:10.1016/j.im.2003.08.019

Solis, I., & Obraczka, K. (2004). FLIP: a flexible interconnection protocol for heterogeneous internetworking. *Mobile Networks and Applications*, *9*(4), 347–361. doi:10.1023/B:MONE.0000031603.28679.6f

Sridhar, T. (2009). Cloud Computing-A Primer. *The Internet Protocol Journal, 12*(3).

Thong, J. (1999). An integrated model of information systems adoption in small businesses. *Journal of Management Information Systems, 15*(4), 187–214.

Williams, M. (2009). *Microsoft loses Sidekick user's personal data.* Network World.

Yap, C., Soh, C., & Raman, K. (1992). Information systems Success Factors in Small Business. *Omega, 20*(506), 597–609. doi:10.1016/0305-0483(92)90005-R

Youseff, L., Butrico, M., & DaSilva, D. (2008). *Toward a unified ontology of cloud computing.* Paper presented at the Grid Computing Environments Workshop (GCE2008).

Yuefa, D., Bo, W., Yaquiang, G., Quan, Z., & Chaojing, T. (2009). Data Security Model for Cloud Computing. In *Proceedings of the IWISA 2009 Conference,* Qingdao, China (pp. 141-145).

This work was previously published in the Information Resources Management Journal, Volume 24, Issue 3, edited by Mehdi Khosrow-Pour, pp. 9-25, copyright 2013 by IGI Publishing (an imprint of IGI Global).

Chapter 13
Information Technology and Supply Chain Collaboration:
Examining the Contingent Role of Environmental Uncertainty

Karthik N. S. Iyer
University of Northern Iowa, USA

ABSTRACT

The utilization of advanced information technologies (IT) in interfirm collaboration has been thematic in current literature. Although conventional wisdom perceives that IT systems facilitate supply chain collaboration, this research provides an alternative perspective. Drawing on resource-based view and contingency 'fit' theory, the study investigates a model of relationships that specify how environmental uncertainty factors influence the nature of the association of two critical but distinctive IT capabilities with collaboration. Findings corroborate the positive association between collaboration and B2B e-commerce and IT analytic capability. However, demand unpredictability enhances the IT analytic capability-collaboration relationship while detracting from the B2B e-commerce-collaboration association. Notably, the study did not find any moderating influence of another critical uncertainty factor, technological turbulence. The findings reveal the complex nature of IT-collaboration relationships and provide managers a framework for understanding the uncertainty contexts under which specific information technologies with various functionalities may be more appropriately leveraged to derive benefits.

INTRODUCTION

The rapid growth of information technology (IT) use in current business practice has captured the imagination of practitioners and academia alike. The use of internet-enabled automated information systems that connect business activities across firms, particularly, has changed the face of business. They have contributed to enhanced business performance (Rosenzweig, 2009; Sanders, 2007). The field of supply chain management (SCM) has especially benefited to such an extent that information technology defines the frontier of current SCM practice (Iyer et al., 2009). Advanced infor-

DOI: 10.4018/978-1-4666-3616-3.ch013

mation technology applications have transformed SCM by enabling the widest 'arc of integration' among supply chain members and orchestrating streamlined value creation operations (Frohlich & Westbrook, 2001; Sanders, 2007). This paper distinguishes the internet-enabled systems that have considerably enhanced information-sharing, real-time dissemination of information and analytic decision-making among collaborative partners, from the more traditional information systems (e.g., traditional EDI, legacy based-information systems that aid basic transactions such as buy/sell, order entry and tracking). Not surprisingly, these advanced IT applications are considered an essential element, the backbone, of current SCM strategy, and thus are the focus of this research. References to information technology from this point on in the paper imply information technologies with advanced capabilities.

SCM is premised on collaboration, the coordinated coupling of processes across partner firms that integrates various facets of business flows. Collaboration engenders extensive cross-firm information sharing and elimination or reduction of non-value activities (Germain & Iyer, 2006). Collaboration among integrated supply chain partners requires extensive information-sharing and globally optimal decisions for staging the development and flow of products through the system, ultimately delivering value to end customers (Rai et al., 2006). IT capabilities provide functionalities such as forward visibility and real-time connectivity. This enables global optimization of resources, streamlined operations and synchronized supply chain flows in tightly coupled cross-firm processes (Sanders, 2007). Collaborative planning and replenishment processes, for example, depend on internet-enabled IT. Scheduling activities also need precise and timely actual usage or point of sales information. Thus, supply chain IT applications with their range of functionalities help partner firms exchange vast amounts of information for rapid decision-making and generating synergistic collaborative outcomes. By enabling development of higher-order capabilities, advanced information technology applications have become essential elements of collaborative operations. They have established themselves as "powerful strategic weapons" for successful supply chains (Ke et al., 2009; Kent & Mentzer, 2003; Rai et al., 2006).

Despite the pervasive managerial view on the impact of information technology and eventual overall performance, the expected benefits from IT-enabled collaboration have materialized albeit inconsistently (Devaraj et al., 2007; Rosenzweig, 2009). Besides, academic literature has paid less attention to the direct facilitating role of information technology has in enhancing cross-firm collaboration (Sanders, 2007). A clear understanding of the IT-collaboration relationship becomes critical since collaboration is a mediating mechanism where the first order impact of information capability manifests, as evident in the following examples. AMR research (now part of Gartner) recently reported a "renaissance" in vendor-managed inventory (VMI) – a form of supply chain collaboration that came into prominence in the 1990s as a means of optimizing inventory levels throughout the distribution system. The driving force is the availability of information technologies that can leverage multiple sources of critical downstream data for collaborative forecasting, optimization of inventory levels, and better matching demand patterns with inventories in the system. Companies like Proctor & Gamble have seen numerous benefits including reduced inventory levels and obsolescence, and enhanced cash-to-cash cycles by deploying advanced information technologies in their collaborative relationships with downstream retail partners. In Dell's case, internet-enabled technologies have created a superior supply chain. Dell has been able to extensively collaborate with supply chain partners – sharing and exchanging information, to provide end customers low-priced higher quality products. Information technologies have enabled Dell to forecast demand with high accuracy, and share updates with all key suppliers several times a day, to shorten the market response times. According to an e-business technology manager at Dell, internet-enabled technologies have allowed Dell's supply chain members including end customers to almost touch each other.

Thus, a purpose of this research is to empirically understand the mostly anecdotal effect of advanced IT applications on the intermediate collaboration variable, in order to provide a better picture of their roles in enhancing supply chain performance (Heim & Peng, 2010). Another notable shortcoming in literature is investigating the effects of information technology using aggregate level measures, i.e., lumping together disparate IT capabilities, and not examining the impact of specific applications (Banker et al., 2006). This research, by studying two classes of advanced IT capabilities with unique functionalities, contributes toward an enriched understanding of the IT-collaboration relationship. B2B e-commerce, the internet based information exchange technology, and IT analytic capability or the class of decision-support application tools, are investigated in this study to examine their specific associations with interfirm collaboration.

Uncertainties in the operating context can be expected to play contingent roles in influencing the impact of IT capabilities on inter-firm collaboration (Rosenzweig, 2009). Recent research has focused attention on the contingency theory idea of 'fit' to unravel the nature of the relationships between information technology and supply chain strategy (collaboration, for example) rather than merely understanding the direct associations. The concept proposes differential outcomes resulting from the interactive 'fit' between information technology, supply chain strategy (i.e., collaboration), and contextual uncertainties (Venkatraman, 1989). However, extant literature on the moderating impact of contextual factors on the IT-collaboration relationship is sparse, despite its acknowledged importance. Clusters of environmental variables have been investigated recently (Premkumar et al., 2005); however, the disentangled roles of critical environmental uncertainty variables are unclear. This study addresses the research gap by investigating ways in which two critical uncertainty variables identified in the strategy literature – technological turbulence and demand unpredictability - moderate the relationships of B2B e-commerce and IT analytic capability with supply chain collaboration. By providing a richer understanding of the dynamic nature of IT-collaboration relationships under contingencies, the study contributes important theoretical and practical insights.

The rest of the paper is organized as follows. The next section elaborates upon the theoretical background and conceptualization of the research framework. The section that follows provides the arguments justifying the direct and contingent relationships embedded in the theoretical framework. An empirical study describing the research sample, the reliability and validity of the measures, and results from the analysis then follow. The final section concludes with a discussion of the analysis results, contributions of the study, research limitations and future opportunities.

BACKGROUND LITERATURE AND RESEARCH MODEL

Supply Chain Collaboration

Supply chain management as a strategy embraces a systems perspective in creating maximum market value. It uniquely captures the synergies among interfirm resources in the network of supply chain partner firms (Lambert, Cooper, & Pagh, 1998; Lummus, Vokurka, & Alber, 1998; Sanders, 2007). Thus understandably, supply chain strategy requires a closely integrated set of partnerships, in essence, inter-firm collaboration as a basis for delivering customer value and achieving a shared market opportunity (Bowersox et al., 1999). Supply chain collaboration can be defined as a process where a firm systematically integrates strategies, synchronizes activities, regularly shares information and other resources, and actively works towards achieving collective goals with supply chain partners (Iyer, 2011). The strategic and synergistic commingling of unique resources and capabilities within and between partners in a firm's collaborative network, has consistently been related to superior performance outcomes (Frohlich & Westbrook, 2001; Germain & Iyer, 2006; Sanders, 2007). From a resource-based view (RBV), the tight coordinated functioning with integrated supply chain partners is a source of competitive advantage (Kandemir et al., 2006; Wang & Wei, 2007).

Information Technology and Supply Chain Collaboration

Current research has focused attention on the role of advanced internet-enabled information technologies in enhancing collaborative exchanges and coordinated decision-making among close-knit supply chain partners (Autry et al., 2010; Frohlich & Westbrook, 2002; Rosenzweig, 2009). These technologies have enabled integrated management of supply chain processes by their decision support ability ranging from day-to-day operations to long-term relationship strategies (Autry et al., 2010). B2B e-commerce, the collection of internet-based information exchange technology applications, has also considerably impacted inter-firm exchanges. Defined as the internet, web, and web-based information resources and infrastructure peculiar to managing interfirm business interactions, B2B e-commerce has facilitated real-time sharing of vast amounts of real-time data including demand information and enhanced visibility of system inventory (Saeed et al., 2005; Sanders, 2007). With its capability of extensive information integration and interoperability, B2B e-commerce has enabled consistent and real-time low-cost sharing of supply chain information among partners and functions (Sanders, 2007). On the supply side, for example, various purchase functions are automated and streamlined, while internet-enabled discussion forums help understand supply requirements and speedier joint-product development. B2B e-commerce is characterized by its ability to enable data consistency and automated accurate data capture and sharing among partners, facilitating cross-firm process integration. It provides the ability to interface function-specific applications, integrating the supply chain network (Rai et al., 2006).

IT analytic capability, on the other hand, enables managers to analyze and resolve short-term and long-term problems. It is defined as a collective of information systems and approaches that provide advanced analytic abilities to solve supply chain management problems by analyzing information, and predicting outcomes (Trkman et al., 2010). The technology's decision-enabling capabilities range from, assisting in optimizing short-term delivery schedules for instance, to medium-term decision-making such as product allocation, to providing strategic level decision capabilities such as configuring the logistics network (Bowersox et al., 2010; Swaminathan & Tayur, 2003). Planning applications, for example, enable generating and processing vast amounts of cross-functional data to develop optimal plans for the entire system as well as for specific critical supply chain functions such as transportation and production (Rai et al., 2006). As another example of an advanced analytic IT, warehouse decision systems enable supply chain managers with various decision capabilities – visual mapping of inventory storage and flow to enhance labor productivity, identification of non-value added activities to better utilize warehouse space, and assessing impact of management actions on future warehouse productivity and costs, to name a few (Min, 2009). From a resource based view, the two IT capabilities have transformed "… commodity-like information technology tools into idiosyncratic and intangible IT capabilities" in integrated supply chains (Iyer et al., 2007, p. 305). Transaction cost perspective also supports the collaboration enabling capabilities of B2B e-commerce and IT analytic capability. The two IT applications with their vast functionalities are shown to considerably reduce both transaction costs that partners incur from coordinated exchanges or integrated decision-making, and risks of opportunistic partner behaviors (Clemens & Row, 1992; Nooteboom, 1992). In sum, the sophistication of IT-enabled collaborative operations help partners share processes, and accelerate and streamline activities. Partner firms can iterate many more product designs enabled by rapid information sharing and decision-making ability or coordinate joint forecasts and business plans, eliminating inefficiencies in delivering market value (Anderson & Lee, 2000). While the thrust of much of supply chain collaborative strategy has been to understand the facilitating role of advanced information systems, there is an acknowledged need for exploring the fit between IT-enabled collaborative strategy and the operating context to delineate the impact on supply chain outcomes. Thus, understanding the role environmental uncertainty context variables play will have significant managerial implications.

Recent literature (Premkumar et al., 2005; Shin, 2006; Tanriverdi, 2006) has gained valuable insights from the contingency 'fit' perspective in its quest for unraveling the so called 'productivity paradox' in information systems literature. The strategic management theoretical lens has provided explanation to the inconsistent linkage between information technology and overall performance by suggesting 'matching fit' between resources, strategy and the environmental context (Venkatraman, 1989). Thus, from an information systems perspective, unconditional associations between IT capabilities and collaboration are insufficient in fully explaining the nature of performance outcomes (Davis-Sramek et al., 2010).

Ultimate performance is contingent upon the interactions and interrelationships among these factors (Venkatraman, 1989). However, there is lack of research on the moderating 'fit' roles of environmental variables on the IT-collaboration relationship. As Davis-Sramek et al. (2010) note, "Literature has not disentangled the effect of environmental variables nor has it examined multiple ITs for differential effects" (p. 44). This study, therefore, contributes to extant literature by examining the interactive influence of two critical environmental uncertainty variables –technological turbulence and demand unpredictability – on the relationship of B2B e-commerce and IT analytic capability with supply chain collaboration.

The research model deriving from the above discussion is shown in Figure 1, and captures the hypothesized relationships of B2B e-commerce and IT analytic capability with supply chain collaboration. The contingency nature of these relationships is investigated by hypothesizing the moderating effects of the two environmental uncertainty factors: technological turbulence and demand unpredictability.

HYPOTHESES

Linking B2B E-Commerce and IT Analytic Capability with Collaboration

Advanced IT capabilities inherently are cross-firm applications. From the relational view theory, they are critical supply chain resources facilitating superior rent generating mechanisms such as inter-firm routines, and generate partnership-specific process

Figure 1. Research framework and hypotheses

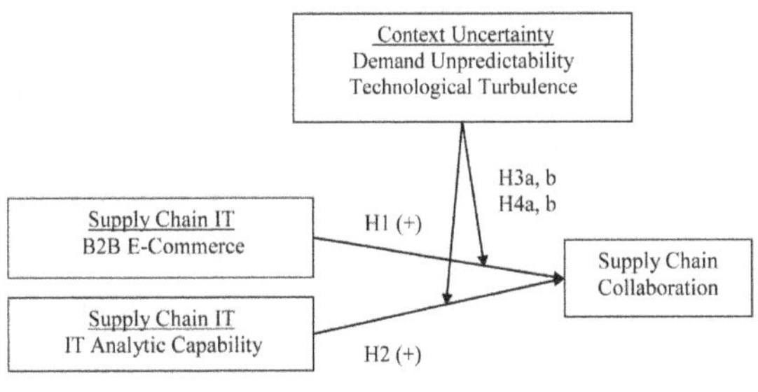

capabilities (Dyer and Singh, 1998). By enabling rapid information access and decision-making, B2B e-commerce and IT analytic capability help supply chain partners work together efficiently and effectively (Mukhopadhyay & Kekre, 2002). Thus, information technology capabilities contribute to close collaborative partnerships. Partners reap the benefits arising from improved supply chain flows, better ways of sharing and exploiting pooled knowledge, and even reapportioned decision-making roles and responsibilities for streamlined functioning (Konsynski & Tiwana, 2004). IT analytic capability enabled decision-making, for example, helps improve collective response to market needs and change, as well as rapidly exploit opportunities leading to sustainable competitive advantage (Bowersox et al., 2010). B2B e-commerce facilitated enhanced ability to process vast data rapidly may help partners develop more organic governing structures. This could enable establishment of integrative mechanisms and re-engineering of processes to improve supply chain flows (Kim & Mahoney, 2006).

At the operational level, partner firms benefit considerably from IT analytic capability. For example, firms can rapidly decide on replacing extensive commitment to inventory throughout the system, reducing costs (Daugherty et al., 1999). Alternately, B2B e-commerce provides access to virtual inventory stores, facilitating collaborative planning among relevant supply chain partners for more efficient shipments and faster order-processing (Croom, 2000). Thus the two classes of advanced information technologies – B2B e-commerce and IT analytic capability - facilitate collaborative exchanges on a range of decision levels.

While there is a lack of studies specifically investigating various classes of advanced information capabilities, extant literature has, to some extent, investigated the general IT use and its relationship with collaboration related variables. The broad consensus is a positive association of information technology with variables such as relationship commitment (Kent & Mentzer, 2003), better coordination among partners (Vickery et al., 2003), or reduced coordination costs (Clemens & Row, 1992), and inter-firm collaboration itself (Subramani, 2004; Sanders, 2007). Collectively, extant literature supports a positive association between the two classes of IT and supply chain collaboration. Thus:

H1: B2B e-commerce has a positive association with supply chain collaboration.

H2: IT analytic capability associates positively with supply chain collaboration.

Contingent Role of Environmental Uncertainty in the IT-Collaboration Relationship

Dynamism and unpredictability in the operating environment represents external forces beyond firm control, and presents threats and opportunities. Supply chain partners require appropriate strategies and collaborative resource configurations as hedges against any negative performance impact of environmental uncertainty (Cannon & Perreault, 1999; Chakravarthy, 1997; Sundaramurthy & Lewis, 2003). Cisco's CEO, John Chambers, on a conference call following the recent quarter's earnings report referred to just such an environment facing the company. While by and large many of the company's business customers were foreseeing a low albeit gradual GDP growth, they were highly unsure about their revenue forecasts and capital expenditure projections for the next one year. Thus for Cisco, there are mixed signals on demand and purchase strategies from business markets. Such an unpredictable market situation calls for appropriate strategy models from Cisco's supply chain to effectively deal with the potential negative impact. In line with process change and innovation adoption literatures which collectively suggest development of technological capabilities as responses to variations in external unpredictability levels (Damanpour, 1991), this research investigates the moderating influence of demand unpredictability and technological turbulence on the IT-collaboration linkage.

Demand unpredictability represents the extent of market volatility and heterogeneity. It is defined as the degree to which markets are fragmented, and customer composition and preferences change (Choudhury, 1997; Kohli & Jaworski, 1990). High levels of demand unpredictability imply that firms are less capable of accurately forecasting market trends. On the other hand, technological turbulence dimension is defined as the rate of change in production, process, and service technologies (Kohli & Jaworski, 1990). Frequent transformations in dominant designs and technology standards and rapid changes in underlying product/service technologies characterize greater levels of technological turbulence (Kandemir et al., 2006). The two uncertainty dimensions are expected to interact with each of the supply chain information capabilities, albeit, in entirely different ways.

Contingency interactive 'fit' in a supply chain partnership context argues for differential impact of B2B e-commerce and IT analytic capability on collaboration due to uncertainties. In predictable environments, SCM strategies favor information systems that contribute toward efficiencies in collaborative activities. Conversely, in chaotic unpredictable environments, information technologies providing flexibilities and market responsiveness are preferred (Beth-Davis et al., 2010). Thus, in a stable and predictable demand and technological environment, as partners focus on efficiency-driven strategy, B2B e-commerce becomes critical in driving integration. Increasing connectivity through B2B e-commerce streamlines supply chain flows among partners, improving operational efficiencies (Lee at al., 2000; Rai et al., 2006). Integrated supply chains are better able to establish simplified process routines, leveraging B2B e-commerce. Simplified routines reduce costs across functions such as manufacturing, material handling, storing or transportation and enable monitoring and responding to markets at lower costs (Fisher, 1997). Low technological turbulence and stable, less fragmented market conditions are characterized by low material and final product prices. Under such conditions, efficient B2B e-commerce enabled collaborative partnerships are desirable due to low opportunity costs (Choudry et al., 1998; Rosenzweig, 2009).

On the other hand, high demand unpredictability and new unique market situations create demand and information idiosyncrasies making it difficult to assimilate, and respond to market situations (Grewal & Tansuhaj, 2001). B2B e-commerce systems with fewer decision-support capabilities are inefficient in contributing to rapid collaborative decision-making in such complex and non-repetitive information sharing conditions (Kendall, 1997; Rai et al., 2006; Saeed et al., 2005). Besides, highly technical information of a short-lived nature may be less amenable for sharing among partners with just B2B e-commerce capabilities. Thus, high environmental uncertainty context situations may detract from the positive relationship between B2B e-commerce and supply chain collaboration.

Environmental uncertainties may, however, strengthen the IT analytic capability-collaboration relationship. IT analytic capability engenders flexibilities in partnerships through information-driven rapid decision-making (Davis-Sramek et al., 2010). The capability increases partners' ability to sense changing external cues to deal with unpredictable conditions effectively (Gatignon & Robertson, 1989). Changing demand patterns and market preferences affect delivery requirements and costs. On the upstream side, unpredictable supply markets necessitate partner firms to frequently re-work the best combinations of cost, quality, and service reliability. Thus, it becomes critical for partners to have the analytics in place to discern requirements upstream and downstream for better performance in unpredictable environments (Norman, 2004). Higher levels of technological turbulence adversely impacts processes leading to greater fluctuations. For example, customer-delivery schedules are negatively affected, lowering customer service levels (Iyer et al., 2004). Developing IT analytic capability counteracts the negative impacts of uncertainty. The ability assists partners to collaborate better and decide more effectively: leveraging pooled resources, making better market forecasts (example collaborative forecasting and replenishment decisions), or bringing more predictability in internal operations (Melville et al., 2004). Thus, environmental uncertainty factors can be expected to positively interact with IT analytic capability in enhancing supply chain collaboration.

H3a,b: Demand unpredictability and technological turbulence moderate inversely the association of B2B e-commerce with supply chain collaboration.

H4a,b: Demand unpredictability and technological turbulence moderate positively the association of IT analytic capability with supply chain collaboration.

METHOD

Sample

A field survey using the council of supply chain management professionals (CSCMP) manufacturers' membership list as sampling frame, was conducted to collect data for testing the hypothesized relationships. Autonomous manufacturing firms or strategic business units formed the unit of analysis. The target population for the survey was US based manufacturing firms. Since the study proposed to generalize the results across a wide variety of manufacturing firms, a broad cross-section of CSCMP member-firms marketing a variety of products in industries spanning the standard industrial classification (SIC) code range (SIC 20 to 39, n= 2,468) was chosen as the sampling frame. SIC system classifies businesses and industries by the type of economic activity using one to four digit codes, and the two digit classification represents the most popular way of classifying various manufacturing industries. Since firms employed multiple CSCMP members, the list was culled to 1,372 firms, retaining members with the highest title levels in each firm. The study ensured that the executives possessed strategic level knowledge and experience in diverse SCM-IT activities in order to respond effectively. In all, 914 randomly drawn potential respondents or two-thirds of the sampling frame were contacted for the study, and 538 of them were sent the questionnaire. Telephonic screening ensured willingness and competency of respondents to effectively complete the questionnaire. Willing key informants were faxed or e-mailed the survey. Respondents who did not reply within two weeks after the original surveys were sent reminders. The final usable sample consisted of a total of 152 surveys, for a 28.3% response rate.

The respondents in the sample represented a wide spectrum of manufacturing firms: food and kindred products (SIC 20), 13%; chemicals and pharmaceuticals (SIC 28), 26%; industrial machinery (SIC 35), 10%; and electronic products (SIC 36), 15%. The majority of respondents stated that logistics was their functional area (51%), followed by distribution (22%), supply chain management (12%), operations (3.9%), information systems, materials management, and purchasing (each with 2.6%), manufacturing (1.3%), and other functional areas such as forecasting (1.9%). They included managers (45%), followed by directors (28%) and vice presidents (15%). Evidently, most of the respondents were in capacities overseeing strategic level decision making in related fields of SCM, logistics and operations. Average sales for firms in the sample are $5.4 billion with an average firm age of 55 years (Table 1).

Representativeness of the sample was assessed using the extrapolation method (Armstrong & Overton, 1977). Mean scores for late respondents,

Table 1. Respondent and organization sample profile

Respondent Profile Number Percentage
Respondent Job Title
Manager 68 45
Director 43 28
Vice-President 23 15
Other 18 12
Respondent Functional Area
Logistics 78 51
Distribution 33 22
Supply Chain Management 18 12
Other 23 15
Organizational Industrial Area
Chemicals 40 26
Electronics 23 15
Food 20 13
Industrial Machinery 15 10
Transportation Equipment 10 7
Furniture 7 5
Other 37 24
Mean Standard Deviation Minimum Maximum
Number of Employees (FTEs) 12,167 24,200 16 120,000
Annual Revenue $4.486 billion $9.84 billion $1 million $52 billion
Organizational Age (years) 55 41 1 195

defined as those completing the survey only after receiving a follow up fax or e-mail two weeks after receiving the original survey (n=31), were compared with the remaining respondents (n=121). T-tests did not yield any significant differences in any of the variables. Secondly, a more rigorous analysis was performed by randomly selecting 300 non-respondents and mailing them ten items culled from the survey. A comparison of these item responses (n=28) with the main sample (n=152) using t-tests revealed no significant differences in means. These assessments alleviate major concerns with non-response bias problems in the study.

Measurement, Reliability, and Validity

The scale to measure supply chain B2B e-commerce was developed as part of the study. Items were generated after a review of SCM and e-commerce literature and an initial set of seven items for the scale was based on suggestions of the Global Supply Chain Forum (Lambert, Cooper, & Pagh, 1998) regarding fundamental cross-firm processes. An exploratory pilot study was conducted to refine the scale. Strategic level managers from a random sample of manufacturing firms representing a wide range of industries formed the key respondents for the pilot survey. Analysis of the results from a usable sample of 36 responses and inputs from industry and academic experts suggested retaining a refined set of five items (See Table 2) for the final scale. Minor wording changes to some items were also made based on the analysis. The scale captures the extent of B2B e-commerce implementation in cross-firm process integration. Respondents rated B2B e-commerce applications using 7-point scales anchored with the endpoints of "rarely" and "frequently" in the following supply chain processes: demand management, order management, materials and finished goods inventory management, and customer management. IT analytic capability was measured using a scale based on the work of Chopra and Meindl (2004). Experts were interviewed about the scale which was then refined further following the pilot test to ensure adequate psychometric properties. The items measured the IT capability in four areas (advanced planning and scheduling, warehouse management systems, transportation and procurement systems) with end points of "low analytic capability" and "high analytic capability". Principal component analysis suggested a uni-dimensional scale.

Supply chain collaboration was measured using a scale adapted from the work of Anthony (2000). The measure captures collaboration ac-

Table 2. Measurement of predictor and moderating variables

Item-to-total correlation
B2B E-Commerce: α=.85; $\bar{x}$=3.89; SD=1.51. Ratings on the extent to which B2B E-commerce has been used to generate cross-firm process integration with key partners: B2B E-commerce defined as including EDI, Web and internet-based applications: 7-point scales with endpoints of "rarely" and "frequently."
Demand management: forecasting .72
Materials inventory management .71
Order management (fulfillment and delivery) .70
Finished goods inventory management .83
Customer management: e.g., customer initiated inquiries .64
IT Analytic Capability: α=.81; $\bar{x}$=4.12; SD=1.73. Ratings on sophisticated applications tied to internet ERP and/or application systems that provide managers with strategic and operational decision-making information: 7-point scales with endpoints of "low analytic capability" and "high analytic capability."
Procurement systems .63
Advanced planning and scheduling (APS) .58
Transportation Management Systems .67
Warehouse Management Systems .64
Demand Unpredictability: α=.74; $\bar{x}$=4.03; SD=1.3. Primary industry; 7-point semantic differential scales.
Sales are predictable...unpredictable .66
Market trends are easy to monitor...difficult to monitor .59
Sales forecasts are likely to be accurate...inaccurate .45
Technological Turbulence: α=.75; $\bar{x}$=3.65; SD=1.54. Primary industry; 7-point semantic differential scales.
Logistics processes change slowly...rapidly .46
Products become obsolete slowly...quickly .58
Core production processes change slowly...rapidly .57
New products are introduced infrequently...frequently .59
Item-to-total correlation
Supply Chain Collaboration: α=.89; $\bar{x}$=3.58; SD=1.76. Ratings on the use of coordination mechanisms with supply chain partners;
7-point scales with endpoints of "rarely" and "often."
Development of joint forecasts with supply chain partners .76
Work with downstream partners to compare actual versus forecasted sales values for proactive action .83
Managing customers' inventory using traditional min/max/EOQ or advanced replenishment models .68
Exchange point of sales information to drive replenishment and billing activities from actual sales data .75

Notes:

- Item-to-total correlations (correlations of each item with the remainder of the items in the sub-scale) are presented in the right column after individual items.
- Cronbach's α or α, is the internal consistency reliability of the scale.
- $\bar{x}$ is the average of the scale item means.
- SD is the mean of scale item standard deviations.

tivities with key partners in areas such as cross-firm forecasting, working on appropriate responses to sales/forecast data, and exchanging point of sales data. The scale was refined prior to data collection, based on inputs from industry experts. Seven-point scales with endpoints of "rarely used" and "often used" were utilized.

The scales for the environmental uncertainty moderators were adapted from established measures. Refinements were made based on conceptual definitions and industry feedback to ensure adequate psychometric properties. Technological turbulence and demand unpredictability measures were adapted from the works of Celly and Frazier (1996), and Miller and Dröge (1986). The variables were measured using four and three items respectively, rating their primary industry on 7-point semantic differential scales. Table 2 summarizes the scales used in the survey.

A principal component analysis was conducted on the variables to establish convergent and discriminant validity of the scales. Using the Eigen value greater than one criterion, the analysis showed five factors: B2B E-commerce, IT analytic capability, supply chain collaboration, technological turbulence, and demand unpredictability. The items loaded strongly (> 0.50) on their respective factors demonstrating convergent validity. Discriminant validity was established with scale items loading strongly on associated factors in comparison to loadings on other factors (Hair et al., 1998). Construct reliability was assessed by using Cronbach's α. As reported in Table 2, the internal consistency measure ranged from 0.74 to 0.89, suggesting adequate reliability for all the measures.

Results

To test for the hypothesized relationships, a stepwise multiple linear regression model was used. The results from the regression analysis are presented in Table 3. Variable means were used for testing the main effects and mean centering was undertaken to create the interaction effects.

Table 3. Regression analysis results

Dependent variable
Standardized estimate (t-value)
Independent variables Supply Chain Collaboration
Independent variables
B2B E-Commerce .470 (6.106a)
IT Analytic capability .166 (2.165b)
B2B E-Commerce x Technological turbulence .042 (0.639)
B2B E-Commerce x Demand Unpredictability -.341 (-4.083a)
IT Analytic capability x Technological turbulence .110 (1.619)
IT Analytic capability x Demand Unpredictability .206 (2.476b)
Overall model
R-square .386
Model F 22.593a
Variables were mean-centered before creating the interaction terms.

a, $p<.01$; b, $p<.05$

Stepwise regression analysis ensures that only those independent variables and interaction terms that significantly affect the dependent variable will be present in the final model. The dependent variable was supply chain collaboration, and the predictor variables were modeled to include B2B e-commerce, IT analytic capability and their interaction terms with each of environmental uncertainty context variables: technological turbulence and demand unpredictability. Multicollinearity was assessed by examining variance inflation factor scores. The largest score was 1.63, well under the acceptable upper bound of 10. The R-square value for the regression model is significant (F=22.593; $p < .01$) and explains 38.6% of the variance in supply chain collaboration.

Hypotheses one and two relating to the main effects stated that B2B e-commerce and IT analytic capability would associate positively with supply chain collaboration. Based on the regression results, both H1 (β=.470; t= 6.106; $p<.01$) and H2 (β=.166; t= 2.165; $p<.05$) are supported. Therefore, the greater the level of B2B e-commerce, the better the supply chain collaboration. Similarly, the greater the IT analytic capability, the higher the collaboration. Of the two interaction effects of demand unpredictability – B2B-ecommerce (β=-.341; t= - 4.083; $p<.01$) and IT analytic capability (β=.206; t= 2.476; $p<.05$), both are significant supporting H3a and H4a. With greater demand unpredictability, the effect of B2B e-commerce on supply chain collaboration is weakened. On the other hand, the greater the demand unpredictability, the better the positive association of IT analytic capability with supply chain collaboration. Hypotheses 3b and 4b stated that B2B e-commerce x technological turbulence, and IT analytic capability x technological turbulence, would associate negatively and positively, respectively, with collaboration. However, both H3b (β=.042; t=.639) and H4b (β=.110; t=1.619) were not supported. Evidently the strength of the relationships of both B2B e-commerce and IT analytic capability with supply chain collaboration are independent of technological turbulence.

DISCUSSION AND IMPLICATIONS

Recent literature has come around to view close collaboration among supply chain partners as the new frontier of competitive advantage. The quality of interactive exchanges and collaborative information sharing emanating from integrated cross-firm processes are touted as contributors to enhanced performance (Rosenzweig, 2009). Given the complexity of operations in integrated supply chain processes, however, accuracy and speed of information sharing and decision-making become paramount. While anecdotal evidence and previous literature have recognized advanced IT capabilities as facilitators of cross-firm collaboration and process integration, the current study advances theoretical development and provides managerial insights into the nature of IT-collaboration relationships. Employing a diverse sample set of manufacturing firms, the study proposed and tested a model of relationships using two critical supply chain IT applications

(B2B e-commerce and IT analytic capability), supply chain collaboration, and two environmental uncertainty factors: demand unpredictability and technological turbulence. The received wisdom in IT-enabled collaboration argues for disaggregating information technology capabilities to enable investigation of any differential impact of various components and capabilities. It is possible that certain information systems have better compatibility with collaborative operations and eventually generate higher returns. The current research, by investigating two specific classes of advanced IT capabilities, i.e., B2B e-commerce and IT analytic capability, contributes towards a comprehensive framework and greater theoretical development of IT-collaboration relationships.

Important findings emerge from the study carrying key theoretical and practical implications. First, much of extant literature has advocated a prescriptive facilitating role of mostly aggregated IT systems in supply chain collaboration. Thus, a fundamental contribution of the research is the empirical investigation of the facilitating role of two critical specific classes of IT capabilities in supply chain collaboration. Both B2B e-commerce and IT analytic capability are shown to have a direct impact on supply chain collaboration. The results underscore the significant impact the two IT capabilities have in collaborative strategies of supply chain partners, while extending the existing knowledge-base by investigating disaggregated specific classes of information technology. Each class of information technology brings in a bundle of specific capabilities. Extensive connectivity and rapid information sharing for B2B e-commerce, and rapid decision capabilities in various supply chain functional areas including warehouse activities and procurement, for example, characterizing IT analytic capability, enable collaboration among partners in unique ways. The research findings also contribute to the unraveling of the so called productivity paradox in extant information systems literature. The inconsistent main effects of information technologies on performance measures characterizing the IT-productivity paradox in previous studies can be explained by the current findings. The findings support collaboration as an intervening mediating mechanism where the first order impact of information technology occurs. For managers in supply chain partnerships, the findings highlight the importance of developing and leveraging various specific IT capabilities with unique functionalities, to enhance collaborative activities. Supply chain managers should realize that beyond just investing in IT resources, partner firms should move towards building specific collaboration-enhancing IT capabilities. This is particularly important since firms may wrongly presume performance gains from just having various information technology applications in place. These IT resources need to be embedded in processes for developing higher-order capabilities in collaborative supply chains to maximize end-customer value. Deployment of B2B e-commerce, a class of advanced IT with capabilities of generating high visibility and rapid sharing of vast data, and advanced analytic decision-support tools such as advanced planning and scheduling systems or warehouse management systems, should thus be the focus of firms to enable collaborative endeavors.

Extant literature, as Davis-Sramek et al. (2010) point out, has "...paid little attention to multiple ITs and how they may dissimilarly interact with environment" (p. 51) in generating payoffs from collaborative strategies. In fact, extant research has struggled with unraveling a clear facilitating role of information technology in strategies to ultimately realize enhanced performance. Various theoretical frameworks including the contingency 'fit' perspective have been explored recently to provide a richer explanation of what has come to be called in information systems literature as the 'IT-productivity' paradox. However, despite the acknowledged serious implications of ignoring the interactive influence of context factors on strategic IT capabilities, there is lack of research on the idiosyncratic role of demand uncertainty and technological turbulence. Thus, another contribution of this paper emanates from investigating the role of these critical environmental uncertainty variables. The study utilized the interactive contingency fit concept as it applies to supply chain strategy and information technology. Given the widespread use of various classes of information systems in integrating supply chains, the current research enriches literature by providing a better understanding on the nature of relationships specific information systems have with collaboration in conditions of uncertainty.

Results provide evidence that the IT-collaboration relationship is more complex than previously understood. Demand unpredictability, while adding to the potency of IT analytic capability in enabling cross-firm collaboration, detracts from the facilitating role of B2B e-commerce. This finding is in line with the strategic 'fit' model as it applies to information systems and supply chain strategy disciplines. The 'fit' model essentially suggests that in stable predictable environmental contexts, efficiency strategies are appropriate. Conversely, in unpredictable contexts, responsive strategies (and therefore capabilities) are a better fit (Fisher, 1997; Venkatraman, 1989). Sharing among partners of straight-forward transactional information such as invoices and shipment or order status, which are of repetitive nature, is well suited for B2B e-commerce under routine and predictable demand conditions. Thus, B2B e-commerce with its ability to share large volumes of routine data, and to provide real-time visibility among partners, is efficient in facilitating collaborative activities when market demand is stable. On the other hand, high market uncertainty conditions favor rapid response capabilities due to custom product specifications, complex semi-structured information sharing, and non-repetitive nature of operations. Therefore, IT analytic capability is more effective under chaotic market conditions. The findings, however, do not support similar interactive 'fit' relationships for technological turbulence. The relationships of B2B e-commerce and IT analytic capability with collaboration are independent of technological turbulence. The two IT capabilities are universal, equally effective in facilitating cross-firm collaboration in conditions where process and product technologies change rapidly as well as conditions where technologies are much more stable. In sum, the study lends credence to the notion that building various information technology capabilities to enhance collaboration, to ultimately realize higher rent payoffs is, in part, contingent upon environmental uncertainty factors.

Managers should understand that there will be differential payoffs from investing in and deploying various classes of information systems as they consider uncertainties in the operating context. Under high demand unpredictability conditions, deploying B2B e-commerce may produce disappointing results in its ability to generate cross-firm integration, while at the same time IT analytic capability is much more effective. Thus, this research offers a basic framework to managers, enunciating the contingencies under which one class of information technology can be more appropriate relative to the other in enabling collaboration. Nevertheless, it is critical for managers to understand that any scaling back on the use of B2B e-commerce in highly unpredictable or fragmented market conditions may be counterproductive because of time-compression diseconomies (Barney, 1991). Considering the positive direct impact on collaboration, the interplay of this specific information capability with other complementary information capabilities has to be evaluated. Managers should leverage the "efficiency" capability in B2B e-commerce and the "responsive" capability in IT analytic capability or other classes of IT to strategically 'fit' various uncertainty levels so as to enhance supply chain collaboration.

LIMITATIONS AND FUTURE RESEARCH

As with any empirical study, the current research has its limitations, which can open up opportunities for future work. An obvious methodological limitation is the cross-sectional nature of the research design that restricts the predictive ability of the findings over time. The limitation could be addressed through rigorous longitudinal studies. Second, the study captures the perceptions of IT and supply chain collaboration from a single firm's (manufacturer) standpoint, which can differ from upstream or downstream partners' views. Such single informant surveys that measure both predictor and criterion variables using the same respondent are susceptible to common method variance. Despite the robustness of the survey design, and the fact that Harman's single factor test using principal component analysis did not reveal any single factor accounting for more than 50% of variance in the data, future researchers can draw data from multiple respondents across the partnership to eliminate any common method bias concerns. Additionally, though the sample size and response rates are in line with current survey research, concerns about adequate representativeness of the sample remain.

Though the research has contributed to literature by extending previous models, internal collaboration, and the dynamics of its relationship with interfirm collaboration needs to be studied to understand the holistic impact various classes of information technologies may have on overall supply chain integration strategies. Future research also needs to incorporate intermediate performance measures such as operational efficiencies and overall financial and market performance measures to fully capture the causal linkages from IT capabilities. Such research endeavors will further clarify the 'mystery' surrounding the IT-productivity paradox.

The current research investigated two classes of information technologies – B2B e-commerce and IT analytic capability, and two environmental uncertainty contingency variables – demand unpredictability and technological turbulence. Despite the richer insights provided by the findings, much work remains to be done in understanding how various advanced information technologies with different functionalities interact with a range of critical contextual contingency factors to impact collaboration and ultimately drive supply chain performance. Future research can investigate various categories of IT capabilities provided in literature (Barki et al., 1993; Kendall, 1997) using frameworks such as Fine's (1998) clockspeed or Fisher's (1997) functional versus innovative supply chains, to better understand the "fit' between supply chain strategy, IT capabilities and environmental contingencies.

CONCLUSION

Investments in advanced IT capabilities are critical decisions for companies, particularly those involved in forging close collaborative relationships with key supply chain partners. Firms increasingly incur large capital outlays in deploying various IT functionalities as it is widely viewed that sophisticated IT capabilities enable close collaboration among supply chain partners to ultimately realize large performance gains. Extant literature has studied the relationship between information technology, collaboration and various performance outcomes, to a good measure. Nevertheless, there is inadequate investigation of specific IT capabilities at the disaggregate level, and any differential impact they may have on collaboration and performance.

The study examined a model of relationships of B2B e-commerce and IT analytic capability with supply chain collaboration. As results show, both the advanced IT capabilities directly associate with collaboration. The findings from the study underscore the importance for firms to invest in various advanced IT functionalities that could promote cross-firm collaboration. The findings of the study support the contingency theory 'fit' notion that provides a framework for understanding the nature of the IT-collaboration relationships. The study provides evidence on the importance of going beyond direct relationships and examining the fit among collaboration strategy, IT capability, and environmental context. Results suggest that stable market conditions favor efficient information capabilities such as B2B e-commerce for enabling interfirm collaboration. On the other hand, chaotic and unpredictable demand conditions favor responsive or flexible IT functionalities as embedded in IT analytic capability. The study findings suggest examining information technology impact on collaboration by modeling disentangled IT functionalities and various environmental variables for a richer understanding of the nature of the relationships.

REFERENCES

Anderson, D. L., & Lee, H. L. (2000). The Internet-enabled Supply Chain: From the 'First Click' to the 'Last Mile. In Anderson, D. L. (Ed.), *Advancing Supply Chain Excellence through Technology* (*Vol. 2*, pp. 15–20). San Francisco, CA: Montgomery Research.

Anthony, T. (2000). Supply Chain Collaboration: Success in the New Internet Economy. In Anderson, D. L. (Ed.), *Advancing Supply Chain Excellence through Technology* (*Vol. 2*, pp. 41–44). San Francisco, CA: Montgomery Research.

Armstrong, S. J., & Overton, T. S. (1977). Estimating Nonresponse Bias in Mail Surveys. *JMR, Journal of Marketing Research*, *14*(3), 396–402. doi:10.2307/3150783

Autry, C. W., Grawe, S. J., Daugherty, P. J., & Richey, R. G. (2010). The Effects of Technological Turbulence and Breadth on Supply Chain Technology Acceptance and Adoption. *Journal of Operations Management*, *28*(6), 522–536. doi:10.1016/j.jom.2010.03.001

Banker, R. D., Bardhan, I., & Asdemir, O. (2006). Understanding the Impact of Collaboration Software on Product Design and Development. *Information Systems Research*, *17*(4), 352–373. doi:10.1287/isre.1060.0104

Barki, H., Rivard, S., & Talbot, J. (1993). A Keyword Classification Scheme For IS Research Literature: An Update. *Management Information Systems Quarterly*, *17*(1), 209–226. doi:10.2307/249802

Barney, J. B. (1991). Firm Resources and Sustained Competitive Advantage. *Journal of Management*, *17*(1), 99–120. doi:10.1177/014920639101700108

Bowersox, D. J., Closs, D. J., & Cooper, M. B. (2010). *Supply Chain Logistics Management*. New York, NY: McGraw Hill/Irwin.

Bowersox, D. J., Closs, D. J., & Stank, T. P. (1999). *21st Century Logistics: Making Supply Chain Integration a Reality*. Oak Brook, IL: Council of Logistics Management.

Cannon, J. P., & Perreault, W. D. Jr. (1999). Buyer-seller Relationships in Business Markets. *JMR, Journal of Marketing Research*, *36*(4), 439–460. doi:10.2307/3151999

Celly, K. S., & Frazier, G. (1996). Outcome-based and Behavior-based Coordination Efforts in Channel Relationships. *JMR, Journal of Marketing Research*, *33*(2), 200–210. doi:10.2307/3152147

Chakravarthy, B. (1997). A New Strategy Framework for Coping with Turbulence. *Sloan Management Review*, *38*(2), 69–82.

Chopra, S., & Meindl, P. (2004). *Supply Chain Management: Strategy, Planning, and Operation*. Upper Saddle River, NJ: Prentice Hall.

Choudhury, V. (1997). Strategic Choices in the Development of Interorganizational Information Systems. *Information Systems Research*, *8*(1), 1–24. doi:10.1287/isre.8.1.1

Choudhury, V., Hartzel, K., & Konsynski, B. (1998). Uses and Consequences of Electronic Markets: An Empirical Investigation in the Aircraft Parts Industry. *Management Information Systems Quarterly*, *22*(4), 471–507. doi:10.2307/249552

Clemons, E., & Row, M. C. (1992). Information Technology and Industrial Cooperation: The changing Economics of Coordination and Ownership. *Journal of Management Information Systems*, *9*(2), 9–28.

Conner, K., & Prahalad, C. K. (1996). A Resource-based Theory of the Firm: Knowledge Versus Opportunism. *Organization Science*, *7*(5), 477–501. doi:10.1287/orsc.7.5.477

Croom, S. R. (2000). The Impact of Web-based Procurement on the Management of Operating Resources Supply. *Journal of Supply Chain Management*, *36*, 4–13. doi:10.1111/j.1745-493X.2000.tb00065.x

Damanpour, F. (1991). Organizational Innovation: A Meta-Analysis of Effects of Determinants and Moderators. *Academy of Management Journal*, *34*(3), 555–590. doi:10.2307/256406

Daugherty, P. J., Myers, M. B., & Autry, C. W. (1999). Automatic Replenishment Programs: An Empirical Examination. *Journal of Business Logistics*, *20*, 63–82.

Davis-Sramek, B., Germain, R., & Iyer, K. (2010). Supply Chain Technology: The Role of Environment in Predicting Performance. *Journal of the Academy of Marketing Science*, *38*(1), 42–55. doi:10.1007/s11747-009-0137-1

Devaraj, S., Krajewski, L., & Wei, J. C. (2007). Impact of E-business Technologies on Operational Performance: The Role of Production Information Integration in the Supply Chain. *Journal of Operations Management*, *25*(6), 1199–1216. doi:10.1016/j.jom.2007.01.002

Dyer, J. H., & Singh, H. (1998). The Relational View: Cooperative Strategy and Sources of Interorganizational Competitive Advantage. *Academy of Management Review*, *23*(4), 660–679. doi:10.2307/259056

Fine, C. H. (1998). *Clockspeed: Winning Industry Control in the Age of Temporary Advantage*. New York, NY: Harper Collins.

Fisher, M. L. (1997). What is the Right Supply Chain for your Product? *Harvard Business Review*, *75*(2), 105–116.

Frohlich, M. T., & Westbrook, R. (2001). Arcs of Integration: An International Study of Supply Chain Strategies. *Journal of Operations Management*, *19*(2), 185–200. doi:10.1016/S0272-6963(00)00055-3

Frohlich, M. T., & Westbrook, R. (2002). Demand Chain Management in Manufacturing and Services: Web-based integration, Drivers and Performance. *Journal of Operations Management*, *20*, 729–745. doi:10.1016/S0272-6963(02)00037-2

Gatignon, H., & Robertson, S. T. (1989). Technology Diffusion: An Empirical Test of Competitive Effects. *Journal of Marketing*, *53*(1), 35–49. doi:10.2307/1251523

Germain, R., & Iyer, K. (2006). The Interaction of Internal and Downstream Integration and its Association with Performance. *Journal of Business Logistics*, *27*(2), 29–52.

Grewal, R., & Tansuhaj, P. (2001). Building Organizational Capabilities for Managing Economic Crisis: The Role of Market Orientation and Strategic Flexibility. *Journal of Marketing*, *65*(2), 67–80. doi:10.1509/jmkg.65.2.67.18259

Hair, J. F., Anderson, R., Tatham, R. L., & Black, W. C. (1998). *Multivariate Data Analysis*. Upper Saddle River, NJ: Prentice Hall.

Heim, G. R., & Peng, D. X. (2010). The Impact of Information Technology Use on Plant Structure, Practices, and Performance: An Exploratory Study. *Journal of Operations Management*, *28*, 144–162. doi:10.1016/j.jom.2009.09.005

Iyer, K. (2011). Demand Chain Collaboration and Operational Performance: Role of IT Analytic Capability and Environmental Uncertainty. *Journal of Business and Industrial Marketing*, *26*(2), 81–91. doi:10.1108/08858621111112267

Iyer, K., Germain, R., & Claycomb, C. A. (2009). B2B E-Commerce Supply Chain Integration and Performance: A Contingency Fit Perspective on the Role of Environment. *Information & Management*, *46*(6), 313–322. doi:10.1016/j.im.2009.06.002

Iyer, K., Germain, R., & Frankwick, G. L. (2004). Supply Chain B2B E-Commerce and Time-based Delivery Performance. *International Journal of Physical Distribution & Logistics Management*, *34*(8), 645–661. doi:10.1108/09600030410557776

Iyer, K., Germain, R., & Frankwick, G. L. (2007). Supply Chain Analytic Capability: Environment and Performance. *International Journal of Integrated Supply Management*, *3*(3), 302–320. doi:10.1504/IJISM.2007.012632

Kandemir, D., Yaprak, A., & Cavusgil, S. T. (2006). Alliance Orientation: Conceptualization, Measurement, and Impact on Market Performance. *Journal of the Academy of Marketing Science*, *34*(3), 324–340. doi:10.1177/0092070305285953

Ke, W., Liu, H., Wei, K. K., Gu, J., & Chen, H. (2009). How Do Mediated and Non-mediated Power Affect Electronic Supply Chain Management System Adoption? The Mediating Effects of Trust and Institutional Pressures. *Decision Support Systems*, *46*, 839–851. doi:10.1016/j.dss.2008.11.008

Kendall, K. E. (1997). The Significance of Information Systems Research on Emerging Technologies: Seven Information Technologies that Promise to Improve Managerial Effectiveness. *Decision Sciences*, *28*(4), 775–792. doi:10.1111/j.1540-5915.1997.tb01331.x

Kent, J. L., & Mentzer, J. T. (2003). The Effect of Investment in Interorganizational Information Technology in a Retail Supply Chain. *Journal of Business Logistics*, *24*(2), 155–176.

Kim, S. M., & Mahoney, J. T. (2006). Mutual Commitment to Support Exchange: Relation-Specific IT System as a Substitute for Managerial Hierarchy. *Strategic Management Journal*, *27*, 401–423. doi:10.1002/smj.527

Kohli, A. K., & Jaworski, B. J. (1990). Market Orientation: The Construct, Research Propositions, and Managerial Implications. *Journal of Marketing*, *54*(2), 1–18. doi:10.2307/1251866

Konsynski, B., & Tiwana, A. (2004). The Improvisation-Efficiency Paradox in Inter-Firm Electronic Networks: Governance and Architecture Considerations. *Journal of Information Technology*, *19*, 234–243. doi:10.1057/palgrave.jit.2000029

Lambert, D. M., Cooper, M. B., & Pagh, J. D. (1998). Supply Chain Management: Implementation Issues and Research Opportunities. *International Journal of Logistics Management*, *9*(2), 1–19. doi:10.1108/09574099810805807

Lee, H. L., Padmanabhan, V., & Whang, S. (1997). Information Distortion in a Supply Chain: The Bullwhip Effect. *Management Science*, *43*, 546–558. doi:10.1287/mnsc.43.4.546

Lee, H. L., So, K., & Tang, C. (2000). The Value of Information Sharing in a Two-Level Supply Chain. *Management Science*, *46*(5), 626–643. doi:10.1287/mnsc.46.5.626.12047

Lummus, R. R., Vokurka, R. J., & Alber, K. L. (1998). Strategic Supply Chain Planning. *Production and Inventory Management Journal*, *39*(3), 49–58.

Melville, N., Kraemer, K., & Gurbaxani, V. (2004). Review: Information Technology and Organizational Performance: An Integrative Model of IT Business Value. *Management Information Systems Quarterly*, *28*(2), 283–322.

Miller, D., & Dröge, C. (1986). Psychological and traditional determinants of structure. *Administrative Science Quarterly*, *31*(4), 539–560. doi:10.2307/2392963

Min, H. (2009). Application of a Decision Support System to Strategic Warehousing decisions. *International Journal of Physical Distribution & Logistics Management*, *39*(4), 270–281. doi:10.1108/09600030910962230

Mukhopadhyay, T., & Kekre, S. (2002). Strategic and Operational Benefits of Electronic Integration in B2B Procurement Processes. *Management Science*, *48*(10), 1301–1313. doi:10.1287/mnsc.48.10.1301.273

Nooteboom, B. (1992). Information Technology, Transaction Costs and the Decision to 'Make or Buy'. *Technology Analysis and Strategic Management*, *4*(4), 339–350. doi:10.1080/09537329208524105

Norman, D. (2004). Supply Chain Analytics Can Drive Financial Performance. *Frontline Solutions*, *5*(1), 25–25.

Premkumar, G., Ramamurthy, K., & Saunders, C. S. (2005). Information Processing View of Organizations: An Exploratory Examination of Fit in the Context of Interorganizational Relationships. *Journal of Management Information Systems*, *22*(1), 257–294.

Rai, A., Patnayakuni, R., & Seth, N. (2006). Firm Performance Impacts of Digitally Enabled Supply Chain Integration Capabilities. *Management Information Systems Quarterly*, *30*(2), 225–246.

Rosenzweig, E. D. (2009). A Contingent View of E-collaboration and Performance in Manufacturing. *Journal of Operations Management*, *27*, 462–478. doi:10.1016/j.jom.2009.03.001

Saeed, K. A., Malhotra, M. K., & Grover, V. (2005). Examining the Impact of Interorganizational Systems on Process Efficiency and Sourcing Leverage in Buyer—Supplier Dyads. *Decision Sciences*, *36*(3), 365–396. doi:10.1111/j.1540-5414.2005.00077.x

Sambamurthy, V., Bharadwaj, A., & Grover, V. (2003). Shaping Agility Through Digital Options: Reconceptualizing the role of Information Technology in Contemporary Firms. *Management Information Systems Quarterly*, *27*(2), 237–263.

Sanders, N. R. (2007). An Empirical Study of the Impact of E-Business Technologies on Organizational Collaboration and Performance. *Journal of Operations Management*, *25*, 1332–1347. doi:10.1016/j.jom.2007.01.008

Shin, N. (2006). The Impact of Information Technology on the Financial Performance of Diversified Firms. *Decision Support Systems*, *41*, 698–707. doi:10.1016/j.dss.2004.10.003

Slater, S. F., & Narver, J. C. (1994). Does Competitive Environment Moderate the Market Orientation-Performance Relationship? *Journal of Marketing*, *58*(1), 46–55. doi:10.2307/1252250

Subramani, M. (2004). How do Suppliers Benefit From Information Technology Use in Supply Chain Relationships? *Management Information Systems Quarterly*, *28*(1), 45–73.

Sundaramurthy, C., & Lewis, M. (2003). Control and Collaboration: Paradoxes of Governance. *Academy of Management Review*, *28*(3), 397–415. doi:10.2307/30040729

Swaminathan, J. M., & Tayur, S. R. (2003). Models for Supply Chains in E-Business. *Management Science*, *49*(10), 1387–1406. doi:10.1287/mnsc.49.10.1387.17309

Tanriverdi, H. (2006). Performance Effects of Information Technology Synergies in Multi-Business Firms. *Management Information Systems Quarterly*, *30*(1), 57–77.

Trkman, P., McCormack, K., De Oliveira, M. P. V., & Ladeira, M. B. (2010). The Impact of Business Analytics on Supply Chain Performance. *Decision Support Systems*, *49*, 318–327. doi:10.1016/j.dss.2010.03.007

Venkatraman, N. (1989). The Concept of Fit in Strategy Research: Toward Verbal and Statistical Correspondence. *Academy of Management Review*, *14*(3), 423–444. doi:10.2307/258177

Vickery, S. K., Jayaram, J., Dröge, C., & Calantone, R. (2003). The Effects of an Integrative Supply Chain Strategy on Customer Service and Financial Performance: an Analysis of Direct Versus Indirect Relationships. *Journal of Operations Management*, *21*(5), 523–539. doi:10.1016/j.jom.2003.02.002

Wang, E. T. G., & Wei, H. (2007). Interorganizational Governance Value Creation: Coordinating for Information Visibility and Flexibility in Supply Chains. *Decision Sciences*, *38*(4), 647–674. doi:10.1111/j.1540-5915.2007.00173.x

This work was previously published in the Information Resources Management Journal, Volume 24, Issue 3, edited by Mehdi Khosrow-Pour, pp. 26-44, copyright 2013 by IGI Publishing (an imprint of IGI Global).

Chapter 14
Integrating OLAP/SOLAP in E-Business Domains:
An Empirical Study

Oualid (Walid) Ben Ali
University of Sharjah, UAE

Samar Mouakket
University of Sharjah, UAE

ABSTRACT

E-business domains have been considered killer domains for different data analysis techniques. Most researchers have examined data mining (DM) techniques to analyze the databases behind E-business websites. DM has shown interesting results, but this technique presents some restrictions concerning the content of the database and the level of expertise of the users interpreting the results. In this paper, the authors show that successful and more sophisticated results can be obtained using other analysis techniques, such as Online Analytical Processing (OLAP) and Spatial OLAP (SOLAP). Thus, the authors propose a framework that fuses or integrates OLAP with SOLAP techniques in an E-business domain to perform easier and more user-friendly data analysis (non-spatial and spatial) and improve decision making. In addition, the authors apply the framework to an E-business website related to online job seekers in the United Arab Emirates (UAE). The results can be used effectively by decision makers to make crucial decisions in the job market of the UAE.

INTRODUCTION

E-business domains, such as E-commerce, E-government, E-learning, E-banking, are growing fast, and with this growth, companies are willing to spend more money and time to analyze the data behind their websites. Based on our literature review, E-business companies have been using either primitive measures to analyze their data or more sophisticated analysis techniques, such as DM or OnLine Analysis Processing (OLAP), to generate useful data and knowledge for decision

DOI: 10.4018/978-1-4666-3616-3.ch014

makers (Kohavi & Provost, 2001; Kohavi et al., 2004). DM and OLAP techniques have shown interesting results, but they present some restrictions concerning the size, the structure, and the type of the data to be analyzed, as well as the level of expertise of end-users who will be interpreting the results. With growing pressure to make E-business companies more profitable, additional analysis techniques are required to analyze the data which are becoming more and more complex.

Current studies have examined the effect of what is called Business Intelligence (BI), which is a combination of data analysis techniques such as DM with OLAP, to analyze fused data coming from different sources. Some researchers have used only textual and numerical data (Codd et al., 1993; Youngworth, 1995; Lau et al., 2008; Zhou et al., 2009) and ignored the geographical features of the data which are presented through text and numbers. In these studies, the analysis lacks visualization or mapping of the analysis results. Other researchers have conducted data analysis based on spatial (geographical) data only, which results in limited and incomplete data analysis (Kouba et al., 2000; Stefanovic et al., 2000; Ferreira et al., 2001; Shekhar et al., 2001; Fidalgo et al., 2004; Bédard et al., 2005; Scotch & Parmanto, 2005; Silva et al., 2005).

Although one cannot deny the importance of previous studies, limited research has considered integrating multiple data analysis techniques to improve the process of decision making and provide comprehensive, easier and friendlier data analysis in an E-business domain. Decision makers, in this rapidly changing world, are demanding faster and more detailed results. To address this issue, more research is needed in investigating the infusion of GIS (Geographic Information System), spatial analysis and non-spatial analysis applications and tools in business. Thus, our research addresses the following question: how can applying different useful analysis techniques to analyze fused and complex data coming from different sources and using different formats (spatial and non-spatial) benefit decision makers? In other words, will the integration of multiple data analysis techniques be more useful and more appropriate in the decision-making process?

In our research, we examine how the infusion of different analysis techniques may be applied in order to help decision makers make better decisions. Thus, we suggest the integration of the following well-known data analysis techniques: OLAP and SOLAP (Spatial OLAP) (for spatial data) in order to analyze fused data coming from E-business websites (non-spatial data) and GIS (spatial/geographical data). First, we have developed a framework which integrates the OLAP and SOLAP analytical techniques to analyze fused data coming from different sources (E-business databases and GIS) to perform comprehensive, easier, and more advanced and sophisticated analyses of E-business websites' databases. Then, we have tested this framework using actual data from an E-business website related to online job seekers in the UAE. Our study provides more comprehensive data analysis of numerical, textual, and spatial data, which can help the decision makers to make better decisions. Based on our review of literature, no similar framework has been proposed, which makes our framework unique and can be considered as a contribution to the fields of E-business, data analysis, and BI.

The remaining sections of the paper are divided as follows. In the next section, we present our review of the literature concerning E-business, DM, OLAP and SOLAP techniques, and BI. We also present in detail our conceptual framework and its components, and then, apply our proposed framework to an E-business website related to online job seekers in the UAE, analyze the data, and interpret the results. In the following section, we present the discussion and the practical implications of our study. In the final section, we present the contributions of our work and suggestions for future research.

LITERATURE REVIEW

Before presenting our proposed framework, we review the literature for the following concepts which we have used in our framework: E-business, DM, OLAP, SOLAP, and BI.

E-Business

E-business is a broader definition of E-commerce that includes not just the buying and selling of goods and services, but also providing services to customers, collaborating with business partners, and conducting electronic transactions within an organization (Phan, 2003; Mokhtarian, 2004). In general, E-business has changed the face of most business functions in competitive enterprises. It has enabled online transactions, and facilitated the generation of large-scale real-time data. The development of online transactions may reflect the compelling advantages of Internet business. The significant benefits to consumers of doing business on the Internet include the vast array of alternative products/services available and quicker access to alternatives. Along with benefits such as a vehicle for purchasing/using, the Internet offers consumers a powerful means of searching out product/services information before doing business (Su et al., 2009).

Data Mining (DM)

By its nature, the Internet can provide rich and interactive information and can increase business efficiency by improving the availability of product/services information, enabling direct, multi-attribute comparisons, and reducing information-search costs (Alba et al., 1997). With data pertaining to various aspects of business transactions being readily available, many studies have applied different analytical tools, such as DM to make sense of the data sets (Agrawal et al., 1993; Kohavi, 2001). Kohavi and Provost (2001) present a survey of some of the recent approaches and architectures where DM has been applied in one domain of the E-business field which is E-commerce. They discuss the importance of integrating DM in business processes. Their study explains how DM is applied to improve the services provided by E-commerce based enterprises, by arguing that it is important to enable the use of data mining in business processes through automated solutions.

Kohavi and Perkh (2003) list ten supplementary analyses that E-business web sites should review after running the common reports provided by most web analytics tools. The recommended analysis is based on the researchers' experience in mining data from different retail E-commerce websites. They have found that while some analyses require architectural support to collect the right data, the effort required is moderate in most cases and should result in a significant return-on-investment (ROI). They suggest that some analyses, such as customer migration, can benefit directly from a wide customer signature, and many analyses may lead to insight that can be investigated through the use of customer signature.

OLAP AND SOLAP ANALYSIS TECHNIQUES

OLAP

OLAP has been defined as the dynamic enterprise analysis required to create, manipulate, animate and synthesize information from exegetical, contemplative and formulaic data analysis models (Lo et al., 2008). OLAP provides multidimensional and summarized views of business data, which can be used for reporting, analysis, modeling and planning to improve decision making (Ranjan, 2009). This includes the ability to recognize new or unanticipated relationships between variables, the ability to identify the parameters necessary to handle large amounts of data, to create an unlimited number of dimensions, and to specify cross-dimensional conditions and expressions (Codd et al., 1993). Other OLAP definitions have since been proposed, including "A software category intended for the rapid exploration and analysis of data based on multidimensional approach with several aggregation levels" (Bédard et al., 2005).

OLAP is a powerful data analysis technique because it allows users to navigate and explore different levels of summarization by interactively changing the set of dimension attributes and their abstraction levels (Lo et al., 2008). In other words, users can navigate from one part of the structured data (cube) to another interactively in order to obtain the most interesting statistics through a set of pre-defined OLAP operations, such as roll-up, drill down, slice, and dice (Lo et al., 2008).

The multidimensional approach which OLAP uses is based on dimensions and measures. Dimensions represent the analysis attributes (axes), while measures are the numerical attributes being analyzed against the different dimensions (Thomsen, 2002). A set of measures aggregated according to a set of dimensions forms what is often called a data cube or hypercube (Thomsen et al., 1999). Inside a data cube, possible aggregations of measures on all the possible combinations of dimension members can be pre-computed. This greatly increases query performance in comparison to the conventional transaction-oriented data structures found in relational and object-relational database management systems (DBMS).

The literature has shown that the multidimensional approach of analysis is more in agreement with the end user's mental model of the data (Codd et al., 1993; Youngworth, 1995; Lau et al., 2008). Based on this approach, the interface of a tool exploring the multidimensional paradigm, such as OLAP, is usually very intuitive and the user can perform analysis ranging from simple to complex, mostly by clicking on the data being organized, in a meaningful way (Youngworth, 1995). This adds to the fact that the multidimensional data structure is optimized for rapid ad hoc information retrieval, which greatly facilitates the data exploration and analysis process.

SOLAP

In various E-business domains, which involve spatial data such as real state, environmental planning, and precision agriculture, participating business may increase their economic returns using knowledge and data extracted from spatial databases. Analyzing this type of data is often not properly exploited and only few applications called Spatial Data Mining (SDM) have been developed in order to analyze such types of data (Bédard et al., 2005).

Traditional OLAP techniques offer good support for simultaneous usage of descriptive, temporal and spatial dimensions in a multidimensional analysis process. Descriptive dimensions are used to describe the data to be analyzed. The temporal ones take into account the temporal aspect of the analysis, and the spatial dimensions allow for the spatial reference of the phenomena under study. However, using traditional OLAP tools, the spatial dimensions are treated like any other descriptive dimension, without consideration for the spatial part of the data. OLAP tools present serious limitations in support of spatio-temporal analysis (no spatial visualization, practically no spatial analysis, no map-based exploration of data).

Data visualization facilitates the extraction of insight from the complexity of the spatio-temporal phenomena and processes being analyzed and also offers a better understanding of the structure and relationships contained within the dataset. In the context of information exploration, maps and graphics do more than make data visible; they are active instruments in the end user's thinking process (Rivest et al., 2001; Salam et al., 2008). Without a cartographic display, OLAP tools lack an essential feature, which could help spatio-temporal exploration and analysis. SOLAP remedies this limitation because it supports the geometric spatial dimensions that can include geometric shapes spatially referenced on a map.

The SOLAP technique is a new type of software tool which allows supporting the exploration and analysis of spatial data in a very unique way. This type of spatial dimension allows the dimension members to be visualized and queried cartographically (on a digital map). SOLAP tools are considered to be a client application tool, offering new and different ways of user interface which can sit on top of multi-scale spatial data warehouses or data cubes (Rivest et al., 2005). As they are based on the multidimensional paradigm, they facilitate the interactive spatio-temporal exploration of data.

The SOLAP system can be defined as a visual platform built especially to support rapid and easy spatio-temporal analysis and exploration of data following a multidimensional approach, comprised of aggregation levels available in cartographic displays (on digital maps) as well as in tabular and diagram displays (Bédard et al., 2005). The cartographic display of a SOLAP tool allows the user to define clusters, correlations and other spatial relationships which cannot be identified when using only non-spatial OLAP tools (Rivest et al., 2005; Salam et al., 2008). Some studies have discussed the fundamental concepts of SOLAP from its historical perspectives (Rivest et al., 2001; Bédard et al., 2005; Tchounikine et al., 2005) while others provide examples of SOLAP applications (Kouba et al., 2000; Stefanovic et al., 2000; Ferreira et al., 2001; Shekhar et al., 2001; Fidalgo et al., 2004; Bédard et al., 2005; Scotch & Parmanto, 2005; Silva et al., 2005).

Integrating OLAP with SOLAP is geared towards decision support as it has the following features:

- **Easy:** The ease comes from the ability to conduct analysis without having to master a query language or to understand the underlying structure of the database, which may be very complex in the particular case of spatio-temporal databases (Rivest et al., 2001). In fact, the analyst interacts directly with the data and focuses on the results of the analysis rather than on the procedures required by the tool to perform the analysis process (Scotch et al., 2007).
- **Rapid:** It is rapid because data are pre-aggregated, computation time is reduced and it is possible to provide very fast answers to complex queries. This allows the user to maintain his flow of thought; his attention is not being distracted by slow response time (Rivest et al., 2001).
- **Multi-Granular:** Decision-support systems typically require access to aggregated information (the global view) as well as more detailed information, typically following several levels of granularity of information. Such levels of granularity apply to the phenomenon being analyzed as well as its time and space dimensions. Combining the thematic dimensions with the spatial and time dimensions allows one to analyze the evolution of phenomenon, to discover trends, to unveil correlations.

Business Intelligence (BI)

BI is the result of a series of improvements in data analysis over the years. Its early applications can be seen in, for example, in the early decision-support systems (Alter, 1980), executive information systems (Watson et al., 1992), the data warehouse (Inmon, 1992), OLAP (Codd et al., 1993), and DM (Fayyad et al., 1996), SOLAP. Today, BI brings many of these parts together in one single system (Figure 1).

BI, which is fully dependent upon OLAP cubes, is a popular concept in the software industry today.

Figure 1. The components of business intelligence

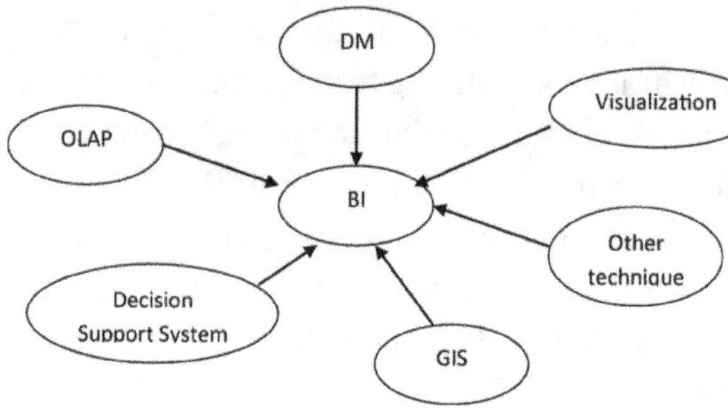

BI is a set of tools used for multidimensional data analysis, which aims to help decision makers obtain a better comprehensive knowledge of their organization's operations, and thereby improve business decisions (Mircea & Andreescu, 2009). In other words, it is the process of taking large amounts of data, analyzing that data, and presenting it to enable management to make business decisions (Stackowiak et al., 2007).

Based on the above definitions of BI, we can decompose BI into three parts: collecting data (based on data fusion), analyzing it and reporting it. First, data is collected for a BI application. This is done by building a data warehouse by fusing data coming from multiple heterogeneous data sources. Typical data sources are relational databases, plain text files and spread sheets. Transferring the data from the data sources to the data warehouse is often referred to as the Extract, Transform and Load (ETL) process. The data is extracted from the sources, transformed to fit, and finally the data is loaded into the warehouse. The ETL process often raises issues of data consistency between data sources; the same data having a different structure, or the same data being found in several data sources without coinciding. In order to load it into the data warehouse the data has to be consistent and the process to accomplish this is called data cleansing.

Second, data is analyzed using different tools. One common tool for analyzing the data is the data cube, a multidimensional data structure built upon the data warehouse. The cube is basically used to group data by several dimensions and to select a subset of interest. Data can be analyzed with tools for DM, which is a concept for finding trends and patterns in the data. Finally, reporting is generated in the form of tables and diagrams. Users can access reports by uploading them to a report server, or the user can connect directly to the data source and create ad hoc reports.

RESEARCH METHODOLOGY

In this section, we first introduce our conceptual framework, and then we apply it using fused data coming from an E-business website's database and GIS sources.

The Proposed Conceptual Framework

In the previous section, we showed that OLAP–SOLAP techniques are easy, rapid and multi-granular. These features have attracted us to combine these techniques in an E-business domain, to analyze the hybrid and fused data behind E-business websites and GIS sources. Thus, we propose a conceptual

Figure 2. The proposed conceptual framework

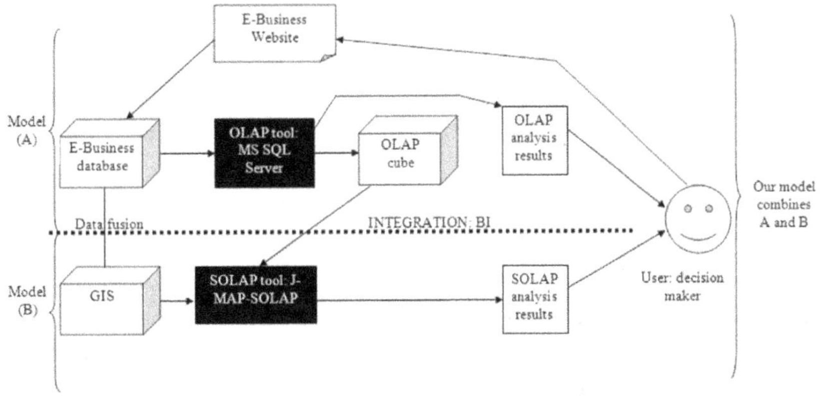

framework in which we combine two well-known techniques (OLAP and SOLAP) to analyze fused data coming from E-business website and GIS sources. This conceptual framework is presented in Figure 2 and is explained in detail.

Our proposed framework combines two different models: A and B (Figure 2). The first model (A) focuses only on analyzing numerical and textual data using OLAP techniques, while the second model (B) focuses only on analyzing spatial/geographical data coming from GIS databases using SOLAP techniques. Most of the data behind E-business websites are comprehensive, textual, numerical and geographical. Thus, both models (A and B) lack capabilities in analyzing such types of comprehensive data. In our research, we proposed combining these two traditional models (A and B) which lead to our conceptual framework to obtain the advantages of both models for more sophisticated and comprehensive data. OLAP stores data in a multidimensional rather than two-dimensional (row-column) format. Most users are more familiar with analyzing data in a two-dimensional setting rather than a multi-dimensional setting. Adding GIS will enable usability issues to occur when additional layers, such as roads and houses, are added to a single view. Combining OLAP and SOLAP techniques would provide organizations with better usability of the data (Matthew et al., 2007).

The components of our framework and the relationships between them are detailed in the following points:

- **The E-Business Website:** this website can be related to any field of the E-business domain: E-commerce, E-government, or E-banking. The website should collect, using some logging applications, some type of data from the users which will be used for further analysis.
- **The E-Business Website Database:** this is the database behind the website database. This database contains the data to be analyzed. This data can be hybrid, which means that it can contain non-spatial data (textual or numerical data) or spatial (geographic data) or both. The analysis results should be used to make important decisions related to the business managed by the website.
- **The GIS:** the spatial data of the E-business website's database can be stored in a GIS which contains the geographic aspect of this spatial data, such as: addresses, street names, regions, countries. GIS can be defined as a spatial analysis system for the organization, storage, transformation, retrieval, analysis, and display of data (Aronoff, 1989), where the location of the data is considered important. Without a cartographic (map-based) user interface to view the spatial data, and without spatial operators to navigate through this type of data, the analysis may be incomplete or may sometimes even lead to the wrong conclusions (Rivest et al., 2005). GIS benefits organizations of all sizes and in almost every industry, therefore, there is a growing interest in and awareness of the economic and strategic value of GIS (Trubint et al., 2006; Murray et al., 2008; Mishra, 2009). In particular, GIS can help decision makers in taking better decisions about location, as more people are beginning to realize that making the correct decision about location is strategic to the success of an organization (Mishra, 2009). Studies have shown how GIS can help in reducing annual operating costs, decreasing travel distance, and improving customer service (Gayialis & Tatsiopoulos, 2004; Murray et al., 2008).
- The non-spatial data of the E-business database are analyzed using an OLAP tool such as the OLAP tool of the SQL-Server. This tool will create an OLAP cube which can be easily browsed by the users and the OLAP analysis results are presented to them.

- The spatial (geographic) data stored in the GIS with the OLAP cube are passed to the SOLAP tool in order to be analyzed and SOLAP analysis results are presented to the users. Spatial analysis lets decision makers analyze patterns, understand relationships and events embedded in geographically referenced data, derive knowledge, and use the knowledge in the decision-making process (O'Sullivan & Unwin, 2002). There are several Internet mapping and web GIS applications that might have been used to support this study, including SAS Web OLAP viewer for Java (SAS), JMap Spatial OLAP v1.0 (K2 Geospatial), and Panorama NovaView GIS (Panorama).
- **The User (Decision-Maker):** The user receives the integrated analysis results from both the OLAP and SOLAP tools in formats which are user-friendly and easy to interpret (tables, graphs, and maps). Examples of decisions made by users include suggesting some enhancements to the form and content of the website, or proposing new business strategies related to the domain of the data. Users can be non-expert since OLAP/SOLAP analysis results are straightforward and can be easily interpreted.

Empirical Study: Job Seekers Website

To show the benefits of our proposed framework, we have used data from a job seekers' website in the UAE. The following steps explain our approach:

Step 1: *Data gathering and fusion.* The first step aims to collect the data behind an E-business job seekers' website within the UAE. In this website, the employers hire consultants and job seekers exchange information. Job seekers from the seven Emirates of the UAE can upload data about themselves, and the employers seek the required employees. The uploaded data contains many attributes such as name, city, nationality, and functional area. This data will be fused with data coming from a GIS which contains the geographical representations of the seven Emirates of the UAE.

Step 2: *OLAP analysis.* To perform an OLAP analysis the data is restructured in a star schema which contains the dimensions and measures (Figure 3). Creating a star schema database is one of the most important steps in creating a data warehouse in order to use OLAP technology to analyze data. The table (person) contains a column for each measure as well as a column for each dimension. Each dimension column has a foreign-key relationship to the related dimension table, and the dimension columns taken together are the key to the fact table (Figure 3).

Using the data collected from the job seekers' website database, we have made some analysis using different dimensions (Figure 3). Figure 4 shows the two-dimensional analysis results of the following dimensions: *city* and *functional areas*. The results presented in Figure 4 show that most job seekers in the Emirate of Ajman are looking for jobs in either the *operations*, *bank office processing* or *data entry* fields. Using OLAP techniques we can combine more than two dimensions in the analysis. Based on this result, the user can make decisions related to job seeking by each Emirate in the UAE.

OLAP analysis is very efficient and can help decision makers make strategic decisions, but it has some limitations. The main limitation of the OLAP technique is that the spatial dimension, namely the city, is just represented by a textual form in the database and it is not possible to store qualitative attributes of the spatial components. The lack of spatial awareness in the OLAP technique means that the location name is the only hint to a geographic or spatial location. So, it is

Figure 3. The data presented in a star schema

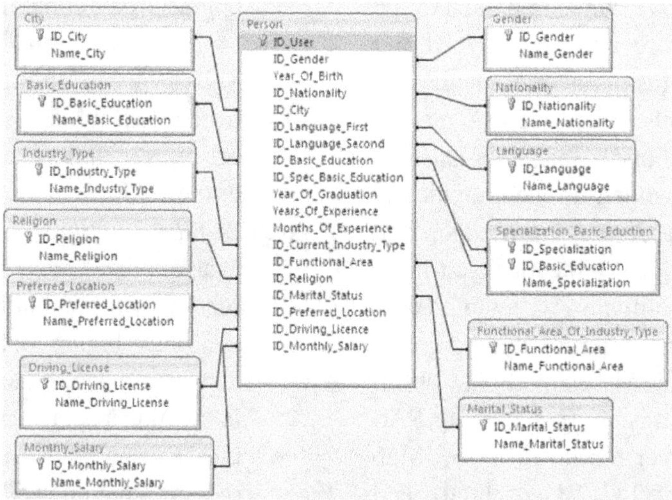

impossible to discover spatial relationships between components of the analysis results. To improve the use of spatial dimensions in decision making, the analysis of multidimensional data should be combined with the visual and analytical capabilities of GIS. The coupling of OLAP and GIS (SOLAP) technology offers better spatial (geographic or cartographic) navigation through the data, for representation in the form of diagrams on maps. In our study, we have coupled OLAP with SOLAP techniques in order to analyze spatial and non-spatial data coming from an E-business website. This coupling, which represents the main contribution of our research, is explained in the next step (step 3).

Step 3: *SOLAP analysis.* Spatial data provide valuable new insight which is invisible and sometimes not even possible to generate using traditional spreadsheets and data processing alone. Our data contains spatial data (city) which can be represented by a geographic element. In our work, we have created a GIS which stores this geographic element, the city. To perform our SOLAP analysis we have used JMap Spatial OLAP developed by a Canadian company called Kheops Technologies, Inc. (http://www.kheops-tech.com/). JMap is a tool that gathers an organization's data and applications on a single platform to improve access to information, making decisions easier. It provides spatial analysis tools and a new level of interactivity and precision for non-technical decision makers. It can be considered a map driven integration platform as well as a Web GIS, allowing easy access to data and systems used by organizations. We have chosen the JMap tool because of the following features:

Figure 4. OLAP analysis results: functional area dimension vs. city dimension

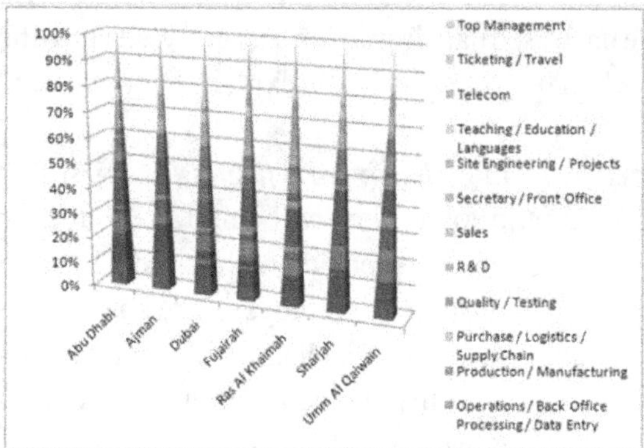

- It aims to support the way humans think and analyze data;
- Its use requires no knowledge of any query language; mouse clicks are used to interact with the data;
- It allows the users to focus on the results of data exploration rather than the analysis process itself (i.e., focus on "what to obtain", rather than "how to obtain it");
- It provides practically instantaneous response times.

To show the benefit of SOLAP over OLAP, we are going to present a SOLAP analysis using the same query which we used for OLAP as presented in Figure 4. In the OLAP query we have used the following two dimensions: functional areas and city. In the SOLAP, since the city dimension (spatial) will be presented using a GIS, we have added another dimension, gender, in order to show the multidimensional benefit of SOLAP. In Figure 5, the user can see in one map that in Abu Dhabi Emirate, most of the people looking for jobs are women, this is also the case for all the other Emirates. Based on this result, the decision makers can adopt some marketing strategies to attract men for particular types of jobs. As you can see in Figure 5, using SOLAP adds more visual advantages when compared with OLAP. Thus, the users can see the whole result on one visual map, zoom in, zoom out, drill down and drill up directly onto the map, etc. This visual flexibility is a remarkable advantage of SOLAP over OLAP technology.

Figure 6 shows the result of a SOLAP analysis using the following two dimensions: *basic education* and *city*. As shown, the user can see the results directly on the map by combining it with other non-spatial dimension presented on charts or diagrams. The user can see from the results that most of the people looking for jobs are Bachelors of Business Administration or Bachelors of Commerce. The results can help the decision makers, for example from the Ministry of Labor, to take actions in creating new job opportunities in the particular Emirates for the people concerned. Also, the government in the UAE can take action by encouraging investors to invest in these fields to create new job opportunities for job seekers in the UAE.

Figure 5. Gender dimension vs. city (GIS) dimension vs. functional area dimension

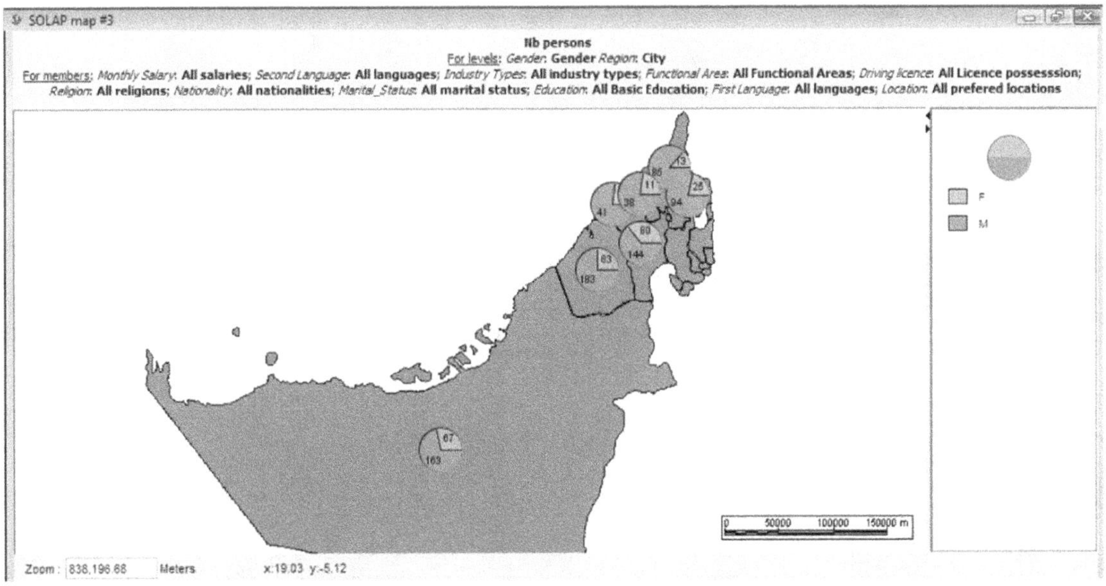

The user can visualize the results in classical visualization modes, such as tables or charts. The same analysis result presented in Figure 6 is presented in tabular form in Figure 7 and as line diagram in Figure 8. This adds more flexibility to the user in terms of result visualization.

DISCUSSION AND PRACTICAL IMPLICATIONS

Several analysis techniques have been used to analyze E-business websites' databases for decision-making purposes. The most famous technique which has been used is DM. This technique has shown its efficiency but it is intended for expert people who can interpret the DM results. In this study, we have proposed combining two data analysis techniques, OLAP and SOLAP, to analyze fused data: non-spatial data coming from an E-business website's database and spatial/geographical data coming from a GIS source. Then, we performed a practical implementation of the proposed conceptual framework using a real E-business website database. As seen from applying our model to an E-business website, a user is able to conduct the analysis without the need to be an expert in a query language or to have knowledge of the structure of the database (Marchand et al., 2004). With a SOLAP tool,

Figure 6. Basic education dimension vs. city (GIS) dimension

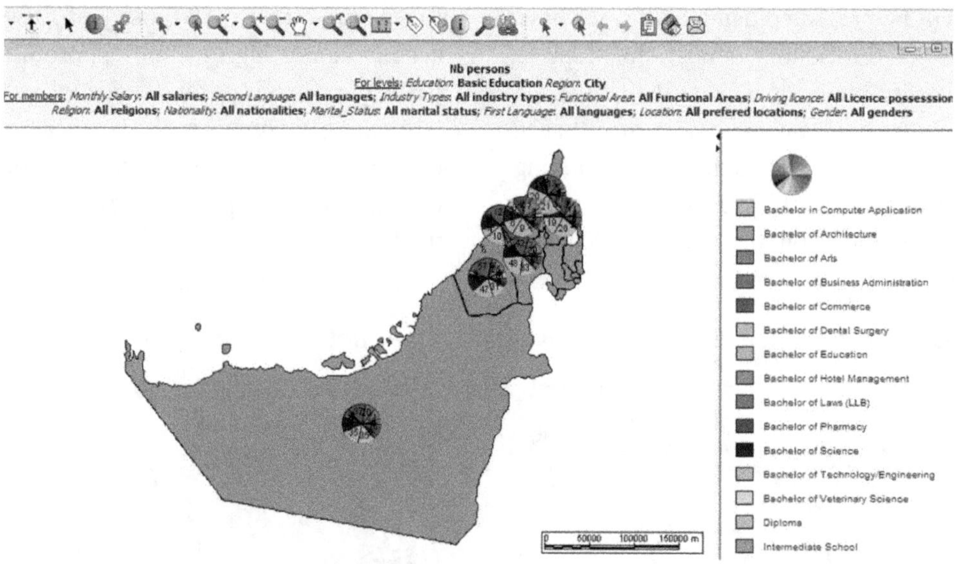

Figure 7. Basic education dimension vs. city (GIS) dimension

Nb persons
For levels: *Education:* **Basic Education** *Region:* **City**
For members: *Monthly Salary:* **All salaries;** *Second Language:* **All languages;** *Industry Types:* **All industry types;** *Functional Area:* **All Functional Areas;** *Driving licence:* **All Licence possesssion;** *Religion:* **All religions;** *Nationality:* **All nationalities;** *Marital_Status:* **All marital status;** *First Language:* **All languages;** *Location:* **All prefered locations;** *Gender:* **All genders**

	Bachelor in ...	Bachelor of ...	Bachelor of ...	Bachelor of ...	Bachelor of ...	Bachelor of ...	Bachelor of ...	Bachelor of ...	Bachelor of ...	Bachelor of ...
Abu Dhabi	6	5	21	20	37	n/a	3	4	8	n/a
Ajman	2	n/a	4	3	12	n/a	n/a	n/a	1	n/a
Dubai	13	5	25	9	57	n/a	5	4	n/a	1
Fujairah	3	3	11	5	13	n/a	5	1	n/a	n/a
Ras Al Khaimah	2	1	4	5	13	n/a	n/a	3	1	n/a
Sharjah	6	1	20	17	42	n/a	4	4	n/a	3
Umm Al Qaiwain	2	2	7	2	4	n/a	3	n/a	n/a	2

Equal range
[1 - 12.2[
[12.2 - 23.4[
[23.4 - 34.6[
[34.6 - 45.8[
[45.8 - 57]

Figure 8. Basic education dimension vs. City (GIS) dimension

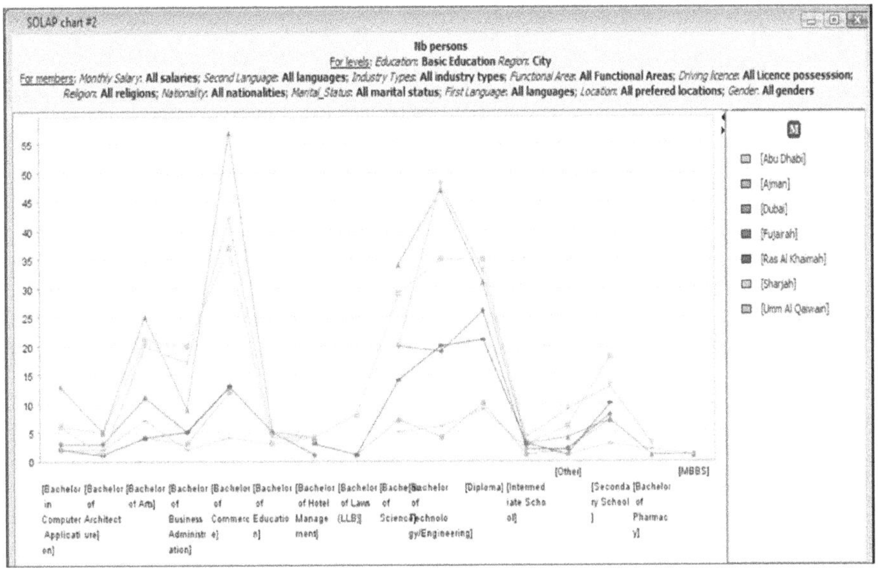

the user can focus on the results of the analysis rather than on the procedures required by the tool to obtain the analysis results. It allows easier and faster navigation within spatial databases. Its multidimensional approach is more user-friendly than the traditional transactional approach typical of GIS (Rivest et al., 2005).

We have applied our framework to data collected from an E-business website for job seekers in the UAE. The data collected is a hybrid as it contains non-spatial data such as demographic information (e.g., gender, age, marital status) and professional information (e.g., education level, work experience), as well as spatial data which refers to each Emirate in the UAE. Also, we have already developed the GIS database of the UAE. This GIS contains only the high level spatial component which is the level of the Emirates in the UAE. We have conducted a SOLAP analysis and connected the GIS with the OLAP in order to perform the SOLAP analysis. The results are very interesting and useful for decision makers since they are presented visually using interactive maps. For example, decision makers in the Ministry of Labor can see the areas of interest to job seekers in the UAE, and decision makers in universities in the UAE can adjust their curricula based on market needs.

CONTRIBUTIONS OF THE RESEARCH

The framework suggested in this study can be considered unique, and thus makes valuable contributions to information systems (IS) research and practice. Our research work has the following contributions. First, it can be considered one of the rare frameworks which integrate OLAP–SOLAP concepts with E-business using hybrid and fused data (spatial and non-spatial) coming from different sources. It is important to mention that OLAP has been integrated in E-business in several previous studies (Figure 2A) (Kohavi & Provost, 2003). SOLAP has also been used alone to analyze geographic data (Figure 2B) (Rivest et al., 2001). But SOLAP has never been used in combination with OLAP in an E-business environment since it is a very recent concept. Thus, our framework has integrated the two different models, which to our knowledge, has not been suggested by any researcher. Second, it is a generic framework and can be applied to any field within E-business domains such as E-commerce, E-government, E-learning, and E-banking, etc. In this study, we have applied our proposed framework to a job seekers website in the UAE. The implementation of the framework is straightforward because it needs only the data related to the application field to be analyzed. Third, when implemented to a specific field such as E-commerce or E-government, the results can be easily interpreted by non-expert users. Finally, the results, which are the outputs of the application of the framework, can be used to make decisions related to the field of such application such as E-commerce, E-government, etc.

CONCLUSION AND SUGGESTIONS FOR FUTURE RESEARCH

In this paper, we have proposed a generic framework which combines OLAP, SOLAP in E-business. We have also applied our framework using the fused data of a job seekers' website and data coming from a GIS representing the seven Emirates of the UAE. Our framework can be considered as original because it is comprehensive (OLAP–SOLAP with non-spatial and spatial data), generic (can be applied to other domains of E-business such as E-commerce or E-government), and expandable (it can integrate other data analysis techniques such as DM or SDM).

In the future, we plan to apply our framework to other fields such as E-government, E-commerce, E-banking, etc. The application of our framework in other fields would make it more generic. We also plan to plug into our framework other analysis techniques, such as DM and SDM, to provide users with different analysis techniques at the same time.

ACKNOWLEDGMENT

The authors are grateful to the anonymous reviewers and the associate editor for their constructive comments on an earlier version of the paper.

REFERENCES

Agrawal, R., Imielinski, T., & Swami, A. (1993). Mining association rules between sets of items in large databases. In *Proceedings of the ACM SIGMOD International Conference on Management of Data (ACM SIGMOD '93)*, Washington, DC (pp. 207–216).

Alba, J., Lynch, J., Webitz, B., Janiszewski, C., Lutrz, R., Sawyer, A., & Woods, S. (1997). Interactive home shopping, consumer, retailer and manufacturer incentives to participate in electronic marketplaces. *Journal of Marketing*, *61*(3), 38–54. doi:10.2307/1251788

Alter, S. (1980). *Decision Support Systems: Current Practices and Continuing Challenges*. Reading, MA: Addison-Wesley.

Aronoff, S. (1989). *Geographical Information Systems: A Management Perspective*. Ottawa, ON, Canada: WDL Publications.

Bédard, Y., Rivest, S., & Proulx, M. J. (2005). Spatial On-Line Analytical Processing (SOLAP): Concepts, architectures and solutions from a geomatics engineering perspective. In Wrembel, R., & Koncilia, C. (Eds.), *Data Warehouses and OLAP: Concepts, Architectures and Solutions* (pp. 298–313). Hershey, PA: Idea Group.

Codd, E. F., Codd, S. B., & Salley, C. T. (1993). *Providing OLAP (On-Line Analytical Processing) to User-Analysts: An IT Mandate*. Retrieved from http://dev.hyperion.com/resource_library/white_papers/providing_olap_to_user_analysts.pdf

Fayyad, U. M., Piatetsky-Shapiro, G., Smyth, P., & Uthurusamy, R. (1996). *Advances in Knowledge Discovery and Data Mining*. Menlo Park, CA: AAAI Press.

Ferreira, A. C., Campos, M. L., & Tanaka, A. (2001). An architecture for spatial and dimensional analysis integration. In *Proceedings of the World Multiconference on Systemics, Cybernetics and Informatics (SCI 2001)*, Orlando, FL (Vol. XIV, pp. 392–395).

Fidalgo, R. N., Times, V. C., Silva, J., & Souza, F. F. (2004). GeoDWFrame: A framework for guiding the design of geographical dimensional schemas. In *Proceedings of the 6th International Conference Data Warehousing and Knowledge Discovery (DaWaK)*, Zaragoza, Spain (pp. 26–37).

Gayialis, S. P., & Tatsiopoulos, I. P. (2004). Design of an IT-driven decision support system for vehicle routing and scheduling. *European Journal of Operational Research, 152*(2), 382–398. doi:10.1016/S0377-2217(03)00031-6

Inmon, W. H. (1992). *Building the Data Warehouse*. New York, NY: Wiley.

Kohavi, R. (2001, August). Mining e-commerce data: The good, the bad, and the ugly (invited industrial track talk). In F. Provost & R. Srikant (Eds.), *Proceedings of the 7th ACM SIGKDD International Conference on Knowledge Discovery and Data Mining*. Retrieved from http://robotics.Stanford.EDU/users/ronnyk/goodBadUglyKDDItrack.pdf

Kohavi, R., Mason, L., Parekh, R., & Zheng, Z. (2004). Lessons and challenges from mining retail e-commerce data. *Machine Learning Journal, 57*(1-2), 83–113. doi:10.1023/B:MACH.0000035473.11134.83

Kohavi, R., & Perkh, R. (2003). Ten supplementary analyses to improve e-commerce web sites. In *Proceedings of the 5th WEBKDD Workshop*, Washington, DC, (pp. 29–36).

Kohavi, R., & Provost, F. (2001). Applications of datamining to electronic commerce. *Data Mining and Knowledge Discovery, 5*(1-2), 115–153.

Kouba, Z., Matouseek, K., & Miksovsky, P. (2000). On data warehouse and GIS integration. In *Proceedings of DEXA 2000* (LNCS 1873, pp. 604–613).

Lau, T. W., Hui, C. L., Ng, S. F., & Moon, K. L. (2008). An implication of e-commerce in textile and clothing industries: A relational online analytical processing (OLAP) approach. *International Journal of Information Technology and Management, 7*(3), 231–243. doi:10.1504/IJITM.2008.017603

Lo, E., Ben, K., Ho, W. S., Lee, S. D., Chui, C. K., & Cheung, D. W. (2008, June 10-12). OLAP on sequence data. In *Proceedings of the ACM SIGMOD International Conference on Management of Data*, Vancouver, BC, Canada.

Marchand, P., Brisebois, A., Bédard, Y., & Edwards, G. (2004). Implementation and evaluation of a hypercube-based method for spatio-temporal exploration and analysis. *ISPRS Journal of Photogrammetry and Remote Sensing, 59*(1-2), 6–20. doi:10.1016/j.isprsjprs.2003.12.002

Matthew, S., Parmanto, B., & Monaco, V. (2007). Usability evaluation of the spatial OLAP visualization and analysis tool (SOVAT). *Journal of Usability Studies, 2*(2), 76–95.

Mircea, M., & Andreescu, A. (2009). Using Business rules in business intelligence. *Journal of Applied Quantitative Methods, 4*(3), 382–393.

Mishra, S. (2009). GIS in Indian retail industry-a strategic tool. *International Journal of Marketing Studies, 1*(1), 50–57.

Mokhtarian, P. L. (2004). A conceptual analysis of the transportation impacts of B2C e-Commerce. *Transportation Journal, 31*(3), 257–284. doi:10.1023/B:PORT.0000025428.64128.d3

Murray, A. T., O'Kelly, M. E., & Church, R. L. (2008). Regional service coverage modeling. *Computers & Operations Research, 35*(2), 339–355. doi:10.1016/j.cor.2006.03.004

O'Sullivan, D., & Unwin, D. J. (2002). *Geographic Information Analysis*. Hoboken, NJ: John Wiley & Sons.

Phan, D. D. (2003). E-business development for competitive advantages: A case study. *Information & Management, 40*(6), 581–590. doi:10.1016/S0378-7206(02)00089-7

Ranjan, J. (2009). Business intelligence: Concepts, components, techniques and benefits. *Journal of Theoretical and Applied Information Technology, 9*(1), 60–70.

Rivest, S., Bédard, Y., & Marchand, P. (2001). Toward better support for spatial decision making: Defining the characteristics of spatial on-line analytical processing (SOLAP). *Geomatica, 55*(4), 539–555.

Rivest, S., Bédard, Y., Proulx, M.-J., Nadeau, M., Hubert, F., & Pastor, J. (2005). SOLAP technology: Merging business intelligence with geospatial technology for interactive spatio-temporal exploration and analysis of data. *ISPRS Journal of Photogrammetry and Remote Sensing, 60*(1), 17–33. doi:10.1016/j.isprsjprs.2005.10.002

Salam, I., Mohajer, M., Talleb, A., & Mohajer, B. (2008). Development of SOLAP patrimony management application system: Fez medina as a case study. *International Journal of Computer Science and Applications, 5*(3a), 57–66.

Scotch, M., & Parmanto, B. (2005, January 3-6). SOVAT: Spatial OLAP visualization and analysis tool. In *Proceedings of the 38th Hawaii International Conference on System Sciences (HICSS-38)* (p. 142b).

Scotch, M., Parmanto, B., & Monaco, V. (2007). Usability evaluation of the spatial OLAP visualization and analysis tool (SOVAT). *Journal of Usability Studies, 2*(2), 76–95.

Shekhar, S., Lu, C. T., Tan, X., Chawla, S., & Vatsavai, R. (2001). Map cube: A visualization tool for spatial data warehouses. In Miller, H. J., & Han, J. (Eds.), *Geographic Data Mining and Knowledge Discovery* (pp. 74–109). London, UK: Taylor & Francis. doi:10.4324/9780203468029_chapter_4

Silva, J., Times, V., Fidalgo, R., & Barros, R. (2005). Providing geographic-multidimensional decision support over the Web. In *APWeb 2005: Proceedings of the 7th Asia-Pacific Web Conference* (LNCS 3399, pp. 477–488).

Stackowiak, R., Rayman, J., & Greenwald, R. (2007). *Oracle Data Warehousing and Business intelligence Solutions*. Indianapolis, IN: Wiley Publishing.

Stefanovic, N., Hanj, J., & Koperski, K. (2000). Object-based selective materialization for efficient implementation of spatial data cubes. *IEEE Transactions on Knowledge Discovery and Data Engineering, 12*(6), 938–958. doi:10.1109/69.895803

Su, Q., Li, L., & Wu, Y. (2009). Analysing relational benefits in e-business environment from behavioural perspective. *Systems Research and Behavioral Science, 26*(2), 129–142. doi:10.1002/sres.965

Tchounikine, A., Miqel, M., Laurini, R., Ahmed, T., Bimonte, S., & Bailot, V. (2005). Panorama de travaux autour de l'intégration de données spatio-temporelles dans les hypercubes. *Revue des Nouvelles Technologies de l'Information,* 21–23.

Thomsen, E. (2002). *OLAP Solutions: Building Multidimensional Information Systems* (2nd ed.). New York, NY: John Wiley & Sons.

Thomsen, E., Spofford, G., & Chase, D. (1999). *Microsoft OLAP Solutions*. New York, NY: John Wiley & Sons.

Trubint, N., Ljubomir, O., & Nebojša, B. (2006). Determining an optimal retail location by using GIS. *Yugoslav Journal of Operations Research, 16*(2), 253–264. doi:10.2298/YJOR0602253T

Watson, H. J., Rainer, R. K., & Houdeshel, G. (1992). *Executive Information Systems: Emergence, Development, Impact*. New York, NY: John Wiley & Sons.

Youngworth, P. (1995). OLAP spells success for users and developers. *Data Based Advisor, 13*(11), 38–49.

Zhou, B., Jiang, D., Pei, J., & Li, H. (2009, June 28-July 1). OLAP on sear logs: An infrastructure supporting data-driven applications in search engines. In *Proceedings of the 15th ACM SIGKDD Conference on Knowledge Discovery and Data Mining,* Paris, France.

This work was previously published in the Information Resources Management Journal, Volume 24, Issue 3, edited by Mehdi Khosrow-Pour, pp. 45-60, copyright 2013 by IGI Publishing (an imprint of IGI Global).

Chapter 15
The Evolution of the Massively Parallel Processing Database in Support of Visual Analytics

Ian A. Willson
The Boeing Company, USA

ABSTRACT

This article explores the evolution of the Massively Parallel Processing (MPP) database, focusing on trends of particular relevance to analytics. The dramatic shift of database vendors and leading companies to utilize MPP databases and deploy an Enterprise Data Warehouse (EDW) is presented. The inherent benefits of fresher data, storage efficiency, and most importantly accessibility to analytics are explored. Published industry and vendor metrics are examined that demonstrate substantial and growing cost efficiencies from utilizing MPP databases. The author concludes by reviewing trends toward parallelizing decision support workload into the database, ranging from within database transformations to new statistical and spatial analytic capabilities provided by parallelizing these algorithms to execute directly within the MPP database. These new capabilities present an opportunity for timely and powerful enterprise analytics, providing a substantial competitive advantage to those companies able to leverage this technology to turn data into actionable information, gain valuable new insights, and automate operational decision making.

Analytics, including the growing field of visual analytics, has an opportunity to significantly expand its effectiveness by leveraging advances in Massively Parallel Processing (MPP) relational databases. Despite a 25-year commercial history, it has been only recently that capabilities have emerged that analytical applications can utilize in effective and economic ways, particularly based upon the Enterprise Data Warehouse (EDW) architecture. Many companies face growing decision support system expenditures, shrinking budgets, increasingly volatile and complex

DOI: 10.4018/978-1-4666-3616-3.ch015

operating environments and yet are unable to integrate and analyze their data to make timely operational, tactical and strategic decisions. The focus of this article is on advances in MPP database technology, representing the decision support system component within the broader Systems of Systems architecture that spans data and information throughout the enterprise. Much of the history of MPP, relational database technology and scientific computing applications of MPP will not be considered, some of which may be better known to readers than MPP database advances. Our focus is on advances in data warehouse technology that represent an historic opportunity for those in the analytics field, who until recently have relied on a variety of purpose-built stand-alone tools or methods of limited capability that increasingly compete for scarce Information Technology (IT) resources. To achieve the full potential of analytics on large or complex data, an examination of recent MPP database trends is in order.

This article presents a brief history of MPP databases and their role in decision support, with an unavoidable focus on Teradata Corporation, which commercialized MPP and remains a market leader (Thoo & Beyer, 2008). Significant downward trends in price per unit of performance, both absolute and relative to transactional non-MPP databases are examined. The synergy of MPP technology and the activated Enterprise Data Warehouse (EDW) make it possible to support wide-ranging analytical queries on a single instance of time-referenced data. The EDW provides an authoritative source of reference ideally suited to analytics, particularly the emerging trend of 'analytics inside', or pushing down parallelized algorithms based on temporal, spatial and statistical primitives executed directly within the MPP database, greatly increasing the accessibility and potential value of these analytical methods. The result is a cost effective delivery system providing powerful analytics to the enterprise, generating business value from IT investments.

THE MASSIVELY PARALLEL PROCESSING DATABASE

With a focus on analytics, most of us have not been concerned with the precise details of the systems that host our data. To start off with, let us define our domain of interest to be broad enterprise-scale relational databases focused on supporting analytics and queries of all types, rather than transaction processing. The focus of this article is on performing a wide variety of valued analytics against such databases using an architecture specifically created to process this workload. MPP technology has been successfully deployed in large database systems for more than 25 years, supporting, with varying degrees of automation, many of the types of analytics we perform today. The author has been working with very large relational databases for decision support and analytical applications since 1986. In an early example, an entire IBM® 4081 mainframe was used to host a Human Resources decision support system. Since that time, what constitutes large has changed, as has the cost per unit of storage or unit of power, but surprisingly the fundamental method of storing and retrieving structured data has changed little.

The storage and retrieval of normalized data in tables first contemplated by Dr. Ted Codd (1970) is increasingly practical now that there is a suitably powerful hardware platform and database architecture available. The various design mitigations previously required for performance are fading in prevalence. The one fundamental change since 1970 is the commercial introduction of the shared-nothing or Massively Parallel Processing (MPP) database by Teradata Corporation, which shipped its first production system in 1984. One important distinction in this application of MPP to relational databases is that the parallelization is being applied to Structured Query Language (SQL) operators, a fundamentally functional language. Better known applications of MPP, at least 20 years ago, were in the scientific computing realm, where massive parallelization was thought to offer the opportunity to speed up calculations for a wide range of high value scientific computing problems.

Thinking Machines Corporation was one of the most widely-known parallel supercomputer manufacturers of the 1980s and early 1990s until its bankruptcy in 1994 (Taubes, 1995). In order to execute scientific calculations in parallel, special language extensions were required to parallelize computing on these MPP systems, such as C* and CM Fortran. Ultimately this approach was not cost-effective, with more economical designs for moderate parallelism utilizing specialized clusters of SMP-based computers succeeding in the commercial market. Fortunately in our case, MPP has proven to be a cost-effective and suitable design for relational databases due to the relative ease and substantial benefit available from parallelizing the functional operations of the SQL, compared with the complex scientific calculations implemented in conventional programming languages. The difficulty of converting other types of algorithms and operators to an efficient massively parallel processing implementation will become clear as we examine statistical and spatial operations and the time it took for these to emerge in MPP databases.

One early discussion of the shared-nothing architecture is a paper by Dr. Michael Stonebraker (1985) at Berkeley which contrasts the shared-nothing architecture with shared memory and shared disk approaches, addressing concerns that shared-nothing would not be able to scale to large transaction volumes. Dr. Stonebraker led the INGRES® project, a foundation for modern relational databases (IEEE Computer Society, 2005) and subsequently created POSTGRES®, which extended the capabilities of relational databases in many application areas and is used within an MPP product from Greenplum in its open source incarnation (Thoo & Beyer, 2008). Dr. Stonebraker also founded Vertica in 2005, designing a grid of commodity Linux servers supporting a columnar parallel database. This approach moves away from the row-based relational database and is targeted at low cost star schema data marts, rather than broad normalized data warehouses.

MPP is a fundamentally different relational database architecture uniquely designed at every level for large-scale decision support, rather than transaction processing. At its core is the concept of a shared-nothing design, in that many, often hundreds of independent units of work, shown as CPU Units in Figure 1, are able to execute tasks concurrently, each entirely owning the data and resources necessary to complete its task. In some systems, these units of work are virtual processors specializing in different tasks (database operations, parsing SQL, session handling), allocated according to the expected workload profile. Each unit of work is capable of managing multiple tasks concurrently, each of which executes independently of any other unit of work in the system, whether a database task or user interaction, so as to maximize parallel throughput.

In order to implement a shared-nothing architecture, both the data and the tasks themselves must be distributed across the system and linked using a highly efficient interconnect bus specifically designed to support many concurrent data requests, as illustrated in Figure 2. The bus illustrated in Figure 2 is a folded banyan switching network which acts as a distributed multi-fabric interconnect to link the various units of work in a fault tolerant manner, bearing some similarity to a telephone switch. This sophisticated interconnect bus must be capable of collectively deliver-

Figure 1. MPP shared-nothing architecture

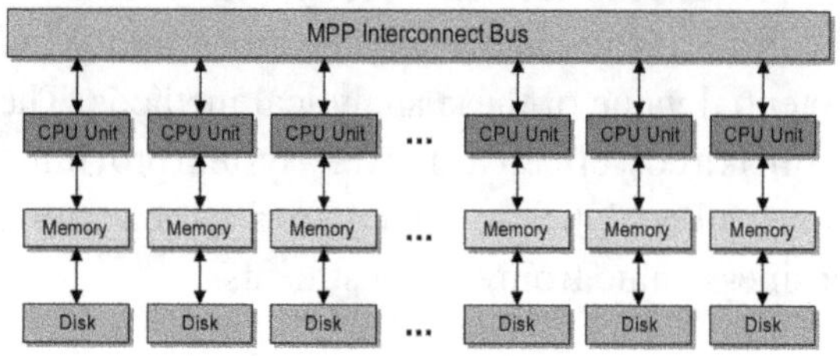

Figure 2. MPP interconnect bus

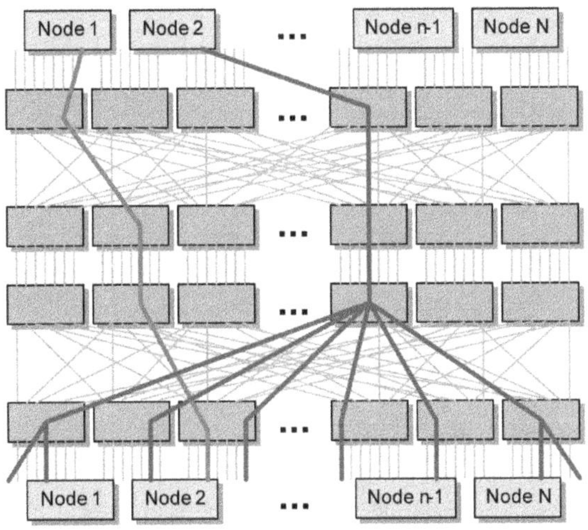

ing large volumes of data with a minimum of overhead added to widely varying data warehouse communications tasks between and within nodes.

The execution plan for all workload in the system is designed by an advanced query optimizer. This critical software component decomposes and parallelizes a query into multiple subtasks designed to maximize the parallel efficiency of both the query and the overall system. Once planned, the workload tasks for a given query must be pro-actively and efficiently managed so as to maximize the parallel throughput of the entire system. Such a database system design parallelizes workload at every level and hence is referred to as massively parallel. Products from Teradata®, HP Neoview®, Netezza®, Oracle® Exadata and IBM DB2® Extended Enterprise Edition are generally regarded as having an MPP design.

Some MPP implementations bypass the expensive and difficult custom design required to parallelize each component, instead choosing to parallelize specific components in a hierarchical (master and many slave nodes) or bounded parallelism (masters and slaves) form (Ballinger & Fryer, 1997; Ballinger, 2006). In most MPP implementations, a key user design decision is to specify the table column or columns that form the basis for evenly distributing the data across the system via hashing. For a normalized design, this is usually the primary key or a subset of the primary key columns if a composite key, such that data is evenly distributed across the system. The MPP system shares this information and other metadata with all units of work such that each knows deterministically which other unit of work owns which hash location of each row in a table. In a simple task to scan an entire table for a partial text match unsupported by any indexing, this would lead to a broadcast message, shown as a blue line in Figure 2, to all database units of work to scan the data for the criteria and to return the result to the requesting node. With an evenly distributed table, this speeds up retrieval by nearly the number of units of work, all else equal. Recent vendor performance claims for identical database software with either conventional non-parallel large table scans or an MPP-based data layer found substantial improvements as high as 2,800% overall (Weiss, 2008).

A nearly opposite use case also illustrates the advantage of the shared-nothing architecture, that of executing n simultaneous queries submitted from different sessions to an n-parallel system. The processes handling sessions, optimizer functions and management are also spread evenly across the MPP machine, allowing all n logins and query plans to be developed at once by n units of work. The query use case is that of a single row lookup where the table is hashed on the lookup value. Each query management process is able to direct only one unit of work to fetch and return the result using the interconnect bus using point-to-point messaging, one instance of which is shown as a red line in Figure 2. On average each unit of work will do a distinct query in parallel, achieving a collective massively parallel execution result of what is known as a tactical query.

MPP AND PARALLEL EFFICIENCY

This MPP database architecture differs fundamentally from Symmetric Multi-Processing architecture (SMP), where resources such as memory are shared and combined across a large system with respect to executing workload. When applied to large-scale analytics, with its very broad and complex database queries, the SMP approach is particularly vulnerable to a variety of bottle-necks and inefficiencies which prevent large scale parallel execution of queries, including long response times for data-intensive queries (full table scans). Parallel efficiency is hampered by CPU's contending for memory and disk I/O resources. Once multiple queries are introduced, parallel efficiency is further reduced. Amdahl's law (Figure 3) shows why full or partial SMP systems seldom can utilize more than 32 CPU's due to the efficiency loss inherent in sharing resources. A single large table query can delay many other smaller queries during its execution. Mitigations such as disk partitioning have been added to address retrieval bottle-necks, but Amdahl's law clearly demonstrates the diminishing overall returns as workload and CPU capacity grows. To a lesser degree the same issue can arise within portions of the MPP workload when workload (or data) is skewed, or not evenly distributed across the units of work. Collectively, well-managed MPP systems are typically able to achieve a very high parallel efficiency in the upper 90% range and hence are uniquely scalable.

From a computational complexity point of view, it is clearly advantageous to reduce the size of n in the complexity order by the hundred fold degree of parallelism present in an average MPP system on any relational database operator such as a join or a sort. 100 parallel executions of an $O((n/100)^2)$ process is much more efficient that one large $O(n^2)$ process, particularly at the million and billion row tables sizes commonly processed during query execution. At $n = 10^6$ data size for an $O(n^2)$ process resulting in a 100 fold reduction

Figure 3. Amdahl's Law

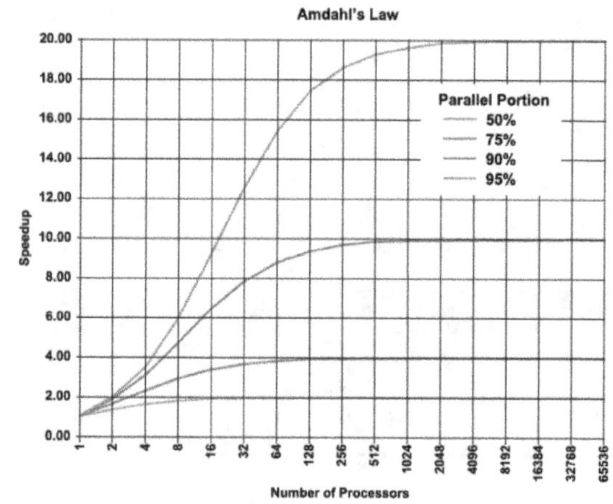

output (e.g., a join), 100 units of parallelism could reduce the cost of the operation 99-fold (1,000 fold reduction per unit provided data from both tables was hashed identically x 100 units less the cost of the combination step on the 1% result across 100 units).

Benchmark tests of SMP-based decision support databases have found substantial efficiency losses in clustering SMP hardware to build out larger system sizes. In practice, companies may have a multitude of growing report-marts implemented on SMP hardware. Additional functionality, data growth and the need to integrate data all drive hardware growth, with clustering utilized when single systems reach their limits. Such efforts suffer system-wide throughput losses result from sharing disk, memory or lacking an appropriate interconnect layer amongst all of the components. On the TPC-H™ decision support benchmark at the 10 Terabyte (TB) scale (Table 1, row 1 and 2), there is a 24.2% performance loss in the Composite Query-per-Hour Performance Metric (QphH) when adding a 2nd SMP node (each with 64 CPU's) to create a cluster of non-MPP database software, with the database and software held constant except for the addition of clustering software. Perhaps not surprisingly, no other published TPC-H benchmarks are available which match identical software on clustered and

Table 1. TPC-H 10TB benchmark per transaction processing performance council™

Hardware/Software	Avail.	Price/Perf.	Throughput	Price
HP SD Itan2/1.5-128p/128 Oracle10g	4/2005	$161/QphH@10TB	86,283 QphH	$13,912,046
HP SD Itan2/1.5-64p/64c Oracle10g	3/2004	$118/QphH@10TB	49,105 QphH	$5,800,675
HP BL25p cluster8P dc2.4 Oracle10g	11/2005	$28/QphH@300GB	18,726 QphH	$523,764
HP BL25p cluster8P 2.6 Oracle10g	10/2005	$34/QphH@300GB	13,284 QphH	$454,283

non-clustered SMP databases. There is one result for the 300 gigabyte (GB) scale TPC-H that compares nearly identical single and dual core processors. The result in rows 3 and 4 in Table 1 appear initially to show a 29.6% performance loss when doubling the cores (16 cores versus 8). However, the dual core system ran at a lower 2.4 GHz clock rate rather than 2.6 GHz, reducing its performance to an unknown degree but certainly less than the 7.7% clock rate difference. This suggests at least an adjusted 22% scalability loss of aggregate performance due to doubling the CPU core count within an SMP design. It should be noted that this analysis only refers to the data load and ad-hoc query oriented TPC-H benchmark. Similar parallel efficiency losses are not seen when considering transactional workloads using TPC-C™ benchmarks (Transaction Processing Performance Council, n.d.). Hardware from a number of vendors demonstrates between 86% and 95% scalability on transactional TPC-C workload tests when doubling the number of CPU's within a given server.

Properly configured MPP systems, by design, show little loss of efficiency within key elements of their architecture (CPU, IO, bus capacity) provided both the overall workload and the data is evenly distributed (not skewed), a potentially serious and significant operational challenge, but one typically managed to a high level in practice. The author's industry experience with hardware expansions of production systems adding more identical units of parallelism have found very high levels of scalability in MPP systems. The lack of very large reference deployments of SMP-based relational databases cited by vendors and industry analysts also supports the finding that large enterprise SMP data warehouse systems are either impractical or uneconomic due to the efficiency loss of sharing components when executing queries against large tables or processing large and varied workloads encountered in a large decision support system.

The basis of MPP performance is the shared-nothing or parallel everything architecture implemented with hardware and software designed around this concept. A single database task, such as a SQL statement of potentially considerable complexity (64-way table joins are possible), is decomposed by a sophisticated optimizer into a number of sequential and parallel sub-tasks in such a way as to avoid execution bottle-necks and leverage the parallel architecture. This process includes generating parallel sub-tasks without inter-dependencies to execute concurrently at a given step of the overall execution plan, if at all possible. A query example is shown in Figure 4, where for the shared-nothing query on the right side, the N size 1/N units of work are all able to execute independently until a final convergence step combines the results each has achieved. Generally a query result set is much smaller than the data used in obtaining the results. This fully parallel plan is contrasted to the shared-everything fully serialized plan on the left of Figure 4, where each step faces resource contention from within. Conditional parallelism, implemented by some vendors, provides a combination of both approaches best illustrated with a more complex example, often using less units of parallelism. Aggregation would be one step not readily executed in parallel, regardless of optimizer design.

Figure 4. Query Parallelism

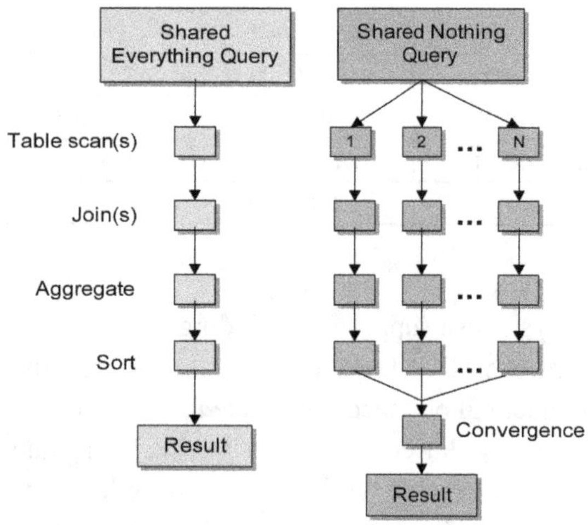

A more typical and complex data warehouse query plan requiring 30 sub-tasks might be executed in 15 sequential steps (some steps with 1 sub-task, others with several) on an MPP system. Note that any of the parallelized sub-tasks may be assigned to all database units of work, such that a step with 4 parallel sub-tasks each assigned to all units of work executed on a 100 unit MPP system would be executing 400 tasks concurrently on a given step of one query system-wide, a considerable parallelization of workload. It is important to note that MPP designs typically use multiple SMP compute nodes with conventional operating system task management employed in the process of executing this workload.

Fundamental to MPP execution is that tasks are evenly distributed amongst physical resources. Communications between tasks occurs only at the beginning and ending of each task, minimizing resource contention and maximizing resource utilization, particularly with a high volume of tasks executing simultaneously as is common on large systems. The design of an effective MPP optimizer is clearly a substantial challenge, with vendors investing significant intellectual property in their designs. MPP optimizers require considerable refinement over many years of real-world tuning in challenging deployments in order to be successful. Leading MPP optimizer designs stand amongst the great practical achievements of computer science.

MPP PRODUCT HISTORY

Teradata Corporation released its first MPP database in 1984, with the company name referring to the capability of storing 1 trillion bytes of data. This was also referenced in the first product name, the DBC 1012, the DataBase Computer capable of storing 10 to the 12th power bytes of data. The author first encountered a Teradata DBC 1012 in 1989 which had previously been used to solve network design problems for our customer AT&T. These early Teradata machines used a physical architecture connecting disk directly to one physical motherboard linked to dozens of identical motherboards using a high-performance interconnect known as the YNET, a critical element of any MPP system. Remarkably, Teradata and a second company stood alone in advancing commercially successful MPP databases for 11 years following the release of the DBC 1012. The other early entrant in the database machine market was Britton Lee Inc., which was founded in 1979 and was later known as ShareBase Corporation. A number of the core engineering team at Britton Lee came of out of the Ingres project. Britton Lee's product, the BD8000, competed with Teradata's DBC 1012 in 1988, with the two representing the entire database machine marketplace (Knight, 1988). Teradata's customers were typically offloading mainframe DBMS processing to Teradata, with Britton Lee's doing the same for smaller host systems such as minicomputers. Britton Lee was purchased by Teradata in 1990, making Teradata the sole parallel decision support database vendor until IBM began shipping DB2 parallel edition in 1995.

At this point in MPP database evolution, the concept of the data warehouse had not yet emerged and there was not a clear delineation between read-only analytical applications of large database queries and transactional OLTP uses. One interesting development was the creation of a distributed parallel high availability architecture for ANSI SQL operations known as NonStop® SQL (Tandem, 1989). The architecture did not share memory amongst processors, relied on a high-speed network interconnect between processors and could be grown in small increments by adding either disk or CPU to clusters and then clusters to a network of clusters. Tandem subsequently released a version of Nonstop focused on large scale data warehousing called NonStop SQL/MX® for deployment on the Windows NT® platform. A number of the key Tandem developers came from the IBM System R project, including Dr. Jim Gray, who subsequently became a Technical Fellow at Microsoft®. Microsoft in turn acquired MPP database vendor DatAllegro in 2008 and is planning an MPP product, currently known as Project Madison, based on this code base for release in 2010. A further note about cross-pollination between database technologies, companies and key individuals, is that Hewlett Packard® released an MPP product called Neoview in 2007 built around a redevelopment of Tandem's NonStop SQL.

The second iteration of Teradata's MPP design (V2) arrived in the 1990s and virtualized the CPU to permit flexible configurations of virtual processors matched to the performance of the components of each model (disk arrays, high speed bus). Interestingly, two recent competitors use a somewhat similar approach to the original DBC 1012, with no virtualized CPU units of work and a fixed number of disks per physical CPU. Netezza, first introduced in 2002 as a low cost data warehouse appliance, combines one disk drive, memory and a specialized CPU onto a single circuit card interconnected within a rack. Hewlett Packard's recent Neoview MPP product uses a single CPU allocated to a fixed amount of disk in a choice of two disk densities.

The evolution of the MPP architecture and specific features uniquely suited to it has allowed companies to obtain substantial benefits when deployed in innovative ways, often demonstrating a positive ROI on IT investments and offering products and services that otherwise would be impossible or uneconomic. In the case of Teradata, more than 900 companies have 2,000 systems in place, with other new entrants also providing MPP-based systems to several hundred companies (e.g., Netezza, IBM DB2 EEE, HP Neoview, Oracle Exadata). The current and future prospects for advanced analytics would be substantially worse without the successful deployment and maturation of the MPP database architecture now widely accepted as fundamental to enterprise decision support.

MPP implementations have tended to borrow some elements of SMP systems and as such are often not entirely massively parallel or pure MPP, even if referred to as such. A number of implementations combine SMP and MPP, such as the use of a 'query director' master node in some designs (Netezza) or the combination of a parallel data and pre-processing layer with an additional SMP layer on top, as in the case of the Oracle Exadata Database Machine (Weiss, 2008). The later system as a whole is not a massively parallel design, as inter-layer communication between the MPP Exadata layer and the Oracle layer is serialized with respect to each task, one of a number of possible bottlenecks in this two layer hybrid approach. In addition, subsequent task steps beyond initial data scans and limited pre-filtering occurs at the upper SMP layer with little or no parallelization, executed entirely by a particular master node.

The use of MPP has evolved as the technology has matured and its capabilities grown, by some measures several hundred-fold, since its first introduction. Early customer focus was on effective usable storage capacity and the new-found ability to query volumes of data that otherwise could not be analyzed without MPP technology. In terms of maximum usable database sizes, Teradata deployments first reached 1 TB at Wal-Mart in January 1992. It should be noted that these large deployments also provide equivalent query, load and backup capabilities and that Teradata systems use proportionally less additional disk space beyond the equivalent size of raw text, unlike other databases (SMP, XML). Subsequent growth in maximum deployed database sizes reached 11 TB in 1996, 24 TB in 1997, 130 TB in 1999, 423 TB in 2003, 1 Petabyte (PB) in 2007 and 2.4 PB in late 2008 (Teradata Corporation, n.d.).

The more than 100-fold growth in system capacity over the past 15 years provides most enterprises with sufficient storage and query capacity to include the majority of their structured data at atomic granularity, even given the number of stores, cell phones, phone calls, trips, or products made. It should be noted that some companies still have vast quantities of data of clear value to analytics (click-stream analysis, dynamic individual web offer optimization) that may not be cost-effectively or practically accommodated on MPP databases. With this background, we proceed to examine three trends uniquely supporting the MPP database architecture that set the stage for pervasive analytics and consider newly emerging trends to integrate statistical and spatial analysis into the MPP database.

THE ENTERPRISE DATA WAREHOUSE (EDW) & ANALYTICS

Recent advances in the performance, cost effectiveness and capability of MPP databases have provided most companies with the opportunity to consolidate hundreds of disparate decision support databases onto a single MPP database system. Data mart consolidation may be achieved through a number of strategies. The Enterprise Data Warehouse approach ultimately favors consolidation in an application-neutral centralized design containing detailed historical data. Light de-normalization and additional summarization can be used as needed, combined with virtual data mart semantic views, to serve a broad variety of query and analytical needs (Thoo & Beyer, 2008). The gains achieved by having a 'single version of the truth' database have been documented by industry research groups for some time and are well accepted, with many companies having already achieved this vision, although certainly not overnight (Eckerson, 2004).

With respect to Teradata customers, a majority have already implemented key components of an active EDW according to a recent survey (Teradata Corporation, 2007). With Teradata being at times the sole MPP database vendor, Teradata customers represent a large segment of the enterprise decision support market and drove the trend to activating the data warehouse by including operational workloads in the same database as traditional business intelligence query and reporting. In late 2007, more than 350 attendees at the Teradata Partners conference from 32 countries responded to a survey in which more than 75% reported having an Active Enterprise Intelligence vision. More than half overall and 75% of manufacturers have implemented active loading, a key capability needed to serve operational users. A majority of respondents also implemented other capabilities such as Active Integration, Active Availability and Active Workload Management, the later being a sophisticated and critical component of the activated EDW which dynamically manages concurrent workloads to maximize throughput and parallel efficiency.

The conversion to the EDW began more than 10 years ago at 3M™ Company, which documented $350 million in global savings in 2001 from their investment in their EDW first deployed in 1998 (Helmaan, 2003). Amongst Teradata customers, many hundreds have already implemented a key component of the EDW, a normalized data model. The normalized structure, used appropriately, can be loaded frequently (mini-batch) or continuously in a non-intrusive manner, leading to the activation of the EDW. This design, in turn, allows a variety of time sensitive functions such as operational reporting to be run off of the EDW, leveraging powerful predictive analytics as well. The temporal data model efficiently represents periods in data and supports any type of time-referenced analysis (latest, as of time X, as of time X without restatement) using temporal extensions to the normalized data model. A broad normalized data model is ideal for advanced analytics, providing direct access to the atomic detail-level data required for statistical analysis or visualization, along with the ability to directly combine all determinants in an analytical model, such as customer, location, financial value and sales.

Cost reduction is also a key driver for deploying a multi-subject normalized data model hosted on MPP, instead of hundreds of disparate report-marts. Any cost-saving assumptions about proliferating data to many smaller low cost hardware platforms have been eclipsed by advances in MPP systems and their cost efficiencies discussed later in this article. This became clear when a major supplier of data mart solutions deployed on SMP databases, Hewlett Packard, did a complete about-face in 2006 (Foley, 2007). Hewlett Packard's introduction of Neoview, a new MPP database, initially was deployed internally at HP to eliminate 750 separate SMP-based data marts, a considerable cost burden even for the hardware manufacturer (Foley, 2007). As most companies have discovered, the application servers, Extract Transform Load tool software licenses and network bandwidth consumed in loading, re-loading and moving data can exceed the cost of the entire EDW. Average data mart costs are in the hundreds of thousands to low millions, multiplied by the many that are usually needed. Even if database administration costs (DBA labor) fall per unit of storage, these costs rise as a percentage of falling hardware prices and also due to rapidly growing data storage, particularly as data volumes and replication increase when data marts proliferate.

While ROI is certainly an important advantage of the EDW, important benefits emerge with respect to analytics. A broad scope normalized database design requires that data elements be well defined with respect to an enterprise data model and generally that data quality be enforced, either in loading, presentation views or through an iterative process working with the source system. The result is a broad consistent database where one can safely join any column of similar or matching domain without detailed knowledge of cryptic codes or system-specific practices. For example, the domain and meaning of a part would be the same in every table referenced, similarly for many other elements of master data. This integrated data model greatly reduces the workload to specify the data to analyze and makes it possible to readily obtain the data with a minimum of effort. With much or all of the data needed available on a single high performance database, the cost and difficulty in obtaining data for analytics can fall by orders of magnitude.

Furthermore, the time-variant nature of the frequently loaded EDW provides fresh consistent data in time for decisions to be taken, enabling operational Business Intelligence (BI) to be performed from the data warehouse (Eckerson, 2007). The era of needing to maintain a separate freshly loaded Operational Data Store (ODS) has long passed in the vast majority of enterprises leveraging the EDW paradigm. The success of the active EDW also addresses the misconception that the data warehouse, by definition, excludes timely data needed for operational decision making. While many decision support systems of 10 or 20 years ago were able to be loaded only daily or weekly, technological developments, both hardware and software, allow data to be loaded continuously or in mini-batch cycles ranging from several minutes to several hours. This largely renders the Operational Data Store (ODS) obsolete. The logical next step from being able to perform operational BI is to automate many operational decisions, a process that falls within the domain of Enterprise Decision Management (EDM). The technological foundation for such automation is the ability to quickly load small amounts of data into the data warehouse via Enterprise Application Integration (EAI), very quickly obtain limited amounts of information (tactical queries) and to connect many decision making components in a Service Oriented Architecture (SOA), all standard infrastructure for the activated EDW.

The substantial benefits of actionable insight from the EDW can be quantified in the ROI and have been carefully documented. One example, from Continental Airlines, has been turned into a business school case from The Center for Customer Relationship Management at the Fuqua School of Business at Duke University (Anderson-Lehman, Watson, Wixom, & Hoffer, 2007). Using its active EDW, Continental Airlines is able to load passenger check-ins and flight detail shortly after departure, which when combined with a broad array of customer data already present, including earlier experiences on the current itinerary, allows the airline to take action prior to the plane landing (e.g., late flight, buy a ticket on a competitor for the non-frequent flyer who already missed 2 prior flights). Many other companies glean insights from a broad database of freshly loaded data, bringing complex analytic tools (customer scoring, near real-time statistical analysis, call center support tools, eCommerce support for web sites and many types of iterative analysis) into the front-lines of tactical decision making for the first time, an exciting prospect indeed.

THE DATA MAY NOT BE TOO LARGE AFTER ALL

It often appears that the quantity of data companies seek to utilize in their data warehouses is growing faster than technology or budgets can keep up with. This over-simplification can be harmful, in that it obscures the fact that the vast majority of data of value, correctly represented, can be readily stored and queried on increasing inexpensive MPP systems. This is not to deny that there are not a great many phone calls made (call detail records) or mouse clicks executed on a busy Internet site, nor to imply it would always make sense to store all obtainable information, particularly in its raw form, in an MPP database for a considerable duration. Nevertheless technology is driving cost reductions that newly enable powerful analytics to be performed, particularly when data is stored in the most accessible and efficient form, the EDW. There is no longer a technological requirement or a cost reason that most valuable business questions which can benefit from advanced analytics cannot be answered on a properly deployed MPP database in a timely manner.

Frequently, the discussion of data size is confounded by deployment practices, which can easily replicate many copies of data throughout the enterprise. Hewlett Packard, for example, found that it had 750 disparate data marts, and not coincidentally was spending a larger percentage of revenue on IT than peer organizations. By definition there is considerable duplication of data in any large collection of reporting systems. Adding the size of all these data marts and reporting systems is not an indication of the true size of the data you seek to analyze. Furthermore, many systems that call themselves a data warehouse or mart are in fact a pre-computed report designed for systems of considerably less power than are available today. Such pre-computed reports may add multiples of additional de-normalized data rows, usually loaded overnight in a batch job, based on the assumption that the database is unable to efficiently perform the complex queries that MPP systems can readily execute. For example, current MPP systems can routinely do sub-second joins of moderate complexity on even the largest table, joining data tables with a calendar table to materialize the latest row for each reporting date during a query, rather than having to replicate the data row for every reporting date in advance. This alone can reduce apparent data size by an order of magnitude or more. It is easy for analysts to become overwhelmed by IT reports of what essentially is many terabytes of replicated, de-normalized and pre-run reports when in fact the real data is considerably smaller. It can be a significant challenge to determine the actual distinct size of the data in order to plan an MPP system, one that only can be overcome with knowledge of the data models and fundamental facts about the data itself.

A further example of the power of the MPP database to reduce persistent storage is to use data modeling to compress data in a way which effectively collapses many similar intersection relationships between objects. In this use case, consider a manufacturer with multiple products made of many parts. A normalized design would consist of a product table, a parts table consisting of parts which may be used on multiple products and an intersection table inheriting the primary key of each. Would anyone really want to store the complete intersection table, part-on-product, particularly multiples of relationships such as designed for, built with, substituted for or maintained by? In a contrived example, the data for 1 million product instances, each of which uses 10,000 part instances of perhaps 30,000 possible parts results in 10 billion rows for each of the 4 intersection tables, with changes over time adding further rows of history, resulting in a total of 100 billion data rows over time. While this size is certainly manageable on a large MPP system, it belies the fact that there is great commonality between instances of products, which over time that can be better represented in an efficiently modeled multi-valued column. This optimization relies on there being a suitable representation or coding of the lowest cardinality parent and that a lookup table is maintained to decode this compressed representation into its atomic components. Multiple compressed columns can be added, one for each intersection relationship type, increasing the row length in the parent part table and also increasing the change rate of the parts table. Since queries rarely require a completely unconstrained scan of every part used on every product in every possible role, the compute capacity of the MPP database can efficiently and in parallel re-assemble the filtered parts of interest on filtered products of interest at run-time, doing so at a much lower overall cost, despite some increase in working space and CPU cost to execute queries. A data storage reduction of nearly 4 orders of magnitude is possible in this use case (~12 million rows in 2 parents and one new lookup table versus 100 billion rows in 2 parent tables and 4 intersection tables).

Database size often drives IT cost discussions and does drive pricing of many database systems, even though it is not an indication of workload capacity, which is central to leveraging the power of the MPP design. It is important to recognize that there can be substantial differences in data size driven by the data model employed (normalized, star, snow-flake) and independently by the hardware platform, with regard to both its compression method and the amount and type of table indexing needed to ensure performance. Each of these factors can vary space requirements 30% to 50%. Newly introduced high compression methods can also use a considerable share of CPU, which should be factored into overall throughput metrics (e.g., 30% CPU lost on data load tasks). A further consideration is the amount of administration work required to administer the database system, particularly its increasingly complex features. Industry analysts and companies have long found substantial amounts of labor required to manage non-MPP reporting systems, particularly to manage clustering and other partial parallelization methods on OLTP databases. Database administrator labor savings switching to an MPP database have in some cases paid for the hardware itself, when factoring in space and CPU efficiency.

With regard to the data model, the normalized model provides substantial space efficiencies compared with hosting multiple data marts, each of which is further de-normalized rather than snow-flaked to limit table joins typically. The space efficiency will vary based on the type of data and the type of business involved. In all cases care must be taken to realistically estimate which additional de-normalizations may be needed. Manufacturers often have complex product structures in which case the product dimension would represent a considerable share of the product data and one would not want to maintain many copies of it across multiple data marts. Other companies with rapid change and a requirement to report across time (instead of building one data mart per facet per time perspective) may face considerable churn in organization and customer areas. Within the normalized model, temporal normalization can collapse many points in time or consecutive periods with identical non-key attribution into a single period row, avoiding repetition between measurements of otherwise identical data. This approach allows for temporal analysis on the unique atomic data without the need for summarization, a substantial convenience and efficiency in conducting time-series analysis.

Technology also provides new options to tune the performance of storage to the expected value of the data. IT departments and more recently MPP vendors make use of a variety of 'hot' to 'cold' storage methods, including tape, file systems, large lower performing disk drives and other lower performance methods appropriate to the cost-benefit of the information. Similarly, the most valued data can migrate to costlier higher performance technologies such as the emergent Solid State Disk (SSD) devices. These advances in systems design have allowed vast quantities of data, into the petabyte range, to be directly accessible for analysis on leading MPP databases on a routine basis. This data otherwise would not be directly accessible in a single location or would languish on disparate file servers and require a heroic, costly and time-consuming effort to extract and assemble for analysis.

MPP COSTS MAY BE FALLING FASTER THAN YOU MAY REALIZE

Those making technical architecture decisions face a challenge with data warehouse acquisition, particularly when considering MPP hardware to support an EDW. A large purchase of a specialized data warehouse platform is more difficult to justify than a succession of smaller purchases of server hardware already utilized for transaction processing, perhaps also leveraging an existing OLTP-oriented DBMS site license. Few organizations can spend the time to conduct costly benchmarks of data warehouse systems and then repeat the process as technology changes. The measurement of system workload capacity across vendors, particularly with varying hardware and software approaches and varying architectures is a substantial challenge. The analysis of performance trends requires us to rely on both industry benchmarks and a vendor metric, Teradata's TPerf. This is not to suggest that other newer MPP vendors may not provide a similar cost-benefit, all else equal. The analysis that follows is an attempt to correlate relevant metrics over time for leading MPP and SMP database systems and should not be viewed as precise or applicable to a given situation.

While industry database benchmarks are available, particularly those published by the non-profit Transaction Processing Performance Council (n.d.), the results may have limited applicability to a given implementation or a specific database. When selecting a TPC benchmark for data warehouse performance, the TPC-H is the logical choice and 10TB an appropriate scale. The first 10TB benchmark was published by Teradata in December 2002, with HP and Oracle systems published starting in 2004 (Table 2). Overall capacity, which is measured in Composite Query-per-Hour Performance Metric (QphH), should be considered carefully and matched between systems if possible. Low concurrent query capacity in SMP hardware is of limited value if it doesn't meet workload requirements, as SMP designs cannot be scaled linearly using clustering methods. Not surprisingly, typical system throughput increases over time, with submissions showing a 400% growth between 2004 and 2008. Since the 2004 HP system had 60% of the 2002 Teradata system's throughput, both HP TPC-H systems would need

Table 2. Metrics per transaction processing performance council and teradata

Hardware/Software	Avail.	Price/Perf.	Throughput	Price
Teradata 5350 64node2cpu, V2R5.0	12/2002	$243/QphH 10TB	81,501 QphH	$19,774,904
HP SD Itanium2/1.5-64p Oracle10g	3/2004	$118/QphH 10TB	49,105 QphH	$5,800,675
HP SD Itanium/1.6-64dc Oracle11g	9/2008	$28/QphH 10TB	208,457 QphH	$5,829,685
Teradata 5250 MP-RAS, V2R4.1	3/2001	$321,888/TPerf	4.66 TPerf/node	$1.5M .4TB/nd
Teradata 5350 MP-RAS, V2R5.0	12/2002	$214,046/TPerf	5.98 TPerf/node	$1.3M .8TB/nd
Teradata 5380 MP-RAS, V2R5.1	3/2004	$158,824/TPerf	8.5 TPerf/node	$1.7M 1.3TB/nd
Teradata 5550H 8 core Linux, TD12	3/2008	$17,978/TPerf	44.5 TPerf/node	$0.8M 4TB/nd
Teradata 2550 8 core Linux, TD12	10/2008	$10,011/TPerf	~31 TPerf/node	$0.3M 3TB/nd

to be doubled or tripled to align with average system growth since Teradata's 2002 submission, with costs per unit rising accordingly due to the scalability losses seen in Table 1.

For the TPC-H data warehouse benchmark, test scenarios lag the complexity and scope of leading implementations. The TPC-H benchmark uses 22 specific and relatively simple SQL queries along with 2 refresh (atomic insert or delete) workloads submitted in a limited number of streams. TPC-H data through 2004 has 9 query streams while the later 2008 data has 24 streams, reflecting one of a number of changes across benchmark specifications that a comparison faces. To the extent changes in benchmark specifications reflect normal practice relating to system capability, such as faster hardware naturally running more concurrent queries, the relative validity of the comparison should hold over time. Conversely, a fixed specified workload test over a period of time when workload capability has grown rapidly would not be meaningful. While industry TPC benchmarks have demonstrated substantial reductions in the cost per unit of performance in recent years, MPP systems have been under represented in this trend. The results for the only terabyte or larger MPP systems tested for TPC-H, a Teradata model 5350, were withdrawn in March of 2004. No subsequent Teradata results have been submitted.

Teradata, however, publishes their own data warehouse capacity metric based on a mix of five categories of workload called TPerf for Traditional Performance (Dietz, 2007). The particular mix of workload categories, while forward-looking in supporting the activated EDW, may not match a given customer's current workload distribution. The workload mix is set at 5% full table scans, 15% tactical queries, 25% for both data loading and simple queries using materialized views and 30% for complex queries with joins. Teradata provides TPerf metrics for 10 generations of hardware dating back to 2000 (Deitz & Poulin, 2007; Tehan, 2008), with hardware pricing based on this TPerf metric. In terms of the quality of the TPerf metric, Teradata customers and the author do have considerable experience validating TPerf as they upgrade hardware and have found it quite predictive of real-world MPP workload capacity. The TPerf metric, however, does not allow comparisons between vendors, may reflect workloads that favor Teradata's architecture, may rely on a configuration not applicable to a specific customer and has not been independently validated in practice. A clear need exists with the emergence of new MPP appliances to have access to comparable capacity and cost metrics to help purchasers understand the often substantial differences between products in the context of the many functions that the modern data warehouse executes.

With regard to the price comparisons, database system pricing includes independent cost components such as disk, CPU, memory, software and maintenance whose relative costs may change over time. Cost-per-unit comparisons over time are thus approximate, particularly across metrics. Provided the system tested is comparable to your needs at that point in time, the individual price components are immaterial. The TPC-H pricing includes hardware, software, 3 years of maintenance and any public or mandatory discounts. The distribution of the cost components of the 2 HP systems considered in Table 2 from 2004 and 2008 is quite similar. One factor that does stand out is that the total price includes a 48% large system discount applied in 2004 and a 44% discount applied in 2008. The 2002 Teradata TPC-H cost component split was similar to the HP systems, however no discount was applied either in TPC-H or TPerf pricing, potentially inflating the Teradata per unit price for the typical large system should Teradata's discount be greater than any additional discounts offered by HP and Oracle in practice. Offsetting this potential over statement of Teradata cost is that Teradata TPerf pricing does not include 3 years of maintenance, which can represent 10% to 20% of system price.

A final caveat is that the appropriate balance of disk and CPU as well as the selection of software components and any per user licensing varies considerably in practice and may not correspond to the configurations selected for pricing, which can be assumed to demonstrate the system at its most efficient configuration. This may introduce variability as the relative cost of disk, CPU and vendor software pricing have varied over the period represented, particularly if your optimal system differs substantially from a typical system, such as being CPU or disk intensive or having few or many users. The data warehouse appliance market is moving towards simplified pricing and bundling of both software and hardware. Teradata's 2550 appliance pricing does include a substantial bundle of software in the base system cost. Trends comparing model 55xx, with cost variations based on the software selected, to model 2550 may thus under-state the trend.

We first examine cost per unit of performance trends within the two respective measures over an identical period. For Teradata's published TPerf metrics, Table 2 data in rows 4 through 7 spans 7 years for Teradata's model 55XX, the high-end member of their product family. List price per TPerf fell 94.41% during this period while throughput per node grew nearly 10-fold, from 4.66 TPerf per node to 44.5. Note that Teradata systems scale linearly with respect to the number of nodes, provided the data size is accommodated and the configuration is less than 1,024 nodes. This creates a theoretical capacity of more than 12 million QphH based on Table 2 row 1 adjusting for the power per node of current model 5550 and the 16-fold increase from 64 to 1,024 nodes. In 2008, Teradata introduced a family of products, with model 2550 providing comparable throughput and capability to most other data warehouse products on the market at a lower price point than the model 55XX (Table 2 Row 8). We must estimate the model 2550 TPerf, as Teradata does not provide this metric. Estimating the model 2550's TPerf at 70% of the model 5550 per node based on available information, the improvement factor over 7.5 years from the 5250 to the 2550 is 32 fold, representing a 96.89% reduction in cost per unit of performance.

With regard to SMP systems on the TPC-H 10TB benchmark, comparable large systems were selected that used Oracle and HP SuperDome hardware as shown in rows 2 and 3 of Table 2, covering availability dates of March 2004 and September 2008. The capacity of the submitted systems grew fourfold during the 4.5-year period while the system cost remained constant. The cost per unit of performance fell 76.32% during the period from $118 to $28 per TPC-H Composite Query-per-Hour, an improvement of 4.22x. Comparing this improvement to other applications of the same hardware and software, the improvement is relatively less than transactional benchmark results during this period. The 5-year trend for TPC-C cost per unit of transactional performance is a factor of 10, with a factor of 14 over the 7 years prior to late 2008 for example.

The more interesting but approximate comparison is between the internal trends within the TPC-H benchmark and TPerf data which, while not directly comparable, do represent the best published data warehouse performance information that we have available to us. Fortunately, the data provided by Teradata for model 5350 provides an anchor point to compare the two measures, as data for both TPC-H and TPerf on this model is available and shown in rows 1 and 5 of Table 2. In order to create a period to match the March 2004 and September 2008 availability dates of the HP Oracle data (rows 2 and 3), we need to average the two Teradata models, 5350 and 5380, to create a 4.5-year time span that overlaps as much of the HP period as possible. By averaging rows 5 and 6 for December 2002 and March 2004, we create a 56-month period from July 2003 to March 2008 for Teradata similar to the 54-month period for HP. During this period, the apparent cost reduction per TPerf within Teradata 55XX models is 59% greater than the cost reduction seen in cost per QphH for SMP-based HP Oracle systems. This corresponds to a 4.22x reduction in cost per QphH for HP relative to a 10.37x reduction in cost per TPerf for Teradata, with the Teradata cost per unit improving at a rate 2.46 times faster.

A second similar trend comparison can be applied to the Teradata model 2550, a more comparable data warehouse to the HP TPC-H results in terms of throughput. In this case, the period of the Teradata model 5380 and 2550 align directly with the HP period. The apparent cost reduction per unit of performance amongst the Teradata models using TPerf is 73% greater than the apparent SMP-based HP Oracle cost TPC-H reduction per unit of performance during the identical period. This corresponds to a 4.22x reduction in cost per QphH for HP relative to a 15.87x reduction in cost per TPerf for Teradata, with the Teradata cost per unit improving at a rate 3.76 times faster. This aligns with practitioner experience suggesting that the Teradata model 2550 has a low cost and a relatively high workload capacity, in part resulting from its software maturity. It should be noted that Teradata's apparent cost leadership is a recent development in low cost appliances. The pioneer in this market, Netezza, is likely to have held a cost advantage for some types of implementations for several years prior.

A final and necessarily more approximate comparison leverages the Teradata TPC-H result and TPerf trends to estimate the price per QphH for Teradata models and thus provide a rough measure of absolute cost trends over time between SMP and MPP systems at a similar scale. The driver for this comparison is the natural tendency of IT departments to seek to leverage common hardware, even if not ideally suited to data warehousing. This comparison can not be projected beyond the 10TB scale and is limited by the relatively simple TPC-H workload and relatively limited throughput of the submitted TPC-H systems. The scalability losses for SMP systems highlighted in Table 1 and the low throughput in QphH of SMP-based TPC-H submissions makes it clear that MPP designs can be expected to show increasing relative cost efficiencies as system size grows and workload increases.

As no other vendor submitted a 10TB TPC-H result until March 2004, the comparison first requires that we adjust Teradata's result from December 2002 forward to March 2004, using the relative cost per TPerf of the Teradata model 5350 and model 5380 of $214,046 and $158,824 respectively. This reduces the imputed cost per QphH as of March 2004 for the model 5380 to $180, a very conservative 26% cost per unit reduction given recent improvement trends. Next we use the relative change in TPerf over the comparable period determined earlier. For the model 5550, the 10.37x TPerf cost reduction over the 54-month period from the $180 starting cost results in an imputed $17 cost per QphH. Similarly for the model 2550, the 15.87x TPerf cost reduction determined earlier results in an imputed $11 cost per QphH. We can now compare the absolute costs to the September 2008 HP Oracle TPC-H benchmark, finding the approximate imputed cost per QphH of the Teradata 5550, at $17, to be 38% less than the HP Oracle system's cost of $28 per QphH. The imputed cost of the Teradata 2550, at $11, is found to be 59% less expensive per unit of performance. Similarly the Teradata 2550 could be expected to perform the TPC-H 10MB benchmark at a throughput of 208,457 QphH at approximately 41% of the cost of the HP system.

A number of factors have combined to give MPP systems a relative advantage, most of which are out of scope for this article. Suffice it to say that low cost high performance multi-core commodity CPU's, improvements in CPU and memory architecture, the ability of the interconnect bus to keep up with the MPP workload and the ability of MPP systems and optimizers to efficiently utilize this shared-nothing architecture have all contributed. A further factor is likely the introduction of vigorous competition in the MPP area (Thoo & Beyer, 2008), which has driven vendors to aggressively compete on price. The result has been a reduction in the cost per unit of performance of 50% in each of the last 3 years for Teradata model 55XX. There has been a cost reduction of 94.4% (17.9 factor) over the period between 2001 and 2008 in the cost per TPerf, from $321,888 to $17,978 on enterprise class hardware. Cost per TPerf falls to an estimated $10,011 representing a 97% reduction (32.2 factor) on the mid-range 2550 platform since 2001. Cost per byte stored has also fallen quickly, with a 96.5% reduction (28.8 ratio) over 7 years, when also including the impact of Teradata's multi-valued data compression.

In practical terms, in 2001 a Teradata system consisting of 10 model 5250 nodes with 4 TB of usable space listed for $15 million and provided a TPerf rating of 46.6. In 2008, a 2 node model 5550H system provided a TPerf rating of 89, stored 8 TB (12 TB with compression), and had a list price of $1.6 million. It should be noted that with a normalized model utilizing database compression and requiring little additional indexing, 12 TB is a considerable amount of data for most enterprises, covering perhaps 50 billion data rows. Cost reductions are even more dramatic if you consider the newer lower-cost data warehouse appliances offered by Teradata and competitors such as Netezza, who popularized the term appliance by releasing a self-contained MPP rack in 2002. While not sufficiently capable to handle high volume complex mixed workloads in the fully activated Enterprise Data Warehouse, they can serve lesser needs cost effectively. One half rack of the Teradata appliance, model 2550, can execute roughly 50 concurrent queries and loads (a capability equivalent to the 2001 system), yet sells for half as much per TB, listing for $99,000, including software. The list price of our example machine falls to $0.6 million using model 2550, providing 6.25 TB of compressed user space and an approximate TPerf rating of 62, 25 times less expensive yet more capable than our 2001 system.

It appears that the MPP database has evolved from being the only database architecture capable of performing analytics against large amounts of relational data, perhaps at considerable cost, to being both a low cost and high capacity platform for large decision support databases. This benefit is further multiplied when data is consolidated and represented in the EDW. Continued replication of systems, infrastructure and data would otherwise capture a growing proportion of the IT budget, threatening the well-being of companies that do not simultaneously increase data warehouse capacity and reduce IT costs. As this recent MPP cost trend becomes recognized, it is expected to drive substantial change as to where analytical data is stored, how it is analyzed, and provide further opportunities to leverage the MPP database architecture.

All of the major DBMS vendors and one hardware supplier are now offering or will soon be offering an MPP product. One software vendor, Oracle, is entering the hardware business for the first time in order to field an MPP product, both indirectly through a pending acquisition (Sun Microsystems, Inc. and Greenplum) and through an alliance with a hardware supplier (Hewlett-Packard) that also sells a competing MPP appliance. Thus in the past 2 years, the database software and hardware vendors most invested in SMP databases, Oracle and HP, have introduced their own MPP systems. Given this clear direction, further IT investments in replicating data, collecting data from disparate sources and using stove-piped analytical systems should decline rapidly. The case for centralization on an efficient MPP database is sufficiently strong that the ROI on conversion covers conversions costs in 12 to 18 months in most cases.

THE MPP DATA WAREHOUSE IN PRACTICE

A fair question to ask is just what benefit to analytics does this apparently low cost high capacity database architecture provide. First and foremost, this capability accelerates the migration of decision support data onto a single or small number of high performance databases. Even without any re-design, such a 'forklift' is compelling given the efficiencies of the MPP database. A key advantage of the MPP database is that its linear scalability eliminates vast amounts of data duplication as well as off-database processing by consolidating the data. If the move to consolidate on MPP is also accompanied by data integration (enterprise data model, data quality, minimum of replication), the result is the single integrated data source that advanced analytics has been seeking for many years. The ability to obtain, on-demand, exactly the data needed from a centralized MPP data warehouse greatly reduces the cost and increases the timeliness and benefits of analytics. The incremental cost of new analytics or Business Intelligence applications becomes significantly less, as additional queries against the MPP database represent incremental CPU usage only, not new infrastructure or new data structures to populate. In the EDW, the substantial amount of work to assemble and present the data has already been done once, representing a fixed cost. This potential to execute SQL-based analytics against the EDW is often not recognized. Even a modest MPP database such as shown in Table 3 has a vast capacity to process information via ANSI-SQL, particularly using ANSI extensions such as ordered analytic

Table 3. Typical 30 TB EDW system (~120 units of work)

Metric	Result	Comment
Insert select, empty table	6.5M rows/sec	134 byte rows, no indexes
Full table scan rate, 1 like operator	6-25M rows/sec	4GB/sec rate for any row length
Worst-case 30KB SQL scan of 1 table	1M rows/sec	125MB/sec rate
2-way SQL minus 13m rows, 134 bytes	18 sec	Change Data Capture (CDC)
Shred into staging tables (load XML)	66 GB/hour	V1 product, not fully parallelized
System - Daily rows loaded	500 million	Not all loaded to target (per cdc)
Single system planned uptime	99.95%	Excludes planned outages
Total daily queries	5 M	Includes load activity, metadata
Outbound daily queries	1.2 M	Excludes metadata
Average outbound query elapsed time	0.3 sec	Web, BI, other user queries
Tactical queries (SOA, parameterized)	0.3 M	Response time of 50ms
BI generated queries (~5-20 table joins)	0.4 M	Direct access, feeds are the rest

functions as well as vendor-specific extensions. Such first order analytics within the EDW is newly practical without any additional external hardware or data replication.

The computational efficiency of relational operators in the cost effective MPP database system should cause re-examination of analytics systems already deployed, particularly alternatives to the MPP relational database. Such systems may have offered cost or performance benefits in the past, but given the rapid reduction in MPP costs per query, may no longer do so today. This is particularly true when the full cost of ownership of all related components is considered (additional servers, replication costs, additional software licenses, labor, etc.). For example, the storage efficiency of MPP databases, in using little more disk space than the normalized atomic text size, stands in contrast to alternative representations such as XML, which when fully deployed use much more space than a normalized representation, perhaps even 10 times as much. Storage efficiency differences can be even greater when considering available techniques in relational database modeling to reduce data size, such as the billion row intersection elimination cited earlier. An XML representation would associate all such intersecting entries separately under a parent, using perhaps 20 bytes for each atomic value and exploding required data storage even more compared to the compressed column approach in the relational model, consequently requiring extensive indexing to query the resulting data.

Moving away from the row-based database, the columnar databases such as Vertica present a special database optimization based on compressing tuples to a small fraction of their presence within rows. As vendors of a type of data warehouse appliance, these new entrants not surprisingly claim that the era of the row-oriented database is largely over and that their product represents a new paradigm (Monash, 2007). Columnar databases do exploit the MPP architecture and some, such as Vertica, meet the criteria to be included in the most well-known industry analysis, the Gartner Magic Quadrant, along with newly listed row-based HP Neoview and Greenplum products (Feinberg & Beyer, 2008). As often occurs when new entrants innovate, MPP vendors are moving to adopt aggressive compression methods as well, ranging from the no cost 35-45% savings row header bit flag method used by Teradata to the Oracle 11 block compression newly applicable to the Exadata layer. While benchmarks are not yet available on the later, at least a 2-4x compression factor seems likely in exchange for a CPU cost of between 10% and 30%, a worthwhile trade-off to speed disk operations. As with any approach, design interacts with the database software, with a model-based approach such as our multi-valued de-normalization example always being an option on any database.

Other specialized data warehouse appliances and software approaches have emerged to process large volumes of data, such as file-based and XML-based databases, MapReduce and Hadoop. While providing particular solutions to very large data problems, these specialized approaches do not appear to provide any benefits for parallelization of analytics nor do they support the wide range of data found in the EDW, a key element in providing a single high performance self-contained analytics system. With near-term technology improvements likely to drive further declines in cost per unit of performance and vigorous competition in the MPP marketplace, the adoption of a mature enterprise-wide MPP-based data warehouse is clearly associated with obtaining a competitive advantage. Assuming an organization has realized this, it can focus on how best to utilize this capability both now and into the future, as the MPP database can provide similar benefits to sophisticated outbound analytics.

DATA TRANSFORMATION MOVES INSIDE

MPP systems have developed capabilities to internally execute more types of workload that can directly benefit analytics. Some of the recent impetus seeks to benefit from the cost and capability trends highlighted in this article, leveraging what has always been an algorithmic opportunity to parallelize workload. This trend began with practitioners driven by increasingly stringent load windows and volumes leveraging SQL to perform transformations in parallel within the database, a capability only now being embraced by the mainstream data load tools. The common transformation operations that were done sequentially in memory with a dedicated application server have largely migrated into the MPP database using ANSI SQL operators and additional functional extensions. A wide variety of common transformations can be translated into set-based SQL, operating within the MPP database a table-at-a-time with full parallel efficiency, instead of being invoked using cursors or traditional programmatic logic in a middle-tier SMP server. However, to avoid having an entire table load or transformation SQL statement fail due to a single error in one row, it is important to carefully pre-filter data or to use bulk error reporting, a difference from the row-at-a-time exception handling used in traditional programming.

The traditional Extract Transform Load (ETL) process has evolved into an ELT process more accurately described as EtLTl that includes the extract, minimal transformation prior to loading, loading to staging tables, major transformations in SQL and finally a low impact load to target tables. Beyond the substantial benefits of running transformations in parallel, the ELT design can also leverage the MPP database by storing and re-using prior transformation results to avoid repeating costlier workload. Transformations, whether done in SQL or requiring external programs, can be stored as persistent data for re-use, joined into the transformation SQL of all subsequent loads. This simple data-oriented re-use optimization is efficiently achieved using SQL operators (outer join, transform matching values, leave nulls for new values) already inherent in the ELT approach. A few additional SQL joins are easily accommodated on modern MPP systems, a fact that may not have been the case several years ago. A daily transaction net change load into a database with 3 years of historical data would add just 0.1% to overall size, with an hourly load into one year of history representing 0.011% of existing data. This further reinforces the advantage of only acting on change, a Change Data Capture (CDC) approach, and using the MPP database to identify change in cases where there is no other method available such as a push publication.

This push down of transformations into MPP-parallelized SQL and other SQL extensions (functions, user-defined code) is increasingly common and illustrates the substantial performance advantages per unit of hardware that MPP systems enjoy when workload leverages this capability. The process involves converting as much as possible of the programmatic transformation code (loops, if-then statements) into the functionally equivalent ANSI SQL code or other database extensions (case statements, joins, set operations, recursion). The central benefit is to convert inherently serial programmatic processes (fetch one row from the database into an ETL server, combine with other information, execute logic, insert or update target database row) into table-at-a-time operations (set SQL). ELT was once the province of large data warehouse operators with application staff able to write the ELT code, typically SQL generators. The data load tool vendors, who previously advocated only an ETL perspective with all workload executed on their middle-tier SMP servers, have recognized the trend and enhanced their products to optimize placement of the transformation logic (transform at the data source, transform on ETL server, transform in the MPP target). One limitation of ELT on an MPP database is that set-SQL statements can lose some of their efficiency on input sets sufficiently small as to not provide a minimum of rows per unit of parallelism. Furthermore, there are still a few transformation processes that do not easily fit into a SQL paradigm, such as complex data cleansing and house-holding analysis.

In terms of reducing costly IT infrastructure, the ELT approach can successfully migrate most data transformation workload into the MPP database at a considerable cost savings. The author has seen ETL environments where the hardware and ETL software licensing costs (often charged per CPU) exceeded that of the MPP database they were loading. Traditional ETL infrastructure costs can represent up to 50% of the target system cost, despite providing no direct end user benefit, unlike additional MPP CPU which can be used as extra capacity for user queries when not performing ELT workloads. ELT workload represents a small percentage of database workload when executed as set-SQL, particularly during the day when throttled to avoid competing with customer queries. The author has seen ELT workload percentages in the single digits for peak times and in the twenty and thirty percentage range off peak for a mature EDW implementation leveraging ELT methods. The positive ROI for ELT migration is generally clear, but the savings will vary based on the exact scenario. Internally written programmatic code leveraging set-SQL executing inside the MPP database is easily the most cost effective solution, requiring only a small application server to invoke using proportionally less ETL licenses or potentially none at all when written directly by application staff. Any ETL server hardware and software savings should be measured against the relative cost of the MPP database and any software licensing costs there. One recent hybrid MPP solution from Oracle and HP requires two software products which together represent 88% of the overall list price (Monash, 2008). The cost and performance benefits of ELT are well established as an efficient time-variant light-weight load process providing a rich source of integrated data available for near real-time analytics.

STATISTICAL ANALYSIS LEVERAGES MPP

An emerging trend is the implementation of advanced statistical primitives directly within MPP databases. Basic statistical functions were added to ANSI SQL-2003 and have been implemented by most database software vendors for some time. On Teradata, the ability to utilize common statistical functions such as correlations and regression functions in SQL queries provides considerable efficiencies when compared to extracting the data from the database and running the statistics function on an external server using a specialized statistical software package. The later approach has been the standard method for many years but is inherently non-parallel and is more cumbersome from a systems perspective. To use this in-database statistics capability and extend it further to parallelize more advanced operators, SAS® and Teradata entered into a strategic alliance in late 2007 (Brobst & Kent, 2008; Webb, 2007).

The SAS application dynamically generates C language code to create and compile Teradata User Defined Functions (UDF) to be dynamically executed within the database at run-time. A similar approach is in development for other areas of SAS functionality. Not surprisingly, this has led to a paradigm shift in how analytics is performed, with more of the computational workload performed directly in the parallel MPP database where the data resides. SAS has launched a 'Managed Server' hosted within the Teradata rack (Webb, 2008a), entirely eliminating other external statistical servers between the end-user's client and the Teradata MPP system. This low cost SAS server blade uses the Teradata appliance's managed Ethernet network to maximize performance between the SAS server and the database. This represents a substantial infrastructure simplification and cost reduction for IT, combined with a large increase in timely analytical power. This evolution mirrors the push down of transformation logic into the database that has lead to a substantial reduction of data load (ETL) servers and serial methods on the inbound side. Statistics software vendors are pushing down the analytic workload of statistical analysis to leverage the high performance and computational efficiency of the MPP database. Other MPP vendors are pursuing similar initiatives to parallelize advanced statistics beyond what the ANSI SQL standard provides for.

One example of performance improvement with statistical push-down is from early 2008. The scoring functionality of SAS was pushed down into Teradata's MPP architecture, with a 4,500% performance improvement (Webb, 2008b) on a benchmark assessing records scored per second (750,000 records scored per second on 6 Teradata nodes, 77,000 scored per second on 1 identical non-database node, 16,400 rows per second via external SAS DATA step). As you would expect, performance scales linearly with the number of Teradata nodes, with test data presented from 1 to 6 nodes in this respect. The entire SAS PROC Freq required the extraction of 39.5 million rows using the external SAS server with a total elapsed time of 1,012 seconds, compared to the SQL push down method, which needed only 32 seconds and returned only the resulting 15,800 rows (Brobst & Kent, 2008). Similar efforts for regression analysis push down are also in work at SAS, providing further statistical intelligence directly within the MPP database.

VISUALIZATION USING INTEGRATED SPATIAL INTELLIGENCE

Most relational database systems have added locational intelligence using geo spatial primitives to extend the SQL language and storage systems of their databases (e.g., Microsoft SQL Server™ in 2008, IBM DB2 Spatial Extender in 2002, Oracle Spatial in 2000, Informix® in 1998). This is particularly interesting in the MPP space, given the need for large volumes of detailed geospatial data which is most effectively stored on an MPP database, as well as the performance potential of this architecture to parallelize spatial operators. Most MPP vendors have only lately started to support spatial operations, with Teradata and Netezza recently releasing products. Netezza launched a spatial feature in late 2008 while Teradata did not launch its first spatial offering until December 2007, and then it was stand-alone product. As of this writing, Teradata plans to release its first integrated spatial product with Teradata 13.0 in the first half of 2009. Both vendors provide support for loading and translating spatial data into an MPP database, native spatial storage types and the ability to use spatial filters in SQL queries. In both cases MPP vendors partner with Geographic Information System (GIS) providers and typically adopt open standards to integrate the visualization component directly with the MPP system. While Oracle has long supported spatial features, it is not clear if the newly released HP Oracle Database Machine can push down spatial or other complex operators from the upper SMP-based Oracle database execution layer into the parallel MPP Exadata layer.

By providing spatial extensions to SQL and spatial data types, MPP vendors make it possible to store and then query large quantities of spatial data, efficiently answering spatial questions on data already in the data warehouse. An example of such a query is to determine the customers within

100 meters of other specified customers, then group them and return data from within the 100 meter buffer around that grouping. The Netezza Spatial implementation claims one to two orders of magnitude reduction in query times in processing geographic location data by pushing down the filtering of spatial queries into a specialized Field Gate Programmable Array (FGPA) processor associated with each parallel unit or SPU (Snippet Processing Unit), consisting of one disk drive, the FGPA and memory on a card.

Various coordinate transformations are supported such as spheroid and spherical transformations and a large number of distance calculations are provided in the case of Teradata's geospatial release. The spatial data types leverage the storage capacity of the MPP database, handling up to 1,000,000 vertices in Teradata 13. Significant challenges do exist in parallelizing spatial relationship operators, particularly since the computation of geometry algorithms is by definition quite costly (Watzke, 2008). Successful parallelization of spatial operators avoids the inherent tendency to duplicate all of the data to each unit of work to in effect compute a relational product join (find the minimum distance by first computing all distances). One common solution to the spatial join problem is a filter-and-refine approach, using the Minimum Bounding Rectangle (MBR) to perform an initial filtering and then use actual geometry to further refine calculations.

Teradata developed a filter approach that involves forming a grid by tessellating a pattern of rectangles over the area of interest and then building an NxM grid where cells are hashed to Teradata's parallel units of work. This allows the use of existing relational operators and maximizes the parallel efficiency of the operation. This is just one example of the need to convert existing algorithms to operate in a massively parallel execution mode to fully leverage the parallel efficiency of the MPP database. The benefits of this approach can be quite substantial, with an insurance use case of determining customer density reduced from hours to one minute (Watzke, 2008). A communication use case cites a reduction in run time from hours to 6 minutes when answering customer location questions relative to store locations. These early results show considerable promise in extending the capabilities of MPP databases via parallel implementation of complex primitives such as spatial methods, which can directly support efficient and timely visual analytics on a frequently updated Enterprise Data Warehouse.

CONCLUSION

A convergence of new capabilities and lower cost products is rapidly pushing Massively Parallel Processing database technology into the mainstream, making available a vast quantity of integrated and timely data. This data warehousing capability is an unprecedented opportunity to expand the scope of advanced analytics. The trend to push down statistics, visualization and other algorithms into the massively parallel MPP database follows recent improvements that pushed data transformations into the MPP database. As we have seen, the MPP database architecture is uniquely suited to large-scale analytics and data manipulation, unlike the SMP architecture which underlies mainstream relational databases. MPP databases have evolved over the past 25 years of deployment to become more sophisticated, more capable and have many large-scale implementations in commercial use. This approach has required multiple advances over many years in order to provide the capability to continuously ingest, integrate and present all of an enterprise's data in a single normalized database, an activated Enterprise Data Warehouse. The EDW has been shown to generate a substantial ROI and for our purposes provides the foundation for powerful near real-time analytics performed at minimal incremental cost.

A key enabler of this trend has been the continuous cost reductions in MPP databases, which appear recently to have over-taken cost reductions in SMP database systems when relating performance measures on cost per unit of performance basis. While MPP systems have always stood alone in being able to host the largest databases, currently in the petabyte range, they can cost-effectively host a wider range of databases previously hosted on SMP systems, which can no longer be regarded as less expensive. An analysis and normalization of two measures of data warehouse performance, one from Teradata and one from an industry group, found dramatic cost reductions in Teradata system cost per unit of performance totaling 96.89% over a 7-year period. While large SMP-based systems also had substantial performance gains and cost reductions on the 10TB TPC-H benchmark, these cost per unit of performance improvements were 59% less than performance metrics for Teradata's enterprise model and 73% less than Teradata's mid-range data warehouse appliance over a similar 4.5-year period. By aligning the two measures on a common test system, we project that Teradata's model 2550 offers absolute cost savings of approximately 59% per unit of performance versus SMP-based hardware based on 10TB TPC-H benchmark data, providing 2.85 times more data warehouse performance per dollar at the 10TB scale factor and concurrency.

Substantial capability improvements simultaneous to large unit cost reductions in MPP systems are particularly welcome at a time when IT is expected, as never before, to deliver insightful analysis quickly and cost effectively. Not only is the parallelization of analytics workload onto the MPP database highly cost effective in most cases, there are also substantial performance gains, enabling near real-time loading and rapid analytics of large quantities of freshly loaded data, providing unprecedented agility in decision making. Analytical tools of many types can be cost-effectively deployed to a broad audience, driving profitable outcomes like never before. This represents a major paradigm shift from how analytics has been done in the past, moving away from costly single-purpose analytics servers to push powerful analytics capability directly into the existing Enterprise Data Warehouse. Organizations and individuals who are aware of this trend and can leverage it successfully, despite the transition involved, are more likely to prosper in the coming years, particularly as IT becomes an enabler of value rather than a center of cost. This revolutionary change is already taking place at the most visionary organizations, building upon the most advanced MPP databases supported by leading analytics vendors.

REFERENCES

Anderson-Lehman, R., Watson, H. J., Wixom, B. H., & Hoffer, J. A. (2007). *Continental Airlines Flies High with Real-time Business Intelligence.* Retrieved from http://www.fuqua.duke.edu/centers/ccrm/datasets/continental/Continental_Airlines_Case_ Study.pdf

Ballinger, C. (2006). *Born To Be Parallel.* Dayton, OH: Teradata Corporation.

Ballinger, C., & Fryer, R. (1997). Born To Be Parallel: Why Parallel Origins Give Teradata an Enduring Performance Edge. *A Quarterly Bulletin of the Computer Society of the IEEE Technical Committee on Data Engineering*, *20*(2), 3–12.

Brobst, S., & Kent, P. (2008). *A New Era of High Performance Analytics.* Dayton, OH: Teradata Corporation.

Codd, E. F. (1970). A relational model for large shared data banks. *Communications of the ACM*, *13*(6), 377–387. doi:10.1145/362384.362685

Deitz, J. (2007). At the core of the Teradata platform. *Teradata Magazine*, *7*(3), 62–65.

Deitz, J., & Poulin, S. (Eds.). (2007). *Proceedings from the 2007 Teradata Partners User Group Conference: Teradata Platform Performance: Higher and Higher*. Retrieved from http://www.teradata.com/teradata-partners/conference/index.cfm

Eckerson, W. (2004). *In Search of a Single Version of the Truth: Strategies for Consolidating Analytical Silos*. Chatsworth, CA: The Data Warehouse Institute (TDWI).

Eckerson, W. (2007). *Best Practices in Operational BI: Converging Analytical and Operational Processes*. Chatsworth, CA: The Data Warehouse Institute (TDWI).

Feinberg, D., & Beyer, M. A. (2008). *Magic Quadrant for Data Warehouse Database Management Systems*. Stamford, CT: Gartner.

Foley, J. (2007). *Exclusive: Inside Hewlett-Packard's Data Warehouse Gamble*. Retrieved from http://www.intelligententerprise.com/showArticle.jhtml?articleID=196801888

Helmaan, P. (2003). 3M: 100 years and processing. *Teradata Magazine*. Retrieved from http://www.teradata.com/td/page/115211

IEEE. Computer Society. (2005). *Michael Stonebraker.* Retrieved from http://www.ieee.org/portal/pages/about/awards/bios/2005vonneumann.html

Knight, R. (1988, April). Some choose a hardware DBMS. *Software Magazine.* Retrieved from http://findarticles.com/p/articles/mi_m0SMG/is_n5_v8/ai_6654621/

Monash, K. (2007). *Are row-oriented RDBMS obsolete?* Retrieved from http://www.dbms2.com/category/michael-stonebraker/

Monash, K. (2008). *Oracle Database Machine and Exadata pricing*. Retrieved from http://www.monash.com/uploads/Oracle-Exadata-pricing-estimates-Sep-30-2008.xls

Stonebraker, M. (1985). *The Case for Shared Nothing*. Retrieved from http://db.cs.berkeley.edu/papers/hpts85-nothing.pdf

Tandem Database Group. (1989). *NonStop SQL, A Distributed, High-Performance, High Availability Implementation of SQL.* Retrieved from http://www.hpl.hp.com/techreports/tandem/TR-87.4.pdf

Taubes, G. (1995, September). The Rise and Fall of Thinking Machines. *Inc.com Magazine.* Retrieved from http://www.inc.com/magazine/19950915/2622.html

Tehan, D. (2008). *Teradata Overview.* Retrieved from http://www.cs.mu.oz.au/351/teradata.pdf

Teradata Corporation. (2007). *2007 Data Warehouse Benchmark Report Prepared for Manufacturing Industry Respondents*. Dayton, OH: Author.

Teradata Corporation. (n.d.). *Teradata history.* Retrieved from http://www.teradata.com/t/history/

Thoo, E., & Beyer, M. A. (2008). *Best Practices for Data Mart Consolidation*. Stamford, CT: Gartner.

Transaction Processing Performance Council. (n.d.). *Complete TPC-H Results List.* Retrieved from http://www.tpc.org/tpch/results/tpch_results.asp?orderby=dbms

Transaction Processing Performance Council. (n.d.). *Complete TPC-C Results List.* Retrieved from http://www.tpc.org/tpcc/results/tpcc_results.asp?orderby=dbms

Transaction Processing Performance Council. (n.d.). *Using Teradata V2R5.0*. Retrieved from http://www.tpc.org/results/individual_results/NCR/NCR5350_ES_10TB.pdf

Walter, T. (2008). *Teradata Architecture – Technology & Differentiation*. Retrieved from http://www.teradata.com/teradata-partners/conference/index.cfm

Watzke, M. (2008). *Teradata GeoSpatial*. Retrieved from http://www.teradata.com/teradata-partners/conference/index.cfm

Webb, B. (2007). *SAS and Teradata Enter into Strategic Partnership*. Cary, NC: SAS Institute. Retrieved from http://www.sas.com/news/preleases/100807/SASandTeradata.html

Webb, B. (2008a). *SAS Speeds Delivery of In-Database Capabilities and Unveils New Software Bundle Program with Teradata*. Cary, NC: SAS Institute. Retrieved from http://www.sas.com/news/preleases/031708/Teradata.html

Webb, B. (2008b). *SAS In-Database Processing with Teradata: An Overview of Foundation Technology*. Cary, NC: SAS Institute. Retrieved from http://support.sas.com/resources/papers/teradata08.pdf

Weiss, W. (2008). *A Technical Overview of the Oracle Exadata Storage Server*. Retrieved from http://www.oracle.com/technology/products/bi/db/exadata/pdf/exadata-technical-whitepaper.pdf

This work was previously published in the Information Resources Management Journal, Volume 24, Issue 4, edited by Mehdi Khosrow-Pour, pp. 1-26, copyright 2013 by IGI Publishing (an imprint of IGI Global).

Chapter 16
3D Object Modeling Using Sketches

Sofia Kyratzi
University of the Aegean, Ermoupolis, Greece

Nickolas S. Sapidis
University of Western Macedonia, Greece

ABSTRACT

In this paper, the authors present a new algorithm for constructing a solid model when the given input is only one partial-view sketch ("natural sketch"). This algorithm is a two-step process, where first a complete (wireframe) sketch is derived, which is then transformed into a 3D polyhedron. The paper details topological and geometric aspects of the process, as well as the essential "user-interaction" components dealing with cases where the sketch-to-solid problem does not have a unique solution.

1. INTRODUCTION

Throughout the history of Computer Graphics and Engineering Visualization it is evident the desire of users to be able to define geometric objects using an interface mimicking as much as possible the traditional "sketching on paper" (Lipson, 1998). Obviously, 3D Geometric Modeling (for engineering, entertainment or artistic applications) is one of the most challenging fields for Sketch-based User Interfaces (SUIs), as in that the SUI must derive from the given 2D sketch the missing 3D information.

This research deals with the problem of defining a Polyhedron from a given Single Sketch (PSS problem) (Lamb & Bandopadhay, 1990; Wang & Grinstein, 1993; Grimstead & Martin, 1995; Schweikardt & Gross, 2000; Varley, 2002; Sapidis, Kyratzi, & Azariadis, 2005; Company, Piquer, Contero, & Naya, 2005; Fahiem, Haq, & Saleemi, 2007; Cao, Liu, & Tang, 2008). A sketch is a set of straight *lines* on a plane that intersect at *junctions*. Loops of lines and junctions form regions of the sketch. The given sketch is either a complete *wireframe sketch* (Figure 1(a)) or a *natural sketch*, i.e., a sketch without hidden lines

DOI: 10.4018/978-1-4666-3616-3.ch016

(Figure 1(b)). The two different types of sketches correspond to two distinct versions of the PSS problem. A given sketch is called *realizable* if it is the correct projection of a polyhedron (Ros & Thomas, 2005).

This paper deals with the PSS problem for the case of a natural sketch, as this is most often involved in industrial applications. Moreover, this investigation is limited to the simplest case of a *trihedral polyhedron* (where exactly three faces meet at each vertex), which is still unsolved (Cao, Liu, & Tang, 2008), and references therein.

The strict majority of published PSS methods are heavily based on the "line labeling" method and on "image regularities", which are known to have significant disadvantages; see an analysis in Section 2. Thus, the present research focuses on a "minimal-completion" algorithm (Kyratzi & Sapidis, 2008, 2009) employing robust tools from Graph Theory, Solid Modeling and Euclidean Geometry. Indeed, these fields offer an abundance of results and algorithmic tools that have found, up to the present time, limited application to the PSS problem. Kyratzi and Sapidis (2009) present the initial part of the "minimal-completion" algorithm focusing on the topological construction of the polyhedron corresponding to a given natural sketch. This paper completes the "minimal-completion" algorithm with its part dealing with the geometric construction of the polyhedron (see sections "Step S5: Geometric construction of the wireframe sketch" and "Step S6: Geometric construction of polyhedron"). Furthermore, this work addresses the issue that, in general, when the PSS problem is solvable, more than one polyhedra correspond to the given natural sketch. In this case, the user should get involved in the polyhedron-construction process to guide it towards a desirable solution; appropriate "user-interaction" methods are developed in the sections "Step S5: Geometric construction of the wireframe sketch" and "Step S6: Geometric construction of polyhedron". Section 5 details application of the "minimal-completion" algorithm on a typical sketch, demonstrating the effectiveness of the proposed methodology.

Figure 1. The two types of sketches involved in the PSS problem

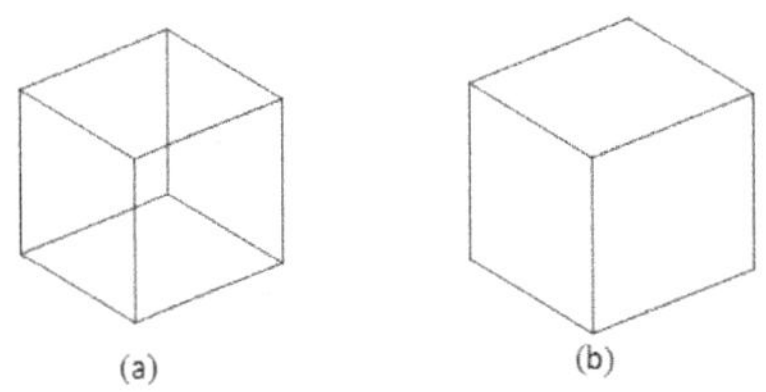

2. CONSTRUCTING A POLYHEDRON FROM A SINGLE SKETCH: A REVIEW OF CURRENT METHODS

The Line Labeling Method

One of the standard tools employed by existing PSS algorithms (Lamb & Bandopadhay, 1990; Grimstead & Martin, 1995; Schweikardt & Gross, 2000; Varley, 2002) is "Line Labeling" (LL) (Sugihara, 1986; Varley, 2002). LL assigns to each line of a sketch one of the four labels {+, −,→,←}. The label "+" ("−") is given to a line in the sketch when the two faces meeting along the corresponding edge form an angle > (<) 180°. The labels "→,←" indicate an occluding line; this means that the corresponding edge is associated to one visible and one hidden face of the polyhedron-to-be-constructed. A sketch is called *labelable* if and only if it can be associated to at least one valid set of labels (Sugihara, 1986). Many algorithms are available for constructing a LL of a sketch; a comprehensive review is given in (Varley, 2002).

The present research completely avoids using the Line Labeling heuristic for the following reasons:

1. The fact that a sketch is labelable is only a necessary condition for the existence of a polyhedron corresponding to this sketch.

Indeed, while both sketches in Figure 2 are labelable and accept exactly the same labeling, only the sketch in Figure 2(b) is the projection of a valid trihedral solid.

2. A sketch may admit different sets of valid labels not all of them corresponding to a valid polyhedron. Indeed, in the example of Figure 3 only the labelings in (a) and (b) result in a correct spatial configuration of lines and in particular only the labeling in a. produces a single-body polyhedron.
3. There is no efficient method to examine whether a labelable sketch is realizable.
4. Given a sketch admitting many different valid labelings, there is no efficient method to identify labelings corresponding to a valid polyhedron.

Finally, it is emphasized that, after presenting in a series of papers (Varley, 2002; Varley, Martin, & Suzuki, 2005) improved versions of LL methods, Varley et al. (2005) reconsider the usefulness

Figure 2. The sketch in (a) is not realizable though labelable, and the sketch in (b) is realizable and admits the same labeling with (a)

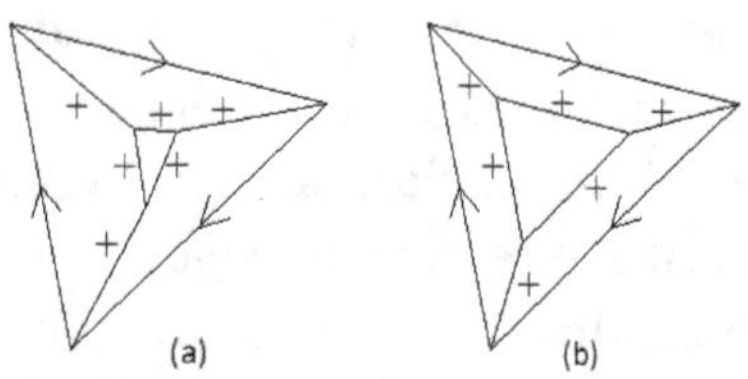

Figure 3. A sketch admitting six different labelings

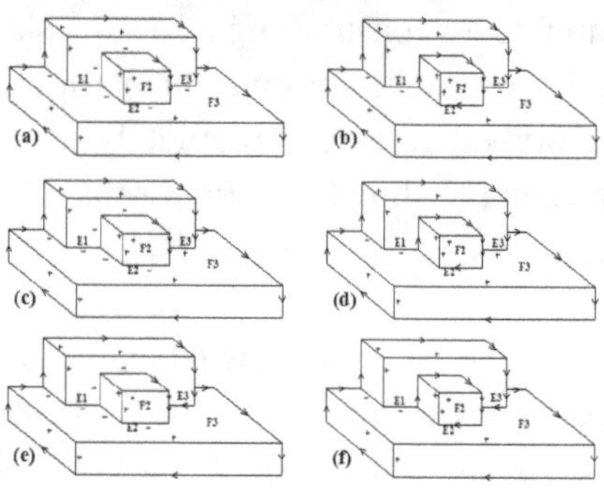

of LL and conclude that this is limited only to distinguishing occluding from non-occluding T-junctions, a case that does not concern sketches of trihedral solids.

Image Regularities

The majority of published works on the PSS problem (Wang & Grinstein, 1993; Grimstead & Martin, 1995; Lipson, 1998; Varley, 2002; Company et al., 2005; Cao, Liu, & Tang, 2008) employ heuristics for the geometric definition of the corresponding solid. These heuristics are based on "correlations" that exist between the geometry of the sketch and the 3D geometry of the corresponding polyhedron (e.g., parallel lines in a sketch correspond to parallel edges of the polyhedron-to-be-constructed) and they are called "*image regularities*". "Image regularities" were first introduced by Lipson (1998) and Lipson and Shpitalni (1996) and then further developed by Company, Contero, Conesa, and Piquer (2004). A detailed description of them can be found in Lipson (1998), Varley and Martin (2002) and Company et al. (2004).

Each "image regularity" detected in the sketch is weighted according to the probability that the identified geometric feature corresponds to a real geometric feature in the polyhedron (e.g., the "parallel lines" regularity is assigned a high "weight", because one usually draws – in orthographic projections – parallel edges of the polyhedron as parallel lines in the sketch). All detected "regularities" are written in mathematical terms forming an "objective function" employed by the optimization method building the geometry of the polyhedron (Lipson, 1998).

The major disadvantages of this methodology are:

1. Its effectiveness depends highly on the set of the employed regularities and the weights assigned to each of them (Lipson, 1998; Company et al., 2004).

2. It does not include solid modeling tools and thus it often results in invalid polyhedra.

3. THE "MINIMAL-COMPLETION" METHODOLOGY

The present research focuses on manifold polyhedra without holes, which are also *trihedral* with planar faces. Adjacent faces (edges) of a polyhedron lie on distinct planes (curves). The user draws a *natural (or partial-view) sketch* in the "*most informative view*", i.e., there is nothing at the "back of the sketch" that cannot be directly inferred from the visible part of it. The given natural sketch is considered to be an *orthographic projection* of a manifold trihedral solid, which is regarded to be in "*general position*" with respect to the given projection plane. This means that (a) no face or edge of the solid is perpendicular to that plane, and (b) no edges or vertices of the object appear to coincide in the projection (Lipson, 1998; Varley, 2002).

The lines (*L*), junctions (*J*) and regions (*R*) of a sketch are called *elements of this sketch*. It is noted that since the PSS problem with T-junctions is still unsolved, we consider in this paper the simplest case, where:

Constraint 1: No element of the natural sketch causes two or more visible regions of it to correspond to one visible region in the wireframe sketch to be constructed; Figure 4(a) depicts an example violating exactly this constraint.

Constraint 2: At most one T-junction exists in each region of the given natural sketch; an example violating this constraint is presented in Figure 4(b).

The ultimate objective of this research is derivation of a valid solid model corresponding to the given natural sketch. This objective, combined with the fact that no information is available regarding the hidden part of the polyhedron, leads to a *"minimal-completion" strategy,* implying that this hidden part should be minimal and at the same time sufficient to define a valid solid model. The present PSS algorithm constructs from the given natural sketch a wireframe sketch, which, according to the above strategy, must include a minimum number of hidden lines, hidden junctions and hidden regions (Figure 5). Our "minimal-completion" algorithm will be detailed in Section 4 following the presentation of the employed mathematical and algorithmic tools in the remainder of Section 3.

Solid Modeling Tools

This research uses the boundary representation method to model a polyhedron (Hoffman, 1989). The vertices (*V*), the edges (*E*) and the faces (*F*) of the polyhedron are called *elements of the polyhedron.* A "one-to-one correspondence" exists between lines/junctions/regions of the wireframe

Figure 4. (a) The bold-marked elements of this natural sketch divide one region of the corresponding wireframe sketch into the regions R_1 and R_2 of the natural sketch, (b) two T-junction in a region

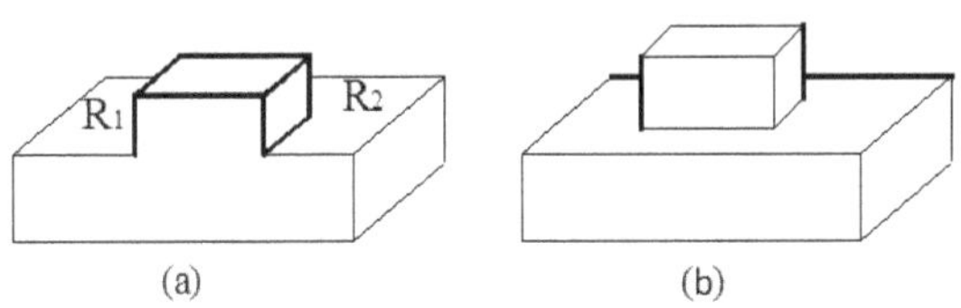

Figure 5. (a-b) Given the natural sketch in (a), the "minimal-completion" strategy results in the wireframe sketch in (b), (c) a non-minimal wireframe sketch for the natural sketch (a)

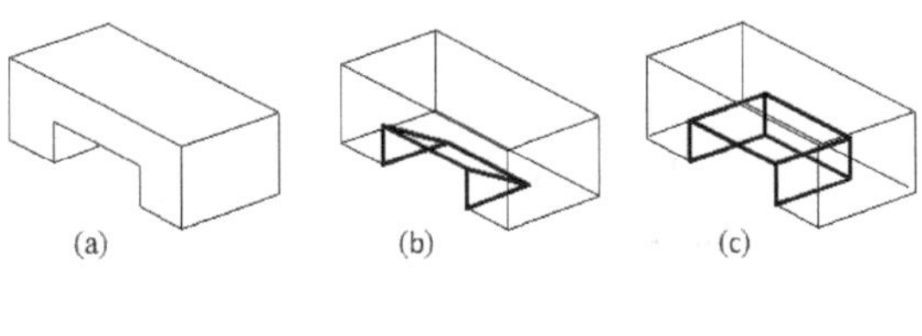

sketch and the edges/vertices/faces (respectively) of the corresponding polyhedron.

For the elements of a trihedral polyhedron of zero genus the Euler formula gives $F - E + V = 2$ (Hoffman, 1989). This formula also holds true for a graph (Diestel, 1997), and since a wireframe sketch (with R regions, L lines, and J junctions) can be modeled as a graph, we obtain:

$$R - L + J = 2. \quad (1)$$

The present research uses extensively, in addition to the boundary representation, also the following:

Theorem 1: *(Face Adjacency Theorem)* (Lipson, 1998). In any planar polyhedron, two adjacent faces have in common only collinear edges.

Topological Analysis of Sketches

The "minimal-completion" algorithm focuses also on the construction of a wireframe sketch, which is defined as follows:

Definition 1: A *valid wireframe sketch* is a sketch such that:

1. Whenever a hidden line intersects a visible line at a point not identical with a junction of the given natural sketch, this point is not considered to be a junction of the wireframe sketch (Figure 6(a)).
2. Every junction is adjacent to three lines; i.e., the degree of each junction j is d(j)=3 (Diestel, 1997).
3. Every line is adjacent to two regions.
4. The sketch is a connected graph (Diestel, 1997).
5. Two adjacent regions of the sketch share exactly one line or two-or-more collinear lines (Lipson, 1998) (as opposed to Figure 6(b)).

Figure 6. (a) The intersection points P_1 and P_2 do not correspond to junctions of the wireframe sketch, (b) this natural sketch does not correspond to a valid wireframe sketch because the lines e_1 and e_2 are not collinear

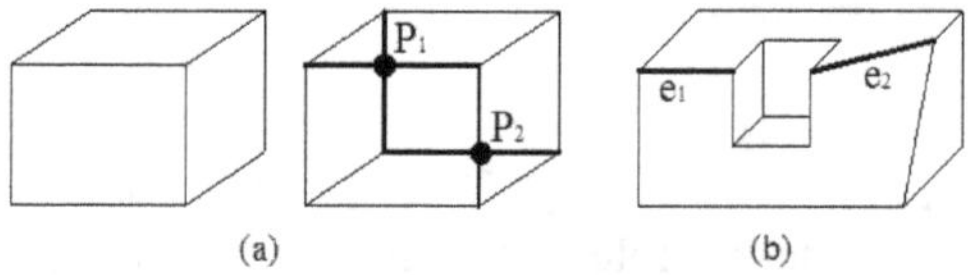

A wireframe sketch is produced from a given natural sketch, when to the latter's boundary elements (elements adjacent to both the interior and the exterior of the sketch) (Diestel, 1997) appropriate hidden lines and junctions are added. The boundary junctions in a natural sketch are classified, according to their degree, into the following three types:

1. **Boundary Junction of Degree:** d(j)=3 (e.g., the junction j in Figure 7(a)) This junction is adjacent to three visible lines, and it belongs to two visible regions and one hidden.
2. **L-junction:** (e.g., the junction j_L in Figure 7(a)) This junction is of degree 2, and it is adjacent to two visible lines and one hidden.
3. **T-junction:** (e.g., the junction j_T in Figure 7(a)) This junction relates to the existence of collinear adjacent lines and it implies depth. In the natural sketch, this junction is detached from the corresponding collinear lines and it is considered to be of degree 1. Thus, a T-junction is adjacent to one visible line (occluded line) and one (or two) *partially visible region(s)*; e.g., the line e and the region R in Figure 7(b). In the wireframe sketch (Figure 7(c)), a T-junction is placed in the hidden part of the object (as required by Constraints 1 & 2; see above) at a location that is calculated by the present "minimal-completion" algorithm.

Given a T-junction in a natural sketch, the corresponding collinear lines define (in the natural as well as in the wireframe sketch) one line called *occluding line* (e.g., line *e* in Figure 7(c)). We note that a natural sketch may include more than one T-junctions; e.g., the sketch in Figure 7(d) includes two T-junctions. Each occluding line and the adjacent to it visible region (occluding region) along with its hidden region (occluded region) are associated to the corresponding T-junction of the sketch. In the example of Figure 7(e), the occluding line *e* belongs to the occluding region R_1 and to the occluded region R_2; the regions R_1, R_2 and the line *e* are associated to the T-junction j_T.

It should be emphasized that, in the present "minimal-completion" algorithm, partially-visible regions are always included in the set of visible regions. This and the fact that T-junctions are considered to be junctions of degree 1, establish that the elements of the natural sketch constitute the visible part of the corresponding wireframe sketch. Thus, a minimal wireframe sketch is a valid wireframe sketch containing the minimum number of hidden elements.

Hidden regions in a minimal wireframe sketch will consist of both hidden and visible lines and junctions. Thus, a "minimal-completion" algorithm should define hidden regions using "L-L paths" and "L-T paths" defined as follows (Figure 8(a-b)):

Definition 2: An *L-L path* in a natural sketch is a path comprised of boundary lines and boundary junctions, where the terminal junctions are L-junctions and the interior junctions (if there are any) all have degree 3.

Definition 3: An *L-T path* in a natural sketch is a path comprised of boundary lines and boundary junctions, where the interior junctions (if there are any) all have degree 3 except for the terminal junctions: these are one L-junction and one T-junction.

The *length* of an L-L or L-T path is the number of lines in it; e.g., the three paths shown in Figure 8(a-c) have length equal to 2, 3, and 1, respectively. The "minimal-completion" algorithm employs the following rule, founded on Theorem 1, Definition 2, and a detailed analysis of a plethora of sketches (Kyratzi, 2007; Kyratzi & Sapidis, 2009):

Rule 1: Each L-L path of the natural sketch corresponds to a distinct hidden region of the wireframe sketch.

"L-L paths" have already been used for the determination of hidden regions (Lamb & Bandopadhay, 1990; Grimstead & Martin, 1995; Varley, 2002) but always in conjunction with the "Line Labeling" heuristic. The present "minimal-completion" algorithm is free of the above heuristic, as it combines L-L paths with L-T paths using a

Figure 7. (a) The junctions j, j_L, and j_T are, respectively, a 3-degree boundary junction, an L-junction, and a T-junction, (b) the occluded line e and the partially-visible region R are associated to the T-junction j_T, (c) in the wireframe sketch corresponding to the natural sketch (b) the T-junction j_T is in the hidden part, (d) a natural sketch with two T-junctions, (e) the regions R_1, R_2 and the line e are associated to the T-junction j_T.

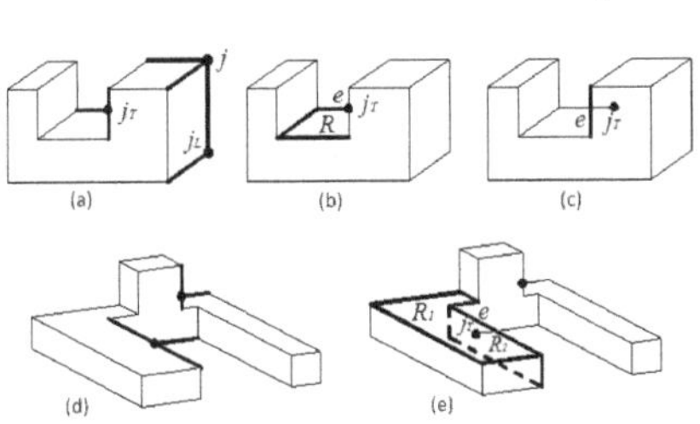

Figure 8. (a) An L-L path, (b) an L-T path, (c) an L-L path of length 1

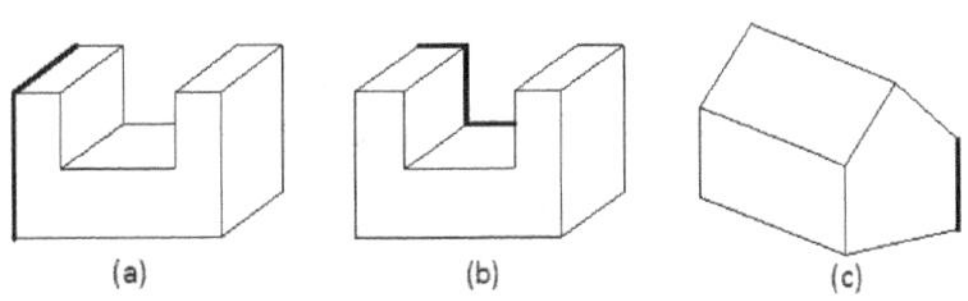

novel "*union operation*" that examines whether a given L-T path and an L-L path should be placed in the same hidden region; see the section "Step S2: Hidden region determination".

Geometric analysis of sketches and the "cross-section" test.

The present research does not employ any "image regularity" heuristics, described in the previous section. Instead, it uses the following two theorems (these are easily proved on the basis of Euclidean geometry) and the "cross-section" criterion (see below) to check the realizability of the under-construction wireframe sketch.

Theorem 2: *Parallel Faces.* Consider two non-adjacent regions R_i and R_j of a sketch that are both adjacent to the regions R_k and R_m (Figure 9(a)). The corresponding to R_i/R_j faces F_i/F_j will be parallel to each other, if (a) lines e_i and e_j of R_m are parallel, and (b) lines e_{i+1} and e_{j+1} of R_k are parallel.

Theorem 3: *Coplanar Faces.* Consider two non-adjacent regions R_i and R_j of a sketch (Figure 9(b)), two lines e_i, e_{i+1} of R_i, and two lines e_j, e_{j+1} of R_j. If the line pairs (e_i, e_j) and (e_{i+1}, e_{j+1}) are non adjacent and respectively collinear, then R_i/R_j correspond to two faces F_i/F_j which are coplanar.

The "cross-section" criterion (Whiteley, 1991; Ros & Thomas, 2005) is a necessary and sufficient condition for a wireframe sketch to be the orthographic projection of a polyhedron. This criterion is described as follows:

Consider the trihedral polyhedron in Figure 10(a). Intersecting the planes of its faces with an arbitrary plane φ produces an arrangement of lines called *cross-section* of the polyhedron. If each pair of *cross-section* lines Lf_i and Lf_j (corresponding to the two faces F_i and F_j) intersect at a point P_{ij} on (the extension of) the common edge e_{ij} of F_i and F_j, the cross-section is called *compatible*. The above concurrence conditions hold true even for

Figure 9. (a) "Parallel Faces" Theorem, (b) "Coplanar Faces" Theorem

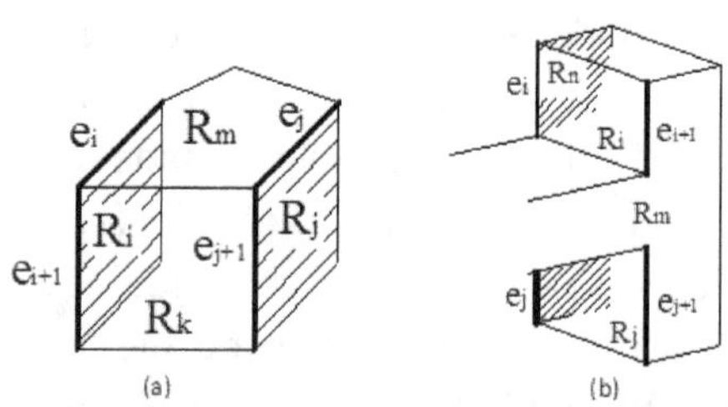

the projection of the polyhedron onto the plane φ (wireframe sketch), because projection preserves collinearity of points and all incidence relations. Thus, given a wireframe sketch S with L lines, J junctions and R regions (Figure 10(b)), a *cross-section* of S is an arrangement of lines $\{Lf_k;\ k = 1, \ldots, R\}$ that represents the regions $\{R_k;\ k = 1, \ldots, R\}$ of S. In complete analogy to the above discussion, if each pair of *cross-section* lines Lf_i and Lf_j intersect at a point P_{ij} on (the extension of) the common line e_{ij} of R_i and R_j, the cross-section is called *compatible with* S (Ros & Thomas, 2005).

Theorem 4: *(Cross-Section Theorem)* (Ros & Thomas, 2005). A wireframe sketch represents the orthographic projection of a trihedral polyhedron if and only if it has a compatible cross-section, such that the cross-section lines Lf_i and Lf_j of each couple of adjacent regions R_i and R_j are not identical.

Below, an equivalent definition (based on Analytic Geometry) of the cross-section criterion is presented which will be used in the development of an algorithmic method for constructing cross-sections.

Definition 4: *(Cross-section of a wireframe sketch).* Let S be a wireframe sketch with R regions, L lines and J junctions. A compatible cross-section with S is a set of lines $\{Lf_i\}$ such that:

Figure 10. (a-b) Cross-section test for a trihedral polyhedron and its projection

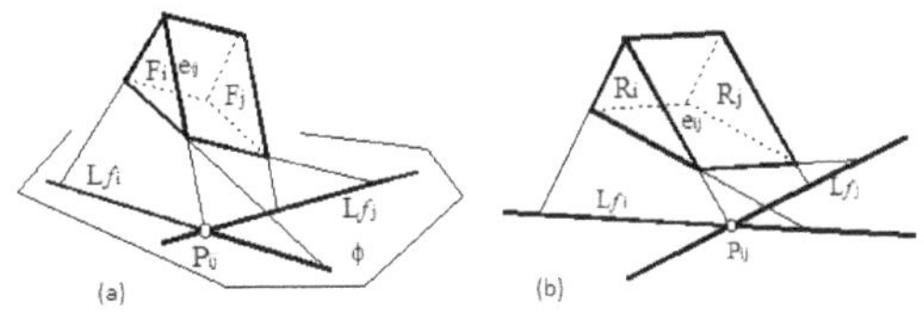

1. Each region R_i of S corresponds to a cross-section line Lf_i: $b_i x + a_i y + 1 = 0$, $i = 1,\ldots, R$ (Whiteley, 1991).
2. For each couple R_i and R_j of adjacent regions, their common line e_{ij} of S and the corresponding cross-section lines Lf_i and Lf_j intersect at a point P_{ij}.
3. The cross-section lines of two adjacent regions are not identical (Theorem 4).
4. For each R_i, its adjacent lines e_{ij} intersect the cross-section line Lf_i.

Given the sketch of Figure 11, the line e_{ij} belongs to the regions R_i and R_j which respectively correspond to the cross-section lines Lf_i and Lf_j. Definition 4 implies that the point $P_{ij}\left(\dfrac{a_j - a_i}{a_i b_j - a_j b_i}, \dfrac{b_i - b_j}{a_i b_j - a_j b_i}\right)$ must be on (the extension of) e_{ij} producing the following equation:

$$(a_j - a_i)k_{ij} + (b_j - b_i)m_{ij} + (a_i b_j - a_j b_i)n_{ij} = 0, \quad (2)$$

Figure 11. A wireframe sketch S and two cross-section lines Lf_i and Lf_j corresponding to the regions R_i and R_j, respectively

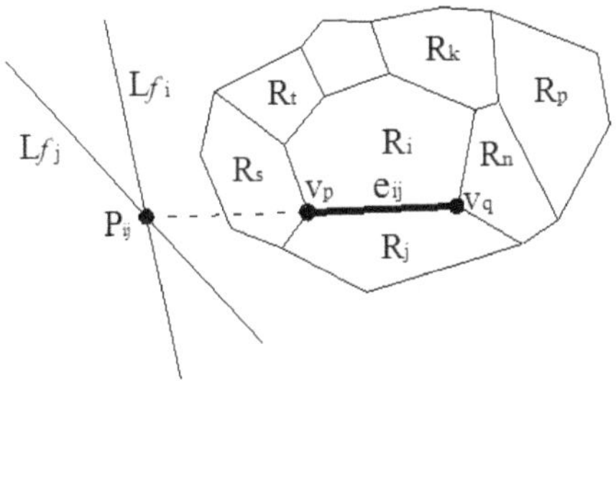

where $k_{ij} = y_p - y_q$, $m_{ij} = x_q - x_p$, and $n_{ij} = x_p y_q - y_p x_q$.

For each line of the wireframe sketch S, a similar equation is obtained. Thus, the following *"Cross-Section" system* is produced:

$$\begin{aligned}
&(a_s - a_t)k_{st} + (b_t - b_s)m_{st} + n_{st}(a_t b_s - a_s b_t) = 0\\
&\cdots\cdots\cdots\cdots\cdots\cdots\cdots\cdots\\
&(a_j - a_i)k_{ij} + (b_i - b_j)m_{ij} + n_{ij}(a_i b_j - a_j b_i) = 0\\
&(a_i - a_n)k_{ni} + (b_n - b_i)m_{ni} + n_{ni}(a_n b_i - a_i b_n) = 0\\
&(a_j - a_n)k_{nj} + (b_n - b_j)m_{nj} + n_{nj}(a_n b_j - a_j b_n) = 0\\
&\cdots\cdots\cdots\cdots\cdots\cdots\cdots\cdots\\
&(a_k - a_p)k_{kp} + (b_p - b_k)m_{kp} + n_{kp}(a_p b_k - a_k b_p) = 0
\end{aligned} \quad (3)$$

For a given sketch, the parameters (a_i, b_i), $i = 1, \ldots, R$, are unknown, to be calculated by the "minimal-completion" algorithm, which exactly solves the above system (3). An analysis of (3) and a solution method for it are the subject of a forthcoming paper.

We conclude this subsection with an important corollary which will be employed by Step S5 of the "minimal-completion" algorithm:

Corollary 1: (Figure 12) Let S be a wireframe sketch and CS/CS′ two compatible cross-sections of it. The intersection point P_{ij} ($i, j \in [1, \ldots, R]$) of two cross-section lines Lf_i and Lf_j in CS, and the intersection point P_{ij}', of the corresponding cross-section lines Lf_i', Lf_j' in CS′, are both on (the extension of) the line e_{ij}.

Graph-Theoretic Tools

Describing sketches as graphs allows employment of a host of graph-theoretic results to estimate the minimum number of hidden elements in a wireframe sketch. These results are presented below.

Theorem 5: (Diestel, 1997). The number of junctions of odd degree in a graph is always even.

Figure 12. Corollary 1- Given two compatible cross-sections CS and CS΄, then all lines of the wireframe sketch are defined by couples of intersection points from CS and CS΄, respectively

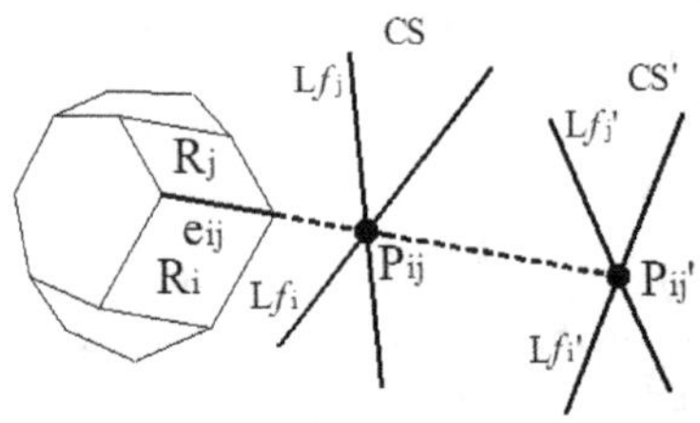

The number of lines in a graph with J junctions is $L = 1/2\sum_{i=1}^{J} d(j_i)$ (20), where d(j_i) is the degree of the junction j_i. This formula establishes the following:

Theorem 6: (Kyratzi & Sapidis, 2009). The number of hidden lines L_h in a wireframe sketch S, derived from a natural sketch S_v, is

$$L_h = (3J_h + 2N_T + N_L) / 2, \quad (4)$$

where J_h is the number of hidden junctions, and N_T /N_L is respectively the number of T- and L-junctions in S_v.

The present research employs the standard "contraction" and "deletion" operators from Graph Theory (Diestel, 1997) to produce the operators *"merge-1"*, *"merge-2"*, and *"delete"*, detailed below. These operators are applied (in Section 4) to the hidden elements of a wireframe sketch when this is found to be not minimal.

"Merge-1" Operator: contracts one junction of degree 2 with a neighboring junction of degree 3 (Figure 13(a)).

"Merge-2" Operator: replaces three, adjacent to each other, junctions of degree 3 with one 3-degree junction (Figure 13(b)).

"Delete" Operator: A line e of an n-angular (n>3) hidden region R is deleted if both the following conditions hold true (Figure 13(c)).

Figure 13. (a) Merge- 1 operator, (b) Merge-2 operator, (c) Delete operator

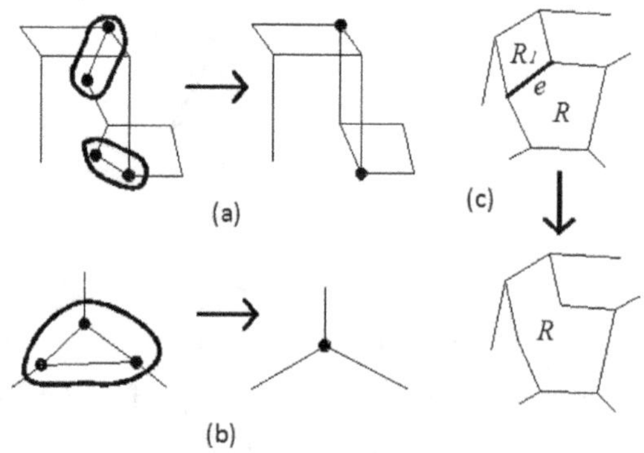

Condition D_1 _ The line e is adjacent to two hidden junctions of degree 3.

Condition D_2 _ There exists at least one triangular visible region, *OR* each line of R adjacent to e belongs also to a second n-angular hidden region (with n>4).

The *"Delete" Operator* aims at eliminating a hidden line in a wireframe sketch without producing a triangular hidden region. This is based on the fact that industrial products seldom include triangular faces. However, when the given natural sketch does include triangular visible regions, the *"Delete" Operator* is allowed to delete hidden lines producing triangular hidden regions.

4. THE "MINIMAL-COMPLETION" ALGORITHM

The proposed "minimal-completion" algorithm solves the problem "Polyhedron from a Single Natural Sketch" (PSS problem) by employing the tools described in the previous section. It includes three major components (Figure 14):

Part A: Topological construction of a minimal wireframe sketch.

Part B: Geometric definition of the minimal wireframe sketch.

Part C: Geometric construction of the polyhedron corresponding to the minimal wireframe sketch.

Part A is divided into four major steps: Steps S1-S3 apply graph-theoretic, solid-modeling and geometric results to the natural sketch in order to estimate the minimum number of hidden junctions/lines/regions that should be added to the "visible topology" to generate the corresponding wireframe sketch. In Step S4 the complete topological-description of the minimal wireframe sketch is produced consistent with the estimated number of hidden elements.

Part B applies geometric tools to the minimal wireframe sketch to obtain its geometric definition and to assure its realizability. In Part C, a polyhedron is defined so that its projection onto the "sketch plane" is identical with the minimal wireframe sketch produced by Part B. More specifically, Part C deals only with the geometric construction of the polyhedron as its topological description is identical with that of the minimal wireframe sketch constructed in Parts A and B. All "steps" included in Parts A, B, and C are presented below.

Figure 14. The "minimal-completion" algorithm

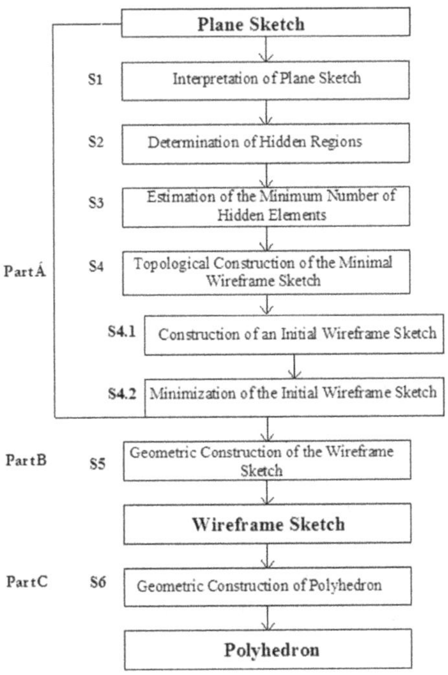

Step S1: Interpretation of the natural sketch

The input natural sketch is a plane graph, and thus the corresponding regions, lines and junctions are identified. Each T-junction becomes a degree-one junction and is associated to its partially-visible region(s), its occluding region and its occluding line. Finally, pairs of parallel lines, collinear lines, and intersecting lines of the natural sketch are identified.

Step S2: Determination of hidden regions

This step employs the *Hidden Region Determination Procedure* (see below) to determine the hidden regions in a minimal wireframe sketch. This procedure is based on Rule 1 and on the following "union operation" procedure:

Union Operation Procedure

Step 1: Rule 1 is applied, generating an *intermediate wireframe sketch.*

Step 2: For each L-T path of the natural sketch, the union with each L-L path is checked with respect to the following:

Topological and Geometric Criteria:

Criterion A: If conditions (2), (3) or (5) of Definition 1 are not satisfied, the union is invalid.

***Criterion* B:** If the L-L path determines the occluded region of the T-junction in the current L-T path, the union is invalid (Figure 15(a)).

***Criterion* C:** If at least one visible region of a line in the L-L path (L-T path) and the hidden region of the L-T path (L-L path) correspond to parallel faces (according to Theorem 2), the union is invalid (Figure 15(b)).

***Criterion* D:** If the visible region of a line in the L-L path and the visible region of a line in the L-T path correspond to coplanar or identical faces (according to Theorem 3), the union is valid (Figure 15(c)).

If all the above criteria are not satisfied, then the union with the current L-L path is labeled "valid".

Step 3: If Steps 1 and 2 have identified more than one possible valid "unions", the geometric validity of each corresponding intermediate wireframe sketch is checked through the "cross-section" criterion: if a "valid" union results in an incompatible cross-section, this union is excluded from the set of "valid unions".

Step 4: For each L-T path and each "valid union" the corresponding intermediate wireframe sketch is constructed. An L-T path is *independent* if the associated set of valid unions is empty otherwise it is a *dependent* path.

Hidden Region Determination Procedure (HRD procedure)

- The "union operation procedure" is applied to the natural sketch.
- The hidden regions of the wireframe sketch are determined: Each L-L path (either united or not with an L-T path) and each independent L-T path corresponds to a distinct hidden region.

Figure 15. (a-b-c) Application of Criteria B, C and D

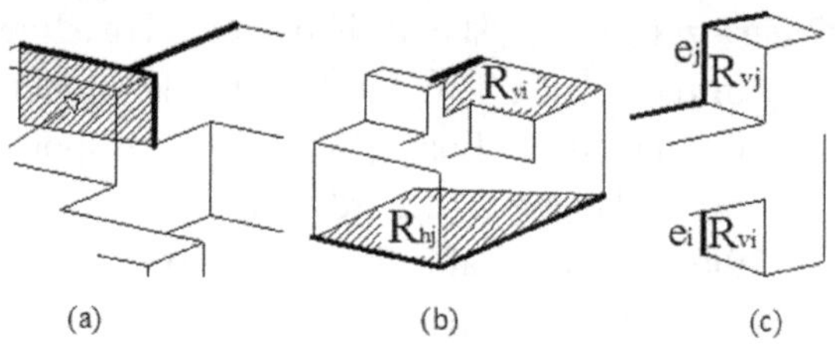

- A lower bound (N_{HR}) for the number of hidden regions adjacent to the boundary elements of the natural sketch is:

$$N_{HR} = N_{LL} + N_{LT} \tag{5}$$

where N_{LL} is the number of L-L paths and N_{LT} is the number of independent L-T paths in the natural sketch.

Step S3: Estimation of the Minimum Number of Hidden Elements

Lower bounds for the number of hidden lines L_h, hidden junctions J_h, and hidden regions R_h in a wireframe sketch are estimated, on the basis of the following system

$$2L_h - 3J_h = 2N_T + N_L \tag{6}$$

$$R_h - L_h + J_h = L_v - J_v - R_v + 2 \tag{7}$$

$$J_h = \begin{cases} 2k, & \text{if } J_v \text{ is even} \\ 2k+1, & \text{if } J_v \text{ is odd} \end{cases} \tag{8}$$

$$N_{HR} \leq R_h, \tag{9}$$

where: L_v, J_v and R_v are the number of visible elements, and N_T / N_L is respectively the number of T- and L-junctions. Relations (6)-(9) have been obtained as follows: (6) is given by Theorem 6, (7) is a direct result of the Euler Formula (eq. (1)) for the under-construction wireframe sketch, and (8) reflects Theorem 5. In (9), the value of N_{HR} is calculated by HRD procedure (eq. (5)).

The "minimal-completion" strategy implies that L_h, J_h and R_h must be as small as possible. System (6)-(7) admits always a solution for L_h and R_h in terms of the independent variable J_h, because the augmented matrix of this system is of rank 2. J_h is calculated using eq. (8), while k is obtained by solving system (6)-(9) for both cases of eq. (8):

$$k \geq \begin{cases} \dfrac{2N_{HR} - \text{“} - 2A}{2}, & \text{if } J_v \text{ is even} \\ \dfrac{2N_{HR} - \text{“} - 2A - 1}{2}, & \text{if } J_v \text{ is odd} \end{cases} \tag{10}$$

with $\Gamma=2N_T+N_L$ and $A=L_v\text{-}J_v\text{-}R_v+2$. Equation (10) and the solution of system (6)-(7) establish the following:

Theorem 7: When k takes the minimum integer value that satisfies relation (10), then L_h, J_h and R_h also admit their minimum values.

Step S4: Topological construction of the minimal wireframe sketch

Construction of the minimal wireframe sketch proceeds in two steps, outlined in the following subsections.

Step S4.1: Construction of an initial wireframe sketch

This step employs the following "Initial Wireframe" procedure to construct an initial wireframe sketch from each intermediate wireframe sketch produced by Step S2. This procedure is outlined below; a detailed description/analysis of it has been presented in Kyratzi and Sapidis (2009).

"Initial Wireframe" Procedure

Step 1: To each L-junction one adds one hidden line and one hidden junction. To each T-junction one adds two hidden lines and two hidden junctions (j_{T1} and j_{T2}) (Figure 16(a-b)).

Step 2: For each T-junction, the corresponding junction j_{T1} is connected to the hidden junction j_{LH} that belongs to this T-junction's partially visible region, by adding one hidden line (Figure 16(c)).

Step 3: For each L-T path:

3a. If it is dependent, the hidden junctions adjacent to it (for the T-junction is used j_{T2}) are connected with the hidden junctions of the corresponding L-L path, by adding two hidden lines respectively (Figure 16(d)),

3b. If it is independent, the hidden junctions adjacent to it are connected to each other with a hidden line (Figure 16(f)).

Step 4: For each unconnected L-L path, the hidden junctions adjacent to it are connected to each other with a hidden line (Figure 16(e)).

The initial wireframe sketch includes hidden regions adjacent to both hidden and visible lines and it also may include *"fully hidden"* regions, i.e., hidden regions adjacent only to hidden lines (e.g., in Figure 16(e) the hidden region $j_1j_2j_3j_4$).

Step S4.2: Minimization of the initial wireframe sketch

If the number of hidden elements in the initial wireframe sketch S_I is greater than the one estimated by system (6)-(9), the sketch is minimized. Fully hidden regions are the first to be eliminated, because they are not inferred by the natural sketch. This step uses the "Wireframe Minimization" procedure, which in turn employs the "Merge-1", "Merge-2" and "Delete" operators (see Section 3).

"Wireframe Minimization" Procedure

Step 1: The "Merge-1" operator is applied to each hidden junction of degree 2 in the initial wireframe sketch S_I.

Step 2: See Figure 17

2a. The number of hidden junctions J_h' in the initial wireframe sketch (generated by step 1) is found, and is compared to the number of hidden junctions J_h estimated by system (6)-(9):

Figure 16. Operations involved in the "Initial Wireframe" procedure

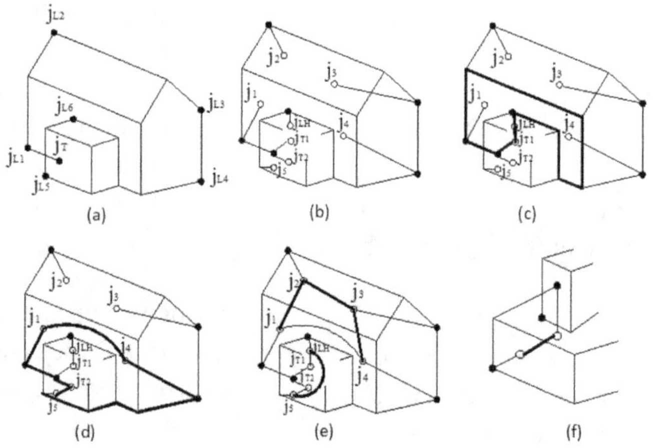

2i. If $J_h'=J_h$, the procedure is terminated, producing one or more minimum wireframe sketches.

2ii. If $J_h' > J_h$, the minimization of the wireframe sketch proceeds as follows:

Case 2ii-a. *There exists at least one triangular fully hidden region*: The "Merge-2" operator is applied to the junctions of this region and the process continues with Step 2(b).

Case 2ii-b. *There exists at least one n-angular (with n>3) fully hidden region*: One such region is eliminated using the "delete" operator, which is applied to each line of the initial wireframe sketch producing, after each deletion, a new simplified sketch. The process continues with Step 2(b).

2b. "Merge-1" operator is applied to each wireframe sketch constructed in (2ii), and the process continues for each new "simplified" sketch with Step 2(a) ("simplified" sketches are considered as "initial" in each iteration).

Step S5: Geometric construction of the wireframe sketch

This part of the algorithm computes the 2D coordinates of each hidden junction and of each T-junction, which are then used to define the corresponding hidden lines. The geometric construction of the wireframe sketch is based on the cross-section criterion and in particular on Theorem 4 (establishing the realizability of a sketch) and on Corollary 1.

Figure 17. (a) An initial wireframe sketch, (a-b) Step 2 – case (2ii-a): elimination of the triangular fully hidden region produces the sketch in (b), (b-c) Step 2 – case (2ii-b): elimination of the 4-angular fully hidden region produces the sketch in (c), (c-d) Step 2(b): elimination of two 2-degree hidden junctions produces the sketch in (d).

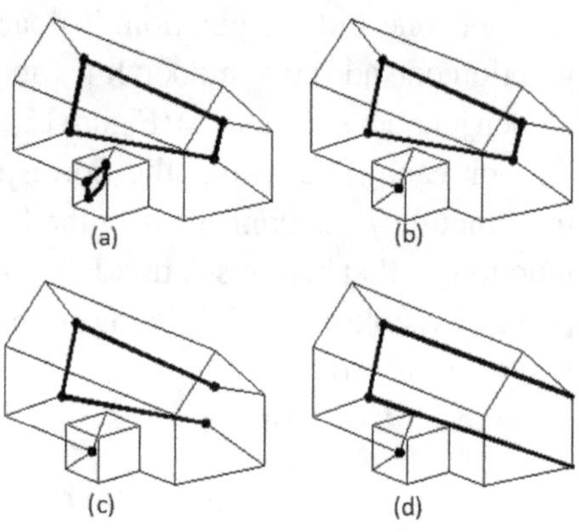

Given the outcome of Step S4, the position of a hidden junction j_h can be obtained as follows: Let R_1, R_2 and R_3 be three adjacent hidden regions that include the hidden junction j_h (Figure 18(a)). For each pair of adjacent hidden regions R_i-R_j, the corresponding cross-section lines intersect at a point P_{ij} which along with the common visible junction of regions R_i-R_j (Figure 18(b)) defines a line e_{ij} that goes through the hidden junction j_h. The intersection point of the three hidden lines, produced by the three adjacent regions, indicates the 2D position of the hidden junction j_h. Corollary 1 ensures that the position of the hidden junction is the same for each cross-section compatible with the sketch.

The present "minimal-completion" algorithm solves the above hidden-junction determination problem algebraically. For each topological description of a minimal wireframe sketch produced by Step S4, the cross-section system (3) is constructed. The unknowns of the system are:

- The pair (a_i, b_i) of each cross-section line, with $i = 1, \dots, R$.
- The coordinates of each hidden junction, and the coordinates of any T-junction.

The system is first solved for the (a_i, b_i) unknowns using these equations that do not include coordinates of the unknown junctions. Then these coordinates are calculated from the unused equations of the system. If these equations do not produce a unique solution (this is the case where L-L paths of length 1 exist in the natural sketch), the user must get involved in the process to help specify a wireframe sketch that best fits the polyhedron envisioned by him/her.

The proposed user-interaction method: The user is informed about which unknown junctions the algorithm is unable to uniquely calculate. Then, the user is invited to determine the direction of at least one of the hidden lines connected to these junctions. Alternatively, the user is invited to determine one of the (x, y) unknown coordinates of a hidden junction. It is noted that the available geometric description of the given natural sketch combined with the "cross-section" system produces permissible ranges for the above quantities (hidden-line directions and/or hidden-junction coordinates) that the user must select. After the user has provided the requested additional geometric information, the algorithm solves the new extended "cross-section" system. The final outcome is presented to the user, who either accepts it or he/she provides new input to refine the obtained solution.

Example: For the natural sketch in Figure 19(a) there are two hidden junction to be specified. As this sketch includes one L-L path of length = 1, the corresponding "cross-section" system does not uniquely determine the 2D coordinates of the hidden junctions. The user is invited to participate in determining j_h and he/she selects to specify the direction of the hidden line e_h. The user provides three different values for the direction of e_h, and the algorithm calculates the corresponding three minimal wireframe sketches presented in Figure 19(b-d).

Figure 18. (a) The cross-section lines Lf_1, Lf_2, and Lf_3 correspond to the hidden regions R_1, R_2, and R_3, (b) the intersection point of lines $e_{1,2}$, $e_{1,3}$, and $e_{2,3}$ is the hidden junction j_h

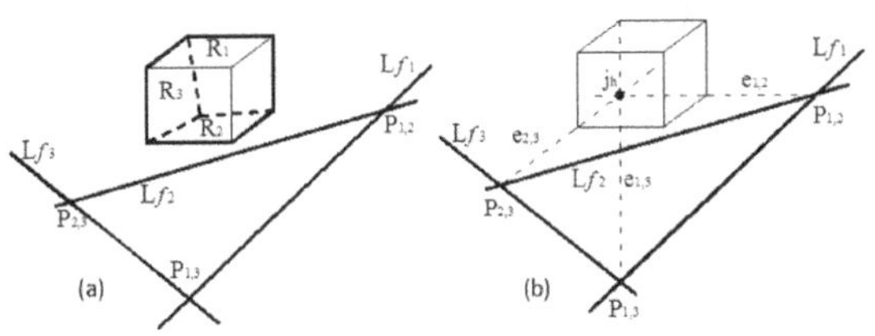

Step S6: Geometric construction of polyhedron

The underlying orthographic projection implies that each vertex of the polyhedron has (x, y) coordinates identical with those of the corresponding junction in the wireframe sketch. Thus, the z coordinates of the vertices are the

Figure 19. (a) A natural sketch with an L-L path of length 1, (b-d) the user has to define the direction of the hidden line e_h in order for the "minimal-completion" algorithm to determine the position of the hidden junction j_h.

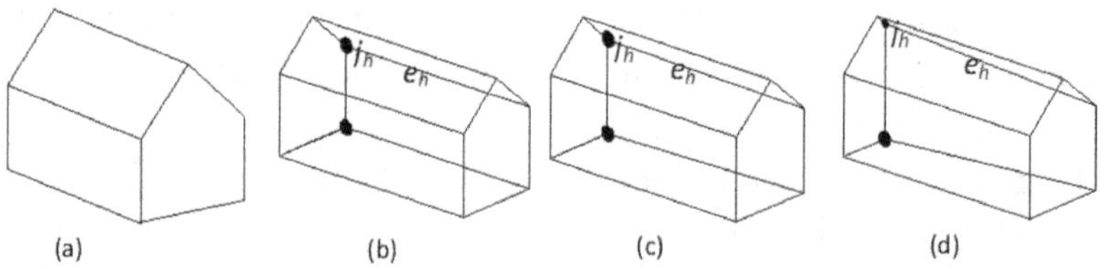

only unknowns to be calculated. At this stage of the "minimal-completion" algorithm user involvement is unavoidable as given a natural or a wireframe sketch, there are, in general, infinite polyhedra that are projected onto the given sketch.

Junctions and lines of the same region correspond to vertices and edges in the same planar face of the polyhedron. Calculation of the unknowns (z coordinates of all vertices) is based on the plane equation of each face. Each edge that is not used for the computation of a plane equation is forced to be located on it. Thus, for each face F_i, one obtains deg(F_i)-2 equations, where deg(F_i) is the number of edges adjacent to F_i. The following linear system is obtained including $\sum_{i=1}^{F}(\deg(F_i)-2)=2V-4$ equations, and V unknowns:

$$
\begin{aligned}
&A_1 z_j + B_1 z_p + C_1 z_q - D_1 z_m + D_1 z_i = 0\\
&A_2 z_j + B_2 z_p + (C_2 + D_2) z_q - D_2 z_i = 0\\
&\dots\dots\dots\dots\dots\dots\dots\dots\dots\dots\\
&A_{2j-3} z_n + B_{2j-3} z_k + (C_{2j-3} + D_{2j-3}) z_m - D_{2j-3} z_i = 0\\
&A_{2j-4} z_n + B_{2j-4} z_k + C_{2j-4} z_m + D_{2j-4} z_r - D_{2j-4} z_i = 0
\end{aligned}
\tag{11}
$$

Ros and Thomas (2005) establish that given a wireframe sketch with a compatible cross-section, one needs to specify only the planes of two adjacent faces F_a and F_b of the polyhedron and then the cross-section method (which is equivalent to the system (11)) specifies a unique polyhedron whose projection is identical with the given wireframe sketch. Specifying the planes of two adjacent faces F_a and F_b is equivalent to specifying four vertices v_i, v_q, v_m and v_r of the polyhedron (Figure 20(a)) where $v_i v_q$ is the common edge of the faces F_a and F_b, and v_r and v_m belong to F_a and F_b, respectively. In conclusion, this analysis establishes that given the z coordinate of the above "independent vertices" v_i, v_q, v_m and v_r, the system (11) produces a unique solution for the given PSS problem.

Since it is impossible for the user to directly select "independent vertices" v_i, v_q, v_m and v_r so that the final polyhedron is to his/her liking, this "user interaction" methodology may be used: the user is required to select a visible vertex v_i, fix the corresponding z_i, and specify values for three of the following six parameters $\left\{\theta,\ \varphi,\ \delta, |\overrightarrow{v_i v_r}|,\ |\overrightarrow{v_i v_m}|,\ |\overrightarrow{v_i v_q}|\right\}$ of the polyhedron to be constructed. Here, θ, φ and δ are the "face angles" around v_i (Figure 20(b)), and $|\overrightarrow{v_i v_r}|$, $|\overrightarrow{v_i v_m}|$, $|\overrightarrow{v_i v_q}|$ are the lengths of the edges adjacent to the selected vertex v_i.

User Interaction Scenario "A": The user specifies the length $|\overrightarrow{v_i v_m}|$ and the angles θ and δ. These will determine z_m, z_q, and z_r on the basis of the following equations:

$$|\overrightarrow{v_i v_m}|^2 = (x_m - x_i)^2 + (y_m - y_i)^2 + (z_m - z_i)^2 \tag{12}$$

$$\left\langle \overrightarrow{v_i v_r}, \overrightarrow{v_i v_m} \right\rangle = |\overrightarrow{v_i v_r}|\,|\overrightarrow{v_i v_m}| \cos\theta \tag{13}$$

Figure 20. (a) The four independent vertices, (b) user interaction scenarios

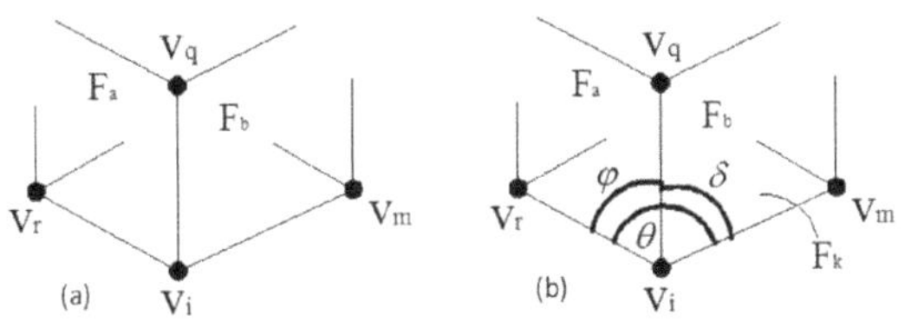

$$\left\langle \overrightarrow{v_i v_m}, \overrightarrow{v_i v_q} \right\rangle = |\overrightarrow{v_i v_m}||\overrightarrow{v_i v_q}| \cos\delta . \qquad (14)$$

Equation (12) always produces a solution for z_m provided that

$$|\overrightarrow{v_i v_m}|^2 \geq (x_m - x_i)^2 + (y_m - y_i)^2 . \qquad (15)$$

Equation (13) is written as a quadratic equation with respect to the unknown $z_r - z_i$, which is solvable if and only if the conditions in Box 1.

Similarly, equation (14) is written as a quadratic equation with respect to the unknown $z_q - z_i$, producing a necessary and sufficient condition for solvability also in terms of $z_m - z_i$: (See Box 2)

If the user-specified $|\overrightarrow{v_i v_m}|$, θ and δ are such that (15)-(17) hold true, then the equations (12)-(14) are solvable and a polyhedron corresponding to the given natural sketch is constructed. When at least one of (15)-(17) is not true, then these equations produce an appropriate range for some of the parameters $|\overrightarrow{v_i v_m}|$, θ and δ. Then, the user is invited to revise the input $|\overrightarrow{v_i v_m}|$, θ and δ, so that the new values satisfy (15)-(17) and directly produce the required polyhedron.

User Interaction Scenario "B": The user specifies the angles θ, φ, and δ. Then, the problem of specifying v_q, v_m and v_r is equivalent to:

$$\left\langle \overrightarrow{v_i v_r}, \overrightarrow{v_i v_m} \right\rangle = |\overrightarrow{v_i v_r}||\overrightarrow{v_i v_m}| \cos\theta \qquad (18)$$

$$\left\langle \overrightarrow{v_i v_r}, \overrightarrow{v_i v_q} \right\rangle = |\overrightarrow{v_i v_r}||\overrightarrow{v_i v_q}| \cos\varphi \qquad (19)$$

$$\left\langle \overrightarrow{v_i v_m}, \overrightarrow{v_i v_q} \right\rangle = |\overrightarrow{v_i v_m}||\overrightarrow{v_i v_q}| \cos\delta . \qquad (20)$$

The system (18)-(20) is analyzed in a similar manner as in Scenario "A" producing appropriate ranges for θ, φ, and δ. In the case that the user-specified θ, φ, and δ disagree with these ranges, the user determines new values so that the problem (18)-(20) is solvable and at the same time it produces a polyhedron as close as possible to that desired by him/her.

5. AN EXAMPLE

Application of the "minimal-completion" algorithm is detailed below:

Step S1: *Sketch Interpretation.* (Figure 21(a-b)) This natural sketch consists of 15 junctions, 19 lines and 6 regions (including one partially visible region), one T-junction and 5 L-junctions. There are four L-L paths (the paths $P_1(L_1\text{-}L_2)$, $P_2(L_2\text{-}L_3)$, $P_3(L_3\text{-}L_4)$, and $P_4(L_1\text{-}L_5)$) and one L-T path (the path $P_5(L_5\text{-}T)$). All paths have length greater than one.

Step S2: *Determination of Hidden Regions.* The "Hidden Region Determination" procedure is applied to the given natural sketch. The "Union operation" procedure, employed by HRD procedure, identifies the set of valid unions for the L-T path P_5: only the union with path P_2 is valid (Figure 21(c)). The union of P_5 with each one of the paths P_1, P_3, and P_4 is invalid because of Criteria C, B, and A, respectively. The minimum number of hidden regions in the corresponding wireframe sketch is $N_{HR} = 4$ (equation (5)).

Box 1.

$$(z_m - z_i)^2 \geq \frac{\cos^2(\theta)[(x_m - x_i)^2 + (y_m - y_i)^2][(x_r - x_i)^2 + (y_r - y_i)^2] - [(x_r - x_i)(x_m - x_i) + (y_r - y_i)(y_m - y_i)]^2}{[(x_r - x_i)^2 + (y_r - y_i)^2]\sin^2(\theta)} \quad (16)$$

Box 2.

$$(z_m - z_i)^2 \geq \frac{\cos^2(\delta)[(x_m - x_i)^2 + (y_m - y_i)^2][(x_q - x_i)^2 + (y_q - y_i)^2] - [(x_q - x_i)(x_m - x_i) + (y_q - y_i)(y_m - y_i)]^2}{[(x_q - x_i)^2 + (y_q - y_i)^2]\sin^2(\delta)} \quad (17)$$

Step S3: *Estimation of the Minimum Number of Hidden Elements.* System (6)-(9) produces the values: $J_h = 1$, $L_h = 5$ and $R_h = 4$.

Step S4: *Topological Construction of the Minimal Wireframe Sketch.* Steps 1-4 of the "Initial Wireframe" procedure are applied to the outcome of Step S2 producing the sketches in Figure 21(d-g). Then, the "Wireframe Minimization" procedure is applied on the sketch of Figure 21(g) producing the sketch in Figure 21(h).

Step S5: *Geometric Construction of the Wireframe Sketch.* For the outcome of Step S4 the corresponding cross-section system is built and resolved. As the given natural sketch includes no L-L path of length 1, Step S5 calculates the coordinates of the hidden junction and those of the T-junction in the sketch without any user involvement. The final output is shown in Figure 21(i).

Step S6: *Geometric Construction of the Polyhedron.* System (11) is constructed and solved, defining the planes of the ten faces of this polyhedron. As explained in section "Step S6: Geometric construction of polyhedron", solution of system (11) involves user interaction. One very probable choice is that the three angles around the vertex v_i are equal

Figure 21. (a-b) A natural sketch with four L-L paths and one L-T path, (c) it is valid for the L-T path L_5-T to be placed in the same hidden region with the L_2-L_3 path, (d-g) topological construction of an initial wireframe sketch, (h) minimization of the initial wireframe sketch, (i) geometric construction of the minimal wireframe sketch, (j-k) two alternative final outcomes (polyhedra) for the same natural sketch (a).

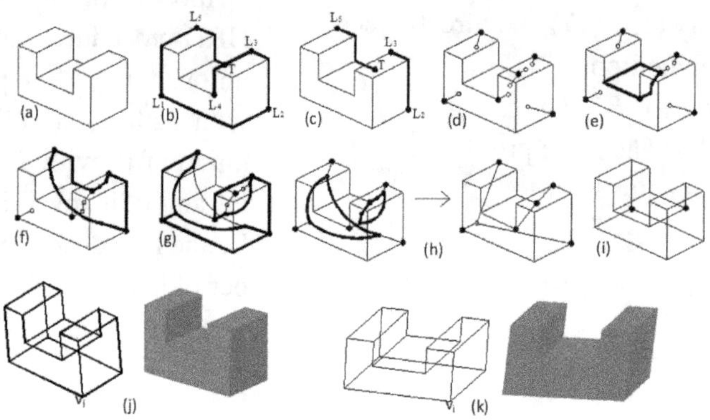

to 90°. For that, the user applies the user-interaction scenario "B" and the final outcome is the polyhedron of Figure 21(j) where all corners are cubic. Figure 21(k) presents an alternative polyhedron corresponding to the case that the user prefers the user-interaction scenario "A" with $\left\{|\overrightarrow{v_i v_m}|, \theta, \delta\right\} = \left\{4.5,\ 120°,\ 90°\right\}$.

6. CONCLUSION

A new solution for the problem of defining a Polyhedron from a given Single Sketch (PSS problem) has been presented. This algorithm is completely free of "Line Labeling" and of other "image understanding" heuristics which have been found highly problematic even by authors who extensively worked on them; see discussion in Sections 1 and 2. Instead, the present method is based on robust tools and models from Graph Theory, Solid Modeling and Euclidean Geometry, combined with appropriate "user interaction" techniques to resolve cases where the PSS problem has more than one possible solutions.

This paper has focused on the geometric construction of a polyhedron corresponding to the given sketch, while topological aspects of the problem have been detailed in (Kyratzi & Sapidis, 2009). In the proposed methodology, "image understanding" heuristics have been replaced by a robust "minimal-completion" strategy combined with appropriate "user-interaction" techniques directly aiming at a "plausible solution". Indeed, the "user-interaction" methods of the sections "Step S5: Geometric construction of the wireframe sketch" and "Step S6: Geometric construction of polyhedron" allow the user to guide the employed geometric constructions towards producing a polyhedron as close as possible to that desired by him/her.

Current research is focusing on extending the present algorithm to the case of more complex natural sketches, e.g., sketches violating Constraint 1 or 2 and sketches depicting polyhedra with through holes.

REFERENCES

Cao, L., Liu, J., & Tang, X. (2008). What the Back of the Object Looks Like: 3D Reconstruction from Line Drawings without Hidden Lines. *IEEE Transactions on Pattern Analysis and Machine Intelligence*, *30*(3), 507–517. doi:10.1109/TPAMI.2007.1185

Company, P., Contero, M., Conesa, J., & Piquer, A. (2004). An Optimisation-Based Reconstruction Engine for 3D Modelling by Sketching. *Computers & Graphics*, *28*(6), 955–979. doi:10.1016/j.cag.2004.08.007

Company, P., Piquer, A., Contero, M., & Naya, F. (2005). A survey on geometrical reconstruction as a core technology to sketch-based modeling. *Computer Graphics*, *29*(6), 892–904. doi:10.1016/j.cag.2005.09.007

Diestel, R. (1997). *Graph Theory*. New York, NY: Springer.

Fahiem, M., Haq, S., & Saleemi, F. (2007). A Review of 3D Reconstruction Techniques from 2D Orthographic Line Drawings. In *Proceedings of the Geometric Modeling and Imaging Conference (GMAI '07)* (pp. 60-66). Washington, DC: IEEE Computer Society.

Grimstead, I. J., & Martin, R. R. (1995). Creating solid models from single 2D sketches. In *Proceedings of the 3rd ACM Symposium on Solid Modeling and Applications* (pp. 323-337). New York, NY: ACM.

Hoffman, C. M. (1989). *Geometric and Solid Modeling: An Introduction.* San Francisco, CA: Morgan Kaufmann.

Kyratzi, S. (2007). *Industrial-Product Concept Development: Geometric and Information Models for Interactive Design.* Unpublished doctoral dissertation, University of the Aegean, Greece.

Kyratzi, S., & Sapidis, N. (2008). An Interactive Sketching Method for 3D Object Modeling. In *Proceedings of the 3rd ACM Conference on Digital Interactive Media in Entertainment and Art (DIMEA'08)* (pp. 335-42). New York, NY: ACM.

Kyratzi, S., & Sapidis, N. (2009). Extracting a polyhedron from a single view sketch: Topological construction of a wireframe sketch with minimal hidden elements. *Computers & Graphics*, *33*(3), 270–279. doi:10.1016/j.cag.2009.03.001

Lamb, D., & Bandopadhay, A. (1990). Interpreting a 3D Object from a Rough 2D Line Drawing. In *Proceedings of the 1st IEEE Conference on Visualization* (pp. 59-66). Los Alamitos, CA: IEEE Computer Society Press.

Lipson, H. (1998). *Computer Aided 3D Sketching for Conceptual Design.* Unpublished doctoral dissertation, Israel Institute of Technology, Israel.

Lipson, H., & Shpitalni, M. (1996). Optimization-Based Reconstruction of a 3D Object from a Single Freehand Line Drawing. *Computer Aided Design*, *28*(8), 651–663. doi:10.1016/0010-4485(95)00081-X

Ros, L., & Thomas, F. (2005). Geometric Methods for Shape Recovery from Line Drawings of Polyhedra. *Journal of Mathematical Imaging and Vision*, *22*(1), 5–18. doi:10.1007/s10851-005-4779-4

Sapidis, N., Kyratzi, S., & Azariadis, F. (2005). Improved Computational Tools for Concept Development Based on Sketches and Advanced CAD Technologies. *Computer-Aided Design and Applications*, *2*(6), 707–716.

Schweikardt, E., & Gross, M. D. (2000). Digital clay: deriving digital models from freehand sketches. *Automation in Construction*, *9*(1), 107–115. doi:10.1016/S0926-5805(99)00052-7

Sugihara, K. (1986). *Machine Interpretation of Line Drawings.* Cambridge, MA: MIT Press.

Varley, P. (2002). *Automatic Creation of Boundary-Representation Models from Single Line Drawings.* Unpublished doctoral dissertation, Cardiff University, UK.

Varley, P., & Martin, R. R. (2002). Estimating Depth from Line Drawing. In *Proceedings of the 7th ACM Symposium on Solid Modeling and Applications* (pp. 180-191). New York, NY: ACM.

Varley, P., Martin, R. R., & Suzuki, H. (2005). Frontal Geometry from Sketches of Engineering Objects: Is Line Labeling necessary. *Computer Aided Design*, *37*(12), 1285–1307. doi:10.1016/j.cad.2005.01.002

Wang, W., & Grinstein, G. (1993). A Survey of 3D Solid Reconstruction from 2D Projection Line Drawings. *Computer Graphics Forum*, *12*(2), 137–158. doi:10.1111/1467-8659.1220137

Whiteley, W. (1991). Weavings, Sections and Projections of Spherical Polyhedra. *Discrete Applied Mathematics*, *32*(3), 275–294. doi:10.1016/0166-218X(91)90004-G

This work was previously published in the Information Resources Management Journal, Volume 24, Issue 4, edited by Mehdi Khosrow-Pour, pp. 27-49, copyright 2013 by IGI Publishing (an imprint of IGI Global).

Chapter 17
On Volume Based 3D Display Techniques

Barry G. Blundell
Auckland University of Technology, New Zealand

ABSTRACT

In the case of certain applications in which a need exists to visualize and interact with voluminous data sets and complex 3-D geometrical models, the conventional computer interface inhibits key human-computer interaction processes. Here, several deficiencies of the standard interface are identified with emphasis on a failure to make optimal use of the complex human sensory systems. Various general forms of interaction modality are outlined together with several types of image space. This provides a basis for brief discussion of emerging 'creative' 3-D display systems with emphasis on computational holography, varifocal techniques, and volumetric systems.

1. INTRODUCTION

The fundamental techniques used in computer graphics to map three-dimensional (3-D) image data onto the conventional two dimensional (2-D) display can be readily traced back to the Renaissance that flourished in Italy from the fourteenth to the sixteenth centuries. The Renaissance is widely viewed as a period of cultural rebirth and scholarly enlightenment in which the coalescence of art and mathematics played a vital role in the development of perspective drawing techniques by means of which artists are able to render (in a geometrically accurate framework) 3-D scenes on 2-D media. Filippo Brunelleschi is generally credited with providing the first demonstration in the Renaissance period of the use of such techniques (*c*1420)[1] and subsequently, in *Della Pittura* (Italian version c1435) Leon Battista Alberti described a formalized methodology (Edgerton, 1976).

DOI: 10.4018/978-1-4666-3616-3.ch017

The Renaissance denotes an important turning point in western culture. During this period scholarly traditions were established, knowledge was widely disseminated, and the image depiction techniques that were gradually refined led to the creation of works which exhibit, and even transcend, photorealism.

The depiction of images on 2-D tableaux, the inclusion of relief through carving and the creation of wholly 3-D representations via sculpture have, from the earliest times, provided outlets for a quest to depict and record our physical surroundings and also as a means of facilitating creative expression. The methodologies outlined by Alberti (coupled with subsequent additions and refinements) are used today in the depiction of 3-D images on the standard computer display. However, various emerging 'creative' 3-D display technologies offer to support true 3-D image depiction thereby enabling the formation of images that possess the attributes that we associate with traditional carving and sculpture.

In the next section we consider the depiction of images on the standard flat screen computer display and emphasize issues relating to the interface between the visible image and the human visual system. Subsequently, we identify three interaction modalities and five forms of image space (the tableau supporting image depiction). In the case of each form of image space, we briefly consider key attributes which impact on the visual characteristics of the depicted image and on interaction opportunities. Subsequently, in Section 4 we focus on three exemplar 3-D display paradigms that are particularly suited to the visualization of volumetric (voluminous) data sets.

2. INTERFACING WITH THE DIGITAL WORLD

In a number of key applications (including medicine, petroleum exploration, education and computer aided design) it is often necessary to visualize and interact with complex voluminous (3-D) data sets. Interaction is most commonly achieved using the conventional flat screen computer display accompanied by the keyboard, mouse and joystick. However, as 3-D applications grow in complexity, these conventional interface tools are inhibiting our ability to efficiently visualize the results of the computational process, and can cause the interaction process to become both clumsy and non-intuitive. In short, in an increasing number of situations conventional interface techniques are limiting the bandwidth of the bi-directional human-computer interface and in turn this reduces the efficiency with which we are able to utilize computer technologies.

This problem primarily arises because conventional interface technologies fail to properly capitalise on the powerful and complex human sensory systems (particularly the full capabilities of our visual sense and aspects of proprioception). We briefly outline some of the limitations of current interface technologies:

1. **The Conventional Display:** The flat screen display supports 3-D image depiction by presenting a number of cues to depth to the visual system. These include linear perspective, height in the visual field, occlusion, shading and aerial perspective. By judiciously employing these cues, Renaissance artists were able to embrace photorealism and because of their association with traditional image depiction techniques, they are referred to as 'pictorial cues' (Boff, Kaufman, & Thomas, 1986; Blundell, 2008). However, when we view our surroundings, we receive additional important information (concerning relative and absolute distances) from other sources. These are commonly classified as oculomotor and parallax cues. The former comprises accommodation and convergence and the latter binocular parallax (stereopsis) and motion parallax. When the conventional flat screen display is used for

3-D image depiction, these cues are absent. This not only makes it more difficult for an operator to interpret spatial relationships but often impacts on the ease with which we can interact with image content.

2. **Interaction Tools:** In the case of the conventional computer interface, the display screen depicts the results of the computational process and also plays a pivotal role in supporting interaction operations. Conventional interaction tools (such as the mouse) are merely unidirectional; they support input *into* the digital domain but do not provide any active haptic sensation (Burdea, 1996; Blundell & Schwarz, 2006) in response to an operator's actions. In contrast, when interacting with our physical surroundings we are able to demonstrate remarkable dexterity as interaction operations are usually accomplished within a complex multi-sensory feedback loop. As indicated in Figure 1, within this loop the brain takes input not only from the visual system but also from various somatosensory and kinaesthetic pathways.

As a result, the conventional computer interface does not properly draw upon natural human dexterity. Furthermore, as indicated above, interactive operations that are carried out on 3-D images depicted on a 2-D screen are supported only by pictorial depth cues; other cues that are of crucial importance in supporting natural interaction are absent. In some situations it therefore becomes necessary to perform interaction operations in a non-intuitive manner; real world practices have to be put to one side and the user must continually adapt to the machine.

3. INTERACTION MODALITIES AND FORMS OF IMAGE SPACE

Three general forms of interaction technique may be identified.[2] These are summarized:

Figure 1. Natural interactive operations are usually performed within a tightly coupled feedback loop which involves visual, somatosensory and kinaesthetic pathways. This effectively supports human dexterity. In the case of the conventional computer interface, only visual feedback is supported (within the context of a limited set of visual cues).

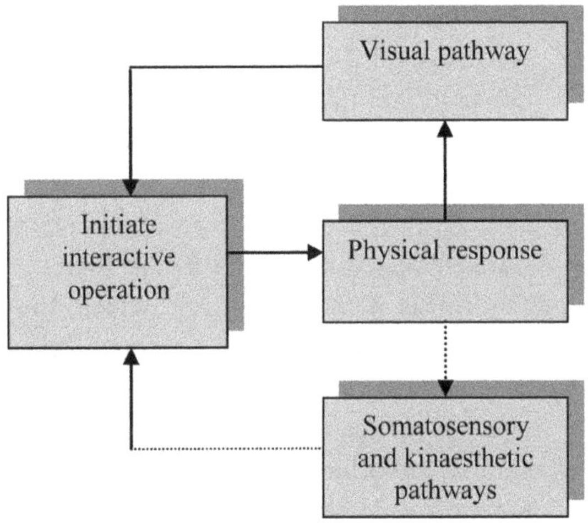

1. **Transferred Interaction:** Here, the interaction tool is used to navigate a virtual cursor within the region in which the image is physically located (or from which it appears to emanate). The conventional computer interface uses this technique – the cursor providing a visual cue by means of which the operator is able to determine the appropriate movement of the interaction tool. Typically there is a direct mapping between the motion of the interaction tool and that of the cursor (although this need not necessarily be the case, e.g., a joystick used in 'rate' mode).
2. **Direct Interaction:** In this scenario, the interaction tool is able to come into direct contact with image components, menus and the like. In the case of the conventional flat screen display, a touch screen provides a simple example of this interaction modality. As discussed below, direct interaction may be used effectively with various forms of creative 3-D display.

3. **Pointer Based Interaction:** Here a visible beam emanating from (or apparently emanating from) the interaction tool provides a visual cue to the pointer's position and orientation relative to the region occupied by an image scene. Thus a virtual cursor is not required and unlike the direct interaction modality, the pointer and image are not coincident. This approach is not appropriate for use with 3-D images depicted via the conventional flat screen display but is well suited to use with several 'creative' 3-D paradigms.

An image space is defined as the region in which an image is located or from which it appears to emanate (Blundell & Schwarz, 2000). The nature of the image space impacts on both the visual attributes and interaction opportunities that may be offered by a display technique. Five forms of image space have been identified (Blundell, 2008) – as summarized:

1. **Planar Image Space:** This form of image space is supported by the conventional flat screen display. Here, an image is formed on a 2-D tableau and as discussed above, the three-dimensionality of images is conveyed by means of various pictorial depth cues.
2. **Physical Image Space:** In this case, image components are depicted within a physical 3-D volume. Since images are able to occupy three physical dimensions they exhibit (to a first approximation) the three-dimensionality that we associate with physical objects and support pictorial, oculomotor and parallax depth cues in a natural manner.
3. **Free Image Space:** The volume associated with a physical image space may comprise a solid, liquid or gaseous media and is assumed to be separated from its surroundings by some form of containing vessel. Thus this image space modality does not support 'direct interaction'. In contrast a free image space corresponds to a region from which an image appears to emanate and into which physical interaction tools may be readily inserted. This form of image space is able to readily support the use of a haptic feedback probe. An optical arrangement may be used to map a physical image space into a free image space (and may also be used to provide magnification, Blundell, 2007). However, the formation of an image that appears to 'float in space' is often non-trivial and any system must conform to the criteria outlined by Halle (1997).
4. **Virtual Image Space:** Here, the image space appears to be located behind some form of optical arrangement comprising, for example, a transparent or mirrored surface (*cf.* the formation of a virtual image by a converging mirror). In the case that a transparent surface is used, an operator may be able to reach around the surface and manipulate a haptic probe. However, the ability of the virtual form of image space to support direct interaction assumes that both the image and interaction probe are concurrently visible to the observer, hence, the requirement for surface transparency. Image space dimensions are determined by the characteristics of the optical arrangement which is juxtaposed between it and the observer. The varifocal form of display can be configured to support this display modality; however, in the case that this employs a varifocal mirror (as opposed to a varifocal lens), direct interaction is not possible. The display system developed by ReachIn Technologies (http://www.reachin.se) in which 3-D images are reflected by a glass plate, is fundamentally based on the Pepper's (Dirck's) Ghost illusion that was used in the 1860s (Blundell, 2006, 2008) and provides a virtual image space able to support direct interaction.
5. **Apparent Image Space:** This is associated with display technologies that are fundamentally based on the principle of the stereoscope (Wheatstone, 1838; Wade, 1983). Here,

for example temporal, spatial or chromatic coding (Blundell, 2006, 2008) techniques may be used to direct a different view onto an image scene into each eye. Disparities between these views are interpreted within the visual cortex as providing a strong sense of *relief*. Although the perceived image appears to occupy a 3-D image space, this is wholly illusionary; the stereoscopic pair of images is located on a plane and the sensation of depth has absolutely no physical basis. The direct interaction technique may, in principle, be used in conjunction with the apparent image space paradigm, although as discussed, a stereoscopic penumbra may occur (Blundell, 2006).

4. VOLUME BASED DISPLAY TECHNIQUES

Volumetric (voluminous) data sets (comprising a set of scalar samples within three spatial dimensions) are frequently large and the computational cost associated with processing such data is often significant. Furthermore, the depiction of voluminous data in order to best support the human visualization and interaction processes is problematic, especially when conventional computer display and interaction interface are employed. Several forms of emerging 'creative' display and interaction techniques offer to significantly advance the visualization and interaction processes.

Although systems fundamentally based on the principle of the stereoscope may be used for this purpose, it is important to note that these systems are usually unable to correctly satisfy the oculomotor cues. Furthermore, although multi-view displays (Okoshi, 1976; McAllister, 1993) are able to support motion parallax[3] in a natural way (across a limited range of vantage positions) other approaches require the inclusion of head-tracking hardware (in which case, latencies occurring between head movement and screen update must be minimized).

In this section we briefly consider three general techniques that are well suited to the depiction of voluminous data – namely the computed holography, varifocal and volumetric approaches.

1. **Computed:** In principle this represents the optimal 3-D display technique as it is able to depict large data sets and has the capability of encoding all depth cue information. However, from a practical standpoint, the implementation of a holographic system able to support real time interaction is daunting. For example, consider a display with height h and width w that is able to support both horizontal and vertical parallax across an angular range of viewing positions (θ). Then the number (N) of digital samples that must be computed is given by St. Hilaire, Benton, and Lucente (1992) as:

$$N = \frac{4wh\sin^2\theta}{\lambda^2}$$

where λ denotes wavelength.

Assuming the generation of a square holographic image with sides of length 20cm, a wavelength of 500nm and a viewing angle extending across 30°, we obtain ~$16\text{x}10^{10}$ digital samples per frame. If each sample is assumed to be represented by 8 bits and the frame update frequency is 30Hz, then the digital bandwidth of the display device is ~$38\text{x}10^{12}$ bits per second. Although a number of approaches may be adopted to reduce this figure (e.g., support for only horizontal parallax), display implementation problems remain daunting. Unfortunately, various 3-D display vendors imply within the naming of their products that they are based on holographic technologies, when in fact this is not the case. As a result there is some confusion as to the current viability of holographic systems able to support real time interaction.

2. **The Varifocal Technique:** Here, for example, a varifocal mirror is formed using a flexible mirrored membrane which cycles

between concave and convex states. Image slices (which are depicted in sequence on a conventional flat screen display) are reflected by this mirror in synchronism with its motion. The image position ($v(t)$) may be related to the mirror diameter (d) and object location (u) by:

$$v(t) \sim \frac{d^2 u}{16u \left| x_{\max} \right| \sin \omega t - d^2}$$

where x_{max} denotes the maximum displacement of the mirror and ω the angular frequency of the mirrors motion (Blundell, 2007, 2008).

Thus the formation of an image space with significant depth requires only a relatively small mirror displacement. This technique supports the majority of pictorial cues, together with the oculomotor and parallax cues. In the case that it is used to support the formation of a 'free image space' (which appears to reside between the mirror and the observer(s)) the direct interaction modality may be employed.

3. **The Volumetric Approach:** This technique usually supports the formation of a physical image space (although the free image space scenario is possible – either directly or via an optical projection system). Volumetric systems can provide limited viewing freedom (and as such give rise to images that may be considered to be the electronic rendition of traditional carving) or may support practically unrestricted freedom of viewing location in which case images can take on properties that we associate with traditional sculpted objects.

A volumetric image space may comprise a uniform transparent solid, liquid or gaseous media in which case, for example, visible voxels may be formed at the intersection of two non-visible directed beam sources (e.g., two step excitation of fluorescence, Schwarz & Blundell, 1993; Downing, Hesselink, Macfarlane, & Barty, 1994). Such systems are referred to as static volume displays (Blundell & Schwarz, 2000). Alternatively, an image space may comprise a set of discrete light emitting elements. Consider a cubic image space comprising N such elements. Doubling the dimensions of the image space results in an eight-fold increase in the number of elements (assuming unchanged voxel resolution). Consequently, in order to permit the formation of an image space with useful dimensions and restrict the number of light emitting elements that must be used (together with the associated interconnections) mechanical motion is often employed (giving rise to the 'swept volume' display technique). Here, each element is moved cyclically through a region of the image space thereby sweeping out a sub-space (Blundell & Schwarz, 2000) and within each sub-space a single element is responsible for the production of multiple voxels. For example, consider the rotation of a planar screen equipped with a rectangular 2-D array of $N_a^{1/3}$ by $N_a^{1/3}$ elements each of which is responsible for voxel production along a circular track (for simplicity we assume these elements are all located on one side of the axis of rotation). Assuming that the elements are separated by a distance ζ in the radial direction, that the minimum inter-voxel spacing in the direction of screen motion is to be defined as χ and that the maximum number of voxels that can be illuminated during a single rotation of the screen is N_a then we can represent the throughput of voxels into the image space as:

$$N_a^{1/3} \sum_{j=1}^{N_a^{1/3}} (1 \rightarrow\approx \frac{2\pi j \zeta}{\chi})$$

Here, j is an integer such that $0 < j \leq N_a^{1/3}$ and the term within the summation denotes the number of voxels that can potentially be formed by each element (integer maths is assumed).

To provide a physical image space of useful dimensions in which images of appropriate resolution can be displayed, it is necessary to permit the formation of voxels at a large number (N_l) locations (typically in excess of 10^8 locations). However, to maintain image clarity the majority of any image space must be void and only a relatively small number voxels are usually active at any one time. We denote the maximum number of voxels that can be addressed by the graphics pipeline during each image refresh period (the 'voxel activation capacity') as (N_a). A key metric, referred to as the 'fill factor' (ψ) (Blundell & Schwarz, 2000), is defined as:

$$\phi(\%) = \frac{N_a}{N_l}.100$$

Typically, and without any compromise in display performance, φ may be several orders of magnitude less than 1%. Some volumetric systems support a high degree of parallelism in terms of the number of voxels that can be activated at any one time and at the other extreme some systems permit only sequential voxel activation. The Perspecta display (Favalora, 2002) provides an example of the former, and the Cathode Ray Sphere (CRS) (Blundell, 2007, 2008) adopts the latter approach. The CRS (Figure 2) employs either two or three electron beams which are able to address a rapidly rotating phosphor coated screen (the electron guns and screen are located in a transparent and evacuated spherical vessel: the electron guns being arranged around the periphery of the image space). Visible voxel production occurs when an electron beam impinges on the screen phosphor and the use of more than one beam compensates for the continuously changing geometry of each electron gun relative to the screen. Images are formed using a dot graphics technique (Schwarz & Blundell, 1997). In this scenario, the total number of voxels that can be activated per image update period is limited by the passage of data to the mechanisms that are responsible for voxel activation. For example, in the case of the CRS, the deflection amplifiers which generate the beam deflection signals (these are applied to the electrostatic deflection plates of each electron gun) impose a restriction on the flow of voxel data to the display and so limit the voxel activation capacity. To ameliorate this problem a further version of the CRS employs electron guns equipped with post deflection acceleration (PDA) electrodes. This greatly reduces the voltages that are needed to obtain a certain deflection of the electron beam. When such electron guns are used, the voxel activation capacity is considerably increased and the next limiting factor is defined by the bandwidth of the electronics responsible for electron beam modulation (i.e., the signals that are supplied to the grid electrodes of each gun.

Figure 2. An animated stick figure displayed on an early Cathode Ray Sphere prototype. The figure is able to move around the physical image space in a natural manner. Little restriction is imposed on viewing angle. Unfortunately, when volumetric images are photographed only the pictorial cues are recorded – accommodation and parallax cues are lost. Consequently, photographs do not effectively depict the true three-dimensionality of volumetric images. This CRS prototype employs two electron guns – PDA is not supported (Photograph © Barry G. Blundell).

5. DIRECT INTERACTION WITH IMAGES DEPICTED IN 'FREE SPACE'

As indicated above, a free image space is able to support the direct interaction modality, enabling, for example, a haptic interaction probe to coexist within the volume occupied by a 3-D image. However, when reviewing this display modality, it is important to consider the impact that the presence of the physical interaction probe may have upon image formation. In this context the presence of the probe may prevent the formation of portions of an image. This results in the creation of a region that can be considered to represent an 'umbra'. In addition, a 'penumbra' may be created in which binocular information is absent. Figure 3 provides a simplified overview of the formation of both umbra and penumbra. This problem occurs when the image source physically lies beyond the interaction probe (relative to the observer). However, when the image source and observer are located on the same side (relative to the interaction probe), neither umbra nor penumbra occur. The system cited previously and developed by ReachIn Technologies provides an example of the latter.

Figure 3. A physical (opaque) interaction tool is used in conjunction with, for example, a temporally coded stereoscopic display. An apparent image space is assumed to lie in front of the stereo plane. The interaction tool is inserted into the image space and gives rise to an umbra, in which no image is visible, and a stereoscopic penumbra, in which only a monocular image is seen (Diagram © Milo Blundell).

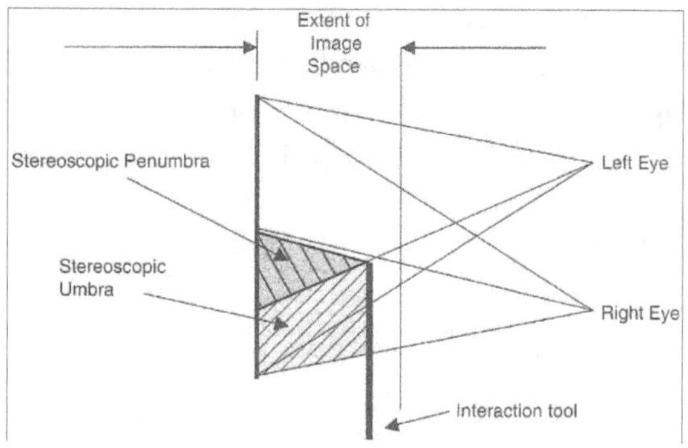

Holographic displays are able to generate both translucent and opaque images. In contrast, images depicted using varifocal systems are inherently translucent. In literature, it is often assumed that volumetric systems are also inherently restricted to the production of translucent images. However, this is not the case but rather is a characteristic of particular embodiments. Opaque images may, in principle, be generated through the use of photochromic materials (Blundell & Schwarz, 2000; Blundell, 2007). Furthermore, almost all volumetric embodiments developed to date give rise to voxels that emit light. In contrast photochromic based displays offer to permit the creation of voxels that scatter ambient light. In this case images are only visible when external light sources are provided. Thus this display modality offers to support the formation of natural shadows and shading. In the case that little restriction is imposed on viewing freedom, this approach may be considered to give rise to images that mimic characteristics of the traditional sculpted image.

6. DISCUSSION

Holographic, volumetric and varifocal techniques give rise to images that satisfy a broad range of pictorial, oculomotor and binocular depth cues. In the case of both holographic and varifocal systems viewing freedom is limited whereas some volumetric embodiments provide essentially unrestricted freedom in viewing position. When an image scene is to be viewed simultaneously by a number of observers, unrestricted viewing freedom is generally beneficial and such displays give rise to images that share many of the properties that are associated with traditional sculpture. All three display modalities are able to support both horizontal and vertical motion parallax.

Volumetric display systems have been researched for many years, the first static volume system being proposed by Emile Luzy and Charles Dupuis in 1912 (Blundell, 2000). The swept-volume technique dates back to the pioneering work of John Logie Baird in the late 1920s (Blundell, 2007). Since that time numerous volumetric systems have been proposed and prototyped. However, many of these embodiments have possessed inherent design flaws. By way of example, consider the implementation of a static volume system in which the image space is formed using a liquid or solid material (Downing *et al.,* 1994). Light emerging from such an image space is subjected to refraction and, as a result, even the most perfectly formed image would appear to be distorted. This impacts our perception of the shape of image components and on our judgment of spatial relationships. Furthermore, should such an image space be employed in conjunction with the pointer based interaction technique, light entering the image space from the pointer would also be subjected to refraction. Thus when considered from an optical standpoint, any volumetric display that employs an image space whose refractive index is significantly greater than its surroundings is unlikely to advance either the visualization or interaction processes. (From a practical perspective, the physical density of the image space would impact display portability and/ or restrict image space dimensions).

Many swept volume volumetric architectures also have associated flaws. For example, should translational motion be used for image space generation, then the mechanical drive tends to be complex (especially as the dimensions of the image space are increased). In contrast, although the use of rotational motion (in conjunction with a planar surface or helical screen) is more readily achieved, the axis of rotation is problematic and results in the formation of a voxel placement 'dead zone' (Blundell, 2007) in which it is not possible to locate voxels.

From the mid 1960s through until the early 1980s, varifocal display technologies were the subject of considerable research interest – activity focusing primarily on medical applications. Unfortunately, due to patent issues, work in this interesting area ceased. In literature, the generation of acoustic noise is generally sited as a major flaw of the varifocal paradigm (the mirror must vibrate at a frequency in excess of the human flicker fusion frequency (~25-30Hz)). However, several approaches may be adopted to ameliorate this problem and the technique continues to offer a practical low cost means of depicting 3-D images that incorporate the three categories of depth cue. In addition, such a display may be used to generate either a virtual or real image space.

The form of image space that is supported by a display technology directly impacts on interaction opportunities. In this sense the driving force behind the development of 'creative' display systems should not simply be based upon the visualization opportunities that a display may offer but also by the display's ability to support intuitive and synergistic interaction. Haptic feedback is best employed in conjunction with forms of free, virtual and apparent image spaces.

An increasing number of interaction interfaces are incorporating limited haptic sensation. Over the coming years we can anticipate that this trend will become more widespread and systems will evolve which provide increasingly realistic haptic effects. In addition we can anticipate greater recognition of the importance of making better use of the complex human visual system, and so 3-D display technologies will become the norm rather than the exception. At present, key manufacturers are focusing upon the development of display technologies which are fundamentally based on the principle of the stereoscope. This does not necessarily mean that the viewer needs to don special glasses as, for example, the multi-view technique enables stereoscopic images to be viewed without recourse to such glasses. Whether this approach will ultimately prove successful is a matter for debate as the decoupling of the accommodation and convergence cues, which is an inherent characteristic of displays that are based on the stereoscope, can cause strain to the human visual system. However, in addition we can also anticipate the production of volume-based displays (of the types discussed above), which more naturally mate with our sense of sight. The development and production of such displays represents a bold step forward, especially as so much of the computing industry (considered from both a hardware and software perspective) is tied so closely to the flat screen display modality.

Currently, internet-based applications are strongly linked to the flat-screen display, and very few image downloads support true 3-D viewing. Perhaps the most likely near-term advances in internet-based interactive graphics will be a migration to true 3-D along with support for haptic interaction tools. The fundamental technologies needed to support the free space image modality are within our grasp. In addition, the complexity of computer applications has grown so that there is a vital need for computer interfaces that make better use of complex human sensory systems. Consequently there can be little doubt that over the coming years we will have the opportunity to interact with the digital world in far more exciting and creative ways.

REFERENCES

Alberti, L. B. (2010). Della pittura e della statua. In Tirabosschi, G. (Ed.), *Della pittura e della statua di Leonbatista Alberti*. Charleston, SC: Nabu Press.

Blundell, B. G. (2007). *Enhanced visualization: Making space for 3-D images*. New York, NY: John Wiley & Sons.

Blundell, B. G. (2008). *An introduction to computer graphics and creative 3-D environments*. New York, NY: Springer. doi:10.1007/978-1-84800-042-1

Blundell, B. G., & Schwarz, A. J. (2000). *Volumetric three-dimensional display systems*. New York, NY: John Wiley & Sons.

Blundell, B. G., & Schwarz, A. J. (2006). *Creative 3-D display and interaction interfaces: A trans-disciplinary approach*. New York, NY: John Wiley & Sons.

(1986). InBoff, K. R., Kaufman, L., & Thomas, J. P. (Eds.). Handbook of perception and human performance: *Vol. I. Sensory processes and perception*. New York, NY: John Wiley & Sons.

Burdea, G. C. (1996). *Force and touch feedback for virtual reality*. New York, NY: John Wiley & Sons.

Downing, E., Hesselink, L., Macfarlane, R. M., & Barty, C. P. J. (1994). *Solid-state three-dimensional computer display*. Paper presented at the Conference on Lasers and Electro-Optics.

Edgerton, S. Y. (1976). *The renaissance rediscovery of linear perspective*. New York, NY: Harper and Row.

Favalora, G. E., Napoli, J., Hall, D. M., Dorval, R. K., Giovinco, M. G., Richmond, M. J., & Chun, W. S. (2002). 100 million voxels volumetric display. In *Proceedings of the 9th SPIE Conference on Cockpit Displays: Displays for Defense Applications* (pp. 300-312).

Halle, M. (1997). Autostereoscopic displays and computer graphics. *ACM SIGGRAPH Computer Graphics*, *31*(2), 58–62. doi:10.1145/271283.271309

Lynes, J. A. (1980). Brunelleschi's perspectives reconsidered. *Perception*, *9*, 87–99. doi:10.1068/p090087

McAllister, D. F. (Ed.). (1993). *Stereo computer graphics and other true 3D technologies*. Princeton, NJ: Princeton University Press.

Okoshi, T. (1976). *Three-dimensional imaging techniques*. New York, NY: Academic Press.

Schwarz, A. J., & Blundell, B. G. (1993). Considerations regarding voxel brightness in volumetric displays utilizing two-step excitation processes. *Optical Engineering (Redondo Beach, Calif.)*, *32*(11), 2818–2823. doi:10.1117/12.148130

Schwarz, A. J., & Blundell, B. G. (1997). Optimising dot-graphics for volumetric displays. *IEEE Transactions on Computer Graphics and Applications*, *17*(3), 72–78. doi:10.1109/38.586020

St. Hilaire, P., Benton, S., & Lucente, M. (1992). Synthetic aperture holography: A novel approach to three-dimensional displays. *Journal of the Optical Society of America. A, Optics and Image Science*, *9*(11), 1969–1977. doi:10.1364/JOSAA.9.001969

Wade, N. J. (Ed.). (1983). *Brewster and Wheatstone on vision*. New York, NY: Academic Press.

Wheatstone, C. (1838). Contributions to the theory of vision – Part the first, on some remarkable, and hitherto unobserved, phenomena of binocular vision. *Philosophical Transactions of the Royal Society of London*, *128*, 371–394. doi:10.1098/rstl.1838.0019

ENDNOTES

1 However, when closely scrutinised, uncertainty surrounds Brunelleschi's demonstration (Lynes, 1980; Blundell & Schwarz, 2006).

2 The interaction modalities selected for introduction here are of particular relevance to subsequent discussion concerning 'creative' 3-D systems.

3 Usually, multi-view and other display paradigms which are fundamentally based on the stereoscope support only horizontal parallax (vertical parallax is absent).

This work was previously published in the Information Resources Management Journal, Volume 24, Issue 4, edited by Mehdi Khosrow-Pour, pp. 50-60, copyright 2013 by IGI Publishing (an imprint of IGI Global).

Chapter 18
Understanding Critical Distance Learning Issues: Toward a Comprehensive Model Predicting Student Satisfaction

Stephen K. Callaway
University of Toledo, USA

Saad M. Alflayyeh
University of Toledo, USA

ABSTRACT

Distance education has been the topic of a substantial amount of research. However, prior studies have shown mixed results when trying to determine if a difference exists in student satisfaction between students in distance courses versus traditional courses. Prior empirical studies have been too narrow in scope, and a more comprehensive model is needed to better explain the factors influencing student satisfaction. Therefore, the current study includes student demographic factors, comprehensive measures of student motivation, and course format, as well as specific course features included, to fully explain student satisfaction. Structural equation modeling is used to test the model. Results indicate a positive association between demographics and motivation, between motivation and course format, between one demographic factor and course format, between course format and preferred features, between course format and satisfaction, and between course features and satisfaction.

INTRODUCTION

Distance education is an increasingly important component of higher education. For example, according to Hatfield (2006), approximately 3.2 million students, or about one in six, completed at least one such class during 2005 (Hatfield, 2006; Jackson & Helms, 2008). As such, distance education has been the topic of a substantial amount of research. However, prior studies have shown mixed results when trying to determine if there is a difference in student satisfaction

DOI: 10.4018/978-1-4666-3616-3.ch018

between students in distance courses versus traditional face-to-face courses (Hara & Kling, 1999; Hirschheim, 2005; Pucel & Stertz, 2005; Storck & Sproull, 1995). Such studies have often simply compared satisfaction between traditional and online students, without considering other important factors influencing satisfaction. Perhaps these empirical studies have been too narrow in scope, and a more comprehensive model is needed to better explain the factors influencing student satisfaction, including demographic factors, comprehensive measures of student motivation, the format of courses selected, as well as specific course features included.

Keegan (1980, 1996, 2002) has proposed various definitions of distance education. One is that distance education can be defined as "use of technical media, such as print, audio, video, or computer, in order to unite teacher and learner and deliver the content of the course" (Keegan, 2002, pp. 22-23). The key points of these definitions are the uniting of teacher and learner, and the two-way communication, which is conducted at a distance. Ultimately, distance education comprises both distance teaching, which focuses on delivering instruction to the learner, and distance learning, which focuses on maximizing learner cognition (Bryant, Kahle, & Schafer, 2005; Keegan, 1996, 2002).

In order to understand satisfaction with distance courses, we must understand the demographics of students who select distance vs. traditional courses and programs, particularly whether they are essentially the same market segment, entirely distinct, or comprise some overlap. Then, the issue is whether these market segments have identical, similar, or distinct motivational factors influencing what courses they select. As such, comprehensive multi-item measures of motivation are required, which encompass the various factors different students may value. Finally, the model needs to assess not only which type of course is selected (distance or traditional), but what specific course features are preferred. Then, a comprehensive multi-item construct for student satisfaction is needed for the predicted variable.

Therefore, the current study has constructed and empirically tested such a model. This study created a comprehensive model showing the mediators that may affect student satisfaction, based upon the literature and upon interviews with university administrators. Specifically, this study collected and examined the chief demographic factors of the market segments, the course format selected (traditional or distance), and the specific course features that may be offered in a course. Moreover, the variables student motivation and student satisfaction comprise comprehensive, multi-item constructs in order to better understand student behavior. That is, customers may be segmented according to certain demographic characteristics, and administrators may use this information to understand customer satisfaction and predict certain customer behaviors, and accordingly create better strategies (Andrews, Brusco, & Currim, 2010; Kumar, Norris, & Sun, 2009). Ultimately, the final model was tested using structural equations modeling (SEM). The model is shown in Figure 1.

In short, the key contribution of this study is presenting a comprehensive model that shows a complete picture that more fully explains the

Figure 1. Comprehensive model predicting student satisfaction

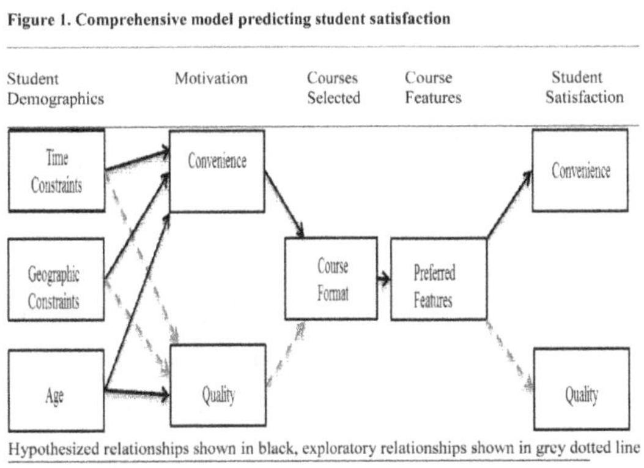

nature of student satisfaction. That is, SEM includes two components: the measurement model and the structural model (Gerbing & Anderson, 1992). As such, this paper addresses each of these components. First, this study creates and measures new comprehensive multi-item constructs (i.e., student motivation, preferred course features, and student satisfaction). Specifically, these constructs had been described in literature but had never previously been this comprehensively operationalized. Second, the current study creates a comprehensive model showing the structure of the relationships between each of these constructs, particularly examining how the relationships between key constructs are mediated by other constructs. In short, while prior studies have revealed some of the most basic relationships (such as predicting student satisfaction or course selection), this study provides a more complete understanding as to why these relationships exist, by identifying and assessing the key mediators in the model.

LITERATURE REVIEW

Demographic Factors

Market segmentation is critical for understanding your consumers. It is essential for administrators developing distance programs and courses to understand the demographics of their customers. According to Dykman and Davis (2008a), many distance education students tend to be older, and they may have experiences that are important to the objectives of an online course, bringing in a 'real world' perspective that may be very beneficial. These professionals likely work full time and cannot afford to take the time from work to pursue a degree in the traditional manner. Research demonstrates that distance education students tend to be older than traditional students, are more likely to be female, married, and employed full-time (Bryant et al., 2005; Gibson & Graff, 1992; Schell, 2001).

The reason for examining the demographic market segmentation and corresponding student motivation is that any new technology, such as radical or disruptive technology, may appeal to a new or different customer niche, whose behaviors and motivations are unlike traditional customers. According to Christensen and Raynor (2003), distance education represents a disruptive technology for full-service, four-year colleges. Disruptive technological innovations offer stripped-down, more convenient and less costly products, which appeal to new or less-demanding customers. This emerging customer segment is initially only a small niche, and as such, is often misunderstood or missed entirely by traditional organizations serving the current mainstream customers (Christensen & Bower, 1996; Christensen & Raynor, 2003).

Moreover, the traditional and the emerging customer segments may demonstrate different motivations and behaviors. Distance programs may offer distinct features, and students enrolled in such programs may have different expectations. According to Hirschheim (2005), some examples of distance education may create a more standardized, minimalist product targeting a mass market which desires a quick certification rather than investing in a long term quality education. As a result, a 'no frills' approach to education may emerge that emphasizes memorization of the most basic content, rather than a high quality educational process of student interaction and learning. If so, there may be a tradeoff between quality, and the flexibility, speed and convenience commonly associated with distance education programs (Hirschheim, 2005).

On the other hand, in the case of distance education versus traditional higher education, these customer segments may or may not be entirely distinct, and may or may not possess different value propositions. There may be substantial overlap between students typically enrolled in traditional physical courses and those enrolled online. Indeed, students may easily switch between programs, or take a mix of both traditional and distance education courses, particularly at traditional universities offering distance education. Understanding these market segments, and what motivates them, is essential for university administration and planning.

Therefore, the first stage of the comprehensive model addresses how student demographic factors will directly impact comprehensive student motivation. Students may be traditional, or they may be non-traditional, meaning some students are older, have families, work full time, and live a greater distance from campus. As such, the three key demographic variables for this model include time constraints (because of work or family life), geographic constraints (distance from campus), and age. These three variables are expected to be directly related to student motivation.

Comprehensive Motivation

Different student segments may reflect different motivations for pursuing distance education, as opposed to traditional education. Research has identified key advantages for distance education to be convenience and flexibility (Hirschheim, 2005; Pucel & Stertz, 2005). That is, distance education delivery methods may be very attractive for non-traditional students who are older, married, have children, work full-time, or otherwise face substantial time constraints, or are located too far away from a campus to attend traditional physical classes (Dykman & Davis, 2008a). Substantial research has identified the convenience of allowing flexible scheduling, as well as the convenience of flexible locations, as important factors for distance students (Pucel & Stertz, 2005). Moreover, Hirschheim (2005) has identified cost as another motivational factor for distance students, whether or not distance courses actually are less costly for the university to offer. Overall, convenience factors include speed, cost, and flexible time and place scheduling.

On the other hand, quality is an essential factor for higher education officials to understand and measure as well (Dykman & Davis, 2008c; Hirschheim, 2005). For example, according to Bryant et al. (2005), the quality of classroom interaction (such as student-instructor or between students) is critical for all college education (Buckley, 2003; Fulford & Zhang, 1993; Vrasidas & McIsaac, 1999). Moreover, Harroff and Valentine (2006) identified critical quality dimensions for understanding distance education.

As such, while all students likely value both quality and convenience; non-traditional students, those who are older, have families, work full time, and live a greater distance from campus, are more likely to value convenience. Ultimately, those facing greater time and geographic constraints will more likely seek convenience, but not at the expense of quality (i.e., not less quality). However, older students, being more demanding overall, will likely prefer both greater quality and convenience. In sum, the following relationship is expected between student demographic factors and student motivation.

H1: Demographic factors (students facing both time and geographic constraints) will be positively associated with convenience motivation factors. Older students will be positively associated both with convenience and quality motivation factors.

Courses Selected

The second stage of this model assesses what factors influence the course format that students are likely to select (i.e., whether students select more traditional courses or more distance courses). Student demographic factors (time constraints, geographic constraints, and student age) as well as student motivation (quality motivation and convenience motivation) are expected to be associated with course selection. Specifically, convenience motivation will be associated with selecting distance education courses. Moreover, student motivation is expected to mediate the relationship between the demographic factors and course selection.

According to Dykman and Davis (2008a), many traditional universities offer a number of degrees mostly or entirely online, including the University of Texas System which offers several bachelors' degrees, masters' degrees, and professional certifications (UT System Telecampus, http://www.telecampus.utsystem.edu/). Many other colleges and universities offer such distance programs as well, and even more offers various distance courses which may fulfill requirements of traditional programs. Clearly distance education is a critical part of the offerings of many traditional schools, and students have a choice of whether to enroll in programs which are entirely distance, entirely traditional, or a mix of the two. Further, students enrolled in distance programs may be able to take individual courses in a traditional format, or vice versa. Students today face many options, and universities must understand the student demographics, and what motivates them, and plan their course format selection accordingly.

Specifically, non-traditional students (i.e., students facing time and geographic constraints as well as older students), arc more likely to enroll in distance education courses. Also, students who are motivated by convenience factors are more likely to enroll in distance education courses. If students value speed, cost, and flexible time and place scheduling, then distance education courses likely offer what they are seeking. That is, convenience motivation is expected to mediate the relationship between demographic factors and course selection. However, quality factors are not expected to be associated with course format selection. That is, students motivated by quality factors may select either distance or traditional courses, indicating that distance students are somewhat more demanding.

H2a: Convenience motivation factors will be positively associated with the selection of distance education courses.

H2b: Demographic factors (older students and students facing both time and geographic constraints) will be positively associated with the selection of distance education courses.

Preferred Course Features

The third stage of this model assesses what factors will influence the specific course features that students are likely to prefer. Selection of course format (traditional or distance courses) as well as student motivation (quality motivation and convenience motivation) are expected to be associated with preferred course features. This stage of the model is necessary to examine in more detail what exactly students are seeking when they select their courses, as the nature of these courses and corresponding student preferences may vary. Specifically, convenience motivation may be associated with a preference for distance course features. Moreover, selection of distance courses is expected to mediate the relationship between convenience motivation and preference for distance course features.

In other words, simply categorizing a course as distance or traditional does not offer enough insight as to what specific course features that students may be seeking based upon their factors of motivation. This level of detail is needed to truly predict student satisfaction. That is, students seeking and enrolled in one type of course may still prefer some course features to be of a specific format more than others. Furthermore, the preferences of students and the format of the course selected may be limited by course availability, advisor recommendation, courses being closed, what features professors are likely to offer, etc. Therefore, it is important to closely examine what specific course features students are most seeking when selecting their courses.

Ultimately, a course comprises a bundle of course features which can be combined in different ways and offered to students. Examples of such course features are described in Dykman and Davis (2008c), Bryant et al. (2005), Dereshiwsky (2001), Hirschheim (2005), Levin (1999), and Wilhelm, Rodehorst, Young, Jensen, and Stepans (2003). Six course features included for this study include lectures on new material, assigned readings and other material, class discussions and participation, examinations, individual tutoring, and group work. Students may have preferences as to which features are offered more traditionally and which more in a distance format. These course features offer a comprehensive look at what students may be seeking when they select their courses.

Buckley (2003), Dykman and Davis (2008c), and Levin (1999) describe the importance of the lecture on new material as well as assigned readings and other subject related material (e.g., books, articles), in terms of student exposure to new material, either in a distance environment or traditionally. Indeed, these course features may easily be offered online by professors, and/or preferred by students, even in a traditional course setting. Next, Dykman and Davis (2008c) and Wilhelm et al. (2003) describe the importance of classroom discussions and participation, as this is where much of the actual learning occurs for students. That is, the quality of classroom interaction (professor-student and between students) is an essential component of the course, and is essential for student satisfaction in any program, particularly distance education (Bryant et al., 2005; Buckley, 2003; Fulford & Zhang, 1993; Vrasidas & McIsaac, 1999).

Finally, Dykman and Davis (2008c) and Dereshiwsky (2001) address testing student comprehension, that is, the examination. However, many professors may hesitate to utilize this feature in a distance environment, even in the context of a distance education course, because of the difficulty in ascertaining the identity of the person taking the exam. Nevertheless, students may indeed strongly prefer that this particular course feature be offered online. Further, individual tutorials are described by Dykman and Davis (2008c) and Littleton and Whitelock (2004) as a way to offer the level of individual attention so important to the success of distance education, by linking the teacher to each student, or students to each other. Finally, Hirschheim (2005) addressed the importance of group work for students in any course. Indeed some studies show a connection between student interaction and the requirement of group work in both the traditional or distance environment, by stimulating student involvement and encouraging students to regulate their group processes (Cohen, 1994; Dewiyanti, Brand-Gruwel, Jochems, & Broers, 2007; Johnson & Johnson, 1994). However, other distance education students may tend to prefer features focusing on individual effort more than teamwork, and have at times been surprised by the requirement of group work in distance courses (Hirschheim, 2005).

Therefore, students who are motivated by convenience factors will likely prefer more of these specific course features in a distance education format (because the distance format is considered to be more convenient), while students motivated by quality factors may prefer either course features (i.e., no relationship expected). Also, selection of distance course format will be positively associated with a preference for specific distance course features. That is, course format selection is expected to mediate the relationship between convenience motivation and the specific course features preferred.

H3a: The selection of distance education courses will be positively associated with a preference for specific distance course features.

H3b: Convenience motivation factors will be positively associated with a preference for specific distance course features.

Student Satisfaction

The final stage of this model explains what factors will influence student satisfaction, particularly satisfaction with convenience and satisfaction with quality. Selection of course format (traditional or distance courses) as well as preference for specific course features (traditional or distance features) are expected to be associated with satisfaction. Specifically, distance course format may be associated with satisfaction with convenience. Moreover, a preference for distance course features is expected to mediate the relationship between distance courses and satisfaction with convenience.

Jackson and Helms (2008) and Pucel and Stertz (2005) reported that the results of studies examining student satisfaction for distance education have been mixed. Klesius, Homan, and Thompson (1997) found that student satisfaction with distance education was equal to satisfaction with traditional instruction, while Ponzurick, France, and Logar (2000) found lower overall satisfaction with the distance education format. Overall, many studies find no significant difference in satisfaction between distance education students and traditional students (Hara & Kling, 1999; Hirschheim, 2005; Storck & Sproull, 1995).

The reason for the inconsistency may well be that studies up to this point have failed to consider a deeper understanding of the concept of student satisfaction. That is, the concept of satisfaction itself is multi-dimensional, and should be measured this way. All factors of satisfaction itself must be considered. Distance education is likely to be associated with greater satisfaction with convenience (such as time and place convenience). However, Hirschheim (2005) and Pucel and Stertz (2005) argued that distance education has at times also demonstrated student dissatisfaction resulting from lack of instructor interaction, difficulty developing student interaction, lack of feedback, as well as confusion about the actual cost of distance education courses. Therefore, a multidimensional construct of student satisfaction, coupled with a comprehensive model of all possible antecedents, should provide us with a complete model predicting student satisfaction.

Ultimately, students enrolled in distance education courses are expected to be more satisfied with convenience factors. Moreover, students that prefer specific distance course features will more likely be satisfied with convenience factors. That is, student preference for specific distance course features will positively mediate the relationship between selection of distance courses and satisfaction with convenience factors. Again, satisfaction with quality factors is not expected to be associated with either course format or preference for specific course features. The comprehensive model predicting student satisfaction is shown in Figure 1. Note that all relationships are positive. In sum,

H4a: A preference for specific distance course features will be positively associated with satisfaction with convenience factors.

H4b: The selection of distance education courses will be positively associated with satisfaction with convenience factors.

METHODOLOGY

The purpose of this study was to examine the impact of student demographics, motivation, course format selection, and specific course features, on student satisfaction at traditional four-year universities (those offering both traditional and distance courses). Therefore, two large public universities located in the Midwestern United States were targeted for this study. Both universities offered courses that were traditional or distance education, that is, a student enrolled in a traditional program could still take some distance education courses, and vice versa.

The data were collected using an online survey targeting students. This survey was designed based upon prior research, specifically prior theoretical studies or reports with anecdotal evidence about motivation, satisfaction and course features. Comprehensive empirical studies of these variables have been lacking in prior studies, according to Farrington and Bronack (2001). Next, semi-structured interviews with administration officials (including admissions officials and advisors) at one of the universities were conducted to further develop the survey. That is, field interviews with key informants helped to establish construct and content validity of the instrument used in this study (Cronbach, 1971; Straub, 1989; Nunnally, 1978).

In the survey, demographic data were gathered from respondents. The demographic variables include age, an index measuring time pressures, and an index measuring distance to travel. For the time pressures index, respondents were asked whether or not they were married (or otherwise part of a cohabitated couple), whether or not they had children, and whether or not they worked full time (answering 1 for 'yes' and 0 for 'no' for each), generating a total score scaled from 0 to 3. For the distance to travel index, respondents were asked whether or not they lived on campus (1 for 'no' and 0 for 'yes'), and then about how many miles from campus (with answers equally divided into 0, 1, 2, or 3 based upon number of miles), leading to a score ranging from 0 to 4. Next, questions asked what proportion of courses taken were taught in a face-to-face physical classroom setting (Q3) – from 1 'none' through 5 'all the classes'. The next question asked what proportion of classes taken were distance learning (Q5) – from 1 'none' through 5 'all the classes'.

Eight specific items representing Motivation Factors were selected according to the literature. These items were based on theoretical studies by Dykman and Davis (2008a, 2008b, 2008c), Hirschheim (2005), and Pucel and Stertz (2005), which depicted both convenience factors and quality factors. Quality factors, according to Bryant et al. (2005), Fulford and Zhang (1993), and Vrasidas and McIsaac (1999), include classroom interaction (instructor-student and between students) as well as university resources and institution reputation. Overall, convenience factors include cost, time convenience, place convenience, and speed to complete a degree; while quality factors include university resources, reputation of degree institution, and interactions with faculty members and with fellow classmates. Students were asked to rate the importance of each of these factors, scaled from one 'not at all important' through five 'very important'.

Next, six specific course features were developed according to Buckley (2003), Dykman and Davis (2008c), Bryant et al. (2005), Dereshiwsky (2001), Littleton and Whitelock (2004), Levin (1999), and Hirschheim (2005), as described. The six features comprise lectures, assigned readings, class discussions, examinations, individualized tutorials, and group work. These specific course features should fully represent the issues pertaining to both quality and convenience for students in either traditional or distance courses. For each course feature, students were asked how they would prefer to receive each of these features, from 1 'entirely in person' through 5 'entirely online'.

Finally, nine items representing Satisfaction Factors were selected, and were based directly on the selected Motivation Factors. However, satisfaction with quality of course instruction (organization, clear course expectations) was added based upon Buckley (2003), Dykman and Davis (2008a, 2008b, 2008c), Pucel and Stertz (2005), Topper (2007), and Young (2006) as an additional key factor that may determine student satisfaction. Again, it is expected that the first five items will represent a single construct indicating satisfaction with quality, and the last four items will represent a construct indicating satisfaction with convenience.

RESULTS AND ANALYSIS

Note that emails were sent to all students informing them of this survey, whether they were enrolled in distance programs or traditional programs, with a link directly to the survey. Since all students use the university email service regularly, results likely would not be skewed toward online usage. Moreover, this methodological approach, the emailed online survey, has been utilized and verified by prior academic research (Ritter, Polnick, Fink, & Oescher, 2010; Robinia & Anderson, 2010). Ultimately 357 usable responses were received. The purpose of this study was to test a model specifying the relationships among student demographics, motivation, course format, preferred course features, and student satisfaction, therefore structural equation modeling was used for model evaluation (Gerbing & Anderson, 1992).

First, for five key constructs (the two motivation constructs, the two satisfaction constructs, and preferred course features), exploratory principal components factor analysis was calculated using SPSS, because the survey included new measures developed in the current study for the corresponding constructs. Factor loadings are shown in Table 1. Confirmatory factor analysis was then used to assess the convergent and discriminant validity of each of the items. As expected, the items exhibited large factor pattern coefficients for the most part with their corresponding latent factors. The observed indicators thus appear to reflect the latent constructs. The goodness of fit of the measurement model (estimated with restricted or confirmatory factor analysis) was adequate (X2

Table 1. Principal component factor analysis with varimax rotation

	ConvMot	QualMot	QualSat	ConvSat	PrefFeat
MotCost	**0.603**	0.285	-0.123	-0.059	-0.018
TimeConv	**0.780**	-0.115	0.024	0.039	0.122
PlaceConv	**0.768**	0.098	0.088	0.049	0.173
MotSpeed	**0.465**	0.211	0.085	-0.187	0.192
Resources	0.230	**0.690**	0.177	-0.070	0.063
Reputation	0.152	**0.705**	0.271	-0.057	0.044
FacInteract	-0.075	**0.828**	0.057	0.137	-0.105
PeerInteract	0.085	**0.739**	0.003	0.219	-0.199
SatCourse	-0.055	0.044	**0.769**	0.188	0.051
SatResources	-0.018	0.088	**0.806**	0.191	0.001
SatReputat	0.147	0.065	**0.766**	0.203	0.076
SatFacInter	-0.067	0.155	**0.734**	0.255	0.015
SatPeerInter	0.112	0.167	**0.675**	0.257	-0.026
SatCost	-0.187	0.140	0.321	**0.603**	-0.022
SatSpeed	-0.057	0.050	0.317	**0.679**	-0.089
SatTimeConv	0.042	0.059	0.206	**0.811**	0.113
SatPlaceConv	0.044	-0.027	0.350	**0.746**	-0.018
Lectures	0.119	-0.051	-0.038	0.030	**0.807**
Readings	0.031	0.068	-0.032	-0.055	**0.712**
Discussion	0.138	-0.059	-0.026	0.084	**0.803**
Exams	0.293	-0.040	0.013	-0.034	**0.704**
Tutoring	-0.008	-0.066	0.116	0.006	**0.585**
TeamWork	0.007	-0.031	0.041	-0.036	**0.719**

= 506.3. df = 220, X^2/df= 2.3, RMSEA = .06, NFI= .84, NNFI= .87, CFI= .90).

The reliability of the multi-item questionnaire scales was tested with Cronbach's alpha. Specifically, the four items (cost, time convenience, place convenience, and speed to degree – labeled Q7, Q8, Q9, Q10) comprising the Convenience Motivation was calculated to be 0.630. While this is less than the .70 rule-of-thumb advocated by Nunnally (1978), alphas as low as .60 are allowed for exploratory research (Cronbach, 1971; Nunnally, 1978; Straub, 1989). The coefficient alpha for the scale containing items Q11, Q12, Q13, and Q14 (quality of resources, reputation of institution, quality of interaction with faculty, and quality of interaction with classmates) was .779. The reliability of the Convenience Satisfaction construct was .782 and the reliability of the Quality Satisfaction construct was .856.

The demographic data comprised the three indexes (time constraints, geographic constraints, and age) described above. Next, all of the indicators were combined into single index measures averaging each of the items' scores. Student selection of traditional and distance courses, as expected, were found to be inversely related, and so the two items were combined into a single construct Course Selection, with the selection of traditional courses item reverse-coded. Table 2 shows the descriptive data (means, standard deviations, and correlations, among the measures in this study). Finally, the structural model was tested using the AMOS software package. The model estimates from this analysis are shown in Table 3. Further, the findings indicate a good fit based on various fit measures (X2/df = 2.21, RMSEA = 0.06, NFI = 0.83, NNFI=0.87, CFI = 0.9).

Hypothesis 1 argues that student demographic factors would influence motivation factors. This hypothesis was supported for two of the three dimensions of demographic factors, and partly supported for the third. As expected, students facing greater time constraints and geographic constraints were indeed more likely motivated by convenience factors, with no significant effects on the quality factors. Older students (age) were also more likely to be motivated by quality factors, as expected. However, unexpectedly, older students did not demonstrate any greater preference for convenience factors. The model statistics are shown in Table 3.

Hypothesis 2a argues that students more motivated by convenience factors will select more distance education courses, while students more motivated by quality factors would not show a greater tendency toward either the traditional

Table 2. Correlations, means and standard deviations of model constructs

	Mean	Std. Dev.	X1	X2	X3	X4	X5	X6	X7	X8
X1 Time Constraints	0.9	1.04	1							
X2 Geog. Constraints	2.8	1	.39**	1						
X3 Age	27.7	9.42	.68**	.44**	1					
X4 Motiv. – Convenience	3.5	0.89	.23**	.19**	.16**	1				
X5 Motiv. – Quality	3.7	0.85	0.02	0.03	.11*	.29**	1			
X6 Course Format	1.9	0.99	-0.03	-.11*	-0.06	0	-0.01	1		
X7 Pref. Course Features	2.5	1.1	.40**	.19**	.32**	.27**	-0.07	0	1	
X8 Satis. – Convenience	3.3	0.84	-.11*	0.01	0.09	-0.02	.20**	-.10*	0	1
X9 Satis. – Quality	3.8	0.82	.18**	.13*	.17*	0.10	.34**	-.14**	0.05	.58**

Significant correlations are in bold.
** significant at $p < 0.01$
* significant at $p < 0.05$

Table 3. Overall results – Model parameter estimates and fit statistics

Estimates and Fit Statistics Standardized Critical P value
Estimate Ratio
Model Parameters
Hypothesis 1
Time Constraints →Motivation-Convenience .236 2.637 .008***
Time Constraints →Motivation-Quality -.106 -1.282 .200
Geographic Constraints → Motivation-Convenience .167 2.363 .018**
Geographic Constraints → Motivation-Quality -.004 -.063 .950
Age→ Motivation-Convenience -.023 -.267 .789
Age→ Motivation-Quality .189 2.197 .028**
Hypothesis 2
Motivation-Convenience→ Course Format .346 4.292 .001***
Motivation-Quality→ Course Format -.122 -2.068 .039**
Time Constraints→ Course Format .274 4.020 .001***
Geographic Constraints→ Course Format .005 .101 .920
Age→ Course Format .085 1.244 .213
Hypothesis 3
Course Format→ Preferred Course Features .493 6.511 .001***
Motivation-Convenience→ Preferred Course Features .187 2.516 .012**
Motivation-Quality→ Preferred Course Features -.177 -2.904 .004***
Hypothesis 4
Preferred Course Features →Satisfaction-Convenience -.099 -1.050 .294
Preferred Course Features →Satisfaction-Quality -.023 -.256 .798
Course Format →Satisfaction-Convenience .255 3.037 .002***
Course Format →Satisfaction-Quality .055 .706 .480
Goodness-of-Fit Statistics
X^2/df = 2.21
RMSEA = 0.06
ECVI= 2.448 (ECVI for Saturated model =2.275)
NFI = 0.83
NNFI(TLI) =0.87
CFI = 0.9

or distance course format. This hypothesis was supported in the case of convenience motivation but not for quality motivation. Indeed, students motivated by convenience were more likely to select the distance course format, but students motivated by quality factors were in fact less likely to select distance (a negative relationship was found). Hypothesis 2b states that demographic factors would influence the course format selected. Students facing time constraints were more likely to select the distance format, as expected, however those facing geographic constraints showed no tendency toward either course format. Likewise, older students did not demonstrate any preference for either the distance or the traditional course format.

Hypothesis 3a argued that students selecting the distance course format would more likely prefer distance course features. This hypothesis was strongly supported. Hypothesis 3b stated that students more likely motivated by convenience factors would show a greater preference for distance course features, which was supported by the data. However, unexpectedly, students more likely motivated by quality factors showed less preference for distance course features (a negative relationship was found).

Hypothesis 4a stated that students showing a greater preference for specific distance course features would be more satisfied with convenience factors. This hypothesis was not supported. As expected, there was no relationship between distance course features and satisfaction with quality factors. Finally, Hypothesis 4b argued that courses selected would influence student satisfaction. As expected, students selecting greater distance courses were more likely satisfied with convenience factors. Also as expected, no relationship was found between distance course format and satisfaction with quality factors. All of the model statistics are shown in Table 3.

DISCUSSION

The current study has presented a comprehensive model explaining several key factors predicting student satisfaction. Clearly, to simply compare student satisfaction between distance and traditional students fails to reveal the deeper factors behind satisfaction, and this study has identified and tested the variables student demographics, student motivation, course format, and specific course features. All are shown to play a role in explaining student satisfaction.

First, time and geographic constraints have been identified as key factors motivating students to seek more convenience factors, but not at the expense of quality factors. Age has been shown to be an important demographic factor, as older students seek more quality factors. Clearly university officials desiring to offer distance learning programs and courses need to understand the demographic factors behind all of their students. Administrators must also understand the competing demands (motivation) of convenience and quality for students as they select such courses. Further, while students selecting more distance courses were more satisfied with the level of convenience, preference for specific distance course features was not strongly associated with that convenience satisfaction, indicating that the tradeoff between convenience and quality may be particularly apparent in these specific features (i.e., presentation of material, testing, tutoring, teamwork, and course interaction).

The study has some limitations, including the limited scope of universities targeted for the study. That is, this study only targeted two schools, and these two schools were similar. For example, some distance learning programs may have trouble generating quality interactions in their distance learning courses, resulting from the prioritization of certain specific course features by faculty, while faculty and administration officials at other universities may invest in a different set of course features in order to achieve a high level of quality interaction. That is, some schools may handle the apparent trade-off between quality and convenience in different ways using different tools. Similarly, student demographic factors may well vary from school to school, indicating different priorities for course selection. Therefore the small number of schools targeted, as well as the lack of variety in the types of institutions included, is one limitation of this study. Furthermore, the fact that this paper did not address student learning outcomes may also be considered a limitation. For example, Buckley (2003) and Reuter (2009) found no difference in overall grade between course formats (distance vs. traditional), but perhaps a more comprehensive model similar to the one posed here would find some key variables predicting differences in student learning as well.

Future research then should include a greater number, and variety, of colleges and universities. Moreover, inclusion of private, online-only colleges would expand the data set, as would inclusion of universities with limited distance education program offerings. Perhaps additional variables explaining student satisfaction can be included, expanding the current comprehensive model. Moreover, inclusion of student learning outcomes (perhaps measured by GPA or test scores), along with student satisfaction, would make this model more complete.

In addition, future research should also investigate whether other factors related to the classification or nature of the colleges and universities themselves would influence or moderate the relationships observed in this study. For example, studies could assess any possible differences according to the demographics of universities, such as between urban vs. non-urban locations. Studies could also specifically target outreach-oriented universities that have historically provided education to military personnel and those in related civilian jobs, as well as examine specialty programs such as Executive MBA programs, nursing, etc., that target specific segments of the educational market. Finally, studies could assess whether differences may exist by accreditation levels and types (e.g., AACSB vs. ACBSP in colleges of business), or according to whether the institution is primarily research-oriented or teaching-oriented.

CONCLUSION

This study is important as it has demonstrated a comprehensive model showing the issues relevant to predicting student satisfaction. Indeed this study has shown the tradeoff between issues of convenience and issues of quality, particularly depending on key student demographics (age, geography, and time constraints). Therefore, the design of online programs and courses should reflect very specific demographic characteristics, where many non-traditional students demand the conveniences of distance programs while older students are more interested in quality. Because time matters more than geography for selecting distance courses, it is important to accommodate the busy schedules of students. The geographic benefit of distance learning, however, apparently is not currently being fully utilized. Apparently the distance programs of traditional colleges have not extended their geographic coverage beyond those of the respective traditional programs. Finally, because distance courses were associated with student satisfaction with convenience, but specific distance course features were not associated with this convenience satisfaction, it is clear that faculty must do a better job in considering how they set up their distance courses, and which course features should be accentuated in this distance environment. Simply creating a generic distance course is not sufficient for today's busy students.

Further, this study can be worked into a model that other schools could use, particularly those that are new to distance learning. That is, the results presented here may be of interest to universities and schools that want to offer distance courses. Specifically, programs customized toward older students must emphasize quality and interaction in the distance programs as well as they do in the traditional programs. Specific course features such as digital classrooms and online discussion boards may achieve this, along with offering occasional face to face meetings to complement the online environment. Further, the importance of time over geography indicates that schools developing new distance programs should consider accommodating busy schedules using other means, such as offering flexible scheduling, while perhaps also expanding the geographic reach for its distance programs, in order to better utilize this benefit of distance courses. Perhaps schools should consider not charging more for out-of-state tuition for online programs. Finally, administrators must consider which types of programs and courses are most suited toward distance learning, and develop courses accordingly that accentuate those specific course features.

Ultimately, university administrators creating new distance programs, or redesigning existing ones, must consider market segmentation (student demographics), the branding of the distance programs, and be able to predict consumer behavior (by focusing on the motivation of the various student segments, and accordingly, student satisfaction). That is, customer (student) satisfaction is important for schools to ensure customer retention and loyalty (Chaudhuri & Verma, 2008; Kabadayi & Gupta, 2005; Shukla, Sharma, & Swami, 2010). Such student satisfaction is critical for schools to ensure customer retention and loyalty, as customers may exhibit significant switching behavior in the online environment (Kabadayi & Gupta, 2005). That is, it is particularly common and easy for students to transfer between programs and schools. The relatively more demanding distance students often may switch from online to traditional programs within a university, may transfer in from other universities (or vice versa), or may mix courses within a program (take distance courses within traditional programs or vice versa).

If these traditional universities were to attempt to compete more directly with online-only schools, they likely would face a substantially different market demographic than they currently do. Therefore, school administrators should carefully consider to what degree they should separate their online programs from their traditional programs (Christensen & Bower, 1996; Christensen & Raynor, 2003). Should they offer only certain programs – those conducive to the conveniences of online coursework? Should they work more closely with other types of institutions, perhaps community colleges? Should such programs be priced lower than traditional programs, as some students expect? Such an approach clearly would not be appropriate for programs targeting older students, would require an expansion of the geographic coverage of their distance programs, and would only be effective for certain courses and programs. Much more research on designing successful strategies for distance programs is warranted.

Ultimately, it is critical for traditional colleges to carefully plan the implementation of their new distance learning programs. At any rate, understanding the complete mix of student demographics and their motivation, as well as the tools and technologies available to enhance specific course functions, in order to strike the right balance between convenience, quality and learning should continue to be a fruitful area for future research in higher education.

REFERENCES

Andrews, R., Brusco, M., & Currim, I. (2010). Amalgamation of partitions from multiple segmentation bases: A comparison of non-model-based and model-based methods. *European Journal of Operational Research*, *201*(2), 608–618. doi:10.1016/j.ejor.2009.03.002

Browne, M. W., & Cudeck, R. (1993). Alternative ways of assessing model fit. In Bollen, K. A., & Long, J. S. (Eds.), *Testing structural equation models* (pp. 136–162). Newbury Park, CA: Sage.

Bryant, S., Kahle, J. B., & Schafer, B. A. (2005). Distance education: A review of the contemporary literature. *Issues in Accounting Education*, *20*(3), 255–272. doi:10.2308/iace.2005.20.3.255

Buckley, K. M. (2003). Evaluation of classroom-based, web-enhanced, and web-based distance learning nutrition courses for undergraduate nursing. *The Journal of Nursing Education*, *42*(8), 367–370.

Chaudhuri, R., & Verma, S. (2008). A framework for determining customer satisfaction: An empirical analysis. *International Journal of Electronic Marketing and Retailing*, *2*(2), 190–201. doi:10.1504/IJEMR.2008.019817

Christensen, C., & Bower, J. (1996). Customer power, strategic investment, and the failure of leading firms. *Strategic Management Journal*, *17*, 197–218. doi:10.1002/(SICI)1097-0266(199603)17:3<197::AID-SMJ804>3.0.CO;2-U

Christensen, C., & Raynor, M. (2003). *The innovator's solution: Creating and sustaining successful growth*. Boston, MA: Harvard Business School Press.

Cohen, E. G. (1994). Restructuring the classroom: Conditions for productive small groups. *Review of Educational Research*, *64*, 1–35.

Cronbach, L. (1971). Test validation. In Thorndike, R. L. (Ed.), *Educational measurement* (2nd ed., pp. 443–507). Washington, DC: American Council on Education.

Dereshiwsky, M. (2001). ''A'' is for assessment: Identifying online assessment practices and perceptions. *Journal of United States Distance Learning Association*, *15*(1), 16–26.

Dewiyanti, S., Brand-Gruwel, S., Jochems, W., & Broers, N. (2007). Students' experiences with collaborative learning in asynchronous computer-supported collaborative learning environments. *Computers in Human Behavior*, *23*, 496–514. doi:10.1016/j.chb.2004.10.021

Dykman, C., & Davis, C. (2008a). Online education forum: Part one -The shift toward online education. *Journal of Information Systems Education, 19*(1), 11–16.

Dykman, C., & Davis, C. (2008b). Online education forum: Part two -Teaching online versus teaching conventionally. *Journal of Information Systems Education, 19*(2), 157–164.

Dykman, C., & Davis, C. (2008c). Online education forum: Part three - A quality online educational experience. *Journal of Information Systems Education, 19*(2), 281–289.

Farrington, G., & Bronack, S. (2001). Sink or swim? *T.H.E. Journal, 28*, 10.

Fulford, C., & Zhang, S. (1993). Perceptions of interaction: The critical predictor in distance education. *American Journal of Distance Education, 7*(3), 8–21. doi:10.1080/08923649309526830

Gerbing, D., & Anderson, J. (1992). Monte Carlo evaluation of goodness fit indices for structural equation models. *Sociological Methods & Research, 21*, 132–160. doi:10.1177/0049124192021002002

Gibson, C. C., & Graff, A. O. (1992). Impact of adults' preferred learning styles and perception of barriers on completion of external baccalaureate degree programs. *Journal of Distance Education, 7*(1), 39–51.

Hara, N., & Kling, R. (1999). Students' frustrations with a web-based distance education course: A taboo topic in the discourse. *First Monday, 4*, 12.

Harroff, P., & Valentine, T. (2006). Dimensions of program quality in web-based adult education. *American Journal of Distance Education, 20*(1), 7–22. doi:10.1207/s15389286ajde2001_2

Hatfield, M. (2006). *Off campus online: Distance learning becoming more popular among students who work, have families* (p. 1). Knight Ridder Tribune Business News.

Hirschheim, R. (2005). The Internet-based education bandwagon: Look before you leap. *Communications of the ACM, 48*(7), 97–101. doi:10.1145/1070838.1070844

Jackson, M., & Helms, M. (2008). Student perceptions of hybrid courses: Measuring and interpreting quality. *Journal of Education for Business, 84*(1), 7–12. doi:10.3200/JOEB.84.1.7-12

Johnson, D. W., & Johnson, F. P. (1994). *Joining together: Group theory and group skills*. Boston, MA: Allyn and Bacon.

Kabadayi, S., & Gupta, R. (2005). Website loyalty: An empirical investigation of its antecedents. *International Journal of Internet Marketing and Advertising, 2*(4), 321–345. doi:10.1504/IJIMA.2005.008105

Keegan, D. (1980). On defining distance education. *Distance Education, 1*(1), 13–56. doi:10.1080/0158791800010102

Keegan, D. (1996). *Foundations of distance education*. New York, NY: Routledge.

Keegan, D. (2002). *The future of leaning: From elearning to m-learning*. Retrieved from http://learning.ericsson.net/mlearning2/project_one/book.html

Klesius, J. P., Homan, S., & Thompson, T. (1997). Distance education compared to traditional education: The students' view. *International Journal of Instructional Media, 24*, 207–222.

Kumar, C., Norris, J., & Sun, Y. (2009). Location and time do matter: A long tail study of website requests. *Decision Support Systems, 47*(4), 500–507. doi:10.1016/j.dss.2009.04.015

Levin, J. (1999). Multiplicity in learning and teaching: A framework for developing innovative online education. *Journal of Research on Computing in Education, 32*(2), 256–270.

Littleton, K., & Whitelock, D. (2004). Guiding the creation of knowledge and understanding in a virtual learning environment. *Cyberpsychology & Behavior*, *7*(2), 173–181. doi:10.1089/109493104323024438

Nunnally, J. D. (1978). *Psychometric theory* (2nd ed.). New York, NY: McGraw-Hill.

Ponzurick, T., France, K., & Logar, C. (2000). Delivering graduate marketing education: An analysis of face-to-face versus distance education. *Journal of Marketing Education*, *22*, 180–187. doi:10.1177/0273475300223002

Pucel, D. J., & Stertz, T. F. (2005). Effectiveness of and student satisfaction with web-based compared to traditional in-service teacher education courses. *Journal of Industrial Teacher Education*, *42*(1), 7–23.

Reuter, R. (2009). Online versus in the classroom: Student success in a hands-on lab class. *American Journal of Distance Education*, *23*(3), 151–162. doi:10.1080/08923640903080620

Ritter, C., Polnick, B., Fink, R., & Oescher, J. (2010). Classroom learning communities in educational leadership: A comparison study of three delivery options. *The Internet and Higher Education*, *13*(1-2), 96–100. doi:10.1016/j.iheduc.2009.11.005

Robinia, K., & Anderson, M. (2010). Online teaching efficacy of nurse faculty. *Journal of Professional Nursing*, *26*(3), 168–175. doi:10.1016/j.profnurs.2010.02.006

Schell, G. P. (2004). Universities marginalize online courses. *Communications of the ACM*, *47*(7), 53–56. doi:10.1145/1005817.1005821

Shukla, A., Sharma, N., & Swami, S. (2010). Website characteristics, user characteristics and purchase intention: Mediating role of website satisfaction. *International Journal of Internet Marketing and Advertising*, *6*(2), 142–167. doi:10.1504/IJIMA.2010.032479

Storck, J., & Sproull, L. (1995). Though a glass darkly, what do people learn in videoconferences. *Human Communication Research*, *22*(2), 197–219. doi:10.1111/j.1468-2958.1995.tb00366.x

Straub, D. (1989). Validating instruments in MIS research. *Management Information Systems Quarterly*, *13*(2), 147–169. doi:10.2307/248922

Topper, A. (2007). Are they the same? Comparing the instructional quality of online and face-to face graduate education courses. *Assessment & Evaluation in Higher Education*, *32*(6), 681–691. doi:10.1080/02602930601117233

Vrasidas, C., & McIsaac, M. (1999). Factors influencing interaction in an online course. *American Journal of Distance Education*, *13*(3), 22–36. doi:10.1080/08923649909527033

Wilhelm, S., Rodehorst, T. K., Young, S., Jensen, L., & Stepans, M. B. (2003). Students' perspectives of the effectiveness of an asynchronous on-line seminar. *Journal of Professional Nursing*, *19*(5), 313–319. doi:10.1016/S8755-7223(03)00102-9

Young, S. (2006). Student views of effective online teaching in higher education. *American Journal of Distance Education*, *20*(2), 65–77. doi:10.1207/s15389286ajde2002_2

Zhang, T., Koehler, M., & Spatariu, A. (2009). The development of the Motivation for Critical Reasoning in Online Discussions Inventory (MCRODI). *American Journal of Distance Education*, *23*(4), 194–211. doi:10.1080/08923640903294411

This work was previously published in the Information Resources Management Journal, Volume 24, Issue 4, edited by Mehdi Khosrow-Pour, pp. 61-76, copyright 2013 by IGI Publishing (an imprint of IGI Global).

Chapter 19
Organizational Citizenship Behavior of Information System Personnel:
The Influence of Leader-Member Exchange

Tzy-Yuan Chou
National Taiwan University, Taiwan

James J. Jiang
The Australian National University, Australia

Gary Klein
University of Colorado, USA

Seng-cho T. Chou
National Taiwan University, Taiwan

ABSTRACT

Leader-member exchange (LMX) represents the quality of interaction between leaders and members of a work unit, such as the information system function within an organization. LMX is expected to improve organizational citizenship behavior, beneficial behaviors not explicitly rewarded, but prior research has failed to establish this link satisfactorily. To determine the influence of LMX in the IS environment, a model is developed based on the background in the IS and management literature that considers LMX an important contributor to job satisfaction and organizational commitment. In turn, organizational commitment influences both work quality and organizational citizenship behaviors in a beneficial way. The model is confirmed with a sample of IS professionals in Taiwan. The results show that effective communication and coordination is crucial between leaders and subordinates at levels within the organization not previously considered.

INTRODUCTION

Information System (IS) leadership is distinctive because of an expectation to combine IS technical skills with an in-depth understanding of functions (Karahanna & Watson, 2006). This characteristic spans all levels within an organization from the operational to the strategic. However, leadership studies in the field tend to focus on the chief information officers' leadership traits as related to specific constructs, processes, structures, and mechanisms that underlie unique IS concerns and

DOI: 10.4018/978-1-4666-3616-3.ch019

organizational benefits of effective leadership of the IS function (Sobol & Klein, 2009). Equally crucial to the success of an organization is the leadership of IS personnel at the operational and development level, where a quality relationship with IS employees influences the driving engine of IS success (Faraj & Sambamurthy, 2006).

It is well established that higher individual performance is generated by the unique skills required of IS personnel and the organizational support provided them (Tesch, Jiang, & Klein, 2003). However, studies of performance do not address the issue of behaviors that promote a more productive work environment. Organizational citizenship behaviors (OCB) reflect positive influences in the environment such as altruism, courtesy, virtue, conscientiousness and sportsmanship (Organ, 1998). These traits are crucial in the success of organizations, perhaps as much so as individual contributions of performance. Yet, IS workers exhibit significantly lower OCBs, along with many other significant differences (Joseph, Ng, Koh, & Ang, 2007; Moore & Love, 2005). What IS leaders do to improve these behaviors for IS personnel without detracting from individual job performance is important to address.

Drawing from employee studies in other disciplines, organizational commitment is a strong indicator of performance and work behavior (Meyer, Stanley, Herscovitch, & Topolnytsky, 2002). Thus, building commitment should have a positive impact on the work and behavior of IS personnel. In particular, consistent support has been found for a positive association between Leader-Member Exchanges (LMX) and organizational commitment, where LMX represents the level and quality of interaction between leaders and employees in a work unit (Wayne, Shore, & Liden, 1997). Likewise, studies find an indirect effect of LMX to commitment through satisfaction (Settoon, Bennett, & Liden, 1996). Creating satisfaction is often viewed as matching the specific interests of employees, which are thought to differ for IS personnel, such as elevated needs for challenges, autonomy, and competent supervision (Beecham, Baddoo, Hall, Robinson, & Sharp, 2008). Unfortunately, no study has determined whether these relationships hold collectively, or where the employees exhibit significantly different traits from the remainder of the employee population or within the IS context. This is crucial because different desires of relationship development by different groups of employees will alter the relationships between LMX and subsequent attitudes (Cogliser, Schriesheim, Scandura, & Gardner, 2009). Will a relationship among LMX, job satisfaction, and organizational commitment hold for IS personnel?

BACKGROUND

Leader-member exchange (LMX) is a relationship-based approach to study leadership (Sherony & Green, 2002). The central premise behind LMX is that, within work units, unique and different types of relationships develop between leaders and subordinates. These relationships are characterized by degrees of physical or mental effort, material resources, information, and/or emotional support exchanged between these two parties. This contrasts greatly with domination methods that appear in the IS literature (Hussain & Cornelius, 2009). LMX is portrayed as one type of exchange that is part of a larger network of social exchanges, which include LMX, co-worker exchange, team-member-exchange, network exchange, and organization-member exchange. In this fashion, LMX represents a set of social approaches rather than a particular style category of leadership (Neufeld, Dong, & Higgins, 2007). Blau (1964) suggests that the basis of any exchange relationship can be described in terms of either social or economic principles and larger relational contexts surround and affect all dyadic exchanges where each exchange is based on a trust that gestures of goodwill will be reciprocated.

Further, lower quality LMX, labelled out-group exchanges involve exchanges basic to the employment contract. High-quality LMX relationships, in-group exchanges, involve mutual exchanges that go beyond those fundamental to the employment contract or those specified in formal job descriptions. In-group exchanges imply preferential treatment from management leaders - such as receiving higher amounts of information, mutual respect and trust, greater autonomy and assistance, latitude, confidence, and concern. Those employees then pay back by with enhanced commitment and loyalty, such as expending extra time and effort, engaging in extra-role behaviors, or helping a co-worker with a task important to the supervisor. Once a relationship forms, the quality of exchange between leader and member remains stable.

Positive, beneficial actions directed at employees by the organization's representatives contribute to the establishment of high-quality exchange relationships. Such actions create obligations for employees to reciprocate in positive, beneficial ways. Individuals engage in different reciprocation efforts depending on the exchange partner. Only when the donor benefits through the effort of the recipient is that sense of indebtedness reduced. It is this interactive building of a relationship that adds to the satisfaction and commitment of the employee as a reciprocal response in high-quality exchange relationships (Humphrey, Nahrgang, & Morgeson, 2007). These potential relationships are represented in the generic model of derived behavior as shown in Figure 1.

Locke (1976) defines job satisfaction as a pleasurable or positive emotional state resulting from the appraisal of one's job as attaining one's important job values, providing these values are congruent with one's basic needs, especially the need for growth resulting from the work itself. Job satisfaction research can be traced to the 1920s where Taylor and the British Industrial Health Research Board emphasized the role of the physical arrangement of the work, physical work-

Figure 1. The eventual impact of LMX on citizenship behaviors

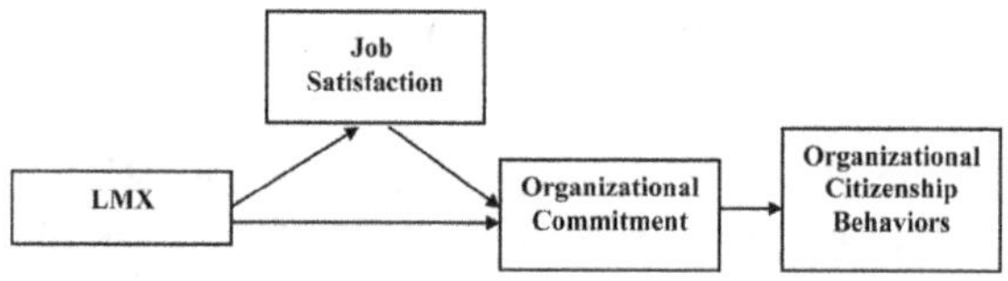

ing conditions, and pay. In the 1930s, leadership research emphasized the 'human relations' role of good supervision, cohesive work groups, and friendly employee-management relations in determining employee satisfaction and productivity. Since then, the emphasis turned to the 'work itself' proponents who argue the attainment of satisfaction through growth in skill, efficacy, and responsibility made possible by mentally challenging work.

Researchers have identified comprehensive antecedents of job satisfaction. Humphrey et al.'s (2007) meta-analytic of work design literature found that motivational characteristics explained 34% of the variance in job satisfaction, social characteristics explained 17%, and work context explained another incremental variance of 4%. Work-related attributes are numerous and include skill variety, task factors, autonomy, role definition issues, enrichment, working conditions, rotation, learning opportunity, amount of work, responsibility, pay, promotion opportunity, and other factors. Agent-related attributes include self-evaluation about self-esteem, general self-efficacy, locus of control, neuroticism, achievement, experience pleasure with success of job, moods, employee involvement, motivations, preferences, intelligence, abilities, values, needs, interaction style, supervision, management style and culture, supervisors' 'considerate' or 'employee centred' tendency, empowerment and autonomous work groups.

Job satisfaction results in reduction of a number of detrimental factors and increase to many positive factors. These include many that directly impact both the employee and organization such as withdrawal, aggression, perceptual distortion, illness, quality, productivity, turnover, absence, sabotage, political stability, illness rates, physical health and longevity, mental health, absences and termination, complaints and grievances (Christen, Iyer, & Soberman, 2006). Job performance is also improved, though many believe the relation contains intervening variables. However, the relationship between job satisfaction and organizational commitment is consistently demonstrated, though the causal direction is disputed (Humphrey et al., 2007).

Organizational commitment (OC) is the strength of an individual's identification with and involvement in a particular organization as characterized by three psychological factors: desire to remain in the organization, willingness to exert considerable effort on its behalf, and belief in and acceptance of its goals and values. In general, three themes are identified in the literature: affective attachment to the organization, perceived costs associated with leaving the organization, and an almost moral obligation to remain with the organization (Meyer & Allen, 1997). An employee can experience all three dimensions of organizational commitment to varying degrees. Results of studies which examine the link between LMX and organizational commitment are mixed. Some find a relationship between LMX and commitment (Lee, 2005), however, others fail to find the same results (Wayne et al., 1997). This mixed result could be due to a lack of focus in a particular context (such as information systems) or failure to consider the differences among the three components of OC.

The affective conceptualization of organizational commitment refers to the employee's attitudinal or emotional attachment to, identification with, and involvement in the organization (Allen & Meyer, 1990). The reason an employee who is affectively committed engages in certain activities is because s/he "wants to". The continuance conceptualization of commitment is based on costs that an employee associates with leaving the organization. Employees engage in a consistent line of activity due to the perceived cost of doing otherwise. Hence, continuance commitment is based on expectations of immediate or future rewards and cost contingencies in comparison to available alternatives. Employees with high continuance commitment engage in certain behaviors, not because they feel that it is the right thing to do or because they want to do it, but because they "need to" and believe that they will derive some reward(s) or minimize some cost(s) from doing so. Normative commitment refers to an employee's feelings of obligation toward the organization (Meyer & Allen, 1997). They behave in accordance with organizational goals because they believe it is the right and moral thing to do. Employees who have been led to believe, via various organizational practices, socialization efforts, or their own personal history, that the organization deserves their loyalty are likely to have a strong normative commitment.

The desired behaviors resulting from the various forms of commitment include organizational citizenship behaviors (OCB). OCBs are extra-role and discretionary behaviors that help co-workers perform their jobs and show conscientious support for the organization (Podsakoff & MacKenzie, 1997). OCBs include simple concepts as being on time, being helpful to others in the organization, and maintaining a positive attitude. It is generally recognized by management and researchers that these behaviors, though not directly or explicitly recognized by formal reward systems, improve the functioning of the organization, reduce friction, cope with interdependencies, provide flexibilities needed to work through contingencies, shape the psychological and organizational context, serve as critical catalysts for task activities and processes, and increase efficiency and effectiveness.

Without employees' OCBs, organization will be a very fragile social system. Based upon Podsakoff and MacKenzie's (1997) meta-analysis, OCBs (1) enhance co-worker and managerial productivity, (2) free up resources to be used in

Figure 2. Research model

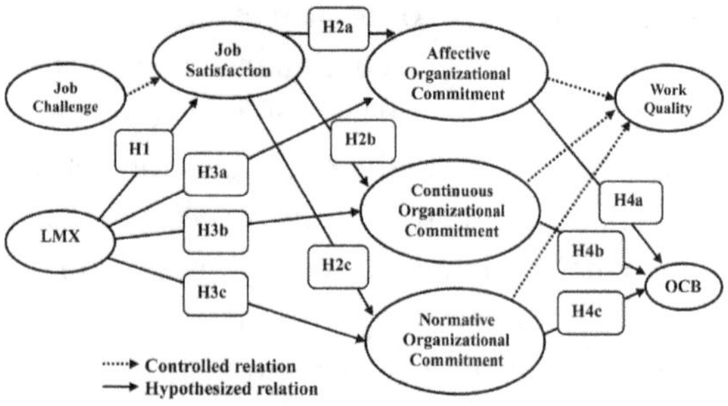

more productive purposes, (3) save the amount of scarce resources dedicated to maintenance functions, (4) help to coordinate activities with others, (5) strengthen the organization's ability to attract and retain the best employees, (6) increase the ability to stabilize the organization's performance, and (7) adapt to environmental changes more effectively.

PROPOSED RESEARCH MODEL AND HYPOTHESES

The primary focus of this study is to examine the relationships among LMX, job satisfaction, organizational commitment, and organizational citizenship behaviors for IS employees. The primary dependent variable is organizational citizenship behaviors to determine if they can be influenced by leadership variables. Work quality is included as a dependent variable to be certain that improvement of one desired property does not detract from other crucial elements of success. Based upon an extensive literature review, we propose the research model shown in Figure 2.

LMX and Job Satisfaction

The Emotional Self-Regulation model developed by Bagozzi (1992) suggests that appraisal results of a situation will incur emotional reactions prior to certain coping responses. LMX can be considered an appraisal of the relationship quality with their supervisor (a part of their work environment) so that job satisfaction can be seen as an emotional response to the appraisal of the work environment. Research on LMX shows a consistent, positive link between LMX quality and overall job satisfaction (Golden & Veiga, 2008). Based on significant, prior evidence, we propose employees with a higher quality of LMX will feel more job satisfaction, or:

H1: Quality of LMX will positively influence Job Satisfaction

Job Satisfaction and Organizational Commitment

According to the Emotional Self-Regulation model, if the emotional response to the job is positive, then organizational commitment should increase (Bagozzi, 1992). IS researchers find positive relationships between organizational commitment and job satisfaction (Igbaria & Guimaraes, 1993). However, the causal direction between organizational commitment and job satisfaction is often disputed. According to Brown and Peterson's (1993) meta-analysis about job satisfaction, the preponderance of conceptual and empirical evidence appears to favour the causal direction from job satisfaction to organizational commitment rather than the reverse. Formally,

H2: Job Satisfaction will positively influence each form of organizational commitment.

H2a: Job Satisfaction will positively influence affective organizational commitment.

H2b: Job Satisfaction will positively influence continuous organizational commitment.

H2c: Job Satisfaction will positively influence normative organizational commitment.

LMX and Organizational Commitment

Studies which examine LMX and organizational commitment find a positive link between LMX quality and OC (Golden & Viega, 2008; Joo, 2010). Studies conclude that high quality LMX relationships result in mutual trust, liking, and respect which tends to enhance organizational commitment, while low quality relationships do not incur such affect (Bowler, Halbesleben, & Paul, 2010). Since individuals with low LMX relationships feel less of a sense of obligation to their supervisors, they tend to perceive their jobs in terms of contractual obligations and exhibit less organizational commitment. LMX is even found to be even more crucial than leadership style (Lo, Ramayah, Min, & Songan, 2010). However, other researchers fail to find the same positive link between LMX and OC. They propose that other variables must mediate the relationship. However, previous research typically used only affective commitment to represent OC. According to the spirit of social exchange theory, individuals might differentiate among the components of organizational commitment, altering the expected relationships.

Considering the relationship between LMX and affective commitment, a high quality of LMX will incur employees' affective commitment to their supervisor because the relationship is dyadic. However, affective commitment (AC) to supervisors doesn't imply affective commitment to the organization. Vandenberghe, Bentein, and Stinglhamber (2004) demonstrate that affective commitment to the organization, the supervisor, and the work group can be reliably distinguished. So, without satisfaction with their jobs, employees' affective commitment to the organization will not readily surface. Employees with a high quality of LMX usually show more loyalty (affective commitment) to their supervisor. Although, supervisors are formal representatives of the organization toward employees, it doesn't mean that the affective commitment to their supervisor definitely will incur affective commitment to their organization. The job is the bridge connecting the employee and organization. Hence, we proposed that under job satisfaction was controlled, LMX will not incur affective commitment. Thus,

H3a: LMX will positively influence affective commitment through job satisfaction.

Continuance commitment (CC) is based on expectations of immediate or future rewards and cost contingencies with leaving the organization in comparison to available alternative jobs (Allen & Meyer, 1990). Both high-quality LMX and job satisfaction will increase CC due to the cost of losing the established relationships in a new organization. Considering the more task-oriented than relationship-oriented characteristics of MIS personnel, we argue that job satisfaction will contribute to MIS personnel's CC more directly. Hence, we propose that under job satisfaction was controlled, LMX will not incur continuance commitment.

H3b: LMX will positively influence continuance commitment through job satisfaction.

Normative commitment (NC) refers to an employee's feelings of obligation toward the organization. According to social exchange theory, employees with high-quality of LMX with their supervisor usually receive preferential treatment such as more latitude, amounts of information, resources, and concern from supervisor and then usually feel obligation to the supervisor (Settoon et al., 1996). Although affective commitment to the supervisor does not necessarily lead to affective commitment to their organization, extra resources belong to the organization and, therefore, obligation to their organization might incur in the form of normative commitment. Especially for exchanges that have evolved beyond pure transactional exchanges to social exchanges (e.g., friendship), employees may have a sense of obligation to the organization. Hence, high-quality LMX should increase employees' normative commitment, or:

H3c: LMX will positively and directly influence normative commitment.

Organizational Commitment and OCB

Organizational commitment is suggested as an antecedent to OCB because it reflects an employee's willingness to aid the organization even if direct reward is not contingent upon that aid (Podsakoff, MacKenzie, Paine, & Bachrach, 2000). However, the relationship between organizational commitment and OCB is not consistent. Perhaps, the relationship reported between commitment and OCB may be overstated or the relationship between OC and OCB depends on the type of organizational commitment. Thus, in this study we divided organizational commitment into affective (AC), continuance (CC), and normative (NC) commitment to examine their relationship with OCB individually. An individual with affective commitment should be expected to engage in behaviors that would help the employing organization achieve its goals regardless of whether or not they are an expected part of the person's role. Researchers have generally concluded that there is a positive relationship between AC and in-role performance (Chen & Francisco, 2003). Thus, we propose employees with higher AC will exhibit higher OCB, or:

H4a: Affective commitment is associated positively with OCB.

A continuance committed individual should be expected to avoid behaviors that might jeopardize organizational membership (Mayar & Schoorman, 1992). Hence, if employees committed to their organization only for "side bet" reasons (e.g., pension, seniority, or special IT/IS skills in this organization) rather than attitudinal reasons, then they may only need to maintain minimum expectations needed to survive in the organization (Chen & Francisco, 2003). Since extra-role performance is not required by the job description, failure to perform OCBs should not jeopardize continued employment. Hence, CC should not contribute to OCB. Empirically, the relationship between CC and OCB is not determined. Significant negative relations were reported in some studies, but not all (Podsakoff et al., 2000). Thus, given that extra-role behavior has no explicit implications for job retention, we would expect continuance commitment to be either unrelated or negatively related to OCB, or:

H4b: Continuance commitment is not associated with OCB.

Normative commitment may be rooted in feelings of indebtedness arising from an organization's providing certain benefits and the feelings of obligation may continue until the employee feels that he or she has 'paid back' the debt (Meyer & Allen, 1997). Hence, NC implies a sense of obligation to contribute to the organization and is formed by early socialization experiences (Chen & Francisco, 2003). When joining an organization, the employee will be subject to a socialization process that promotes an expected level of loyalty to that particular organization. Obligations in a relational exchange are broad and open-ended and employees with a strong sense of normative commitment feel personally responsible for discretionary behaviors (such as OCB). Hence, we propose that employees with strong NC may feel a more deep seated obligation to be a good organizational citizen, or:

H4c: Normative commitment is positively associated with OCB.

Controls

Work quality is important as a factor of success in the development and operations of IS, and complements OCBs. Job performance is defined as a total expected value to his/her organization of the discrete behavioral episodes that an employee carries out over a period of time. Empirical and theoretical reports in the performance literature identify variables such as knowledge, skill, motivation, and habits as direct determinants of the expected value of an individual's performance. It is important that work quality not be offset by promoting OCBs, thus we include work quality as an outcome to control for a detrimental impact. Thus, the links from OC to work quality are established in the literature, serving the purpose of confirming external validity of the study and controlling for potential ill effects of the antecedents to OCB. Further, IS employees are somewhat unique when compared to many other employee groups and have a higher need for challenging work and a lower need for social interaction (Reid, Allen, Riemenschneider, & Armstrong, 2008). Both the content of the work and the context of the work can improve satisfaction (Galup, Klein, & Jiang, 2008). Motivated IS personnel will increase their productivity and remain longer in the organization (Beecham et al., 2008). In this fashion, job challenge is a critical motivator for IS personnel and serves as a control variable.

RESEARCH METHODS

Sampling

Target respondents of this study are IS personnel from 3 public organizations, 4 private organizations and 1 non-profit organization in Taiwan. All private organizations are publicly listed, one of them is in financial industry and the others are information service providers. The 3 public organizations are charged with planning, analyzing, designing, and maintaining information systems and processing financial data. For each organization, we contacted one first-line or middle-level manager and asked him/her as our contact person to distribute blank and collect filled in questionnaires within his/her organization. Once they agreed to participant, we made an appointment with them to introduce our research purpose and instruments and pass on the blank questionnaires. Confidentiality was assured to participants. Follow up calls were made two weeks after original distribution. A total of 304 questionnaires were returned. Except for 6 questionnaires with incomplete data, the remaining questionnaires were retained for advanced analysis. The demographics are summarized in Table 1.

Constructs

All constructs were utilized in past research and measured by multi-item scales. Because all respondents are located in Taiwan, a Chinese

Table 1. Sample demographics

Categories		Percentage (%)
Organization type	Public	42
	Private	58
Education Level	Master or above	21
	Bachelor degree	78
	High School or Associate Degree	1
Gender	Male	47
	Female	53
Age	< 30	24
	31~35	24
	36~40	14
	41~45	15
	46~50	8
	> 50	14
Position	Contractor	3
	Assistant system analyst (SA)	49
	System analyst	36
	Senior system analyst	11

translated version was employed. The translation work was done by one of the researchers and a piloted Chinese version was conducted by 5 practitioners. According to their feedback we reworded some statements. Likert-type scales, with anchors ranging from 1 (strongly disagree) to 7 (strongly agree) were used for each item.

The measurement of job satisfaction and job challenge are adopted from Igbaria (1991). All three components of organizational commitment are composed of items from Meyer, Allen, and Smith (1993). LMX-7 is a commonly-used measure for the LMX construct (Scandura & Graen, 1984) and was adopted for this study. The 10-item measure from Randall, Fedor, and Longenecker (1990) is adopted for OCB. The measure of work quality is adopted from Randall et al. (1990) is adopted. Items of each construct in this study are shown in Table 2.

A partial least squares (PLS) methodology was adopted to verify measurements and relationships with PLS-Graph Version 3.01. PLS uses ordinary least squares as its estimation technique. It performs an iterative set of factor analysis and applies a bootstrap approach to estimate the significance of the paths. The two-step approach includes measurement validation and path analysis. For measurement validity, item reliability, convergent validity, and discriminant validity tests to examine the measurement model in PLS. Individual item reliability is represented by observing factor loadings. A high loading implies the shared variance between constructs and its measurement is higher than the error variance (Hulland, 1999). Factor loadings higher than 0.7 are viewed as having high reliability and factor loading less than 0.5 were dropped.

Table 2. Final component items

Measures	Loadings	ITC
Leader-Member-exchange (LMX) (Composite Reliability = 0.94, AVE = 0.70)		
1. You usually feel that you know where you stand you usually know how satisfied your immediate supervisor is with what you do.	0.74	0.65
2. You feel that your immediate supervisor understands your problems and needs.	0.88	0.82
3. You feel that your immediate supervisor recognizes your potential.	0.80	0.73
4. Regardless of how much formal authority your immediate supervisor has built into his or her position, he or she would be personally inclined to use power to help you solve problems in your work.	0.86	0.80
5. Again, regardless of the amount of formal authority your immediate supervisor has, you can count on him or her to 'bail you out' at his or her expense when you really need it.	0.87	0.82
6. I have enough confidence in my immediate supervisor that I would defend and justify his or her decisions if he or she were not present to do so	0.86	0.80
7. You characterize your working relationship with your immediate supervisor as effective.	0.86	0.80
Affective Commitment (Composite Reliability = 0.87, AVE = 0.53)		
1. I would be very happy to spend the rest of my career with this organization.	0.85	0.66
2. I really feel as if this organization's problems are my own.	0.87	0.67
3. I do not feel 'emotionally attached' to this organization. (reverse-coded)	0.63	0.61
4. This organization has a great deal of personal meaning for me.	0.81	0.60
5. I do not feel a strong sense of belonging to my organization. (reverse-coded)	0.64	0.63
Continuance Commitment (Composite Reliability = 0.84, AVE = 0.64)		
1. Right now, staying with my organization is a matter of necessity as much as desire.	0.84	0.34
2. It would be very hard for me to leave my organization right now, even if I wanted to.	0.79	0.53

continued on following page

Table 2. Continued

Measures	Loadings	ITC
3. Too much in my life would be disrupted if I decided I wanted to leave my organization now.	0.75	0.63
Normative Commitment (Composite Reliability = 0.87, AVE = 0.57)		
1. Even if it were to my advantage, I do not feel it would be right to leave my organization now.	0.67	0.50
2. I would feel guilty if I left my organization now.	0.74	0.61
3. This organization deserves my loyalty.	0.81	0.64
4. I would not leave my organization right now because I have a sense of obligation to the people in it.	0.81	0.61
5. I owe a great deal to my organization.	0.74	0.61
Job Challenge (Composite Reliability = 0.89, AVE = 0.67)		
1. Work with competent colleagues.	0.69	0.43
2. Work on technically challenging tasks.	0.85	0.69
3. Work on organizationally important projects.	0.85	0.79
4. Work on professionally important projects	0.86	0.80
Job Satisfaction (Composite Reliability = 0.92, AVE = 0.84)		
1. Generally speaking, I am very satisfied with my job.	0.92	0.55
2. I am generally satisfied with the kind of work I do on in my job.	0.91	0.38
OCB (Composite Reliability = 0.90, AVE = 0.70)		
1. Being willing to volunteer for tasks.	0.79	0.68
2. Being willing to take on additional responsibility.	0.70	0.57
3. Being willing to give personal time to the organization.	0.62	0.46
4. Working well without supervision.	0.73	0.67
5. Often sharing knowledge and information with others.	0.66	0.58
6. Frequently offering suggestions.	0.63	0.53
7. Not being late for work.	0.50	0.47
8. Not being absent from work.	0.58	0.59
9. Not wasting any time.	0.77	0.72
10. Showing enthusiasm about my work.	0.83	0.74
Work Quality (Composite Reliability = 0.91, AVE = 0.68)		
1. Usually paying attention to details at work.	0.80	0.73
2. Doing your work completely and thoroughly.	0.85	0.79
3. Having a concern for quality.	0.87	0.81
4. Being cost-conscious.	0.80	0.65
5. Typically following company policy.	0.78	0.61

Note: ITC is the Item-total correlation

Convergent validity is examined by item-total correlation (ITC), composite reliability, and variance extracted by constructs (AVE) (Fornell & Larcker, 1981). To meet required convergent validity, ITC should not be lower than 0.3, composite reliability should higher than 0.7, and AVE higher than 0.5. A higher value of AVE means the variance captured by the construct is higher than the measurement error and, thus, more credible. Discriminant validity focuses on testing whether the measures of constructs differentiate from each other (Messick, 1980). To meet required discriminant validity, the correlation between pairs of construct should be lower than 0.80 and the square root of AVE should higher than correlation coefficients (Bagozzi, Yi, & Phillips, 1991).

Means, standard deviations, square root of AVE and correlations among constructs are shown in Table 3. All items in this study have loadings higher than 0.5, all constructs have AVE values higher than 0.5, the minimum composite reliability is 0.845 (Table 2). Hence, reliability and validity of measurements are assured and adequate.

RESULTS

PLS was adopted to examine the path model depicted in Figure 2. All variables were entered into the model simultaneously, and a bootstrap re-sampling procedure was performed to assess the effects proposed in the hypotheses. Table 4 reports summary results for the hypotheses; standardized path coefficients (β), standard errors, and significances. Likewise, the relationships for the control variables were all significant and included in the final model.

A mediator must satisfy certain conditions for its effect to be significant. For this study, the requirements are that LMX be positively related to JS and that LMX be positively related to AC, CC and NC. This pattern holds and satisfies Kenny, Kashy, and Bolger's (1998) first two conditions required to provide evidence consistent with mediation, stating that the exogenous variable (LMX) should be related to both the mediator (JS) and the outcome variable (AC). Further requirements are then that JS should be associated with each OC component while controlling for LMX and the relationship between LMX and OC is reduced when JS is entered into the model. If the relationship becomes non-significant, then JS is a full mediator. If the relationship is lessened and still significant, then JS is a partial mediator. The results shown in Table 4 confirm hypotheses 1, 2a-2c, and 3a-3c. Job satisfaction is a full mediator between LMX and AC and CC. However, job satisfaction is a partial mediator between LMX and NC. LMX retains a direct effect on NC.

CONCLUSION

As shown in Table 4, all hypotheses were supported in this study. By separating organizational commitment into affective, continuous, and normative commitment, we confirm that job satisfaction mediates the relationship between LMX and organizational commitment and the effects of mediating are different for different type of organizational commitment. From an academic perspective this study yields additional insights into relationships among LMX, Job satisfaction, and organizational commitment, which should

Table 3. Descriptive statistics of constructs

Variable	Mean	SD	LMX	JS	AC	CC	NC	JC	WQ	OCB
LMX	4.63	1.06	**0.84**							
Job Satisfaction (JS)	4.66	0.99	0.52	**0.92**						
Affective Commitment (AC)	4.48	0.98	0.38	0.63	**0.73**					
Continuance Commitment (CC)	4.65	1.11	0.24	0.50	0.50	**0.80**				
Normative Commitment (NC)	4.16	1.06	0.55	0.54	0.55	0.41	**0.76**			
Job Challenge (JC)	4.97	1.01	0.43	0.52	0.37	0.35	0.43	**0.82**		
Work Quality (WQ)	5.53	0.84	0.32	0.42	0.37	0.33	0.25	0.39	**0.82**	
OCB	5.17	0.81	0.46	0.54	0.50	0.37	0.48	0.50	0.78	**0.71**

Notes: Diagonal elements (bold) are the square root of AVE between the constructs and their measures, off-diagonal elements are correlations between constructs.

Table 4. Summary of path analysis

Model	Beta Coefficient	Standard Error	T-Statistic	Result
H1: LMX → Job Satisfaction (JS)	0.36*	0.08	4.83	Supported
H2a: JS → Affective commitment	0.63*	0.05	11.85	Supported
H2b: JS → Continuance commitment	0.56*	0.06	9.53	Supported
H2c: JS → Normative commitment	0.37*	0.08	4.86	Supported
H3a: LMX → Affective commitment	0.08	0.06	1.34	Fully Mediated
H3b: LMX → Continuance commitment	0.00	0.07	0.01	Fully Mediated
H3c: LMX → Normative commitment	0.37*	0.06	5.93	Partially Mediated
H4a: AC → OCB	0.41*	0.07	6.05	Supported
H4b: CC → OCB	0.10	0.07	1.35	Supported
H4c: NC → OCB	0.23*	0.07	3.21	Supported

* significant at p-value < .05;

contribute to the future development of this line of research. LMX could directly incur normative commitment due to perceived obligations to the supervisor and organization. However, affective and continuance commitment do not directly result from LMX, but indirectly from LMX through job satisfaction. This phenomenon might provide a way to explain why previous research results are inconsistent in examining the relationship between LMX and organizational commitment.

This study also provides several implications for practitioners. IS personnel are valuable, intangible, and important resources to a contemporary organization. This study highlighted the importance of LMX, job satisfaction and job challenge to IS personnel by showing its impact on organizational commitment. Improving IS personnel's satisfaction and organizational commitment might have more aggressive impact for IS success than just avoiding IS personnel turnover.

Second, there are certain unchangeable constraints or cost for organizations to improve the work environment, atmosphere, context, or climate for employees. LMX is a role making process that can transcend bureaucratic formats. Hence, LMX could be an important resource for companies to employ. Managers do have some control over employees' perceptions of LMX quality. Especially, the ways managers interact with their employees will deeply influence perceived LMX quality. To change managers' attitudes and behaviors might improve LMX quality. Once IS employees perceive higher LMX quality with their supervisors, enhanced job satisfaction and organizational commitment can be expected.

Third, LMX, as a source of significant satisfaction and OC, is a dyadic relationship between supervisor and subordinate. Enhancing and cultivating the relationship depends on both of their ability and efforts. This suggests how to manage MIS personnel resources and enhance quality of LMX:

1. Provide leadership training for all employees. For IS managers, leadership training that emphasizes the importance of mentoring, human relations skills, joint development of goals, and effective interpersonal communications would be helpful.
2. Build a corporate culture in which open two-way communication occurs because open communication is necessary to establish a sense of trust in the exchange relationship. This careful consideration of establishing

mutual trust relationships with subordinates will improve LMX quality and benefit the organization due to increased OC.

3. IS managers should provide equal training and career development plans to all subordinates, and recognize each employee's potential and capabilities. Career planning and development seminars and workshops would benefit subordinates.
4. Opportunities to leave the dyad and be independent of the relationship with their supervisors are rare for employees. To improve the manager's impressions, subordinates should improve their capacities, knowledge, and demonstrate their strong learning motivation. Subordinates should be afforded training to increase their knowledge, skills, and self-confidence on the job.

Fourth, as an IS manager you need to understand employees' values and attitudes, communicate clearly, and hold respect their wishes. Especially in leading IS personnel from the baby boom, generation X, and Internet generation cohorts, management must appreciate cross-generational differences in order to adapt to the information-based environments.

There are limitations to this study, as with every study. First, the data was collected from one Asian county only. Implications generated from this study should be carefully interpreted and more studies conducted before extending the study results to other contexts or settings. Second, only employees remaining with the organization are sampled, those having left may represent a population that is under-sampled. Third, this is a cross-sectional study. The actual causal relationships between variables are not established as is a longitudinal study. However, we use several common models to justify our direction of inference. Fourth, since all measures used are self-reported, common method variance and social desirability effects might be a potential problem. Several factors, however, applicable to this research may reduce these potential biases. Duchon, Green, and Taber (1986) show self-reports about vertical exchange correlate significantly with other measures and sources of information about the LMX construct. Further, a longitudinal study shows that relationships between exchange scores and job satisfaction exhibit substantial consistency over time and method variance typically does not emerge as a bias in analyses involving questionnaires with widely demonstrated reliabilities and validities (Seers & Graen, 1984). The fifth weakness is that only the subordinate's perspective about LMX is measured in this study. Although the original approach of LMX includes the idea of assessing LMX from both the subordinate and the leader perspectives, research showed lower reliabilities for leader responses (Gerstner & Day, 1997).

REFERENCES

Allen, N. J., & Meyer, J. P. (1990). The measurement and antecedents of affective, continuance and normative commitment to the organization. *Journal of Occupational Psychology*, *63*(1), 1–18.

Bagozzi, R. P. (1992). The self-regulation of attitudes, intentions, and behavior. *Social Psychology Quarterly*, *55*(2), 178–204. doi:10.2307/2786945

Bagozzi, R. P., Yi, Y., & Phillips, L. W. (1991). Assessing construct validity in organizational research. *Administrative Science Quarterly*, *36*(3), 421–458. doi:10.2307/2393203

Beecham, S., Baddoo, N., Hall, T., Robinson, H., & Sharp, H. (2008). Motivation in software engineering: A systematic literature review. *Information and Software Technology*, *50*(9-10), 860–878. doi:10.1016/j.infsof.2007.09.004

Blau, P. M. (1964). *Exchange and power in social life*. New York, NY: John Wiley & Sons.

Bowler, W. M., Halbesleben, R. B., & Paul, J. R. B. (2010). If you're close with the leader, you must be a brownnose: The role of leader-member relationships in follower, leader, and co-worker attributions of organizational citizenship behavior motives. *Human Resource Management Review*, *20*(4), 309–316. doi:10.1016/j.hrmr.2010.04.001

Brown, S. P., & Peterson, R. A. (1993). Antecedents and consequences of salesperson job satisfaction: Meta-analysis and assessment of causal effects. *JMR, Journal of Marketing Research*, *30*(1), 63–77. doi:10.2307/3172514

Chen, Z. X., & Francesco, A. M. (2003). The relationship between the three components of commitment and employee performance in China. *Journal of Vocational Behavior*, *62*(3), 490–510. doi:10.1016/S0001-8791(02)00064-7

Christen, M., Iyer, G., & Soberman, D. (2006). Job satisfaction, job performance, and effort: A reexamination using agency theory. *Journal of Marketing*, *70*(1), 137–150. doi:10.1509/jmkg.2006.70.1.137

Cogliser, C. C., Schriesheim, C. A., Scandura, T. A., & Gardner, W. L. (2009). Balance in leader and follower perceptions of leader-member exchange: Relationships with performance and work attitudes. *The Leadership Quarterly*, *20*, 452–465. doi:10.1016/j.leaqua.2009.03.010

Duchon, D., Green, S. G., & Taber, T. D. (1986). Vertical dyad linkage: A longitudinal assessment of antecedents, measures and consequences. *The Journal of Applied Psychology*, *71*(1), 56–60. doi:10.1037/0021-9010.71.1.56

Faraj, S., & Sambamurthy, V. (2006). Leadership of information systems development projects. *IEEE Transactions on Engineering Management*, *53*(2), 238–249. doi:10.1109/TEM.2006.872245

Fornell, C., & Larcker, D. F. (1981). Evaluating structural equations with unobservable variables and measurement error. *JMR, Journal of Marketing Research*, *18*(1), 39–50. doi:10.2307/3151312

Galup, S. D., Klein, G., & Jiang, J. J. (2008). The impacts of job characteristics on IS employee satisfaction: A comparison between permanent and temporary employees. *Journal of Computer Information Systems*, *48*, 58–68.

Gerstner, C. R., & Day, D. V. (1997). Meta-analytic review of leader-member exchange theory: Correlates and construct issues. *The Journal of Applied Psychology*, *82*(6), 827–844. doi:10.1037/0021-9010.82.6.827

Golden, T. D., & Veiga, J. F. (2008). The impact of superior-subordinate relationships on the commitment, job satisfaction, and performance of virtual workers. *The Leadership Quarterly*, *19*(1), 77–88. doi:10.1016/j.leaqua.2007.12.009

Hulland, J. (1999). Use of partial least squares (PLS) in strategic management research: A review of four recent studies. *Strategic Management Journal*, *20*(2), 195–204. doi:10.1002/(SICI)1097-0266(199902)20:2<195::AID-SMJ13>3.0.CO;2-7

Humphrey, S. E., Nahrgang, J. D., & Morgeson, F. P. (2007). Integrating motivational, social, and contextual work design features: A meta-analytic summary and theoretical extension of the work design literature. *The Journal of Applied Psychology*, *92*(5), 1332–1356. doi:10.1037/0021-9010.92.5.1332

Hussain, Z. I., & Cornelius, N. (2009). The use of domination and legitimation in information systems implementation. *Information Systems Journal*, *19*(2), 197–224. doi:10.1111/j.1365-2575.2008.00322.x

Igbaria, M. (1991). Job performance of MIS professionals: An examination of the antecedents and consequences. *Journal of Engineering and Technology Management*, *8*(2), 141–171. doi:10.1016/0923-4748(91)90027-O

Igbaria, M., & Guimaraes, T. (1993). Antecedents and consequences of job satisfaction among information center employees. *Journal of Management Information Systems*, *9*(4), 145–174.

Joo, B. K. (2101). Organizational commitment for knowledge workers: The roles of perceived organizational learning culture, leader-member exchange quality, and turnover intention. *Human Resource Development Quarterly*, *21*(1), 69–85. doi:10.1002/hrdq.20031

Joseph, D., Ng, K. Y., Koh, C., & Ang, S. (2007). Turnover of information technology professionals: A narrative review, meta-analytic structural equation modelling, and model development. *Management Information Systems Quarterly*, *31*(3), 547–577.

Karahanna, E., & Watson, R. T. (2006). Information systems leadership. *IEEE Transactions on Engineering Management*, *53*(2), 171–176. doi:10.1109/TEM.2006.872247

Kenny, D. A., Kashy, D. A., & Bolger, N. (1998). Data analysis in social psychology. In Gilbert, D. T., Fiske, S., & Lindzey, G. (Eds.), *The handbook of social psychology* (pp. 233–265). New York, NY: McGraw-Hill.

Lee, J. (2005). Effects of leadership and leader-member exchange on commitment. *Leadership and Organization Development Journal*, *26*(8), 655–672. doi:10.1108/01437730510633728

Lo, M. C., Ramayah, T., Min, H. W., & Songan, P. (2010). The relationship between leadership styles and organizational commitment in Malaysia: Role of leader-member exchange. *Asia Pacific Business Review*, *16*(1), 79–103. doi:10.1080/13602380903355676

Locke, E. A. (1976). The nature and causes of job satisfaction. In Dunnette, M. (Ed.), *Handbook of industrial and organizational psychology* (pp. 1297–1350). Chicago, IL: Rand McNally.

Mayer, R., & Schoorman, D. (1992). Predicting participation and production outcomes through a two dimensional model of organizational commitment. *Academy of Management Journal*, *35*(3), 671–684. doi:10.2307/256492

Messick, S. (1980). Test validity and the ethics of assessment. *The American Psychologist*, *35*(11), 1012–1027. doi:10.1037/0003-066X.35.11.1012

Meyer, J. P., & Allen, N. J. (1997). *Commitment in the workplace: Theory research and application*. Thousand Oaks, CA: Sage.

Meyer, J. P., Allen, N. J., & Smith, C. A. (1993). Commitment to organizations and occupations: Extension and test of a three-component conceptualization. *The Journal of Applied Psychology*, *78*(4), 538–551. doi:10.1037/0021-9010.78.4.538

Meyer, J. P., Stanley, D. J., Herscovitch, L., & Topolnytsky, L. (2002). Affective, continuance, and normative commitment to the organization: A meta-analysis of antecedents, correlates, and consequences. *Journal of Vocational Behavior*, *61*(1), 20–52. doi:10.1006/jvbe.2001.1842

Moore, J. E., & Love, M. S. (2005). IT professionals as organizational citizens. *Communications of the ACM*, *48*(6), 88–93. doi:10.1145/1064830.1064832

Neufeld, D. J., Dong, L., & Higgins, C. (2007). Charismatic leadership and user acceptance of information technology. *European Journal of Information Systems*, *16*(4), 494–510. doi:10.1057/palgrave.ejis.3000682

Organ, D. W. (1998). *Organizational citizenship behavior: The good soldier syndrome*. Lexington, MA: Lexington Books.

Podsakoff, P., MacKenzie, S., Paine, J., & Bachrach, D. (2000). Organizational citizenship behaviors: a critical review of the theoretical and empirical literature and suggestions for future research. *Journal of Management*, *26*(3), 513–563. doi:10.1177/014920630002600307

Podsakoff, P. M., & MacKenzie, S. B. (1997). Impact of organizational citizenship behavior on organizational performance: A review and suggestion for future research. *Human Performance*, *10*(2), 133-151.

Randall, D. M., Fedor, D. B., & Longenecker, C. O. (1990). The behavioral expression of organizational commitment. *Journal of Vocational Behavior*, *36*(2), 210–224. doi:10.1016/0001-8791(90)90028-Z

Reid, M. F., Allen, M. W., Riemenschneider, C. K., & Armstrong, D. J. (2008). The role of mentoring and supervisor support for state IT employees' affective organizational commitment. *Review of Public Personnel Administration*, *28*(1), 60–78. doi:10.1177/0734371X07311703

Scandura, T. A., & Graen, G. B. (1984). Moderating effects of initial leader-member exchange status on the effects of a leadership intervention. *The Journal of Applied Psychology*, *69*(3), 428–436. doi:10.1037/0021-9010.69.3.428

Seers, A., & Graen, G. B. (1984). The dual attachment concept: A longitudinal investigation of the combination of task characteristics and leader-member exchange. *Organizational Behavior and Human Performance*, *33*(3), 283–306. doi:10.1016/0030-5073(84)90025-4

Settoon, R. P., Bennett, N., & Liden, R. C. (1996). Social exchange in organizations: Perceived organizational support, leader-member exchange, and employee reciprocity. *The Journal of Applied Psychology*, *81*(3), 219–227. doi:10.1037/0021-9010.81.3.219

Sobol, M., & Klein, G. (2009). Relation of CIO background, IT infrastructure, and economic performance. *Information & Management*, *46*(5), 271–278. doi:10.1016/j.im.2009.05.001

Tesch, D., Jiang, J. J., & Klein, G. (2003). The impact of information system personnel skill discrepancies on stakeholder satisfaction. *Decision Sciences*, *34*(1), 107–129. doi:10.1111/1540-5915.02371

Vandenberghe, C., Bentein, K., & Stinglhamber, F. (2004). Affective commitment to the organization, supervisor, and work group: Antecedents and outcomes. *Journal of Vocational Behavior*, *64*(1), 47–71. doi:10.1016/S0001-8791(03)00029-0

Wayne, S. J., Shore, L. M., & Liden, R. C. (1997). Perceived organizational support and leader-member exchanges: a social exchange analysis. *Academy of Management Journal*, *40*(1), 82–111. doi:10.2307/257021

This work was previously published in the Information Resources Management Journal, Volume 24, Issue 4, edited by Mehdi Khosrow-Pour, pp. 77-93, copyright 2013 by IGI Publishing (an imprint of IGI Global).

Compilation of References

Abbasi Shahkooh, K., Abbasi Shahkooh, S., & Abdollahi, A. (2008). Corruption Reduction in Developing Countries Based on E-government. *World Applied Science Journal*, *4*(2), 1–7.

Ad Hamid, N. R. (2005). E-CRM: Are we there yet? *Journal of American Academy of Business*, *6*(1), 51–57.

Adamides, E. D., & Karacapilidis, N. (2006). A knowledge centred framework for collaborative business process modeling. *Business Process Management Journal*, *12*(5), 557–575. doi:10.1108/14637150610690993

Adamson, I., & Shine, J. (2003). Extending the New Technology Acceptance Model to Measure the End User Information Systems Satisfaction in a Mandatory Environment: A Bank's Treasury. *Technology Analysis & Strategic Management*, *15*(4), 441-455.

Admiraal, E., & Lockhorst, D. (2009). E-Learning in Small and Medium-sized Enterprises across Europe. *International Small Business Journal*, *27*(6), 743–767. doi:10.1177/0266242609344244

Agarwal, R., & Karahanna, E. (1998). On The Multi-Dimensional Nature Of Compatibility Beliefs In Technology Acceptance. In *Proceedings of the Annual Meeting of the Diffusion Interest Group in Information Technology (DIGIT)*, Tulsa, OK (pp. 1-16). Retrieved May 16, 2008, from http://disc-nt.cba.uh.edu/chin/digit98/first.pdf

Agarwal, R., & Karahanna, E. (2000). Time flies when you're having fun: cognitive absorption and beliefs about information technology usage. *Management Information Systems Quarterly*, *24*(4), 665–694. doi:10.2307/3250951

Agarwal, R., Sarkar, M. B., & Echambadi, R. (2002). The Conditioning Effect of Time on Firm Survival: An Industry Life Cycle Approach. *Academy of Management Journal*, *45*, 971–994. doi:10.2307/3069325

Aghion, P., & Tirole, J. (1997). Formal and real authority in organizations. *The Journal of Political Economy*, *105*(1), 1–29. doi:10.1086/262063

Agrawal, R., Imielinski, T., & Swami, A. (1993). Mining association rules between sets of items in large databases. In *Proceedings of the ACM SIGMOD International Conference on Management of Data (ACM SIGMOD '93)*, Washington, DC (pp. 207–216).

Ajzen, I. (1985). From Intention to actions: a theory of planned behavior. In Kuhl, J., & Beckmann, J. (Eds.), *Action control: from cognition to behavior* (pp. 11–39). New York: Springer-Verlag. doi:10.1007/978-3-642-69746-3_2

Akamai. (2009). *Contest Data processing from the Edge*. Retrieved April 12, 2010, from http://www.akamai.com/dl/brochures/contest_brochure.pdf

Akhter Shareef, M., Kumar, V., & Kumar, U. (2011). e-Government Adoption Model (GAM): Differing service maturity levels Original Research Article. *Government Information Quarterly*, *28*(1), 17–35. doi:10.1016/j.giq.2010.05.006

Alavi, M. (2000). Managing Organizational Knowledge. In Zmud, R. (Ed.), *Framing the Domains of IT Management*. Cincinnati, OH: Pinnaflex Educational Resources.

Alba, J., Lynch, J., Webitz, B., Janiszewski, C., Lutrz, R., Sawyer, A., & Woods, S. (1997). Interactive home shopping, consumer, retailer and manufacturer incentives to participate in electronic marketplaces. *Journal of Marketing*, *61*(3), 38–54. doi:10.2307/1251788

Albert, G. (2009). Enhancing Dynamic Cloud-based Services using Network Virtualization. In *Proceedings of the 1st ACM Workshop on Virtualized Infrastructure and Systems and Architectures*, Barcelona, Spain (pp. 37-44). New York, NY: ACM.

Alberti, L. B. (2010). Della pittura e della statua. In Tirabosschi, G. (Ed.), *Della pittura e della statua di Leonbatista Alberti*. Charleston, SC: Nabu Press.

Alberts, C., & Dorofee, A. (2003). *Managing Information Security Risks: The OCTAVE Approach*. Boston: Addison-Wesley.

Al-Busaidy, M., & Weerakkody, V. (2009). E-government diffusion in Oman: a public sector employees' perspective. *Transforming Government: People. Process and Policy*, *3*(4), 375–393.

Allen, M. (2006). *Social Engineering: A Means to Violate a Computer System*. Bethesda, MD: SANS Institute.

Allen, N. J., & Meyer, J. P. (1990). The measurement and antecedents of affective, continuance and normative commitment to the organization. *Journal of Occupational Psychology*, *63*(1), 1–18.

Al-Mashari, M., & Zairi, M. (1999). BPR implementation process: an analysis of key success and failure factors. *Business Process Management Journal*, *5*(1), 87–112. doi:10.1108/14637159910249108

Alpar, P., & Olbrich, S. (2005). Legal requirements and Modelling of Processes in e-Government. *Electronic. Journal of E-Government*, *3*(3), 139–148.

Altaf, F., & Schuff, D. (2010). Taking a Flexible Approach to ASPs. *Communications of the ACM*, *53*(2), 141–143. doi:10.1145/1646353.1646389

Altameem, T., Zairi, M., & Alshawi, S. (2006). Critical Success Factors of E-Government: A Proposed Model for E-Government Implementation. In *Proceedings of the Innovations in Information Technology Conference* (pp. 1-5).

Alter, S. (1980). *Decision Support Systems: Current Practices and Continuing Challenges*. Reading, MA: Addison-Wesley.

Amiri, M., & Nejati Ajibisheh, M. (2008). Role of empowerment and youth involvement in poverty eradication. *Annals of University of Bucharest. Economic and Administrative Series*, *2*, 163–167.

Andersen, K. (2004). *E-government and public sector process rebuilding: dilettantes, wheel barrows, and diamonds*. Dordrecht, The Netherlands: Kluwer Academic Publishers.

Anderson, D. L., & Lee, H. L. (2000). The Internet-enabled Supply Chain: From the 'First Click' to the 'Last Mile. In Anderson, D. L. (Ed.), *Advancing Supply Chain Excellence through Technology* (*Vol. 2*, pp. 15–20). San Francisco, CA: Montgomery Research.

Anderson, E. E., & Choobineh, J. (2008). Enterprise information security strategies. *Computers & Security*, *27*, 22–29. doi:10.1016/j.cose.2008.03.002

Anderson-Lehman, R., Watson, H. J., Wixom, B. H., & Hoffer, J. A. (2007). *Continental Airlines Flies High with Real-time Business Intelligence*. Retrieved from http://www.fuqua.duke.edu/centers/ccrm/datasets/continental/Continental_Airlines_Case_ Study.pdf

Anderson, R. E., & Srinivasan, S. (2003). E-satisfaction and e-loyalty: A contingency framework. *Psychology and Marketing*, *20*(3), 123–138. doi:10.1002/mar.10063

Andrews, R., Brusco, M., & Currim, I. (2010). Amalgamation of partitions from multiple segmentation bases: A comparison of non-model-based and model-based methods. *European Journal of Operational Research*, *201*(2), 608–618. doi:10.1016/j.ejor.2009.03.002

Anthony, T. (2000). Supply Chain Collaboration: Success in the New Internet Economy. In Anderson, D. L. (Ed.), *Advancing Supply Chain Excellence through Technology* (*Vol. 2*, pp. 41–44). San Francisco, CA: Montgomery Research.

Antonio Muñoz-Cañavate, A., & Hípola, P. (2011). Electronic administration in Spain: From its beginnings to the present Original Research Article. *Government Information Quarterly*, *28*(1), 74–90. doi:10.1016/j.giq.2010.05.008

Antonucci, Y. L., Boykin, D., & Donahue, K. (2009). Wyeth Pharmaceuticals: In pursuit of process excellence. In Snabe, J. H., Rosenberg, A., Moller, C., & Scavillo, M. (Eds.), *Business process management: The SAP roadmap* (pp. 319–344). Boston: Galileo Press.

Ardagna, D., Mirandola, R., Trubian, M., & Zhang, L. (2009). Run-time resource management in SOA virtualized environments. In *Proceedings of the 1st International Workshop on Quality of Service-Oriented Software Systems,* Amsterdam, The Netherlands.

Ardakani, M. H. (2006). *Economic development & planning*. Tehran, Iran: Avaye Noor Publications.

Arduini, D., Belotti, F., Denni, M., Giungato, G., & Zanfei, A. (2010). Technology adoption and innovation in public services the case of e-government in Italy. *Information Economics and Policy*, *22*(3), 257–275. doi:10.1016/j.infoecopol.2009.12.007

Armstrong, S. J., & Overton, T. S. (1977). Estimating Nonresponse Bias in Mail Surveys. *JMR, Journal of Marketing Research*, *14*(3), 396–402. doi:10.2307/3150783

Aronoff, S. (1989). *Geographical Information Systems: A Management Perspective*. Ottawa, ON, Canada: WDL Publications.

Arrington, M. (2009). *In Our Inbox: Hundreds of Confidential Twitter Documents.* Retrieved April 12, 2010, from http://techcrunch.com/2009/07/14/in-our-inbox-hundreds-of-confidential-twitter-documents/

Assuncao, D. D., Costanzo, A., & Buyya, R. (2009). Evaluating the Cost-Benefit of Using Cloud Computing to Extend the Capacity of Clouds. In *Proceedings of the HPDC'09 Conference,* Munich, Germany (pp. 141-150).

Autry, C. W., Grawe, S. J., Daugherty, P. J., & Richey, R. G. (2010). The Effects of Technological Turbulence and Breadth on Supply Chain Technology Acceptance and Adoption. *Journal of Operations Management*, *28*(6), 522–536. doi:10.1016/j.jom.2010.03.001

Backhouse, J., & Dhillon, G. (1996). Structures of responsibility and security of information systems. *European Journal of Information Systems*, *5*, 2–9. doi:10.1057/ejis.1996.7

Bagozzi, R. P. (1992). The self-regulation of attitudes, intentions, and behavior. *Social Psychology Quarterly*, *55*(2), 178–204. doi:10.2307/2786945

Bagozzi, R. P., Yi, Y., & Phillips, L. W. (1991). Assessing construct validity in organizational research. *Administrative Science Quarterly*, *36*(3), 421–458. doi:10.2307/2393203

Ballinger, C. (2006). *Born To Be Parallel*. Dayton, OH: Teradata Corporation.

Bandura, A. (1982). Self-efficacy mechanism in human agency. *The American Psychologist*, *37*(2), 122–147. doi:10.1037/0003-066X.37.2.122

Banker, R. D., Bardhan, I., & Asdemir, O. (2006). Understanding the Impact of Collaboration Software on Product Design and Development. *Information Systems Research*, *17*(4), 352–373. doi:10.1287/isre.1060.0104

Banker, R. D., Charnes, A., & Cooper, W. W. (1984). Some Models for Estimating Technical and Scale Inefficiencies in Data Envelopment Analysis. *Management Science*, *30*(9), 1078–1092. doi:10.1287/mnsc.30.9.1078

Barki, H., Rivard, S., & Talbot, J. (1993). A Keyword Classification Scheme For IS Research Literature: An Update. *Management Information Systems Quarterly*, *17*(1), 209–226. doi:10.2307/249802

Barney, J. B. (1991). Firm Resources and Sustained Competitive Advantage. *Journal of Management*, *17*(1), 99–120. doi:10.1177/014920639101700108

Baron, M., Pettit, P., & Slote, M. (1997). *Three Methods of Ethics: A Debate*. Oxford, UK: Blackwell.

Barrick, M. R., & Mount, M. K. (1991). The Big Five personality dimensions and job performance: A meta-analysis. *Personnel Psychology*, *44*(1), 1–26. doi:10.1111/j.1744-6570.1991.tb00688.x

Barrick, M. R., & Mount, M. K. (2000). Select on conscientiousness and emotional stability. In Locke, E. A. (Ed.), *Handbook ofprinciples of organizational behavior*. Malden, MA: Blackwell Publishing.

Barrick, M. R., Mount, M. K., & Gupta, R. (2003). Meta-analysis of the relationship between the five-factor model of personality and Holland's occupational types. *Personnel Psychology*, *56*, 45–74. doi:10.1111/j.1744-6570.2003.tb00143.x

Barrick, M. R., Mount, M. K., & Judge, T. A. (2001). Personality and Performance at the Beginning of the New Millennium: What Do We Know and Where Do We Go Next? *International Journal of Selection and Assessment*, *9*(1-2), 9–30. doi:10.1111/1468-2389.00160

Barrick, M. R., Stewart, G. L., Neubert, M. J., & Mount, M. K. (1998). Relating member ability and personality to work-team process and team effectiveness. *The Journal of Applied Psychology*, *83*(3), 377–391. doi:10.1037/0021-9010.83.3.377

Bass, B. M., & Bass, R. (2008). *Bass & Stogdill's handbook of leadership: Theory, research, and managerial applications* (4th ed.). New York: Free Press.

Becker, J., Algermissen, L., & Niehaves, B. (2006). A procedure model for process oriented e-government projects. *Business Process Management Journal*, *12*(1), 61–75. doi:10.1108/14637150610643760

Bédard, Y., Rivest, S., & Proulx, M. J. (2005). Spatial On-Line Analytical Processing (SOLAP): Concepts, architectures and solutions from a geomatics engineering perspective. In Wrembel, R., & Koncilia, C. (Eds.), *Data Warehouses and OLAP: Concepts, Architectures and Solutions* (pp. 298–313). Hershey, PA: Idea Group.

Beecham, S., Baddoo, N., Hall, T., Robinson, H., & Sharp, H. (2008). Motivation in software engineering: A systematic literature review. *Information and Software Technology*, *50*(9-10), 860–878. doi:10.1016/j.infsof.2007.09.004

Behrens, S., Jamieson, K., Jones, D., & Cranston, M. (2005). *Predicting System Success using the Technology Acceptance Model: A Case Study.* Paper presented at the 16th Australasian Conference on Information Systems Predicting Success using TAM, Sydney, Australia.

Bélanger, F., & Carter, L. (2008). Trust and risk in e-government adoption. *The Journal of Strategic Information Systems*, *17*(2), 165–176. doi:10.1016/j.jsis.2007.12.002

Benamati, J., & Lederer, A. (2010). Managing the Impact of Rapid IT Change. *Information Resources Management Journal*, *23*(1), 1–16. doi:10.4018/irmj.2010102601

Benamati, J., & Rajkumar, T. (2008). An Outsourcing Acceptance Model: An Application of TAM to Application Development Outsourcing Decisions. *Information Resources Management Journal*, *21*(2), 80–102. doi:10.4018/irmj.2008040105

Bentler, P. M., & Hu, L. T. (1995). Evaluating model fit. In Hoyle, R. H. (Ed.), *Structural Equation Modeling* (pp. 76–99). Thousand Oaks, CA: Sage.

Berdrow, I., & Lane, H. W. (2003). International joint ventures: Creating value through successful Knowledge Management. *Journal of World Business*, *38*, 15–30. doi:10.1016/S1090-9516(02)00106-2

Berente, N., Vandenbosch, B., & Aubert, B. (2009). Information flows and business process integration. *Business Process Management Journal*, *15*(1), 119–141. doi:10.1108/14637150910931505

Berger, A. N., & Humphrey, D. B. (1997). Efficiency of Financial Institutions: International Survey and Directions for Future Research. *European Journal of Operational Research*, *98*, 175–212. doi:10.1016/S0377-2217(96)00342-6

Bhattacherjee, A. (2000). Acceptance of e-commerce services: the case of electronic brokerages. *IEEE Transactions on Systems, Man, and Cybernetics. Part A, Systems and Humans*, *20*(4), 411–420. doi:10.1109/3468.852435

Bias, R. (2009). *Cloudcenters are Datacenters in the Sky*. Retrieved April 12, 2010, from http://blog.gogrid.com/2009/01/08/cloudcenters-are-datacenters-in-the-sky/

Blackburn, W. R. (2007). *The Sustainability Handbook: The Complete Management Guide to Achieving Social, Economic and Environmental Responsibility*. Washington, DC: Environmental Law Institute.

Blanchard, K. (1987). Ethical Management. *Executive Excellence*, *11*(4), 3–4.

Blau, P. M. (1964). *Exchange and power in social life*. New York, NY: John Wiley & Sons.

Blundell, B. G. (2007). *Enhanced visualization: Making space for 3-D images*. New York, NY: John Wiley & Sons.

Blundell, B. G. (2008). *An introduction to computer graphics and creative 3-D environments*. New York, NY: Springer. doi:10.1007/978-1-84800-042-1

Blundell, B. G., & Schwarz, A. J. (2000). *Volumetric three-dimensional display systems*. New York, NY: John Wiley & Sons.

Blundell, B. G., & Schwarz, A. J. (2006). *Creative 3-D display and interaction interfaces: A trans-disciplinary approach*. New York, NY: John Wiley & Sons.

Boh, W. F. (2007). Mechanisms for sharing knowledge in project-based organizations. *Information and Organization, 17*, 27–58. doi:10.1016/j.infoandorg.2006.10.001

Bollen, K. A. (1989). *Structural Equations with Latent Variables*. New York, NY: Wiley.

Bowersox, D. J., Closs, D. J., & Stank, T. P. (1999). *21st Century Logistics: Making Supply Chain Integration a Reality*. Oak Brook, IL: Council of Logistics Management.

Bowersox, D. J., Closs, D. J., & Cooper, M. B. (2010). *Supply Chain Logistics Management*. New York, NY: McGraw Hill/Irwin.

Bowler, W. M., Halbesleben, R. B., & Paul, J. R. B. (2010). If you're close with the leader, you must be a brownnose: The role of leader-member relationships in follower, leader, and co-worker attributions of organizational citizenship behavior motives. *Human Resource Management Review, 20*(4), 309–316. doi:10.1016/j.hrmr.2010.04.001

Bozeman, B. (1987). *All organizations are public: Bridging public and private organizational theories*. San Francisco, CA: Jossey-Bass.

Braa, J., & Hedberg, C. (2000). *Developing district-based health care information systems, Information Flows, Local Improvisations and Work Practices*. Paper presented at the IFIPWG9.4 Conference, Cape Town, South Africa.

Brancheau, J. C., Janz, B. D., & Wetherbe, J. C. (1996). Key issues in information systems management: 1994–95 SIM Delphi results. *Management Information Systems Quarterly, 20*(2), 225–242. doi:10.2307/249479

Brandtzeg, P. B., Heim, J., & Karahasanovic, A. (2011). Understanding the new digital divide—A typology of Internet users in Europe Original Research Article. *International Journal of Human-Computer Studies, 69*(3), 123–138. doi:10.1016/j.ijhcs.2010.11.004

Briggs, S. R. (1992). Assessing the five-factor model of personality description. *Journal of Personality, 60*(2), 253–293. doi:10.1111/j.1467-6494.1992.tb00974.x

Brobst, S., & Kent, P. (2008). *A New Era of High Performance Analytics*. Dayton, OH: Teradata Corporation.

Brodkin, J. (2009). *Cloud computing outages: Amazon customers the latest to suffer downtime*. Retrieved from http://www.networkworld.com/community/node/48961

Brown, M. M., & Brudney, J. L. (2001). *Achieving advanced electronic government services: An examination of obstacles and implications from an international perspective*. Paper presented at the National Public Management Research Conference, Bloomington, IN.

Browne, M. W., & Cudeck, R. (1993). Alternative ways of assessing model fit. In Bollen, K. A., & Long, J. S. (Eds.), *Testing structural equation models* (pp. 136–162). Newbury Park, CA: Sage.

Brown, G. H. (1952). Brand loyalty – fact or fiction? *Advertising Age, 23*, 53–55.

Brown, S. P., & Peterson, R. A. (1993). Antecedents and consequences of salesperson job satisfaction: Meta-analysis and assessment of causal effects. *JMR, Journal of Marketing Research, 30*(1), 63–77. doi:10.2307/3172514

Bryant, S., Kahle, J. B., & Schafer, B. A. (2005). Distance education: A review of the contemporary literature. *Issues in Accounting Education, 20*(3), 255–272. doi:10.2308/iace.2005.20.3.255

Buckley, K. M. (2003). Evaluation of classroom-based, web-enhanced, and web-based distance learning nutrition courses for undergraduate nursing. *The Journal of Nursing Education, 42*(8), 367–370.

Burdea, G. C. (1996). *Force and touch feedback for virtual reality*. New York, NY: John Wiley & Sons.

Cachin, C., Keidar, I., & Shraer, A. (2009). Trusting the Cloud. *SIGACT News, 40*(2), 81–87. doi:10.1145/1556154.1556173

Campbell-Kelly, M. (2009). The Rise, Fall, and Resurrection of Software as A Service. *Communications of the ACM, 52*(5), 28–30. doi:10.1145/1506409.1506419

Cannon, J. P., & Perreault, W. D. Jr. (1999). Buyer-seller Relationships in Business Markets. *JMR, Journal of Marketing Research, 36*(4), 439–460. doi:10.2307/3151999

Cao, L., Liu, J., & Tang, X. (2008). What the Back of the Object Looks Like: 3D Reconstruction from Line Drawings without Hidden Lines. *IEEE Transactions on Pattern Analysis and Machine Intelligence, 30*(3), 507–517. doi:10.1109/TPAMI.2007.1185

Carr, N. (2008). *The Big Switch*. New York, NY: Norton.

Carroll, A., & Scherer, R. (1999). Models of management morality for new millennium. *Business Ethics Quarterly*, *11*(2), 365–371. doi:10.2307/3857754

Carter, L., & Bélanger, F. (2005). The utilization of e-government services: citizen trust, innovation and acceptance factors. *Information Systems Journal*, *15*(1), 5–25. doi:10.1111/j.1365-2575.2005.00183.x

Cascio, W. F. (2006). *Managing Human Resources: Productivity, Quality of Work Life, Profits* (7th ed.). New York: McGraw-Hill/Irwin.

Cattell, R. B., Cattell, A. K., & Cattell, H. E. P. (1993). *16 Personality Factor Inventory* (5th ed.). Champaign, IL: The Institute for Personality and Ability Testing.

Cegielski, C. G. (2001). *A Model of the Factors that Affect the Integration of Emerging Information Technology into Corporate Strategy*. Unpublished doctoral dissertation, University of Mississippi.

Celly, K. S., & Frazier, G. (1996). Outcome-based and Behavior-based Coordination Efforts in Channel Relationships. *JMR, Journal of Marketing Research*, *33*(2), 200–210. doi:10.2307/3152147

Cernea, M. M. (1994). Making development sustainable. In Serageldin, I., & Steer, A. (Eds.), *Making development sustainable: form concepts to action* (pp. 7–10). Washington, DC: World Bank.

Chakravarthy, B. (1997). A New Strategy Framework for Coping with Turbulence. *Sloan Management Review*, *38*(2), 69–82.

Chaudhuri, A., & Holbrook, M. B. (2001). The chain of effects from brand trust and brand affect to brand performance: the role of brand loyalty. *Journal of Marketing*, *65*(2), 81–93. doi:10.1509/jmkg.65.2.81.18255

Chaudhuri, R., & Verma, S. (2008). A framework for determining customer satisfaction: An empirical analysis. *International Journal of Electronic Marketing and Retailing*, *2*(2), 190–201. doi:10.1504/IJEMR.2008.019817

Chau, P. (1995). Factors used in the selection of packaged software in small businesses: Views of owners and managers. *Information & Management*, *29*, 71–78. doi:10.1016/0378-7206(95)00016-P

Chau, P. Y. K., & Hu, P. J. (2001). Information technology acceptance by individual professionals: a model comparison approach. *Decision Sciences*, *32*(4), 699–717. doi:10.1111/j.1540-5915.2001.tb00978.x

Cheng, R. (2010, February 8). *'Cloud Computing': What Exactly is it, Anyway?* Retrieved May 5, 2010, from http://online.wsj.com/article/SB10001424052748703580904574638391318085158.html

Chen, H. M., Chen, Q., & Kazman, R. (2007). The affective and cognitive impacts of perceived touch on online customers' intention to return in the Web-based eCRM environment. *Journal of Electronic Commerce in Organizations*, *5*(1), 69–91. doi:10.4018/jeco.2007010104

Chen, Q., & Chen, H. M. (2004). Exploring the success factors of eCRM strategies in practice. *Journal of Database Marketing & Customer Strategy Management*, *11*(4), 333–343. doi:10.1057/palgrave.dbm.3240232

Chen, Z. X., & Francesco, A. M. (2003). The relationship between the three components of commitment and employee performance in China. *Journal of Vocational Behavior*, *62*(3), 490–510. doi:10.1016/S0001-8791(02)00064-7

Chong, S.C., & Choi, Y.S. (2005). Critical factors in the successful implementation of knowledge management. *Journal of Knowledge Management Practice, 6.*

Chong, A. Y. L., & Ooi, K. B. (2008). Adoption of interorganizational system standards in supply chains: an empirical analysis of RosettaNet standards. *Industrial Management & Data Systems*, *108*(4), 529–547. doi:10.1108/02635570810868371

Chong, A. Y. L., Ooi, K. B., Lin, B., & Tan, B. I. (2010). Online banking adoption: an empirical analysis. *International Journal of Bank Marketing*, *28*(4), 267–287. doi:10.1108/02652321011054963

Chong, A. Y. L., Ooi, K. B., & Sohal, A. (2009). The relationship between supply chain factors and adoption of e-Collaboration tools: An empirical examination. *International Journal of Production Economics*, *122*(1), 150–160. doi:10.1016/j.ijpe.2009.05.012

Chong, S. (2006). KM critical success factors: A comparison of perceived importance versus implementation in Malaysian ICT companies. *The Learning Organization*, *13*(3), 230–256. doi:10.1108/09696470610661108

Chopra, S., & Meindl, P. (2004). *Supply Chain Management: Strategy, Planning, and Operation.* Upper Saddle River, NJ: Prentice Hall.

Choudhury, V. (1997). Strategic Choices in the Development of Interorganizational Information Systems. *Information Systems Research, 8*(1), 1–24. doi:10.1287/isre.8.1.1

Choudhury, V., Hartzel, K., & Konsynski, B. (1998). Uses and Consequences of Electronic Markets: An Empirical Investigation in the Aircraft Parts Industry. *Management Information Systems Quarterly, 22*(4), 471–507. doi:10.2307/249552

Chourabi, H., Mellouli, S., & Bouslama, F. (2009). Modeling e-government business processes: New approaches to transparent and efficient performance. *Information Polity, 14*(1), 91–109.

Christen, M., Iyer, G., & Soberman, D. (2006). Job satisfaction, job performance, and effort: A reexamination using agency theory. *Journal of Marketing, 70*(1), 137–150. doi:10.1509/jmkg.2006.70.1.137

Christensen, C., & Bower, J. (1996). Customer power, strategic investment, and the failure of leading firms. *Strategic Management Journal, 17*, 197–218. doi:10.1002/(SICI)1097-0266(199603)17:3<197::AID-SMJ804>3.0.CO;2-U

Christensen, C., & Raynor, M. (2003). *The innovator's solution: Creating and sustaining successful growth.* Boston, MA: Harvard Business School Press.

Chun, B., & Maniatis, P. (2009). Augmented Smartphone Applications Through Clone Cloud Execution. In *Proceedings of the HotOS 2009 Conference,* Monte Verita, Switzerland.

Chun, S. W. (2007). Change that attitude: The ABCs of a persuasive security awareness program. In Tipton, H. F., & Krause, M. (Eds.), *Information Security Management Handbook* (pp. 521–530). Boca Raton, FL: Auerbach Publications. doi:10.1201/9781439833032.ch43

Clemons, E. K., & Weber, B. W. (1990). Strategic Information Technology Investments: Guidelines for Decision Making. *Journal of Management Information Systems, 7*(2), 9–28.

Clemons, E., & Row, M. C. (1992). Information Technology and Industrial Cooperation: The changing Economics of Coordination and Ownership. *Journal of Management Information Systems, 9*(2), 9–28.

Cloud Security Alliance. (2009). *Security Guidance for Critical Areas of Focus in Cloud Computing.* Retrieved April 12, 2010, from http://www.cloudsecurityalliance.org/csaguide.pdf

Codd, E. F., Codd, S. B., & Salley, C. T. (1993). *Providing OLAP (On-Line Analytical Processing) to User-Analysts: An IT Mandate.* Retrieved from http://dev.hyperion.com/resource_library/white_papers/providing_olap_to_user_analysts.pdf

Codd, E. F. (1970). A relational model for large shared data banks. *Communications of the ACM, 13*(6), 377–387. doi:10.1145/362384.362685

Cogliser, C. C., Schriesheim, C. A., Scandura, T. A., & Gardner, W. L. (2009). Balance in leader and follower perceptions of leader-member exchange: Relationships with performance and work attitudes. *The Leadership Quarterly, 20*, 452–465. doi:10.1016/j.leaqua.2009.03.010

Cohen, E. G. (1994). Restructuring the classroom: Conditions for productive small groups. *Review of Educational Research, 64*, 1–35.

Company, P., Contero, M., Conesa, J., & Piquer, A. (2004). An Optimisation-Based Reconstruction Engine for 3D Modelling by Sketching. *Computers & Graphics, 28*(6), 955–979. doi:10.1016/j.cag.2004.08.007

Company, P., Piquer, A., Contero, M., & Naya, F. (2005). A survey on geometrical reconstruction as a core technology to sketch-based modeling. *Computer Graphics, 29*(6), 892–904. doi:10.1016/j.cag.2005.09.007

Conley, J. J. (1985). Longitudinal stability of personality traits: A multitrait-multimethod-multioccasion analysis. *Journal of Personality and Social Psychology, 49*(5), 1266–1282. doi:10.1037/0022-3514.49.5.1266

Conner, K., & Prahalad, C. K. (1996). A Resource-based Theory of the Firm: Knowledge Versus Opportunism. *Organization Science, 7*(5), 477–501. doi:10.1287/orsc.7.5.477

Cook, T. D., & Campbell, D. T. (1979). *Quasi-Experimentation: Design and Analysis Issues for Field Settings*. Boston: Houghton-Mifflin.

Coplien, J. O. (1998). A generative development - Process pattern language. In Rising, L. (Ed.), *The Patterns Handbook: Techniques, Strategies, and Applications* (pp. 243–300). Cambridge, UK: Cambridge University Press.

Costa, P., Zahn, T., Rowston, A., O'Shea, G., & Schubert, S. (2009). Why should we integrate services, servers, and networking in a data center? In *Proceedings of the 1st ACM Workshop on Research on Enterprise Networking*, Barcelona, Spain (pp. 111-118).

Costa, P. T., & McCrae, R. R. (1988). Personality in adulthood: A 6-year longitudinal study of self-reports and spouse ratings on the NEO Personality Inventory. *Journal of Personality and Social Psychology*, *54*(5), 853–863. doi:10.1037/0022-3514.54.5.853

Criado, J. I., & Ramilo, M. C. (2003). E-government in practice: An analysis of Web site orientation to the citizens in Spanish municipalities. *International Journal of Public Sector Management*, *16*(3), 191–218. doi:10.1108/09513550310472320

Cronbach, L. (1971). Test validation. In Thorndike, R. L. (Ed.), *Educational measurement* (2nd ed., pp. 443–507). Washington, DC: American Council on Education.

Croom, S. R. (2000). The Impact of Web-based Procurement on the Management of Operating Resources Supply. *Journal of Supply Chain Management*, *36*, 4–13. doi:10.1111/j.1745-493X.2000.tb00065.x

Cuieford, J. P. (1965). *Fundamental Statistics in Psychology and Education* (4th ed.). New York, NY: McGraw Hill.

Cunningham, P., & Wilkins, J. (2009). A Walk in the Cloud. *Information Management Journal*, *43*(1), 22–30.

Cunningham, R. M. (1956). Brand-Loyalty-What, where, how much. *Harvard Business Review*, *34*(1), 116–128.

Curtis, D. (2006). Mind sets and methods: poverty strategies and the awkward potential of the enabling state. *International Journal of Public Sector Management*, *19*(2), 150–164. doi:10.1108/09513550610650419

Da Veiga, A., & Eloff, J. H. P. (2007). An information security governance framework. *Information Systems Management*, *24*, 361–372. doi:10.1080/10580530701586136

Dalkey, N., & Helmer, O. (1963). An experimental application of the Delphi method to the use of experts. *Management Science*, *9*(3), 458–467. doi:10.1287/mnsc.9.3.458

Damanpour, F. (1991). Organizational Innovation: A Meta-Analysis of Effects of Determinants and Moderators. *Academy of Management Journal*, *34*(3), 555–590. doi:10.2307/256406

Dancy, J. (1991). An Ethics of Prima Facie Duties. In Singer, P. (Ed.), *A Companion to Ethics* (pp. 225–226). Oxford, UK: Blackwell.

Daugherty, P. J., Myers, M. B., & Autry, C. W. (1999). Automatic Replenishment Programs: An Empirical Examination. *Journal of Business Logistics*, *20*, 63–82.

Davenport, T. H. (1993). Integrate process reengineering and TQM. *Planning Review*, *21*(3), 6–12.

Davenport, T. H., & Beers, M. C. (1995). Managing information about processes. *Journal of Management Information Systems*, *12*(1), 57–80.

Davenport, T. H., & Short, J. E. (1990). The new industrial engineering: Information technology and process redesign. *Sloan Management Review*, *31*(4), 11–27.

Davis, F. D. (1989). Perceived usefulness, perceived ease of use, and user acceptance of information technology. *Management Information Systems Quarterly*, *13*(3), 319–339. doi:10.2307/249008

Davis, J. (2007). Overview of an IT corporate security organization. In Tipton, H. F., & Krause, M. (Eds.), *Information Security Management Handbook* (pp. 567–577). Boca Raton, FL: Auerbach Publications. doi:10.1201/9781439833032.ch47

Davis-Sramek, B., Germain, R., & Iyer, K. (2010). Supply Chain Technology: The Role of Environment in Predicting Performance. *Journal of the Academy of Marketing Science*, *38*(1), 42–55. doi:10.1007/s11747-009-0137-1

Day, G. S. (1969). A two-dimensional concept of brand loyalty. *JMR, Journal of Marketing Research*, *9*, 29–36.

Day, G. S. (1994). The capabilities of market-driven organizations. *Journal of Marketing*, *58*(4), 37–52. doi:10.2307/1251915

Deane, F., Podd, J., & Henderson, R. (1998). Relationship between self-report and log data estimates of information system usage. *Computers in Human Behavior*, *14*(4), 621–636. doi:10.1016/S0747-5632(98)00027-2

Deelman, E., Singh, G., Livny, M., Berriman, B., & Good, J. (2008). The cost of doing science on the Cloud: The Montage Example. In *Proceedings of the ACM/IEEE Conference on Supercomputing*, Piscataway, NJ (pp. 1-12).

Deitz, J., & Poulin, S. (Eds.). (2007). *Proceedings from the 2007 Teradata Partners User Group Conference: Teradata Platform Performance: Higher and Higher*. Retrieved from http://www.teradata.com/teradata-partners/conference/index.cfm

Deitz, J. (2007). At the core of the Teradata platform. *Teradata Magazine*, *7*(3), 62–65.

Dekimpe, M. G., Pierre, F., Srinath, G., Gary, L. L., & Christophe, V. B. (1997). Generalizing about trade show effectiveness: A cross-national comparison. *Journal of Marketing*, *61*(4), 55–64. doi:10.2307/1252086

Delic, K., & Walker, M. (2008). Emergence of the Academic Computing Clouds. *ACM Ubiquity*, *9*(31).

DeMarco, T. (1978). *Structured Analysis and System Specification*. New York, NY: Yourdon Press.

Demming, W. E. (1986). *Out of the crisis*. Cambridge, MA: MIT Press.

den Butter, F. A. G., de Graaf, M., & Nijsen, A. (2009). *The Transaction Costs Perspective on Costs and Benefits of Government Regulation*. Rotterdam, The Netherlands: Tinbergen Institute.

Dereshiwsky, M. (2001). ''A'' is for assessment: Identifying online assessment practices and perceptions. *Journal of United States Distance Learning Association*, *15*(1), 16–26.

Devaraj, S., Krajewski, L., & Wei, J. C. (2007). Impact of E-business Technologies on Operational Performance: The Role of Production Information Integration in the Supply Chain. *Journal of Operations Management*, *25*(6), 1199–1216. doi:10.1016/j.jom.2007.01.002

Deveraj, S., Easley, R. F., & Crant, J. M. (2008). How does personality matter? Relating the Five-Factor model to technology acceptance and use. *Information Systems Research*, *19*(1), 93–105. doi:10.1287/isre.1070.0153

Dewiyanti, S., Brand-Gruwel, S., Jochems, W., & Broers, N. (2007). Students' experiences with collaborative learning in asynchronous computer-supported collaborative learning environments. *Computers in Human Behavior*, *23*, 496–514. doi:10.1016/j.chb.2004.10.021

Dick, A. S., & Basu, K. (1994). Customer loyalty: Toward an integrated conceptual framework. *Journal of the Academy of Marketing Science*, *22*, 99–113. doi:10.1177/0092070394222001

Diestel, R. (1997). *Graph Theory*. New York, NY: Springer.

DMTF. (2009). *Open Virtualization Format Specification*. Retrieved April 13, 2010, from http://www.dmtf.org/standards/published_documents/DSP0243_1.0.0.pdf

Downing, E., Hesselink, L., Macfarlane, R. M., & Barty, C. P. J. (1994). *Solid-state three-dimensional computer display*. Paper presented at the Conference on Lasers and Electro-Optics.

Drucker, P. F. (1993). *Post-Capitalist Society*. Oxford, UK: Butterworth Heinemann.

Duchon, D., Green, S. G., & Taber, T. D. (1986). Vertical dyad linkage: A longitudinal assessment of antecedents, measures and consequences. *The Journal of Applied Psychology*, *71*(1), 56–60. doi:10.1037/0021-9010.71.1.56

Dunn, W. S., Mount, M. K., Barrick, M. R., & Ones, D. S. (1995). Relative importance of personality and general mental ability in manager's judgements of applicant qualifications. *The Journal of Applied Psychology*, *80*(4), 500–509. doi:10.1037/0021-9010.80.4.500

Dyer, J. H., & Singh, H. (1998). The Relational View: Cooperative Strategy and Sources of Interorganizational Competitive Advantage. *Academy of Management Review*, *23*(4), 660–679. doi:10.2307/259056

Dykman, C., & Davis, C. (2008). Online education forum: Part one -The shift toward online education. *Journal of Information Systems Education*, *19*(1), 11–16.

Dykman, C., & Davis, C. (2008). Online education forum: Part two -Teaching online versus teaching conventionally. *Journal of Information Systems Education, 19*(2), 157–164.

Dykman, C., & Davis, C. (2008). Online education forum: Part three - A quality online educational experience. *Journal of Information Systems Education, 19*(2), 281–289.

Eckerson, W. (2004). *In Search of a Single Version of the Truth: Strategies for Consolidating Analytical Silos.* Chatsworth, CA: The Data Warehouse Institute (TDWI).

Eckerson, W. (2007). *Best Practices in Operational BI: Converging Analytical and Operational Processes.* Chatsworth, CA: The Data Warehouse Institute (TDWI).

Economist Intelligence Unit. (2004). *World investment prospects: The revival of globalisation?* Retrieved November 21, 2010, from http://graphics.eiu.com/files/ad_pdfs/WIP_2004.pdf

Edgerton, S. Y. (1976). *The renaissance rediscovery of linear perspective*. New York, NY: Harper and Row.

Edwards, A., Fischer, A., & Lain, A. (2009). Diverter: a new approach to networking within virtualized infrastructures. In *Proceedings of the ACM Workshop on Research on Enterprise Networking,* Barcelona, Spain (pp. 103-110).

Egan, M. (2005). *The Executive Guide to Information Security: Threats, Challenges, and Solutions.* Indianapolis, IN: Addison-Wesley.

Eicker, S., Kochbeck, J., & Schuler, P. (2008). *Employee competencies for business process management.* Paper presented at the International Conference on Business Information Systems, Innsbruck, Austria.

Eldridge, D. (2007). Optimal allocation of decision rights for value-adding in venture capital. *Management Decision, 45*(5), 897–909. doi:10.1108/00251740710753701

Fahiem, M., Haq, S., & Saleemi, F. (2007). A Review of 3D Reconstruction Techniques from 2D Orthographic Line Drawings. In *Proceedings of the Geometric Modeling and Imaging Conference (GMAI '07)* (pp. 60-66). Washington, DC: IEEE Computer Society.

Families, U. S. A. (2008). *America's Health Care Crisis: Cities on the front lines.* Retrieved November 21, 2010, from http://www.familiesusa.org/assets/pdfs/cities-on-the-front-lines.pdf

Fang, Z. (2002). E-government in digital era: concept, practice, and development. *International Journal of the Computer, the Internet and Management, 10*(2), 1-22.

Faraj, S., & Sambamurthy, V. (2006). Leadership of information systems development projects. *IEEE Transactions on Engineering Management, 53*(2), 238–249. doi:10.1109/TEM.2006.872245

Farrington, G., & Bronack, S. (2001). Sink or swim? *T.H.E. Journal, 28,* 10.

Favalora, G. E., Napoli, J., Hall, D. M., Dorval, R. K., Giovinco, M. G., Richmond, M. J., & Chun, W. S. (2002). 100 million voxels volumetric display. In *Proceedings of the 9th SPIE Conference on Cockpit Displays: Displays for Defense Applications* (pp. 300-312).

Fayyad, U. M., Piatetsky-Shapiro, G., Smyth, P., & Uthurusamy, R. (1996). *Advances in Knowledge Discovery and Data Mining.* Menlo Park, CA: AAAI Press.

FCC. (2009). *FCC Public Notice.* Retrieved April 14, 2010, http://hraunfoss.fcc.gov/edocs_public/attachmatch/DA-09-2433A1.pdf

Feinberg, D., & Beyer, M. A. (2008). *Magic Quadrant for Data Warehouse Database Management Systems.* Stamford, CT: Gartner.

Ferreira, A. C., Campos, M. L., & Tanaka, A. (2001). An architecture for spatial and dimensional analysis integration. In *Proceedings of the World Multiconference on Systemics, Cybernetics and Informatics (SCI 2001),* Orlando, FL (Vol. XIV, pp. 392–395).

Festa, P. (1999, June 30). Destop.com joining Web-based applications market. *Cnet News.* Retrieved from http://news.cnet.com/Desktop.com-joining-Web-based-applications-market/2100-1023_3-227919.html

Fidalgo, R. N., Times, V. C., Silva, J., & Souza, F. F. (2004). GeoDWFrame: A framework for guiding the design of geographical dimensional schemas. In *Proceedings of the 6th International Conference Data Warehousing and Knowledge Discovery (DaWaK),* Zaragoza, Spain (pp. 26–37).

Fine, C. H. (1998). *Clockspeed: Winning Industry Control in the Age of Temporary Advantage.* New York, NY: Harper Collins.

Fingar, P. (2006). The MBA is dead, long live the MBI. *BPTrends*, *4*(12), 1–7.

Fisher, M. L. (1997). What is the Right Supply Chain for your Product? *Harvard Business Review*, *75*(2), 105–116.

Fitzgerald, T. (2007). Information security governance. In Tipton, H. F., & Krause, M. (Eds.), *Information Security Management Handbook* (pp. 15–34). Boca Raton, FL: Auerbach Publications. doi:10.1201/9781439833032.ch2

Foley, J. (2007). *Exclusive: Inside Hewlett-Packard's Data Warehouse Gamble*. Retrieved from http://www.intelligententerprise.com/showArticle.jhtml?articleID=196801888

Fonseca, B., & Nobel, C. (2005, September 19). Katrina's wrath: Gulf coast business take on daunting task of restoring IT operations after storm. *eWeek*, 22-24.

Fornell, C., & Larcker, D. F. (1981). Evaluating structural equations models with unobservable variables and measurement error. *JMR, Journal of Marketing Research*, *18*, 39–50. doi:10.2307/3151312

France, C. (2010). *Business Information Modeling and the Cloud.* Retrieved April 14, 2010, from http://www.aecbytes.com/feature/2010/BIM_Cloud.html

Fredriksson, O. (2005). *Relationship and Loyalty Attitude Differences Among Swedish Retail Bank Clients: E-banking Versus Branch Office Users*. New York: Free Press.

Frohlich, M. T., & Westbrook, R. (2001). Arcs of Integration: An International Study of Supply Chain Strategies. *Journal of Operations Management*, *19*(2), 185–200. doi:10.1016/S0272-6963(00)00055-3

Frohlich, M. T., & Westbrook, R. (2002). Demand Chain Management in Manufacturing and Services: Web-based integration, Drivers and Performance. *Journal of Operations Management*, *20*, 729–745. doi:10.1016/S0272-6963(02)00037-2

Fulford, C., & Zhang, S. (1993). Perceptions of interaction: The critical predictor in distance education. *American Journal of Distance Education*, *7*(3), 8–21. doi:10.1080/08923649309526830

Fumy, W., & Sauerbrey, J. (Eds.). (2006). *Enterprise Security*. Erlangen, Germany: Publicis Corporate Publishing.

Galbraith, J. R. (1973). *Designing Complex Organizations*. Reading, MA: Addison-Wesley.

Galbraith, J. R. (1993). *Competing with Flexible Lateral Organizations* (2nd ed.). Reading, MA: Addison-Wesley.

Galup, S. D., Klein, G., & Jiang, J. J. (2008). The impacts of job characteristics on IS employee satisfaction: A comparison between permanent and temporary employees. *Journal of Computer Information Systems*, *48*, 58–68.

Gammelgaard, J., & Ritter, T. (2000). *Knowledge retrieval process in multinational consulting firms*. Frederiksberg, Denmark: Danish Social Sciences Research Council. Retrieved from http://web.cbs.dk/departments/int/seminarpapers/JG-Knowledge.pdf

Garcia, A. C. B., Maciel, C., & Pinto, F. B. (2005). A Quality Inspection Method to Evaluate E-Government Sites. In M. Wimmer, R. Traunmüller, Å. Grönlund, & K. Andersen (Eds.), *Electronic Government* (LNCS 3591, pp. 198-209).

Garfinkel, S. (2007). *An evaluation for Amazon's Grid Computing Services: EC2,S3,SQS*. Retrieved April 14, 2010, from http://simson.net/clips/academic/2007.harvard.s3.pdf

Garvin, D. A. (1995). Leveraging processes for strategic advantage. *Harvard Business Review*, *73*(5), 76–90.

Gatewood, B. (2009). Clouds on the Information Horizon: How to Avoid the Storm. *Information & Management*, 32–36.

Gatignon, H., & Robertson, S. T. (1989). Technology Diffusion: An Empirical Test of Competitive Effects. *Journal of Marketing*, *53*(1), 35–49. doi:10.2307/1251523

Gayialis, S. P., & Tatsiopoulos, I. P. (2004). Design of an IT-driven decision support system for vehicle routing and scheduling. *European Journal of Operational Research*, *152*(2), 382–398. doi:10.1016/S0377-2217(03)00031-6

Gefen, D., & Straub, D. (2000). The relative importance of perceived ease of use in IS adoption: A study of e-commerce adoption. *Journal of the Association for Information Systems.* Retrieved from http://jais.isworld.org?articles/1-8/article.htm

Gefen, D., Karahanna, E., & Straub, D. W. (2003). Trust and TAM in online shopping: an integrated model. *Management Information Systems Quarterly*, *27*(1), 51–90.

Geng, X., Stinchcombe, M. B., & Whinston, A. B. (2006). Product Bundling. In Hendershott, T. (Ed.), *Handbook of Economics and Information Systems* (pp. 499–525). Amsterdam, The Netherlands: Elsevier.

Gerbing, D., & Anderson, J. (1992). Monte Carlo evaluation of goodness fit indices for structural equation models. *Sociological Methods & Research*, *21*, 132–160. doi:10.1177/0049124192021002002

Germain, R., & Iyer, K. (2006). The Interaction of Internal and Downstream Integration and its Association with Performance. *Journal of Business Logistics*, *27*(2), 29–52.

Gerstner, C. R., & Day, D. V. (1997). Meta-analytic review of leader-member exchange theory: Correlates and construct issues. *The Journal of Applied Psychology*, *82*(6), 827–844. doi:10.1037/0021-9010.82.6.827

Geva, A. (2006). A typology of moral problems in business: A framework for ethical management. *Journal of Business Ethics*, *69*, 134–147. doi:10.1007/s10551-006-9072-y

Gibson, S. (2001, September 17). Terrorism puts nation and human spirit to extreme test. *eWeek*, 1.

Gibson, S. (2006, August 28). Lessaons learned. *eWeek*, 20-23.

Gibson, C. C., & Graff, A. O. (1992). Impact of adults' preferred learning styles and perception of barriers on completion of external baccalaureate degree programs. *Journal of Distance Education*, *7*(1), 39–51.

Giddings, B., Hopwood, B., & O'Brien, G. (2002). Environment, economy and society: fitting them together into sustainable development. *Sustainable Development*, *10*(4), 187–196. doi:10.1002/sd.199

Gilbert, D., Balestrini, P., & Littleboy, D. (2004). Barriers and benefits in the adoption of e-government. *International Journal of Public Sector Management*, *17*(4), 286–301. doi:10.1108/09513550410539794

Glaser, B. G., & Strauss, A. L. (1967). *The Discovery of Grounded Theory: Strategies for Qualitative Research*. Chicago, IL: Aldine Publishing Company.

Goehring, J. (2007). *Nations in Transit 2007. Democratization from Central Europe to Eurasia*. New York, NY: Freedom House.

Gohring, N. (2010, September 28). Cloud Services Empower Startups. *New York Times*. Retrieved September 28, 2010, from http://www.nytimes.com

Goldberg, L. R. (1981). Language and individual differences: The search for universals in personality lexicons. In Wheeler, L. (Ed.), *Review of personality and social psychology* (*Vol. 2*, pp. 141–166). Beverly Hills, CA: Sage.

Goldberg, L. R. (1990). An alternative "description of personality": The Big Five factor structure. *Journal of Personality and Social Psychology*, *59*(6), 1216–1229. doi:10.1037/0022-3514.59.6.1216

Goldberg, L. R. (1992). The development of markers for the Big-Five factor structure. *Psychological Assessment*, *4*(1), 26–42. doi:10.1037/1040-3590.4.1.26

Golden, T. D., & Veiga, J. F. (2008). The impact of superior-subordinate relationships on the commitment, job satisfaction, and performance of virtual workers. *The Leadership Quarterly*, *19*(1), 77–88. doi:10.1016/j.leaqua.2007.12.009

Gonzalez, R. G., & Llopis, J. (2006). Information systems outsourcing: A literature analysis. *Information & Management*, *43*, 821–834. doi:10.1016/j.im.2006.07.002

Google. (2009). *Google apps and government*. Retrieved April 14, 2010, from http://googleenterprise.blogspot.com/2009/09/google-apps-and-government.html

Gordon, L. A., & Loeb, M. P. (2002). Return on information security investments: Myths vs. reality. *Strategic Finance*, *11*, 26–31.

Gordon, L. A., & Loeb, M. P. (2006). Budgeting process for information security expenditures. *Communications of the ACM*, *49*(1), 121–125. doi:10.1145/1107458.1107465

Gough, H. (1988). *Manual for the California Psychological Inventory*. Palo Alto, CA: Consulting Psychologists Press.

Gough, H. (1990). Testing for leadership with the California Psychological Inventory. In Clark, K. E., & Clark, M. B. (Eds.), *Measures of leadership* (pp. 355–379). West Orange, NJ: Leadership Library of America.

Gragg, D. (2003). *A Multi-Level Defense Against Social Engineering*. Bethesda, MD: SANS Institute.

Graziano, W. G., & Eisenberg, N. G. (1997). Agreeableness: A dimension of personality. In Hogan, R., Johnson, J., & Briggs, S. R. (Eds.), *Handbook of Personality Psychology* (pp. 795–824). San Diego, CA: Academic Press. doi:10.1016/B978-012134645-4/50031-7

Greenberg, A., Hamilton, J., Jain, N., Kandula, S., Kim, C., & Lahiri, P. (2009). VL2: A scalable and Flexible Data Center Network. *ACM SIGCOMM Computer Communication Review*, *39*(4), 51–62. doi:10.1145/1594977.1592576

Grewal, R., & Tansuhaj, P. (2001). Building Organizational Capabilities for Managing Economic Crisis: The Role of Market Orientation and Strategic Flexibility. *Journal of Marketing*, *65*(2), 67–80. doi:10.1509/jmkg.65.2.67.18259

Grimstead, I. J., & Martin, R. R. (1995). Creating solid models from single 2D sketches. In *Proceedings of the 3rd ACM Symposium on Solid Modeling and Applications* (pp. 323-337). New York, NY: ACM.

Grover, V., Henry, R. M., & Thatcher, J. B. (2007). Fix IT-business relationships through better decision rights. *Communications of the ACM*, *50*(12), 80–86. doi:10.1145/1323688.1323699

Grover, V., Jeong, S., Kettinger, W., & Teng, J. (1995). The implementation of business process reengineering. *Journal of Management Information Systems*, *12*(1), 109–144.

Guadagno, R. E., & Cialdini, R. B. (2002). Online Persuasion: An Examination of Gender Differences in Computer-Mediated Interpersonal Influence. *Group Dynamics*, *6*(1), 38–51. doi:10.1037/1089-2699.6.1.38

Guru, B., Shanmugam, B., Alam, N., & Perera, C. (2003). An evaluation of Internet banking sites in Islamic countries. *Journal of Internet Banking and Commerce*, *8*(2), 3–11.

Hair, J. F., Anderson, R. E., Tatam, R. L., & Black, W. C. (1998). *Multivariate Data Analysis* (5th ed.). Upper Saddle River, NJ: Prentice-Hall.

Halle, M. (1997). Autostereoscopic displays and computer graphics. *ACM SIGGRAPH Computer Graphics*, *31*(2), 58–62. doi:10.1145/271283.271309

Hammer, M. (1990). Reengineering work: Don't automate, obliterate. *Harvard Business Review*, *68*(4), 104–112.

Hammer, M. (2007). The process audit. *Harvard Business Review*, *85*(4), 111–123.

Hammer, M., & Champy, J. (1993). *Reengineering the corporation: A manifesto for reengineering business revolution*. New York: Harper.

Hand, E. (2007). Head in the Clouds. *Nature*, *449*(7165), 963–963. doi:10.1038/449963a

Hansche, S. D. (2007). Making security awareness happen. In Tipton, H. F., & Krause, M. (Eds.), *Information Security Management Handbook* (pp. 541–553). Boca Raton, FL: Auerbach Publications. doi:10.1201/9781439833032.ch45

Hansche, S. D., Berti, J., & Hare, C. (2004). *Official (ISC)^2 Guide to the CISSP Exam*. Boca Raton, FL: Auerbach Publications.

Hara, N., & Kling, R. (1999). Students' frustrations with a web-based distance education course: A taboo topic in the discourse. *First Monday*, *4*, 12.

Harmon, P. (2004). Evaluating an organization's business process maturity. *BP Trends*, *2*(3), 1–11.

Harroff, P., & Valentine, T. (2006). Dimensions of program quality in web-based adult education. *American Journal of Distance Education*, *20*(1), 7–22. doi:10.1207/s15389286ajde2001_2

Hasanali, F. (2002). *Critical Success Factors of Knowledge Management*. Houston, TX: APQC.

Hatfield, M. (2006). *Off campus online: Distance learning becoming more popular among students who work, have families* (p. 1). Knight Ridder Tribune Business News.

Hayne, S., & Pollard, C. (2000). A comparative analysis of critical issues facing Canadian information systems personnel: a national and global perspective. *Information & Management*, *38*(2), 73–86. doi:10.1016/S0378-7206(00)00056-2

Hazlett, S. A., & Hill, F. M. (2003). E-government: The realities of using IT to transform the public sector. *Managing Service Quality*, *13*(6), 445–452. doi:10.1108/09604520310506504

Heeks, R. (2004). *E-government as a Carrier of Context*. Manchester, UK: Institute for Development Policy and Management, University of Manchester.

Heeks, R. (2004). *E-government for development, transparency definition*. Manchester, UK: Institute for Development Policy and Management, University of Manchester.

Heim, G. R., & Peng, D. X. (2010). The Impact of Information Technology Use on Plant Structure, Practices, and Performance: An Exploratory Study. *Journal of Operations Management*, *28*, 144–162. doi:10.1016/j.jom.2009.09.005

Helmaan, P. (2003). 3M: 100 years and processing. *Teradata Magazine*. Retrieved from http://www.teradata.com/td/page/115211

Hidding, G. J., Wilson, T., Williams, J. R., & Kuncheria, T. (2008). Complementary Resources' Role in First Movers and Followers in I.T. Industries. *Journal of Information Science and Technology*, *5*(3), 3–23.

Hill, T., & Lewicki, P. (2006). *Statistics. Method and applications: A comprehensive reference for science, industry and data mining*. Retrieved May 21, 2008, from http://www.statsoft.com/textbook/stathome.html

Hill, Z., & Humphrey, M. (2009). Applicability of the Willow Architecture for Cloud Management. In *Proceedings of the 1st Workshop on Automated Control for Datacenters and Clouds (ACDC'09),* Barcelona, Spain (pp. 31-36).

Hill, J. B., Sinur, J., Flint, D., & Melenovsky, M. J. (2006). *Gartner's position on business process management (Rep. No. G00136533).* Stamford, CT: Gartner Research.

Hirschheim, R. (2005). The Internet-based education bandwagon: Look before you leap. *Communications of the ACM*, *48*(7), 97–101. doi:10.1145/1070838.1070844

Ho, A. T., & Ni, A. Y. (2004). Explaining the adoption of e-government features: A case study of Iowa county treasurers' offices. *American Review of Public Administration*, *34*(2), 164–180. doi:10.1177/0275074004264355

Hoffman, C. M. (1989). *Geometric and Solid Modeling: An Introduction*. San Francisco, CA: Morgan Kaufmann.

Holland, J. L. (1985). *Making vocational choices: A theory of vocational personalities and work environments*. Englewood Cliffs, NJ: Prentice-Hall.

Holliday, I., & Kwok, R. C. W. (2004). Governance in the information age: Building e-government in Hong Kong. *New Media & Society*, *6*, 549–570. doi:10.1177/146144804044334

Holsapple, P., & Josh, I, K. (2002). Knowledge manipulation activities: results of a Delphi study. *Information & Management*, *39*(6), 477–490. doi:10.1016/S0378-7206(01)00109-4

Hoover, J. (2008). *Outages force Cloud Computing Users to Rethink Tactics*. Retrieved from http://www.informationweek.com/news/services/saas/showArticle.jhtml?articleID=210004236

Horst, M., Kuttschreuter, M., & Gutteling, J. M. (2007). Perceived usefulness, personal experiences, risk perception and trust as determinants of adoption of e-government services in The Netherlands. *Computers in Human Behavior*, *23*(4), 1838–1852. doi:10.1016/j.chb.2005.11.003

Hosein, I. (2005). *Researching the ethics of Knowledge Management: the case of Data-mining*.

Hough, L. M., & Furnham, A. (2002). Importance and use of personality variables in work settings. In Borman, W. C., Ilgen, D. R., & Klimoski, R. J. (Eds.), *Comprehensive Handbook of Psychology* (pp. 131–169). New York: Wiley.

Hughes, O. E. (2003). *Public Management and Administration* (3rd ed.). New York, NY: Palgrave Macmillan.

Hulland, J. (1999). Use of partial least squares (PLS) in strategic management research: A review of four recent studies. *Strategic Management Journal*, *20*(2), 195–204. doi:10.1002/(SICI)1097-0266(199902)20:2<195::AID-SMJ13>3.0.CO;2-7

Humphrey, S. E., Nahrgang, J. D., & Morgeson, F. P. (2007). Integrating motivational, social, and contextual work design features: A meta-analytic summary and theoretical extension of the work design literature. *The Journal of Applied Psychology*, *92*(5), 1332–1356. doi:10.1037/0021-9010.92.5.1332

Hung, R. Y.-Y. (2006). Business process management as competitive advantage: A review and empirical study. *Total Quality Management*, *17*(1), 21–40. doi:10.1080/14783360500249836

Hung, S.-Y., Ku, C.-Y., & Chang, C.-M. (2003). Critical factors of WAP services adoption: an empirical study. *Electronic Commerce Research and Applications*, *2*(1), 42–60. doi:10.1016/S1567-4223(03)00008-5

Hunter, J. E. (1980). *Test validation for 12,000 jobs: An application of synthetic validity and validity generalization to the General Aptitude Test Battery*. Washington, DC: U.S. Department of Labor.

Hunter, J. E. (1983). A causal analysis of cognitive ability, job knowledge, job performance, and supervisory ratings. In Landy, F., Zedeck, S., & Cleveland, J. (Eds.), *Performance measurement and theory* (pp. 257–266). Hillsdale, NJ: Erlbaum.

Hunter, J. E. (1986). Cognitive ability, cognitive aptitudes, job knowledge and job performance. *Journal of Vocational Behavior*, *29*(3), 340–362. doi:10.1016/0001-8791(86)90013-8

Hunter, J. E., & Hunter, R. F. (1984). Validity and utility of alternative predictors of job performance. *Psychological Bulletin*, *96*(1), 72–98. doi:10.1037/0033-2909.96.1.72

Hussain, Z. I., & Cornelius, N. (2009). The use of domination and legitimation in information systems implementation. *Information Systems Journal*, *19*(2), 197–224. doi:10.1111/j.1365-2575.2008.00322.x

IBM. (2009). *Safer citizens of a smarter planet*. Retrieved December 5, 2010, from http://www.ibm.com/smarterplanet/us/en/public_safety/visions/index.html

IEEE. Computer Society. (2005). *Michael Stonebraker*. Retrieved from http://www.ieee.org/portal/pages/about/awards/bios/2005vonneumann.html

Igbaria, M. (1991). Job performance of MIS professionals: An examination of the antecedents and consequences. *Journal of Engineering and Technology Management*, *8*(2), 141–171. doi:10.1016/0923-4748(91)90027-O

Igbaria, M., & Guimaraes, T. (1993). Antecedents and consequences of job satisfaction among information center employees. *Journal of Management Information Systems*, *9*(4), 145–174.

InBoff, K. R., Kaufman, L., & Thomas, J. P. (1986). (Eds.). Handbook of perception and human performance: *Vol. I. Sensory processes and perception*. New York, NY: John Wiley & Sons.

Inmon, W. H. (1992). *Building the Data Warehouse*. New York, NY: Wiley.

Institute for Trade Studies and Research (ITSR). (2004). *Electronic commerce, concepts and applications*. Tehran, Iran: Author.

International Energy Agency. (2006). *World Energy outlook 2006*. Retrieved November 21, 2010, from http://www.iea.org/textbase/nppdf/free/2006/weo2006.pdf

InWEnt. (2007). *Governing Emerging Megacities - Challenges and Perspectives*. Retrieved November 21, 2010, from http://www.germany-wuf4.de/dokumente/06_inwent/06.02_en_inwent_governing_emerging_megacities.pdf

Iske, P., & Boersma, W. (2005). Connected brainsquestion and answer systems for knowledge sharing: concepts, implementation and return on investment. *Journal of Knowledge Management*, *9*(1), 126–145. doi:10.1108/13673270510583018

Iyer, K. (2011). Demand Chain Collaboration and Operational Performance: Role of IT Analytic Capability and Environmental Uncertainty. *Journal of Business and Industrial Marketing*, *26*(2), 81–91. doi:10.1108/08858621111112267

Iyer, K., Germain, R., & Claycomb, C. A. (2009). B2B E-Commerce Supply Chain Integration and Performance: A Contingency Fit Perspective on the Role of Environment. *Information & Management*, *46*(6), 313–322. doi:10.1016/j.im.2009.06.002

Iyer, K., Germain, R., & Frankwick, G. L. (2004). Supply Chain B2B E-Commerce and Time-based Delivery Performance. *International Journal of Physical Distribution & Logistics Management*, *34*(8), 645–661. doi:10.1108/09600030410557776

Iyer, K., Germain, R., & Frankwick, G. L. (2007). Supply Chain Analytic Capability: Environment and Performance. *International Journal of Integrated Supply Management*, *3*(3), 302–320. doi:10.1504/IJISM.2007.012632

Jackson, M., & Helms, M. (2008). Student perceptions of hybrid courses: Measuring and interpreting quality. *Journal of Education for Business*, *84*(1), 7–12. doi:10.3200/JOEB.84.1.7-12

Jacoby, J., & Kyner, D. B. (1973). Brand loyalty vs. repeat purchasing behavior. *JMR, Journal of Marketing Research*, *10*(1), 1–9. doi:10.2307/3149402

Janoff, N. (1998). Organizational patterns at AG Communication Systems. In Rising, L. (Ed.), *The Patterns Handbook: Techniques, Strategies, and Applications* (pp. 131–140). Cambridge, UK: Cambridge University Press.

Janssen, M., & Cresswell, A. M. (2005). An enterprise application integration methodology for e-government. *The Journal of Enterprise Information Management*, *18*(5), 531–547. doi:10.1108/17410390510623990

Jarvenpaa, S. L., & Todd, P. A. (1997). Consumer reactions to electronic shopping on the world wide web. *International Journal of Electronic Commerce*, *1*(2), 59–88.

Jennex, M., & Olfman, L. (2005). Assessing Knowledge Management success. *International Journal of Knowledge Management*, *1*(2), 33–49. doi:10.4018/jkm.2005040104

Jeyaraj, A., Rottman, J. W., & Lacity, M. C. (2006). A review of the predictors, linkages, and biases in IT innovation adoption research. *Journal of Information Technology*, *21*(1), 1–23. doi:10.1057/palgrave.jit.2000056

Jih, W. J., Lee, S. F., & Fang, S. R. (2006). Investigating the impact of customer relationship management practices of e-commerce on online customers' website satisfaction: A model-building approach. *International Journal of E-Business Research*, *2*(4), 61–77. doi:10.4018/jebr.2006100104

Jih, W. J., Wong, S., & Chang, C. B. (2004). Effect of perceived risk on adoption of internet banking: An empirical investigation. *International Journal of Electronic Business Research*, *1*(1), 91–105.

Jimba, S. W. (2000). Information technology and the dialectics of poverty in Africa. *New Library World*, *101*(1158), 253–262. doi:10.1108/03074800010348714

Johnson, D. W., & Johnson, F. P. (1994). *Joining together: Group theory and group skills*. Boston, MA: Allyn and Bacon.

Johnston, A. C., & Hale, R. (2009). Improved security through information security governance. *Communications of the ACM*, *52*(1), 126–129. doi:10.1145/1435417.1435446

Joo, B. K. (2101). Organizational commitment for knowledge workers: The roles of perceived organizational learning culture, leader-member exchange quality, and turnover intention. *Human Resource Development Quarterly*, *21*(1), 69–85. doi:10.1002/hrdq.20031

Joseph, D., Ng, K. Y., Koh, C., & Ang, S. (2007). Turnover of information technology professionals: A narrative review, meta-analytic structural equation modelling, and model development. *Management Information Systems Quarterly*, *31*(3), 547–577.

Josephson, M. (2001). *Making ethical decisions*. Retrieved from http://www.josephsoninstitute.org/MED/medtoc.htm

Judge, T. A., & Bono, J. E. (2000). Five-Factor model of personality and transformational leadership. *The Journal of Applied Psychology*, *85*(5), 751–765. doi:10.1037/0021-9010.85.5.751

Judge, T. A., Bono, J. E., Ilies, R., & Gerhardt, M. W. (2002). Personality and leadership: A qualitative and quantitative review. *The Journal of Applied Psychology*, *87*(4), 765–780. doi:10.1037/0021-9010.87.4.765

Judge, T. A., Higgins, C. A., Thoresen, C. J., & Barrick, M. R. (1999). The Big Five personality traits, general mental ability and career success across the life span. *Personnel Psychology*, *52*(3), 621–652. doi:10.1111/j.1744-6570.1999.tb00174.x

Jurisch, M., Wolf, P., & Krcmar, H. (2010). Toward a Formal Approach to Process Bundling in Public Administrations. In M. Wimmer, J.-L. Chappelet, M. Janssen, & H. Scholl (Eds.), *Electronic Government* (LNCS 6228, pp. 412-423).

Kabadayi, S., & Gupta, R. (2005). Website loyalty: An empirical investigation of its antecedents. *International Journal of Internet Marketing and Advertising*, *2*(4), 321–345. doi:10.1504/IJIMA.2005.008105

Kairab, S. (2005). *A Practical Guide to Security Assessments*. Boca Raton, FL: Auerbach Publications.

Kandemir, D., Yaprak, A., & Cavusgil, S. T. (2006). Alliance Orientation: Conceptualization, Measurement, and Impact on Market Performance. *Journal of the Academy of Marketing Science, 34*(3), 324–340. doi:10.1177/0092070305285953

Kant, I. (1997). *Critique of Practical Reason* (Gregor, M., Trans.). Cambridge, UK: Cambridge University Press.

Karahanna, E., & Watson, R. T. (2006). Information systems leadership. *IEEE Transactions on Engineering Management, 53*(2), 171–176. doi:10.1109/TEM.2006.872247

Karmakar, U. S., & Apte, U. M. (2007). Operations Management in the Information Economy: Information Products, Processes and Chains. *Journal of Operations Management, 25*(2), 438–453. doi:10.1016/j.jom.2006.11.001

Katzenstein, G., & Lerch, F. J. (2000). Beneath the Surface of Organizational Processes: A Social Representation Framework for Business Process Redesign. *ACM Transactions on Information Systems, 18*(4), 383–422. doi:10.1145/358108.358111

Keegan, D. (2002). *The future of leaning: From elearning to m-learning.* Retrieved from http://learning.ericsson.net/mlearning2/project_one/book.html

Keegan, D. (1980). On defining distance education. *Distance Education, 1*(1), 13–56. doi:10.1080/0158791800010102

Keegan, D. (1996). *Foundations of distance education.* New York, NY: Routledge.

Kelly, K. (1999). *New rules for the new economy: 10 radical strategies for a connected world.* New York, NY: Penguin Books.

Kendall, K. E. (1997). The Significance of Information Systems Research on Emerging Technologies: Seven Information Technologies that Promise to Improve Managerial Effectiveness. *Decision Sciences, 28*(4), 775–792. doi:10.1111/j.1540-5915.1997.tb01331.x

Kennedy, A. (2006). Electronic customer relationship management (eCRM): Opportunities and challenges in a digital world. *Irish Marketing Review, 18*(1-2), 58–68.

Kenny, D. A., Kashy, D. A., & Bolger, N. (1998). Data analysis in social psychology. In Gilbert, D. T., Fiske, S., & Lindzey, G. (Eds.), *The handbook of social psychology* (pp. 233–265). New York, NY: McGraw-Hill.

Kent, J. L., & Mentzer, J. T. (2003). The Effect of Investment in Interorganizational Information Technology in a Retail Supply Chain. *Journal of Business Logistics, 24*(2), 155–176.

Kerlinger, F. N., & Lee, H. B. (2000). *Foundations of Behavioral Research* (4th ed.). Fort Worth, TX: Harcourt College Publishers.

Kettinger, W. J., Teng, J. T. C., & Guha, S. (1997). Business Process Change: A Study of Methodologies, Techniques, and Tools. *Management Information Systems Quarterly, 21*(1), 55–80. doi:10.2307/249742

Ke, W., Liu, H., Wei, K. K., Gu, J., & Chen, H. (2009). How Do Mediated and Non-mediated Power Affect Electronic Supply Chain Management System Adoption? The Mediating Effects of Trust and Institutional Pressures. *Decision Support Systems, 46*, 839–851. doi:10.1016/j.dss.2008.11.008

Khazanchi, D. (2005). Information Technology (IT) Appropriateness: The Contingency Theory of "FIT" and IT implementation in Small and Medium Enterprises. *Journal of CIS, 45*(3), 88–94.

Kim, S. M., & Mahoney, J. T. (2006). Mutual Commitment to Support Exchange: Relation-Specific IT System as a Substitute for Managerial Hierarchy. *Strategic Management Journal, 27*, 401–423. doi:10.1002/smj.527

Kincad, J. W. (2003). *Customer Relationship Management: Getting It Right!* Upper Saddle River, NJ: Prentice-Hall PTR.

Kitiyadisai, K. (2000). *The implementation of IT in reengineering the Thai Revenue Department, Information Flows, Local Improvisations and Work Practices.* Paper presented at the IFIPWG9.4 Conference, Cape Town, South Africa.

Kleijnen, M., Wetzels, M., & de Ruyter, K. (2004). Consumer acceptance of wireless finance. *Journal of Financial Services Marketing, 8*(3), 206–217. doi:10.1057/palgrave.fsm.4770120

Klesius, J. P., Homan, S., & Thompson, T. (1997). Distance education compared to traditional education: The students' view. *International Journal of Instructional Media, 24*, 207–222.

Klischewski, R. (2004). Information Integration or Process Integration? How to Achieve Interoperability in Administration. In R. Traunmüller (Ed.), *Electronic Government* (LNCS 3183, pp. 57-65).

Knight, R. (1988, April). Some choose a hardware DBMS. *Software Magazine*. Retrieved from http://findarticles.com/p/articles/mi_m0SMG/is_n5_v8/ai_6654621/

Kohavi, R. (2001, August). Mining e-commerce data: The good, the bad, and the ugly (invited industrial track talk). In F. Provost & R. Srikant (Eds.), *Proceedings of the 7th ACM SIGKDD International Conference on Knowledge Discovery and Data Mining*. Retrieved from http://robotics.Stanford.EDU/users/ronnyk/goodBadUglyKDDItrack.pdf

Kohavi, R., & Perkh, R. (2003). Ten supplementary analyses to improve e-commerce web sites. In *Proceedings of the 5th WEBKDD Workshop*, Washington, DC, (pp. 29–36).

Kohavi, R., Mason, L., Parekh, R., & Zheng, Z. (2004). Lessons and challenges from mining retail e-commerce data. *Machine Learning Journal*, *57*(1-2), 83–113. doi:10.1023/B:MACH.0000035473.11134.83

Kohavi, R., & Provost, F. (2001). Applications of datamining to electronic commerce. *Data Mining and Knowledge Discovery*, *5*(1-2), 115–153.

Kohli, A. K., & Jaworski, B. J. (1990). Market Orientation: The Construct, Research Propositions, and Managerial Implications. *Journal of Marketing*, *54*(2), 1–18. doi:10.2307/1251866

Konstantinou, A., Eilam, T., Kalantar, M., Totok, A., Arnold, W., & Snible, E. (2009). An architecture for virtual solution composition and deployment in infrastructure clouds. In *Proceedings of the 3rd International Workshop on Virtualization Technologies in Distributed Computing (VTDC'09)*, Barcelona, Spain (pp. 9-18).

Konsynski, B., & Tiwana, A. (2004). The Improvisation-Efficiency Paradox in Inter-Firm Electronic Networks: Governance and Architecture Considerations. *Journal of Information Technology*, *19*, 234–243. doi:10.1057/palgrave.jit.2000029

Korhonen, K., & Pirttilä, T. (2003). Cross-functional decision0making in improving inventory management decision procedures. *International Journal of Production Economics*, *81*, 195–203. doi:10.1016/S0925-5273(02)00286-4

Kossick, R. M. (2002). Mexico's emerging E-government program: The role of the Internet in promoting economic development, democratic governance and the Rule of the Law. *Law and Business Review of the Americas*, 141-187.

Kouba, Z., Matouseek, K., & Miksovsky, P. (2000). On data warehouse and GIS integration. In *Proceedings of DEXA 2000* (LNCS 1873, pp. 604–613).

Kovacich, G. L. (2003). *The Information Systems Security Officer's Guide: Establishing and Managing an Information Protection Program*. Woburn, MA: Butterworth-Heinemann.

Krcmar, H., Dold, G., Fischer, H., Strobel, M., & Seifert, E. (2000). *Informationssysteme für das Umweltmanagement - Das Referenzmodell ECO-Integral*. Munich, Germany: R. Oldenbourg Verlag.

Kuehn, A. (1962). Consumer brand choice as a learning process. *Journal of Advertising Research*, *2*, 10–17.

Kumar, C., Norris, J., & Sun, Y. (2009). Location and time do matter: A long tail study of website requests. *Decision Support Systems*, *47*(4), 500–507. doi:10.1016/j.dss.2009.04.015

Kyratzi, S. (2007). *Industrial-Product Concept Development: Geometric and Information Models for Interactive Design*. Unpublished doctoral dissertation, University of the Aegean, Greece.

Kyratzi, S., & Sapidis, N. (2008). An Interactive Sketching Method for 3D Object Modeling. In *Proceedings of the 3rd ACM Conference on Digital Interactive Media in Entertainment and Art (DIMEA'08)* (pp. 335-42). New York, NY: ACM.

Kyratzi, S., & Sapidis, N. (2009). Extracting a polyhedron from a single view sketch: Topological construction of a wireframe sketch with minimal hidden elements. *Computers & Graphics*, *33*(3), 270–279. doi:10.1016/j.cag.2009.03.001

Lacerda, D. P., Cassel, R. A., & Rodrigues, L. H. (2010). Service process analysis using process engineering and the theory of constraints thinking process. *Business Process Management Journal, 16*(2), 264–281. doi:10.1108/14637151011035598

LaFollette, H. (1997). Theorizing about Morality. In LaFollette, H. (Ed.), *Ethics in Practice: an Anthology* (pp. 3–10). Oxford, UK: Blackwell.

Lamb, D., & Bandopadhay, A. (1990). Interpreting a 3D Object from a Rough 2D Line Drawing. In *Proceedings of the 1st IEEE Conference on Visualization* (pp. 59-66). Los Alamitos, CA: IEEE Computer Society Press.

Lambert, D. M., Cooper, M. B., & Pagh, J. D. (1998). Supply Chain Management: Implementation Issues and Research Opportunities. *International Journal of Logistics Management, 9*(2), 1–19. doi:10.1108/09574099810805807

Lam, W., & Shankararaman, V. (2004). An Enterprise Integration Methodology. *IT Professional, 6*(2), 40–48. doi:10.1109/MITP.2004.1278864

Land, F., Amjad, U., & Nolas, S. (2004). *Knowledge management: The dark side of KM.* Paper presented at the ETHICOMP Conference.

Land, F., Amjad, U., & Nolas, S. (2007). The ethics of Knowledge Management. *Journal of Knowledge Management, 3*(1), 1–9. doi:10.4018/jkm.2007010101

Lau, T. W., Hui, C. L., Ng, S. F., & Moon, K. L. (2008). An implication of e-commerce in textile and clothing industries: A relational online analytical processing (OLAP) approach. *International Journal of Information Technology and Management, 7*(3), 231–243. doi:10.1504/IJITM.2008.017603

Layne, K., & Lee, J. (2001). Developing fully functional E-government: A four stage model. *Government Information Quarterly, 18*(2), 122–136. doi:10.1016/S0740-624X(01)00066-1

Lee, H. L., Padmanabhan, V., & Whang, S. (1997). Information Distortion in a Supply Chain: The Bullwhip Effect. *Management Science, 43*, 546–558. doi:10.1287/mnsc.43.4.546

Lee, H. L., So, K., & Tang, C. (2000). The Value of Information Sharing in a Two-Level Supply Chain. *Management Science, 46*(5), 626–643. doi:10.1287/mnsc.46.5.626.12047

Lee, I. (2004). Evaluating business process-integrated information technology investment. *Business Process Management Journal, 10*(2), 214–233. doi:10.1108/14637150410530271

Lee, J. (2005). Effects of leadership and leader-member exchange on commitment. *Leadership and Organization Development Journal, 26*(8), 655–672. doi:10.1108/01437730510633728

Lee, S. F., Jih, W. J., & Fang, S. R. (2006). Investigating the impact of customer relationship management practices of e-commerce on online customers' website satisfaction: A model-building approach. *International Journal of E-Business Research, 2*(4), 61–77. doi:10.4018/jebr.2006100104

Lester, C. (2000). *Building Wealth: The New Rules for Individuals, Companies, and Nations in a Knowledge-Based Economy.* New York, NY: Harper Business.

LeVeque, V. (2006). *Information Security: A Strategic Approach.* Hoboken, NJ: Wiley-Interscience.

Levine, E. L., & Flory, A. (1975). Evaluation of job applicants: A conceptual framework. *Public Personnel Management, 4*, 378–385.

Levin, J. (1999). Multiplicity in learning and teaching: A framework for developing innovative online education. *Journal of Research on Computing in Education, 32*(2), 256–270.

Levy, M., Powell, P., & Worrall, L. (2005). Strategic Intent and E-Business in SMEs: Enablers and Inhibitors. *Information Resources Management Journal, 18*(4), 1–20. doi:10.4018/irmj.2005100101

Liao, S., Shao, Y. P., Wang, H., & Chen, A. (1999). The adoption of virtual banking: an empirical study. *International Journal of Information Management, 19*(1), 63–74. doi:10.1016/S0268-4012(98)00047-4

Lichtman, J. (1998). Invoke employee loyalty. *Workforce, 77*, 121–122.

Liebermann, Y., & Stashevsky, S. (2002). Perceived risks as barriers to Internet and e-commerce usage. *Qualitative Market Research: An International Journal, 5*(4), 291–300. doi:10.1108/13522750210443245

Lim, H., Babu, S., Chase, J., & Parekh, S. (2008). Automated Control in Cloud Computing: Challenges and Opportunities. In *Proceedings of the 1st Workshop on Automated Control Datacenters and Clouds (ACSC'09)*, Barcelona, Spain (pp. 13-18).

Lim, K. S., & Razzaque, M. A. (1997). Brand loyalty and situational effects: An interactionist perspective. *Journal of International Consumer Marketing, 9*(4), 95–115. doi:10.1300/J046v09n04_06

Linstone, H., & Turoff, M. (1975). *The Delphi Method. Techniques and Applications*. Reading, MA: Addison-Wesley.

Lipson, H. (1998). *Computer Aided 3D Sketching for Conceptual Design*. Unpublished doctoral dissertation, Israel Institute of Technology, Israel.

Lipson, H., & Shpitalni, M. (1996). Optimization-Based Reconstruction of a 3D Object from a Single Freehand Line Drawing. *Computer Aided Design, 28*(8), 651–663. doi:10.1016/0010-4485(95)00081-X

Lipstein, B. (1959). The dynamics of brand loyalty and brand switching. In *Proceedings of the Fifth Annual Conference of the Advertising Research Foundation* (pp. 101-108). New York, NY: Advertising Research Foundation.

Littleton, K., & Whitelock, D. (2004). Guiding the creation of knowledge and understanding in a virtual learning environment. *Cyberpsychology & Behavior, 7*(2), 173–181. doi:10.1089/109493104323024438

Lo, E., Ben, K., Ho, W. S., Lee, S. D., Chui, C. K., & Cheung, D. W. (2008, June 10-12). OLAP on sequence data. In *Proceedings of the ACM SIGMOD International Conference on Management of Data*, Vancouver, BC, Canada.

Locke, E. A. (1976). The nature and causes of job satisfaction. In Dunnette, M. (Ed.), *Handbook of industrial and organizational psychology* (pp. 1297–1350). Chicago, IL: Rand McNally.

Lo, M. C., Ramayah, T., Min, H. W., & Songan, P. (2010). The relationship between leadership styles and organizational commitment in Malaysia: Role of leader-member exchange. *Asia Pacific Business Review, 16*(1), 79–103. doi:10.1080/13602380903355676

Lowry, P. B., Albrecht, C. C., & Nunamaker, J. F. (2003). Evolutionary development and research on Internet-based collaborative writing tools and processes to enhance e-Writing in an e-Government setting. *Decision Support Systems, 34*, 229–252. doi:10.1016/S0167-9236(02)00119-7

Luftman, J., & Brier, T. (1999). Achieving and sustaining business-IT alignment. *California Management Review, 42*(1), 109–122.

Lummus, R. R., Vokurka, R. J., & Alber, K. L. (1998). Strategic Supply Chain Planning. *Production and Inventory Management Journal, 39*(3), 49–58.

Lynes, J. A. (1980). Brunelleschi's perspectives reconsidered. *Perception, 9*, 87–99. doi:10.1068/p090087

MacMenamin, S. M., & Palmer, J. F. (1988). *Strukturierte Systemanalyse*. Munich, Germany: Hanser.

Magal, S., & Lewis, C. (1995). Determinants of Information Technology Success in Small Business. *Journal of CIS, 35*(3), 75–83.

Magnusson, P., Westjohn, S. A., & Boggs, D. J. (2009). Order-of-Entry Effects for Service Firms in Devleoping Markets: An Examination of Multinational Advertising Agencies. *Journal of International Marketing, 17*(2), 23–41. doi:10.1509/jimk.17.2.23

Mahajan, V., Muller, E., & Bass, F. M. (1990). New Product Diffusion in Marketing: A Review and Directions for Research. *Journal of Marketing, 54*, 1–26. doi:10.2307/1252170

Maiwald, E., & Sieglein, W. (2002). *Security Planning and Disaster Recovery*. Berkeley, CA: McGraw-Hill/Osborne.

Maleki, M., & Anand, D. (2008). Service Outsourcing: Information Technology. *SCMS Journal of Indian Management, 5*(3), 42–52.

Marchand, P., Brisebois, A., Bédard, Y., & Edwards, G. (2004). Implementation and evaluation of a hypercube-based method for spatio-temporal exploration and analysis. *ISPRS Journal of Photogrammetry and Remote Sensing, 59*(1-2), 6–20. doi:10.1016/j.isprsjprs.2003.12.002

Mason, R., Collins, C., & Cox, E. (1986). Four ethical issues of the Information Age. *Management Information Systems Quarterly*, 5–12. doi:10.2307/248873

Mathi, K. (2004). *Key Success Factors for Knowledge Management*. Unpublished master's thesis, University of Applied Sciences/FH Kempten.

Matthews, J., Garfinkel, T., Hoff, C., & Wheeler, J. (2009). Virtual machine Contracts for Datacenter and Cloud Computing Environments. In *Proceedings of the 1st Workshop on Automated Control for Datacenters and Clouds (ACDC'09),* Barcelona, Spain (pp. 23-30).

Matthew, S., Parmanto, B., & Monaco, V. (2007). Usability evaluation of the spatial OLAP visualization and analysis tool (SOVAT). *Journal of Usability Studies*, *2*(2), 76–95.

Mayer, R. J., Davis, J. H., & Schoorman, F. D. (1995). An integrative model of organizational trust. *Academy of Management Review*, *20*(3), 709–734.

Mayer, R., & Schoorman, D. (1992). Predicting participation and production outcomes through a two dimensional model of organizational commitment. *Academy of Management Journal*, *35*(3), 671–684. doi:10.2307/256492

McAllister, D. F. (Ed.). (1993). *Stereo computer graphics and other true 3D technologies*. Princeton, NJ: Princeton University Press.

McCann, J. E., & Gilmore, T. N. (1983). Diagnosing organizational decision making through responsibility charting. *Sloan Management Review*, *24*(2), 3–15.

McCrae, R. R. (1987). Creativity, divergent thinking, and openness to experience. *Journal of Personality and Social Psychology*, *52*(6), 1258–1265. doi:10.1037/0022-3514.52.6.1258

McCrae, R. R. (1996). Social consequences of experiential openness. *Psychological Bulletin*, *120*(3), 323–337. doi:10.1037/0033-2909.120.3.323

McCrae, R. R., & Costa, P. T. (1991). Adding liebe und arbeit: The full five-factor model and well-being. *Personality and Social Psychology Bulletin*, *17*(2), 227–232. doi:10.1177/014616729101700217

McDaniel, M. A., Schmidt, F. L., & Hunter, J. E. (1988). Job experience correlates of job performance. *The Journal of Applied Psychology*, *73*(2), 327–330. doi:10.1037/0021-9010.73.2.327

McFarlan, F. (1984). Information Technology Changes the Way You Compete. *Harvard Business Review*, *62*(3), 98–103.

McKeithen, K. B., Reitman, J. S., Rueter, H. H., & Hirtle, S. C. (1981). Knowledge organization and skill differences in computer programmers. *Cognitive Psychology*, *13*(3), 307–325. doi:10.1016/0010-0285(81)90012-8

McNaughton, D. (2002). An Unconnected Heap of Duties? In Stratton-Lake, P. (Ed.), *Ethical Intuitionism: Re-evaluations* (pp. 76–91). Oxford, UK: Clarendon Press.

Melenovsky, M. J. (2005). *Align roles and responsibilities to make BPM work(Rep. No. G00127680)*. Stamford, CT: Gartner Research.

Melenovsky, M. J., & Hill, J. B. (2006). *Role definition and organizational structure: Business Process Improvement (Rep. No. G00141487)*. Stamford, CT: Gartner Research.

Mell, P., & Grance, T. (2009). *The NIST Definition of Cloud Computing*. Retrieved April 12, 2010, from http://csrc.nist.gov/groups/SNS/cloud-computing/cloud-def-v15.doc

Melville, N., Kraemer, K., & Gurbaxani, V. (2004). Review: Information Technology and Organizational Performance: An Integrative Model of IT Business Value. *Management Information Systems Quarterly*, *28*(2), 283–322.

Messick, S. (1980). Test validity and the ethics of assessment. *The American Psychologist*, *35*(11), 1012–1027. doi:10.1037/0003-066X.35.11.1012

Meyer, J. P., & Allen, N. J. (1997). *Commitment in the workplace: Theory research and application*. Thousand Oaks, CA: Sage.

Meyer, J. P., Allen, N. J., & Smith, C. A. (1993). Commitment to organizations and occupations: Extension and test of a three-component conceptualization. *The Journal of Applied Psychology*, *78*(4), 538–551. doi:10.1037/0021-9010.78.4.538

Meyer, J. P., Stanley, D. J., Herscovitch, L., & Topolnytsky, L. (2002). Affective, continuance, and normative commitment to the organization: A meta-analysis of antecedents, correlates, and consequences. *Journal of Vocational Behavior*, *61*(1), 20–52. doi:10.1006/jvbe.2001.1842

Migdadi, Y. K. A. (2008). Quantitative Evaluation of the Internet Banking Service Encounter's Quality: Comparative Study between Jordan and the UK Retail Banks. *Journal of Internet Banking and Commerce*, *13*(2), 1–8.

Miller, D., & Hazel, G. (2007). *Megacity Challenges: A stakeholder perspective.* Retrieved November 21, 2010, from http://www.siemens.com/press/pool/en/events/megacities/media_mrc_globe_170107_d_1431329.pdf

Miller, D., & Dröge, C. (1986). Psychological and traditional determinants of structure. *Administrative Science Quarterly*, *31*(4), 539–560. doi:10.2307/2392963

Min, H. (2009). Application of a Decision Support System to Strategic Warehousing decisions. *International Journal of Physical Distribution & Logistics Management*, *39*(4), 270–281. doi:10.1108/09600030910962230

Min, S., Song, S., & Keebler, J. S. (2002). An Internet-mediated market orientation (IMO): Building a theory. *Journal of Marketing Theory and Practice*, *10*(2), 1–11.

Mircea, M., & Andreescu, A. (2009). Using Business rules in business intelligence. *Journal of Applied Quantitative Methods*, *4*(3), 382–393.

Mishra, S. (2009). GIS in Indian retail industry-a strategic tool. *International Journal of Marketing Studies*, *1*(1), 50–57.

Mitnick, K., & Simon, W. (2002). *The Art of Deception: Controlling the Human Element of Security*. New York, NY: John Wiley & Sons.

Mokhtarian, P. L. (2004). A conceptual analysis of the transportation impacts of B2C e-Commerce. *Transportation Journal*, *31*(3), 257–284. doi:10.1023/B:PORT.0000025428.64128.d3

Monash, K. (2007). *Are row-oriented RDBMS obsolete?* Retrieved from http://www.dbms2.com/category/michael-stonebraker/

Monash, K. (2008). *Oracle Database Machine and Exadata pricing*. Retrieved from http://www.monash.com/uploads/Oracle-Exadata-pricing-estimates-Sep-30-2008.xls

Monroe, K. B., & Guiltinan, J. P. (1975). A path-analytic exploration of retail patronage influences. *The Journal of Consumer Research*, *2*, 19–28. doi:10.1086/208612

Moon, J., & Kim, W. Y. G. (2001). Extending the TAM for World Wide Web Context. *Information & Management*, *38*(4), 217–230. doi:10.1016/S0378-7206(00)00061-6

Moore, G. C., & Benbasat, I. (1991). Development of an Instrument to Measure the Perceptions of Adopting an Information Technology Innovation. *Information Systems Research*, *2*(3), 192–223. doi:10.1287/isre.2.3.192

Moore, J. E., & Love, M. S. (2005). IT professionals as organizational citizens. *Communications of the ACM*, *48*(6), 88–93. doi:10.1145/1064830.1064832

Moorhouse, J. R. (2002). *Desired characteristics of ethical leaders in business, educational, political, and religious organizations from East Tennessee: A Delphi investigation*. Johnson City, TN: East Tennessee State University.

Morris, M. G., & Venkatesh, V. (2000). Age differences in technology adoption decisions: Implications for a changing work force. *Personnel Psychology*, *53*(2), 375–403. doi:10.1111/j.1744-6570.2000.tb00206.x

Mount, M. K., & Barrick, M. R. (1995). The big five personality dimensions: Implications for research and practices in human resource management. In Ferris, G. (Ed.), *Research in personnel and human resources management* (*Vol. 13*, pp. 153–200). Greenwich, CT: JAI Press.

Mount, M. K., Barrick, M. R., & Strauss, J. P. (1994). Validity of observer ratings of the Big Five personality factors. *The Journal of Applied Psychology*, *79*(2), 272–280. doi:10.1037/0021-9010.79.2.272

Mukhopadhyay, T., & Kekre, S. (2002). Strategic and Operational Benefits of Electronic Integration in B2B Procurement Processes. *Management Science*, *48*(10), 1301–1313. doi:10.1287/mnsc.48.10.1301.273

Murray, A. T., O'Kelly, M. E., & Church, R. L. (2008). Regional service coverage modeling. *Computers & Operations Research*, *35*(2), 339–355. doi:10.1016/j.cor.2006.03.004

Mwenda, K. K., & Muuka, G. N. (2004). Towards best practices for micro finance institutional engagement in African rural areas; selected cases and agenda for action. *International Journal of Social Economics*, *31*(1-2), 143–158. doi:10.1108/03068290410515475

Nehmzow, C. (1997). The Internet Will Shake Banking's Medieval Foundations. *Journal of Internet Banking and Commerce, 2*.

Nejati, M. (2010). Knowledge Management Performance Evaluation: Challenges and Requirements for Organizations. *Technics Technologies Education Management*, *5*(1), 251–254.

Nejati, M., Md Shahbudin, A. S., & Amran, A. (2010). Sustainable development: a competitive advantage or a threat? *Business Strategy Series*, *11*(2), 84–89. doi:10.1108/17515631011026407

Nelson, M. (2009). The Cloud, The Crowd, and Public Policy. *Issues in Science and Technology*, *25*(4), 96–106.

Netchaeva, I. (2002). E-government and e-democracy: A comparison of opportunities in the North and South. *Gazette*, *64*(5), 467–477. doi:10.1177/17480485020640050601

Neufeld, D. J., Dong, L., & Higgins, C. (2007). Charismatic leadership and user acceptance of information technology. *European Journal of Information Systems*, *16*(4), 494–510. doi:10.1057/palgrave.ejis.3000682

Newcastle City Council. (2006). *Newcastle in 2021- A Regeneration Strategy for Newcastle*. Retrieved November 21, 2010, from http://www.newcastle.gov.uk/wwwfileroot/regen/ppi/RegenStrategyFinalDoc.pdf

Newman, J. W., & Werbel, R. A. (1973). Multivariate analysis of brand loyalty for major household appliances. *JMR, Journal of Marketing Research*, *10*(4), 404–409. doi:10.2307/3149388

Ngai, E. W. T. (2005). Customer relationship management research (1992-2002): An academic literature and classification. *Marketing Intelligence & Planning*, *23*(6-7), 582–605. doi:10.1108/02634500510624147

Nijsen, A. (2009). SCM to Measure Compliance Costs. In *Business Regulation and Public Policy* (*Vol. 20*, pp. 1–22). New York, NY: Springer. doi:10.1007/978-0-387-77678-1_5

Nolan, R., & McFarlan, F. (2005). Information Technology and the Board of Directors. *Harvard Business Review*, *83*(10), 96–106.

Nolle, T. (2009). *Identifying Applications for Public and Private Clouds*. Retrieved April 14, 2010, from http://searchcloudcomputing.techtarget.com/tip/0,289483,sid201_gci1358701,00.html?track=NL-1329&ad=710605&asrc=EM_NLT_7835341&uid=8788654

Nooteboom, B. (1992). Information Technology, Transaction Costs and the Decision to 'Make or Buy'. *Technology Analysis and Strategic Management*, *4*(4), 339–350. doi:10.1080/09537329208524105

Norman, D. (2004). Supply Chain Analytics Can Drive Financial Performance. *Frontline Solutions*, *5*(1), 25–25.

North, K. (2009). *The Many Flavors of Platform Services for Cloud Computing*. Retrieved April 14, 2010, from http://www.drdobbs.com/windows/220300737

Nunes, M. B., Annansingh, F., Eaglestone, B., & Wakefield, R. (2006). Knowledge management issues in knowledge-intensive SMEs. *The Journal of Documentation*, *62*(1), 101–119. doi:10.1108/00220410610642075

Nunnally, J. (1978). *Psychometric Theory*. New York, NY: McGraw-Hill.

Okoli, C., & Pawlowski, S. D. (2004). The Delphi method as a research tool: an example, design considerations and applications. *Journal of International Management*, *42*, 15–29.

Okoshi, T. (1976). *Three-dimensional imaging techniques*. New York, NY: Academic Press.

O'Neill, P., & Sohal, A. S. (1999). Business Process Reengineering. A review of recent literature. *Technovation*, *19*(9), 571–581. doi:10.1016/S0166-4972(99)00059-0

Open Cloud. (2010). *Open Cloud Manifesto*. Retrieved April 12, 2010, from http://opencloudmanifesto.org/Cloud_Computing_Use_Cases_Whitepaper-3_0.pdf

Organ, D. W. (1998). *Organizational citizenship behavior: The good soldier syndrome*. Lexington, MA: Lexington Books.

Osborne, M. (2006). *How to Cheat at Managing Information Security*. Rockland, MA: Syngress Publishing.

O'Sullivan, D., & Unwin, D. J. (2002). *Geographic Information Analysis*. Hoboken, NJ: John Wiley & Sons.

Paim, R., Caulliraux, H. M., & Cardoso, R. (2008). Process management tasks: a conceptual and practical view. *Business Process Management Journal*, *14*(5), 694–723. doi:10.1108/14637150810903066

Palankar, M., Iamnitchi, A., Ripeanu, M., & Garfinkel, S. (2008). Amazon S3 for science Grids: A viable soulution? In *Proceedings of the International Workshop on Data-aware Distributed Computing (DADC'08)*, New York, NY (pp. 55-64).

Paliwoda, S. J. (1983). Predicting the future using Delphi. *Management Decision*, *21*(1), 31–38. doi:10.1108/eb001309

Palvia, P. (1996). A model and instrument for measuring small business user satisfaction with information technology. *Information & Management*, *31*(3), 151–163. doi:10.1016/S0378-7206(96)01069-5

Paré, G., & Elam, J. J. (1995). Discretionary use of personal computers by knowledge workers: testing of a social psychological theoretical model. *Behaviour & Information Technology*, *14*(4), 215–228. doi:10.1080/01449299508914635

Parsons, G. L. (1983). *Fitting Information Systems Technology to the Corporate Needs: The Linking Strategy*. Boston, MA: HBS Case Services.

Parsons, G. L. (1983). Information technology: a new competitive weapon. *Sloan Management Review*, *25*(1), 3–14.

Parvatiyar, A., & Sheth, J. N. (2001). Customer relationship management: Emerging practice, process, and discipline. *Journal of Economic & Social Research*, *3*(2), 1–34.

Pavlou, P. A. (2003). Consumer acceptance of electronic commerce: Integrating trust and risk with the technology acceptance model. *International Journal of Electronic Commerce*, *7*(3), 101–131.

Pearlman, K., Schmidt, F. L., & Hunter, J. E. (1980). Validity generalization results for tests used to predict job proficiency and training criteria in clerical positions. *The Journal of Applied Psychology*, *65*(4), 373–407. doi:10.1037/0021-9010.65.4.373

Pearson, S. (2009). Taking account of privacy when designing cloud computing services. In *Proceedings of the 2009 ICSE Workshop on Software Engineering Challenges of Cloud Computing*, Vancouver, BC (pp. 44-52).

Peltier, J., Schibrowsky, J., & Zhao, Y. (2009). Understanding the Antecedents to the Adoption of CRM Technology by Small Retailers. *International Small Business Journal*, *27*(3), 307–336. doi:10.1177/0266242609102276

Peltier, T. (2006). Social Engineering: Concepts and Solutions. *Information System Security*, *15*(5), 13–21. doi:10.1201/1086.1065898X/46353.15.4.20060901/95427.3

Peltier, T. R. (2004). *Information Security Policies and Procedures: A Practitioner's Reference* (2nd ed.). Boca Raton, FL: Auerbach Publications. doi:10.1201/9780203488737

Peppard, J. (2000). Customer Relationship Management (CRM) in financial services. *European Management Journal*, *18*(3), 312–326. doi:10.1016/S0263-2373(00)00013-X

Peters, R., Jansen, M., & Engers, T. (2004). Measuring e-government impact: existing practices. In *Proceedings of the Sixth International Conference on Electronic Commerce*, Delft, The Netherlands (pp. 480-488).

Peterson, A. H. (2001). Customer Relationship Management. *Credit Union Magazine*, *67*(7), 4a–6a.

Peterson, R. A. (2000). *Constructing effective questionnaires*. Thousand Oaks, CA: Sage.

Petty, R. E., Brinol, P., & Tormala, Z. L. (2002). Thought Confidence as a Determinant of Persuasion: The Self-Validation Hypothesis. *Journal of Personality and Social Psychology*, *82*(5), 722–741. doi:10.1037/0022-3514.82.5.722

Phan, D. D. (2003). E-business development for competitive advantages: A case study. *Information & Management*, *40*(6), 581–590. doi:10.1016/S0378-7206(02)00089-7

Phang, C. W., Li, Y., Sutanto, J., & Kankanhalli, A. (2005). Senior citizens' adoption of Egovernment: In quest of the antecedents of perceived usefulness. In *Proceedings of the 38th Hawaii International Conference on System Science* (pp. 1-8).

Phil, B. (1997). Pennsylvania Professor Touts Personnel Investment. *America's Community Banker*, *6*(8).

Pinsonneault, A., & Kraemer, K. L. (2002). Exploring the Role of Information Technology in Organizational Downsizing: A Tale of Two American Cities. *Organization Science*, *13*(2), 191–208. doi:10.1287/orsc.13.2.191.537

Podsakoff, P. M., & MacKenzie, S. B. (1997). Impact of organizational citizenship behavior on organizational performance: A review and suggestion for future research. *Human Performance,10*(2), 133-151.

Podsakoff, P. M., MacKenzie, S. B., Lee, J. Y., & Podsakoff, N. P. (2003). Common method biases in behavioral research: A critical review of the literature and recommended remedies. *The Journal of Applied Psychology, 88*(5), 879–903. doi:10.1037/0021-9010.88.5.879

Podsakoff, P., MacKenzie, S., Paine, J., & Bachrach, D. (2000). Organizational citizenship behaviors: a critical review of the theoretical and empirical literature and suggestions for future research. *Journal of Management, 26*(3), 513–563. doi:10.1177/014920630002600307

Ponzurick, T., France, K., & Logar, C. (2000). Delivering graduate marketing education: An analysis of face-to-face versus distance education. *Journal of Marketing Education, 22*, 180–187. doi:10.1177/0273475300223002

Poore, R. S. (2007). Information security governance. In Tipton, H. F., & Krause, M. (Eds.), *Information Security Management Handbook* (pp. 89–94). Boca Raton, FL: Auerbach Publications. doi:10.1201/9781439833032.ch8

Pope, J. (2000). *Transparency International Sourcebook 2000: Confronting Corruption, The Elements of a National Integrity System* (3rd ed.). Berlin, Germany: Transparency International.

Porter, M. E., & Millar, V. E. (1985). How Information Gives You Competitive Advantage. *Harvard Business Review*, 149–174.

Pourezzat, A. A., Nejati, M., & Nejati, M. (2008). E-Government and Empowerment: Impacts on Equal Access to Information and Developing Public Language. *Lex et Scientia, 15*(1), 123–127.

Prasad, B., & Harker, P. T. (1997). *Examining the Contribution of Information Technology Toward Productivity and Profitability in U.S. Retail Banking (No. 97-09)*. Philadelphia: The Wharton School, University of Pennsylvania.

Premkumar, G. (2003). A Meta-Analysis of Research on Information Technology Implementation in Small Business. *Journal of Organizational Computing and Electronic Commerce, 13*(2), 91–121. doi:10.1207/S15327744JOCE1302_2

Premkumar, G., Ramamurthy, K., & Saunders, C. S. (2005). Information Processing View of Organizations: An Exploratory Examination of Fit in the Context of Interorganizational Relationships. *Journal of Management Information Systems, 22*(1), 257–294.

PricewaterhouseCoopers. (2005). *Cities of the Future.* Retrieved November 21, 2010, from http://www.pwc.com/en_GX/gx/government-public-sector-research/pdf/cities-final.pdf

Pucel, D. J., & Stertz, T. F. (2005). Effectiveness of and student satisfaction with web-based compared to traditional in-service teacher education courses. *Journal of Industrial Teacher Education, 42*(1), 7–23.

Quin, J., Anderson, P., & Finkelstien, S. (1996). Managing professional intellect: Making the most of the best. *Harvard Business Review*, 71–80.

Ragowsky, A., & Geffen, D. (2008). What makes the competitive contribution of ERP strategic. *Database, 39*(2), 33–49.

Rai, A., Patnayakuni, R., & Seth, N. (2006). Firm Performance Impacts of Digitally Enabled Supply Chain Integration Capabilities. *Management Information Systems Quarterly, 30*(2), 225–246.

Ramsey, M. (2010, October 17). Bumpy Road for Electrics. *The Wall Street Journal*. Retrieved November 21, 2010, from http://online.wsj.com/article/SB10001424052748704654004575517891616896222.html

Randall, D. M., Fedor, D. B., & Longenecker, C. O. (1990). The behavioral expression of organizational commitment. *Journal of Vocational Behavior, 36*(2), 210–224. doi:10.1016/0001-8791(90)90028-Z

Ranganathan, C., Seo, D., & Babad, Y. (2006). Switching behavior of mbile users: do users' relational investments and demographics matter? *European Journal of Information Systems, 15*(3), 269–276. doi:10.1057/palgrave.ejis.3000616

Ranjan, J. (2009). Business intelligence: Concepts, components, techniques and benefits. *Journal of Theoretical and Applied Information Technology, 9*(1), 60–70.

Ravesteyn, P., Batenburg, R., & deWaal, B. (2008). In search of competencies needed in BPM projects. *Communications of the IIMA, 8*(2), 23–30.

Regan, P. (2003). Safe Harbors or Free Frontiers? Privacy and Transborder Data Flows. *The Journal of Social Issues*, *59*(2), 263–282. doi:10.1111/1540-4560.00064

Reid, M. F., Allen, M. W., Riemenschneider, C. K., & Armstrong, D. J. (2008). The role of mentoring and supervisor support for state IT employees' affective organizational commitment. *Review of Public Personnel Administration*, *28*(1), 60–78. doi:10.1177/0734371X07311703

Rellermeyer, J., Duller, M., & Alonso, G. (2009). Engineering the cloud from software modules. In *Proceedings of the 2009 ICSE Workshop on Software Engineering Challenges of Cloud Computing*, Vancouver, BC.

Reuter, R. (2009). Online versus in the classroom: Student success in a hands-on lab class. *American Journal of Distance Education*, *23*(3), 151–162. doi:10.1080/08923640903080620

Reynolds, F. D., & Darden, W. R. (1974). *Constructing Life Style and Psychograghics*. Chicago, IL: AMA.

Reynolds, F. D., Darden, W. R., & Martin, W. (1974). Developing an image of the store-loyal customer. *Journal of Retailing*, *50*(4), 73–84.

Rhee, K. Y., & Kim, W. B. (2004). The adoption and use of the Internet in South Korea. *Journal of Computer-Mediated Communication, 9*(4). Retrieved December 2, 2010, from http://jcmc.indiana.edu/vol9/issue4/rhee.html

Richardson, R. (2008). *CSI Computer Crime and Security Survey*. San Francisco: Computer Security Institute.

Riemenschneider, C., & Mykytyn, P. (2000). What small business executives have learned about managing information technology. *Information & Management*, *37*(5), 257–269. doi:10.1016/S0378-7206(99)00052-X

Riquelme, H., & Kam, B. H. (2007). Online Converstion Rates Among Australian Financial Institutions: A Qualitative Exploration. *Jouranl of Financial Services Marketing*, *11*(4), 290–300. doi:10.1057/palgrave.fsm.4760047

Ristenpart, T., Tromer, E., Shacham, H., & Savage, S. (2009). Exploring Information Leakage in Third Party Clouds. In *Proceedings of the CCS '09 Conference*, Chicago, IL.

Ritter, C., Polnick, B., Fink, R., & Oescher, J. (2010). Classroom learning communities in educational leadership: A comparison study of three delivery options. *The Internet and Higher Education*, *13*(1-2), 96–100. doi:10.1016/j.iheduc.2009.11.005

Rivest, S., Bédard, Y., & Marchand, P. (2001). Toward better support for spatial decision making: Defining the characteristics of spatial on-line analytical processing (SOLAP). *Geomatica*, *55*(4), 539–555.

Rivest, S., Bédard, Y., Proulx, M.-J., Nadeau, M., Hubert, F., & Pastor, J. (2005). SOLAP technology: Merging business intelligence with geospatial technology for interactive spatio-temporal exploration and analysis of data. *ISPRS Journal of Photogrammetry and Remote Sensing*, *60*(1), 17–33. doi:10.1016/j.isprsjprs.2005.10.002

Robinia, K., & Anderson, M. (2010). Online teaching efficacy of nurse faculty. *Journal of Professional Nursing*, *26*(3), 168–175. doi:10.1016/j.profnurs.2010.02.006

Robinson, H. S., Anumba, C. J., Carrillo, P. M., & Al-Ghassani, A. M. (2006). STEPS: a knowledge management maturity roadmap for corporate sustainability. *Business Process Management Journal*, *12*(6), 793–808. doi:10.1108/14637150610710936

Rockart, J. (1979). Chief executives define their own information needs. *Harvard Business Review*, 81–92.

Rodenhagen, J., Diekhans, B., & Rieckmann, P. (2009). Prozessmanagement im Kontext des E-Government 2.0 - Einsatzfelder, Rahmenbedingungen, und aktuelle Maßnahmen. *Praxis der Wirtschaftsinformatik*, *265*(265), 36–50.

Rogers, E. M. (1995). *Diffusion of innovations*. New York, NY: Free Press.

Rosemann, M., & deBruin, T. (2005). Application of the holistic model for determining BP maturity. *BP Trends*, 1-21.

Rosemann, M., deBruin, T., & Power, B. (2006). BPM Maturity. In Jeston, J., & Nelis, J. (Eds.), *Business Process Management: Practical guidelines to successful implementation* (pp. 299–315). Amsterdam, The Netherlands: Elsevier.

Rosen, G. (2010). The business of Clouds. *Crossroads, 16*(3), 26–28. doi:10.1145/1734160.1734169

Rosenzweig, E. D. (2009). A Contingent View of E-collaboration and Performance in Manufacturing. *Journal of Operations Management, 27*, 462–478. doi:10.1016/j.jom.2009.03.001

Ros, L., & Thomas, F. (2005). Geometric Methods for Shape Recovery from Line Drawings of Polyhedra. *Journal of Mathematical Imaging and Vision, 22*(1), 5–18. doi:10.1007/s10851-005-4779-4

Ross, D. (2005). E-CRM from a study chain management perspective. *Information Systems Management, 22*(1), 37–44. doi:10.1201/1078/44912.22.1.20051201/85737.5

Ross, D. T., & Schoman, K. E. Jr. (1977). Structured analysis for requirements definition. *IEEE Transactions on Software Engineering, 3*(1), 6–15. doi:10.1109/TSE.1977.229899

Rowley, J. (2011). e-Government stakeholders—Who are they and what do they want? *International Journal of Information Management, 31*(1), 53–62. doi:10.1016/j.ijinfomgt.2010.05.005

Ruggles, R. (1998). The state of the notion: knowledge management in practice. *California Management Review, 40*(3), 80–89.

Rusch, J. (1999). *The Social Engineering of Internet Fraud.* Paper presented at the INET'99 Conference, San Jose, CA.

Saeed, K. A., Malhotra, M. K., & Grover, V. (2005). Examining the Impact of Interorganizational Systems on Process Efficiency and Sourcing Leverage in Buyer—Supplier Dyads. *Decision Sciences, 36*(3), 365–396. doi:10.1111/j.1540-5414.2005.00077.x

Salam, I., Mohajer, M., Talleb, A., & Mohajer, B. (2008). Development of SOLAP patrimony management application system: Fez medina as a case study. *International Journal of Computer Science and Applications, 5*(3a), 57–66.

Sambamurthy, V., Bharadwaj, A., & Grover, V. (2003). Shaping Agility Through Digital Options: Reconceptualizing the role of Information Technology in Contemporary Firms. *Management Information Systems Quarterly, 27*(2), 237–263.

Sambamurthy, V., & Zmud, R. W. (2000). The organizing logic for an enterprise's IT activities in the digital era - A prognosis of practice and a call for research. *Information Systems Research, 11*(2), 105–114. doi:10.1287/isre.11.2.105.11780

Sanders, N. R. (2007). An Empirical Study of the Impact of E-Business Technologies on Organizational Collaboration and Performance. *Journal of Operations Management, 25*, 1332–1347. doi:10.1016/j.jom.2007.01.008

Sapidis, N., Kyratzi, S., & Azariadis, F. (2005). Improved Computational Tools for Concept Development Based on Sketches and Advanced CAD Technologies. *Computer-Aided Design and Applications, 2*(6), 707–716.

Sarantis, D., Charalabidis, Y., & Askounis, D. (2011). A goal-driven management framework for electronic government transformation projects implementation. *Government Information Quarterly, 28*(1), 117–128. doi:10.1016/j.giq.2009.10.006

Saraph, J. V., Benson, P. G., & Schroeder, R. G. (1989). An instrument for measuring the critical factors of quality management. *Decision Sciences, 20*, 810–829. doi:10.1111/j.1540-5915.1989.tb01421.x

Scandura, T. A., & Graen, G. B. (1984). Moderating effects of initial leader-member exchange status on the effects of a leadership intervention. *The Journal of Applied Psychology, 69*(3), 428–436. doi:10.1037/0021-9010.69.3.428

Scheer, A.-W., Nüttgens, M., & Zimmermann, V. (Eds.). (1996). *Business Process Reengineering in der Verwaltung*. Wiesbaden, Germany: Gabler.

Schell, G. P. (2004). Universities marginalize online courses. *Communications of the ACM, 47*(7), 53–56. doi:10.1145/1005817.1005821

Schmidt, F. L. (2002). The role of general cognitive ability and job performance: Why there can be no debate. *Human Performance, 15*(1), 187–210. doi:10.1207/S15327043HUP1501&02_12

Schmidt, F. L., & Hunter, J. E. (1998). The validity and utility of selection methods in personnel psychology: Practical and theoretical implications of 85 years of research findings. *Psychological Bulletin, 124*(2), 262–274. doi:10.1037/0033-2909.124.2.262

Schmidt, F. L., & Hunter, J. E. (2004). General mental ability in the world of work: Occupational attainment and job performance. *Journal of Personality and Social Psychology, 86*(1), 162–173. doi:10.1037/0022-3514.86.1.162

Schmidt, F. L., Hunter, J. E., & Outerbridge, A. N. (1986). Impact of job experience and ability on job knowledge, work sample performance, and supervisory ratings of performance. *The Journal of Applied Psychology, 71*(3), 432–439. doi:10.1037/0021-9010.71.3.432

Schmidt, F. L., Hunter, J. E., Outerbridge, A. N., & Goff, S. (1988). Joint relation of experience and ability with job performance: Test of three hypotheses. *The Journal of Applied Psychology, 73*(1), 46–57. doi:10.1037/0021-9010.73.1.46

Schumacher, M., Fernandez-Buglioni, E., Hybertson, D., Buschmann, F., & Sommerlad, P. (2006). *Security Patterns*. Chichester, UK: John Wiley & Sons.

Schwabe, G., & Krcmar, H. (1996). Der Needs Driven Approach - eine Methode zur Gestaltung von Telekooperation. In Schwabe, G., Krcmar, H., & Lewe, H. (Eds.), *Herausforderung Telekooperation*. Berlin, Germany: Springer.

Schwartz, E. (2007). *Salesforce.com launches SaaS platform*. Retrieved from http://www.infoworld.com/t/architecture/salesforcecom-launches-saas-platform-724

Schwartz, E. (2008). The dangers of cloud computing. *Network World Asia, 4*(7), 10–12.

Schwartz, M. (2007). The Business ethics of management theory. *Journal of Management History, 13*(1), 43–54. doi:10.1108/17511340710715160

Schwarz, J. P., & Hoffmann, S. (2009). *Behörden und Unternehmen entlasten - Bürokratiekosten senken*. Retrieved February 11, 2010, from http://www.egovernment-computing.de/index.cfm?pid=7476&pk=202981&print=true&printtype=article

Schwarz, A. J., & Blundell, B. G. (1993). Considerations regarding voxel brightness in volumetric displays utilizing two-step excitation processes. *Optical Engineering (Redondo Beach, Calif.), 32*(11), 2818–2823. doi:10.1117/12.148130

Schwarz, A. J., & Blundell, B. G. (1997). Optimising dot-graphics for volumetric displays. *IEEE Transactions on Computer Graphics and Applications, 17*(3), 72–78. doi:10.1109/38.586020

Schweikardt, E., & Gross, M. D. (2000). Digital clay: deriving digital models from freehand sketches. *Automation in Construction, 9*(1), 107–115. doi:10.1016/S0926-5805(99)00052-7

Scotch, M., & Parmanto, B. (2005, January 3-6). SOVAT: Spatial OLAP visualization and analysis tool. In *Proceedings of the 38th Hawaii International Conference on System Sciences (HICSS-38)* (p. 142b).

Scotch, M., Parmanto, B., & Monaco, V. (2007). Usability evaluation of the spatial OLAP visualization and analysis tool (SOVAT). *Journal of Usability Studies, 2*(2), 76–95.

Scullin, S. S., Fjermestad, J., & Romano, N. C. Jr. (2004). E-relationship marketing: changes in traditional marketing as an outcome of electronic customer relationship management. *Journal of Enterprise Information Systems, 17*(6), 410–415.

Seers, A., & Graen, G. B. (1984). The dual attachment concept: A longitudinal investigation of the combination of task characteristics and leader-member exchange. *Organizational Behavior and Human Performance, 33*(3), 283–306. doi:10.1016/0030-5073(84)90025-4

Settoon, R. P., Bennett, N., & Liden, R. C. (1996). Social exchange in organizations: Perceived organizational support, leader-member exchange, and employee reciprocity. *The Journal of Applied Psychology, 81*(3), 219–227. doi:10.1037/0021-9010.81.3.219

Shahidehpour, M., Yamin, H., & Li, Z. (2002). *Market Operations in Electric Power Systems*. New York, NY: John Wiley & Sons. doi:10.1002/047122412X

Shani, D., & Chalasani, S. (1992). Exploiting niches using relationship marketing. *Journal of Consumer Marketing, 9*(3), 33–42. doi:10.1108/07363769210035215

Shanteau, J. (1992). Competence in experts: The role of task characteristics. *Organizational Behavior and Human Decision Processes, 53*(2), 252–266. doi:10.1016/0749-5978(92)90064-E

Shanteau, J. (1992). How much information does an expert use? Is it relevant? *Acta Psychologica*, *81*(1), 75–86. doi:10.1016/0001-6918(92)90012-3

Sharafi, A., Wolf, P., & Krcmar, H. (2010). Process and Data-Oriented Approach for Bundling Corporate Reporting Duties to Public Authorities – A Case Study on the Example of Waste Management Reporting. In M. Wimmer, J.-L. Chappelet, M. Janssen, & H. Scholl (Eds.), *Electronic Government* (LNCS 6228, pp. 400-411).

Shekhar, S., Lu, C. T., Tan, X., Chawla, S., & Vatsavai, R. (2001). Map cube: A visualization tool for spatial data warehouses. In Miller, H. J., & Han, J. (Eds.), *Geographic Data Mining and Knowledge Discovery* (pp. 74–109). London, UK: Taylor & Francis. doi:10.4324/9780203468029_chapter_4

Shin, N. (2006). The Impact of Information Technology on the Financial Performance of Diversified Firms. *Decision Support Systems*, *41*, 698–707. doi:10.1016/j.dss.2004.10.003

Shukla, A., Sharma, N., & Swami, S. (2010). Website characteristics, user characteristics and purchase intention: Mediating role of website satisfaction. *International Journal of Internet Marketing and Advertising*, *6*(2), 142–167. doi:10.1504/IJIMA.2010.032479

Siemens. (2009). *Sustainable Urban Infrastructure; Munich Edition – paths toward a carbon-free future*. Retrieved November 30, 2010, from http://www.mobility.siemens.com/shared/data/pdf/www/corporate/sustainable_munich_2009_e.pdf

Silva, J., Times, V., Fidalgo, R., & Barros, R. (2005). Providing geographic-multidimensional decision support over the Web. In *APWeb 2005: Proceedings of the 7th Asia-Pacific Web Conference* (LNCS 3399, pp. 477–488).

Simmons, G., Armstrong, G., & Durkin, M. (2008). A Conceptualization of the Determinants of Small Business Website Adoption. *International Small Business Journal*, *26*(3), 351–389. doi:10.1177/0266242608088743

Simon, H. A. (1960). *The New Science of Management Decision*. New York: Harper & Brothers Publishers.

Sivo, S. A., Saunders, C., Quing, C., & Jiang, J. (2006). How low should you go? Response rates and the validity of inference in IS questionnaire research. *Journal of the Association for Information Systems*, *7*(6), 351–413.

Slater, S. F. (1997). Developing a customer value-based theory of the firm. *Journal of the Academy of Marketing Science*, *25*(2), 162–167. doi:10.1007/BF02894352

Slater, S. F., & Narver, J. C. (1994). Does Competitive Environment Moderate the Market Orientation-Performance Relationship? *Journal of Marketing*, *58*(1), 46–55. doi:10.2307/1252250

Smart Cities. (2007). *Smart cities: Ranking of European medium-sized cities*. Retrieved November 30, 2010, from http://www.smart-cities.eu/download/smart_cities_final_report.pdf

Smart, P. A., Maddern, H., & Maull, R. S. (2009). Understanding business process management: Implications for theory and practice. *British Academy of Management*, *20*(4), 491–507.

Smith, H., & Fingar, P. (2002). *Business process management (BPM): The third wave*. Tampa, FL: Meghan-Kiffer Press.

Smith, M., & Kumar, R. (2004). A theory of Application Service Provider (ASP) use from a client perspective. *Information & Management*, *41*(8), 977–1002. doi:10.1016/j.im.2003.08.019

Snedaker, S. (2006). *IT Security Project Management Handbook*. Rockland, MA: Syngress.

Sobol, M., & Klein, G. (2009). Relation of CIO background, IT infrastructure, and economic performance. *Information & Management*, *46*(5), 271–278. doi:10.1016/j.im.2009.05.001

Solis, I., & Obraczka, K. (2004). FLIP: a flexible interconnection protocol for heterogeneous internetworking. *Mobile Networks and Applications*, *9*(4), 347–361. doi:10.1023/B:MONE.0000031603.28679.6f

Spanyi, A. (2006). *More for less*. Tampa, FL: Meghan-Kiffer Press.

Spreier, S. W., Fontaine, M. H., & Malloy, R. L. (2006). Leadership run amok: The destructive potential of overachievers. *Harvard Business Review*, *84*(6), 72–82.

Sridhar, T. (2009). Cloud Computing-A Primer. *The Internet Protocol Journal, 12*(3).

Srinivasan, S. S., Anderson, R., & Ponnavolu, K. (2002). Customer loyalty in E-commerce: An exploration of its antecedents and consequences. *Journal of Retailing*, *78*(1), 41–50. doi:10.1016/S0022-4359(01)00065-3

St. Hilaire, P., Benton, S., & Lucente, M. (1992). Synthetic aperture holography: A novel approach to three-dimensional displays. *Journal of the Optical Society of America. A, Optics and Image Science*, *9*(11), 1969–1977. doi:10.1364/JOSAA.9.001969

Stackowiak, R., Rayman, J., & Greenwald, R. (2007). *Oracle Data Warehousing and Business intelligence Solutions*. Indianapolis, IN: Wiley Publishing.

Stefanovic, N., Hanj, J., & Koperski, K. (2000). Object-based selective materialization for efficient implementation of spatial data cubes. *IEEE Transactions on Knowledge Discovery and Data Engineering*, *12*(6), 938–958. doi:10.1109/69.895803

Stewart, T. A. (1997). *Intellectual Capital: The new Wealth of Organizations*. New York, NY: Doubleday.

Stonebraker, M. (1985). *The Case for Shared Nothing*. Retrieved from http://db.cs.berkeley.edu/papers/hpts85-nothing.pdf

Storck, J., & Sproull, L. (1995). Though a glass darkly, what do people learn in videoconferences. *Human Communication Research*, *22*(2), 197–219. doi:10.1111/j.1468-2958.1995.tb00366.x

Straub, D. (1989). Validating instruments in MIS research. *Management Information Systems Quarterly*, *13*(2), 147–169. doi:10.2307/248922

Strejcek, G., & Theil, M. (2004). Technology push, legislation pull? E-government in the European Union. *Decision Support Systems*, *34*(1), 305–313.

Suarez, F., & Lanzolla, G. (2007). The Role of Environmental Dynamics in Building a First Mover Advantage Theory. *Academy of Management Review*, *22*(2), 377–392.

Subramani, M. (2004). How do Suppliers Benefit From Information Technology Use in Supply Chain Relationships? *Management Information Systems Quarterly*, *28*(1), 45–73.

Sugihara, K. (1986). *Machine Interpretation of Line Drawings*. Cambridge, MA: MIT Press.

Suh, B., & Han, I. (2002). Effect of trust on customer acceptance of Internet banking. *Electronic Commerce Research and Applications*, *1*(4), 247–263. doi:10.1016/S1567-4223(02)00017-0

Sundaramurthy, C., & Lewis, M. (2003). Control and Collaboration: Paradoxes of Governance. *Academy of Management Review*, *28*(3), 397–415. doi:10.2307/30040729

Sundarraj, R. P., & Wu, J. (2005). Using information-systems constructs to study online- and telephone-banking technologies. *Electronic Commerce Research and Applications*, *4*(4), 427–443. doi:10.1016/j.elerap.2004.12.001

Su, Q., Li, L., & Wu, Y. (2009). Analysing relational benefits in e-business environment from behavioural perspective. *Systems Research and Behavioral Science*, *26*(2), 129–142. doi:10.1002/sres.965

Swaminathan, J. M., & Tayur, S. R. (2003). Models for Supply Chains in E-Business. *Management Science*, *49*(10), 1387–1406. doi:10.1287/mnsc.49.10.1387.17309

Swift, R. S. (2001). *Accelerating Customer Relationships Using CRM and Relationship Technologies*. Upper Saddle River, NJ: Prentice-Hall PTR.

Szymanski, D. M., & Hise, R. T. (2000). E-satisfaction: An initial examination. *Journal of Retailing*, *76*(3), 309–322. doi:10.1016/S0022-4359(00)00035-X

Tandem Database Group. (1989). *NonStop SQL, A Distributed, High-Performance, High Availability Implementation of SQL*. Retrieved from http://www.hpl.hp.com/techreports/tandem/TR-87.4.pdf

Tan, M., & Teo, T. (2000). Factors influencing the adoption of Internet banking. *Journal of the Association for Information Systems*, *1*(5), 1–42.

Tanriverdi, H. (2006). Performance Effects of Information Technology Synergies in Multi-Business Firms. *Management Information Systems Quarterly*, *30*(1), 57–77.

Taubes, G. (1995, September). The Rise and Fall of Thinking Machines. *Inc.com Magazine*. Retrieved from http://www.inc.com/magazine/19950915/2622.html

Taylor, F. W. (1911). *Scientific management*. New York: Harper & Brothers.

Taylor, S., & Todd, P. (1995). Understanding information technology usage: A test of competing models. *Information Systems Research*, *6*(2), 144–176. doi:10.1287/isre.6.2.144

Tchounikine, A., Miqel, M., Laurini, R., Ahmed, T., Bimonte, S., & Bailot, V. (2005). Panorama de travaux autour de l'intégration de données spatio-temporelles dans les hypercubes. *Revue des Nouvelles Technologies de l'Information,* 21–23.

Tehan, D. (2008). *Teradata Overview*. Retrieved from http://www.cs.mu.oz.au/351/teradata.pdf

Teo, T. S. H. (2001). Demographic and motivation variables associated with Internet usage activities. *Internet Research*, *11*(2), 125–137. doi:10.1108/10662240110695089

Teo, T. S. H., & Pok, S. H. (2003). Adoption of WAP-enabled Mobile Phones Among Internet Users. *Omega*, *31*(6), 483–498. doi:10.1016/j.omega.2003.08.005

Teradata Corporation. (2007). *2007 Data Warehouse Benchmark Report Prepared for Manufacturing Industry Respondents*. Dayton, OH: Author.

Teradata Corporation. (n.d.). *Teradata history*. Retrieved from http://www.teradata.com/t/history/

Tesch, D., Jiang, J. J., & Klein, G. (2003). The impact of information system personnel skill discrepancies on stakeholder satisfaction. *Decision Sciences*, *34*(1), 107–129. doi:10.1111/1540-5915.02371

Thomas, J. C., Kellogg, W. A., & Erickson, T. (2001). The Knowledge Management puzzle: Human and social factors in knowledge management. *IBM Systems Journal*, *40*(4), 863–884. doi:10.1147/sj.404.0863

Thomsen, E. (2002). *OLAP Solutions: Building Multidimensional Information Systems* (2nd ed.). New York, NY: John Wiley & Sons.

Thomsen, E., Spofford, G., & Chase, D. (1999). *Microsoft OLAP Solutions*. New York, NY: John Wiley & Sons.

Thong, J. (1999). An integrated model of information systems adoption in small businesses. *Journal of Management Information Systems*, *15*(4), 187–214.

Thoo, E., & Beyer, M. A. (2008). *Best Practices for Data Mart Consolidation*. Stamford, CT: Gartner.

Thoresen, C. J., Bradley, J. C., Bliese, P. D., & Thoresen, J. D. (2004). The Big Five personality traits and individual job performance growth trajectories in maintenance and transitional job stages. *The Journal of Applied Psychology*, *89*(5), 835–853. doi:10.1037/0021-9010.89.5.835

Thornburgh, T. (2004). *Social Engineering: the "dark art"*. Paper presented at the 1st Annual Conference on Information Security Curriculum Development, Kennesaw, GA.

Toffler, A. (1990). *The Third Wave*. New York, NY: Morrow.

Topper, A. (2007). Are they the same? Comparing the instructional quality of online and face-to face graduate education courses. *Assessment & Evaluation in Higher Education*, *32*(6), 681–691. doi:10.1080/02602930601117233

Tornatzky, L. G., & Klein, R. J. (1982). Innovation characteristics and innovation adoption-implementation: A meta-analysis of findings. *IEEE Transactions on Engineering Management*, *29*(1), 28–45.

Towers, S., & Schurter, T. (2005). *Building on experience: An executive report*. Business Process Management Group.

Transaction Processing Performance Council. (n.d.). *Complete TPC-C Results List*. Retrieved from http://www.tpc.org/tpcc/results/tpcc_results.asp?orderby=dbms

Transaction Processing Performance Council. (n.d.). *Using Teradata V2R5.0*. Retrieved from http://www.tpc.org/results/individual_results/NCR/NCR5350_ES_10TB.pdf

Transparency International. (2008). *Global Corruption Report 2008, Corruption in the water sector*. Cambridge, UK: Cambridge University Press.

Transportation Research Board. (1996). *Transportation Options for Megacities in the Developing World*. Retrieved November 30, 2010, from http://trb.org/publications/admin/megacities.pdf

Trkman, P., McCormack, K., De Oliveira, M. P. V., & Ladeira, M. B. (2010). The Impact of Business Analytics on Supply Chain Performance. *Decision Support Systems*, *49*, 318–327. doi:10.1016/j.dss.2010.03.007

Trubint, N., Ljubomir, O., & Nebojša, B. (2006). Determining an optimal retail location by using GIS. *Yugoslav Journal of Operations Research*, *16*(2), 253–264. doi:10.2298/YJOR0602253T

Tudor, J. K. (2001). *Information Security Architecture*. Boca Raton, FL: Auerbach Publications.

Tung, F. C. (2007). Using the e-CRM information system in the hi-tech industry: Predicting salesperson intentions. *Journal of American Academy of Business*, *11*(2), 131–136.

Turban, E., King, D., Lee, J., & Viehland, D. (2004). *Electronic Commerce: A Managerial Perspective*. Upper Saddle River, NJ: Prentice-Hall.

Tushman, M., & Anderson, M. L. (1990). Technological Discontinuities and Dominant Designs: A Cyclical Model of Technological Change. *Administrative Science Quarterly*, *35*, 604–633. doi:10.2307/2393511

Ullah, A., & Routray, J. K. (2007). Rural poverty alleviation through NGO interventions in Bangladesh: how far is the achievement? *International Journal of Social Economics*, *34*(4), 237–248. doi:10.1108/03068290710734208

UN-HABITAT. (2006). *Our Future: Sustainable Cities – Turning Ideas into Action*. Retrieved November 21, 2010, from http://www.unhabitat.org/downloads/docs/3040_94379_background-final.pdf

United Nations and American Society for Public Administration (ASPA). (2002). *Benchmarking e-government: A global perspective*. New York, NY: UN Publications.

United Nations Development Programme (UNDP). (2007). *Human Development Report 2007/2008*. New York, NY: Author.

United Nations Human Settlement Programme (UNHSP). (2007). *United Nations Human Settlement Programme Report*. New York, NY: Author.

United Nations. (2004). *Global E-Government Readiness Report*. New York, NY: Department of Economic and Social Affairs, United Nations.

United Nations. (2008). *UN E-Government Survey 2008 form e-government to connected governance*. New York, NY: Department of Economic and Social Affairs, Division for Public Administration and Development Management, United Nations.

United Nations. (2010). *The Millennium Development Goals Report*. New York, NY: Author.

Van der Haar, H., & Von Solms, R. (2003). A model for deriving information security control attribute profiles. *Computers & Security*, *22*(3), 233–244. doi:10.1016/S0167-4048(03)00311-0

Van Der Heijden, H. (2004). User acceptance of hedonic information systems. *Management Information Systems Quarterly*, *28*(4), 695–704.

Van Slyke, C., Belanger, F., & Comunale, C. L. (2004). Factors influencing the adoption of web-based shopping: The impact of trust. *The Data Base for Advances in Information Systems*, *35*(2), 32–49.

Vandenberghe, C., Bentein, K., & Stinglhamber, F. (2004). Affective commitment to the organization, supervisor, and work group: Antecedents and outcomes. *Journal of Vocational Behavior*, *64*(1), 47–71. doi:10.1016/S0001-8791(03)00029-0

Varley, P. (2002). *Automatic Creation of Boundary-Representation Models from Single Line Drawings*. Unpublished doctoral dissertation, Cardiff University, UK.

Varley, P., & Martin, R. R. (2002). Estimating Depth from Line Drawing. In *Proceedings of the 7th ACM Symposium on Solid Modeling and Applications* (pp. 180-191). New York, NY: ACM.

Varley, P., Martin, R. R., & Suzuki, H. (2005). Frontal Geometry from Sketches of Engineering Objects: Is Line Labeling necessary. *Computer Aided Design*, *37*(12), 1285–1307. doi:10.1016/j.cad.2005.01.002

Venkatesh, V., & Davis, F. D. (2000). A theoretical extension of the technology acceptance model: Four longitudinal field studies. *Management Science*, *46*(2), 186–204. doi:10.1287/mnsc.46.2.186.11926

Venkatesh, V., Morris, M., Davis, G., & Davis, F. (2003). User Acceptance Of Information Technology: Toward A Unified View. *Management Information Systems Quarterly*, *27*(3), 425–437.

Venkatraman, N. (1989). The Concept of Fit in Strategy Research: Toward Verbal and Statistical Correspondence. *Academy of Management Review*, *14*(3), 423–444. doi:10.2307/258177

Venkatraman, N., & Zaheer, A. (1990). Electronic Integration and Strategic Advantage: A Quasi-Experimental Study in the Insurance Industry. *Information Systems Research*, *1*(4), 377–393. doi:10.1287/isre.1.4.377

Vernadat, F. B. (2002). Enterprise modeling and integration (EMI): Current status and research perspectives. *Annual Reviews in Control*, *26*(1), 15–25. doi:10.1016/S1367-5788(02)80006-2

Vickery, S. K., Jayaram, J., Dröge, C., & Calantone, R. (2003). The Effects of an Integrative Supply Chain Strategy on Customer Service and Financial Performance: an Analysis of Direct Versus Indirect Relationships. *Journal of Operations Management*, *21*(5), 523–539. doi:10.1016/j.jom.2003.02.002

von Lucke, J. (2008). *Hochleistungsportale für die öffentliche Verwaltung*. Cologne, Germany: Joseph Eul Verlag GmbH.

Von Solms, B. (2005). Information security governance - Compliance management vs operational management. *Computers & Security*, *21*(4), 356–371.

Vrasidas, C., & McIsaac, M. (1999). Factors influencing interaction in an online course. *American Journal of Distance Education*, *13*(3), 22–36. doi:10.1080/08923649909527033

Wade, N. J. (Ed.). (1983). *Brewster and Wheatstone on vision*. New York, NY: Academic Press.

Walter, T. (2008). *Teradata Architecture – Technology & Differentiation*. Retrieved from http://www.teradata.com/teradata-partners/conference/index.cfm

Wang, E. T. G., & Wei, H. (2007). Interorganizational Governance Value Creation: Coordinating for Information Visibility and Flexibility in Supply Chains. *Decision Sciences*, *38*(4), 647–674. doi:10.1111/j.1540-5915.2007.00173.x

Wang, W., & Grinstein, G. (1993). A Survey of 3D Solid Reconstruction from 2D Projection Line Drawings. *Computer Graphics Forum*, *12*(2), 137–158. doi:10.1111/1467-8659.1220137

Watson, D. L., & Clark, A. (1997). Extraversion and its positive emotional core. In Hogan, R., Johnson, J., & Briggs, S. R. (Eds.), *Handbook of Personality Psychology* (pp. 767–793). San Diego, CA: Academic Press. doi:10.1016/B978-012134645-4/50030-5

Watson, H. J., Annino, D. A., Wixom, B. H., Avery, K. L., & Rutherford, M. (2001). Current practices in data warehousing. *Information Systems Management*, *18*(1), 47–55. doi:10.1201/1078/43194.18.1.20010101/31264.6

Watson, H. J., Rainer, R. K., & Houdeshel, G. (1992). *Executive Information Systems: Emergence, Development, Impact*. New York, NY: John Wiley & Sons.

Watzke, M. (2008). *Teradata GeoSpatial*. Retrieved from http://www.teradata.com/teradata-partners/conference/index.cfm

Wayne, S. J., Shore, L. M., & Liden, R. C. (1997). Perceived organizational support and leader-member exchanges: a social exchange analysis. *Academy of Management Journal*, *40*(1), 82 111. doi:10.2307/257021

Webb, B. (2007). *SAS and Teradata Enter into Strategic Partnership*. Cary, NC: SAS Institute. Retrieved from http://www.sas.com/news/preleases/100807/SASandTeradata.html

Webb, B. (2008). *SAS Speeds Delivery of In-Database Capabilities and Unveils New Software Bundle Program with Teradata*. Cary, NC: SAS Institute. Retrieved from http://www.sas.com/news/preleases/031708/Teradata.html

Webb, B. (2008). *SAS In-Database Processing with Teradata: An Overview of Foundation Technology*. Cary, NC: SAS Institute. Retrieved from http://support.sas.com/resources/papers/teradata08.pdf

Weber, K., Otto, B., & Österle, H. (2009). One size does not fit all - A contigency approach to data governance. *ACM Journal of Data and Information Quality*, *1*(1), 4:1-4:27.

Wechsler, D. (1997). *Wechsler Adult Intelligence Scale (WAIS-III)* (3rd ed.). New York: Psychological Corporation.

Weill, P. (2004). Don't jut lead, govern: How top-performing firms govern IT. *MIS Quarterly Executive*, *3*(1), 1–17.

Weill, P., & Ross, J. W. (2004). *IT Governance: How Top Performers Manage IT Decision Rights for Superior Results*. Boston: Harvard Business School Press.

Weill, P., & Vitale, M. (2002). What IT infrastructural capabilities are needed to implement e-business models. *MISQ Executive*, *1*(1), 17–34.

Weiss, W. (2008). *A Technical Overview of the Oracle Exadata Storage Server*. Retrieved from http://www.oracle.com/technology/products/bi/db/exadata/pdf/exadata-technical-whitepaper.pdf

Wei, T. T., Marthandan, G., Chong, A. Y. L., Ooi, K. B., & Arumugam, S. (2009). What drives Malaysian m-commerce adoption? An empirical analysis. *Industrial Management & Data Systems*, *109*(3), 370–388. doi:10.1108/02635570910939399

Werhane, P., & Freeman, E. (2003). Business Ethics. In Frey, R. G., & Wellman, C. (Eds.), *A Companion to Applied Ethics* (pp. 537–552). London, UK: Blackwell.

Wheatstone, C. (1838). Contributions to the theory of vision – Part the first, on some remarkable, and hitherto unobserved, phenomena of binocular vision. *Philosophical Transactions of the Royal Society of London*, *128*, 371–394. doi:10.1098/rstl.1838.0019

Whiteley, W. (1991). Weavings, Sections and Projections of Spherical Polyhedra. *Discrete Applied Mathematics*, *32*(3), 275–294. doi:10.1016/0166-218X(91)90004-G

Whitman, M. E., & Mattord, H. J. (2008). *Management of Information Security* (2nd ed.). Florence, KY: Course Technology.

Whitman, M. E., & Mattord, H. J. (2009). *Principles of Information Security* (3rd ed.). Florence, KY: Course Technology.

Wilhelm, S., Rodehorst, T. K., Young, S., Jensen, L., & Stepans, M. B. (2003). Students' perspectives of the effectiveness of an asynchronous on-line seminar. *Journal of Professional Nursing*, *19*(5), 313–319. doi:10.1016/S8755-7223(03)00102-9

Williams, M. (2009). *Microsoft loses Sidekick user's personal data*. Network World.

Winter, S., & Taylor, S. L. (1996). The Role of IT in the Transformation of Work: A Comparison of Post-industrial, Industrial, and Proto-industrial Organization. *Information Systems Research*, *7*(1), 5–22. doi:10.1287/isre.7.1.5

Witt, L. A., Burke, L. A., Barrick, M. R., & Mount, M. K. (2002). The interactive effects of conscientiousness and agreeableness on job performance. *The Journal of Applied Psychology*, *87*(1), 164–169. doi:10.1037/0021-9010.87.1.164

Wixom, B. H., & Watson, H. J. (2001). An empirical investigation of the factors affecting data warehousing success. *Management Information Systems Quarterly*, *25*(1), 17–41. doi:10.2307/3250957

Wolf, P., Jurisch, M., & Krcmar, H. (2010). *Analyse und Design von Prozessketten*. Paper presented at the Fachtagung Verwaltungsinformatik (FTVI) Conference.

Wolf, P., & Krcmar, H. (2005). Prozessorientierte Wirtschaftlichkeitsuntersuchung für E-Government. *Wirtschaftsinformatik*, *47*(5), 337–346.

Wong, K. Y. (2005). Critical success factors for implementing knowledge management in small and medium enterprises. *Industrial Management & Data Systems*, *105*(3), 261–279. doi:10.1108/02635570510590101

Wong, W., & Welch, E. (2004). Does e-government promote accountability? A comparative analysis of Website openness and government accountability. *Governance: An International Journal of Policy. Administration and Institutions*, *17*(2), 275–297.

Workman, M. (2007). Gaining Access with Social Engineering: An Empirical Study of the Threat. *Information System Security*, *16*(6), 315–331. doi:10.1080/10658980701788165

Workman, M. (2008). Wisecrackers: A theory-grounded investigation of phishing and pretext social engineering threats to information security. *Journal of the American Society for Information Science and Technology*, *59*(4), 662–674. doi:10.1002/asi.20779

World Bank. (2006). *A practitioner's guide - Health Financing Revisited*. Washington, DC: Author.

World Commission on Environment and Development (WCED). (1987). *Our Common Future*. Oxford, UK: Oxford University Press.

World Health Organization. (2005). *Celebrating Water for Life – The International Decade for Action 2005 – 2015.* Washington, DC: Author.

World Water Assessment Programme. (2006). *Water: a shared responsibility – The United Nations World Water Development Report 2.* Retrieved November 21, 2010, from http://unesdoc.unesco.org/images/0014/001444/144409e.pdf

Worthington, A. C. (1999). Measuring Technical Efficiency in Australian Credit Unions. *The Manchester School, 67*(2), 231–248. doi:10.1111/1467-9957.00144

Wu, I. L., & Chen, J. L. (2005). An extension of Trust and TAM model with TPB in the initial adoption of on-line tax: An empirical study. *International Journal of Human-Computer Studies, 62*(6), 784–808. doi:10.1016/j.ijhcs.2005.03.003

Wu, J.-H., & Wang, S.-C. (2005). What drives mobile commerce? An empirical evaluation of the revised technology acceptance model. *Information & Management, 42*(5), 719–729. doi:10.1016/j.im.2004.07.001

Wylder, J. (2004). *Strategic Information Security.* Boca Raton, FL: Auerbach Publications.

Yang, K. C. C. (2005). Exploring factors affecting the adoption of mobile commerce in Singapore. *Telematics and Informatics, 22*(3), 257–277. doi:10.1016/j.tele.2004.11.003

Yap, C., Soh, C., & Raman, K. (1992). Information systems Success Factors in Small Business. *Omega, 20*(506), 597–609. doi:10.1016/0305-0483(92)90005-R

Yildiz, M. (2007). E-government research: Reviewing the literature, limitations, and ways forward. *Government Information Quarterly, 24*(3), 646–665. doi:10.1016/j.giq.2007.01.002

Young, S. (2006). Student views of effective online teaching in higher education. *American Journal of Distance Education, 20*(2), 65–77. doi:10.1207/s15389286ajde2002_2

Youngworth, P. (1995). OLAP spells success for users and developers. *Data Based Advisor, 13*(11), 38–49.

Youseff, L., Butrico, M., & DaSilva, D. (2008). *Toward a unified ontology of cloud computing.* Paper presented at the Grid Computing Environments Workshop (GCE2008).

Yu, S., Kim, Y., & Kim, M. (2004). Linking Organizational Knowledge Management Drivers to Knowledge Management Performance: An Exploratory Study. In *Proceedings of HICSS37.* Washington, DC: IEEE Computer Society.

Yuefa, D., Bo, W., Yaquiang, G., Quan, Z., & Chaojing, T. (2009). Data Security Model for Cloud Computing. In *Proceedings of the IWISA 2009 Conference,* Qingdao, China (pp. 141-145).

Zarei, B., Ghapanchi, A., & Sattary, B. (2008). Toward national e-government development models for developing countries: A nine-stage model. *The International Information & Library Review, 40*(3), 199–208. doi:10.1016/j.iilr.2008.04.001

Zhang, T., Koehler, M., & Spatariu, A. (2009). The development of the Motivation for Critical Reasoning in Online Discussions Inventory (MCRODI). *American Journal of Distance Education, 23*(4), 194–211. doi:10.1080/08923640903294411

Zhou, B., Jiang, D., Pei, J., & Li, H. (2009, June 28-July 1). OLAP on sear logs: An infrastructure supporting data-driven applications in search engines. In *Proceedings of the 15th ACM SIGKDD Conference on Knowledge Discovery and Data Mining,* Paris, France.

Zhu, K., & Kraemer, K. L. (2002). E-Commerce Metrics for Net-Enhanced Organizations: Assessing the Value of E-Commerce to Firm Performance in the Manufacturing Sector. *Information Systems Research, 13*(3), 275–295. doi:10.1287/isre.13.3.275.82

Zuboff, S. (1988). *In the Age of the Smart Machine: The Future of Work and Power.* New York: Basic Books.

Zucker, L. G. (1986). Production of trust: institutional source of economic structure, 1840–1920. In Staw, B. M., & Cummings, L. L. (Eds.), *Research in Organizational Behavior* (pp. 53–111). Greenwich, CT: JAI Press.

About the Contributors

Mehdi Khosrow-Pour (DBA) received his Doctorate in Business Administration from the Nova Southeastern University (FL, USA). Dr. Khosrow-Pour taught undergraduate and graduate information system courses at the Pennsylvania State University – Harrisburg for 20 years where he was the chair of the Information Systems Department for 14 years. He is currently president and publisher of IGI Global, an international academic publishing house with headquarters in Hershey, PA (www.igi-global.com). He also serves as executive director of the Information Resources Management Association (IRMA) (www.irma-international.org) and executive director of the World Forgotten Children's Foundation (www.world-forgotten-children.org). He is the author/editor of over twenty books in information technology management. He is also the editor-in-chief of the *Information Resources Management Journal*, the *Journal of Cases on Information Technology*, the *Journal of Electronic Commerce in Organizations* and the *Journal of Information Technology Research* and has authored more than 50 articles published in various conference proceedings and journals.

* * *

Akbar Kary Dolat Abadi is a faculty member of Shahid Sattari University. He holds a BSc in electrical engineering and MSc in opto electronic optic branch of electrical engineering. He has been teaching in University for about 15 years and led more than 100 theses. Her main research interests include WDM, DWDM, network, Information technology and its applications. He had some printed articles in these subjects.

Saad Alflayyeh is a Ph.D. student of Manufacturing and Technology Management at the College of Business and Innovation, University of Toledo. He received his MBA degree from the University of Toledo. His research interests are global supply chain management, technology transfer, innovation, e-business and manufacturing strategy. His current work focuses on the economics of alternative energy.

Oualid Ben Ali has obtained a Ph.D. degree in Computer Science from Laval University (Quebec, Canada) (supervised by Bernard Moulin since 2001). He is mainly interested in using multiagent systems to simulate behaviors and phenomena in 2D-3D geographic virtual spatial environments. Then he received a 2 years - MARIE-CURIE scholarship to work in the Hull York Medical School (York, UK) and in the Hull Immersive Virtual Environment (HIVE) (Hull, UK) as an EVAN post-doctoral fellow. Currently, he is an assistant professor at the University of Sharjah, in the College of Business Administration, MIS Department. His current research interests include Modeling and Simulation, E-Government, Geographic Information Systems, Data Analysis (OLAP and Data Mining), Artificial Intelligence, MultiAgent Systems, etc.

Yvonne Lederer Antonucci received her Ph.D. in Information Systems from Drexel University. She is an Associate Professor at Widener University in the Accounting and Information Management Department in addition to being the SAP Alliance Coordinator and Director of the Business Process Innovation Center of Excellence. Yvonne teaches graduate and undergraduate level classes in information systems, enterprise systems, and business process management. She has published in numerous international journals, books, and conferences in the areas of business process management, information technology outsourcing, inter-organizational trust and collaboration, workflow management, and enterprise systems.

Ali Assadian is currently an MBA student at University of California, San Diego. He has a Master's degree in Urban Affair Management from University of Tehran. He, also, has a bachelor degree in Electrical Engineering from K.N. Toosi University of Technology. His areas of interest and research include sustainable development, social and environmental development, energy management/conservation, and technology development. He has publications in different journals addressing sustainability, urban affairs, and energy management.

Barry Blundell is a physicist and chartered engineer with broad ranging transdisciplinary research interests. His main areas of research activity relate to the development and characterisation of innovative 3-D display and haptic interfaces, sustainable computing, the ethical application of digital technologies, and the social impact and history of data gathering and analysis technologies. In relation to his work concerning 3-D systems, he has particular interests in medical, engineering, and educational applications. He has held academic positions in a several countries and is the author of twelve books.

Richard Brody is the Rutledge Professor of Accounting in the Anderson School of Management at the University of New Mexico. He earned his Ph.D. from Arizona State University, his M.S. from Colorado State University and his B.S. from the University of Delaware. He is a Certified Public Accountant, a Certified Fraud Examiner and a Forensic Certified Public Accountant. Professor Brody's research addresses issues related to forensic accounting, auditing and corporate governance. Recent research has focused on issues such as corporate fraud, identity theft, mandatory auditor rotation, the outsourcing of income tax returns to India and the impact of corporate governance structure on auditor judgment.

Stephen Burd is an Associate Professor of Management in the Anderson School of Management at the University of New Mexico. He earned his Ph.D. from Purdue University in 1983. His teaching and research interests include computer and software architecture, system and network administration, healthcare technology and cost-effectiveness, and database management. He is Associate Director for UNM's Center for Information Assurance Research and Education and is Secretary and Treasurer of the New Mexico Telehealth Alliance. He is a Certified Public Accountant licensed in Maryland.

Stephen K. Callaway is an Assistant Professor in the Department of Management at the University of Toledo, where he teaches courses in strategic management and entrepreneurship. His research interests include technology management and entrepreneurship. He has multiple publications, including journals such as Journal of High Technology Management Research and International Journal of Organizational Analysis.

Alain Yee-Loong Chong is currently a postdoctoral fellow in the Department of Industrial and Systems Engineering, The Hong Kong Polytechnic University. He received his BSc and MSc (Distinction) from Coventry University, UK, and PhD from the Multimedia University, Malaysia. His research interests include supply chain management, e-business adoption and service science. To date, he has published in more than 50 peer reviewed international journal and conference papers. He is a Member of the Institute of Electrical and Electronics Engineers (IEEE). He is also the editor of the *International Journal of Modelling in Operations Management* and *International Journal of Network and Mobile Technologies.*

Seng-cho T. Chou is Professor of Information Management at National Taiwan University. He received his Ph.D. in Computer Science from the University of Illinois at Urbana-Champaign. Before joining NTU, he had worked at Jet Propulsion Lab in Pasadena and the Chinese University of Hong Kong. He has been an advisor on a number of IT projects in both the public and private sectors. His research interests include information and knowledge management, service science and innovation, and Web technologies and applications.

Tzy-Yuan Chou is a deputy division chief in the Financial Data Center of the Ministry of Finance in Taiwan. She was awarded her Ph.D in 2009 by the National Taiwan University in Taiwan. With more than fifteen years of practicing information systems project management; she has significant experience in systems projects, programs, and development. Tzy-Yuan Chou has been awarded several prizes from her government for successful completion of critical projects, including the best Application Certification prize from the Ministry of Interior of Taiwan in 2007-2008 for a tax e-filing system. Currently, she is in charge of major tax system for the Taiwan government budgeted at over 3 billion USD. Her research involves aspects of he profession that have presented unique challenges, including the motivation of IS personnel and program management. James Jiang is the Distinguish Professor of IS in the Research School of Business and School of Accounting and Business Information Systems, The Australian National University (ANU), Australia. Currently, he is also an honorary Distinguished Chair Professor of Management, National Taiwan University, Taiwan. Prior to join the ANU, he was in the academic positions in the U.S. Professor Jiang's research interests are IS Project/Program Management and Service Quality. He has published over 150 academic journal articles on these areas. He has served as on the editorial boards of Information Resources Management Journal, International Journal of IT Project Management, Information & Management, and MIS Quarterly.

Hossein Dabbagh has a bachelor's degree in "Management", a master's degree in "Philosophy". His current major research interests are in "Western Philosophy" and "Ethics".

Richard J. Goeke received his Ph.D. in Management Systems from Kent State University. He is an Assistant Professor in the Accounting and Information Management Department at Widener University, where he teaches undergraduate and graduate level classes in information systems, systems analysis, and database management. Prior to joining Widener, Richard spent 17 years in industry in information systems, accounting, marketing, and management. His research has been published in *Quality Management Journal, International Journal of Operational Research, Business Process Management Journal, Information Resources Management Journal,* and *Communications of the ACM.* His current research interests include business process management, enterprise resource planning, and data warehousing.

Christian Ikas has been an analyst at the Chair for Information Systems, Technische Universitaet Muenchen, since 2009. His research focuses on issues pertaining to the fields of E-Government and process management. He takes special interest in facilitating a resource-efficient and citizen-oriented provision of public services. He has assisted in the design of an E-Government maturity model as well as a publication concerning E-Government services tailored to the needs of expatriates.

Karthik N. S. Iyer is an Associate Professor of Marketing at the College of Business, University of Northern Iowa. He earned his Ph.D. from Oklahoma State University. His current research focuses on assessing the impact of IT on supply chain management, supply chain collaboration and capabilities, alliances and organizational learning. Dr. Iyer's research has been published in scholarly journals including *Industrial Marketing Management, Transportation Research Part E: Logistics and Transportation Review, Journal of Business Logistics, International Journal of Physical Distribution and Logistics Management, Information & Management, and the Journal of the Academy of Marketing Science.*

Wen-Jang (Kenny) Jih is a professor of Computer Information Systems in the Jennings A. Jones College of Business, Middle Tennessee State University. He recently has conducted research in the areas of knowledge management, information strategy, and e-commerce. His papers have been published in International Journal of E-Business Research, Information Resource Management Journal, International Journal of Information Management, International Journal of Knowledge Management Studies, Journal of Information Systems Education, Journal of Computer Information Systems, Computers in Industry, International Journal of Enterprise Information Systems, and others. He received his doctorate degree in Business Computer Information Systems from the University of North Texas in 1985.

Marlen Jurisch is a doctoral candidate in Information Systems at the Department of Informatics, Technische Universitaet Muenchen. She has executed several qualitative and quantitative studies in process management and E-Government. Since 2010, she is a co-project leader for a study funded by the German Federal Ministry of the Interior which examines the efficient design of interorganizational eGovernment processes. Prior to joining her PhD program, she worked for Booz Allen Hamilton and SAP Research in their American and German offices. She has research interests in E-Government, process management and organizational change management.

Gary Klein is the Couger Professor of Information Systems at the University of Colorado in Colorado Springs. He obtained his Ph.D. in Management Science from Purdue University. His research interests include project management, technology transfer, and mathematical modeling with over 150 academic publications in these areas. He served as Director of Education for the American Society for the Advancement of Project Management, is a Fellow of the Decision Sciences Institute, and is an active member of the Project Management Institute. He serves on the editorial board of the International Journal of Information Technology Project Management and the Journal of the Association of Information Systems and serves as an AE for MIS Quarterly and SE for the Pacific Asia Journal of the Association of Information Systems.

Helmut Krcmar holds the Chair for Information Systems at the Department of Informatics at Technische Universitaet Muenchen (TUM) since 2002. He is a member of the Department of Informatics and the Faculty of Business Administration as well as a member of the "Carl von Linde-Akademie". Since 2004, he is a member of the Program Faculty of the Elite Graduate Program "Finance and Information Management (FIM)" in the Elitenetzwerk Bayern. Until May 2007, he was Academic Director of the Executive Training Program ¡communicate!. Since January 2004, he is Board Member of the Center for Digital Technology and Management (CDTM) at Technische Universitaet Muenchen. His research interests include Information and Knowledge Management, IT-enabled Value webs, Service Management, Computer Supported Cooperative Work, Information Systems in Health Care and E-Government.

Sofia Kyratzi received her PhD (2007) degree in Computer Graphics and Geometric Modeling from the Department of Product and Systems Design Engineering of the University of the Aegean, and her MSc (2002) in Medical Informatics from Aristotle University of Thessaloniki. She also holds a BSc (2000) in Mathematics from Aristotle University of Thessaloniki. From 2001 to 2002, she worked as a researcher in the Informatics and Telematics Institute of CERTH in Thessaloniki. The last two years she has been employed as an instructor in the Department of Product and Systems Design Engineering (University of the Aegean). Her research interests include geometric and solid modeling, computer graphics, computer aided sketching, image understanding and computer vision.

Brett J. L. Landry, PhD, CISSP is the Ellis Endowed Chair of Technology Management, Associate Professor and Director of the Center for Cybersecurity Education at the University of Dallas. Over the last twenty years, Landry has worked in infosec in the public and private sectors and has published numerous journal articles in the *ACM Journal of Educational Resources in Computing (JERIC), Communications of the ACM (CACM), Decision Sciences Journal of Innovative Education, International Journal of Services and Standards, Journal Business Ethics, Journal of Organizational Change Management*, and others.

Xin (Robert) Luo is an Assistant Professor of Management Information Systems and Information Assurance in the Anderson School of Management at the University of New Mexico, USA. He earned his Ph.D. in Information Systems from Mississippi State University. His teaching and research interests include information assurance, e-commerce/m-commerce, and cross-cultural management. His research has been published in journals including *Journal of the Association for Information Systems, European Journal of Information Systems, Communications of the ACM, Decision Support Systems, Communication of the Association for Information Systems, Journal of Organizational and End User Computing, Information Management and Computer Security, Cross-Cultural Management, Journal of Information Privacy and Security, International Journal of Information Security & Privacy, Information Systems Security,* and *Journal of Internet Banking and Commerce, etc.*

Sathiadev Mahesh is a Professor in the College of Business at the University of New Orleans. He received his Ph.D. from Purdue University. He has an M.B.A. from Oklahoma State University and degrees in Engineering from the I.I.T. Madras and University of Madras, India. His research has been published in many journals including *Decision Sciences, Omega*, the *Journal of Organizational Change Management*, and the *Journal of Health & Human Services Administration*. His primary interest lies in the area of systems development. He has worked on many systems development projects and has experience with a wide range of business applications. In addition, Dr. Mahesh has worked in process improvement, including process quality improvement.

Nick-Naser Manochehri received his Ph.D. (2001) in Applied Technology, from the University of North Texas, USA, his MS in Software Engineering and bachelor's in Computer Science. He has several years of industrial experience as a software developer and senior instructor in the area of IT at SBC Communications Inc. in Dallas Texas. He also worked as an assistant professor in the department of IS at SQU in Oman. He is currently an assistant professor in the college of Business and Economics, department of Accounting & Information Systems at the Qatar University. His research area of interest includes: IT, TQM, e/mobile Commerce, e-learning & educational Technology.

Samar Mouakket is an associate professor in the MIS department at the University of Sharjah, UAE. She received her Ph.D. in 1996 in Management Information Systems from Sheffield University, UK. Her research interests include systems analysis and user requirements determination during systems development, Geographic Information Systems, Data Analysis (OLAP and Data Mining), and the deployment and utilization of different business information systems, such as ERP systems, as well as web-based business applications, such as e-commerce, e-government and e-banking.

Mostafa Nejati is an industrial engineer (Isfahan University of Technology), Master of Urban Affairs Management (University of Tehran), and currently a PhD researcher in the School of Management, Universiti Sains Malaysia (USM). His research areas of interest include (but are not limited to) sustainable development, knowledge management, project management, healthcare, youth and poverty research. He has had numerous publications in renowned international journals including ISI and Scopus indexed ones. Mr. Nejati is also the Editor-in-Chief of *Global Business and Management Research Journal*, and acts as an executive editor, editorial board member or reviewer of some esteemed journals published by renowned publishers including Elsevier, Emerald, and IGI Global.

H. Jim Nelson is an assistant professor of Management Information Systems at Southern Illinois University, Carbondale. He received his BS in Computer Science from California Polytechnic State University, San Luis Obispo, and his MS and PhD in Information Systems from the University of Colorado, Boulder. His research interests include developing theoretically grounded models of information systems quality, investigating how people make IT paradigm shifts, and determining the business value of information technology. Dr. Nelson generally teaches the more technical courses in information systems including object oriented technology, systems analysis and design, database theory and practice, and business data communications.

Roshanak Rouzbehani has a bachelor's degree in "Management", a master's degree in "IT Management". Her current major research interests are in "Knowledge Management" and "Business Ethics".

Fatemeh Saghafi is an assistant professor at the Iran Telecommunication Research Center (ITRC). She holds a BSc in Communication engineering and MSc & PhD in Industrial engineering. She has been working for about 15 years in ITRC. Her main research interests include e-government development and implementation, system simulation, foresight, performance management systems, knowledge management, social network and decision-making science.

Nickolas S. Sapidis is currently a Professor of "Computational Design and Analysis of Machine Elements" with the Department of Mechanical Engineering of the University of Western Macedonia (Kozani, Greece). Prior to that, he was a faculty member with the Department of Product and Systems Design Engineering of the University of the Aegean (Syros, Greece). He holds a Diploma in Naval Architecture & Marine Engineering (1985), an M.A. in Applied Mathematics (1987) and an M.S. in Mechanical Engineering (1988). He received his PhD in Mechanical and Aerospace Sciences from the University of Rochester in 1993. N. Sapidis is on the editorial board of these international scientific journals: International Journal of Visual Analytics for Advanced Information Management, Computer-Aided Design, Virtual and Physical Prototyping, International Journal of Product Lifecycle Management, Computer-Aided Design and Applications, Mathematical Problems in Engineering, International Journal of Product Development, Computer Graphics and CAD/CAM, International Journal of Design Engineering, and International Journal of Computer Aided Engineering and Technology. N. Sapidis has been pursuing research on "Design of Mechanical Products", "Computer-Aided Design (CAD)", "Computer-Aided Engineering (CAE)", "Solid Modeling", "Geometric Modeling of Surfaces", "Geometric Algorithms", "Virtual Engineering", and "Computer Graphics". He is the author of more than 50 papers on the above subjects. His research has been implemented in industrial CAD/CAE-software systems by the Massachusetts Institute of Technology (MIT) and companies including General Motors (GM), Intergraph and Tribon Solutions. N. Sapidis has taught at the Hellenic Air Force Academy, the National Technical University of Athens, the University of Athens and the Polytechnic University of Catalunya (Spain). Also, he has been providing education/training services to MIT as well as to major Greek corporations like Elefsis Shipyards and the Bank of Greece. His industrial experience on CAD/CAE includes GM R&D Center and GM Design Center (USA), as well as the Marine Technology Development Co (Greece). N. Sapidis has served on the Program Committee of more than 40 international conferences, and was an "invited Keynote Speaker" for 7 international conferences. N. Sapidis has given "invited lectures" at numerous conferences, Universities and corporations in Asia, Europe and the US.

Carol Saunders is currently Professor of Management at the University of Central Florida. She served as General Conference Chair of ICIS'99 and Telecommuting '96. She is an AIS Fellow and has served on a number of editorial boards, including a three-year term as Editor-in-Chief of *MIS Quarterly.* She currently is the Senior Editor of the IS Research Perspectives section of *Journal of the Association of Information Systems (JAIS).* She recently returned from Austria as the Distinguished Fulbright Scholar at the Wirtschafts Universitaet – Wien (WU). Her current research interests include the organizational impacts of information technology, overload, backsourcing, virtual teams, virtual worlds, and time. Her research is published in *MIS Quarterly, Information Systems Research, Journal of MIS, Journal of AIS, Communications of the ACM, Information Resources Management Journal, Academy of Management Journal, Academy of Management Review,* and *Organization Science.*

Alessandro Seazzu is the director of UNM's Center for Information Assurance Research and Education (CIARE). Through CIARE, UNM has been designated by the NSA and DHS as a Center of Academic Excellence in Information Assurance and was recently selected as the host site for one of the FBI's Regional Computer Forensics Laboratory. He has been a faculty member with the Anderson School since 1995. His areas of research and study have been in virtual environments in security and human behavior in security.

Kolsoom Abbasi Shahkooh received her MSc in Information Technology from University of West England Bristol in the UK. She has been working at the Iran Telecommunication Research Center (ITRC) as a researcher for about 7 years. Her main research interests include e-government development and implementation, enterprise interoperability, foresight, information technology, e-commerce and decision-making science.

Armin Sharafi is a doctoral candidate in Information Systems at the Department of Informatics, Technische Universitaet Muenchen. He has carried out research on IT-related areas such as process management, evaluation of workflow systems and E-Government. During that time he worked in and acquired several projects funded by public authorities (German Federal Ministry of the Interior, Bavarian Research Alliance etc.) and industry. Prior to joining his PhD program, he worked for Axel Springer, Pirelli Tyres and DaimlerChrysler. His recent research and teaching interests are data mining, knowledge discovery in databases, new product development, engineering change management and business games.

T. Sridhar has over 20 years of experience in the Networking domain where his work has involved technology consulting, software architecture and development. He received his BE in Electronics and Communications Engineering from the College of Engineering, Guindy, Anna University, Madras, India, and his Master of Science in Electrical and Computer Engineering from the University of Texas at Austin.

R. P. Sundarraj is currently a Professor of Information Systems at Qatar University's Accounting and Information Systems department. Prior to that, he has held tenured faculty positions at the University of Waterloo, Canada, and at Clark University, USA. Professor Sundarraj obtained his Bachelors in Electrical Engineering from the University of Madras, India, and his MS and Ph.D. in Management and Computer Sciences from the University of Tennessee, Knoxville. His teaching and research encompass the development of methodologies for the efficient design and management of emerging information systems, as well as the use of parallel computing for solving large-scale problems. His work has been supported by grants and research contracts in different countries. Professor Sundarraj has published in various national and international journals such as *Mathematical Programming, IEEE Transactions, ACM Transactions and European Journal of Operational Research.* In addition, he has provided e-commerce solutions for marketing and inventory-management problems arising in Fortune 100 companies.

Kenneth R. Walsh is an Associate Professor in the Department of Management, Information Systems Group at University of New Orleans. Before returning to academia, Dr. Walsh was a Senior Systems Analyst at Exxon Corporation where he developed database software for oil well support and maintenance and other management applications. He received a Ph.D. in Information Systems from the University of Arizona in 1996. His research has been published in *Information & Management*, *Communications of the ACM*, and a number of other information systems journals. His research interests include network computing models, structured modeling group support systems (SM-GSS), Internet support for education, and applications of virtual reality technology. Dr. Walsh has taught a wide variety of management information systems courses at both the graduate and undergraduate levels.

Ian A. Willson, currently a Technical Fellow with The Boeing Company, is an associate editor of the International Journal of Visual Analytics (IJVA). He received his Ph.D. in Artificial Intelligence and Management Sciences from the University of Toronto where he also held a SSHRC post-doctoral fellowship. Ian's dissertation and national post-doctoral fellowship culminated in the publication of many research papers in refereed journals such as the European Journal of Operational Research, Fuzzy Sets and Systems and The International Society for Optical Engineering. He taught undergraduate and graduate courses at the University of Toronto and has been an invited speaker at numerous conferences and universities worldwide. He has advanced the state of the art in data and analytics, first at the IBM Software Laboratory and then at Management Science Associates, where he created innovative analytical software for the first Massively Parallel Processing computer. His research interests also include psychology, marketing, management science and computer science domains such as artificial intelligence, userinterface design, heuristics, visualization and many aspects of analytics and relational database technology. Ian also serves as Vice-Chairperson of the Teradata Product Advisory Council.

Petra Wolf heads the public information management Research Group at the Chair for Information Systems of the Technische Universitaet Muenchen. Among her main research interests are business process management for E-Government, public sector reengineering and knowledge management. She has been involved in numerous research projects dealing with information needs of managers in public administration, questions of IT governance in public sector, business to government processes or methods for efficiency assessment of E-Government solution. Currently her research group focuses on questions concerning the efficient design of interorganizational E-Government processes.

Yu "Andy" Wu is an assistant professor in the Department of Information Technology and Decision Sciences, College of Business at the University of North Texas. He received a Ph.D. in Management Information Systems from the University of Central Florida. Andy's primary research interests include social networks and information security. His articles appeared in journals such as *Informing Science*, *Journal of Organizational and End User Computing*, *Communication of the Association for Information Systems*, *International Journal of Networking and Virtual Organizations*, and the proceedings of a number of international conferences. Before his academic career, Andy had seven years' experiences in various business and management positions.

Mehdi Shami Zanjani is Assistant Professor of Information Technology Management at the Faculty of Management, University of Tehran. He has a bachelor's degree in "Industrial Management", a master's degree in "Information Technology Management", and a PhD in "Systems Management" from the University of Tehran. His professional experience includes ten years, three of which were spend as senior consultant of "Programme Management" at "Iran Tax Administration Reform Programme". He also has several consulting experiences to SMEs and government agencies in the field of "Knowledge Management". He has been teaching "Knowledge Management Process", "Project & Programme Management", "Systems Analysis & Design" and "Management Information Systems" for six years. His current major research interests are in "Knowledge Management Mechanisms" and "Programme Management".

Index

F

G

H

I

L

M

N

O

P

Q

R

S

T

U

V

W

www.ingramcontent.com/pod-product-compliance
Lightning Source LLC
LaVergne TN
LVHW080057220926
848484LV00007BA/1851